T0320133

Financial Risk Management

Founded in 1807, John Wiley & Sons is the oldest independent publishing company in the United States. With offices in North America, Europe, Australia, and Asia, Wiley is globally committed to developing and marketing print and electronic products and services for our customers' professional and personal knowledge and understanding.

The Wiley Finance series contains books written specifically for finance and investment professionals as well as sophisticated individual investors and their financial advisors. Book topics range from portfolio management to e-commerce, risk management, financial engineering, valuation, and financial instrument analysis, as well as much more.

For a list of available titles, visit our Web site at www.WileyFinance.com.

Financial Risk Management

Models, History, and Institutions

ALLAN M. MALZ

WILEY

John Wiley & Sons, Inc.

Published by John Wiley & Sons, Inc., Hoboken, New Jersey.
Published simultaneously in Canada.

For general information on our other products and services or for technical support, please contact our Customer Care Department within the United States at (800) 762-2974, outside the United States at (317) 572-3993 or fax (317) 572-4002.

Wiley also publishes its books in a variety of electronic formats. Some content that appears in print may not be available in electronic books. For more information about Wiley products, visit our Web site at www.wiley.com.

Library of Congress Cataloging-in-Publication Data:

Malz, Allan M.
   Financial risk management: models, history, and institution : models, history, and institution / Allan M. Malz.
      p.   cm. – (Wiley finance series)
   Includes bibliographical references and index.
   ISBN 978-0-470-48180-6 (cloth); ISBN 978-1-118-02291-7 (ebk);
   ISBN 978-1-118-02290-0 (ebk); ISBN 978-1-118-02289-4 (ebk)
   1. Financial risk management.   I. Title.
   HD61.M256 2011
   332–dc22
                                                      2010043485

10 9 8 7 6 5 4 3 2 1

To
Karin, Aviva, and Benjamin
with love

Contents

List of Figures

Preface

Financial Risk Management started as one thing and has ended as another. I took up this project with the primary aim of making risk measurement and management techniques accessible, by working through simple examples, and explaining some of the real-life detail of financing positions. I had gotten fairly far along with it when the subprime crisis began and the world changed.

I had already begun to appreciate the importance of liquidity and leverage risks, which are even harder to measure quantitatively than market and credit risks, and therefore all the more important in practice. In the subprime crisis, liquidity and leverage risks were dominant. Had the subprime crisis never occurred, they would have had an honorable place in this text. After the crisis erupted, it became hard to think about anything else. To understand why liquidity and leverage are so important, one needs to understand the basic market and credit risk models. But one also needs to understand the institutional structure of the financial system.

One aim of Financial Risk Management is therefore to bring together the model-oriented approach of the risk management discipline, as it has evolved over the past two decades, with economists' approaches to the same issues. There is much that quants and economists can learn from one another. One needs to understand how financial markets work to apply risk management techniques effectively.

A basic aim of the book is to provide some institutional and historical context for risk management issues. Wherever possible, I've provided readers with data from a variety of public- and private-sector sources, for the most part readily accessible by practitioners and students. One of the blessings of technology is the abundance of easily obtainable economic and financial data. The particular phenomena illustrated by the data in the figures are important, but even more so familiarity with data sources and the habit of checking impressions of how the world works against data.

Some themes are developed across several chapters, but can be read in sequence for a course or for individual study:

- Recent financial history, including postwar institutional changes in the financial system, developments in macroeconomic and regulatory policy, recent episodes of financial instability, and the global financial crisis are the focus of all or part of Chapters 1, 9, 11, 12, 14, and 15.
- Market risk is studied in Chapters 2 through 5 on basic risk models and applications. Chapter 7 discusses spread risk, which connects market and credit risks, Chapter 11 discusses model validation, and Chapters 12 through 15 discuss liquidity risk, risk capital, the behavior of asset returns during crises, and regulatory approaches to market risk.
- Credit risk is studied in Chapters 6 through 9, which present basic concepts and models of the credit risk of single exposures and credit portfolios, and in Chapters 11, 12, and 15, which study credit risk in the context of leverage, liquidity, systemic risk and financial crises.
- Structured credit products and their construction, risks, and valuation, are the focus of Chapter 9. Chapter 11 continues the discussion of structured credit risk, while Chapters, 12, 14, and 15 discuss the role of structured products in collateral markets and in financial system leverage.
- Risk management of options is developed in Chapters 4 and 5 in the context of nonlinear exposures and portfolio risk. Chapter 14 discusses the role of option risk management in periods of financial stress.
- Extraction of risk measures based on market prices, such as risk-neutral return and default probabilities and equity and credit implied correlations, is studied in Chapters 7, 9 and 10, and applied in Chapters 1, 11, and 14.

Financial Risk Management is intermediate in technical difficulty. It assumes a modicum, but not a great deal, of comfort with statistics and finance concepts. The book brings a considerable amount of economics into the discussion, so it will be helpful if students have taken an economics course.

Each chapter contains suggestions for further reading. Most of the texts cited provide alternative presentations or additional detail on the topics covered in *Financial Risk Management*. Some of them treat topics that couldn't be covered adequately in this book, or in some way take the story further. Others are suggested basic readings on statistics, finance, and economics.

I've had the good fortune of working with wonderful, smart people for the past quarter-century. The Federal Reserve System is home to some of the brightest and most hardworking people I've known, and the citizenry is lucky to have them in its employ. RiskMetrics Group was a unique company built on brains, quirkiness, and a sense of mission. Working at two hedge funds added considerably to my human capital as well as my life experience.

Many of my former colleagues, and others, made extremely helpful comments on early drafts. I thank Alan Adkins, Adam Ashcraft, Peter Benson, Harold Cline, Emanuel Derman, Christopher Finger, Alan Laubsch, Jorge Mina, Jonathan Reiss, Joshua Rosenberg, Peruvemba Satish, Barry Schachter, David Spring, Eugene Stern, Peter Went, and an anonymous reviewer. Students in my risk management course at Columbia asked many excellent questions. My editors at Wiley, Bill Falloon and Vincent Nordhaus, have been helpful in countless ways. I absolve them all of responsibility for the myriad errors that surely remain. I would also like to thank Karin Bruckner for designing the dust jacket, and for marrying me.

The views expressed in this book are entirely my own and are not necessarily reflective of views at the Federal Reserve Bank of New York or of the Federal Reserve System. Any errors or omissions are my responsibility.

Financial Risk Management

CHAPTER 1

Financial Risk in a Crisis-Prone World

R isk has become a focal point for anyone thinking about, or acting in, financial markets. The financial market crisis that began in 2007 confirmed the centrality of risk analysis in finance and in public policy vis-à-vis the financial markets. The crisis, which we'll refer to going forward as the "subprime crisis," will be the reference point for thinking about risk for decades to come.

The name itself is a bit of a misnomer for a crisis that now extends far beyond the subprime residential mortgage sector in the United States to the entire world and most sectors of the economy and financial system. It has highlighted grave shortcomings in public policy toward the economy, business and financial practices, and in previous analyses and prescriptions. It will be a recurrent and inescapable theme in this book.

In order to adequately analyze, or even describe, the subprime crisis, we need an analytical toolkit, which this textbook will provide. In this chapter, we survey the landscape of financial risk historically, sketch the financial world of our time, and provide an overview of different types of financial risk. We have two main objectives: to get a basic sense of the subject matter of financial risk analysis, and of the financial world in which we live and which market participants try to understand and influence. But a fuller description of the crisis itself will have to wait until later chapters.

1.1 SOME HISTORY: WHY IS RISK A SEPARATE DISCIPLINE TODAY?

To understand why risk management became a major focus in finance in the 1990s, we need to understand something of the history of the financial services industry during the preceding decades. We'll look at a few broad themes in this evolution, focusing on the United States, in which these changes have tended to occur earlier. But it is important to understand that the financial system evolved as a whole, and that these themes are analytical constructs meant to help us understand the financial system, not realities in their own right.

1.1.1 The Financial Industry Since the 1960s

Financial services firms engage primarily in originating or trading in financial instruments. They hold long and short positions in loans, securities, and other assets, either to trade or as an investment, though some financial service providers just provide advice, or facilitate trades without using their own balance sheets. These firms are often called *financial intermediaries*, since their primary role is to move funds from ultimate savers to ultimate investors. Over the past half-century, the financial services industry has undergone a large transformation from a bank-centered world to one in which credit is intermediated in a wide variety of ways. Because of these changes, the credit intermediation process has become decentralized and takes place in forms that can be hard to measure and understand. For this reason, particularly since the onset of the subprime crisis, observers have spoken of the emergence of a "shadow banking system."

Banking Since the 1960s: From Intermediation to Fees   At the core of this evolution lies the banking industry, which from the medieval era until just a few decades ago was by far the most important part of the financial services industry. Banks or *depository institutions*, in their classic form, take deposits and make loans, and profit from the spread between the higher lending interest rate and generally low deposit rates. Their risks are mainly those that arise from intermediating between short-term liabilities and longer-term assets. Banks have increasingly diversified their business away from the classic deposit-taking and lending function and engage in other activities from which they earn fees in addition to net interest. Often, these activities are carried out by subsidiaries within a holding company structure.

In 1960, banking was a heavily regulated industry focused on lending to nonfinancial corporations. Under the U.S. Glass-Steagall Act of 1933, *commercial banks* took deposits and made commercial loans, while *investment banks* bought and sold securities (the *broker-dealer* function) and helped companies issue stock and debt securities (the *underwriting* function).[1]

---

[1]This distinction was peculiar to the United States. In Europe, the universal bank model combined commercial and investment banking, as in the post–Glass-Steagall United States.

Large companies could borrow directly from commercial banks through commercial and industrial (C&I) loans (and to a smaller extent insurance companies), or directly from the public through bond and commercial paper issues. Smaller companies usually had no alternative to C&I loans.

One way to compare the different types of risks to which commercial and investment banks are exposed is by looking at the typical structure of their balance sheets. Commercial banks specialized in maturity intermediation between deposits, which are very short-term loans, and C&I loans, which are generally medium- to long-term. Hence, they were fragile, since depositors could demand the return of their money, while the corporate borrower was generally neither obligated nor able to unwind projects and turn invested capital back into cash nearly fast enough to meet the demand. In the extreme, banks could suffer bank runs that potentially ended their existence. In the 1960s, banking was nonetheless considered a simple business, often and probably unfairly described by the "3-6-3 rule": Pay depositors 3 percent, lend at 6 percent, and be on the golf course by 3 P.M.

Investment banks had very different balance sheets. They, too, had plenty of short-term debt, but their assets were inventories of securities, most of them quite liquid. They were capitalized and regulated to be unwound quickly in the event of financial distress. As discussed in Chapter 12, the balance sheets of both commercial and investment banks changed drastically over the past few decades in ways that led to greater risk. There was a degree of convergence between the two types of firms, although they remained under distinct legal and regulatory regimes. Banks began to hold *trading books* of securities and loans held for potential sale, in addition to their traditional *banking books* of commercial and mortgage whole loans that were presumed to be held until repayment. Broker-dealers began to hold less liquid securities in their inventories.

Figure 1.1 illustrates these changes by tracing bond issuance and bank borrowing by U.S. companies over the past half-century. Nonfinancial corporations have always had sources of lending, such as trade receivables, commercial paper, and mortgages, apart from the capital markets and bank loans. Even before the capital market expansion of the 1980s, nonfinancial firms relied on bank loans for only 15 to 20 percent of their debt funding, and company debt via bond issuance was generally about one-and-a-half times to twice as large as bank debt. The creation of the *high-yield* or *junk bond market* opened a new channel for borrowing directly from investors, which we describe presently. The share of bank lending has declined to under 5 percent, with the ratio of bonds to bank loans increasing steadily to over 5-to-1.

Since 2005, and during the subprime crisis, bank lending has had a fleeting revival, due to increased bank lending to private equity firms buying

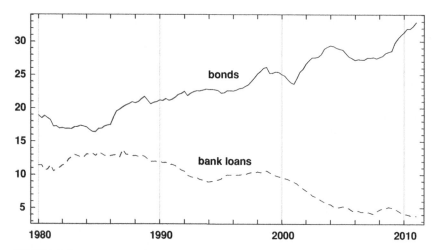

FIGURE 1.1   Disintermediation in the U.S. Financial System 1980–2010
The graph plots the shares, in percent, quarterly through end-2010, of borrowing
via the corporate bond market and of nonmortgage borrowing from banks in total
liabilities of U.S. nonfarm nonfinancial corporations. Bank lending is comprised
mostly of commercial and industrial loans (C&I loans).
Source: Federal Reserve Board, Flow of Funds Accounts of the United States (Z.1),
Table L.102.

public companies as well as increased borrowing by smaller companies directly from banks. However, most of this debt was distributed to investors
outside the originating bank. Large bank loans trade somewhat like corporate bonds in secondary markets and differ primarily in having, in most
cases, a claim prior to bonds on the assets of the firm in the event of default.

The role of finance in the economy has grown substantially in the
postwar era and especially during recent years. Figure 1.2 displays the share
of the financial services industry in U.S. gross domestic product (GDP) since
1947. During that time, it has grown from about 2.3 to about 8 percent of
output, with the most rapid growth occurring between 1980 and 2000. The
finance share has fallen a bit in the most recent data, and may fall further
as the subprime crisis plays out and intermediaries fail or merge.

Another viewpoint on the magnitude of finance's role in the economy
comes from estimates of the cost of financial intermediation. According to
John Bogle, who developed low-cost index mutual funds in the 1970s, the
aggregate cost of intermediation rose 20-fold.[2]

---

[2]See Bogle (2008), p. 36.

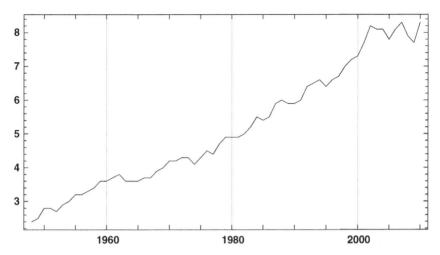

FIGURE 1.2 Share of Financial Services Industry in U.S. Output 1947–2009
Share of value added in GDP of the finance and insurance industry, as defined by
the North American Industrial Classification System (NAICS), annual, in percent.
Source: Bureau of Economic Analysis of the U.S. Department of Commerce, U.S.
Economic Accounts Data, Gross-Domestic-Product-(GDP)-by-Industry Data,
available at www.bea.gov/industry/gdpbyind_data.htm.

Financial Innovation   Financial innovation describes the introduction and
wide use of new types of financial instruments. These innovations have been
made possible by general technical progress in the economy, particularly
the radical cheapening of communication, computation, and data storage.
These factors have interacted with technical progress in finance, primarily
the invention of new types of securities.

The wave of innovation began at a relatively slow pace in the 1960s
in the money markets, with the introduction of negotiable certificates of
deposit (CDs). There had long been time deposits, bank deposits repaid to
the depositor at the end of a fixed interval rather than on demand, but
negotiable CDs could be sold prior to maturity at a market-adjusted interest
rate in a secondary market, rather than "broken," at a cost.

Financial innovation also affected retail and private investors directly.
Investment companies such as *mutual funds* and *hedge funds* pool investments and make shares in the pools available to the public. In contrast to
other institutional investors, their capital is placed directly with them by the
public. Mutual funds are an old form of investment vehicle, dating back in
various forms to the nineteenth century. In the United States, most mutual
funds are organized and regulated under the Investment Company Act of

1940 (the "1940 Act"), which restricts both what mutual funds may invest in and how they advertise. They experienced tremendous growth over the past quarter-century. Their growth was driven mainly by wealth accumulation, but also by the introduction of *index funds*, funds that track securities indexes such as the S&P 500 and permit even small investors to have diversified investment portfolios and reduce risk with low transaction costs.

A new form of mutual fund, the *exchange-traded fund* (ETF), was introduced in 1993; the first was the SPDR traded on the American Stock Exchange. An ETF tracks a well-defined index, like many mutual funds, but can be traded intraday, in contrast to a mutual fund, which can only trade at its end-of-day *net asset value* (NAV). To gain this ability, certain institutional investors are tasked with creating and unwinding unit of the ETF from the index constituents.

We focused in our discussion of disintermediation on the ability of public markets to compete with banks' lending activity. But banks have another important function, called *liquidity transformation*, of providing liquid means of payment to the public. Their lending function is to own a certain type of asset, classically C&I loans and real estate loans. Their liquidity function is to provide a certain type of liability, namely *demand deposits*.

Just as access to the public capital markets and other forms of credit intermediation have reduced banks' intermediation share, a new type of liquid means of payment, money market mutual funds (MMMFs), have reduced banks' role in providing the public with means of payment. The first MMMF was introduced in 1972 and they have grown rapidly over the past three decades. Competition from MMMFs obliged the Federal Reserve to completely remove limits on interest paid by banks on demand deposits in the 1980. Although they were initially conceived as a product for retail investors, institutional investors now account for over two-thirds of MMMF assets and their behavior plays the decisive role in the stability of MMMFs in stress periods. MMMFs have been crucial purchasers of the liabilities of the shadow banking system, providing its necessary link to the public's demand for liquidity. We discuss securitization and related financial innovations in Chapters 9 and 12, and discuss the role these structures played during the subprime crisis in Chapter 14. These innovations played an important role in the transformation of banking by creating alternatives for depositors and thus reducing the extent to which banks could rely on a quiescent deposit base for funding. But it also created new loci for instability in stress periods.

The other major innovations of the 1970s and 1980s were in derivatives markets, especially the introduction of swaps and the expansion of futures and options trading. A *derivative security* or *contract* is one whose payoff is entirely determined by the values or payoffs of some other security; as the price of the underlying asset or risk factors change, the value of a derivative on the asset changes. The security that drives the derivative's payoffs is called the *underlying*.

The first swaps were *currency swaps*, introduced in the mid-1970s. In 1981, a transaction said to be the first *interest-rate swap* was concluded between IBM Corp. and the World Bank.

Forwards are an old market mechanism that has been in use in some form for many centuries. Futures markets date to the post–Civil War era in the United States, when the first agricultural futures began trading in Chicago. The breakdown of the Bretton Woods system of fixed exchange rates created demand for currency risk management tools; the first financial—as opposed to commodities—futures were on currencies, introduced in 1972.

The expansion of options markets was unusual in that it was facilitated enormously by an innovation in finance theory, the development of the *Black-Scholes-Merton option pricing model*. The first exchange-traded options were introduced in 1973.

In the early to mid-1980s, a major focus of financial innovation was on *exotic options*. Variants such as *barrier options*, which pay off only if a threshold value is attained by the underlying asset price, were introduced. But exotic options have never become as widely used as the banking industry hoped.

We've mentioned the growth in issuance of high-yield bonds. "Speculative-grade" or high-yield bonds had existed for many years prior to the 1980s. But they were typically "fallen angels," formerly investment-grade bonds issued by companies that had become financially weak. The innovation was to enable small or financially weaker firms to issue new high-yield bonds. Many of these firms had previously been unable to borrow in capital markets at all. The growth in the high-yield market was supported by the easing of certain restrictions on securities firm activities, which we describe later in this chapter.

Another innovation of the 1970s was the *securitization* of mortgage loans. Bonds collateralized by real estate had existed at least since 1770, when the first precursor of the German *Pfandbriefbanken* was organized in Silesia as a Seven Years' War reconstruction measure. In these *covered bonds*, a single bond is collateralized by the value of a pool of real estate loans. In 1970, the first *pass-through certificates* were issued by the Government National Mortgage Association (GNMA, also known as "Ginnie Mae"), a federally owned housing-finance company. These went beyond merely collateralizing the bond issue; the cash flows to the pass-through bondholders are, apart from fees and other costs, those actually generated by the mortgage collateral.

Since a mortgage borrower in the United States generally must amortize a loan, and always has the option to repay the loan early, pass-throughs are partially redeemed or "factored down" as the loans are repaid. Homeowners are particularly apt to prepay when interest rates decline, as they can then refinance and reduce their monthly payments. Pass-through investors therefore face *prepayment risk*, the risk of a capital loss resulting from losing a higher-coupon cash flow in a lower-yield environment.

These bonds were among the earliest *mortgage-backed securities* (MBS). The next step in the evolution of securitization was the issuance of the first *collateralized mortgage obligation* (CMO) in 1983. The essentials of later securitization innovations were all here: The collateral was placed in a trust, and the cash flows were distributed to three different bond classes, called *tranches*, under the terms of a structure. A *sequential-pay structure* was used in this and other early CMOs: After coupon payments, all prepayment cash flows went to the first tranche until it was fully redeemed, then to the second tranche, and finally to the third.

Other changes involved, not new security types, but changes in market lending practices. For example, lending via *repurchase agreements* or "repo," a form of secured credit, had historically been limited to government bond markets. From the 1990s, repo was increasingly used to finance mortgage bond positions. We discuss these developments in detail in Chapter 12.

Major changes also took place in trading technology. A *securities exchange* is an organized locus of securities trading to which only exchange members have direct trading access. Exchanges are an old institution, dating back to the early seventeenth century in the Low Countries. Initially, only underlying assets were traded on exchanges. Exchanges now include futures, options, and other derivatives. Until relatively recently, traders had to be physically present at the exchange's location. With the improvement of communication and computing technology, *electronic trading* has become the dominant form of trading on exchanges. Electronic trading has made transacting far cheaper, but has also introduced new complexities into markets.

Trading can also take place outside of exchanges, in *over-the-counter* (OTC) markets. For some asset, such as U.S. government and corporate bonds, real estate, as well as many types of derivatives, OTC trading is typical. Large volumes of electronic trading also take place in OTC markets. The differences between exchange-traded and OTC markets are important in understanding liquidity risk, discussed in Chapter 12. Swaps and other OTC derivatives have grown enormously in size: The Bank for International Settlements (BIS) has collected data on OTC derivatives since 1998 (see Figure 1.3).

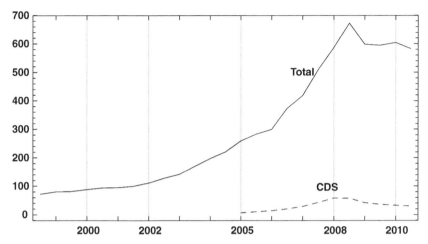

FIGURE 1.3   OTC Derivatives Markets 1998–2010
The solid line plots the total for all derivatives types; the dashed line displays the volume of CDS. Notional amounts outstanding, G10 countries including Switzerland, trillions of U.S. dollars, semiannual through June 2010.
Source: BIS, Semiannual Over-The-Counter (OTC) Derivatives Markets Statistics, Table 19, downloaded at www.bis.org/statistics/derstats.htm.

1.1.2   The "Shadow Banking System"

The combination of disintermediation on the part of banks and financial innovation has given rise to what is sometimes called the "shadow banking system." The term means that intermediation between savers and borrowers occurs largely outside of the classic banking system, at least in the traditional sense of banks owning, servicing, and monitoring loans until maturity or default. But it is also meant to convey that the channels of credit intermediation and the exposures of participants in the intermediation process are difficult to identify and measure. The more neutral terms "market-based" and "arm's-length" lending are also commonly used to describe innovative forms of credit in which much of the risk is taken by nonbank financial firms in the form of tradable assets.

We have already seen one important aspect of disintermediation, the substitution of financing via the capital markets for financing via bank loans. The shadow banking system amplified the disintermediation of traditional bank lending to firms and individuals, but also extended it to new types of lending such as subprime mortgages. Most importantly, as the subprime crisis deepened, it became clear that the shadow banking system had obscured both the poor credit quality of much recently originated debt, and the extensive borrowing or *leverage* of some market participants. The financial fragility induced by this leverage did not become apparent until the assets began to evidence credit deterioration.

The shadow banking system has its origins in the 1960s, but did not come fully to fruition until just before the subprime crisis. Much of it is being dismantled, or at least has been frozen, during the crisis. Several interrelated financial innovations fostered its development:

Securitization enables more credit risk to be taken outside the banking system. We discuss securitization in Chapter 9.

Markets for collateral gave additional economic value to securitized products. The securities not only paid a coupon financed by the underlying loans, but could also be pledged by the bondholders to themselves obtain credit. We describe these markets in detail in Chapter 12.

Off-balance-sheet vehicles permit financial institutions to take on more risk while remaining within regulatory capital rules.

Money market mutual funds are important lenders in the short-term credit markets. An MMMF invests in a wide range of short-term assets, including some with material market and credit risk, and provides checkable accounts to investors.

Risk transfer via credit derivatives has led to the replacement of *funding* by *guarantees*. This permits banks and other institutions to move their risks off their balance sheets. This does not necessarily reduce the risks, but potentially makes them more difficult to identify and measure.

Up until the mid-1980s, securitizations were focused primarily on residential mortgages guaranteed by one of the federal housing finance agencies. Repayment of the loans was guaranteed by the U.S. government, so the securities exposed investors mainly to interest rate risk, but in some cases a great deal of it and in complex, option-like forms. In the late 1980s, *asset-backed securities* (ABS) were introduced, in which bonds were issued that distributed cash flows and credit losses from a pool of non-mortgage loans in order of bond seniority. Initially, bonds were issued against collateral pools containing credit card debt and auto loans. The idea was later extended to student loans, leases, loans to auto, equipment, and truck dealers, and a wide variety of other debt types.

In the 1990s, the introduction of credit derivatives made possible new types of securitized products. The most widely used credit derivative, the *credit default swap* (CDS), was introduced in the early 1990s. CDS are important in many ways: as widely used derivatives, in their capacity as a rich source of data on market perceptions of credit risk, and because of the operational and systemic risk issues their rapid growth has raised. Figure 1.3 displays the BIS data on the size of the CDS market, which remains small by comparison with the staggering size of the overall OTC derivatives market. We discuss CDS further in Section 7.3.

The CMO idea was extended to collateral types other than mortgages with the introduction of the *collateralized debt obligation* (CDO). The collateral pool could now contain just about any asset with a cash flow, including securitizations and credit derivatives. In 1997, J.P. Morgan created a security called the Broad Index Secured Trust Offering (BISTRO), in which credit derivatives were used to achieve the economic effects of moving underlying collateral off the bank's balance sheet. BISTRO is regarded as the first *synthetic CDO*.

Traditional accounting rules found it hard to accommodate these innovations. Were options an "asset," and should they be placed on the firm's balance sheet? Similar questions arose around banks' and brokerages' responsibility for the securitizations they originated. In addition to derivatives, a growing portion of the universe of investment objects were off-balance-sheet securities.

The shadow banking system fostered the growth of yet another "old-new" institution, *specialty finance companies*. They make a wide variety of loans, primarily to businesses. The companies exist because their parent firms are considered highly creditworthy and can borrow at relatively low interest rates in capital markets, or because they sold the loans they made into securitizations (the *originate-to-distribute* business model). This access to relatively inexpensive funding gives them a competitive advantage as lenders. Among the largest such firms is GE Capital, the lending arm of industrial firm General Electric, CIT Group, and General Motors Acceptance Corp. (GMAC); only the first-named has survived the subprime crisis in its original form.

These financial innovations amplified the disintermediation of the banking system. We have already seen how the share of banking was reduced by the growing importance of capital markets in providing credit. The shadow banking system was also responsible for an increasing share of intermediation over the past quarter-century. Figure 1.4 displays the shares of credit market assets (that is, liabilities of others as opposed to buildings and copy machines) held by different types of institutions and investors. The shares of traditional intermediaries—banks, insurance companies, and retirement funds—have declined over the past three decades, while the shares of new types of intermediaries have risen.

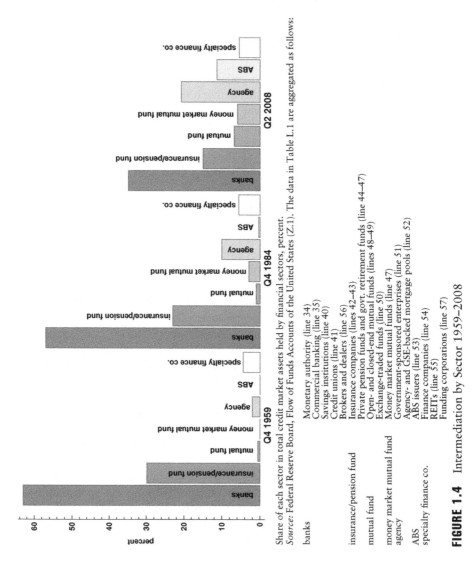

Share of each sector in total credit market assets held by financial sectors, percent.
Source: Federal Reserve Board, Flow of Funds Accounts of the United States (Z.1). The data in Table L.1 are aggregated as follows:

banks	Monetary authority (line 34) Commercial banking (line 35) Savings institutions (line 40) Credit unions (line 41) Brokers and dealers (line 56)
insurance/pension fund	Insurance companies (lines 42–43) Private pension funds and govt. retirement funds (line 44–47)
mutual fund	Open- and closed-end mutual funds (lines 48–49) Exchange-traded funds (line 50)
money market mutual fund	Money market mutual funds (line 47)
agency	Government-sponsored enterprises (line 51) Agency- and GSE-backed mortgage pools (line 52)
ABS	ABS issuers (line 53)
specialty finance co.	Finance companies (line 54) REITs (line 55) Funding corporations (line 57)

FIGURE 1.4 Intermediation by Sector 1959–2008

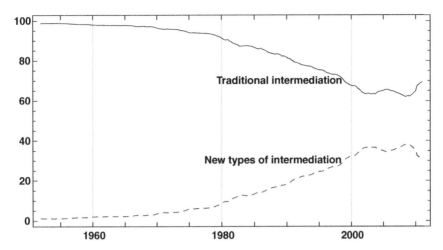

FIGURE 1.5   Traditional and Innovative Intermediation 1951–2010
Shares of traditional and innovative intermediation in total credit market assets
held by financial sectors, quarterly, percent.
The sectors displayed in Figure 1.4 are aggregated as follows: "Traditional
intermediation" includes "banks," "insurance/pension fund," "mutual fund," and
"specialty finance co." "New types of intermediation" includes "money market
mutual fund," "agency," and "ABS."
Source: Federal Reserve Board, Flow of Funds Accounts of the United States (Z.1).

Of particular note are the proportions of intermediation accounted
for by money market mutual funds, by mortgage debt intermediated by
government-sponsored enterprises, and by ABS. These sectors together had
a share in intermediation of less than 9 percent at the end of the 1970s; their
share had risen to over 37 percent by the end of 2007.

Between 1980 and 2007, as the "innovative" sectors of the financial
system, including those at the center of the shadow banking system, grew to
nearly 40 percent of total intermediation, traditional intermediation shrank
to just over 60 percent. The broader trend can be seen in Figure 1.5.

The introduction of *commercial mortgage-backed securities* (CMBS)
around 1990 as a new source of funding for commercial real estate is a good
example of the impact innovation had on a particular sector of the financial
system. These are a type of securitized credit product in which commercial
real estate loans used to finance the purchase or development of commercial
properties, such as apartment and office buildings, retail shopping malls,
hotels, and industrial developments are pooled, and bonds backed by the
loans are sold to investors. They are much like mortgage-backed securities,

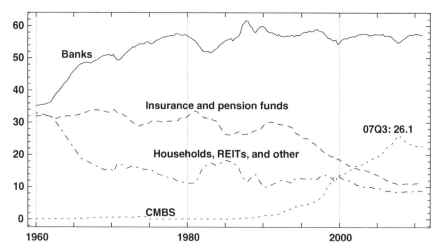

FIGURE 1.6   Financing of Commercial Real Estate Lending 1960–2010
Shares of total commercial real estate lending loans held by financial sectors,
quarterly, percent.
Banks include commercial banks and savings institutions. Institutional investors
include insurance companies and pension funds. Other includes finance companies.
Source: Federal Reserve Board, Flow of Funds Accounts of the United States (Z.1),
Table L.220.

except that the typical residential mortgage loan is much smaller than the
typical commercial real estate loan. A CMBS therefore generally has far
fewer loans in the pools supporting the bonds, at most a few hundred,
compared to MBS, in which the collateral pool of a large deal can contain
many thousands of residential mortgage loans.

Figure 1.6 displays the sources of funding for commercial real estate
loans over the past 60 years. In the middle of the twentieth century,
the main sources of funds were about evenly divided between banks, insurance companies, and other sources such as wealthy households. Over
time, the latter became less important as a source, while banks became more
important, so that by the late 1980s, banks were the source of about 60 percent of commercial real estate lending. In part, banks were making up for
the slowing of growth in more traditional C&I lending to companies.

The volume of CMBS grew rapidly throughout the 1990s and until the subprime crisis, reaching a share of 26 percent of total commercial real estate lending in mid-2007. The share of banks remained high,
while the share of insurance companies and other institutional investors
as direct lenders continued to decline. Instead, they became large investors
in CMBS.

1.1.3 Changes in Public Policy Toward the Financial System

Beginning in the 1970s, public policy toward the financial system changed in may ways. These changes are often summarized, somewhat misleadingly, as "deregulation." But they were less a deliberate attempt to give market forces a greater role in the financial system than part of the process of adapting to the broader changes taking place in the financial world. Changes in regulation often occurred in response to short-term financial stresses and had long-term consequences that were quite different from those intended. We discuss approaches to and techniques of financial regulation in more detail in Chapter 15.

Geographical Segregation within and Across National Borders   In the United States, until 1994, a bank chartered in one state could not open branches in another, and in some states, under *unit banking*, could not open multiple branches even within a state. Interstate branching was permitted by the Riegle–Neal Interstate Banking and Branching Efficiency Act of 1994.

In international finance, capital controls, which we describe in more detail in a moment, kept residents of many countries from investing in foreign securities or holding foreign exchange. Capital controls were lifted by many countries beginning in the 1970s.

Removal of Price and Interest Rate Controls   Historically, interest rates and prices of financial services have often been capped. In the United States, the trend toward lifting these restrictions began in 1970 with the lifting of limits on certain U.S. deposit interest rates that had been capped under Regulation Q since 1933. The remaining caps were gradually removed by the Monetary Control Act of 1980.

In the brokerage industry, fixed commissions for stock trades on the New York Stock Exchange were abolished in 1975. Other countries followed, such as the United Kingdom with its "Big Bang" reform of 1986.

Limits on foreign exchange rates have been the most persistent area of price control. Fixed foreign exchange rates are different from other price controls. The exchange rate can be seen not only as the price, say, of an asset called "U.S. dollars." It is also the relative price of the locally issued money in terms of dollars. A fixed exchange rate vis-à-vis the dollar can serve as a key mechanism by which a central bank controls money and credit.

In order to maintain fixed exchange rates, most countries imposed controls on international flows of capital. Examples of such controls are prohibitions or controls on capital imports and exports, that is, investments abroad by domestic residents and domestically by foreign residents, and a public monopoly of the right to conduct foreign exchange transactions. Early financial innovations, such as the development of swap markets, were in part adaptations by market participants to these controls.

Fixed foreign exchange rates between major currencies ended in the mid-1970s (see Chapter 14). Within Europe, many important exchange rates remained fixed, or pegged within narrow limits, until they were merged into one currency, with one central bank, in the European Monetary Union.

Competition Between Types of Financial Intermediaries More competition between different types of financial market participants was permitted, loosening the division of labor among them. A milestone was the Depository Institutions Deregulation and Monetary Control Act of 1980, which permitted savings and loan associations to provide checking accounts like those of commercial banks.

Underwriting, or arranging issues of bonds for corporate and other capital markets borrowers, had been carried out by only a small number of firms prior to the 1970s. It was typically slow and expensive, due in part to the elaborate *registration* process by which information about securities was conveyed to the public. In a more highly regulated financial system, most bonds are permitted to be traded in public markets. *Public securities* are subject to many rules, especially regarding disclosure of information about the issuer and its financial condition, and to restrictions on who may invest in them and how they may be traded. *Private securities* are subject to fewer disclosure requirements, but to more restrictions on trading and ownership.

Two regulatory innovations eased registration requirements and contributed to the massive expansion in both the fixed-income and equity markets that began in the 1980s:

Shelf registration enabled underwriters to bring issues to market more rapidly, and introduced "economies of scale" into the process by which one issuer could issue a number of bonds over time without repeating all steps in the registration process. Shelf registration proved particularly important in the development of the securitization markets.

Rule 144a introduced the notion of a private security with lower disclosure requirements. Rule 144a issues could be sold to and traded only among *qualified institutional buyers*, essentially institutional investors.

Broker-dealers, in contrast to banks, buy and sell securities. Their risks are primarily those arising from holding inventories of securities. They are designed to be less fragile, since they can be wound down and liquidated by selling off inventories of stocks and bonds, rather than hard-to-sell loans to businesses and individuals. When broker-dealers fail, a smaller potential for problems to spread to the broader financial system is expected than when banks fail.

This presumption about the differences in the public policy issues raised by broker-dealers was shockingly violated during the subprime crisis. A number of large financial institutions failed, but among them were two of the largest U.S. broker-dealers, Bear Stearns and Lehman Brothers. Bear Stearns was not obliged to file for bankruptcy and liquidate; Lehman was. In subsequent chapters, we study the reasons for the breakdown of the presumption that broker-dealers can "fail quietly."

The paradigmatic restriction on competition between banks and broker-dealers, the Glass-Steagall Act, was rolled back in stages, culminating in the Gramm-Leach-Bliley Financial Services Modernization Act of 1999. These regulatory changes interacted with the development of nonbank intermediation to change the competitive landscape in financial services. For example, nonbank lenders became important in the origination of mortgage loans. Subsidiaries of insurance companies called *monoline insurers* became credit guarantors of asset-backed and municipal bonds.

1.1.4 The Rise of Large Capital Pools

As wealth grew during the postwar era, increasing quantities of capital became available to take advantage of investment opportunities. Most of this new capital flowed into traditional repositories such as pension funds and insurance companies. Public and private occupational pension funds receive "contributions," that is, savings by individuals or by companies, trade unions, or the public sector on their behalf, and invest them. These investments can be managed directly by the firm or other entity that sponsors the plan, or by outside managers hired by the sponsor. Insurance companies insure property against damage or loss, and families against loss of a major source of income. Insurers must deal with the nonfinancial risks of losses on policies they issue, and also face financial risk on the investments they make with their insurance reserves. Capital also flowed into "old-new" vehicles such as mutual funds.

In the 1980s, two new types of investment fund became much more significant, hedge funds and sovereign wealth funds. *Hedge funds* are a loosely defined group of investment companies that are distinguished by restrictions on who can invest in them. In general, they are open only to other institutional investors and wealthy individuals. Because the fund is not open to the general public, it is not subject to many of the restrictions on investment style and technique constraining publicly offered mutual funds or pension funds under the 1940 Act. Such constraints include the ability to trade derivatives, take short positions, and use leverage. This permits hedge funds to take different risks from other fund types and to engage in strategies that cannot be carried out at all without these tools.

A hedge fund is essentially a set of accounts that deploys capital received from investors. Hedge funds are often organized in an onshore-offshore structure, in which paired accounts have nearly identical investments. The offshore account is organized as a corporation and domiciled in a country that does not tax trading profits. The investors are then responsible for paying taxes where they reside. The onshore account, typically organized as a limited partnership, is domiciled onshore. Its investors are entities such as pension funds that are not obliged to pay profit taxes. Both accounts are managed in parallel by a hedge fund management company, which employs the portfolio managers, makes the investment decisions, and receives management fees.

Hedge funds are an old form of investment company, dating back (at least anecdotally) to the late 1940s. But they have increased quite rapidly, in both numbers and assets under management, over the past two decades. According to Hedge Fund Research, Inc. (HFR), there were 610 hedge funds in 1992; that number grew to 10,096 at its peak in 2007, just before the subprime crisis. Figure 1.7 displays HFR's estimates of assets under management by hedge funds, which have reached nearly $2 trillion. At these levels,

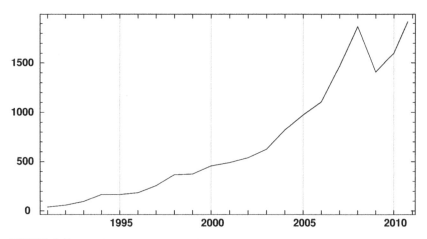

FIGURE 1.7 Hedge Fund Assets under Management 1992–2010
Estimated assets of the hedge fund industry, annual.
Source: HFR.

hedge fund assets have become comparable in volume to international reserves.

The data in Figure 1.7 represent the capital or equity placed with hedge funds by investors. As we see in Chapter 12, market participants can use derivatives, short positions, and leverage to greatly magnify the potential risks as well as returns on investors' capital. The direct impact of hedge funds' trading on particular financial markets at particular times can therefore be quite intense. Examples of the strategies used by hedge funds include:

> *Equity long-short trading* involves taking long positions in equities that are expected to outperform the stock market as a whole and selling other equities that are expected to underperform. The portfolio then has little overall exposure to the stock market. If the manager is correct in his forecasts, the portfolio will outperform the market.

> *Convertible bond arbitrage* exploits the persistent gaps between the values of *convertible bonds*, bonds that can be converted into equity, and other securities that, when assembled into a portfolio in the right proportions, approximately replicate the exposures embedded in the convertible.

> *Statistical arbitrage* is an "advanced" form of the equity long-short strategy. It uses a combination of technology and valuation and risk models to take advantage of small, high-frequency, transitory gaps between current and forecast values of equities. It usually is carried out using frequent, automated trades, and short holding periods, and can rapidly switch from long to short positions in the same stock.

Investment companies are closely related, but not identical, to *financial advisors*, who only provide advice and don't offer investments. Typically, a large firm operating mutual or hedge funds is an advisor, but the funds are invested in accounts which are some form of investment company. The asset-management divisions of large banks act as advisors, but generally also operate investment companies.

Another important form of capital pool are *private equity funds*. These are similar to hedge funds in some respects; the funds are raised from institutional investors and wealthy individuals, they take the legal form of limited partnerships, and the funds are managed by specialized management companies, the private equity firms. They differ, however, in that they have a fixed size of committed funds, and a fixed duration, usually 10 years, prior to which investors cannot withdraw funding, and at the end of which the capital and profits are to be distributed to the investors. Private equity funds generally specialize in *leveraged buyouts* (LBOs), in which the fund buys all the stock of a company, "taking it private," operates and restructures the acquisition, and reintroduces the company to the public markets some years later, usually via an *initial public offering* (IPO). LBOs derive their name from the typical practice of financing the acquisition largely through borrowed funds.

Sovereign wealth funds (SWFs) are a byproduct of the large postwar international capital flows in which a number of countries invest at least part of their international reserves. As with hedge funds, there is no universally agreed-upon definition of a SWF. They are typically owned and managed by a sovereign, separately from its currency reserves, and in a risk-seeking style similar to that of a private asset pool. The International Monetary Fund (IMF) has estimated the aggregate size of SWFs as of 2008 at between $2.1 and 3.0 trillion. This compares to about $1.5 trillion in hedge fund assets and $4.5 trillion in international reserves (the latter figure intersecting to some extent with SWF assets).

1.1.5   Macroeconomic Developments Since the 1960s: From the Unraveling of Bretton Woods to the Great Moderation

Increases in Wealth and Income   We've discussed changes in the financial markets over the past half-century. These changes are one aspect of vast changes in the world economy, particularly the growth of incomes and wealth in most parts of the world.

Measuring world income growth is hard, and any estimates are rough at best. Two efforts to do so are Angus Maddison's, conducted under the auspices of the Organization for Economic Development and Cooperation (OECD), and the Penn World Table. Maddison's data on per capita world output, astoundingly, cover the past 2,000 years, with annual data since 1950. Overall, the world today enjoys far higher income than a half century ago; the average annual compounded growth rate from 1950 to 2008 has been 2.2 percent, that is, average per capita income in 2008 was over $3\frac{1}{2}$ times its level of 1950 (see Figure 1.8). The most rapid growth occurred in the quarter-century following the end of World War II, and the decade preceding the subprime crisis.

This aggregate growth figure conceals huge, but declining, regional disparities, with East Asia, Western Europe, and North America at the higher end of the income growth distribution, and Africa at the other end. Income disparity has increased within many countries, but overall world income

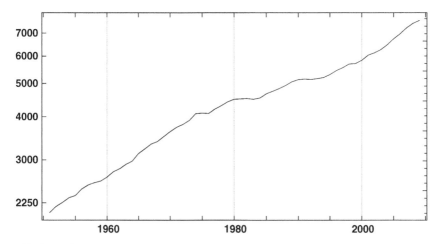

FIGURE 1.8 Growth of World Income 1950–2008
The graph displays the logarithm of world per capita income, annually. Although the graph is on a logarithmic scale, the vertical axis tick labels are in 1990 U.S. dollars.
Source: Statistics on World Population, GDP and Per Capita GDP, 1-2008 AD (Angus Maddison).

disparity has been driven lower by the large increase in incomes of large countries such as China and India.[3]

Along with incomes, international trade and capital flows have increased dramatically over the past half-century. Trade has increased because income and output have increased, and because the international division of labor has intensified. Trade barriers were lowered under the General Agreement on Tariffs and Trade (1947–1995) and its successor the World Trade Organization (since 1995). These efforts have endeavored to replace bilateral trade agreements, which tend to discriminate against third world countries and therefore create smaller gains from trade, with multilateral ones.

Figure 1.9 displays one measure of the increasing volume of international trade since 1971. The average growth rate has been just over 6 percent per annum, but with the onset of the subprime crisis, there was an unprecedented drop of nearly 12 percent in 2009.

Progress in communication and information technology have been an important part of income growth. Technical progress has been one of the

---

[3]Maddison's data is available at www.ggdc.net/maddison/. The Penn World Table data is available at http://pwt.econ.upenn.edu/php_site/pwt_index.php.

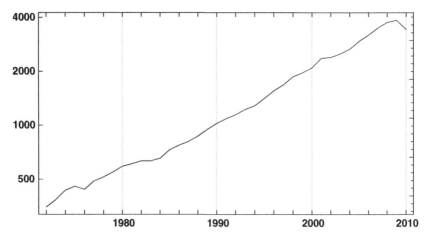

FIGURE 1.9   Growth of World International Trade 1971–2009
Annual volume of world trade in goods and services, calculated as an arithmetic average of the volume of world imports and exports, in billions of 2005 U.S. dollars. The graph is plotted on a logarithmic scale, but vertical axis tick labels are expressed as levels.
Source: Organisation for Economic Co-operation and Development (OECD), International Trade (Main Economic Indicators).

enabling factors in financial innovation, and has probably also been an important factor in the past 15 years' increase in productivity, illustrated for the United States in Figure 1.10. Two periods of high productivity growth, well over $2\frac{1}{2}$ percent per annum, were separated by the period 1973–1995, during which output per hour grew by less than $1\frac{1}{2}$ percent.

Wealth accumulation has increased as a consequence of rising incomes. Ownership of more assets by households has been accompanied, at least in developed countries, by more widespread ownership of financial assets as well as residential real estate (see, for example, Figure 15.1).

The Keynesian Moment and the Stagflation Crisis   Economic policy in the early postwar period centered on high employment and economic growth in the United States, and on reconstruction and recovery in Europe. Macro-economic policy was informed by the view that there was a stable trade-off, called the *Phillips curve*, between the two. Inflation was a secondary concern. The United States and Europe enjoyed both rapid growth and low inflation in the first two postwar decades, a time of high confidence in the ability of policy makers to "fine-tune" economic policy to achieve multiple goals.

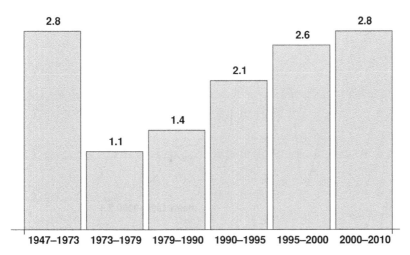

FIGURE 1.10 U.S. Labor Productivity 1947–2010
Nonfarm business sector labor productivity (output per hour), average percent
change at an annual rate.
Source: U.S. Bureau of Labor Statistics, http://www.bls.gov/lpc/prodybar.htm.

The framework for international economic policy was the Bretton
Woods system, under which the U.S. dollar served as the linchpin of a
system of fixed exchange rates and rules for addressing international financial flows. In such a system, only the United States could conduct a truly
independent monetary policy.

Doubts about this framework grew in response to two disturbing phenomena that grew into a crisis in the 1970s:

- U.S. inflation rates were gradually rising and by the early 1970s had
  reached alarming levels. As seen in Figure 1.11, U.S. inflation rose
  from 1.2 percent in 1965 to 6.3 percent in 1970, eventually peaking at
  12.4 percent in 1980.
- The United States was also running growing trade deficits and capital
  outflows that made it increasingly difficult to maintain fixed exchange
  rates. During the 1960s, these outflows had been a minor blot on the pic-
  ture of macroeconomic policy success, rather than a center of concern.
  By the 1970s, the deficits had become a full-blown crisis.

In a sequence of increasingly radical steps beginning in 1968 and culminating in March 1973, when it permitted the dollar to float against other
major currencies, the United States led the way in dismantling the Bretton
Woods system. The European Common Market countries immediately

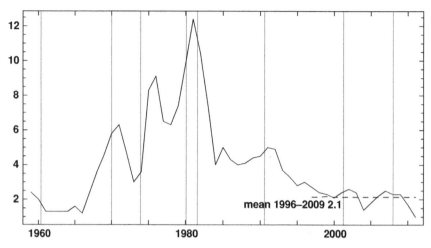

FIGURE 1.11   U.S. Inflation 1958–2010
Annual percent change in the consumer price index—all urban consumers (CPI-U),
all items less food and energy. Vertical grid lines represent the dates of NBER
business cycle peaks.
Source: U.S. Bureau of Labor Statistics, series CUUR0000SA0L1E.

introduced measures to limit foreign exchange rate fluctuations between
their currencies. The Common Market evolved into the European Union, and
its efforts to "peg" European currencies to one another eventually evolved
into a single currency, the euro, introduced in 1998. The currency crises that
beset this evolution are described in Chapter 14.

The major industrial countries have from time to time intervened in
currency markets by buying or selling dollars against other currencies to
counteract volatility or exchange rate levels that were perceived as unacceptable, hence the name *managed floating* for the exchange-rate system,
such as it is, today. The U.S. dollar nonetheless remains prominent in trade
and capital flows, in global investment portfolios, and in the reserves of
other central banks.

Capital flows have increased rapidly since the breakdown of the Bretton
Woods system, though the degree of integration has precedents in earlier
periods of history. International differences in savings rates manifest themselves in current account surpluses and deficits, or differences in the value of
the goods and services a country imports and exports. The United States has
a low savings rate (see Figure 1.16) and runs large current account deficits
(Figure 1.12). By this means, the world is provided with dollar balances.
Countries with high savings rates tend to run current account surpluses, unless their domestic investment rates are also high, since their output is greater

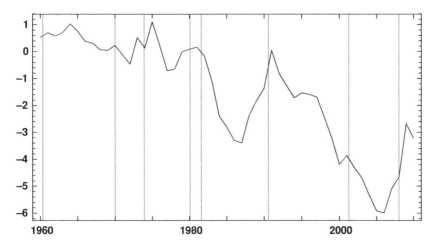

FIGURE 1.12   U.S. Current Account Balance 1960–2010
Ratio of the U.S. balance on current account to gross domestic product in current dollars, percent, annual.
Source: Bureau of Economic Analysis, U.S. International Transactions Accounts, Table 1, line 77; National Income and Product Accounts, Table 1.1.5, line 1.

than their consumption and investment. Current account surpluses are offset by equal capital flows in the opposite direction. Countries saving more than they invest internally must invest in foreign assets. The surpluses—or the corresponding overseas investments—are additions to the net assets of the surplus country vis-à-vis the rest of the world, and are frequently accumulated in the form of foreign assets of the central bank, that is, central bank reserves.

Figure 1.13 displays IMF estimates of international monetary reserves. The growth in reserves has been rapid and steady since the end of the Bretton Woods era. Two periods of especially rapid growth stand out. The first occurred in the immediate aftermath of the transition in 1973 to the managed-float exchange-rate system that prevails today, as countries equipped themselves with the international reserves they felt necessary to cope with potential instability. The second occurred after 1998; reserves increased almost four-fold in the decade 2001–2010. This increase followed the Asian Crisis in emerging markets, lasting from mid-1997 to early 1999, during which a number of countries were forced to devalue their currencies and endure severe, if brief, recessions. In its aftermath, a number of developing countries determined not only to restore, but to significantly increase their foreign-exchange reserves. Other reasons for the increase, which was concentrated in East Asia and in oil-exporting countries,

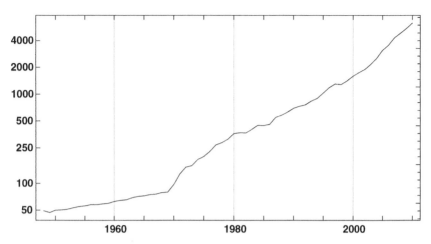

FIGURE 1.13   Growth of International Monetary Reserves 1948–2010
International reserves, annual, billions of Special Drawing Rights (SDRs),
logarithmic scale. SDRs are a currency unit introduced by the IMF in 1969 as a
means of increasing its flexibility to provide liquidity to countries experiencing
balance of payments problems. Today, it serves primarily as a unit of account. In
early 2010, one SDR was worth about $1.57.
Source: International Monetary Fund.

include the increase in oil prices and export-led development in East Asian
countries.

The "Great Moderation"   During the 1970s, a new orientation in macroeconomic policy placed expectations about the future, especially concerning
economic policy, at the center of economic models. In this approach, a credible commitment by central banks to low inflation could help maintain price
stability at much lower cost in growth and employment than the Phillips
curve suggested. In the new approach, central banks focused more on managing inflation expectations, explicitly or implicitly targeting low inflation
and revising their earlier emphasis on employment and growth.

The new orientation was initially a dramatic success. U.S. inflation
dropped rapidly throughout the 1980s and 1990s. The annual increase in
the core urban consumer price index (CPI-U), a standard inflation measure,
fell below 3 percent in 1994, fell below 2 percent in 2003, and has not been
higher than 2.5 percent since (Figure 1.11).

Interest rates dropped even more rapidly. The Federal Reserve initiated
the new policy by dramatically increasing nominal short-term interest rates,
but was able to lower them rapidly once inflation began to decline. The
renewed focus on low inflation, and disappointment with the results of

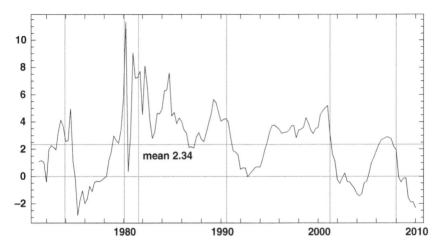

FIGURE 1.14   Real Fed Funds Rate 1971–2009
The graph displays a simple approach to measuring the real Fed funds rate. For the
period from Q1 1971 through Q3 1997, the real Fed funds rate is estimated as the
quarter-end nominal target rate less the average of the four preceding and four
subsequent quarterly estimates of the GDP personal consumption expenditure
deflator, an inflation estimate. For the period from Q4 1997 through Q3 2009, the
real Fed funds rate is estimated as the quarter-end nominal target rate less the
five-year forward breakeven rate, a market-adjusted inflation estimate based on
Treasury Inflation-Protected Securities (TIPS).
Source: Bloomberg Financial L.P.

"Phillips-curve Keynesianism," was shared by a number of central banks
around the world.

The Federal Reserve was able eventually to lower real, or inflation-
adjusted, interest rates by definitively removing inflation fears from the
economy's wage- and price-setting. It did the latter by initially cutting interest rates more slowly than the inflation rate was falling. This can be seen
in Figure 1.14 in the behavior of the real *target federal funds rate*, the rate
on overnight central bank reserves the Fed endeavors to achieve through its
daily operations in the money market. The real Fed funds rate was extremely
volatile in the 1970s, reaching double-digit levels at the time of the Fed's
major effort against inflation around 1980. Following the onset of the dot-
com bust in 2000, real short-term interest rates fell to extremely low levels,
and were below zero for the first time since the mid 1970s. The difference
was that in the 1970s, real rates were negative because inflation was so high;
after 2000 it reflected the low level of nominal interest rates.

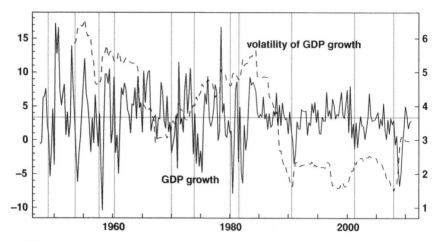

FIGURE 1.15 U.S. Growth Rate and Its Volatility 1947–2009
The solid line (left y-axis) plots U.S. GDP growth, Q2 1947 to Q3 2009, seasonally
adjusted at an annual rate, percent. The dashed line (right y-axis) plots the rolling
standard deviation of the past 5 years' quarterly growth rates in percent. Vertical
gridlines represent the dates of NBER business cycle peaks and the horizontal
gridline the mean GDP growth rate over the entire period.
Source: U.S. Bureau of Labor Statistics, series CUUR0000SA0.

The small decline in employment and growth attendant on the disinflation of the early 1980s, once the initial interest-rate shock had been
absorbed, was a surprise. A dampening of business cycles over the past half-
century had been noted, but a decline in fluctuations in output, prices, and
other economic indicators was now unmistakable. The standard deviation
of U.S. output growth, for example, dropped rapidly from around 6 percent
to about 2 percent, as seen in Figure 1.15. This change has sometimes been
called the "Great Moderation."

The benign economic and financial environment was reflected in many
ways. For example, the disinflation of the early 1980s made it possible for corporations to finance growth through capital-markets borrowing, leading to an increase in balance sheet that outstripped the increase
in firm value. This trend reversed in the early 1990s, as can be seen in
Figure 1.17, when nonfinancial corporate business began to see strong
profit growth, and leverage ratios declined rapidly until the onset of the
subprime crisis.

But shadows did appear on the horizon. One worry was the decline in
the U.S. household savings rate. Figure 1.16 shows that, once the immediate

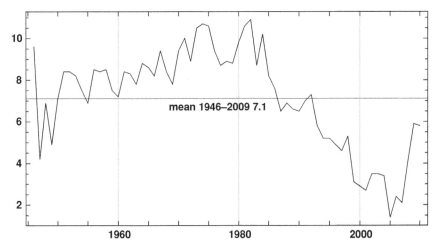

FIGURE 1.16 U.S. Savings Rate 1946–2010
Personal saving as a percentage of disposable personal income, annual.
Source: Bureau of Economic Analysis, National Income and Product Accounts,
Table 2.1, line 34.

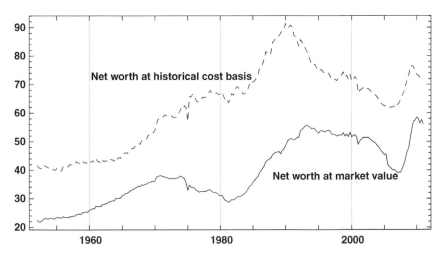

FIGURE 1.17 Corporate Leverage in the United States 1950–2010
Ratio of debt instruments to net worth, nonfinancial corporations, quarterly.
Source: Federal Reserve Board, Flow of Funds Accounts of the United States (Z.1),
Table B.102.

postwar consumption boom had ended (the savings rate had approached 25 percent during the war years), the savings rate was typically near 10 percent until about 1982. It declined steadily thereafter, and households became steadily more indebted, until the financial crisis spurred a sharp increase in savings. One reason commonly advanced for the decline is households' choice to rely on asset appreciation rather than forgone consumption to build wealth. The sudden disappearance of confidence in that approach led to the rise in savings in 2008. We further explore these macroeconomic phenomena and their relationship to the subprime crisis in Chapter 14.

Perhaps most worrisome was the apparently increasing frequency of episodes of financial stress. There were many types, most of them affecting only one or a small number of financial firms, but with at least the potential for wider effects. Table 1.1 lists a few of the financial mishaps of recent decades that preceded the subprime crisis. By no means is the table comprehensive.

By way of contrast, let's get a perspective from a time when the world seemed a financially more secure and stable place. Stefan Zweig provides this description of the placid financial environment of late nineteenth century Europe:

> *There were no revolutions, no sharp destruction of wealth in the calm of that epoch; if securities lost even four or five percent on the exchanges, it was called a "crash," and one spoke with wrinkled brow of the "catastrophe." ... Wills stipulated precisely how one's grandchildren and great-grandchildren were to be protected from even the smallest loss in asset value, as though an invisible debt instrument guaranteed safety from the eternal Powers. And in the meantime, one lived contentedly, and stroked one's petty worries like good, obedient house pets one did not, fundamentally, really fear* [Zweig, 1944].

The era was not as stable as appeared, and in its aftermath Keynes (1920) provided one diagnosis of the forces undermining it: "the instability of an excessive population dependent for its livelihood on a complicated and artificial organization, the psychological instability of the laboring and capitalist classes, and the instability of Europe's claim, coupled with the completeness of her dependence, on the food supplies of the New World." In the century since it ended, financial risk and instability have been recognized as persistent features of the economic system. All the more surprising, then, that the study of financial risk is a relatively new discipline in finance and economics.

TABLE 1.1 Financial Mishaps of the Past Four Decades

Event	Date	Description
Penn Central	1970	Hitherto-largest U.S. bankruptcy. Nonfinancial firm unable to roll commercial paper funding, contagion fears lead to widening of other commercial paper spreads.
Herstatt Bank	1974	Collapse of German bank exposes foreign counterparties, particularly banks, to foreign exchange settlement risk.
Franklin National Bank	1974	Collapse of a U.S. commercial bank. Underlying factors include foreign-exchange and loan losses, and short-term wholesale funding. Posed systemic risk in fragile environment.
Drysdale Government Securities	1982	Collapse of government securities dealer with highly leveraged positions. Its custodian and accounting firm suffered reputational damage and financial losses.
Penn Square Bank	1982	Collapse of Oklahoma bank on bad loans to energy industry, occasions largest payoff of insured depositors to date by FDIC.
Continental Illinois	1984	Collapse of commercial bank dependent on brokered rather than retail deposits. Remains among largest resolutions of a commercial bank; all depositors were made whole.
Stock market correction	1987	Largest one-day drop in U.S. stock market history; remained localized.
Citibank	1987	Near-failure, by a narrow margin, on sovereign lending ("petrodollar recycling") to Latin American countries during the 1970s and early 1980s.
Savings and loan crisis	1989	Failure of hundreds of banks on bad loans. Losses began in the mid-1980s and failures peaked in 1989, when a comprehensive bailout plan was passed by Congress.
Gulf War I	1990	Crude oil prices skyrocket.
Drexel Burnham Lambert	1990	Collapse of broker-dealer that had been prominent in the nascent high-yield bond market. Smooth unwind following Chapter 11 bankruptcy filing with little spillover.

(*Continued*)

31

TABLE 1.1 (*Continued*)

Event	Date	Description
Hammersmith and Fulham	1991	U.K. local government avoids interest-rate swap losses after a legal ruling that it had had no legal power to enter the transactions.
Bank of Credit and Commerce International (BCCI)	1991	Large and complex international bank unwound with creditor and depositor losses after fraudulent dealings revealed, including secret ownership of U.S. banks.
Exchange Rate Mechanism (ERM) crisis	1992	"Black Wednesday," sterling leaves ERM, September 16, 1992. ERM disbanded after second wave of attacks breaks French franc band in 1993.
Metallgesellschaft	1993	Hedging strategy leads to margin calls and large mark-to-market losses.
Askin Capital	1994	Collapse of large highly leveraged mortgage bond fund amid general turmoil in Treasury and MBS markets following surprisingly timed and aggressive monetary tightening.
Gibson Greetings	1994	Large losses on plain vanilla and exotic interest-rate swap transactions.
Procter and Gamble	1994	Large losses on plain vanilla and exotic interest-rate swap transactions. P&G did not prevail in a lawsuit against its counterparty, Bankers Trust, for compensation on grounds of its fiduciary duty to P&G.
Kidder Peabody	1994	Trades not properly entered into books and records ("ticket in the drawer") by "rogue trader" result in losses and sale of firm's assets to PaineWebber.
Orange County, CA	1994	Municipality suffers large loss on interest-rate swaps and repo, leading to municipal bankruptcy.
Mexican peso crisis	1994	Mexican peso devaluation follows difficulty rolling over short-term foreign currency debt. Contagion fears lead to large-scale internationally coordinated financial support.
Daiwa Bank	1995	Trades not properly entered into books and records by rogue trader over an extended period generate large losses and regulatory penalties. Daiwa survived.

Barings Bank	1995	Rogue-trader ticket-in-the-drawer episode generates large losses and leads to collapse of Barings.
Asian crisis	1997	Contagion event, begins with breaking the USD-THB peg, eventually forces Korea and other East Asian nations to break U.S. dollar pegs. Continues through 1998 with Russia and Long-Term Capital crises; last shudders in Latin America in early 1999.
Long Term Capital Management	1998	Collapse of large hedge fund. Negotiated assumption of assets by major banks and brokers.
Russian debt crisis	1998	Russian debt restructuring and currency devaluation following inability to roll over short-term bonds.
Enron bankruptcy	2001	Risk positions in off-balance-sheet vehicles were not disclosed in accounting statements. Once disclosed, creditors withdrew.
9/11 terrorist attack	2001	Destruction of people and physical infrastructure.
Credit correlation event	2005	Spreads widen on downgrades of auto manufacturers and volatility in credit derivatives markets.
Amaranth Advisors	2006	Collapse of hedge fund on large losses in commodities futures markets.
Société Generale	2007	Rogue trader ticket-in-the-drawer episode. Large losses cause reputational damage but do not jeopardize firm.
Bernard Madoff	2008	Exposure of unusually long-running and large-scale Ponzi scheme.
Jefferson County, AL	2009	Municipality suffers large loss on interest-rate swap transactions, files for bankruptcy protection.

1.2   THE SCOPE OF FINANCIAL RISK

Risk can be defined informally in different ways, but the central notions are those of uncertainty about meeting goals or about potential loss, and of incomplete control over the outcomes of decisions. Risk management is the effort to understand these uncertainties in order to make better choices among goals and meet them more effectively.

A meaningful distinction was been drawn by American economist Frank H. Knight (1921) between two types of surprises. "Risk," on the one hand, refers to situations or problems that are quantifiable, and which one can reasonably describe with a probability distribution. "Uncertainty," on the other hand, refers to situations in which no quantitative estimates can be made; the outcomes are unknown or can only be guessed at, "because the situation dealt with is in a high degree unique" (p. 231).

Knight drew this distinction in an attempt to understand entrepreneurial rewards and their relationship to the interest rate. He attributed profit to the businessman's willingness to make choices under uncertainty, rather than as a reward to taking "risk," which is tamer: "Profit arises out of the inherent, absolute unpredictability of things, out of the sheer brute fact that the results of human activity cannot be anticipated and then only in so far as even a probability calculation in regard to them is impossible and meaningless" (p. 311).

This is a relevant distinction for financial risk. We often employ models that assume we can summarize the behavior asset returns, defaults, or some other quantity in a probability distribution. But many of the most important determinants of loss can't be quantified this way. We are then in danger of falling into the drunk's trap of looking for his lost keys where the light is, rather than where they might actually have fallen. Many large financial losses are due to circumstances that are very hard to model. But models and quantitative analysis are nonetheless required for an understanding the issues involved and for posing relevant questions.

We can summarize the major types of financial risk in Table 1.2, which also provides a road map of much of the rest of this book.

1.2.1   Risk Management in Other Fields

Fields outside of finance, such as engineering, public security, the military, public health, and the environment have been studying risk for a long time. Similar questions to those posed by risk analysis in finance arise in these disciplines: Which events cause the most harm? Which are the most likely? What does it cost to mitigate different types of harm? These disciplines have

TABLE 1.2 Types of Financial Risk

Type	Description
Market risk	Risk of loss arising from changes in market prices. It takes many forms:
Price risk	The risk that the market price of a security goes the wrong way. Price risk can arise for a single security, or for a portfolio. In the latter case, the price risk of the portfolio is influenced by the *return correlations* of the securities, in addition to their returns taken individually. We discuss single-security price risk in Chapter 3 and that of portfolios in Chapter 5.
	Securities prices can also include those of derivative securities, including options. Option prices are exposed to the risk of changes in *implied volatility*, which we cover in Chapter 4.
	Price risk arises not only from changes in the price *levels* of securities. Positions may be hedged with offsetting positions in similar securities, so their *relative* price changes are more important than overall price changes. For example, a *long-short equity* portfolio may have little exposure to the general direction of stock prices, but a large exposure to the relative prices of certain stocks. In fixed-income securities, this risk is called *spread risk*, which we discuss in Chapters 4 and 7.
	Multinational manufacturing firms typically face commodity and currency risk, and risks arising from long-term project planning. One measure of the impact is called *Earnings at Risk* (EaR).
Execution risk	The risk that you cannot execute a trade quickly enough or skillfully enough to avoid a loss. An important example is *stop-loss risk*, the risk that you cannot exit a trade at the worst price you were willing to accept. This risk cannot be entirely mitigated by prearrangements such as *stop-loss orders*.
Mark-to-market risk	The risk that the market value of a security or a portfolio declines, even if that loss is not realized through a sale or unwinding. Mark-to-market risk is closely connected to credit and liquidity risk, and we discuss it in Chapter 12.
Credit risk	The risk that the creditworthiness of the issuer of a debt obligation you own deteriorates. Debt obligations include myriad varieties of securities, but also include nonsecurity obligations, such as those of a trading counterparty. Credit risk also arises from positions in *credit derivatives*, such as CDS.

(Continued)

TABLE 1.2 (*Continued*)

Type	Description
Default risk	The risk that the debtor becomes insolvent, that is, unable to pay timely. The credit risk of single securities will be covered in Chapter 6. Chapter 8 extends the analysis to portfolios, and, as with the price risk of portfolios, it requires that we take account of coincident losses. In the case of credit portfolios, the relevant correlation concept is not return, but *default correlation*. Default correlation becomes even more important in assessing the risk of *structured credit products*, which we discuss in Chapter 9. In a structured credit product, the cash flows and the credit losses from a pool of underlying assets are distributed to a set of bonds according to contractually stipulated rules.
Credit migration risk	The risk of the issuer or the security receiving a lower credit rating.
Counterparty risk	The risk that a trading counterparty will not fulfill an obligation to pay or deliver securities. We discuss counterparty risk in Chapter 6
Clearing and settlement risk	The operational side of credit risk. *Clearing* is the process of matching trade records with counterparties, making sure they are accurate, reconciling trades with the books and records of the firm, and *netting*, that is, cancelling offsetting trades where appropriate. *Settlement* is the process of transfering securites and making final payment for them. Settlement risk is a type of very short-term credit risk that also has elements of operational risk. In most financial transactions, the two counterparties send payment or securities at the same time, or at least as close as business hours in different time zones permit. But what if you send your value but the counterparty doesn't send his? This risk is called *Herstatt risk* after an episode in 1974 in which the Herstatt Bank in Germany became insolvent. When it shut down, it had received payments earlier in the 24-hour trading day on a large volume of foreign exchange trades for which it had not yet made payment of the countervalue. Some of its counterparty banks were in danger of insolvency as a result.

Liquidity risk	This falls between market and credit risk, partly because it has several meanings. We discuss liquidity risk in Chapter 12.
Market liquidity risk	The risk that the market is not deep enough, at the time you have to buy or sell, for you to trade without pushing the price against yourself.
Funding liquidity risk	The risk that credit becomes unavailable, or is offered only on more stringent terms, and that as a result, you cannot continue to finance a position. Some positions may lose money because *other* market participants have similar positions, lose funding, and have to sell, depressing prices. During the subprime crisis, for example, banks' desire to keep ample cash balances, and their reluctance to lend to other banks, led to an unusual widening of the spread between Libor, the interbank lending rate, and riskless Treasury bills (see Figure 14.9).
Model risk	The potential for loss arising from incorrect models. It can take many forms, depending on whether the errors are due to data, parameterization, omitted variables, or other issues. The subprime crisis provides an important example of model risk. Risk models for subprime securities, whether those of the rating agencies that provided AAA ratings for large portions of the bonds, or those of at least some investors, were based on the only historical data available; subprime residential mortgage loans were not made prior to the last two decades (see Chapter 11). One source of model risk is *correlation risk*. The risk of applying the "wrong" return correlation arises frequently because correlation is hard to estimate. We discuss correlation in Chapters 8 and 9, and provide an extended example of correlation risk in Chapter 11.
Operational risk	The potential for loss arising from breakdowns in policies and controls that ensure the proper functioning of people, systems, and facilities. This is sometimes called "everything else that can go wrong," because it is a large and diffuse category. But it is nonetheless extremely important. One example of operational risk is risk of loss because of inadequate internal controls. For example, a trader may not enter a trade properly into the books and records of his firm, although he has entered the firm into a legally binding contract. Several episodes of extremely large losses, including the failure of two-century old Barings Bank, have resulted from "rogue trader" actions.

(Continued)

TABLE 1.2 *(Continued)*

Type	Description
Legal risk	The risk that a firm may be sued for its financial practices, or find that a contract that is valuable to it cannot be enforced. Legal risk has several variants:
Fraud risk	The risk that a contract to which one is a party was entered into fraudulently, or that an asset's value has been fraudulently manipulated. Financial fraud often comes to light during a financial crisis, and the subprime crisis is no exception. Two well-known examples illustrate the types of loss caused by fraud. During the peak years of subprime mortgage origination in the years 2002–2006, many subprime loans were "stated income" loans, in which the income stated on the loan application was not verified by the loan originator. In many of these, the stated income was false. The borrower, the originator, or the bank purchasing the loan from a nonbank originator may have been responsible for the falsification. The fraud victim was the lender, or the investor in residential mortgage-backed securities backed by the loans. The appearance of lenders on both sides is an example of how complex legal risk can be. An example of fraudulent manipulation of asset values, the Bernard Madoff investment scam, also illustrates a classic form of fraud, the *Ponzi scheme*. In a Ponzi scheme, initial investors are drawn in by high promised returns, and paid out as promised. However, they are not paid out of investment returns, but out of later investors' equity. The later investors are not repaid at all once the scheme is exposed and ends.
Regulatory risk	This is the risk that an activity will be found to be out of compliance with regulations, or that a currently sanctioned activity will be prohibited. Losses can arise from having to exit or reorganize a line of business. We study the rationale and practice of regulatory policy in Chapter 15.

An example from the subprime crisis is the Securities Exchange Commission's September 18, 2009 temporary prohibition on establishing *short positions* in the equities of many financial companies. Short positions are positions in which the security is not purchased, but borrowed and sold, with the intention of buying it back later at a lower price and returning it to the source of the borrow. Whether the prohibition had its intended effect is a matter of debate. But one unanticipated outcome was to induce a near-complete halt in the trading of convertible bonds, since that business depends on the ability to establish short positions in the equity of the issuing company.

Compliance risk   A form of regulatory risk in which a firm experiences losses from the behavior of its employees rather than corporate behavior.

Reputational risk   The potential for loss of revenue, loss of share value, exit of key employees, or costly litigation arising from bad publicity regarding an institution's business practices, whether true or not. It is sometimes called *headline risk*, because of the dramatic way in which adverse news can surface.

During the subprime crisis, the rating agencies' reputation for objectivity and freedom from conflict of interest suffered. In particular, they are widely believed to have granted higher ratings than warranted to securities whose values were based on the creditworthiness of subprime loans.

Systemic risk   The risk that the payments or credit intermediation system as a whole become impaired, with serious macroeconomic consequences. Such episodes are called *financial crises*, and we discuss them throughout, but particularly in Chapters 12, 14, and 15.

developed a structured approach that distinguishes between the following overlapping tasks:

Risk assessment identifies the potential sources of harm or loss and attempts to quantify the extent of loss, taking into account uncertainty, and how it is affected by different actions.

Risk management operates on the basis of the assessment to weigh alternative policies toward the mitigation of risk.

Communication transmits this information to end-users, analysts, and decision makers.

Financial risk management involves the same tasks, in the context of the financial assets and liabilities of individuals and firms.

In engineering, issues that involve risk range from the fraction of defective light bulbs resulting from different production techniques, to the traffic loads bridges and roads should be designed to withstand. One contrast to financial risk is that small errors can lead to very large consequences. To take an example from software engineering, it has been reported that errors in a number-rounding algorithm led to the failure of a Patriot missile defence system to intercept the Iraqi Scud that killed 28 U.S. soldiers in Saudi Arabia during the first Gulf War. In the financial arena, such a mishap would be an example of model risk, in particular, the risk of underestimated risks or inaccurate asset valuations arising from programming errors.

Financial risks are more forgiving in the sense that it usually takes a gross error to produce grossly adverse results, and the results of individual errors are rarely directly life-threatening. But errors by many market participants simultaneously, possibly as a result of shared models, or by policy makers, can cause sustained and grievous harm.

The nonfinancial risk disciplines have taken the quantitative and, especially, the statistical study of risk quite far. But the application of quantitative methods does not settle matters in risk management in nonfinancial any more than in financial matters. Risk management can be tremendously controversial in the financial as well as nonfinancial fields when they are part of a public policy debate. Some examples of contentious nonfinancial risk issues that are susceptible to a quantitative analysis include:

- Is nuclear power safe enough to rely on it for any part of our energy supply?
- What should public policy be toward residential construction in areas prone to natural disasters such as flooding?
- What levels of environmental pollution or food contamination should be deemed acceptable?

FURTHER READING

Introductory risk management textbooks covering some of the same material as the present one, include Hull (2006), Crouhy, Mark and Galai (2000*b*) and Marrison (2002).

Landes (1998) and Kindleberger (1993) are good starting points for general economic and financial history. Bernstein (1996) is a history of risk and probability theory. Knight's distinction between risk and uncertainty is laid out in Knight (1921). Black (1986) is an aphoristic but fascinating essay on the impact of randomness. For an example of how the field of risk management is viewed outside of finance, see Modarres (2006).

Allen and Santomero (2001) is a conceptual survey of the financial innovation wave of the 1970s to 1990s. Frederiksen (1894) describes the early stages of securitization in Germany. The early postwar history of the repo market and its relationship to the money markets is presented in Willis (1972).

Levine (2005) provides a survey of the role of financial development in overall economic development. Blume (2002) discusses the evolution of equity markets. Pozsar, Adrian, Ashcraft, and Boesky (2010) is the indispensable introduction and guide to the development of non bank intermediation in the decades preceding the subprime crisis. Benston and Kaufman (1997) discusses changes in financial regulation during the 1980s and early 1990s.

Introductions to hedge funds are provided by Fung and Hsieh (1999), Agarwal and Naik (2005), Brown and Goetzmann (2003), and Lo (2005). Kaplan and Stromberg (2009) describe the private equity business. See Jen (2006, 2007) and Butt, Shivdasani, Stendevad, and Wyman (2008) on sovereign wealth funds.

Eichengreen (2008) is a history of postwar international monetary relations. Goodfriend (2007) and Clarida, Gali, and Gertler (1999, 2000) articulate developed countries' approach to monetary policy over the past three decades, including the implicit or explicit use of feedback rules and attentiveness to market expectations. They also provide evidence that this approach has changed since the 1970s.

For more detail on some of the mishaps catalogued in Table 1.1, see Calomiris (1994) on Penn Central, Schwert (1990*b*) on the 1987 stock market correction, Overdahl and Schachter (1995) on Gibson Greetings, and Jorion (1996*a*) on Orange County. Pyle (1995) is an analytical history of the U.S. savings and loan crisis. McAndrews and Potter (2002) and Fleming and Garbade (2002) discuss financial market effects of 9/11. See also the references at the end of Chapter 14.

CHAPTER 2

Market Risk Basics

In this chapter, we begin studying how to quantify *market risk*, the risk of loss from changes in market prices, via statistical models of the behavior of market prices. We introduce a set of tools and concepts to help readers better understand how returns, risk, and volatility are defined, and we review some basic concepts of portfolio allocation theory.

The statistical behavior of asset returns varies widely, across securities and over time:

- There is enormous variety among assets, as we saw in Chapter 1, ranging from simple cash securities, to fixed-income securities, which have a time dimension, to derivative securities, whose values are functions of other asset prices, to, finally, a bewildering array of indexes, basket products, tradeable fund shares, and structured credit products.
- The market risks of many, if not most, securities must be decomposed into underlying *risk factors*, which may or may not be directly observable. In addition to statistical models, therefore, we also need models and algorithms that relate security values to risk factors. We also need to accurately identify the important risk factors.

  We discuss the relationship between asset prices and risk factors further in Chapter 4. For now, we will be a bit loose and use the terms "asset prices" and "risk factors" synonymously.
- Some risk factors are far from intuitive. It is relatively straightforward to understand fluctuations in, say, equity prices. But options and option-like security returns are driven not only by price fluctuations, but also by the actual and anticipated behavior of volatility. Markets can even, as we see in Chapter 14, be affected by the volatility of volatility.

It is impossible to capture the variety of real-life security price fluctuations in a single, simple model. But the standard model we develop in this and the next chapter is useful as a starting point for quantitative modeling. It will also help us understand the issues and pitfalls involved in security price modeling. *Nobody* believes in the standard model literally, but it provides a framework for thinking about problems. If we study the standard model, and come away more conscious of its flaws than of its virtues, we will have accomplished a great deal. Finally, as we see in Chapter 15, the standard model informs to a large extent the regulatory approach to major financial institutions.

We want to understand the relationship between risk and security price behavior. Finance theory has developed a framework for this called *modern finance theory*. It has plagued researchers with far more questions than answers, but it helps organize thinking about the subject. Modern finance theory has its roots in economic theory, where much of the theoretical apparatus it employs, such as constrained expected utility maximization and the conditions for a set of prices and quantities to be mutually consistent and individually and socially optimal, were developed.

Choices are made through time, and the environment in which choices are made is subject to uncertainty. To characterize uncertainty, modern finance theory has made extensive use of tools, particularly certain classes of *stochastic processes*, that describe uncertain environments over time and permit tractable models to be developed.

2.1 ARITHMETIC, GEOMETRIC, AND LOGARITHMIC SECURITY RETURNS

We begin by laying out the algebra of returns. Returns on an asset can be defined two different ways, as a proportional change called the *arithmetic* or *simple rate of return*, or as a logarithmic change, called the *logarithmic rate of return*. Let's assume for now that the asset pays no cash flows between t and $t + \tau$. The two definitions are expressed in the following pair of identities:

$$S_{t+\tau} \equiv (1 + \tau r_{t,\tau}^{\text{arith}}) S_t$$

$$S_{t+\tau} \equiv e^{\tau r_{t,\tau}} S_t$$

where $r_{t,\tau}^{\text{arith}}$ is the time-t, τ-period arithmetic rate of return, and $r_{t,\tau}$ the time-t τ-period rate of logarithmic rate of return on the asset. Time is usually measured in years. If returns did not vary over time, we could simplify the notation by dropping the first subscript, t. If the periodic rate of return did not vary with the horizon τ, we could drop the second subscript, t, and write r_t^{arith} and r_t. In this book, we'll generally adhere to a convention that Roman symbols such as t, T, and t_1, represent dates, while Greek symbols such as τ and τ_1 represent an elapsed time.

The rates of return are the increments to the asset's value. The quantities $1 + r_{t,\tau}^{\text{arith}}$ and $e^{r_{t,\tau}}$ are called the *gross rates of return*, since they include the value of the asset, not just the increment. The gross return is just the proportional change in the asset price:

$$\frac{S_{t+\tau}}{S_t} = 1 + \tau r_{t,\tau}^{\text{arith}} = e^{\tau r_{t,\tau}}$$

The change in the asset price itself is

$$S_{t+\tau} - S_t = \tau r_{t,\tau}^{\text{arith}} S_t = (e^{\tau r_{t,\tau}} - 1)S_t$$

The logarithmic return is the logarithmic change in asset price or the increment to the logarithm of the price:

$$r_{t,\tau} = \frac{1}{\tau} \log\left(\frac{S_{t+\tau}}{S_t}\right) = \frac{1}{\tau}[\log(S_{t+\tau}) - \log(S_t)]$$

Putting these definitions together gives us two equivalent ways of expressing the relationship between arithmetic and log returns:

$$r_{t,\tau}^{\text{arith}} = \frac{1}{\tau}(e^{\tau r_{t,\tau}} - 1)$$

$$r_{t,\tau} = \frac{1}{\tau} \log(1 + \tau r_{t,\tau}^{\text{arith}})$$

The choice of units is a common source of confusion. In the definitions above, and in most computations, we treat $r_{t,\tau}$ and $r_{t,\tau}^{\text{arith}}$ as decimals. We have to multiply by 100 to get a return in percent, the format in which returns are most often reported. Yet another unit for expressing returns is *basis points*, 0.0001 or hundredths of a percent, typically used to report changes, spreads, or differences in returns. A full percentage point is often called a "point" in market jargon. The gross return and the change in asset price are measured in currency units. For example, if the price was 100 a year ago, and 103 today, we have $103 = (1.03)100$, so the arithmetic rate of return is 0.03 expressed as a decimal, or 3 percent, or 300 bp. The logarithmic rate of return is $\log\left(\frac{103}{100}\right) = 0.02956$, as a decimal.

In the end, we care primarily about profit and loss (P&L) in dollars, so it doesn't really matter whether we describe returns as arithmetic or logarithmic. But there can be practical advantages to using one rather than the other, and logarithmic returns also have a conceptual advantage over arithmetic. Logarithmic returns represent the constant proportional rate at which an asset price must change to grow or decline from its initial to its terminal level, taking into account the growth in the "base" on which returns are measured. We'll discuss this in the context of stochastic processes shortly.

It is therefore easier to aggregate returns over time when they are expressed logarithmically, using the rule $e^{r_1 \tau_1} e^{r_2 \tau_2} = e^{r_1 \tau_1 + r_2 \tau_2}$. Suppose we are interested in monthly and in annual returns, and are measuring time in months. We have a series of month-end asset prices $S_0, S_1, S_2, \ldots, S_{12}$, with S_0 the asset price at the end of the last month of the prior year. The one-month logarithmic returns are

$$r_{t,t+1} = \log(S_t) - \log(S_{t-1}) \quad t = 1, 2, \ldots, 12$$

The one-year logarithmic return is the sum of the one-month logarithmic returns:

$$\log\left(\frac{S_{12}}{S_0}\right) = \log(S_{12}) - \log(S_0) = \sum_{t=1}^{12} r_{t,t+1}$$

The arithmetic rates of return are not conveniently additive in this way. The one-year arithmetic rate of return is the geometric average of one-month rates:

$$\frac{S_{12}}{S_0} - 1 = \frac{S_1}{S_0}\frac{S_2}{S_1} \cdots \frac{S_{12}}{S_{11}} - 1 = \prod_{t=1}^{12}(1 + r_{t,t+1}^{\text{arith}}) - 1$$

This is a more cumbersome calculation than for logarithmic returns. For example, if we know that an investment had quarterly logarithmic returns of 1, 1.5, −0.5, and 2.0 percent in successive quarters, we can see immediately that its logarithmic return for the year was 4.0 percent. If an investment had quarterly arithmetic returns of 1, 1.5, −0.5, and 2.0 percent, the annual arithmetic return is a harder-to-compute 4.0425 percent.

An even more striking example is this: If you have a positive logarithmic return of 10 percent one day, and negative 10 percent the next, you get back to the original asset price; that is, the gross two-day return is zero. If you have a positive arithmetic return of 10 percent one day, and negative 10 percent the next, the gross two-day return is *negative*. One context in which the distinction between arithmetic and logarithmic returns is quite important when returns are compounded is *leveraged ETFs*, ETFs that are constructed using derivatives contracts and pay a multiple of the daily arithmetic return on an index. Because their returns are defined daily, in a volatile market there can be a large difference between the average daily return on a leveraged ETF and the return over longer periods of time.

However, arithmetic returns are easier to aggregate over positions. Let's introduce a bit of notation we'll use frequently. Let $S_{t,n}, n = 1, 2, \ldots, N$ represent the prices of N securities and $x_n, n = 1, 2, \ldots, N$ the amounts (e.g., the number of shares or ounces of gold) of those N securities in a portfolio. To keep things simple, assume all the positions are long. The time-t value of the portfolio is

$$V_t = \sum_{n=1}^{N} x_n S_{t,n}$$

and the arithmetic return between time t and $t + \tau$ is

$$\frac{V_{t+\tau}}{V_t} - 1 = \frac{1}{V_t} \sum_{n=1}^{N} x_n (S_{t,n} - S_{t+\tau,n})$$

$$= \frac{1}{V_t} \tau \sum_{n=1}^{N} x_n r_{t,\tau,n}^{\text{arith}} S_{t,n}$$

$$= \frac{1}{V_t} \tau \sum_{n=1}^{N} \omega_n r_{t,\tau,n}^{\text{arith}}$$

where

$$\omega_n = \frac{x_n S_{t,n}}{V_t} \quad n = 1, 2, \ldots, N$$

are the weights of the positions in the portfolio. (Yes, we needed three subscripts on $r_{t,\tau,n}^{\text{arith}}$ to distinguish the date, the time horizon, and the security.) The portfolio return can be expressed as a weighted average of the arithmetic returns of the assets. There is no corresponding simple relationship between the logarithmic returns of the portfolio and those of the positions.

Another advantage of logarithmic returns becomes clearer later in this chapter when we discuss the standard asset pricing model. No matter how large in magnitude a logarithmic return is, an asset price will remain

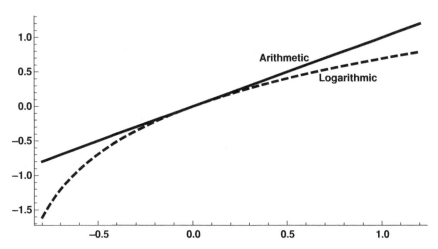

FIGURE 2.1   Approximating Logarithmic by Arithmetic Returns
Arithmetic (x) and logarithmic $(\log(1+x))$ returns for x between 0 and 80 percent.

positive; as the return approaches negative infinity, the asset price will approach, but never reach, zero. An arithmetic return less than -100 percent, in contrast, leads to a negative asset price, which generally makes no sense. This convenient property of logarithmic returns is on motivation for the typical assumption in financial modeling that asset returns are *lognormally distributed*.

For small values of $r_{t,\tau}$ or $r_{t,\tau}^{\text{arith}}$ (that is, small increments $S_{t+\tau} - S_t$), the approximate relationship

$$r_{t,\tau} \approx r_{t,\tau}^{\text{arith}}$$

holds. This approximation of logarithmic by arithmetic returns is a useful and usually innocuous simplification that is widely used in risk measurement practice. As seen in Figure 2.1, the approximation breaks down for large positive or negative values of r_t, which arise when the time interval τ is large, or the return volatility is high. We discuss the approximation further in the context of risk measurement in Chapters 3 and 5.

To see the accuracy of the approximation more exactly, express the log return by expanding $\log(1 + r_{t,\tau}^{\text{arith}})$ around the point $r_{t,\tau}^{\text{arith}} = 0$ to get

$$r_{t,\tau} = r_{t,\tau}^{\text{arith}} - \frac{1}{2}(r_{t,\tau}^{\text{arith}})^2 + \frac{1}{3}(r_{t,\tau}^{\text{arith}})^3 + \cdots$$

The Taylor expansion is equal to the arithmetic return, plus a series in which negative terms are succeeded by smaller-magnitude positive terms.[1]

The log return is smaller than the log of the arithmetic gross return. Thus treating log returns as though they were arithmetic results in a smaller-magnitude estimate of the change in asset price. The opposite is true for negative returns. The table in Example 2.1 compares return computations.

Example 2.1 (Accuracy of Arithmetic Return Approximation) The return in the first column is an arithmetic return. The corresponding log return, that is, the log return that would produce the same change in asset price $S_{t+\tau} - S_t$, is displayed in the second column, and is always a smaller number.

$r_{t,\tau}^{\text{arith}}$	$\log(1 + r_{t,\tau}^{\text{arith}})$
−0.50	−0.693
−0.10	−0.105
−0.01	−0.010
0.01	0.010
0.10	0.095
0.50	0.405

2.2 RISK AND SECURITIES PRICES: THE STANDARD ASSET PRICING MODEL

The standard model in finance theory begins by relating security prices to people's preferences and to security payoffs via an *equilibrium model* of asset prices and returns. Such a model explains observed asset price behavior as the outcome of a market-clearing process rooted in fundamentals: investor preferences and the fundamental productivity and risks of the economy. The mechanisms behind this relationship are individual portfolio optimization and equilibrium relationships. A common approach is the *representative agent model*, which abstracts from differences among individuals or households by defining equilibrium as a state of affairs in which prices have adjusted so that the typical household is just content to hold its asset portfolio and has no incentive to trade assets.

---

[1]If $r_{t,\tau} < 0$, all the terms are negative.

2.2.1   Defining Risk: States, Security Payoffs, and Preferences

Investing can be thought of as choices among distributions. To reduce uncertainty to probability distributions is a gross oversimplification, since many of the most important uncertainties are "Knightian," and not susceptible to quantification. But in modeling with a distributional hypothesis, even if the distribution is not normal, or not even explicitly stated, this is an oversimplification we have to make.

To set up the standard model, we define the "primitives," the facts about the world. Preferences, in the model world of standard theory, are about two things:

Intertemporal consumption decisions People can be motivated to defer consumption now only in exchange for higher consumption in the future.

Risk aversion People prefer a sure thing to any risky prospect with the same expected value.

In this model world, choices are predictable and take place in a well-specified environment. Outside this world, preferences may include other motivations, such as avoiding losses, and behavior can be surprisingly susceptible to influences that have little bearing on getting "more," and which the standard theory can only consider distractions. These phenomena are studied by *behavioral finance*, and there is a lively debate on whether they are incidental to the more important regularities identified by the standard theory, or are in fact central to explaining financial phenomena in the real world.

We need a probability model, that is, a *state space* and probabilities assigned to each state and all their possible combinations. This tells us what states of the world are possible. State spaces can be discrete and finite, discrete and countable, or continuous. If the state space is finite, with I possible states, we can denote the probability of each by $\pi_i, i = 1, \ldots, I$. Security returns or payoffs are different in each state, that is, they have a probability distribution, with the probabilities of particular values equal to the probabilities of the states in which the payoffs have those values. Risk is then defined as the positive probability of ending up in a state of the world in which returns or consumption are low.

As clear as this definition of risk seems, one immediately runs into knotty problems, particularly that of ranking securities that have different return probability distributions. Suppose we're comparing two securities. If one has a higher payoff than the other in every state of the world, it is clearly preferable. But what if it has a higher payoff in some, but a lower payoff in other states? There are a few common approaches to ranking securities:

Mean-variance dominance provides a partial ordering of investments, ranking those with the same variance but a higher mean, or those with the same mean but a lower variance, as preferable. But this approach doesn't rank securities with both a different mean and variance. Also, the next section describes why the correlation of a security's returns with the general state of the economy in the future is important. A security that pays off when times are bad can be preferred to another that has a higher expected return and lower volatility but pays off most in good times when you least need the extra income.

Stochastic dominance focuses on the entire distribution of payoffs, and stipulates says that payoff distributions that are skewed more to high payoffs are ranked higher. Comparing two payoff distributions, if one generally has a lower probability of very low returns and a higher probability of very high payoffs than the other, it may be ranked higher, even if it has a lower mean and higher variance. We examine "fat-tailed" and skewed distributions in Chapter 10.

Expected utility is an approach in which investments are ranked by the expected value of the investor's *utility function*, a measure of the satisfaction or welfare he derives from different amounts consumption.

Preferences can be summarized in an *expected utility function*, the arguments of which are consumption or wealth, now and at future dates. For simplicity, we will deal with utility as a function of consumption at a set of discrete dates $t = 0, 1, \ldots$ Time 0 represents the present, and $u(c_t)$ represents utility at time t as a function of consumption c_t. This leads to a *time-separable* utility function, in which expected utility is a sum of current and expected utilities. There is no money in this asset pricing model: the units of c_t, the consumption good, are called the *numéraire* for the model.

To be consistent with the basic premises of the model, the utility function has to *discount* future consumption relative to consumption in the present. We do this via a parameter $0 < \delta < 1$ representing the *pure rate of time preference*. In our examples, we'll set $\delta = 0.95$, meaning a risk-free interest rate of about 5 percent makes the individual barely indifferent between a little additional utility now and later.

The utility function, of course, must have positive marginal utility $u'(c_t) > 0$ for any value of c_t; more is better. To display *risk aversion*, the marginal utility of consumption also has to decline as the level of consumption rises, that is, utility is a *concave* function of consumption, $u''(c_t) < 0$. With such a utility function, the prospect of consuming either two meatballs or no meatballs, with a 50-50 chance of each, will be less attractive than consuming one meatball for sure. More is still better, but much more is not quite that much better. The *Arrow-Pratt measure of risk aversion* is a standard measure equal to $-cu''(c)/u'(c)$.

Example 2.2   A simple example is *logarithmic utility*:

$$u(c) = \log(c)$$

Marginal utility is

$$u'(c) = \frac{1}{c}$$

which is positive but declining as c gets larger, that is, $u''(c_t) < 0$. The Arrow-Pratt measure of risk aversion for logarithmic utility is

$$-c\frac{u''(c)}{u'(c)} = c\frac{1}{c^2}c = 1$$

In a two-period model, consumption today is a quantity c_0 that is known with certainty once savings decisions are taken. Consumption tomorrow is a random quantity $c_1^{(i)}, i = 1, \ldots, I$. The expected utility function is

$$u(c_0) + \delta E\left[u(c_1)\right] = u(c_0) + \delta \sum_i^I \pi_i u(c_1^{(i)})$$

where $E[x]$ represents the mathematical expected value of the random variable x. The future payoff of a security is a random variable, that is, it varies by state. It can be a relatively simple one, such as a two-state model in which a coin toss determines whether the security will have a low or a high payoff, or a relatively complex one, for example, a normally distributed variate with a payoff anywhere on $(-\infty, +\infty)$, but with small-magnitude outcomes much more likely than extreme ones.

Let's flesh out the simpler example, a two-state, two-period model with two securities, one risky and one risk-free. The two periods are labeled 0 and 1. The payoff on one unit of the security at $t = 1$ can be represented as a random variable y_1, and the payoff in each state by $y_1^{(i)}, i = 1, 2$. We're giving the payoffs a subscript "1" because, while we're only looking at one risky security at the moment, in most contexts we study several risky securities or risk factors. The risk-free security has a payoff of 1 in each state. The prices at time 0 of the risky and risk-free securities are denoted S_1 and S_f.

We also need to stipulate what resources are available to the individual. The simplest assumption is that in each period and in each state, a certain "endowment" of the consumption good is settled upon him like manna. This is called the *endowment process*, denoted $(e_0, e_1, \ldots)$, and with the $e_1, e_2, \ldots$ random variables. There is no uncertainty about consumption in the present, only about the future. The endowment process is the model's representation of the output fundamentals of the economy. In this highly stylized model, there is no concept of investment in real productive capacity. The time-t endowment in each state is denoted $e_t^{(i)}, i = 1, 2$.

We can compute returns from the asset prices. Any risky asset has a state-dependent arithmetic rate of return r_n, with realizations

$$r_n^{(i)} = \frac{y_n^{(i)}}{S_n} - 1 \qquad n = 1, 2, \ldots; i = 1, \ldots, I$$

$$r_f = \frac{1}{S_f} - 1$$

The second equation describes the relationship between the price S_f of the risk-free asset and its return r_f. (We are sticking to arithmetic rates in the examples of this section because we are dealing with a discrete-time problem. We can also simplify the subscripts because both the date [0] and the period [1] are unambiguous.)

As we will see shortly, we can always calculate a risk-free rate, even if there isn't really a tradeable risk-free asset. So we can define the *excess returns* of asset n as

$$r_n - r_f \qquad n = 1, \ldots$$

The excess return $r_n - r_f$ is a random variable, with realizations $r_n^{(i)} - r_f$ in different states. The *expected return* of an asset is defined as $\mu_n = \mathrm{E}[r_n]$.

The expected value of the excess return of asset n

$$\mathrm{E}[r_n - r_f] = \mu_n - r_f \qquad n = 1, \ldots, N$$

is the *risk premium* of asset n, the expected spread between the equilibrium return on asset n and the risk-free rate.

Example 2.3 In the two-state, two-period version, the individual receives a known amount e_0 of the consumption good at $t = 0$ and a random amount e_1 at $t = 1$. We can summarize the setup of the example in this table:

State	$e_1^{(i)}$	$y_1^{(i)}$	π_i
$i = 1$	1.25	1.50	0.90
$i = 2$	0.50	0.25	0.10

In State 2, consumption is very low, but it also has a low probability. The risky security behaves like "nature," but is even more generous in the high-probability state and even stingier in the low-probability state.

2.2.2 Optimal Portfolio Selection

The next step is to set up the individual's optimization problem. The individual is to maximize the expected present value of utility $u(c_0) + \delta E[u(c_1)]$, subject to budget constraints

$$c_0 = e_0 - x_f S_f - x_1 S_1$$
$$c_1 = e_1 + x_f + x_1 y_1$$

The choice variables are x_1 and x_f, the amounts of the risky and risk-free securities purchased. The individual is a price taker in this problem; that is, he responds to asset prices as given by the market and can't influence them. We will see shortly how the equilibrium prices are determined.

To solve the problem, substitute the constraints into the utility function to get a simple, rather than constrained, optimization problem

$$\max_{\{x_1, x_f\}} u(e_0 - x_f S_f - x_1 S_1) + \delta E\left[u(e_1 + x_f + x_1 y_1)\right]$$

The first-order conditions for solving this problem are:

$$S_1 u'(e_0 - x_f S_f - x_1 S_1) = \delta \mathrm{E}\left[y_1 u'(e_1 + x_f + x_1 y_1)\right]$$

$$= \delta \sum_i^s \pi_i y_1^{(i)} u'\left(e_1^{(i)} + x_f + x_1 y_1^{(i)}\right)$$

$$S_f u'(e_0 - x_f S_f - x_1 S_1) = \delta \mathrm{E}\left[u'(e_1 + x_f + x_1 y_1)\right]$$

$$= \delta \sum_i^s \pi_i u'\left(e_1^{(i)} + x_f + x_1 y_1^{(i)}\right)$$

Each of these first-order conditions has the structure

$$S_n = \delta \frac{\mathrm{E}\left[y_n u'(c_1)\right]}{u'(c_0)} \qquad n = 1, f$$

setting the asset price equal to the trade-off ratio between present and expected future satisfaction. This ratio is called the *marginal rate of substitution* or *transformation*.

Example 2.4   If utility is logarithmic, the individual solves

$$\max_{\{x_1, x_f\}} \log(e_0 - x_f S_f - x_1 S_1) + \delta \mathrm{E}\left[\log(e_1 + x_f + x_1 y_1)\right]$$

leading to the first-order conditions

$$\delta \mathrm{E}\left[y(e_1 + x_f + x_1 y_1)^{-1}\right] = S_1(e_0 - x_f S_f - x_1 S_1)^{-1}$$

$$\delta \mathrm{E}\left[(e_1 + x_f + x_1 y_1)^{-1}\right] = S_f(e_0 - x_f S_f - x_1 S_1)^{-1}$$

Substituting the parameters of our example, we have

$$0.95[0.9 \cdot 1.50(1.25 + x_f 1.50 + x_1)^{-1} + 0.1 \cdot 0.25(0.50 + x_f + x_1 0.25)^{-1}]$$
$$= S_1(1 - x_f S_f - x_1 S_1)^{-1}$$
$$0.95[0.9(1.25 + x_f 1.50 + x_1)^{-1} + 0.1(0.50 + x_f + x_1 0.25)^{-1}]$$
$$= S_f(1 - x_f S_f - x_1 S_1)^{-1}$$

We can solve these two equations numerically for the asset demand functions $x_f(S_f, S_1)$ and $x_1(S_f, S_1)$. For example, for $S_f = 0.875$ and $S_1 = 1.05$—which are not necessarily the equilibrium prices—we have

$x_f(0.875, 1.05) = -0.066$ and $x_1(0.875, 1.05) = 0.062$. At those prices, the individual will borrow at the (arithmetic) risk-free rate of $0.875^{-1} - 1 = 0.1429$ to invest in more of the risky asset. The latter, at the stipulated prices, would have an expected return of

$$0.9 \left(\frac{1.50}{1.05} - 1 \right) + 0.1 \left(\frac{0.25}{1.05} - 1 \right) = 0.3095$$

and a risk premium of 16.67 percent.

The two asset demand functions are each downward-sloping in its own price and upward-sloping in the price of the other asset. A rise in the price of each asset decreases demand for it, but increases demand for the other asset.

2.2.3 Equilibrium Asset Prices and Returns

The final step is to nail down the equilibrium asset prices S_f and S_1. In the model environment we have set up, there is an easy way to do this. Since we have specified the individual's endowment, we can dispense with setting up a model of the production and supply side of the economy. Instead, we cast the individual as a representative agent, imagining him as either the one individual in the economy or as one of myriad identical individuals.

Equilibrium prevails if the net demand for each asset is zero. The supply of the consumption good is already set by the endowment process, and there are no positive quantities of any other assets. The securities in our example are shadow entities, and their prices must adjust so the representative agent desires to hold exactly zero amounts of them.

In this model, therefore, we know the individual will eat exactly his endowment, that is,

$$c_t^{(i)} = e_t^{(i)} \qquad t = 1, \ldots; i = 1, \ldots, I$$

so we know not only the endowment process, but the *consumption* process. This leads to a solution of the equilibrium problem. It also provides a simple approach to asset pricing that has had enormous influence on academic and practitioner work.

Each asset price is a similar function of the same set of arguments, namely, the marginal rate of substitution between utility now and utility later. For the two-security, two-period problem, the first-order conditions are

$$\delta E\left[y_1 u'(e_1)\right] = \delta \sum_i^I \pi_i y_1^{(i)} u'\left(e_1^{(i)}\right) = S_1 u'(e_0)$$

$$\delta E\left[u'(e_1)\right] = \delta \sum_i^I \pi_i u'\left(e_1^{(i)}\right) = S_f u'(e_0)$$

or

$$S_1 = \delta \frac{E\left[y_1 u'(e_1)\right]}{u'(e_0)}$$

$$S_f = \delta \frac{E\left[u'(e_1)\right]}{u'(e_0)}$$

Example 2.5 In our example, the first-order conditions simplify in equilibrium to discounted expected values of the marginal utilities of the future payoffs of each security:

$$S_1 = \delta e_0 E\left[y_1 e_1^{-1}\right] = 0.95\left(0.9\frac{1.50}{1.25} + 0.1\frac{0.25}{0.50}\right) = 1.0735$$

$$S_f = \delta e_0 E\left[e_1^{-1}\right] = 0.95\left(0.9\frac{1}{1.25} + 0.1\frac{1}{0.50}\right) = 0.874$$

When we first looked at the first-order conditions, these trade-offs were seen to depend on the individual's portfolio choices; given the prices S_1 and S_f, we know what the household will choose. But in the no-trade equilibrium of the representative agent model, given agent preferences and the endowment process, choices and prices mutually adjust. Thus, given future consumption, state-by-state, we know what the shadow asset prices must be.

This leads to a set of pricing arguments that varies by state, and combines information about both pure time discounting and risk aversion. It is called the *stochastic discount factor* (SDF), *pricing kernel, pricing functional,* or the *state prices,* depending on which of its characteristics you want to emphasize. We'll denote it κ. State prices are a random variable

$$\kappa_i = \delta \frac{u'\left(c_1^{(i)}\right)}{u'(c_0)} \qquad i = 1, \ldots, I$$

The SDF is a state-by-state list of marginal rates of transformation of present for future consumption, in equilibrium and given the current and future endowments.

The first-order conditions can be rewritten so as to display the asset prices as simple linear functions of κ, the payoffs, and their probabilities:

$$S_1 = \mathbf{E}\,[y_1\kappa] = \sum_i^I \pi_i y_1^{(i)} \kappa_i$$

$$S_f = \mathbf{E}\,[\kappa] = \sum_i^I \pi_i \kappa_i$$

The state-price approach simplifies asset pricing because the state prices come directly out of the pure intertemporal optimization problem, in which there are no assets, only a consumption process over time. First we identify the "pricing calculator"; information about individual asset payoffs can then be added in a later step. The pricing formulas hold for any riskless or risky asset n, and can be computed as long as we know its payoffs $y_n^{(i)}$, $i = 1, \ldots, I$:

$$S_n = \mathbf{E}\,[y_n\kappa] = \sum_i^I \pi_i y_n^{(i)} \kappa_i \qquad n = 1, 2, \ldots$$

The payoffs are different, but the state price density κ is the same for all n. That's what we mean by "shadow" assets. They don't really have to exist for us to price them this way, and we don't need a complete list of assets in advance of pricing any individual one of them. In particular, there does not have to actually be a riskless asset for us to know what its price would be if such a thing were to exist. That is convenient, because, as we see in Section 2.5, it is hard to find an asset that is truly riskless.

The pricing formula can be expressed equivalently in terms of returns as

$$1 = \mathbf{E}\,[(1 + r_n)\kappa] = \sum_i^I \pi_i \left(1 + r_n^{(i)}\right) \kappa_i$$

$$1 = \mathbf{E}\,[(1 + r_f)\kappa] = (1 + r_f) \sum_i^I \pi_i \kappa_i$$

The risk-free rate is higher when future consumption is higher on average and less uncertain. The price of the risk-free asset is the expected value of the SDF, and is related to r_f, the risk-free rate of return, by

$$S_f = \frac{1}{1 + r_f} = E[\kappa] = \delta E\left[\frac{u'(e_1)}{u'(e_0)}\right]$$

$$= \sum_i^I \pi_i \kappa_i = \delta \frac{1}{u'(c_0)} \sum_i^I \pi_i u'\left(c_1^{(i)}\right)$$

Example 2.6 The state prices in our example are

State	κ_i
$i = 1$	0.76
$i = 2$	1.90

The state price for state 1, $\kappa_1 = 0.76$, is much smaller than $\kappa_2 = 1.90$, because consumption is higher in state 1, lowering its marginal utility and thus the value of an additional unit of it.

The risk-free return is $(0.874)^{-1} - 1$ or 14.4 percent, and the returns and excess returns of the risky asset in each state are

State	$r_1^{(i)}$	$r_1^{(i)} - r_f$
$i = 1$	39.7	25.3
$i = 2$	−76.7	−91.1

The expected risky return and excess return are 28.1 and 13.7 percent.

The risk premium is just a different way of expressing the price of a risky asset, but has an illuminating relationship to the stochastic discount factor. Subtract the equilibrium pricing condition of risky asset n from that of the risk-free asset:

$$E\left[(r_n - r_f)\kappa\right] = 0$$

The expected value of the excess return on any risky asset times the SDF equals zero. In other words, at equilibrium prices, you are exactly compensated for the risk you take.

We'll transform this expression using the *covariance*, which measures the extent to which fluctuations in two random variables coincide. For any random variables x and y, the covariance is defined as

$$\text{Cov}(x, y) = \text{E}\left[(x - \text{E}[x])(y - \text{E}[y])\right]$$

Next, use the relationship $\text{Cov}(x, y) = \text{E}[xy] - \text{E}[x]\text{E}[y]$ for any random variables x and y to get

$$\text{E}\left[(r_n - r_f)\kappa\right] = \text{Cov}(r_n - r_f, \kappa) + \text{E}\left[r_n - r_f\right]\text{E}[\kappa] = 0$$

implying

$$\text{E}\left[r_n - r_f\right]\text{E}[\kappa] = -\text{Cov}(r_n - r_f, \kappa)$$

Now, r_f is not random, but known at $t = 0$, so $\text{Cov}(r_n - r_f, \kappa) = \text{Cov}(r_n, \kappa)$ and

$$\text{E}\left[r_n - r_f\right] = -\frac{\text{Cov}(r_n, \kappa)}{\text{E}[\kappa]} = -\frac{\text{Cov}(r_n, \kappa)}{\text{Var}(\kappa)}\frac{\text{Var}(\kappa)}{\text{E}[\kappa]}$$

The first term, $\frac{\text{Cov}(r_n, \kappa)}{\text{Var}(\kappa)}$, is the regression coefficient of the risky security's returns on the SDF and is called the *beta* of the risky security to the SDF κ. The beta is often interpreted as the variation in the risky security's return that can be "explained by" or "predicted from" the SDF's variation across states. The beta depends on the return distribution of the specific security as well as—via the SDF—preferences and the endowment. It is positive when the risky security has high payoffs in high-SDF states, that is, states in which consumption is low and its marginal utility is high.

The second term,

$$\frac{\text{Var}(\kappa)}{\text{E}[\kappa]} = (1 + r_f)\,\text{Var}(\kappa)$$

is a measure of aggregate risk called the *price of risk*. It is the same for all assets and is driven by preferences (via δ and the type of utility function) and the variance of future consumption across states. The variance of the SDF can be high either because the dispersion of future consumption, that is, the fundamental risk in the economy, is high, or because risk aversion is high, pulling apart the marginal rates of transformation for a given distribution of future consumption.

If the beta is negative, that is, the risky security tends to pay off more when the SDF is low and the endowment is plentiful, and the SDF also has high dispersion, then prices of risky assets will be driven lower, and their risk premiums higher; hence the minus sign.

Example 2.7 Continuing our example, we have $\text{Var}(\kappa) = 0.650$ and $\text{Cov}(r_n, \kappa) = -0.7125$, so the beta is

$$\frac{\text{Cov}(r_n, \kappa)}{\text{Var}(\kappa)} = -1.0965$$

and the price of risk is

$$\frac{\text{Var}(\kappa)}{\text{E}\,[\kappa]} = 0.7435$$

The risky security has a positive risk premium, since it has a high payoff in the high-consumption state, when you need that high payoff the least, and vice versa.

2.2.4 Risk-Neutral Probabilities

There is an alternative point of view on this approach to pricing via utility and endowments. Instead of taking the expected value of the asset's payoffs, weighted by the stochastic discount factor, we'll ask an "inverse" question: What probabilities do we need to be able to derive the equilibrium asset price, but now as an expected present value discounted at *the risk-free rate*? These new probabilities are called *risk-neutral probabilities* $\tilde{\pi}_i, i = 1, \ldots, I$, in contrast to the real-life *subjective* or *physical probabilities* we have used up until now to compute expected values. Substituting the risk-neutral for the physical probabilities, but leaving the state space and the set of outcomes unchanged, leads to the *risk-neutral probability measure*.

In the two-period model, the risk neutral probabilities are defined as

$$\tilde{\pi}_i = \frac{\pi_i \kappa_i}{\sum_i^I \pi_i \kappa_i} = \frac{\pi_i \kappa_i}{1 + r_f} \qquad i = 1, \ldots, I$$

This gives us a way of expressing security prices as a straightforward expected present value of the payoffs, weighted using the risk-neutral probabilities, discounting by the risk-free rate. The standard pricing equation can be rewritten

$$S_n = \mathrm{E}\,[y_n \kappa] = \frac{\tilde{\mathrm{E}}\,[y_n]}{1 + r_f} = \frac{1}{1 + r_f} \sum_i^I \tilde{\pi}_i\, y_n^{(i)} \qquad n = 1, 2, \ldots$$

The notation $\tilde{\mathrm{E}}\,[x]$ denotes the expected value of x, using risk-neutral rather than physical probabilities.

To provide some intuition on risk-neutral probabilities, think for a moment about how asset pricing works in our model. The assets are traded in the market, and the price of each claim will depend on the payoffs of the asset in different states, the endowment or "market" payoff in each state, the probability of each state, and the desirability of getting an additional payoff in that state via investment in the asset. If there are many traders or agents, "desirability" is aggregated through the market. In a representative agent model, it depends on endowments; the marginal utility of future consumption is higher in states in which the endowment is low.

Desirability is important. If two claims have the same payoff in two equiprobable states, they won't have the same price if consumption goods are scarcer in one state than in the other. The impact of return distributions is blended with that of the market's risk preferences.

If there is no arbitrage, the prices of the assets therefore imply a probability distribution of states. It may be quite different from the "true" or physical distribution, but *all the claims will be priced consistently with it.* Conversely, if this is not true, that is, if the prices of two claims reflect different risk-neutral probabilities of some states, then an arbitrage profit is available.

We can also see that the risk-neutral expected return is equal to the risk-free rate:

$$1 = \mathrm{E}\,[(1 + r_n)\kappa] = \frac{\tilde{\mathrm{E}}\,[(1 + r_n)]}{1 + r_f}$$
$$\Rightarrow \tilde{\mathrm{E}}\,[r_n] \quad = \quad r_f$$

Suppose we have a set of securities that each provide a payoff of $1 in one of the I future states, and 0 otherwise. These securities are called *elementary* or *contingent claims* or *state price securities*. There is an elementary claim for each state $i = 1, \ldots, I$, with a price ε_i.

Even without knowing the individual prices of the elementary claims, we can make some statements about them. If you had a portfolio of 1 unit of each of the elementary claims, you would receive 1 unit of the consumption good regardless of the future state, so it would be equivalent to having a risk-free bond. The sum of the prices of the elementary claims must therefore equal the price of a risk free-bond $S_f = \frac{1}{1+r_f}$.

To find the individual prices of the elementary claims, write out the pricing formula for a security that pays off one unit in one state, say i:

$$\varepsilon_i = \pi_1 \kappa_1 \cdot 0 + \cdots + \pi_i \kappa_i \cdot 1 + \cdots + \pi_I \kappa_I \cdot 0 = \pi_i \kappa_i \qquad i = 1, \ldots, I$$

But then the risk-neutral probabilities are also equal to the present values of the elementary claims prices:

$$\tilde{\pi}_i = (1 + r_f) \pi_i \kappa_i = (1 + r_f) \varepsilon_i \qquad i = 1, \ldots, I$$

These properties also provide an equivalent way of valuing any asset as the price of a bundle of elementary claims.

Example 2.8   In our two-state log utility example, the risk-neutral probabilities and elementary claim prices are

State	π_i	$\tilde{\pi}_i$	ε_i
$i = 1$	0.90	0.78	0.68
$i = 2$	0.10	0.22	0.19

The risk-neutral probability for "bad" state 2 is more than double the physical probability, reflecting the desire of the risk-averse individual to insure a higher level of consumption in that state.

Risk-neutral probabilities combine information about the physical probabilities with information about preferences. They are important for two reasons. First, they provide an alternative pricing approach for securities that can be hedged by other securities, plain-vanilla options providing the classic example. Second, as we see in Chapters 10 and 14, we can not only compute asset prices using risk-neutral probabilities. We can also use observed asset prices to estimate risk-neutral probabilities. A risk-neutral probability distribution can be extracted from forward and option prices, and can shed a great deal of light on market sentiment regarding risk.

2.3   THE STANDARD ASSET DISTRIBUTION MODEL

The standard risk measurement model we describe in this section is focused not so much on the asset price itself, or even its mean, as on its potential range of variation; we are interested in the volatility, not the trend. The standard model says little on the trend of asset prices.

The starting point for the model is the *geometric Brownian motion* or *diffusion* model of the behavior over time of an asset price or risk factor S_t. This model is also the basis for the Black-Scholes option pricing model, and is generally a point of departure for analysis of asset return behavior.

In this standard model, returns are normally distributed. The standard model can be useful when overall or "main body" risk is important, as opposed to extreme moves. The model can also serve as a building block, or a teaching tool. But there is extensive evidence, which we review in Chapter 10, that returns are not normally distributed.

First, we will show how this model is built, so that we can understand its implications. We are interested in price fluctuations, so it is the asset *returns* that we ultimately need to understand. We start with a model of asset returns, and show how to derive the geometric Brownian motion model of the asset price from it. Finally, we see how to measure return volatility using the model.

To model the variability of risk factors over time, we look for a stochastic process that, for a suitable choice of parameters, will mimic the behavior seen in real-world risk factors. A stochastic process is an indexed set of random variables; the index is taken to be time. If we could model an observable risk factor exactly using a particular stochastic process, the historical time series of risk factor values would still not itself *be* the stochastic process. Rather, it would be a *sample path* of the stochastic process. The number of possible sample paths depends on the sample space of the stochastic process.

2.3.1 Random Walks and Wiener Processes

We'll set out a model of r_t, the logarithmic asset return, and then build on that to derive a model of asset price behavior. The geometric Brownian motion model builds on a stochastic process called the *random walk*. A random walk is a random variable that

- Is a function of "time" t, which runs from zero (or some arbitrary positive number) to infinity
- Starts at $(0, 0)$
- Adds increments to its level at time steps of length Δt
- Moves up or down at each time step by an amount $\sqrt{\Delta t}$
- Moves up with probability π and down with probability $1 - \pi$

Let's denote the steps or increments to the random walk by Y_i and its position or state after n steps by

$$X_n = \sum_{i=1}^{n} Y_i$$

If we chop t into finer and finer steps, that is, make Δt smaller, n will be larger. The Y_i are independent and identically distributed. The number of moves up ($Y_i > 0$) is therefore a binomially distributed random variable with parameters n and π. Denoting by k the number of up-moves in the first n steps, the state or position of the random walk X_n can be written as

$$X_n = [k - (n - k)]\Delta t = (2k - n)\Delta t$$

since the number of down-moves ($Y_i < 0$) in the first n steps is $n - k$.

There are 2^n possible paths $(Y_1, \ldots, Y_n)$, each with a probability $\frac{1}{2^n}$. There are $2n + 1$ possible values $(-n\Delta t, \ldots, -\Delta t, 0, \Delta t, \ldots, n\Delta t)$ of the position X_n, with the probability of each equal to the that of the corresponding binomially distributed number of up-moves. Apart from the extreme "straight up" and "straight down" paths that lead to $X_n = -n\Delta t$ and $X_n = -n\Delta t$, there is more than one way to reach each possible value of X_n.

It's convenient to set $\pi = \frac{1}{2}$. The mean of each step is then

$$E[Y_i] = E\left[\frac{1}{2}\sqrt{\Delta t} + \frac{1}{2}\left(-\sqrt{\Delta t}\right)\right] = 0 \quad i = 1, \ldots, n$$

and its variance is

$$\mathrm{Var}[Y_i] = E\left[Y_i^2\right] - (E[Y_i])^2 = \frac{1}{2}\left(\sqrt{\Delta t}\right)^2 + \frac{1}{2}\left(-\sqrt{\Delta t}\right)^2 = \Delta t \quad i = 1, \ldots, n$$

From these facts, together with the independence of the steps, we can compute the variance of the position after n steps:

$$E[X_n] = 0$$

$$\mathrm{Var}[X_n] = n\Delta t$$

The time elapsed after n steps is $t = n\Delta t$, so one property we can see right away is that the variance of the state of a random walk is equal to the time elapsed t, and thus its standard deviation is equal to $\sqrt{t}$. This is an

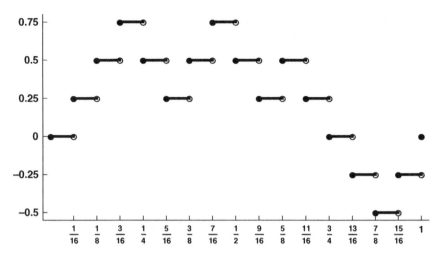

FIGURE 2.2 Sample Path of a Random Walk

Plot shows the first 16 positions of one simulation of a random walk. The total time elapsed in the first 16 steps is set to $t = 1$, so the time interval between adjacent steps is $\Delta t = \frac{1}{16}$ and the magnitude of the increments is $|Y_i| = \frac{1}{\sqrt{\Delta t}} = \frac{1}{\sqrt{16}} = \frac{1}{4}, i = 1, \ldots$ The solid dots show the value the position takes on at the start of each time interval, and the open circles show the points of discontinuity.

important relationship between volatility and the passage of time that we will see repeatedly in different forms.

The random walk is a discrete time or discontinuous stochastic process, as illustrated in Figure 2.2. Any value of t will do, so let's set $t = 1$, so that $\Delta t = \frac{1}{n}$. But now let the number of the time steps go to infinity by holding $t = n\Delta t = 1$ constant, letting $n \to \infty$ and $\Delta t \to 0$. As the number of time steps grows, the mean and variance of the position X_n remain unchanged at 0 and 1, respectively.

The magnitude of the low-probability extreme states $X_n = \pm n\Delta t = \pm 1$ remains constant, but the probability of reaching them decreases as the number of time steps increases, even though the total time elapsed and the variance of the state X_n are *not* increasing. Figure 2.3 displays the distribution of the terminal position X_n for an increasing fineness of the time steps between time 0 and 1.

But computing the probabilities under the binomial distribution of the number of up moves, and thus of X_n, becomes difficult as the number of time steps grows. It is also not necessary. Figure 2.3 suggests that the distribution of the terminal position X_n converges to the normal. In fact, we can invoke the central limit theorem to show that the distribution of X_n converges to a

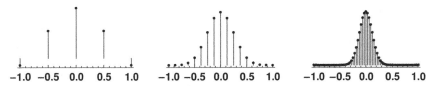

FIGURE 2.3 Convergence of a Random Walk to a Brownian Motion
The plots display the probability density of X_n, the terminal position of a random walk over an interval of length 1, with $n = 4, 16, 64$ time steps and with the probability of a step in either direction set to $\pi = \frac{1}{2}$.

standard normal random variable. The mean and variance haven't changed, but we have an easier distribution than the binomial to work with.

The stochastic process to which the state X_n of the random walk converges is called a *Brownian motion* or *Wiener process* W_t. The value of W_t is a zero-mean normal variate with a variance equal to t:

$$W_t \sim N(0, \sqrt{t})$$

We have defined an increment to a Brownian motion as the limit of a random walk as its time steps shrink to zero, but this is technically not necessary. A Brownian motion is defined uniquely by the following properties:

1. It starts at $W_0 = 0$.
2. For any $t \geq 0$ and $\tau > 0$, the increment to the process over the period $t + \tau$ is normally distributed:

$$W_{t+\tau} - W_t \sim N(0, \sqrt{\tau})$$

Each such increment can be thought of as composed of infinitely many random walk steps.
3. The increment $W_{t+\tau} - W_t$ is independent of the history of the process up to time t. In other words, the random variables W_t and $W_{t+\tau} - W_t$ are independent. This is called the *martingale property*. In fact, if we chop all of history into intervals such that $0 \leq t_1 < t_2 < \cdots < t_n < \infty$, the increments $W_{t_1}, W_{t_2} - W_{t_1}, \cdots, W_{t_n} - W_{t_{n-1}}$ are all independent.
4. Every sample path is continuous.

All other properties of Brownian motion can be derived from this definition. The last one is a major difference from the random walk, which, as we saw, is discontinuous.

Some of Brownian motion's properties are initially counterintuitive, such as the fact that its *total variation process*, the expected value of the total distance a Brownian motion moves over any interval, no matter how short, is infinite. To see this, recall that the magnitude of the random walk step is $|\sqrt{\Delta t}| = \sqrt{\Delta t}$ with certainty, so that is also its expected magnitude. But then the total distance traveled over the interval t is, with certainty, equal to

$$n\sqrt{\Delta t} = \frac{t}{\Delta t}\sqrt{\Delta t} = \frac{t}{\sqrt{\Delta t}}$$

and its limit as $\Delta t \to 0$ is infinity. This is one aspect of Brownian motion's "urge to wander." It is constantly vibrating, so if you take the path it has traveled, even over a very short time, and uncurl it, it is infinitely long, and composed of infinitely many tiny, sharp, up or down moves. For this reason, although continuous, Brownian motion is not smooth. In fact, it cannot be differentiated: $\frac{\partial W_t}{\partial t}$ does not exist.

Yet its *quadratic variation process*, the expected value of the sum of the *squared* distances it moves over any interval, no matter how many, is *finite* and equal to the length of the interval. The quadratic variation of a Brownian motion is another form that the relationship between volatility and the passage of time takes. Although it has a strong urge to wander "in the small"—infinite total variation—it wanders in a contained way "in the large."

To gain intuition about these properties, let's look at Figure 2.4, which illustrates the convergence of a random walk to a Brownian motion. It shows a *single* sample path of a Brownian motion, sampled at progressively finer subintervals of the interval $(0, 1)$. It starts in the upper left hand panel by dividing $(0, 1)$ into 16 subintervals, and ends in the lower right with 1,024 subintervals. In other words, we are approximating the continuous Brownian motion with a sequence of discrete random walks.

Because we are plotting a single sample path, the value of W_t must be the same in each panel for any point in time, such as $\frac{1}{16}$. For example, in the upper right panel, the interval $(0, 1)$ is divided into 64 subintervals. The values of the Brownian motion at times $\frac{1}{16}, \frac{1}{8}, \ldots, \frac{15}{16}, 1$ must be the same as in the upper left panel. But we can't just generate the 64-step version and connect every fourth value with a straight line to get the 16-step version. This would violate the requirement that the random walk move up or down at each time step.

Rather, we generate the 16-step version, and interpolate a 4-step discrete *Brownian bridge* between neighboring points. A Brownian bridge is just a Brownian motion that is constrained to end at a certain point at a certain

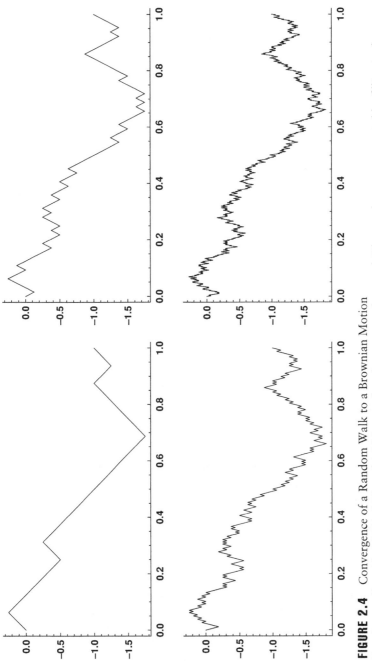

FIGURE 2.4 Convergence of a Random Walk to a Brownian Motion
Random walks with 16, 64, 256, and 1,024 steps, but the same random seed. The graphs are constructed by filling in the intermediate steps with discrete Brownian bridges.

time. In simulation, one uses a Brownian bridge to "thicken up" Brownian motion sample points in a way that is true to the Brownian motion's tendency to wander, while still getting it to the next, already-known, sample point. Let's take a closer look at the construction of a Brownian bridge in order to better understand the variation properties of Brownian motion.

Denote up-moves in the random walk representations by a 1 and down-moves by a 0. The 16-step random walk can then be represented as a random sequence of 0s and 1s. In our example, we are increasing the fineness of the random walk by subdividing each time interval into four equal subintervals in each step of the convergence to a Brownian motion. Since each time step is divided into four, and $2 = \sqrt{4}$, the magnitude of the up- and down-moves is divided by two. If the next step in the coarser random walk is a down-move, there are then four different ways the finer random walk could get there in four steps, with each increment just half the size of the coarser random walk's increments. They can be represented by the 4-dimensional identity matrix

$$\begin{pmatrix} 1 & 0 & 0 & 0 \\ 0 & 1 & 0 & 0 \\ 0 & 0 & 1 & 0 \\ 0 & 0 & 0 & 1 \end{pmatrix}$$

The four possible bridging paths if there is an up-move are

$$\begin{pmatrix} 0 & 1 & 1 & 1 \\ 1 & 0 & 1 & 1 \\ 1 & 1 & 0 & 1 \\ 1 & 1 & 1 & 0 \end{pmatrix} = \begin{pmatrix} 1 & 1 & 1 & 1 \\ 1 & 1 & 1 & 1 \\ 1 & 1 & 1 & 1 \\ 1 & 1 & 1 & 1 \end{pmatrix} - \begin{pmatrix} 1 & 0 & 0 & 0 \\ 0 & 1 & 0 & 0 \\ 0 & 0 & 1 & 0 \\ 0 & 0 & 0 & 1 \end{pmatrix}$$

Note that the required bridge does not depend on the last step or on the position, but only on the next step. This is an expression of the martingale property, or "memorylessness," of Brownian motion. To generate the finer random walk, at each step of the coarser random walk, depending on whether it is an up or down move, we randomly pick one of the four rows of the appropriate one of these matrices to generate the intermediate four steps.

We can now see how increasing the fineness of the random walk increases the total distance traveled. Each time we refine the random walk by dividing the time steps by a factor of four, multiplying the number of time steps by four, and connecting the steps with a Brownian bridge, we double the distance traveled compared to one step of the coarser random walk. As the random walk becomes finer and finer, and converges to a Brownian motion, the distance traveled—the total variation—approaches infinity. But the quadratic variation has remained at unity.

2.3.2 Geometric Brownian Motion

The Wiener process W_t, with a few changes, provides our model of *logarithmic returns* on the asset:

- We add a *drift* μ, expressed as a decimal per time period t. We can do this by adding a constant $\mu \Delta t$ to each step of the random walk as it converges to W_t.
- We scale the random walk by a *volatility* term σ by multiplying each time step of the original random walk by σ. The volatility will be assumed for now to be a constant parameter, not dependent on the current level of the asset price and not dependent on time.

The convergence results of the last subsection remain the same, but the value of the Brownian motion is now a normally distributed random variable with mean μt and variance $\sigma^2 t$:

$$W_t \sim N(\mu t, \sigma \sqrt{t})$$

This completes the model of *increments to the logarithm* of the asset price or risk factor. A standard way to write this is as a *stochastic differential equation* (SDE):

$$d \log(S_t) = \mu dt + \sigma d W_t$$

The random value of an increment to the log of the asset price over some time interval $(t, t + \tau)$ can be expressed as

$$\log(S_{t+\tau}) = \log(S_t) + \mu \tau + \sigma (W_{t+\tau} - W_t)$$

So we now have a model of log returns:

$$r_{t,\tau} = \mu \tau + \sigma (W_{t+\tau} - W_t)$$

Logarithmic returns are therefore normally distributed:

$$r_{t,\tau} \sim N(\mu \tau, \sigma \sqrt{\tau})$$

Based on this model, we build a model of the *increments to the level* of the asset price. We can't simply take exponents to characterize the level of the asset price itself. Rather, we must apply Itô's Lemma, using the relationship $S_t = e^{\log(S_t)}$. We get the SDE

$$dS_t = \left(\mu + \frac{1}{2}\sigma^2\right) S_t dt + \sigma S_t dW_t \qquad (2.1)$$

Intuitively, this makes perfect sense. If the logarithm of the asset price moves randomly up or down in proportion to a volatility factor σ, the random increases will accelerate the exponential growth more than the equally probable random decreases will decelerate them. The reason is that the positive returns increase the asset price level, the base for the next vibration, while the negative returns decrease the base. So the exponent of the process, the asset price level, will grow on average just a bit faster than μ, quite apart from its random fluctuations. Itô's Lemma tells us exactly how much: $\frac{1}{2}\sigma^2$ per time unit.

Another way to see this is to go back to the discrete-time model for a moment and imagine an asset price moving up or down each period by the same proportional amount σ. The asset price starts at some arbitrary positive level S_0, and

$$S_t = \begin{cases} S_{t-1}(1+\sigma) & \text{for} \quad t-1 \quad \text{odd} \\ S_{t-1}(1-\sigma) & \text{for} \quad t-1 \quad \text{even} \end{cases}$$

The volatility of logarithmic changes in the asset is approximately σ if σ is low. For any $\sigma > 0$, S_t will eventually go to zero; how quickly depends on how large is σ. If, however, we adjust the process to

$$S_t = \begin{cases} S_{t-1}\left(1+\sigma+\frac{\sigma^2}{2}\right) & \text{for} \quad t-1 \quad \text{odd} \\ S_{t-1}\left(1-\sigma+\frac{\sigma^2}{2}\right) & \text{for} \quad t-1 \quad \text{even} \end{cases}$$

it will stay very close to S_0 almost indefinitely.

The solution to the SDE, Equation (2.1), for the asset price level is

$$S_t = S_0 e^{\mu dt + \sigma dW_t} \qquad (2.2)$$

Figure 2.5 illustrates the behavior of an asset price following geometric Brownian motion, and Figure 2.6 illustrates the behavior of log returns. The

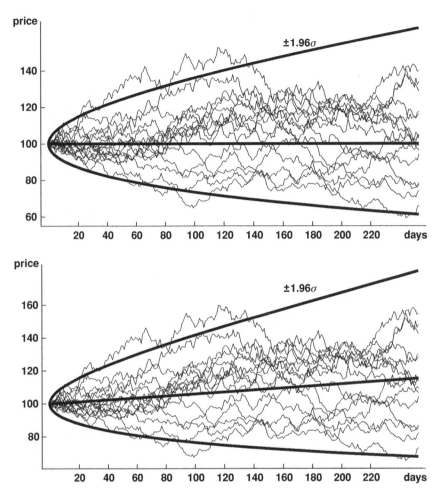

FIGURE 2.5 Geometric Brownian Motion: Asset Price Level
Upper panel (zero drift) Fifteen simulations of the price level over time of an asset
following a geometric Brownian motion process with $\mu = 0$ and $\sigma = 0.25$ at an
annual rate. The initial price of the asset is $S_0 = 100$. The hyperbola plots the 95
percent confidence interval over time: at any point in time, 95 percent of the
simulated path should be within it.
Lower panel (positive drift) This panel is identical to the one above but with
$\mu = 0.20$ at an annual rate.

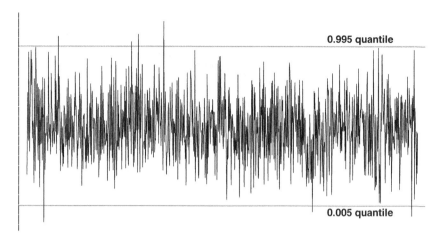

FIGURE 2.6 Geometric Brownian Motion: Daily Returns
Simulation of 1,000 sequential steps of a geometric Brownian motion process with $\mu = 0$ and $\sigma = 0.25$ at an annual rate. The horizontal grid lines mark the 99 percent confidence interval. There should be about five occurrences of returns above and below the grid lines. In most samples of 1,000, however, this will not be exactly the case. This becomes important when we try to assess the quality of model-based risk measures.

asset price has these properties if it follows a geometric Brownian motion process:

- The asset price is equally likely to move up or down.
- The further into the future we look, the likelier it is that the asset price will be far from its current level.
- The higher the volatility, the likelier it is that the asset price will be far from its current level within a short time.
- The time series of daily logarithmic asset *returns* are independent draws from a normal distribution.

Example 2.9 (Distribution of Asset Price Under Standard Model) Using the stochastic process illustrated in Figure 2.5, with $S_0 = 100$, $\mu = 0$, and $\sigma = 0.125$, the expected value of the asset price after 128 business days ($t = 0.5$) is 100, and the 95 percent confidence interval for $S_{0.5}$ is $(83.7659, 118.451)$.

2.3.3 Asset Return Volatility

As we have seen, in the standard model, logarithmic returns on an asset that follows a geometric Brownian motion with a drift μ and volatility σ

are normally distributed as $N(\mu\tau, \sigma\sqrt{\tau})$. Expected return and variance are proportional to the time interval over which the returns are measured:

$$E[r_{t,\tau}] = \mu\tau$$
$$\text{Var}(r_{t,\tau}) = E[(r_{t,\tau} - E[r_{t,\tau}])^2]) = \sigma^2\tau$$

The return volatility or standard deviation is proportional to the square root of the interval:

$$\sqrt{\text{Var}(r_{t,\tau})} = \sigma\sqrt{\tau}$$

This is called the *square-root-of-time rule*. It is commonly used to convert volatilities and covariances from one interval, such as daily, to another, such as annual, and vice versa. In computing volatility for shorter periods than one year, we usually take only trading days rather than calendar days into account. Once holidays and weekends are accounted for, a typical year in the United States and Europe has a bit more than 250 trading days (52 five-day weeks, less 8 to 10 holidays). A convenient rule of thumb is to assume 256 trading days. Converting from annual to daily volatility is then a simple division by $\sqrt{256} = 16$.

Our notation for return doesn't indicate the period over which returns are measured. In the standard model, this doesn't matter, because the square-root-of-time tells us how to move back and forth between measurement intervals. In a different model, the measurement period can be very important. For example, in a mean-reverting volatility model, measuring return volatility over a short period such as one day might lead to a wild overestimate of volatility over a longer period such as one year.

2.4 PORTFOLIO RISK IN THE STANDARD MODEL

The standard model, as we've presented it so far, is a world with just one risk factor: The only source of uncertainty is the randomness of the future endowment. But the world may have more than one "ultimate" source of risk, and portfolios typically contain exposures to many securities. So we need to think about how the risks of the individual securities or risk factors relate to one another. First, of course, we introduce even more notation. We have a portfolio with x_n units, priced at S_n, of each of the N assets in the portfolio, $n = 1, \ldots, N$. The units might be the number of shares of stock or the bond par value or the number of currency units.

We need a model of the joint or multivariate probability distribution of the N returns. The natural extension of the standard model we just outlined is to stipulate that risk factors follow a multidimensional geometric Brownian motion process. The portfolio's logarithmic returns are then jointly normally distributed. In the joint normal model, each of the N assets has a log return distribution

$$r_{t,\tau,n} \sim N(\mu_n\tau, \sigma_n\sqrt{\tau}) \qquad n = 1, \ldots, N$$

In a normal model, we can discuss "risk" and "volatility" nearly interchangeably. We therefore have to repeat our warning that returns are not, in fact, joint normal, so that the theories and tools laid out here should be thought of as expository devices or approximations.

2.4.1 Beta and Market Risk

Suppose we want to know how one asset's return varies with that of another asset or portfolio. The return covariance measures the variance of one asset's return that is associated with another asset's return variance. It is expressed in squared return units:

$$\sigma_{mn} = E\left[(r_m - E\left[r_m\right])(r_n - E\left[r_n\right])\right] \qquad m, n = 1, \ldots$$

where r_m and r_n now represent returns on two different assets as random variables rather than at a point in time.

The return correlation also measures the extent to which the asset returns move together. While the covariance will be affected by typical size of the returns of the two assets, and is hard to compare across asset pairs with different volatilities, correlation is always on $(-1, 1)$ and therefore easy to compare and interpret. The correlation ρ_{mn} is related to volatility $\sigma_n = \sqrt{E\left[(r_n - \mu_n)^2\right]}$ and covariance by

$$\rho_{mn} = \frac{\sigma_{mn}}{\sigma_m\sigma_n} \qquad m, n = 1, \ldots$$

We previously introduced beta as a measure of the comovement of a security's returns with aggregate economic risk. Beta is also used as a statistical measure of the comovement of the returns of two different assets. The beta of asset m to asset n is defined as the ratio of the covariance of asset m's and asset n's excess returns to the variance of asset n's excess return:

$$\beta_{mn} = \frac{\sigma_{mn}}{\sigma_n^2}$$

The beta is often interpreted as the variation in asset m return that can be "explained by" or "predicted from" asset n's variation. Typically, asset

n is a portfolio representing a major asset class such as stocks or bonds, or a major subclass, such as a national or industry index. Beta is then used as a relative risk measure; it can be viewed as telling you what the risk is of, say, a single stock relative to the stock market as a whole.

The standard way to estimate beta is to run a regression between the two assets' excess returns. The regression equation is:

$$r_{mt} - r_f = \alpha + \beta_{mn}(r_{nt} - r_f) + u_t$$

In the joint normal model, the error terms u_t in this equation are also normally distributed. The direction of the regression matters: in general $\beta_{mn} \neq \beta_{nm}$.

When we look at the beta of one asset's returns to another's or to an index, we are interested not only in "how much beta" there is—is the beta near unity, or negative, well above unity, or near zero?—but also the extent to which variation in the asset's return is attributable to variation in the index return. To measure this, we can look at the *R-squared* or R^2 of the regression, which is equal to the square of the correlation between the dependent and independent variables. Let $\hat{\rho}_{x,y}$ denote the sample correlation coefficient between x and y:

$$R^2 \equiv \hat{\rho}_{x,y}^2$$

We have $0 \leq R^2 \leq 1$. An R^2 close to 1 indicates that the index returns do much to explain movements in the asset. The R^2 of the regression is often interpreted as a measure of the explanatory power of beta.

The beta coefficient is related to the correlation by

$$\rho_{mn} = \beta_{mn}\frac{\sigma_n}{\sigma_m} \qquad \Leftrightarrow \qquad \beta_{mn} = \rho_{mn}\frac{\sigma_m}{\sigma_n}$$

So the beta is close to the correlation if the two variables are about the same in variability. If the dependent variable, say an individual stock, has a low volatility compared to the independent variable, say, a stock index, then even if the correlation is close to unity, the beta will be low.

Example 2.10 (Descriptive Statistics for EUR-USD and USD-JPY) For EUR-USD and JPY-USD price returns, November 1, 2005, to October 31, 2006, we have the following descriptive statistics. An estimate of their joint return distribution, under the assumption the pair of currency returns is a bivariate normal, is illustrated in Figure 2.7. A scatter plot of the returns and the estimated regression line of USD-JPY on EUR-USD are displayed in Figure 2.8. The ellipse plotted in Figure 2.8 contains 95 percent of the

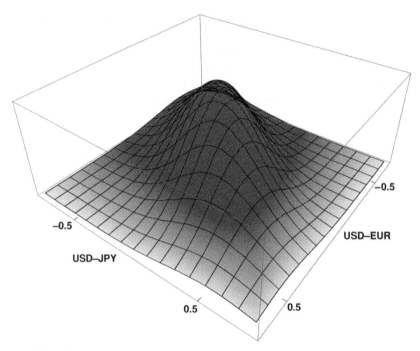

FIGURE 2.7 Joint Distribution of EUR and JPY Returns
Estimated joint normal density of logarithmic daily EUR-USD and JPY-USD price
returns, January 2, 1996, to October 6, 2006. Prices are expressed as the dollar
price of the non-USD currency. A slice parallel to x, y-plane corresponds to
confidence region for the two returns.
Source: Bloomberg Financial L.P.

observed returns. The volatilities are, using $\sqrt{252} = 15.8745$ as the square-
root-of-time factor:

	EUR-USD	JPY-USD
Daily return volatility	0.61	0.68
Annual return volatility	9.69	10.79

The statistics relating the two currencies to one another are

Covariance of daily returns	14.80×10^{-5}
Correlation of daily returns	0.357
Beta of EUR-USD to JPY-USD	0.320
Beta of JPY-USD to EUR-USD	0.398

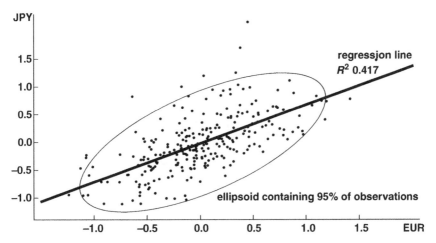

FIGURE 2.8 Correlation and Beta
Scatter plot of logarithmic daily EUR-USD and JPY-USD price returns, Nov. 1, 2005, to Oct. 31, 2006, and regression of USD-JPY on EUR-USD. Exchange rates are expressed as the dollar price of the non-USD currency.
Source: Bloomberg Financial L.P.

Conversely, one can easily have a high beta, but a low correlation and thus a low R^2, if the dependent variable has a very high volatility compared to the index. This will happen if an individual stock's return has only a loose association with the market's return, but, when the individual stock price moves, it moves a lot.

Figure 2.9 illustrates this possibility. In constructing the graph, we model the dependent and independent variables—the asset and index returns—as jointly normally distributed variates with zero mean. Once we have a model, we can state the population α, β, and R^2. The population α is zero, while the population β is given by the covariance matrix—that is, the volatilities and correlation—of the asset returns.

Suppose we fix the index return volatility at 15 percent. There are many ways to get, say, $\beta = 1$. If we set $\sigma_y = 2\sigma_x$, then we must have $\rho_{x,y} = 0.5$ and $R^2 = (0.5)^2 = 0.25$:

$$1 = \frac{2\sigma_x}{\sigma_x}0.5$$

Similarly, if $\sigma_y = 4\sigma_x$, that is, the dependent variable is highly volatile, the correlation must be only $\rho_{x,y} = 0.25$ and $R^2 = (0.25)^2 = 0.0625$. The slope of the line doesn't change, but the goodness-of-fit is much lower.

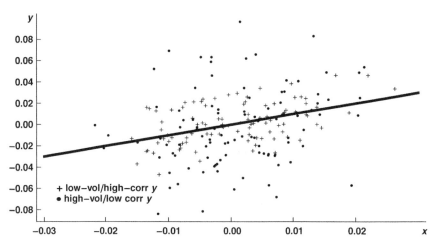

FIGURE 2.9 Volatility and Beta

Scatter plot of daily returns of joint realizations of a low-volatility and high volatility dependent and independent variates, and the common population regression line. The dependent variable volatility is set at $\sigma_x = 0.15$ per annum. The high-volatility dependent variable has $\sigma_x = 0.60$ and $\rho_{x.y} = 0.25$, and is represented by points. The low-volatility dependent variable has $\sigma_x = 0.30$ and $\rho_{x.y} = 0.50$, and is represented by +'s.

The population regression line has a slope $\beta = 1$ and intercept $\alpha = 0$ in both cases. If we did enough simulations, the sample regression lines would very likely coincide almost exactly with the population regression line. However, the high-volatility observations are vertically strewn very widely around the regression line compared to the low-volatility simulations.

Beta is often used in the context of the *capital asset pricing model* (CAPM), an equilibrium model framed in terms of security returns rather than consumption and endowments. The CAPM makes a strong assumption, mean-variance optimization, about investor preferences. In this model, a household's utility is a function of portfolio return and volatility rather than of consumption, and it seeks to maximize return for a given level of volatility. Like the consumption-based model developed above, the CAPM's major results can be expressed in terms of beta. The equilibrium return r_n of any security n can be expressed as

$$ \mathrm{E}\left[r_n - r_f\right] = \beta_n \mathrm{E}\left[r_{\mathrm{mkt}} - r_f\right] \qquad n = 1, 2, \ldots $$

where r_{mkt} represents the *market portfolio*. The market portfolio can be interpreted as an aggregate measure of risk, or as an aggregate of all the risky securities outstanding. In practical applications, it is represented by a broad market index such as the S&P 500 stock market index or a global stock market index such as the MSCI.

The beta relationship states that the expected excess return on any asset is proportional to the excess return of the market portfolio. The ratio of single-asset to market excess returns depends on security n's beta. This relationship is similar to that derived above in the standard asset pricing model. In both models, the risk premium of any individual security is a function of two components: a beta, which depends on the risk characteristics of the security itself, and a second component, the risk premium of the market portfolio, which is the same for all securities. In both models, there is single risk factor, whether the price of risk derived from the SDF, or the risk premium of the market portfolio, that embodies equilibrium prices, given preferences and fundamentals.

There are, however, important differences between β_n and $\frac{\text{Cov}(r_n, \kappa)}{\text{Var}(\kappa)}$. The CAPM beta is *positive* for securities that pay off in prosperous times, when the market portfolio is high, while $\frac{\text{Cov}(r_n, \kappa)}{\text{Var}(\kappa)}$ is positive for securities that pay off in lean times when consumption is low. That is why the CAPM beta relationship omits the minus sign.

A further major result of the CAPM is that, in equilibrium, asset prices must have adjusted so that the market portfolio is the optimal mix of risky assets for everyone. Portfolio choice is not about choosing securities, since prices will adjust in equilibrium so that households are content to own the mix of securities outstanding in the market. Rather, it is about choosing the mix of the risky market portfolio and a riskless asset. The latter choice depends on preferences and may differ across households with different utility functions.

The CAPM is not completely satisfying, because it relies on the very specific mean-variance optimization assumption about preferences, and because the concept of a market portfolio is both nebulous and unobservable. The *arbitrage pricing theory* (APT) is one response. Rather than making strong assumptions about preferences, it assumes that returns are linearly related to a set of (possibly unobservable) factors, and that arbitrage opportunities are competed away, at least for the most part.

The APT starts with a linear factor model of security n's returns:

$$r_n = \text{E}[r_n] + \beta_{n1} f_1 + \beta_{n2} f_2 + \cdots + \beta_{nK} f_K + \epsilon_n \qquad n = 1, 2, \ldots$$

The factors $f_1, \ldots, f_K$ are random variables, representing surprises or "news" such as a higher-than-expected inflation rate, or lower-than-expected profits in a particular industry. The β_{nk} are betas or sensitivities to the factors f_k. The model imposes these restrictions:

$$E[f_k] = 0 \quad \forall n = 1, \ldots, K$$
$$E[f_j f_k] = 0 \quad \forall j, k = 1, \ldots, K$$
$$E[\epsilon_n] = 0 \quad \forall n = 1, 2, \ldots$$
$$E[\epsilon_m \epsilon_n] = 0 \quad \forall m, n = 1, 2, \ldots$$

The first two restrictions state that, on average, there are no surprises in the factors and that the factors are independent of one another. The last two restrictions state that security prices adjust, up to a random error, so that expected excess returns are just what the factor model says they should be.

This model of expected returns is similar to, but more plausible than, the CAPM's single ultimate source of risk, embodying all the fundamental risks in the economy. The assumption of no or limited arbitrage possibilities is more attractive than a specific hypothesis on preferences. Using the factor-based return model, together with the no-arbitrage assumption, the APT arrives at this representation of equilibrium returns:

$$\mathrm{E}\left[r_n - r_f\right] \approx \beta_{n1}\lambda_1 + \beta_{n2}\lambda_2 + \cdots + \beta_{nK}\lambda_K \quad n = 1, 2, \ldots$$

where the β_{nk} are the same factor sensitivities as in the return model, and the λ_k are the expected excess returns or risk premiums on each of the K factors. The intuition behind the arbitrage pricing model is that asset and portfolio returns line up "more or less" with the returns on the factors that govern them, apart perhaps from random noise. We use a model like this to generate credit risk in Chapters 6 and 8

From a risk measurement standpoint, one limitation of the CAPM and arbitrage pricing models is that they explain return in terms of a "snapshot" of factors, while in practice returns may be generated by varying a portfolio over time. Gamma trading, which we discuss in Chapters 5 and 13, is the classic example of such a *dynamic strategy*. It is also very hard in practice to distinguish genuine alpha from harvesting of risk premiums.

2.4.2 Diversification

Diversification is reduction in risk from owning several different assets. We will explore diversification further in Chapter 13, when we discuss portfolio market and credit risk. For now, let's get a sense of the interaction between risk, volatility, and correlation in the simple model in which returns are jointly normally distributed.

It's easier at this point to work with the *weights* rather than the *number of units* of the assets. The market value of each position is $x_n S_n$. Each asset has a portfolio weight, related to the market values by

$$\omega_n = \frac{x_n S_n}{\sum_{n=1}^{N} x_n S_n} \qquad n = 1, \ldots, N$$

The volatility of a portfolio depends on the volatilities of the components and their correlations among one another. If a portfolio contains N assets, its volatility is

$$\sigma_p = \sum_{n=1}^{N} \omega_n^2 \sigma_n^2 + \sum_{n=1}^{N} \sum_{m=1}^{N} \omega_n \omega_m \sigma_n \sigma_m \rho_{nm}$$

Suppose we have a portfolio consisting of long positions in two assets. The assets themselves can also be portfolios in their own right, as long as we have good estimates—or at least estimates for which we are prepared to suspend disbelief—of their expected return, volatilities, and correlation. For concreteness, let's imagine the two assets are well-diversified portfolios of equities (asset 1) and bonds (asset 2).

Assume there is a fixed dollar amount that can be invested in the two assets, and that we can only take long positions in the portfolios, so it is unambiguous to speak of portfolio weights based on market values. Denote the expected returns by μ_n, the return volatilities by σ_n, $n = 1, 2$, the asset 1 weight by ω, and the returns correlation between the two assets by ρ. The portfolio return is

$$\mu_p = \omega \mu_1 + (1 - \omega)\mu_2$$

and the portfolio volatility is

$$\sigma_p = \sqrt{\omega^2 \sigma_1^2 + (1 - w)^2 \sigma_2^2 + 2\omega(1 - \omega)\sigma_1 \sigma_2 \rho}$$

In this simple setup with long positions only, there is (almost) always a diversification effect which reduces risk. Figure 2.10 illustrates the impact of the asset return volatilities and correlation and the allocation among the two assets on the diversification benefit:

- If correlation is +1 (perfect correlation), any portfolio that is long one or both assets has same risk. The diversification effect is zero, but you also don't add risk as the weight changes.

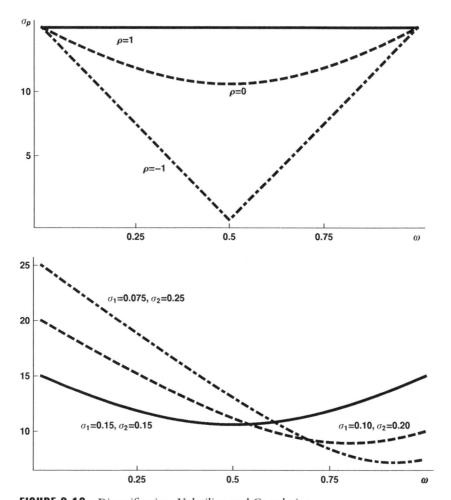

FIGURE 2.10 Diversification, Volatility, and Correlation
Upper panel: Volatility of a portfolio consisting of long positions in two assets with identical volatilities. Perfect correlation: any long-long portfolio has same risk. Zero correlation: one asset might have large loss while other does not. Diversification benefit in terms of vol. Greatest diversification benefit from negative (positive) correlation.
Lower panel: Volatility of a portfolio consisting of long positions in two assets with different volatilities and zero correlation. If the two volatilities are very different, the opportunity to diversify is more limited.

- If correlation is 0, one asset might have a loss while other does not. There is some diversification effect, unless one of the allocations and/or one of the volatilities is very large compared to the other.
- If correlation is –1 and the weights are the same ($\omega = 0.5$), the positions are a perfect offset, and portfolio risk is zero.
- If correlation is somewhere in between, there is a diversification benefit, but it may be small. If correlation is near zero then the diversification benefit will be small if the volatilities are very close to one another.

2.4.3 Efficiency

Not every diversified portfolio is *efficient*. An efficient portfolio is one in which the investments are combined in the right amounts, so that you cannot get extra return from a different combination without also getting some extra volatility. We distinguish between efficient portfolios and *minimum-variance portfolios*, which are portfolios with the lowest possible volatility for a given portfolio return. There generally are several minimum-variance portfolios with the same volatility, one of which has a higher portfolio return than the others. Only the latter is efficient. Figure 2.11 plots minimum-variance and efficient portfolios constructed from stocks and bonds for varying correlations between the two asset classes.

It is easy to plot these curves for just two assets; every combination of the two has minimum variance. If there is a third asset, things are more complicated. Substituting a high-volatility asset with a low or negative correlation to the other two, for a lower-volatility asset with a high correlation to the third asset, might reduce the portfolio volatility. So for more than two assets, mathematical programming techniques are required to plot the minimum-variance curve.

But once we identify any two minimum-variance portfolios, we "revert" to the two-asset case: We can plot the entire minimum-variance locus from just these two. So long as the stock and bond portfolios in our example are themselves minimum-variance portfolios, that is, well-diversified portfolios that can't be reshuffled to provide a higher return without also increasing volatility, the example is a good representation of the minimum-variance locus for the entire universe of stocks and bonds.

The efficient portfolios are the ones to the north and right of the *global minimum-variance portfolio*, the one combination of the assets that has the lowest volatility of all. Figure 2.10 displays an example of the efficient

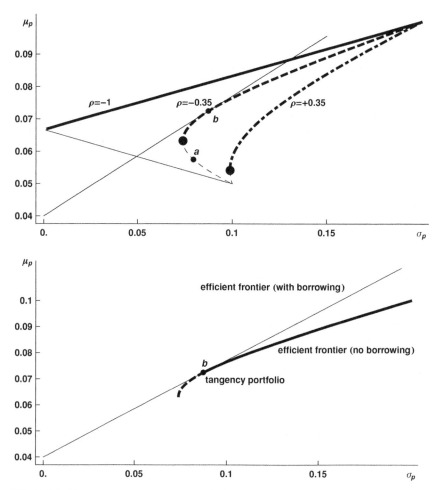

FIGURE 2.11   Minimum-Variance and Efficient Portfolios
Efficient frontier for portfolios that can be created from long positions in two
assets, for different correlations between the two assets.
Upper panel: Each curve shows the entire locus of minimum-variance portfolios.
The global minimum-variance portfolios are marked by black dots. The thick part
of each curve shows the efficient minimum-variance portfolios.
Lower panel: Efficient frontier with a risk-free rate of 0.04 and correlation −0.35.

frontier for portfolios that can be created from long positions in two assets (or portfolios) with expected returns and volatilities given by

	Return	Volatility
Stock portfolio	0.10	0.10
Bond portfolio	0.05	0.20

and correlations as noted in the graphs. The global minimum-variance portfolios correspond to the minima of the plots in the upper panel of Figure 2.10 and are marked with large dots in the upper panel of Figure 2.11. For a given covariance matrix of returns, the asset weights at this unique point don't depend on expected returns, though the resulting expected return does.

How can a portfolio be minimum-variance but inefficient? The dot marked "a" identifies one. It contains more bonds and less stocks than its efficient twin directly north of it on the same minimum-variance locus. Since bonds have a lower expected return, the portfolio has sacrificed return for no reward in lower volatility.

The upper panel of Figure 2.11 shows only the return-volatility combinations available by mixing long positions in stocks and bonds. If we are allowed to go short bonds, that is, borrow bonds, sell what we borrow, and use the proceeds to buy more stocks, we can get higher returns and higher volatility. The locus of available combinations with shorting would be the continuation of the hyperbola plots in the upper panel of Figure 2.10, northeast of the point at which the allocation to stocks is 100 percent. With shorting permitted, extremely high expected returns can be obtained, albeit with extremely high volatility. In addition, the ratio of return to volatility deteriorates at higher returns.

The availability of a risk-free rate changes the problem of finding efficient portfolios. The new efficient frontier is now no longer the upper arm of the hyperbola, but rather the straight line through the point r_f on the y-axis that is tangent to the locus of efficient portfolios without a risk-free rate. As in the case in which there is no borrowing at the risk-free rate, every efficient portfolio is a combination of two other "portfolios," the risk-free investment and the combination of stocks and bonds defined by the tangency point.

The efficient frontier with a risk-free investment, for a stock-bond return correlation of –0.35, is displayed as a thin solid line in the upper panel of Figure 2.11. The lower panel of Figure 2.11 focuses on the case of a stock-bond return correlation of –0.35. Again, the locus of the efficient frontier depends on whether it is possible to short. If shorting is excluded, the efficient frontier is the straight line segment connecting the point $(0, r_f)$ to the tangency point and the segment of the upper arm of the hyperbola between the tangency point and the point at which the entire allocation is to stocks. If shorting is possible, the efficient frontier is the ray from $(0, r_f)$ through the tangency portfolio.

Expected returns on individual assets in an efficient portfolio have this relationship to one another:

$$\frac{\mu_n - r_f}{\sigma_{np}} = \frac{\mu_p - r_f}{\sigma_p^2} \qquad n = 1, \ldots, N$$

It states that the ratio of expected excess return of each asset to its return covariance with the portfolio is equal to the portfolio's excess return ratio to its variance. The right-hand side expression is the *Sharpe ratio* $\frac{\mu_p - r_f}{\sigma_p}$ of the portfolio. The tangency portfolio is the unique portfolio for which the Sharpe ratio is maximized.

This relationship can also be defined in terms of beta:

$$\mu_n - r_f = \frac{\sigma_{np}}{\sigma_p^2}(\mu_p - r_f) = \beta_{np}(\mu_p - r_f) \qquad n = 1, \ldots, N \qquad (2.3)$$

If the portfolio is a broad index, representing the "market," the CAPM tells us it is not only minimum-variance but efficient (ignoring the Roll critique).

2.5 BENCHMARK INTEREST RATES

The term *risk-free rate* is something of a misnomer: there are no truly riskless returns in the real-world economy. The term is usually used to mean "free of default risk." There are two types of interest rates that are conventionally taken as proxies for a riskless return. Which of these types of risk-free rate is used depends on the context. In any case, we should be aware that these are conventions or benchmarks, used for pricing and analytics, but not to be taken literally as riskless returns.

Government Bond Interest Rates   Government bonds are often considered riskless assets. The reason is that the issuer of the bonds, the central government, is also the issuer of the currency of denomination of the bonds, which is also generally the only legal tender.

This analysis, however, leaves out several risks:

- Longer-term government bills and bonds have price risk arising from *fluctuations in interest rates*, even if there is no credit risk. For example, the owner of a three month U.S. T-bill will suffer a capital loss if the three month rate rises. This risk is small for very short-term bills, but most government debt issues, including those of the United States, have initial maturities of at least a month. We discuss market risk due to interest rate volatility in Chapter 4.
- At the point of default, a government may have the alternative of issuing sufficient currency to meet its debt obligations. Government bonds are denominated in nominal currency units, that is, they are not routinely indexed for inflation. Investors therefore face *inflation risk*, the risk that the inflation rate in the currency of issue over the life of the bond will exceed the market expectation that was incorporated in the price of the bond at the time the investment is made.

  Many industrialized countries issue inflation-protected bonds, with coupons and principal payments that are indexed to inflation. These are generally longer-term issues, though, and have considerable interest-rate market risk.
- Foreign investors may face *exchange-rate risk*. The government can guarantee repayment in its own currency units, but cannot eliminate exchange-rate risk or guarantee the value of the bonds in terms of other currencies.
- Government issues may in fact have non-trivial *credit risk*. Bonds issued by most countries have higher yields than similar bonds issued by highly industrialized countries, such as the United States, the United Kingdom, and Germany. And even the latter countries' credit risk carries a positive price, as seen in prices of sovereign CDS. Government bonds are also subject to credit migration risk (see Chapter 6), the risk of an adverse change in credit rating, for example the August 5, 2011 downgrade by Standard and Poors of the U.S. long-term rating.

  Central government debt is more prone to default if it is denominated in foreign currency. If the sovereign entity is also the issuer of the currency in which the bond is denominated, it has the ability to redeem the bonds in freshly issued local currency, expanding the domestic money supply, no matter how large the debt. Whether it chooses to do so depends on the degree of central bank independence and its monetary policy choices.[2] A government might not, however, choose this course of

---

[2]The U.S. Treasury has issued few foreign currency–denominated liabilities. Almost all of these exceptions related to exchange rate policy and were obligations to other developed-country central banks.

action if redemption at par would entail an extreme inflation outcome. In contrast, U.S. dollar-denominated debt issued by other countries, or U.S. municipal bonds, cannot avoid default by issuing dollars.

There are, however, examples of countries defaulting on domestic currency–denominated obligations. For example, on August 17, 1998, Russia restructured its short-term ruble-denominated bonds in an attempt to avoid a massive expansion of its monetary supply and a devaluation of the ruble. Russia was forced nonetheless on September 2 to devalue.

Money Market Rates Short-term interest rates, those on obligations with a year or less to maturity, are called *money market rates*. Some money market rates serve as benchmarks for risk-free rates. The *Libor*, or London Interbank Offered Rate, curve are the rates paid for borrowing among the most creditworthy banks. There is a distinct Libor curve for each of ten major currencies. Libor rates are proxies for risk-free rates because of the central role the banking system plays. Many investors can obtain financing for their own trading activities at interest rates close to the Libor curve. We study the financing of investment positions in the contemporary financial system in Chapter 12. The British Bankers' Association (BBA) compiles and posts an estimate of the prevailing Libor rates for each currency at 11:00 every morning in London, based on a poll of major banks, making Libor a convenient reference point.

However, Libor rates incorporate a significant degree of credit risk. For major currencies, there is always a substantial spread between these rates and those on government bonds of that currency's issuing authority. For example, the spread between 10-year U.S. dollar swap par rates and the yield on the 10-year U.S. Treasury note is generally on the order of 50 bps and can occasionally be much higher (see Figure 14.15 and the accompanying discussion in Chapter 14).

Another type of money market rate that is also often used as an indicator of the general level of short-term rates is the repo rate, or rates payable on repurchase agreements, introduced in the previous chapter. We discuss repo in more detail in Chapter 12, but for now we can describe it as a short-term rate that is relatively free of credit risk. It, too, is often used as a proxy for risk-free rates.

The spread between Libor and other money market rates that serve as proxies fluctuates, and at times it is extremely unstable, as we see in Chapter 14. This has, for example, been the case during the subprime crisis. Even more than government bond yields, then, the Libor curve is not a risk-free rate, but rather a benchmark for interest rates.

FURTHER READING

Danthine and Donaldson (2005) is a textbook introduction to modern finance theory. Campbell (2000) is a review of the state of play and open questions in asset pricing and return behavior. Cochrane (2005), Dybvig and Ross (2003), and Ross (2005) are clear introductions to the state-price density approach to asset pricing. Drèze (1970) is an early paper identifying the risk-neutral probabilities embedded in equilibrium asset prices.

The first few chapters of Baxter and Rennie (1996) and Chapter 3 of Dixit and Pindyck (1994) are clear and accessible introductions to stochastic processes. Duffie (1996) is more advanced, but covers both the asset pricing and the return behavior material in this chapter, and is worth struggling with. Černý (2004) combines explication of models of return behavior and asset pricing with programming examples.

Elton and Gruber (2003) is a textbook covering the portfolio allocation material presented in this chapter. Huberman and Wang (2008) is an introduction to arbitrage pricing theory. The original presentation of the theory is Ross (1976).

Lo (1999) discusses risk management in the context of decision theory and behavioral economics. Barberis and Thaler (2003) is a survey of behavioral finance.

See Houweling and Vorst (2005) on the Libor curve as a risk-free benchmark.

CHAPTER 3

Value-at-Risk

Value at Risk (VaR) is a technique for analyzing portfolio market risk based on a known—or at least posited—return model. VaR has dreadful limitations, both as a model and as a practice of risk managers in real-world applications. We talk about these at length in Chapters 10 and 11. And VaR has come under ferocious, and to a large extent justified, attack from many quarters. But it is nonetheless an extremely important technique, for a number of reasons. It is worth laying these out carefully, lest the poor reputation of VaR lead to the neglect of an important analytical tool:

- Uniquely among risk measures, VaR provides a single number summarizing the risk of even large and complex portfolios. That number may be inaccurate. But in situations that require at least an order-of-magnitude estimate of the potential loss of a portfolio, or in which a comparison must be made as to which of two portfolios is riskier, it is hard to avoid using some sort of VaR estimate, at least as one among other risk measures.
- Examining VaR, its assumptions, the different ways to compute it, and its pitfalls, is an excellent way to understand the issues involved in risk measurement. We study VaR techniques not because we believe in them or in any particular distributional hypothesis literally, but so that we can learn to ask the right questions.
- VaR is a reasonably accurate guide to the "main body" risks of most portfolios, that is, losses that are large, but nonetheless routine. There are, of course, important exceptions to the information value of VaR even as a general indicator of riskiness, such as option portfolios and dynamic strategies. We discuss these cases in Chapters 4 and 13. But that VaR is a poor guide to extreme losses and for some types of portfolios does not diminish its value as a measure of overall risk in many cases.
- As we see in Chapter 13, there are risk measures related to VaR that give insights into the contributions of different positions to the total risk

of a portfolio. These measures can be of value in the process of portfolio construction.

- Criticism of VaR is often bundled with criticism of modeling assumptions, such as normally distributed returns, that are not inherent in VaR, but are made in specific implementations of VaR. As we will see below, these are distinct issues and should be distinguished in critical review.
- Finally, VaR was developed because there was need for it. Before VaR, there were risk measures that pertained to equity portfolios, or to fixed income, and so on, but no way to summarize the risk of a portfolio containing different asset classes. As first banks and then other types of financial firms became more heavily involved in trading activities, VaR was an early response to this gap.

3.1 DEFINITION OF VALUE-AT-RISK

Let's start by defining VaR formally. We denote portfolios by x. We can think of x as a vector, with elements representing the amounts of different securities or risk factors, or as a scalar, representing the exposure of a single position to a single risk factor. For most of the rest of this chapter, we stick to the simplest case: We assume the portfolio consists of a single long position, x shares or par amount of an asset, or units of exposure to a single risk factor, with an initial price of S_t. Section 3.4 below discusses short positions.

We have already been using S_t interchangeably for risk factors and simple asset prices that are captured by the standard model and its near relations. Later in this and subsequent chapters, we discuss some of the issues around *mapping*, that is, deciding how to represent a risky position with specific observable data. We will extend the discussion to portfolios and to positions that are more difficult to represent in Chapters 4 and 5.

The value of the position at time t is

$$V_t = xS_t$$

The current, time-t value of the position is a known value V_t, but the future value $V_{t+\tau}$ is a random variable. The dollar return or *mark-to-market* (MTM) profit or loss (P&L) $V_{t+\tau} - V_t$ is also a random variable:

$$V_{t+\tau} - V_t = x(S_{t+\tau} - S_t)$$

VaR is, in essence, a quantile of the distribution of this P&L. That is, VaR is a loss level that will only be exceeded with a given probability in a given time frame. If we know the distribution of returns on S_t, we can compute the VaR of the position. In measuring VaR, we hold the portfolio, that is, x, constant, and let the risk factor or asset price fluctuate.

As noted in the introduction to this chapter, the way the term "VaR" is used can be misleading. VaR is often thought of as a particular model and procedure for estimating portfolio return quantiles. We describe this standard model in detail in a moment. Right now, we are presenting a more general definition of VaR as a quantile. It is not tied to a particular model of risk factor returns, or to a particular approach to estimating quantiles or other characteristics of the portfolio return.

As a quantile of $V_{t+\tau} - V_t$, VaR is the expected worst case loss on a portfolio with a specific confidence level, denoted α, over a specific holding period; one minus the confidence level is the probability of a loss greater than or equal to the VaR over the specified time period:

$$\mathrm{VaR}_t(\alpha, \tau)(x) \equiv -(V^* - V_t) \quad \text{s.t.} \quad 1 - \alpha = \mathbf{P}\left[V_{t+\tau} - V_t \leq V^* - V_t\right]$$

The minus sign in this definition serves to turn a loss into a positive number, the way VaR is typically expressed. A negative VaR means that the worst P&L expected at the given confidence level is a profit, not a loss.

We can also express the P&L in terms of returns. Let $r_{t,\tau}$ denote the τ-period logarithmic return on the risk factor at time t. To simplify notation, we set the compounding interval of the return equal to the time horizon of the VaR. Thus, for example, if we are computing a one-day VaR, we will express the return at a daily rate. The return is a random variable, related to the P&L $V_{t+\tau} - V_t$, as we saw in the previous chapter, by

$$V_{t+\tau} - V_t = x(S_{t+\tau} - S_t) = xS_t\left(\frac{S_{t+\tau}}{S_t} - 1\right) = xS_t(e^{r_{t,\tau}} - 1)$$

That is, P&L is equal to the initial value of the position times a proportional shock to the risk factor.

From this definition, we can derive r^*, the risk factor return corresponding to the VaR:

$$V^* = xS_t e^{r^*}$$

We'll call V^*, the position value at which a loss equal to the VaR is realized, the *VaR scenario*, and r^*, the logarithmic change in S_t at which the VaR scenario occurs, the *VaR shock*. The VaR shock, in other words, is a quantile of the return distribution. The VaR itself is

$$\text{VaR}_t(\alpha, \tau)(x) = -(V^* - V_t) = -xS_t(e^{r^*} - 1) = xS_t(1 - e^{r^*}) \tag{3.1}$$

Note that, in the definition thus far, we haven't made any assumptions about the distribution of risk factor returns. A common misconception about VaR is that it always assumes log returns are normally distributed. It is true that in practice, for a number of good and bad reasons, the normal return model is, in fact, usually assumed. But that is not inherent in VaR. VaR can be computed in a number of ways, and can be based on any tractable hypothesis about return distributions; a quantile does not have to be a quantile of the normal distribution.

Figure 3.1 illustrates, with a simple example, a single long position in one unit of AMEX SPDR shares, an ETF that represents a tradable version of the S&P 500 index. The date on which the calculations are made is November 10, 2006, with the closing value of the S&P 500 index at 1376.91. The graph plots the probability distribution of the next-day index level. The one-day

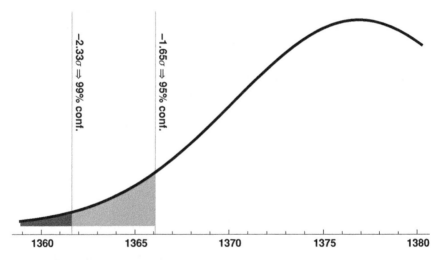

FIGURE 3.1 Definition of VaR
Overnight (1-day) VaR for one unit of the S&P 500 index on November 10, 2006. The drift is set equal to zero, and the volatility is computed using the EWMA technique, described in Section 3.2.2, with 250 days of data and a decay factor if 0.94. The vertical grid lines represent the VaR scenarios corresponding to $\alpha = 0.95$ and 0.99. The VaR is the difference between the index value in the VaR scenario and 1376.91, the closing value of the index.

VaR is the difference between the 1- and 5-percent quantiles of the next-day price, represented by vertical grid lines, and the closing price.

3.1.1 The User-Defined Parameters

Regardless of the distributional hypothesis, the risk manager determines two parameters when computing a VaR. They are set pragmatically, with reference to the type of investor and its activities, or by a financial intermediary's regulatory overseer, rather than being determined by other model elements:

The time horizon or holding period. We will denote this τ, measured in days or years. For a portfolio of short-term positions, it is typically 1 day to 1 month. Longer-term investors, such as individuals and pension funds, will be more interested in a VaR with a time horizon of one year or more. For a given portfolio, VaR for a longer time horizon (say, 1 month) is greater than VaR for short horizon (say, overnight).

When treating periods less than one year, as is typical in VaR calculations, we usually consider only trading days rather than calendar days. This convention is consistent with that used in calculating, say, daily from annual volatilities.

The confidence level (typically 95, 99, or 99.9 percent), that is, what is the probability of the quantile being exceeded? For a given portfolio, VaR at a higher confidence level is greater than VaR for lower confidence interval. This can be seen in Figure 3.1; the worst case loss at a 99 percent confidence level is higher than that at a 95 percent confidence level.

The choice of confidence level is a difficult problem in using VaR. On the one hand, one would like to use VaR at a high confidence level, since it then provides an estimate of the extremely high, unusual and infrequent losses that the investor seeks to avoid. At a lower confidence level, the VaR provides an estimate of "main body" risks, the smaller, more regularly occurring losses that, while interesting, are not as crucial an element of risk management. For example, VaR at a confidence level of 95 percent and with an overnight time horizon provides an estimate of losses that can be expected to occur once a month. Such losses could be considered a recurrent fact of investing life or a cost of doing business, rather than an extreme loss absolutely to be avoided.

On the other hand, in our current state of knowledge, the accuracy of VaR tends to decrease as the confidence level rises. While one would like to use VaR at a 99.99 percent confidence level, and obtain estimates of the worst loss to be expected on average every 10,000 trading days, or about 40 years, such estimates are likely to be devoid of predictive, and thus practical, value.

3.1.2   Steps in Computing VaR

Having defined VaR, we now describe how to compute it. At this point, more needs to be said about maintained hypotheses concerning return distributions. At an "outline" level, the choices and steps in computing VaR are

Establish a return distribution. In this step, based on some combination of real conviction about the actual distribution and mere convenience, we stipulate a distributional hypothesis, that is, we state what family of distributions the returns are drawn from. We can then estimate the parameters of the distribution. Or we may instead let the data speak more directly for themselves and rely on the quantiles of the returns, without imposing a distributional hypothesis. Either way, a judgement call is required. Nothing in theory or the data will tell the risk manager unambiguously which approach is better.

Choose the horizon and confidence level. This choice will be based both on the type of market participant using the VaR, and on limitations of data and models.

Mapping. This step relates positions to risk factors. It is as important as the distributional hypothesis to the accuracy of the results. To actually compute a VaR, we need return data. For any portfolio, we have to decide what data best represent its future returns. Sometimes this is obvious, for example, a single position in a foreign currency. But most often it is *not* obvious, for reasons ranging from paucity of data to the complexity of the portfolio, and choices must be made.

Compute the VaR. The last step, of course, is to put data and models together and compute the results. Many implementation details that have a material impact on the VaR estimates are decided in this stage. For this reason, software, whether internally developed or obtained from a vendor, is so important, as we see in Chapter 11's discussion of model risk.

Each of these steps requires judgement calls; none of these choices will be dictated by something obvious about the models or in the environment.

3.2 VOLATILITY ESTIMATION

The typical assumption made in VaR estimation is that logarithmic returns are normally distributed, generally with a mean of zero. The key parameter to be estimated therefore is the volatility. There are a number of techniques for estimating volatility. Most are based on historical return data, but one can also use implied volatility, which we discuss in Chapters 4, 5 and 10.

Criteria for a "good" volatility estimator include:

- We want to capture the true behavior of risk factor returns. Recall that in the geometric Brownian motion model, the volatility for an asset is a constant, never changing over time. This is far from characteristic of real-world asset returns.
- We also want a technique that is easy to implement for a wide range of risk factors.
- The approach should be extensible to portfolios with many risk factors of different kinds.

3.2.1 Short-Term Conditional Volatility Estimation

Next, we describe the standard approach to estimating a VaR. We do so in the following steps:

- Posit a statistical model for the joint distribution of risk factor returns.
- Estimate the parameters of the model.
- Estimate the portfolio return distribution.

If we posit that logarithmic returns are jointly normally distributed, risk factors follow a geometric Brownian motion. As we saw in Chapter 2, the level of the risk factor is then a random variable that can be described by Equation (2.2), reproduced here:

$$S_{t+\tau} = S_0 e^{\mu \, dt + \sigma \, dW_t}$$

We look at several ways to use historical return data to estimate the volatility. As we do so, bear in mind that VaR is oriented towards short-term risks. It is harder to forecast short-term expected return than short-term volatility. In fact, short-term volatility forecasts are relatively accurate, compared to forecasts of returns, or to longer-term volatility forecasts. Over short time horizons, the drift term μ is likely to make a much smaller contribution to total return than volatility. Practitioners make a virtue of necessity and typically restrict VaR estimates to a time horizon over which forecasting can have some efficacy.

What does "short-term" mean in this context? There is no fixed standard of the longest time horizon for which a VaR estimate is useful. It depends partly on one's views on the true underlying model to which the lognormal is an approximation, and what that model says about the forecastability of volatility and the unimportance of the drift. The practice is to neutralize the drift, which is likely to be comparatively small. In the geometric Brownian motion model outlined above, we set

$$\mu = -\frac{\sigma^2}{2}$$

so as to zero out the slight acceleration of growth resulting from continuous compounding, and keep the drift over discrete intervals equal to zero.

To see why we can safely ignore the mean, consider the potential range of returns for varying levels of the drift and volatility, and over long and short time intervals, if the asset price follows a geometric Brownian motion. The table below shows the 1 percent quantile of the logarithmic return, for time horizons of one day and one year, and for varying assumptions on the drift and volatility parameters. In other words, for each set of assumed parameters, there is a 1 percent chance that the return will be even lower than that tabulated below:

	$\tau = \frac{1}{252}$ (1 day)			
	$\mu = 0.00$	$\mu = 0.10$	$\mu = 0.20$	$\mu = 0.30$
$\sigma = 0.10$	−0.015	−0.014	−0.014	−0.013
$\sigma = 0.50$	−0.074	−0.073	−0.073	−0.073

	$\tau = 1$ (1 year)			
	$\mu = 0.00$	$\mu = 0.10$	$\mu = 0.20$	$\mu = 0.30$
$\sigma = 0.10$	−0.233	−0.133	−0.033	0.067
$\sigma = 0.50$	−1.163	−1.063	−0.963	−0.863

The comparison is similar to that in Figure 2.5. We see that, for short time horizons, the drift makes very little difference, since it is linear in time ($\mu\tau$) and small for a short time horizon, even for a high value of μ. The potential loss is greater when volatility is high, 50 percent as compared to

10 percent per annum, but the difference, for either volatility, between a drift of zero and a drift of 30 percent per annum is small. In contrast, for a time horizon of one year, the drift can make a substantial difference. At a low volatility of 10 percent, increasing the drift from zero to 30 percent raises the worst-case outcome with a 99 percent confidence level from a loss of 23.3 percent to a gain of 6.7 percent. The upward shift in worst-case outcomes arising from a higher drift is the same at a higher volatility, but stands out less against the backdrop of the higher potential loss the higher volatility makes possible.

With the drift set to zero, we have

$$S_{t+\tau} = S_t e^{\sigma\, dW_t} = S_t e^{r_t}$$

where

$$r_t \sim N\left(-\frac{\sigma^2}{2}\tau, \sigma\sqrt{\tau}\right)$$

For a long position of x units of an exposure to a single risk factor, the P&L

$$V_{t+\tau} - V_t = xS_t\left(e^{r_t} - 1\right)$$

is lognormally distributed. Assume for now that we know the value of the portfolio or asset return volatility σ. In fact, of course, we don't; it has to be estimated.

The P&L is negative when $r_t < 0$. The VaR at a confidence level α is the 1-α quantile of the P&L distribution. This corresponds to a return equal to $z_*\sigma\sqrt{\tau}$,

where α is the confidence level of the VaR, e.g., 0.99 or 0.95,
  z_* is the ordinate of the standard normal distribution at which $\Phi(z) = 1 - \alpha$,
  σ is the time-t annual volatility estimate,
  τ is the time horizon of the VaR, measured as a fraction of a year.

Note that for any $\alpha > 0.50$, $z_* < 0$. Figure 3.1 illustrates how VaR is calculated and how it is affected by the confidence interval. The VaR shock is related to volatility by

$$r^* = z_*\sigma\sqrt{\tau}$$

so the α percentile of $V_{t+\tau} - V_0$ is

$$xS_t \left(e^{z_* \sigma \sqrt{\tau}} - 1 \right)$$

and the VaR is estimated as

$$\mathrm{VaR}_t(\alpha, \tau)(x) = -xS_t \left(e^{z_* \sigma \sqrt{\tau}} - 1 \right)$$

The logarithmic change in the asset price at which a loss equal to the VaR is incurred, $z_* \sigma \sqrt{\tau}$, is the VaR shock, and $e^{z_* \sigma \sqrt{\tau}} xS_t$, the position value at which a loss equal to the VaR is incurred, is the VaR scenario.

Example 3.1 At a 99 percent confidence level, we have $1 - \alpha = 0.01$ and $z_* = -2.33$. Suppose time is measured in years, the time horizon of the VaR estimate is one day or overnight, portfolio value is lognormally distributed, and the volatility is estimated at $\sigma = 0.24$ per annum. The daily volatility, using the rule of thumb described in Chapter 2, is then $\sigma\sqrt{\tau} = 0.24\frac{1}{16} = 0.015$, or 1.5 percent. The VaR shock, finally, is $z_* \sigma \sqrt{\tau} = -2.33 \cdot 0.015$ or approximately -3.5 percent. In other words, the overnight, 99 percent VaR is about 3.5 percent of the initial portfolio value.

Note that for this simple long position, $z_* < 0$. As we will see below, for short positions or for securities whose values decrease as the risk factor increases, we may have $z_* > 0$ at the same confidence level.

In the model as presented so far, the volatility parameter σ is a constant. Volatility, however, varies over time. *Time-varying volatility* is observed in the returns of all financial assets. Volatility changes over time in a certain particular way. Periods of lower and higher volatility are persistent. If the magnitude of recent returns has been high, it is likelier that returns in the near future will also be of large magnitude, whether positive or negative.

The phenomenon, also described as *volatility clustering*, presents a number of challenges in interpreting financial markets. In empirical research, it is difficult to "explain" asset prices by associating them with fundamental factors in the economy via a model. The observed variations in asset return volatility cannot be persuasively linked to variations in fundamental drivers of asset returns. For example, stock market return volatility is a well-documented phenomenon over centuries of available historical price data, but cannot be satisfactorily explained by the behavior of earnings, dividends, economic growth, and other fundamentals, which are far less variable.

From one point of view, this presents an obstacle to validating the theory that financial markets are efficient. The difficulty of explaining asset return volatility via fundamentals has been described as the problem of *excess volatility* and has given rise to a large literature attempting to explain this excess with models of how traders put on and unwind positions over time. However, it is also difficult to find fundamentals-based return models that outperform simple short-term return forecasts such as one based on the random walk, that is, essentially, a coin toss.

We put time-varying volatility in the context of other departures from the standard geometric Brownian motion return model, such as "fat tails," in Chapter 10. Here, we will present techniques for forecasting time-varying volatilities.

Future volatility can be forecast from recent volatility with some accuracy, at least over short horizons, even though returns themselves are hard to predict. We can obtain a current estimate of volatility, using recent data on return behavior, denoted $\hat{\sigma}_t$ to remind us that we are computing an estimate of the *conditional volatility* dependent on information available at time t.

A first approach is to use the sample standard deviation, the average square root of daily return deviations from the mean over some past time period:

$$\hat{\sigma}_t = \sqrt{\frac{1}{T} \sum_{\tau=1}^{T} (r_\tau - \bar{r})^2}$$

where T is the number of return observations in the sample, and $\bar{r}$, the sample mean, is an estimator of μ.

Since we've decided that, for short periods at least, we can safely ignore the mean, we can use the *root mean square* of r_t:

$$\hat{\sigma}_t = \sqrt{\frac{1}{T} \sum_{\tau=1}^{T} r_\tau^2}$$

This statistic is the second sample moment and the maximum likelihood estimator of the standard deviation of a normal, zero-mean random variable. This estimator adapts more or less slowly to changes in return variability, depending on how long an observation interval T is chosen.

3.2.2 The EWMA Model

The sample standard deviation does too little to take the phenomenon of time-varying volatility into account. An alternative approach is the "Risk-Metrics model," which applies an *exponentially weighted moving average* (EWMA) to the return data. A *decay factor* $\lambda \in (0, 1)$ is applied to each observation so that more recent observations are given greater weight in the volatility estimate than observations in the more remote past.

The decay factor is typically close to, but less than unity. As long as the decay factor is less than unity, the resulting volatility estimator is stable. The decay factor is chosen so as to be consistent with the long-term behavior of short-term volatility. For quite short horizons—a few days—a value of about 0.94 has found considerable empirical support. For somewhat longer periods, such as one month, a "slower" decay factor of 0.97 has been recommended, among others, by bank regulators.[1]

The user chooses a number T of daily time series observations $\{r_1, r_2, \ldots, r_T\}$ on risk factor returns. The weight on each return observation is

$$\frac{1 - \lambda}{1 - \lambda^T} \lambda^{T-\tau} \qquad \tau = 1, \ldots, T$$

The weight is composed of two parts:

- $\lambda^{T-\tau}$ is the impact of the decay factor on the $T - t$-th observation. The most recent observation is the last (i.e., sequence number T) in a time series in standard ascending order by date. It has a weight of $\lambda^{T-T} = 1$; as the most recent, it carries a "full weight." For the first, that is, the observation furthest in the past, the value is λ^{T-1}. As $T \to \infty$, this tends to zero.
- $\frac{1-\lambda}{1-\lambda^T}$ "completes the weight" and ensures all the weights add up to unity. From the formula for the sum of a geometrical series, we have

$$\sum_{\tau=1}^{T} \lambda^{T-\tau} = \sum_{\tau=1}^{T} \lambda^{\tau-1} = \frac{1 - \lambda^T}{1 - \lambda}$$

so the sum of the weights is unity.

---

[1]Fleming, Kirby, and Ostdiek (2001) find a decay factor of 0.94 fits a wide range of assets well. The use of VaR is used in setting regulatory capital in some developed countries and is discussed in Chapter 15.

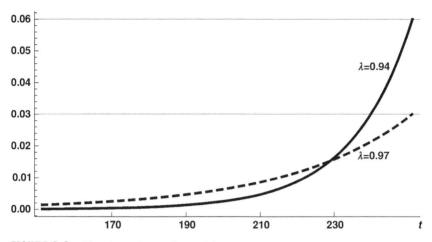

FIGURE 3.2 The EWMA Weighting Scheme
The graph displays the values of the last 100 of $T = 250$ EWMA weights $\frac{1-\lambda}{1-\lambda^T}\lambda^{T-t}$ for $\lambda = 0.94$ and $\lambda = 0.97$.

Figure 3.2 displays the behavior of the weighting scheme. The weights decline smoothly as the return observations recede further into the past. If the decay factor is smaller, more recent observations have greater weight, and past observations are de-emphasized more rapidly.

If you start out with a time series of asset prices, you lose one observation for the return calculations and T observations for the EWMA calculation, for a total of $T + 1$ fewer observations on the EWMA volatility than on the asset prices themselves.

As $T \to \infty$, $\lambda^T \to 0$, so if T is large, the weights are close to $(1 - \lambda)\lambda^{T-\tau}$. The EWMA estimator can then be written

$$\hat{\sigma}_t = \sqrt{(1 - \lambda) \sum_{\tau=1}^{t} \lambda^{t-\tau} r_\tau^2}$$

If T is large, the EWMA estimator can also be written in *recursive form* as

$$\hat{\sigma}_t^2 = \lambda \hat{\sigma}_{t-1}^2 + (1 - \lambda) r_t^2 \qquad (3.2)$$

To use the recursive form, you need a starting value $\hat{\sigma}_0$ of the estimator, which is then updated using the return time series to arrive at its current value $\hat{\sigma}_t$. If $\hat{\sigma}_0$ is not terribly far from $\hat{\sigma}_t$, it will rapidly converge to the correct value of $\hat{\sigma}_t$.

The recursive form provides additional intuition about the procedure:

- The smaller is λ, the faster the EWMA estimator adapts to new information.
- The larger the absolute value of the latest return observation, the larger the change in the EWMA estimator. The sign of the return doesn't matter, only its magnitude.
- The EWMA estimator is not that different from the sample moment; it merely adapts faster to new information. But if you believe that volatility is time-varying, you should not use the sample moment.

Example 3.2 (Computing the EWMA Volatility Estimator) Suppose we wish to find the value of the EWMA volatility estimator for the S&P 500 index on November 10, 2006, using closing values of the index and setting $T = 250$ and $\lambda = 0.94$. We need 251 observations on the index, giving us 250 return observations. The table displays the weights, index values, and returns for the last 11 observations used.

Obs	Date	λ^{T-t}	$\frac{1-\lambda}{1-\lambda^T}\lambda^{T-t}$	S_t	$100r_t$
240	27Oct06	0.539	0.032	1377.34	−0.849
241	30Oct06	0.573	0.034	1377.93	0.043
242	31Oct06	0.610	0.037	1377.94	0.001
243	01Nov06	0.648	0.039	1367.81	−0.738
244	02Nov06	0.690	0.041	1367.34	−0.034
245	03Nov06	0.734	0.044	1364.30	−0.223
246	06Nov06	0.781	0.047	1379.78	1.128
247	07Nov06	0.831	0.050	1382.84	0.222
248	08Nov06	0.884	0.053	1385.72	0.208
249	09Nov06	0.940	0.056	1378.33	−0.535
250	10Nov06	1.000	0.060	1376.91	−0.103

3.2.3 The GARCH Model

The *generalized autoregressive conditionally heteroscedastic* (GARCH) model can be seen as a generalization of EWMA. It places the time series of conditional volatility estimates in the spotlight rather than the return series. The return series plays the role of the randomly generated shocks or innovations to the process that generates the conditional volatility series.

We will look at GARCH(1,1), the simplest version of the model. The returns are assumed to follow a process

$$r_t = \epsilon_t \sigma_t$$

with $\epsilon_t \sim N(0, 1)$ and independent $\forall t$; that is, successive shocks to returns are independent. The conditional volatility process, the equation that describes how the estimate of the current level of volatility is updated with new return information, is

$$\sigma_t^2 = \omega + \alpha \sigma_{t-1}^2 + \beta r_t^2$$

We want this to be a stationary process, that is, we don't want volatility to be able to wander far from ω, since that would admit the possibility of implausibly high or low volatility levels. We therefore impose the assumption $\alpha + \beta \leq 1$.

The conditional volatility process then looks remarkably like the recursive form of the EWMA estimator, and in fact has the same interpretation: it shows how the current estimate of volatility is updated with new information about the magnitude of returns.

Figure 3.3 illustrates the relationship between the GARCH(1,1) and EWMA estimators with estimated volatilities over a 10-year period for

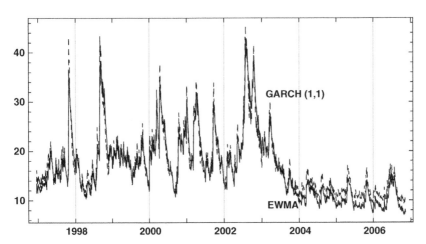

FIGURE 3.3 Comparison of Volatility Estimators
Volatility estimates for the S&P 500 index, January 3, 1996, to November 10, 2006. The GARCH(1,1) volatilities (dotted line) use the following parameter estimates: $\omega = 0.000002$, $\alpha = 0.091$, $\beta = 0.899$. The GARCH parameter estimates are based on the observation range May 16, 1995, to April 29, 2003. The EWMA estimates (solid line) use a decay factor of 0.94 and 250 days of data. *Data source:* Bloomberg Financial L.P.

the S&P 500 index. The GARCH(1,1) estimates are those presented as background information for the 2003 Nobel Prize in Economics.[2] The GARCH(1,1) estimates up to April 29, 2003, are fitted values, while those later, are forecasts. The EWMA estimates use a decay factor $\lambda = 0.94$.

We can see, first, that the EWMA and GARCH(1,1) estimates are very close to one another. The main difference between the two is that, when conditional volatility abruptly spikes, the GARCH(1,1) estimate is somewhat more reactive, updating more drastically. Overall, the EWMA estimates mimic GARCH(1,1) closely. The estimates begin to diverge as the forecast period gets further from the end of the observation period on which they were based, but remain reasonably close for a long time, indicating that the GARCH(1,1) parameters are fairly stable and that, with a suitable decay factor, EWMA is a good approximation to GARCH(1,1).

3.3   MODES OF COMPUTATION

Let's look next at how to estimate VaR and how the estimate varies with the time horizon of the VaR. We continue the example of a single long position in the S&P 500 index with an initial value of $1,000,000 as of Nov. 10, 2006. We'll set the time horizon to one day and the confidence level to 99 percent.

3.3.1   Parametric

Parametric VaR relies on algebra rather than simulation to compute an estimate of the VaR. For a portfolio x consisting of a single position, linear in the underlying risk factor, that estimate is

$$\text{VaR}_t(\alpha, \tau)(x) = -xS_t \left(e^{z_* \hat{\sigma}_t \sqrt{\tau}} - 1 \right)$$

This expression is the same as that we developed above, only now $\hat{\sigma}_t$ represents an *estimate* of the unobservable volatility parameter.

For our example, using the the RiskMetrics/EWMA estimate $\hat{\sigma}_t = 7.605\%$, we have

$$\text{VaR}\left(0.99, \frac{1}{252}\right) = -1,000,000 \left(e^{\frac{-2.33 \cdot 0.07605}{\sqrt{252}}} - 1 \right)$$
$$= 1,000,000 \cdot (1 - e^{-0.0111})$$
$$= \$11,084$$

---

[2]See Royal Swedish Academy of Sciences (2003).

Practitioners sometimes apply the approximation $e^r \approx 1 + r$, leading to the VaR estimate

$$\text{VaR}_t(\alpha, \tau) = -z_* \hat{\sigma}_t \sqrt{\tau} x S_t \qquad (3.3)$$

This approximation of logarithmic by arithmetic returns (see Chapter 2 for more detail) is particularly common in calculating VaR for a portfolio, as we will see in Chapter 4.

In our example, we have the slightly greater VaR estimate

$$\text{VaR}\left(0.99, \frac{1}{252}\right) = -1,000,000 \frac{(-2.33) \cdot 0.07605}{\sqrt{252}} = \$11,146$$

3.3.2 Monte Carlo Simulation

Our model of returns is

$$r_t = \sqrt{t}\sigma \epsilon_t$$

where ϵ_t is a standard normal random variate. To estimate the VaR via Monte Carlo simulation:

1. Generate I independent draws from a standard normal distribution. We'll label these $\tilde{\epsilon}_1, \ldots, \tilde{\epsilon}_I$.
2. For each of the I draws, we get a single simulation thread for the return by calculating

$$\tilde{r}_i = \sqrt{t}\hat{\sigma}\tilde{\epsilon}_i \qquad i = 1, \ldots, I$$

where $\hat{\sigma}$ is an estimate of the volatility.
3. The corresponding estimate of the asset price is

$$\tilde{S}_i = S_0 e^{\tilde{r}_i} = S_0 e^{\sqrt{t}\hat{\sigma}\tilde{\epsilon}_i} \qquad i = 1, \ldots, I$$

4. For each of the I simulation threads, we now revalue the portfolio, either by multiplying the number of shares x, or equivalently by multiplying the portfolio value xS_0 by $e^{\tilde{r}_i} - 1$. This gives us the P&L $\tilde{V}_i - V_0$ of the portfolio in the scenario corresponding to the i-th simulation.
5. Reorder the simulated P&Ls $\tilde{V}_i - V_0$ by size. This gives us the order statistics $\tilde{V}^{(i)} - V_0$, with $\tilde{V}^{(1)} - V_0$ corresponding to the largest loss and $\tilde{V}^{(I)} - V_0$ to the largest profit.

6. Finally, for the stipulated confidence level α, we identify the P&L $i^* = (1 - \alpha)I$ corresponding to the VaR. We have

$$\text{VaR}(\alpha, \tau) = -(\tilde{V}_{i^*} - V_0) = -V_0(e^{\tilde{r}_{i^*}} - 1)$$
$$= xS_0(1 - e^{\tilde{r}_{i^*}})$$

If i^* is not an integer, we average the neighboring simulation results.

In the example, as set out in Table 3.1, the 99 percent overnight VaR would be estimated as the tenth worst scenario out of $I = 1,000$ simulation trials, or $10,062. This is fairly close to the parametric VaR; the differences can be accounted for by simulation noise.

The virtues of Monte Carlo are that it can accommodate a lot of troublesome characteristics of models and portfolios, such as multiple risk factors, options, or non-normal returns. We discuss these issues in subsequent chapters. All we need for Monte Carlo to work is a return distribution that we either believe in or are willing to stipulate. The main drawback of Monte

TABLE 3.1 Example of Monte Carlo Simulation

i	$\tilde{r}^{(i)}$	$\tilde{S}^{(i)}$	$\tilde{V}^{(i)} - V_0$
1	−0.01538	1,355.89	−15,263.83
2	−0.01300	1,359.13	−12,913.46
3	−0.01279	1,359.42	−12,705.08
4	−0.01254	1,359.75	−12,465.97
5	−0.01159	1,361.04	−11,524.08
6	−0.01097	1,361.89	−10,911.72
7	−0.01087	1,362.02	−10,814.77
8	−0.01081	1,362.11	−10,750.62
9	−0.01071	1,362.24	−10,655.52
10	−0.01011	1,363.06	−10,061.59
11	−0.01008	1,363.10	−10,032.39
12	−0.00978	1,363.50	−9,735.93
...	...	...	...
997	0.01281	1,394.66	12,894.69
998	0.01288	1,394.76	12,964.92
999	0.01355	1,395.70	13,644.34
1,000	0.01597	1,399.07	16,093.82

The example computes VaR via Monte Carlo simulation for a single position in the S&P 500 index with an initial value of $1,000,000, with a time horizon of one day, and a confidence level of 99 percent, as of Nov. 10, 2006. The portfolio's initial value is $1,000,000. The horizontal lines mark the VaR scenario. The $\tilde{V}^{(i)} - V_0$ and $\tilde{r}^{(i)}$ are the order statistics of $\tilde{V}_i$ and $\tilde{r}_i$, and $\tilde{S}^{(i)} \equiv S_0 e^{\tilde{r}^{(i)}}$.

Carlo simulation is that it can be computationally slow or "expensive," and is less of a drawback as computing time cheapens.

3.3.3 Historical Simulation

Historical simulation relies on the "natural experiment" of historical returns to estimate VaR. It does not depend on any distributional hypotheses and does not require the estimation of distribution moments.

To estimate the VaR via historical simulation:

1. Select a historical "look-back" period of I business days. Compute the price return for each day in this interval, for which we'll reuse the notation $\tilde{r}_1, \ldots, \tilde{r}_I$. Each i corresponds to a particular date.
2. The corresponding estimate of the asset price is

$$\tilde{S}_i = S_0 e^{\tilde{r}_i}$$

3. The rest of the procedure is identical to that for Monte Carlo simulation: Order the $\tilde{S}_i$ (or the $\tilde{r}_i$) as in step 5 of the Monte Carlo procedure. The VaR corresponds to the historical return in the $i^* = (1 - \alpha)I$-th order statistic, that is, the i^*-th worst loss

Table 3.2 shows how the data are to be arranged and identifies the VaR shock, VaR scenario, and VaR. The VaR computed using historical simulation is \$17,742, or about 60 to 70 percent higher than estimated via Monte Carlo or parametrically.

Let's compare the two simulation approaches in more detail. Figure 3.4 displays the histograms of simulation results for the Monte Carlo and historical simulations. We can read it in conjunction with the tabular display of the extreme simulation results. The VaR shocks in the two simulation approaches are quite different, but the behavior of the most extreme returns, in ordered simulation threads numbered 1 to 3 or 998 to 1,000, are even more different from one mode of computation to the other. The historical simulation data show that the equity return behavior is fat-tailed; on the 0.5 percent of days on which the return is most extreme, returns have a magnitude of about 1.5 percent in the Monte Carlo simulations, but about 3.5 percent in the historical simulations.

The results of historical simulation can depend heavily on the observation interval. There is no prescribed amount of history one should take into account. Rather, it is a risk manager choice, but a difficult one; there is no right answer, only trade-offs. If one takes a longer historical period, one is likelier to capture low-probability, large-magnitude returns and obtain a

TABLE 3.2 Example of VaR Computed via Historical Simulation

i	Date	$\tilde{r}^{(i)}$	$\tilde{S}_i$	$\tilde{V}^{(i)} - V_0$
1	24Mar03	−0.0359	1,328.40	−35,231.47
2	24Jan03	−0.0297	1,336.66	−29,233.44
3	10Mar03	−0.0262	1,341.34	−25,829.72
4	19May03	−0.0252	1,342.60	−24,917.93
5	30Jan03	−0.0231	1,345.45	−22,849.28
6	24Sep03	−0.0193	1,350.62	−19,095.65
7	24Feb03	−0.0186	1,351.60	−18,380.75
8	20Jan06	−0.0185	1,351.68	−18,326.28
9	05Jun06	−0.0180	1,352.40	−17,799.75
10	31Mar03	−0.0179	1,352.48	−17,741.75
11	05Aug03	−0.0178	1,352.59	−17,663.46
12	17May06	−0.0170	1,353.72	−16,841.06
...	...	...	...	...
997	21Mar03	0.0227	1,408.55	22,976.69
998	02Apr03	0.0258	1,412.87	26,115.93
999	13Mar03	0.0339	1,424.35	34,457.03
1,000	17Mar03	0.0348	1,425.69	35,426.69

The example computes VaR via historical simulation for a single position in the S&P 500 index with an initial value of USD 1,000,000, with a time horizon of one day and a confidence level of 90 percent, as of Nov. 10, 2006. The portfolio's initial value is USD 1,000,000. The horizontal lines mark the VaR scenarios. The $\tilde{V}^{(i)} - V_0$ and $\tilde{r}^{(i)}$ are the order statistics of $\tilde{V}_i$ and $\tilde{r}_i$, and $\tilde{S}^{(i)} \equiv S_0 e^{\tilde{r}^{(i)}}$.

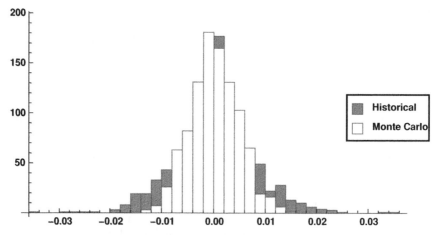

FIGURE 3.4 Comparison of Simulation Approaches
Histograms of Monte Carlo and historical simulated return results displayed in Tables 3.1 and 3.2.

more accurate estimate of the tail risks in the portfolio. But, as noted in discussing short-term conditional volatility estimation, estimates based on longer history are less likely to do a good job estimating a short-term VaR. If the focus is on the main-body, rather than tail risks, longer history may be counterproductive.

Much depends on whether the fat-tailed behavior manifests itself in the short or long term. Do large returns appear routinely? Or do the returns behave close to normally most of the time, but subject to infrequent large shocks? We explore these issues further in Chapter 10. Boudoukh, Richardson, and Whitelaw (1997) have proposed a hybrid approach in which the historical data are weighted, as in the EWMA volatility estimation procedure, but then used in historical simulation, rather than in a volatility estimate. A more-recent large-magnitude return will then have more impact on the VaR than a less-recent one.

3.4 SHORT POSITIONS

For a short position, the number of units x of exposure, say, shares borrowed and sold, is negative. The P&L can still be written

$$V_{t+\tau} - V_t = xS_t \left(e^{r_t} - 1\right)$$

but it is negative when $r_t > 0$. The parametric VaR at a confidence level α therefore corresponds to a return equal to $z_* \sigma \sqrt{\tau}$, with z_* now the ordinate of the standard normal distribution at which $\Phi(z) = \alpha$, rather than $\Phi(z) = 1 - \alpha$. In other words, it corresponds to a right-tail rather than left-tail quantile of the normal distribution. The VaR is still estimated as

$$\text{VaR}_t(\alpha, \tau)(x) = xS_t \left(e^{z_* \hat{\sigma}_t \sqrt{\tau}} - 1\right)$$

but we have $z_* > 0$, not $z_* < 0$.

In our example, if we have a short rather than long S&P position, the parametric VaR is computed as

$$\text{VaR}\left(0.99, \frac{1}{252}\right) = -1,000,000(e^{0.0111} - 1) = \$\,11,208$$

which is slightly higher than for a long position; if we use the approximation of Equation (3.3), $-z_* \hat{\sigma}_t \sqrt{\tau} x S_t$, the result is identical to that for a long position.

Short positions provide a good illustration of some inadequacies of VaR as a risk measure. There is no difficulty computing VaR for short positions; in fact, as we have just seen, the results are essentially the same as for a long position. However, there are a number of crucial differences between long and short positions. Long positions have limited "downside," or potential loss, since the market value of the asset can go to zero, but no lower. But short positions have unlimited downside, since prices can rise without limit. Short positions are thus inherently riskier, and this additional risk is not captured by VaR.

No matter which approach is used to compute VaR or estimate volatility, the risk manager has to decide how to represent the risk of a position with a risk factor S_t. He can then determine how many units x of this exposure are in the position. In many cases, it is fairly straightforward to associate positions with risk factors. A spot currency position, for example, should be associated with the corresponding exchange rate, and the number of units is just the number of currency units in the position.

But it is surprising how few cases are actually this straightforward. Most individual securities are exposed to several risk factors. To continue the currency example, currency positions are usually taken via forward foreign exchange, which are exposed to domestic and foreign money-market rates as well as exchange rates. We continue the discussion of mapping in discussing portfolio VaR in Chapter 5.

Even in the simplest cases, mapping a security to a single risk factor neglects the *financing risk* of a position. This, too, is a particularly glaring omission for short positions, as we see in Chapter 12.

3.5 EXPECTED SHORTFALL

VaR provides an estimate of a threshold loss. That is, it is a loss level that is unlikely to be exceeded, with "unlikely" defined by the confidence level. Another measure of potential loss, called *expected shortfall* (ES), *conditional value-at-risk* (CVaR), or *expected tail loss*, is the expected value of the loss, given that the threshold is exceeded. In this section, we define this risk measure and discuss why it is useful.

Expected shortfall is a conditional expected value. If x is a well-behaved continuous random variable with density function $f(x)$, the conditional expected value of x given that $x \leq x^*$ is

$$\frac{\int_{-\infty}^{x^*} x f(x) dx}{P[x \leq x^*]}$$

To understand this expression, let's compare its numerator, $\int_{-\infty}^{x^*} xf(x)dx$, to the very similar expression $\int_{-\infty}^{\infty} xf(x)dx$ for the mean of x. We can see that the numerator gives the expected value, not over the whole range of x, but only of values at or below x^*. In other words, it represents the average of low values of x, multiplied by the correspondingly low probabilities of occurring.

The denominator is the probability of some value below x^* occurring. In Figure 3.1, this is illustrated for the value of a long position as the shaded areas in the left tail of the density. To obtain the conditional expected value of this tail event, we apply its definition as the ratio of the expected value $\int_{-\infty}^{x^*} xf(x)dx$ to its probability.

Similarly, the formal expression for ES is also composed of two parts. The expected value of the position value, if it ends up at or below the VaR scenario V^*, is $\int_0^{V^*} vf_\tau(v)dv$, where $f_\tau(v)$ is the time-t density function of the position value. Note that the value of a long position can't go lower than zero. By definition, the probability of a loss greater than or equal to the VaR is $1 - \alpha$, where α is the confidence level of the VaR. So the conditional expected value of the position is

$$\frac{1}{1-\alpha} \int_0^{V^*} vf_\tau(v)dv$$

The conditional expected loss, treated as a positive number, is just the initial position value less this quantity:

$$V_t - \frac{1}{1-\alpha} \int_0^{V^*} vf_\tau(v)dv$$

Expected shortfall is always larger than the VaR, since it is an average of the VaR and loss levels greater than the VaR.

Example of Expected Shortfall			
Mode	VaR	ES	$\frac{\text{ES}}{\text{VaR}}$
Parametric	11,083.57	12,686.68	1.145
Monte Carlo	10,061.59	11,806.67	1.173
Historical	17,741.75	22,940.60	1.293

In the standing example of this chapter, the expected shortfall can be computed using any of the modes of computation we have laid out. For the parametric approach, the expected shortfall is computed as

$$\frac{1}{1-\alpha} x S_t \mathrm{E}\left[1 - e^{z\sigma_t\sqrt{\tau}} | z < z_*\right]$$

For the Monte Carlo and historical simulation approaches, the expected shortfall is computed as the average of $x S_t \left[1 - \exp\left(\tilde{r}^{(i)}\right)\right]$, where the averaging is over the i^* simulated returns that are as bad as or worse than the VaR scenario. In our example, in which the number of simulations is set to $I = 1{,}000$, we average over the 10 worst simulation threads.

Just as we saw for VaR itself, Monte Carlo simulation gives results for expected shortfall that are not very different from those of the parametric approach assuming normally distributed returns. However, the historical simulation approach is better able to capture the extremes of the distribution, so not only is the VaR larger, but the expected value of outcomes worse than the VaR is even larger relative to the VaR than for approaches relying on the normal distribution.

If we compute VaR parametrically, using the convenient approximation of Equation (3.3), we have a similarly convenient way to compute the expected shortfall; it is equal to

$$\frac{\phi(-\alpha)}{(1-\alpha)z_*} \, \mathrm{VaR}_t(\alpha, \tau)(x)$$

where $\phi(\cdot)$ represents the standard normal probability density function.

Expected shortfall is useful for a number of reasons, which will be discussed in greater detail below:

- Expected shortfall can be a more useful risk measure than VaR when the standard model is wrong in certain ways, in particular when the return distribution has fat tails (see Chapter 10).
- Expected shortfall via historical simulation can be compared with the VaR to obtain clues as to how far from the standard model the true distribution actually is.
- Expected shortfall has theoretical properties that occasionally have a useful practical application (see the discussion of "coherent" risk measures in Chapter 11).

FURTHER READING

Jorion (2007) and Dowd (2005) are general risk management textbooks with a focus on market risk measurement. Introductions to VaR models are provided by Duffie and Pan (1997), Morgan Guaranty Trust Company (1996), Mina and Xiao (2001), and Gourieroux and Jasiak (2010). Culp, Miller, and Neves (1998) is an end-user-focused introduction. Second-generation developments in VaR modeling are described in Engle and Manganelli (2001) and Pearson and Smithson (2002). Basel Committee on Banking Supervision (2011) is a literature survey from a regulatory point of view.

See Black (1993) and Merton (1980) on the difficulty of estimating expected return.

Comparative surveys of approaches to forecasting volatility are presented by Brailsford and Faff (1996), Tay and Wallis (2000), Engle and Patton (2001), Brooks and Persand (2003), Andersen, Bollerslev, Christoffersen, and Diebold (2010), and Poon and Granger (2003, 2005). Christoffersen and Diebold (2000) focuses on longer-term volatility forecasts. Schwert (1990*b*) and (1990*a*) present the results of studies of the macroeconomic influences on U.S. stock market volatility using a long historical data set going back to the late 19th century.

Vlab is a web site maintained at New York University Stern School of Business presenting updated volatility and correlation forecasts for a range of assets. It can be accessed at http://vlab.stern.nyu.edu/.

CHAPTER 4

Nonlinear Risks and the Treatment of Bonds and Options

In the previous chapter, we discussed risk measurement for single "well-behaved" securities, with returns that can appropriately be mapped to returns of one risk factor. In this basic case, the asset also has returns that move *linearly*, that is, one-for-one or in a constant proportion to some underlying asset or risk factor return. But many securities are not at all well-behaved in this sense. Rather, they have *nonlinear* returns that have much larger or smaller responses to some other asset returns, depending on the asset price level.

Nonlinearity can vitiate risk measurement techniques such as VaR that are designed primarily for linear exposures. In this chapter, we discuss nonlinearity, and how to measure risk in its presence. We'll focus on two important examples of nonlinear securities, options and bonds. Another reality that we will have to address is that many assets are complex, and are exposed to multiple risk factors, and that most real-world portfolios contain many positions and are exposed to multiple risk factors. In the next chapter, studying risk measurement for portfolios, we focus on assets that are sensitive to multiple risk factors.

Options and option-like exposures depart in both ways from the previous chapter's model: nonlinearity and dependence on several risk factors. First, the P&L of an option is a nonlinear function of returns on the underlying asset. A relatively small return on the underlying asset can have a large impact on option P&L. The P&L would therefore not be normally distributed, even if risk factor changes were. Options are not unique in this regard. Bond prices are also nonlinearly related to interest rates or yields. Bond traders refer to this nonlinear sensitivity as *convexity*.

Second, option returns depend jointly on several market risk factors, the underlying asset price, the financing or risk-free interest rate, and the underlying asset's dividend, interest yield, or storage cost. There is also a type of volatility risk that is peculiar to options and option-like securities.

Options are a species of derivatives. As noted in Chapter 1, derivatives are securities with values that are functions of the values of other assets or risk factors. But not all derivatives are nonlinear. There are two basic types of derivatives: futures, forwards, and swaps on the one hand, and options on the other.

> *Futures, forwards, and swaps* have a linear and symmetric relationship to the underlying asset price and can be hedged statically. *Static hedging* means that the derivatives position can be hedged with a one-time trade in the underlying asset. This does not mean their values move one-for-one with those of the underlying, but rather that their responsiveness to changes in the underlying is constant.
>
> The possibility of static hedging means that only the value of the underlying asset and not its volatility determines the value of the derivative, so futures, forwards, and swaps generally have zero *net present value* (NPV) at initiation. We note this here, since it is a direct consequence of linearity; it becomes important when we study counterparty credit exposure in Chapter 6.
>
> *Options* have a nonlinear relationship to the underlying asset price and must be hedged dynamically to minimize their risks. *Dynamic hedging* means that the amount of the underlying asset that neutralizes changes in the derivative's value itself changes over time, so repeated trades are needed to stay hedged. For some values of the underlying asset, the option value may move close to one-for-one with the underlying, while for other values of the underlying it may hardly change at all. In general, volatility is an important element in the value of an option, so an option contract cannot have zero NPV at initiation.

Nonlinearity is also important because it is one of two ways that the P&L distribution can have fat tails, that is, a tendency toward very large positive and/or negative values:

- The payoff function of the security may lead to disproportionately large-magnitude returns for modest changes in the underlying asset price or risk factor. For example, a given change in the value of the underlying price may lead to a much larger or smaller change in the value of an option at different levels of the underlying. Nonlinearity is the focus of this chapter.
- The distribution of risk factor or asset price returns may be non-normal. We discuss this possibility in more detail in Chapter 10.

4.1 NONLINEAR RISK MEASUREMENT AND OPTIONS

A number of approaches to modeling option risk have been developed. We'll focus on two relatively simple approaches. The first applies the simulation techniques we developed in Chapter 3 in a way that takes account of the special problems raised by the nonlinearity of options. The second, called *delta-gamma*, uses a quadratic approximation to option returns. We'll discuss these for plain-vanilla options, but they can be applied to exotic options, convertible bonds, and other structured products. Both techniques can help address the difficulties in accurately measuring risk generated by nonlinearity, but neither completely solves them. After describing the delta-gamma technique for options, we'll show how it can be applied to fixed-income securities.

This section assumes some, but not terribly much, familiarity with option pricing models, and readers can see the textbooks cited at the end of the chapter to brush up. In this chapter, we simplify things by talking about options in the context of the standard Black-Scholes-Merton pricing model. We denote the Black-Scholes theoretical or model value of a plain-vanilla *European call option* by $v(S_t, T - t, X, \sigma, r, q)$ and that of a *put option* by $w(S_t, T - t, X, \sigma, r, q)$,

where $S_t =$ is the time-t underlying price
$\sigma =$ is the time-t asset return volatility
$X =$ is the exercise price
$T =$ is the maturity date, and $\tau = T - t$ the time to maturity
$r =$ is the financing rate.
$q =$ is the cash flow yield, such as a dividend or coupon, on the underlying asset.

A European option is one that can only be exercised at maturity, in contrast to an *American option*, which can be exercised anytime prior to expiration. We define "one option" as an option on one unit—share, ounce, or currency unit—of the underlying asset.

The formulas are spelled out in Appendix A.3. Option value depends on its "design parameters," the things that are part of the option contract: whether it is a put or a call, its time to maturity, and the exercise price. It also depends on market risk factors: the underlying asset price, the financing or risk-free interest rate, the underlying asset's cash-flow yield, and the asset return volatility. The cash flow yield can be the interest paid by a foreign-currency bank deposit, the coupon yield of a bond, a negative rate representing the cost of storing oil or gold, or the dividend yield paid by common stock.

In the Black-Scholes model, we assume that interest rates and the cash flow yield are constant and nonrandom. Most importantly, we assume that the return volatility σ of the underlying asset is constant, nonrandom, and that we have a reliable estimate of it, so the risk of the option is related only to fluctuations in the underlying asset price. Let's highlight two important aspects of the constant-volatility assumption. First, in the last chapter, we treated return volatility as a time-varying quantity, and sought to obtain an accurate short-term forecast of its future value, conditional on recent return behavior. Here, we treat volatility as constant. If this were only true, we would, after a relatively short time interval, be able to estimate the volatility with near-perfect accuracy. It would then matter little whether we treat σ as a known or an estimated parameter.

Second, note that the volatility parameter is the only one that can't be observed directly. In many applications, we take σ to be the *implied volatility*, that is, an estimate of volatility that matches an observed option price to the Black-Scholes formula, given the observed values of the remaining arguments, S_t, τ, X, r, and q. But there are crucial gaps between the Black-Scholes model and actual option price behavior. Implied volatility fluctuates over time, and not only because the conditional volatility of the underlying is time-varying. Market participants' desire to buy and sell options fluctuates, too, because of their changing appetite for risk in general, because their hedging needs change over time, and because of their changing views on future returns on the underlying asset, among other reasons. Implied volatility risk, which we discuss in Chapters 5 and 10, is a key risk factor for option positions.

Staying in the Black-Scholes world for now will help us discuss the risk measurement issues arising from nonlinearity. The volatility σ is then both the actual and implied volatility. For the rest of this chapter, the risk of the option is understood to be driven by the risk of the underlying asset, that is, changes in S_t, alone.

For concreteness, let's look at a foreign-exchange option, specifically, a European call on the euro, denominated in U.S. dollars, struck *at-the-money forward*, with an initial maturity of one week. The long option position is unhedged, or "naked." The spot rate at initiation is $1.25 per euro, the domestic (U.S.) one week money market rate (r) is 1 percent, and the euro deposit rate (q) is 28 basis points, both per annum. "At-the-money forward" means that the strike price of the option is set equal to the current one-week forward foreign exchange rate. This is a standard way of setting option strikes in the OTC currency option markets. Given the domestic and foreign deposit rates, the one-week forward rate, the exercise price of the option, is slightly higher than the spot rate; the euro trades at a small premium of about two ticks, that is, the forward rate "predicts" a slight dollar depreciation to \$1.2502 over the subsequent week. This is consistent with *covered interest rate parity* and the absence of forward arbitrage, since the domestic interest rate is slightly higher than the foreign one. We assume finally, that the actual and implied volatility σ is 12 percent per annum.

In the Black-Scholes model, logarithmic exchange rate returns follow the probability distribution:[1]

$$\log(S_{t+\tau}) \sim N\left[\log(S_t) + \left(r - q - \frac{\sigma^2}{2}\right)\tau, \sigma\sqrt{\tau}\right]$$

This distributional hypothesis is consistent with the parametric VaR examples of Chapter 3. The mean of the time-$T = t + \tau$ spot rate is equal to the forward rate, and its standard deviation is equal to the constant volatility, adjusted for the time horizon $t + \tau$. Just as in Chapter 3, we have set the parameters in our example so that the drift over discrete time periods is equal to zero:

$$r - q = \frac{\sigma^2}{2} = 0.0072$$

In the case of forward foreign exchange, under covered interest parity, the drift is equal to the spread between the two interest or deposit rates involved, minus the volatility adjustment. In our example, we've set the spread so as to zero out the drift. The value of a one-week European call is then \$0.00838, or a bit more than $\frac{8}{10}$ of a U.S. cent for each euro of underlying notional amount.

4.1.1 Nonlinearity and VaR

Now that we've set up the model and the example, let's start by imagining the simplest possible way to compute a one-day VaR for the one-week European call on the euro. The upper panel of Figure 4.1 shows the P&L of a long position in one euro call after one day as a function of the underlying exchange rate, including one day of *time decay*, the perfectly predictable change in value of the option as its remaining maturity is shortened by the passing of time. The 1 and 99 percent quantiles of the one-day ahead exchange rate, given the posited probability distribution, are marked in the graph with vertical grid lines. The points at which those grid lines intersect the P&L plot mark the 1 and 99 percent quantiles of the next-day P&L.

---

[1]See Appendix A.3 for more detail on this distribution and its relationship to the Black-Scholes model.

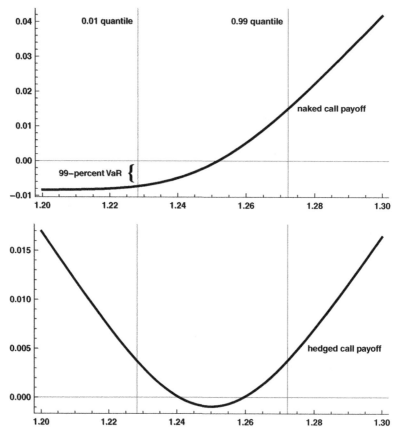

FIGURE 4.1   Monotonicity and Option Risk Measurement
One-day P&L in dollars of an at-the-money forward call on the euro,
denominated in U.S. dollars, as a function of the next-day USD-EUR exchange
rate. The option parameters and the spot rate's probability distribution are as
described in the text. Vertical grid lines denote the 1st and 99-th percentiles of
the exchange rate.
Upper panel: One-day P&L of a position in one euro call as a function of the
underlying exchange rate.
Lower panel: One-day P&L of a position in one euro call, delta-hedged at the
beginning of the period, as a function of the underlying exchange rate.

If the value of a position is a nonlinear function of a single risk factor,
and we know or stipulate its P&L distribution, it looks fairly straightforward
to compute any of its P&L quantiles, including the VaR, directly from the
P&L distribution. The 99 percent VaR of the call position in our example
is equal to about $0.0065.

Let's try to generalize this approach, which we'll refer to as "analytical," to other types of option positions. We denote the pricing or value function of the position or security by $f(S_t, \tau)$, where S_t is the sole risk factor. For the specific case of a European option, we set $f(S_t, \tau) = v(S_t, \tau, X, \sigma, r, q)$ or $f(S_t, \tau) = w(S_t, \tau, X, \sigma, r, q)$, since σ is a parameter for now, and S_t the only random driver of value. The number of options in the position is denoted x, so the time-t value of the portfolio is $V_t = xf(S_t, \tau)$, and the random P&L over the VaR time horizon θ is

$$V_{t+\theta} - V_t = x\left[\, f(S_{t+\theta}, \tau - \theta) - f(S_t, \tau)\,\right]$$

The function arguments in the first term inside the square brackets reflect the fact that the VaR will be determined by the exchange rate one day ahead, and its impact on the value of an option with a maturity that is now one day shorter. We would like to be able to calculate, say, the one day, 99 percent VaR, by setting it equal to

$$f(S^*, \tau - \theta) - f(S_t, \tau)$$

per option, where S^* is the, say, 1st or 99-th percentile of S_t, depending on whether the position is long or short. The VaR shock, the asset return at which the VaR is just reached, is then

$$r^* = \log\left(\frac{S^*}{S_t}\right) \quad \Leftrightarrow \quad S^* = S_t e^{r^*}$$

But this only works if the position value or P&L is a *monotonic* or *monotone function* of the underlying risk factor. The function $f(S_t, \tau)$ is called *monotone increasing* in S_t if and only if

$$S_1 > S_2 \quad \Leftrightarrow \quad f(S_1, \tau) > f(S_2, \tau) \qquad \forall S_1, S_2$$

A function $f(S_t, \tau)$ is called *monotone decreasing* in S_t if and only if

$$S_1 > S_2 \quad \Leftrightarrow \quad f(S_1, \tau) < f(S_2, \tau) \qquad \forall S_1, S_2$$

Plain-vanilla options fulfill this requirement. The long call shown in the upper panel of Figure 4.1, for example, is monotone increasing; its slope or "delta" (to be defined in a moment) is never negative. A put is a nonincreasing function; its delta is never positive.

The lower panel of Figure 4.1 illustrates a case in which this "analytical" method of VaR calculation won't work, because the portfolio value is not a monotone function of the underlying asset price. It displays the next-day P&L on a *delta-hedged* position in the call. Here, the first percentile of the exchange rate doesn't tell us the VaR, because there is another, higher, exchange rate realization, close to the 99th percentile, that has *exactly the same P&L*.

The lower panel suggests that the VaR shock is zero or just a small fluctuation away from the initial exchange rate. The delta-hedged call is a "long volatility" or "long gamma" trade, and is most profitable if there are large exchange-rate fluctuations in either direction.

So there is a crucial additional requirement, monotonicity, if we are to take the simple "analytical" approach to risk measurement for an option position. Monotonicity also enters into the standard theory behind the distribution of a transformation of a random variable with a known distribution. This standard theory, discussed in Appendix A.5, requires that the *inverse function* of the transformation exist, and only monotone functions are "one-to-one" and thus invertible. Monotonicity is thus a requirement for being able to "pass through" the probability distribution of S_t to the probability distribution of $V_t - V_{t+\tau}$.

4.1.2 Simulation for Nonlinear Exposures

Since we can't assume the P&L is a monotonic function of the underlying asset, the "analytical" approach doesn't work in general. In the example above, monotonicity didn't hold even for a position exposed to a single risk factor. Very few portfolios are that simple, and the invertibility condition is very hard to meet in practice. An approach that uses the same model for the underlying return behavior, but doesn't fail in the face of nonmonotonicity, is *Monte Carlo* or *historical simulation with full repricing*. This procedure is similar to that laid out in Chapter 3. But we have here the additional step of computing the P&L via $f(S_t, \tau)$ in each simulation thread, rather than simply ascertaining the value of S_t in each simulation thread.

The first two steps of either of these simulation approaches are to prepare the simulated returns. These are identical to the first two steps of the Monte Carlo and historical simulation techniques as laid out for linear positions in Chapter 3. The difference for nonlinear positions is in how the simulated returns are treated next, in the "repricing" step. Instead of multiplying the position value by the simulated returns, we enter the simulated return into the pricing or value function $f(S_t, \tau)$.

For the Monte Carlo simulation technique, and still assuming the normal distribution, the simulated exchange rates are

$$\tilde{S}^{(i)} = S_t \exp\left(\sigma\sqrt{\tau}\tilde{\epsilon}^{(i)}\right) \qquad i = 1, \ldots, I$$

where $\tilde{\epsilon}^{(i)}, i = 1, \ldots, I$ are a set of independent draws from a $N(0, 1)$ distribution. We set the VaR time horizon $\theta = \frac{1}{252}$ and $I = 10{,}000$ in our examples.

The 99 percent VaR is found by substituting the $\tilde{S}^{(1)}, \ldots, \tilde{S}^{(I)}$ into the P&L function $x[f(S_{t+\theta}, \tau - \theta) - f(S_t, \tau)]$ to get

$$x\left[f(\tilde{S}^{(i)}, \tau - \theta) - f(S_t, \tau)\right] \qquad i = 1, \ldots, I$$

and taking the 1st percentile, or 10th worst outcome. The result in our example is a VaR estimate of \$0.0065, or about $\frac{65}{100}$ of one cent per euro of underlying notional, and about the same as that obtained with the "analytical" approach. The result is not identical to that of the "analytical" approach because of simulation noise: the distribution of the $\tilde{S}^{(i)}$ is only approximately equal to that of S_t.

Monte Carlo with full repricing is often impractical for computing risk for large portfolios. It can be slow if there are many positions, and if enough of those positions are priced via complicated models, though this is becoming less of a problem as computing power increases. Many derivative and structured credit pricing models are implemented via simulation rather than analytical solution. That means that if we want to know what the security is worth for a given value of the underlying asset or other market inputs, we don't plug the $\tilde{S}^{(i)}$ into a formula, but rather simulate the security value using the inputs as parameters. We give a detailed example of such a procedure in Chapter 9. In many cases, each simulation of a security value can be quite "expensive" in computer time. In order to do risk computations with $I = 10,000$ for such an asset, we must repeat this pricing process 10,000 times. If each repricing requires, say, 1,000 simulations to be accurate, a total of 10,000,000 simulation threads have to be computed. Even a great deal of sheer computing power may not speed it up enough to be practicable.

But if we stipulate the distribution of the underlying returns, Monte Carlo can be made as accurate as we like, as long we use as much computing time and as many simulations as are needed for that level of accuracy and the pricing model we are using. It therefore serves as the typical benchmark for assessing the accuracy of other approaches, such as delta-gamma, which we discuss next. Of course, to use Monte Carlo as a benchmark, you have to run it, at least in studies, if not in practice.

4.1.3 Delta-Gamma for Options

So far, we have developed a simple approach that fails in the absence of monotonicity, and a simulation approach that is too slow to be practicable in general. The next approach we will explore, delta-gamma, does not help at all with the monotonicity problem, but it can speed up calculations compared to full repricing. It raises new statistical issues, and, more importantly, it is based on an approximation that hedging can be wildly wrong. But when delta-gamma is safe to use, it can be very useful.

The starting point for the delta-gamma approach is to approximate the exposure of a call to fluctuations in the underlying asset price, using a quadratic approximation in S_t, by

$$
\begin{aligned}
\Delta v(S_t, \tau, X, \sigma, r, q) &= v(S_t + \Delta S, \tau - \Delta t, X, \sigma, r, q) \\
&\quad - v(S_t, \tau, X, \sigma, r, q) \\
&\approx \theta_{c,t} \Delta t + \delta_{c,t} \Delta S + \frac{1}{2} \gamma_t \Delta S^2
\end{aligned}
\tag{4.1}
$$

The *theta* of the call option is

$$
\theta_{c,t} \equiv \frac{\partial}{\partial t} v(S_t, \tau, X, \sigma, r, q)
$$

The theta of a long position in a put or call option is negative, and represents the predictable loss of option value as its maturity shortens.

The *delta* of the option, the slope of the option pricing function we referred to above, is

$$
\delta_{c,t} \equiv \frac{\partial}{\partial S_t} v(S_t, \tau, X, \sigma, r, q)
$$

The delta is also the amount of the underlying asset that must be bought or sold to hedge the option against small fluctuations in the underlying price. Corresponding definitions can be provided for a put. The *gamma* is

$$
\gamma_t \equiv \frac{\partial^2}{\partial S_t^2} v(S_t, \tau, X, \sigma, r, q)
$$

and is the same for both a call and put with the same strike and maturity. The delta and gamma change with the underlying price, the implied volatility, and the other market and design parameters of the options, but we are not spelling out this dependency in the notation, except to put a time subscript on the sensitivities.

We have two ways now to use the quadratic approximation to compute the one day, 99 percent VaR:

- "Analytical," that is, find the quantile of the future exchange rate corresponding to the 0.01 quantile of the P&L function, and substitute it into the delta-gamma approximation to the P&L function. This approach will not solve the monotonicity problem, but it is fast.

■ Simulation, that is, use the same simulated values of the future exchange rate as in full repricing, but use the delta-gamma approximation to compute each simulation thread's P&L. The first percentile (times −1) is the VaR. This approach *will* solve the monotonicity problem, and it is much faster than full repricing. But it can be inaccurate, as we will see in a moment.

We can also compare the quadratic to a linear approximation using delta alone:

$$\Delta v(S_t, \tau, X, \sigma, r, q) \approx \theta_{c,t}\Delta t + \delta_{c,t}\Delta S$$

As we will see, there are tricky issues in choosing between a linear and higher-order approximation.

Let's look at examples that cover a range of option position types frequently encountered in practice. For each one, we'll graph the P&L function itself as a solid curve, and the delta (linear) and delta-gamma (quadratic) approximations to the P&L function. For each option prtfolio, we will also display the histogram of simulated P&Ls using the P&L function itself and the delta-gamma approximation. The one-day, 99 percent confidence level VaR results are summarized in Table 4.1 for the three option position types and the three approaches to VaR estimation.

Unhedged Long Call The upper panel of Figure 4.2 illustrates the delta-gamma approximation for an unhedged, or "naked," long call. The solid plot shows the one-day change in value of the one week euro call of our standing example as the spot exchange rate varies.

The analytical approach can be used, since the payoff profile is monotonic. The analytical as well as the simulation approaches using the delta-gamma approximation or full repricing all give roughly equal VaR estimates of about $0.0073. Any of these are much more accurate than the delta approximation, which substantially overestimates the VaR.

TABLE 4.1 Comparison of Option VaR Estimates

	Analytical	Delta	Delta-Gamma	Full Repricing
Long call	0.00731	0.01178	0.00736	0.00726
Delta-hedged long call	NA	0.00092	0.00092	0.00092
Risk reversal	0.01178	0.01073	0.00410	0.01152

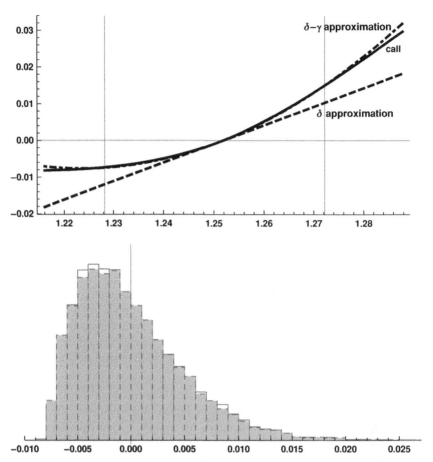

FIGURE 4.2　Delta-Gamma and Full-Repricing VaR for an Unhedged Long Call
Upper panel: One-day P&L in dollars of a long call option position as a function
of the next-day USD-EUR exchange rate. The solid curve plots the exact P&L
function, the dashed curve the delta approximation, and the dot-dashed curve the
delta-gamma approximation.
Lower panel: Histogram of simulated P&Ls using the exact P&L function
(unshaded bars), and the delta-gamma approximation (shaded bars).

Hedged Long Call　For a hedged long call, we can't use the analytical approach at all, since the P&L function is notmonotone. The hedged call has a
delta of zero when the hedge is first put on, so the quadratic approximation
becomes

$$\Delta v(S_t, T - t, X, \sigma, r, q) \approx \theta_{c,t}\Delta t + \frac{1}{2}\gamma_t \Delta S^2$$

As can be seen from Figure 4.3, the worst losses on this long gamma strategy—a strategy for which the position gamma is positive—occur when the exchange rate doesn't move at all. A short gamma position has its worst losses when there is a large exchange-rate move. This is an important point: A delta-hedged option position still has a potentially large gamma exposure to the underlying price, since it cannot be hedged continuously in time. Rather, the hedge is rebalanced at discrete intervals.

At the 1st and 99th percentiles of the exchange rate's next-day distribution, the P&L of the long gamma trade is positive. The nonrandom one day time decay of $0.00092 is the largest possible loss, and is offset to a greater or lesser extent by gamma gains from any exchange rate fluctuations. About two-thirds of the simulation scenarios are losses, but within the narrow range $(-0.00092, 0)$.

All three simulation approaches give almost exactly the same result. The reason is that a small loss, very close to the time decay of the option, is the likeliest outcome. Under the normal distribution, most fluctuations are small, and the gamma is therefore a very small positive number. So the lower quantiles of the P&L distribution are equal to the time decay, minus a tiny gamma gain.

Option Combinations   Before describing the next option position, involving several options, we need to introduce some terminology. An *option combination* is a portfolio of options containing both calls and puts. An *option spread* is a portfolio containing only calls or only puts. A combination or a spread may contain either short or long option positions, or both.

One of the most common option combinations is the *straddle*, consisting of a call and a put, both either long or short, both struck at-the-money spot or forward, and both with the same maturity. In the options on futures markets, the exercise price is generally chosen to be close to the price of the current futures with the same expiration date as the options.

Almost as common are combinations of out-of-the-money options, particularly the *strangle* and the *risk reversal*. Both consist of an out-of-the-money call and out-of-the-money put. In these two combinations, the exercise price of the call component is higher than the current spot or forward asset price (or futures), and the exercise price of the put is lower. In a risk reversal, an out-of-the-money call is exchanged for an out-of-the-money put, with a net premium paid by one to the other counterparty. In a strangle, one counterparty sells both an out-of-the-money call and an out-of-the-money put to the other. Figure 4.4 displays the payoff profiles of these combinations.

In the OTC foreign exchange option markets, risk reversals and strangles are usually standardized as combinations of a 25-delta call and a 25-delta put (or 10-delta). The exercise prices of the call and put are both set so

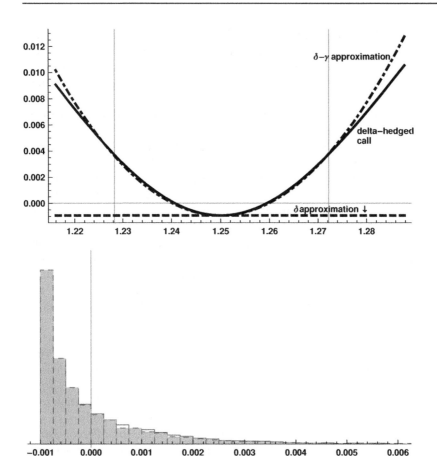

FIGURE 4.3 Delta-Gamma and Full-Repricing VaR for a Hedged Call
Upper panel: One-day P&L in dollars of a delta-hedged long call option position as a function of the next-day USD-EUR exchange rate. The solid curve plots the exact P&L function, the dashed curve the delta approximation, and the dot-dashed curve the delta-gamma approximation.
Lower panel: Histogram of simulated P&Ls using the exact P&L function (unshaded bars), and the delta-gamma approximation (shaded bars).

that their forward deltas are equal to 0.25 or 0.10. We describe the quoting conventions of these instruments in more detail in Section 5.5.

Risk reversals provide a good illustration of the relationship between nonlinearity in the pricing function and the pitfalls of relying on linear or quadratic approximations to the pricing function to measure risk. The risk reversal's P&L function is monotone, but alternates between concave and convex segments. This renders the delta-gamma approach much less accurate; in fact, it is significantly worse than using delta alone, as can be seen

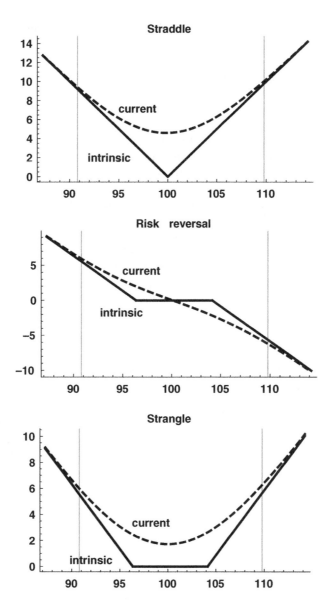

FIGURE 4.4 Option Combinations
Each panel shows the intrinsic and current values of an option combination. The current price of the underlying asset is 100, the annual implied volatility is 20 percent, the time to maturity of all the options is 1 month, and the risk-free rate and dividend rate on the underlying asset are both set at 1 percent. The forward asset price is therefore also 100. In each panel, the solid line represents the intrinsic and the dashed line the current value of the combination as a function of the terminal or current price of the underlying. The vertical grid lines mark the 1 and 99 percent quantiles of the risk-neutral distribution of the underlying asset.

in Figure 4.5. Surprisingly, using the "less accurate" linear approximation is in fact *less* misleading than using the quadratic approximation, which underestimates the VaR by over one-half.

The risk reversal is similar to a delta-hedged option in that it has an initial net delta that is close to zero. Its initial gamma is much lower, though, since there are two offsetting options; the long option position has positive and the short option has negative gamma. Moreover, each of the component options has a lower-magnitude gamma at the initial exchange rate than an at-the-money option with the same maturity.

An alternative approach to VaR measurement would be to compute the variance of the change in value of the option $\Delta v(S_t, T - t, X, \sigma, r, q)$. In other words, we would treat the option value itself, rather than the underlying asset price, as the risk factor. But this involves an additional statistical issue. The quadratic approximation gives us $\Delta v(S_t, T - t, X, \sigma, r, q)$ as a function of the change in the value of the underlying asset and the squared change. To compute its variance, we would have to take into account the joint distribution of a normal variate, and its square. Other analytical approximations to delta-gamma have also been proposed, but none appear to be decisively superior in accuracy over a wide range of position types and asset classes.

4.1.4 The Delta-Gamma Approach for General Exposures

The delta-gamma approach can be applied to any security with payoffs that are nonlinear in a risk factor. For simplicity, let's continue to look at securities that are functions $f(S_t, \tau)$ of a single risk factor S_t and time. Just as we did for an option in Equation (4.1), we can approximate changes in value by the second-order Taylor approximation:

$$\Delta f(S_t, \tau) = f(S_t + \Delta S, \tau - \Delta t) - f(S_t, \tau) \approx \theta_t \Delta t + \delta_t \Delta S + \frac{1}{2} \gamma_t \Delta S^2$$

The *theta* of the security is the perfectly predictable return per time period:

$$\theta_t \equiv \frac{\partial f(S_t, \tau)}{\partial \tau}$$

For a bond or a dividend-paying stock, for example, the theta is the coupon or other cash flow, and is a positive number.

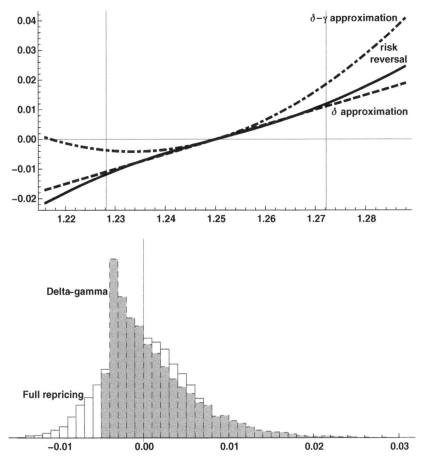

FIGURE 4.5 Delta-Gamma and Full-Repricing VaR for a Risk Reversal
Upper panel: One-day P&L in dollars of a risk reversal position as a function of the next-day USD-EUR exchange rate. The solid curve plots the exact P&L function, the dashed curve the delta approximation, and the short-long dashed curve the delta-gamma approximation.
Lower panel: Histogram of simulated P&Ls using the exact P&L function (unshaded bars), and the delta-gamma approximation (shaded bars).

The *delta* of any security, just as for an option, is the first derivative of the value $f(S_t, \tau)$ per unit or per share with respect to the risk factor S_t:

$$\delta_t \equiv \frac{\partial f(S_t, \tau)}{\partial S_t}$$

The *gamma* of the security is

$$\gamma_t \equiv \frac{\partial^2 f(S_t, \tau)}{\partial S_t^2}$$

As with options, in order to apply the delta-gamma approach without being misleading, the function $f(S_t, \tau)$ must be monotonic in S_t, that is, its first derivative does not change sign, no matter how high or low the value of the risk factor S_t. We assume that the risk factor S_t is lognormally distributed with zero mean. Recall that the parametric VaR for a long position in a single security is estimated as

$$\text{VaR}_t(\alpha, \tau)(x) = -\left(e^{z_*\sigma\sqrt{\tau}} - 1\right) x S_t$$

We now have to be careful with determining z_*, the standard normal ordinate corresponding to the VaR shock. If the delta is negative, then z_* is in the right rather than the left tail of the normal distribution. The most important example is VaR of a bond when we map bond prices to interest rates. We study this approach to bond VaR estimation in the rest of this chapter.

Under the delta-gamma approach, VaR is estimated as

$$\text{VaR}_t(\alpha, \tau)(x) = -x\left\{\left(e^{z_*\sigma\sqrt{\tau}} - 1\right) S_t\delta_t + \frac{1}{2}\left[\left(e^{z_*\sigma\sqrt{\tau}} - 1\right) S_t^2\right]^2 \gamma_t\right\}$$

where z_* is the ordinate of the standard normal distribution for

$$\left\{\begin{matrix} \alpha \\ 1-\alpha \end{matrix}\right\} \quad \text{for} \quad \delta_t \left\{\begin{matrix} <0 \\ >0 \end{matrix}\right\}$$

and α is the VaR confidence level. If $\delta_t > 0$, as in the examples up until now, then z_* is a negative number such as -2.33, and $e^{z_*\sigma\sqrt{\tau}} - 1 < 0$. If $\delta_t < 0$, as in the example we develop in the next section, then z_* is a positive number such as $+2.33$, and $e^{z_*\sigma\sqrt{\tau}} - 1 > 0$. Either way, the VaR estimate is a positive number.

4.2 YIELD CURVE RISK

This chapter on nonlinear risks may seem an odd place to discuss yield curve risk. The reason we do so is that, while bonds have a price expressed in currency units, they are more frequently viewed as exposures to interest rate rather than bond price fluctuations. Interest rate exposure is nonlinear, though much less drastically so than for options and other derivatives.

We start by focusing on default-free bonds, that is, bonds with deterministic future cash flows; their size and timing are known with certainty. The only thing that is risky about them is the discounted value the market will place on a dollar of cash flow delivered in the future. In subsequent chapters, we introduce credit spreads and discuss the risks of defaultable bonds when both risk-free and credit-risky interest rates can fluctuate. In practice, of course, as we noted in Chapter 2, no security is perfectly free of default risk.

Bond and other fixed-income security values are generally expressed for trading purposes as either a dollar/currency unit price, as a yield, or as a spread. However, none of these price metrics completely describe the *yield curve* the bond value depends on. Bond prices are not appropriate risk factors because

- Bonds vary in maturity. *Ceteris paribus*, longer-maturity bonds have a greater volatility than shorter-maturity bonds. In fact, as bonds near their maturity date, the volatility declines to zero, a phenomenon known as *pull-to-par*. So the risk of a bond changes merely because of the passing of time.
- Interest rates vary by the term over which the use of money is granted. Bond prices are determined, not by one interest rate, but by the yield curve, that is, interest rates of many different maturities. Interest rates are more truly the underlying risk factor than bond prices themselves. By focusing on the yield curve, we capture the differences in the sensitivity of a bond's value to changes in interest rates with different terms to maturity.

There are three common approaches to computing the VaR of a bond:

1. *Cash-flow mapping.* The value of any default-free bond can be decomposed into a set of zero-coupon bonds corresponding to each of the cash-flows associated with it. The prices of zero-coupon bonds can be used as risk factors. This approach can involve a large number of zero-coupon bonds if there are many cash flows and/or the bond has a long term to maturity. In such cases, we can bucket the cash flows into a smaller number of zero-coupon *nodes* or *vertexes*.

2. *Duration* of a bond can be measured and used together with the yield history of bonds of that maturity to derive an estimate of the bond's return volatility.

3. *Factor models* for bonds are focused on parsimonious sets of drivers
    of interest-rate risk. These can be interpreted statistically, for ex-
    ample, as *principal components* of interest rates, or economically,
    related to changes in the level, slope, and curvature of the yield
    curve.

The rest of this chapter introduces basic yield-curve concepts and focuses
on the duration approach to measuring the interest-rate risk of a bond. Bonds
denominated in a currency other than that of the portfolio owner's domicile
have currency risk in addition to that generated by fluctuating interest rates.

4.2.1 The Term Structure of Interest Rates

This section gives a brief overview of yield curve concepts. The term structure
can be described in three ways which have equivalent information content,
the *spot* and *forward curves* and the *discount function*.

Any interest rate, including a spot rate, can be expressed numerically
using any compounding interval, that is, the period during which interest
accrues before interest-on-interest is applied. Interest rates with any compounding interval can be easily transformed into rates with any other compounding interval. Therefore, the choice of compounding interval is purely
a choice of units, and is made for convenience only. We'll focus on continuously compounded rates, that is, interest rates expressed as though they were
paid as a continuous flow, equal in every instant to the same fraction of the
principal. The mathematics of the yield curve are simplest when expressed
in continuously compounded terms, but real-world interest rates are rarely
set this way. Interest rates are expressed as a rate per unit of time. We will
express all interest rates at annual rates unless otherwise indicated.

We start with the notion of a *zero-coupon* or *discount bond*, a bond
with only one payment, at maturity. We denote the time-t price per dollar
of *principal amount* (also called *par* or *notional amount* or *face value*) of
a discount bond maturing at time T by p_τ, where $\tau \equiv T - t$ is the time to
maturity (a time interval rather than a date). The price at maturity of a
risk-free discount bond is $p_0 \equiv 1$.

Spot and Forward Rates   The *spot rate* r_τ is the continuously compounded
annual rate of interest paid by a discount bond, that is, the rate of interest paid for the commitment of funds from the current date t until the
maturity date T. The *continuously compounded spot rate* is the interest
rate paid from time t to time T. The *continuously compounded spot* or
zero-coupon curve is the function r_τ relating continuously compounded

spot rates to the time to maturity or maturity date. This function changes as interest rates fluctuate. But for the rest of this section, we'll omit the "as-of" date subscript and keep only the time-to-maturity subscript, since our focus for now is on the properties of the yield curve at a point in time, rather than on its evolution over time.

The relationship between p_τ and r_τ is given by

$$
\begin{aligned}
p_\tau e^{r_\tau \tau} &= 1 \\
\Rightarrow \ln(p_\tau) + r_\tau \tau &= 0 \\
\Rightarrow \qquad r_\tau &= -\frac{\ln(p_\tau)}{\tau}
\end{aligned}
\tag{4.2}
$$

that is, r_τ is the constant annual exponential rate at which the bond's value must grow to reach \$1 at time T.

Example 4.1 Let the price of a discount bond expiring in nine months be $p_{\frac{3}{4}} = 0.96$. The continuously compounded nine-month spot rate is

$$
r_{\frac{3}{4}} = -\frac{\ln\left(p_{\frac{3}{4}}\right)}{\dfrac{3}{4}} = 0.054429
$$

or 5.44 percent. In this, as in our other examples, we ignore the refinements of *day-count conventions*, which dictate how to treat such matters as variations in the number of days in a month or year, and the fact that the number of days in a year is not an integer multiple of 12.

A *forward rate* is the rate of interest paid for the commitment of funds from one future date T_1, called the *settlement date*, until a second future date T_2, called the *maturity date*, with $t \leq T_1 < T_2$. We now have two time intervals at work: the time to settlement $\tau_1 = T_1 - t$ and the time to maturity $\tau_2 = T_2 - T_1$. (Note that $T_2 = t + \tau_1 + \tau_2$.)

The *continuously compounded forward rate from time T_1 to time T_2*, denoted $f_{\tau_1, \tau_1 + \tau_2}$, is the continuously compounded annual interest rate contracted at time t to be paid from time T_1 to time T_2. The *continuously compounded τ_2-period forward curve* is the function $f_{\tau_1, \tau_1 + \tau_2}$ relating forward rates of a given time to maturity to the time to settlement or the settlement date. An example of a forward curve is the curve of three-month U.S. dollar money market rates implied by the prices of Chicago Mercantile Exchange (CME) Eurodollar futures contracts, for which we have $\tau_2 = \frac{1}{4}$.

We can relate continuously compounded forward rates to discount bond prices and spot rates. The forward rate is defined by

$$\frac{1}{p_{\tau_1}} p_{\tau_1+\tau_2} e^{f_{\tau_1,\tau_1+\tau_2}\tau_2} = 1$$

$$\Rightarrow \quad \ln\left(\frac{p_{\tau_1+\tau_2}}{p_{\tau_1}}\right) + f_{\tau_1,\tau_1+\tau_2}\tau_2 = 0 \tag{4.3}$$

$$\Rightarrow \quad f_{\tau_1,\tau_1+\tau_2} = -\frac{1}{\tau_2}\ln\left[\frac{p_{\tau_1+\tau_2}}{p_{\tau_1}}\right] = \frac{1}{\tau_2}\ln\left[\frac{p_{\tau_1}}{p_{\tau_1+\tau_2}}\right]$$

The first line of Equation (4.3) defines the forward rate as the constant rate at which the price of a bond maturing on the forward maturity date must grow so as to equal the price of a bond maturing on the forward settlement date. From the last line of Equation (4.3), together with the last line of (4.2), we see that forward rates can also be calculated directly from spot rates:

$$f_{\tau_1,\tau_1+\tau_2} = \frac{r_{\tau_1+\tau_2}(\tau_1+\tau_2) - r_{\tau_1}\tau_1}{\tau_2}$$

The *instantaneous forward rate* with settlement date T, denoted f_τ, is the limit, as $T_1 \to T_2$, of $f_{\tau_1,\tau_1+\tau_2}$:

$$f_\tau = \lim_{\tau_2 \to 0} f_{\tau_1,\tau_1+\tau_2} = \lim_{\tau_2 \to 0} \frac{r_{\tau_2}(\tau_1+\tau_2) - r_{\tau_1}\tau_1}{\tau_2} = r_\tau + \frac{dr_\tau}{d\tau}\tau$$

after simplifying notation by setting $\tau \equiv \tau_1$. The instantaneous forward rate is the interest rate contracted at time t on an infinitely short forward loan settling τ periods hence. For concreteness, one can think of it as a forward on the overnight rate prevailing at time T. The *instantaneous forward curve* is the function f_τ relating instantaneous forward rates to the time to settlement or the settlement date.

A forward rate with a finite time to maturity can be viewed as the average of the instantaneous forward rates over the time to maturity. Integrating over a range of settlement dates, we have

$$f_{\tau_1,\tau_1+\tau_2} = \frac{1}{\tau_2}\int_{\tau_1}^{\tau_1+\tau_2} f_s\, ds$$

A τ-year continuously compounded spot rate, that is, the constant annual rate at which a pure discount bond's value must grow to reach one currency unit at time T, can be expressed by integrating the instantaneous forward curve over the time to maturity:

$$r_T = \frac{1}{T} \int_0^T f_t dt$$

The relationship between spot and forward rates has an important implication: the forward curve is higher than the spot curve for maturity intervals in which the spot curve is upward sloping, and vice versa.

Spot curves and forward curves are two equivalent ways of expressing the term structure of interest rates as a function of the time to maturity. A third is the discount function or *discount factor curve*, which relates the prices of zero-coupon bonds to their times to maturity. Unlike either spot curves or forward curves, the discount function has no compounding intervals. As we saw in defining them, forward rates can be viewed as logarithmic changes along the discount function. Discount factors are very close to 1 for short maturities, and close to 0 for long maturities. The discount function must slope downwards.

4.2.2 Estimating Yield Curves

None of the yield curve concepts we've just defined are, in general, directly observable. This is a pity, because modeling and implementing risk measures for fixed-income securities requires them. Apart from a small number of short-term bonds such as U.S. Treasury bills and strips, there are not many zero-coupon bonds. And while many bond prices are expressed in yield terms, money-market instruments are among the only single cash-flow securities that would permit one to easily convert the yield into a continuously compounded spot rate. Forward rates are expressed in money market futures and *forward rate agreements*, the OTC analogue of money market futures.

In other words, yield curves have to be extracted or estimated from the actually traded mishmash of diverse fixed-income security types. Aside from the diversity of cash flow structures and quoting conventions, there are other problems with the market data used in estimating yield curves, for example,

Liquidity. Different securities on what seems to be the same yield curve can have very different liquidity, so that effectively, their prices are generated by different yield curves. For example, *on-the-run* or freshly issued U.S. Treasury notes have lower yields and higher prices than *off-the-run* notes, that is, issues from less recent auctions, which tend to have lower prices and a liquidity premium.

Embedded options. Some bonds are callable or have other option-like features. In fact, some U.S. Treasury notes issued prior to 1985 were

callable. These options can have value, and if they do, their prices
do not coincide with the discount factors for similar bonds without
options.

Taxes. Different types of bonds have different tax treatment. For example, in the United States, income from U.S. Treasury issues is not
taxed at the state and local level, and the income from most bonds
issued by state and local governments is not taxed at all, while income from corporate bonds is taxable at the federal, state, and local
level. These tax differences have a large impact on prices that has
to be taken into account in estimating yield curves.

To get around these problems, one can filter the data so that they are
uniform with respect to their tax, liquidity, and optionality characteristics.
Alternatively, one can estimate the impact of these characteristics and adjust
the data for them.

Another set of issues making it difficult it construct yield curves is that
the estimated yield curves can behave strangely in several ways:

Asymptotic behavior. If we extrapolate yield curves to much longer
maturities than the data provide, in itself a problematic exercise,
the prices or spot rates may become negative or infinite.

Violations of no-arbitrage conditions. Estimated yield curves may display discontinuities, spikes, and other oddities. Intermediate points
on the spot and forward curves falling between actual observations
may then be much higher or lower than neighboring points. Lack
of smoothness may lead to the apparent possibility of instantaneous
arbitrage between bonds or forward contracts with different maturities as computed from the curve.

The discount, spot, and forward curves are different ways of expressing
the same time value of money, so any of these forms of the yield curve can
be estimated and transformed into any of the others, with the form chosen
for a particular purpose a matter of convenience or convention.

Bootstrapping and Splines   A common approach "connects the dots" between observed yields, spot rates, or forward rates:

Bootstrapping. Each security is stripped down to its individual cash
flows, which are arranged in maturity order. Starting with the
shortest maturity, and using the results of each step to support the
subsequent step, the discount factors or spot rates corresponding to

each maturity are computed. Futures and forwards as well as cash securities can be included.

Spline interpolation is a process for connecting data points by passing polynomial functions through them. Polynomials have the advantage that, depending on their degree, they lead to smooth curves in the sense that they have finite derivatives. For example, cubic splines have finite first, second, and third derivatives.

The bootstrapping and spline approaches have the advantage that the price or yield of each of the securities used to estimate the yield curve can be recovered exactly from the estimated curve. But both approaches tend to produce curves that are spiky or excessively wavy, or extrapolate out to infinity or zero. In practice, these problems can be addressed by preprocessing the data or by additional smoothing techniques.

Parametric Estimates   Parametric approaches begin with a model that limits the forms the yield curve can take. For example, the *Nelson-Siegel* specification of the instantaneous forward rate is similar in spirit to a delta-gamma approach and is given by

$$f(\tau; \beta_0, \beta_1, \beta_2, \theta) = \beta_0 + \beta_1 e^{-\frac{\tau}{\theta}} + \beta_2 \frac{\tau}{\theta} e^{-\frac{\tau}{\theta}} \qquad (4.4)$$

where $(\beta_0, \beta_1, \beta_2, \theta)$ is a vector of parameters to be estimated and τ, representing the time to maturity, is the single argument of the function. The corresponding representation of the spot rate is the definite integral of this instantaneous forward rate over τ, Equation (4.4) or

$$\begin{aligned}
r(\tau; \beta_0, \beta_1, \beta_2, \theta) &= \beta_0 + (\beta_1 + \beta_2)\left(\tfrac{\tau}{\theta}\right)^{-1}\left(1 - e^{-\frac{\tau}{\theta}}\right) - \beta_2 e^{-\frac{\tau}{\theta}} \\
&= \beta_0 + \beta_1\left(\tfrac{\tau}{\theta}\right)^{-1}\left(1 - e^{-\frac{\tau}{\theta}}\right) \\
&\quad + \beta_2\left[\left(\tfrac{\tau}{\theta}\right)^{-1}\left(1 - e^{-\frac{\tau}{\theta}}\right) - e^{-\frac{\tau}{\theta}}\right]
\end{aligned}$$

With different values of the parameters, the function is capable of fitting a wide range of typical yield curve shapes. Each term and parameter in the function contributes a distinct element to these typical patterns:

- β_0 is the asymptotic value of the forward rate function and represents the forward rate or futures price prevailing at very long maturities.
- As $\tau \downarrow 0$, the forward and spot rates tend toward $\beta_0 + \beta_1$, which thus more or less represents the overnight rate. To constrain the very

short-term interest rate to nonnegative values, the condition $\beta_1 > -\beta_0$ is imposed. If $\beta_1 > 0$ (< 0), the very short-term value of the function is higher (lower) than the long-term value.

■ The term $\beta_1 e^{-\frac{\tau}{\theta}}$ imposes exponential convergence to the long-term value β_0. If $\beta_1 > 0$ (< 0), the convergence is from above (below).

■ The term $\beta_2 \frac{\tau}{\theta} e^{-\frac{\tau}{\theta}}$ permits hump-shaped behavior of the yield curve. If $\beta_2 > 0$ (< 0), the function rises above (falls below) its long-term value before converging.

■ The speed of convergence of both the simple and humped exponential terms to the long-term value is governed by θ. A higher value of θ corresponds to slower convergence. That is, for a given gap between very short- and long-term rates, a higher value of θ lowers any other term spread.

We use the Nelson-Siegel specification in the examples in the rest of this chapter. The reason is that the parameters have a nice interpretation as three yield curve risk factors:

1. β_0 is the yield curve *level* factor and has a constant factor loading of unity.
2. β_1 is the yield curve *curvature* factor. It has a factor loading of $\left(\frac{\tau}{\theta}\right)^{-1}\left(1 - e^{-\frac{\tau}{\theta}}\right)$.
3. β_2 is a factor representing an "overshoot-and-converge" pattern in the yield curve level, and has a factor loading of $\left(\frac{\tau}{\theta}\right)^{-1}\left(1 - e^{-\frac{\tau}{\theta}}\right) - e^{-\frac{\tau}{\theta}}$.

In particular, by changing β_0, we can induce parallel shifts up or down in the yield curve in a simple way. We use this property in the rest of this chapter. The Nelson-Siegel is used more in academic work than in the practical work of financial intermediaries, since it doesn't exactly replicate the input security prices. But it is a very practical tool for explicating risk measurement techniques for fixed income.

Figure 4.6 illustrates the Nelson-Siegel function. It is estimated using unweighted least squares and data on Libor, eurodollar futures, and plain-vanilla swap rates on Nov. 3, 2007.

4.2.3 Coupon Bonds

A coupon bond is an interest-bearing instrument that makes regular payments, called *coupons*, at contractually specified times $t_1 < t_2 < \ldots < t_n = T$, and a final payment of the principal or face value at maturity date T. For most coupon bonds, the coupons are all the same amount c per dollar of

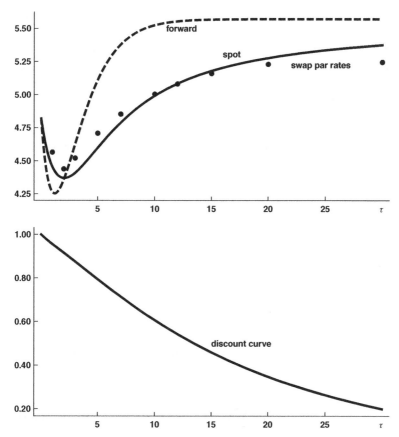

FIGURE 4.6   Spot, Forward, and Discount Curves
Three equivalent representations of the yield curve, as spot, forward, and discount curves, USD swaps, Nov. 1, 2007, maturities in years.
Upper panel: Continuously compounded spot curve and corresponding instantaneous forward curve, interest rates in percent. The dots represent the U.S. dollar swap par rate prevailing on Nov. 3, 2007.
Lower panel: Discount curve, expressed as dollars per dollar of face value or as a decimal fraction of face value.

face value, and the payment intervals are all equal: $t_{i+1} - t_i = t_i - t_{i-1} = h$, $i = 1, 2, \ldots, n-1$. We'll denote by $p_{t,h}(c)$ the price at time t of a bond maturing at time T, with an annual coupon rate c, paid $\frac{1}{h}$ times annually.

For a newly issued bond, the first coupon payment is h years in the future, so $t_1 = t + h$ and $T = nh$. For example, a 10-year bond with semiannual coupons has $n = \frac{10}{\frac{1}{2}} = 10 \cdot 2 = 20$ coupon payments. Not only the time to maturity of the bond, but also the coupon and the frequency of coupon payments affect the bond's value.

A coupon bond can be viewed as a package of discount bonds, with each coupon payment and the principal payment at maturity is viewed as a discount bond. This lets us relate coupon bond prices to the continuously compounded spot curve:

- The i-th coupon payment is equivalent to an $i \times h$-year discount bond with a face value of c. If it were traded separately, its price would be $c \times e^{-r_{ih}ih}$.
- The principal payment is equivalent to a T-year discount bond with a face value of \$1. If it were traded separately, its price would be $e^{-r_\tau \tau}$.

The value of the coupon bond is the arithmetic sum of these values. This identity can be expressed in terms of spot rates:

$$p_{\tau,h}(c) = ch \sum_{i=1}^{\frac{\tau}{h}} e^{-r_{ih}ih} + e^{-r_\tau \tau}$$

The continuously compounded *yield to maturity* of a coupon bond $y_\tau(c)$ is defined by

$$p_{\tau,h}(c) = ch \sum_{i=1}^{\frac{\tau}{h}} e^{-y_\tau(c)ih} + e^{-y_\tau(c)\tau} \qquad (4.5)$$

The yield can be interpreted as the constant (over maturities) spot rate that is consistent with the value of the bond. There is a one-to-one relationship between the price and the yield of a coupon bond, given a specific coupon, maturity, and payment frequency. Given a price, the formula can be solved for $y_\tau(c)$ using numerical techniques. We can therefore express the bond price as $p(y_t)$, expressed as a percent of par (or dollars per \$100 of notional value), with specific parameters τ, h, and c.

A *par bond* is a bond trading at its face value \$1. For a par bond, the yield to maturity is equal to the coupon rate.

Example 4.2 Let's price a 10-year coupon bond using the yield curve represented in Figure 4.6. We assume the bond has annual payments ($h = 1$) of 5 percent ($c = 0.05$). The spot rates and discount factors are:

Maturity	Spot rate r_t	Discount factor	Coupon PV
1	4.4574	0.95640	0.04782
2	4.3702	0.91631	0.04582
3	4.4083	0.87612	0.04381
4	4.4967	0.83538	0.04177
5	4.5989	0.79458	0.03973
6	4.6983	0.75435	0.03772
7	4.7881	0.71522	0.03576
8	4.8666	0.67751	0.03388
9	4.9342	0.64142	0.03207
10	4.9919	0.60702	0.03035

The last column displays the present value of the coupon payment for each maturity, expressed in dollars per \$1 of face value. The sum of these present values is 0.388716. Including the present value of the principal at maturity, we have

$$p_{\tau,h}(c) = 0.05 \sum_{t=1}^{10} e^{-r_t t} + e^{-r_\tau \tau}$$

$$= 0.388716 + 0.60702$$

$$= 0.995737$$

per \$1 of face value, or 99.5737 par value. The bond's yield to maturity is 4.9317 per annum.

A simple example of a coupon bond curve is the swap curve. For U.S. dollar–denominated swaps, the compounding convention is semiannual, while for most other currencies it is annual. For a flat swap curve, that is, a swap curve on which swap rates for any maturity are equal to a constant, there is a simple formula for the spot rate:

$$r_t = h \log(r^s) \qquad \forall t > 0$$

where r^s is the swap rate. For example, with a flat semiannual swap curve of 3.5 percent, the spot rate is a constant 3.470 percent.

4.3   VAR FOR DEFAULT-FREE FIXED INCOME SECURITIES USING THE DURATION AND CONVEXITY MAPPING

We have now seen that a fixed-income security can be decomposed into a set of cash flows occurring on specific dates in the future and that its value can be computed as the value of that set of discount bonds. We can therefore measure the VaR and other distributional properties of a fixed-income security using the distributions of its constituent discount bonds; the return distribution of the bond is the return distribution of the portfolio of zeroes. The security is treated as a portfolio consisting of the discount bonds. To carry out this cash-flow mapping approach to computing VaR, we require time series of returns on all the discount bonds involved. From these time series, we can compute the volatilities and correlations needed for the parametric and Monte Carlo approaches, and the historical security returns needed to carry out the historical simulation approach.

This section lays out a simpler approach to measuring VaR for a bond using the *duration-convexity* approximation. It is a specific application of the delta-gamma approach to VaR measurement. The single risk factor in this case is the yield to maturity of the bond. It is straightforward to apply delta-gamma to coupon bonds, since bond values are monotonically decreasing functions of yield.

We will treat the price of the bond as a function of its time-t yield to maturity y_t. In the notation of this chapter, $p(y_t)$ plays the role of the general function $f(S_t, \tau)$, but we will ignore explicit dependence on the time to maturity other than through the yield. For fixed-income securities with very short times to maturities, this would introduce a material bias, but "roll-down" can be ignored for most bonds. We assume that $p(y_t)$ can be differentiated twice with respect to y_t.

By reducing the number of factors that influence bond prices to a single yield rather than an entire term structure of interest rates, this approach implicitly assumes that any change in bond value is caused by a *parallel shift* in the yield curve. This approach thus ignores the impact of changes in the shape of the yield curve to which the yield to maturity is invariant. A curve steepening or flattening that leaves the level of yield unchanged may impact the value of the bond, so this duration-convexity approximation can understate risk.

In order for us to use the yield as a risk factor, we need an additional ideal condition, namely, the existence of a liquid market in which freshly issued bonds of precisely the same maturity trade daily. This condition is not always met for the plain-vanilla swap market as well as the government bond market, as we see in Chapters 12 and 14.

With all these caveats, the duration-convexity approach is a reasonably accurate approximation for most bonds. It is also relatively easy to compute, and it is intuitive for fixed-income traders. For these reasons, it has become quite standard.

4.3.1 Duration

We start by defining two related concepts, the DV01 and modified duration of a bond. The *DV01* is the change in value that results from a one basis point (0.0001) change in yield. It is multiplied by -1 for the convenience of working with a positive number:

$$\text{DV01} \equiv -dy_t \frac{dp}{dy_t} = -0.0001 \frac{dp}{dy_t}$$

The concept of DV01 applies to any interest-rate sensitive security, including options. It can be defined to encompass changes in any yield curve concept, such as spot or forward rates, as long as the change is a parallel shift, that is, a uniform 1bp shift of the entire curve. We can get the DV01 of the position by multiplying the quantity we just defined by the par amount of the security.

In many textbooks on fixed income, DV01 and duration are calculated by algebraically differentiating Equation 4.5, which defines the relationship between bond price and yield with respect to the yield. Nowadays, it is generally easier to use numerical approaches. The DV01 of a bond can be easily and accurately calculated as the difference in the value of the coupon bond with the entire yield curve shifted up and down, in parallel, by 0.5bp:

$$\text{DV01} \approx \Delta p = -0.0001 \frac{p(y_t + 0.00005) - p(y_t - 0.00005)}{0.0001}$$
$$= p(y_t - 0.00005) - p(y_t + 0.00005)$$

where Δp has been specified as the change for a 1bp change in yield.

The *modified duration* of a bond is defined as

$$\text{mdur}_t \equiv -\frac{1}{p}\frac{dp}{dy_t} = \frac{1}{p}\frac{1}{dy_t}\text{DV01} \qquad (4.6)$$

DV01 is expressed in dollars per $100, that is, dollars per par value of the bond, per 1bp of yield change, while modified duration is a proportional measure, specifically, the percent change in the bond's value for a 1 percent

(100 basis point) change in yield. Like DV01, modified duration is usually computed numerically:

$$\text{mdur}_t \approx -\frac{1}{p}\frac{\Delta p}{\Delta y_t} = \frac{1}{p}\frac{\text{DV01}}{0.0001}$$

Example 4.3 (DV01 and Duration) We illustrate the duration and convexity approach by continuing Example 4.2 of a default-free plain vanilla 10-year "bullet" bond paying an annual coupon 5 percent and priced using the yield curve displayed in Figure 4.6. To make notation a bit easier and avoid lots of zeroes, we'll express bond par values as $100.

The DV01 is $0.080466 per $100 of notional value:

$$\text{DV01} = -0.0001\frac{99.5335175 - 99.6139834}{0.0001} = 99.6139834 - 99.5335175$$

$$= 0.080466$$

The modified duration of the bond in our example is 8.08104. So if the interest rate falls by 1 percentage point, the value of the bond will rise by approximately 8.08 percent. If the interest rate falls by 1 basis point, the value of the bond will rise by approximately 0.0808 percent. A $1,000,000 notional value position in the bond will decline by $804.66 per basis point: At a price of 99.5737, the position value is $995,737, relative to which the decline in value is $804.66.

4.3.2 Interest-Rate Volatility and Bond Price Volatility

To compute the VaR, we assume we have a trusted estimate $\hat{\sigma}_t$ of the volatility of daily changes in the bond yield. This is called a yield or *basis point volatility*, as opposed to return or price volatility.

There are two generally accepted ways to compute interest-rate volatility:

> *Yield volatility.* In this definition, we treat the yield as though it were a price and state the volatility as the standard deviation of proportional changes in the yield. For example, if the yield level is 5 percent and the yield volatility is 15 percent, then the annualized standard deviation of yield changes is $0.15 \times 0.05 = 0.0075$ or 75 basis points.

Yield volatility, like return volatility, can be historical, based on historically observed yields, or implied, based on fixed-income option prices. When discussing implied rather than historical volatility, yield volatility is often called *Black volatility*. Prices of OTC interest rate options such as swaptions, are typically quoted as Black vols, although there are readily available screens on Reuters and other market information providers that translate the entire grid of option and underlying swap maturities and maturities into basis point volatilities as well as dollar prices per option unit.

In expressing these interest-rate option prices, the yield is treated as lognormally distributed. As in the case of other option implied volatilities, this is not so much an authentic modeling assumption as a pricing convention that can be translated into currency unit prices via the Black-Scholes formulas. The empirical underpinning for the lognormality assumption is even weaker than for asset prices. However, it does, at least, prevent negative interest rates from appearing.

Basis-point volatility. In this definition of volatility, we state the volatility of changes in the yield itself, equal to $y_t \sigma_y$. In the example we just gave, the basis-point volatility corresponding to a yield level of 5 percent and an annual yield volatility of 15 percent is 75 basis points per annum. It is, however, generally not expressed in annual terms, but rather at a daily rate, using the square-root-of-time rule. With a day count of 252 days per year, we have a daily basis-point volatility of 4.72 basis points.

The same choice of definitions applies to the computation of any across-the-curve interest-rate volatility.

The relationship between bond price volatility σ_p and yield volatility σ_y is derived from the definition of modified duration, which we can rewrite as

$$\frac{dp}{p(y_t)} = - \operatorname{mdur}_t dy_t$$

As can be seen in Figure 4.7, the relationship is nearly linear. When volatility is defined as yield volatility, the change in yield, measured in interest-rate units such as basis points, is $dy_t = \sigma_y y_t$, so

$$\sigma_p = \operatorname{mdur}_t y_t \sigma_y$$

This expression for bond price volatility will be used in the VaR computation examples that follow.

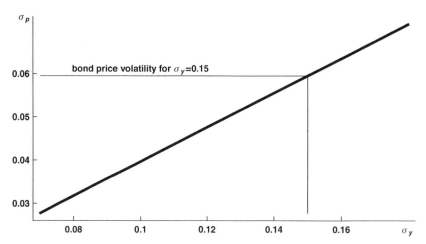

FIGURE 4.7 Bond Price and Yield Volatility
Bond price volatility is a linear function of yield volatility for a given term structure. Volatilities are expressed as decimals at an annual rate.

Example 4.4 (Yield and Bond Price Volatility) Continuing Example 4.3 of a default-free plain vanilla 10-year "bullet" bond paying an annual coupon of 5 percent, let the Black (yield) volatility equal 15 percent. The price volatility is then

$$\sigma_p = \text{mdur}_t \, y_t \sigma_y = 8.08104 \times 0.04932 \times 0.15 = 0.0598$$

or 5.98 percent.

4.3.3 Duration-Only VaR

We'll begin by calculating VaR for the bond position using duration only. This is essentially a delta approximation. For many purposes, using duration only is accurate enough.

Given an estimate of the yield volatility, whether based on historical data or an implied volatility, we can say that, with confidence level α, the change in yield over the period t to $t + \tau$ will be less than

$$\left(e^{z_* \sigma_y \sqrt{\tau}} - 1 \right) y_t$$

with a probability of α, where z_* is the ordinate of the standard normal distribution at which $\Phi(z) = \alpha$.

A VaR estimate for a long position of x units of the bond is then

$$\text{VaR}_t\,(\alpha, \tau) = x\left(e^{z_* \sigma_y \sqrt{\tau}} - 1\right) y_t \times \text{mdur}_t \times p(y_t)$$

where x is the par value of the bonds. The VaR is thus equal to the size of the position times the absolute value of the decline in price in the VaR scenario. This can be equivalently expressed as

$$\text{VaR}_t\,(\alpha, \tau) = x\left(e^{z_* \sigma_y \sqrt{\tau}} - 1\right) y_t \times \text{DV01}$$

This is a simpler expression, but isn't typically encountered because modified duration is the more common metric for expressing bond price sensitivity.

Note that we take the ordinate of α rather than $1 - \alpha$. Why? In the terminology of the delta-gamma approach, we identify

$$\frac{dp}{dy_t} = \delta_t = -p\,\text{mdur}_t$$

as the delta of the bond. Since $\delta_t < 0$, we have used the right-tail rather than the left-tail ordinate of the standard normal distribution. This corresponds to the fact that the bond loses value when the yield rises.

Example 4.5 (Duration-Only VaR) In our standing example, the market parameters for the estimate are

Initial notional value	$1,000,000
Initial market value	$995,737
Initial yield	4.9317%
mdur	8.08104 bp per bp of yield
Yield vol σ_y	15% p.a. (0.945% per day)

The VaR parameters are

Time horizon	1 day
Confidence level	99%
z_*	2.33

The duration-only VaR is then:

$$\text{VaR}_t\,(\alpha,\tau) = x\left(e^{z_\alpha \sigma_y \sqrt{\tau}} - 1\right) y_t \, \text{mdur}_t \, p(y_t)$$

$$= 10^6 \times (e^{0.02198} - 1) \times 0.04932 \times 8.081 \times 0.995737$$

$$= 10^6 \times 0.022253 \times 0.396835$$

$$= 8819.78$$

4.3.4 Convexity

We can make the VaR estimate somewhat more precise by approximating the bond's nonlinear exposure to yield. To do this, we measure the bond's *convexity*, the second derivative of its value with respect to the yield, normalized by the price:

$$\text{conv}_t \equiv \frac{1}{p(y_t)} \frac{d^2 p}{dy_t^2}$$

Like DV01 and duration, convexity can be computed for all interest-rate sensitive securities and using across-the-curve interest-rate concepts other than yield to maturity.

Convexity is always positive for plain-vanilla bonds, but it can be negative for some structured products. Mortgage-backed securities are an important example of bonds with negative convexity. We will see some structured credit examples in Chapters 9 and 11, and an example of the difficulty of managing negative convexity in Chapter 14.

The convexity of a bond, like the DV01, can be computed numerically by shifting the yield curve up and down, in parallel, by 0.5 bp, twice. We have

$$\Delta^2 p \equiv \Delta[\Delta(p)] = \Delta[p(y_t + 0.00005) - p(y_t - 0.00005)]$$

$$= p(y_t + 0.0001) - p(y_t) - [p(y_t) - p(y_t - 0.0001)]$$

$$= p(y_t + 0.0001) + p(y_t - 0.0001) - 2p(y_t)$$

This computation is identical to measuring the bond's DV01 for yields that are 0.5 basis points higher and lower than the current yield, and taking their difference.

Convexity is then measured as

$$\text{conv}_t \approx \frac{1}{p}\frac{\Delta^2 p}{\Delta y_t^2} = \frac{1}{0.0001^2 p}[p(y_t + 0.0001) + p(y_t - 0.0001) - 2p(y_t)]$$

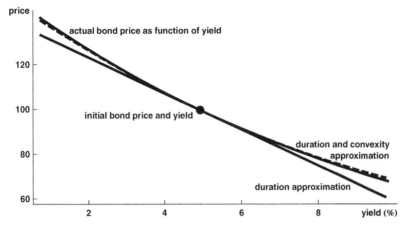

FIGURE 4.8 Approximating the Bond Price-Yield Relationship
Using duration alone provides a linear approximation to the sensitivity of the
bond price to changes in yield. For small changes in yield, this is fairly close.
Using convexity provides a linear-quadratic approximation. It's an
improvement, but still not quite exact.

Example 4.6 (Convexity) Continuing Example 4.5, the duration and convexity approximation is illustrated in Figure 4.8. The convexity of the bond
is 74.2164. We can compute this result as follows. The DV01 measure at
a yield 0.5 basis points lower (higher) than the current yield is 0.0805029
(0.0804290). The difference between these DV01s is 0.0000739. Dividing
this result by $0.0001^2 \times p$ gives the result for convexity.

There is an alternative convention for expressing duration. It is in fact
more widely used than the one presented here, appearing for example on
Bloomberg bond analysis screens and in the published research of most
banks and brokerages; the textbooks are mixed. This alternative convention
doesn't affect duration, but does make a difference for convexity. It expresses the yield as a decimal ($1\mathrm{bp} \equiv 0.0001$) in the pricing formula (there
is no alternative), but as a percent in the denominator, so $1\mathrm{bp} \equiv 0.01$. The
DV01 or Δp or $\Delta^2 p$ we just defined is multiplied by 100. In the alternative
convention, modified duration is the same, but convexity is expressed in
units one-hundredth the size of those here.

4.3.5 VaR Using Duration and Convexity

We can now apply the full delta-gamma approach to compute VaR for a
bond. The gamma is represented by convexity:

$$\frac{d^2 p}{dy_t^2} = \gamma = p \, \mathrm{conv}_t$$

With duration and convexity, we have a linear-quadratic or second-order approximation to the bond's value:

$$\Delta p \approx - \text{mdur}_t \, \Delta y_t + \frac{1}{2} \, \text{conv}_t (\Delta y_t)^2$$

The convexity term increases the gain from a decline in yield and reduces the loss from a rise in yield. The VaR estimate for the bond is now

$$\text{VaR}_t \,(\alpha, \tau) = x \left(e^{z_\alpha \sigma_y \sqrt{\tau}} - 1 \right) y_t \, p \, \text{mdur}_t - \frac{1}{2} x \left[\left(e^{z_\alpha \sigma_y \sqrt{\tau}} - 1 \right) y_t \right]^2 p \, \text{conv}_t$$

Example 4.7 (VaR for a Default-Free Plain-Vanilla Coupon Bond) The additional parameter, compared to the previous example of duration-only VaR, is

conv$_t$ 74.2164bp per squared bp of yield

The convexity adjustment, which attenuates the loss in the VaR scenario and is therefore subtracted from the linear loss term, is:

$$x \frac{1}{2} \left[\left(e^{z_\alpha \sigma_y \sqrt{\tau}} - 1 \right) y_t \right]^2 \text{conv}_t \, p(y_t)$$

$$= 10^6 \times \frac{1}{2} (0.022253 \times 0.04932)^2 \times 74.2164 \times 0.995737$$

$$= 10^6 \times \frac{1}{2} \times 1.20141 \times 10^{-6} \times 74.2164 \times 0.995737$$

$$= 44.39$$

The VaR is thus

$$\text{VaR}_t \left(0.99, \frac{1}{252} \right) = 8,819.78 - 44.39 = 8,775.39$$

FURTHER READING

Taleb (1997) and Hull (2000) are textbook introductions to option modeling and risk management. Allen (2003) is a general risk management textbook with a strong focus on derivatives. See Rubinstein (1994) on derivatives and nonlinear risk.

VaR for nonlinear portfolios is discussed by Britten-Jones and Schaefer (1999). Alternative ways of carrying our delta-gamma are explored in Mina and Ulmer (1999), and methods for speeding up simulations when repricing are discussed in Mina (2000).

Tuckman (2002) is a textbook covering fixed-income modeling. Shiller and McCulloch (1990) provides a compact but accessible introduction to term-structure concepts. The yield-curve fitting technique employed in this chapter was originally developed by Nelson and Siegel (1987). The interpretation of the Nelson-Siegel approach as a factor model is presented in Diebold and Li (2006). See Chance and Jordan (1996) on the duration-convexity approach. Cash flow mapping alternatives to duration-convexity VaR are discussed in Mina (1999).

CHAPTER 5

Portfolio VaR for Market Risk

The previous chapter took one step in the direction of addressing the real-world complexities of many assets, namely, the nonlinearity of their returns with respect to some underlying risk factor. This chapter deals with another source of complexity, the dependence of returns jointly on several risk factors. With these two enhancements, the simple VaR techniques we studied in Chapter 3 become applicable to a far wider range of real-world portfolios.

A simple example of a security with several risk factors, which we mentioned in Chapter 3, is foreign exchange, which is typically held either in the cash form of an interest-bearing foreign-currency bank deposit, or the over-the-counter (OTC) derivatives form of a foreign exchange forward contract. In either form, foreign exchange is generally exposed not only to an exchange rate, but to several money-market rates as well. Another example is a foreign equity. If you are, say, a dollar-based investor holding the common stock of a foreign company, you are exposed to at least two risk factors: the local currency price of the stock and the exchange rate. As yet another example, if a long domestic equity position is hedged by a short index futures position, in an effort to neutralize exposure to the stock market, a small exposure to risk-free interest rates as well as the risk of poor hedging performance are introduced. Similar issues arise for most commodity and stock index positions, which are generally established via futures and forwards.

As we set forth these simple examples, it becomes clear that exposure to a single risk factor is the exception, not the rule. Many other derivatives and credit products also have joint exposure to several risk factors and nonlinearity with respect to important risk factors, so we need techniques for measuring VaR for multiple risk factors. These characteristics are closely related to the issue of how best to map exposures to risk factors.

In addition, most real-world portfolios contain several assets or positions. The techniques developed in Chapter 3 work for portfolios with several assets or positions if they are exposed to only one risk factor. One can conjure up a example, say, a long or short position in the cash equity of a single firm plus long or short positions in the stock via total return swaps (to be discussed in Chapter 12). There is still only one market risk factor, the equity price, but even this portfolio bears counterparty credit risk (to be discussed in Chapter 6). And it is hard to imagine what sort of investor would have this as their entire portfolio, rather than just one trade idea among others.

We beg in this chapter by introducing a framework that accommodates multiple risk factors, whether generated by a single security or in a portfolio. In this framework, the risk of the portfolio is driven by the volatilities of the individual risk factors and their correlation with one another. In the second part of this chapter, we discuss one important example of a single security exposed to several risk factors: Options are exposed, among other risk factors, to both the underlying asset and its implied volatility. This advances the discussion of option risk and nonlinearity begun in the previous chapter.

5.1 THE COVARIANCE AND CORRELATION MATRICES

We'll start by developing some concepts and notation for a portfolio exposed to several risk factors; we require not only the standard deviations of risk factor log returns, but also their correlations. Suppose our portfolio contains N risk factors $S_{1t}, \ldots, S_{Nt}$. We represent this list of risk factors as a vector

$$\mathbf{S}_t = (S_{1t}, \ldots, S_{Nt})$$

The vector of log returns is

$$\mathbf{r}_t = (r_{1t}, \ldots, r_{Nt}) = \left[\log\left(\frac{S_{1,t+\tau}}{S_{1,t}}\right), \ldots, \log\left(\frac{S_{N,t+\tau}}{S_{N,t}}\right) \right]$$

The vector of volatilities is $(\sigma_1, \sigma_2, \ldots, \sigma_N)$; each σ_n is the volatility of the return r_{nt} of the nth risk factor. The correlation matrix of the returns is

$$\begin{pmatrix} 1 & \rho_{12} & \cdots & \rho_{1N} \\ \rho_{12} & 1 & \cdots & \rho_{2N} \\ \vdots & \vdots & \ddots & \vdots \\ \rho_{1N} & \rho_{2N} & \cdots & 1 \end{pmatrix}$$

where ρ_{mn} is the correlation coefficient of log returns to risk factors m and n. This matrix is symmetric, since $\rho_{nm} = \rho_{mn}$.

The *covariance matrix* is computed from the vector of volatilities and the correlation matrix as the following *quadratic form*:

$$\Sigma = (\sigma_{mn})_{m,n=1,\dots,N} = \begin{pmatrix} \sigma_1^2 & \sigma_1\sigma_2\rho_{12} & \cdots & \sigma_1\sigma_N\rho_{1N} \\ \sigma_1\sigma_2\rho_{12} & \sigma_2^2 & \cdots & \sigma_2\sigma_N\rho_{2N} \\ \vdots & \vdots & \ddots & \vdots \\ \sigma_1\sigma_N\rho_{1N} & \sigma_2\sigma_N\rho_{2N} & \cdots & \sigma_N^2 \end{pmatrix}$$

$$= \text{diag}(\sigma_1, \sigma_2, \dots, \sigma_N) \begin{pmatrix} 1 & \rho_{12} & \cdots & \rho_{1N} \\ \rho_{12} & 1 & \cdots & \rho_{2N} \\ \vdots & \vdots & \ddots & \vdots \\ \rho_{1N} & \rho_{2N} & \cdots & 1 \end{pmatrix} \text{diag}(\sigma_1, \sigma_2, \dots, \sigma_N).$$

The notation $\text{diag}(x)$ means a square matrix with the vector x along the diagonal and zeroes in all the off-diagonal positions, so $\text{diag}(\sigma_1, \sigma_2, \dots, \sigma_N)$ represents:

$$\begin{pmatrix} \sigma_1 & 0 & \cdots & 0 \\ 0 & \sigma_2 & \cdots & 0 \\ \vdots & \vdots & \ddots & \vdots \\ 0 & 0 & \cdots & \sigma_N \end{pmatrix}$$

It is often easier in programming to use matrices rather than summation, and this notation lets us express the covariance matrix as a product of matrices.

In order to construct a covariance matrix, the correlation matrix must be *positive semi-definite*. A matrix $\mathbf{A}$ is positive semi-definite if for any vector x, we have $x'\mathbf{A}x \geq 0$. The covariance matrix is then positive semi-definite, too. This means that for any portfolio of exposures, the variance of portfolio returns can't be negative.

To see how all this notation fits together, take the simple case of two risk factors $\mathbf{S}_t = (S_{1t}, S_{2t})$. The covariance matrix is

$$\Sigma = \begin{pmatrix} \sigma_1 & 0 \\ 0 & \sigma_2 \end{pmatrix} \begin{pmatrix} 1 & \rho_{12} \\ \rho_{12} & 1 \end{pmatrix} \begin{pmatrix} \sigma_1 & 0 \\ 0 & \sigma_2 \end{pmatrix} = \begin{pmatrix} \sigma_1^2 & \sigma_1\sigma_2\rho_{12} \\ \sigma_1\sigma_2\rho_{12} & \sigma_2^2 \end{pmatrix}$$

5.2 MAPPING AND TREATMENT OF BONDS AND OPTIONS

Mapping is the process of assigning risk factors to positions. Chapter 3 alluded to these issues in the context of short positions, as did the last chapter in the context of options and fixed-income securities. In order to compute risk measures, we have to assign risk factors to securities. How we carry out this mapping depends on many things and is in the first instance a modeling decision.

In the last chapter, we gave an example of such a modeling choice: Bond risk can be measured using a duration-convexity approximation, or by treating a coupon bond as a portfolio of zero-coupon bonds. This modeling choice corresponds to a choice of mappings. In carrying out the duration-convexity approximation, we mapped the bond to a single risk factor, the yield. Bond prices can also be seen as depending jointly on several risk factors, namely, those determining the term structure of interest rates, by treating the bond as a portfolio of zero-coupon bonds. We then have to map it to multiple risk factors, a set of zero-coupon interest rates. The modeling choice brings with it a mapping, which in turn brings with it the need to adopt a portfolio approach to risk measurement. A related, but more complex example is corporate bond returns, which are driven not only by default-free interest rates or yields, but also depend on the additional risk factors that determine the credit spread.

Single domestic common equities are among the few assets that can readily be represented by a single risk factor, the time series of prices of the stock. But for portfolios of equities, one often uses factor models, rather than the individual stock returns. This is again a modeling decision. The value of the asset may be assumed to depend on some "fundamental" factors, in the sense of the arbitrage pricing model. Equities are often modeled as a function of the market factor, firm size, and valuation, to name only the classic Fama-French factors. The fundamental factors will capture common aspects of risk, and thus more accurately model return correlation than treating each equity's return stream as a risk factor in its own right.

Questions about mapping often boil down to what data are available from which we can draw inferences about risk. The data we have are, as a rule, not nearly as variegated as the risks. Data on individual bond spreads, for example, are hard to obtain. Some data, such as data on equity risk factors, have to be manufactured in a way that is consistent with the factor model being applied.

In Chapter 4, we expressed the value of a position with a nonlinear pricing function as $xf(S_t)$ (omitting then time argument for simplicity). We now let $\mathbf{x}$ represent a vector of M securities or positions, each a function of the N risk factors: $x_1 = f_1(S_t), \ldots, x_M = f_M(S_t)$.

The portfolio can then be written

$$V_t = \sum_{m=1}^{M} x_m f_m(\mathbf{S}_t)$$

where $\mathbf{S}_t$ is the time-t value of the vector of risk factors. Any one of the M securities, however, may be exposed to only a small subset of the N risk factors.

The P&L over the time interval τ is then approximately equal to the change in V_t:

$$V_{t+\tau} - V_t = \sum_{m=1}^{M} x_m \left[f_m(\mathbf{S}_{t+\tau}) - f_m(\mathbf{S}_t) \right]$$

The asset may be treated as linear: that is, an equity, an equity index, a commodity, a currency, or a default risk-free zero-coupon bond. The mapping in this case is straightforward. We treat each equity (or currency pair, etc.) as representing a risk factor. Many assets, however, have a more complicated nonlinear relationship with risk factors.

The gravity of the mapping choice in risk measurement is hard to overstate. As we see in Chapter 11, it is closely related to some of the difficult problems in risk measurement encountered during the subprime crisis.

5.3 DELTA-NORMAL VAR

For a single position with returns driven by a single risk factor, as we saw in Chapter 3, the VaR is easy to compute via a parametric formula. But for portfolios with more than one risk factor, there is no exact closed-form solution for calculating VaR.

The *delta-normal approach* is an approximate, parametric, closed-form approach to computing VaR. One of its virtues is that it is simple to compute. That means we don't have to do simulations, with all the programming and data manipulation burden that entails, or reprice securities, which can involve expensive repeated numerical solutions, as described in Chapter 4. Instead, we compute the value of an algebraic expression, just as in parametric VaR with a single risk factor. Another advantage is that we can exploit certain properties of the closed-form solution to get information about the risk contributions of particular securities or risk factors to the overall risk of the portfolio. We explore these properties and how to use the associated "drill-downs" in Chapter 13.

In the delta-normal approach, there are two approximations, in addition to the model's joint normal distributional hypothesis. We:

1. *Linearize* exposures to risk factors. This obviates the need for repricing. However, we cannot use a quadratic approximation, only a linear one.
2. Treat *arithmetic*, not log returns, as normally distributed.

5.3.1 The Delta-Normal Approach for a Single Position Exposed to a Single Risk Factor

To see how this approach is carried out, let's start with the simplest possible example, a single security exposed to a single risk factor, so $M = N = 1$. We'll do this to illustrate the techniques: Such simple portfolios don't really benefit from the shortcuts involved in delta-normal. Among the few examples of such positions are foreign currency positions held in non–interest bearing accounts or banknotes, common stocks, if mapped to the stock price rather than using a factor model, and short-term government bond positions.

Linearization In Chapter 4, we defined the delta of a *security* as the first derivative of its value $f(S_t)$ with respect to a risk factor S_t:

$$\delta_t \equiv \frac{\partial f(S_t)}{\partial S_t}$$

The *delta equivalent* of a *position* is its delta times the number of units or shares in the position x, evaluated at the most recent realization of the risk factor:

$$x S_t \delta_t = x S_t \frac{\partial f(S_t)}{\partial S_t}$$

The delta equivalent has approximately the same dollar P&L, but not necessarily even approximately the same market value as the position itself. It shows more or less the same sensitivity to risk factor fluctuations, but does not have the same value as the position. For example, an option's delta equivalent may be a good hedge, even though it has a market value quite different from that of the option itself.

For risk factors that are identical to non-derivative assets, such as currencies and stocks, and for exposures that move linearly with some set of risk factors, this is not an approximation, but exact. When the risk factor is identical to the security, we have

$$\delta_t = \frac{\partial f(S_t)}{\partial S_t} = 1$$

and the delta equivalent has the same market value as the position.

Arithmetic Return Approximation   The VaR shock $z_* \sigma \sqrt{\tau}$, where

α is the confidence level of the VaR, e.g. 0.99 or 0.95
z_* is the ordinate of the standard normal distribution at which $\Phi(z) = 1 - \alpha$
σ is the time-t annual volatility estimate
τ is the time horizon of the VaR, measured as a fraction of a year

is a basic building block of a parametric VaR estimate, as we saw in Chapter 3. In parametric VaR for a long position in a single risk factor, we model P&L as lognormally distributed, so the VaR shock is $z_* \sigma \sqrt{\tau}$. In the delta-normal approach, we treat the P&L as *normally* distributed, so the arithmetic return corresponding to the VaR shock is $z_* \sigma \sqrt{\tau}$ rather than $e^{z_* \sigma \sqrt{\tau}} - 1$, even though the underlying asset price model is one of logarithmic returns. The same caveats apply here as in Chapter 3, where we introduced this approximation of parametric VaR for a single risk factor as Equation (3.3); if the return shock is not more than a few percentage points, the difference will be small, but for combinations of a higher confidence level, a longer horizon, and a higher volatility, the difference can be large.

Putting together the linearization of the value function and the arithmetic return approximation, the P&L shocks for a single risk factor are measured by

$$V_{t+\tau} - V_t \approx r_t x \delta_t S_t$$

and the VaR is estimated as

$$\mathrm{VaR}_t(\alpha, \tau)(x) = -z_* \sigma \sqrt{\tau} x \delta_t S_t$$

Example 5.1 (VaR of a Foreign Currency) Suppose a U.S. dollar–based investor holds a position in euros worth \$1 million. We'll compute its 1-day, 99 percent VaR via the delta normal approach as of November 10, 2006, using the root mean square estimate of volatility. The portfolio value can be represented as

$$V_t = 1,000,000 = xS_t$$

where S_t represents the dollar price of the euro, equal on November 10, 2006, to 1.2863. The number of units of the euro is $x = \frac{1000000}{S_t}$, or € 777,424, and the delta is $\delta_t = 1$. In this mapping, we ignore the interest-rate market risk that arises from fluctuations in euro and U.S. dollar money market rates if the position is held as a forward or as a euro-denominated bank deposit.

Using the 91 business days (90 return observations) of data ending November 10, 2006, the annualized root mean square of the daily log changes in the euro exchange rate is 6.17 percent. The VaR is then just over 0.9 percent:

$$\mathrm{VaR}_t \left(0.99, \frac{1}{252}\right)(x) = -z_* \sigma \sqrt{\tau} x \delta_t S_t$$

$$= 2.33 \times 0.0617 \sqrt{\frac{1}{252}} \times 777,424 \times 1.2863$$

$$= 2.33 \times 0.0617 \sqrt{\frac{1}{252}} \times 1,000,000$$

$$= \$9,044$$

5.3.2 The Delta-Normal Approach for a Single Position Exposed to Several Risk Factors

In the next example, we use the delta-normal approach to measure the risk of a single position that is a function of several risk factors. The number of securities or positions is still $M = 1$, so x is still a scalar rather than a vector, but the number of risk factors is $N > 1$. So S_t now represents a vector and we also represent delta equivalents by the vector

$$\mathbf{d}_t = x \begin{pmatrix} S_{1t}\delta_{1t} \\ \dots \\ S_{nt}\delta_{Nt} \end{pmatrix}$$

where x is the number of units of the security. The VaR is

$$\text{VaR}_t(\alpha, \tau)(x) = -z_* \sqrt{\tau} \sqrt{\mathbf{d}'_t \Sigma \mathbf{d}_t} \tag{5.1}$$

For a two-factor position $(N = 2)$,

$$\text{VaR}_t(\alpha, \tau)(x) = -z_* \sqrt{\tau} x \sqrt{S_{1t}^2 \delta_{1t}^2 \sigma_1^2 + S_{2t}^2 \delta_{2t}^2 \sigma_2^2 + 2 S_{1t} S_{2t} \delta_{1t} \delta_{2t} \sigma_1 \sigma_2 \rho_{12}}$$

Consider, for example, a position in a foreign stock. The risk will not be the same for an overseas investor as for a local investor. For the overseas investor, value is a function of two risk factors:

$$f(\mathbf{S}_t) = S_{1t} \times S_{2t}$$

where S_{1t} is the local currency stock price and S_{2t} the exchange rate, in units of the overseas investor's currency per foreign currency unit. The position is equivalent to a portfolio consisting of a long position in the stock, denominated in the local currency, plus a long position in foreign exchange.

Example 5.2 (VaR of a Foreign Stock) Suppose a U.S. dollar–based investor holds $1 million worth of the Istanbul Stock Exchange National 100 Index (also known as the ISE 100, Bloomberg ticker XU100). We'll consider the 1-day, 99 percent VaR of this portfolio as of November 10, 2006, using EWMA volatility and correlation estimates. We denote the local currency price of XU100 by S_1, while S_2 represents the exchange rate of the Turkish lira against the dollar, in USD per TRL; the time-t U.S. dollar value of the index is thus $S_{1t} S_{2t}$.

The portfolio value can be represented as

$$V_t = 1{,}000{,}000 = x f(\mathbf{S}_t) = x S_{1t} S_{2t}$$

Since we have set the value of the portfolio at $1,000,000, the number of units of XU100 x is

$$x = \frac{1{,}000{,}000}{S_{1t} S_{2t}} = 3.65658 \times 10^7$$

using market data for November 10, 2006:

n	Description	S_{nt}	δ_{nt}	$d_{nt} = xS_{nt}\delta_{nt}$	σ_n
1	long XU100	39627.18	6.9013×10^{-7}	1,000,000	20.18
2	long TRL	6.9013×10^{-7}	39627.18	1,000,000	12.36

The deltas, delta equivalents, and EWMA volatilities (annualized, in percent) are also displayed. Note that both delta equivalents are equal to the $1,000,000 value of the portfolio. The EWMA return correlation is 0.507.
   In matrix notation, we have:

$$
\Sigma = \begin{pmatrix} \sigma_1 & 0 \\ 0 & \sigma_2 \end{pmatrix} \begin{pmatrix} 1 & \rho_{12} \\ \rho_{12} & 1 \end{pmatrix} \begin{pmatrix} \sigma_1 & 0 \\ 0 & \sigma_2 \end{pmatrix}
$$

$$
= \begin{pmatrix} 0.2018 & 0 \\ 0 & 0.1236 \end{pmatrix} \begin{pmatrix} 1 & 0.5066 \\ 0.5066 & 1 \end{pmatrix} \begin{pmatrix} 0.2018 & 0 \\ 0 & 0.1236 \end{pmatrix}
$$

$$
= \begin{pmatrix} 0.04074 & 0.012633 \\ 0.01263 & 0.015269 \end{pmatrix}
$$

and

$$
\mathbf{d}_t = 1000000 \begin{pmatrix} 1 \\ 1 \end{pmatrix}
$$

The VaR is then about 4.2 percent:

$$
\text{VaR}_t\left(0.99, \frac{1}{252}\right)(x) = -z_* \sqrt{\tau} \sqrt{\mathbf{d}_t' \Sigma \mathbf{d}_t}
$$

$$
= 2.33 \times 10^6 \sqrt{\frac{1}{252}} \sqrt{\begin{pmatrix} 1 \\ 1 \end{pmatrix}' \begin{pmatrix} 0.04074 & 0.01263 \\ 0.01263 & 0.01527 \end{pmatrix} \begin{pmatrix} 1 \\ 1 \end{pmatrix}}
$$

$$
= \$41,779
$$

5.3.3 The Delta-Normal Approach for a Portfolio of Securities

Now let's apply the delta-normal approach to general portfolios of $M > 1$ securities, exposed to $N > 1$ risk factors. Recall that the value of a portfolio can be represented

$$V_t = \sum_{m=1}^{M} x_m\, f_m(\mathbf{S}_t)$$

where $f_m(\mathbf{S}_t)$ is the pricing function for the m-th security. The delta equivalent of the portfolio is the sum of the delta equivalents of the positions. The number of units of each of the M positions is now a vector

$$\mathbf{x} = \begin{pmatrix} x_1 \\ \vdots \\ x_M \end{pmatrix}$$

In measuring portfolio risk, we are interested in the portfolio's total exposure to each risk factor. So first, we need to add up exposures of different securities to each risk factor. The delta equivalent for each risk factor is

$$\sum_{m=1}^{M} x_m S_{nt} \frac{\partial f_m(\mathbf{S}_t)}{\partial S_{nt}} = \sum_{m=1}^{M} x_m S_{nt} \delta_{mnt} \qquad n = 1, \ldots, N$$

The vector of delta equivalents of the portfolio is thus

$$\mathbf{d}_t = \begin{pmatrix} \sum_{m}^{M} x_m S_{1t} \delta_{m1t} \\ \cdots \\ \sum_{m}^{M} x_m S_{Nt} \delta_{mNt} \end{pmatrix}$$

We want to express this in matrix notation, again because it is less cumbersome in print and because it gets us closer to the way the procedure might be programmed. We now have a $N \times M$ matrix of deltas:

$$\Delta_t = \begin{pmatrix} \delta_{11t} & \delta_{21t} & \cdots & \delta_{M1t} \\ \delta_{12t} & \delta_{22t} & \cdots & \delta_{M2t} \\ \vdots & \vdots & \ddots & \vdots \\ \delta_{1Nt} & \delta_{2Nt} & \cdots & \delta_{MNt} \end{pmatrix}$$

If security m is not exposed to all the risk factors in S_t, then some of its first derivatives will be zero, that is, $\delta_{nmt} = 0$, and make no contribution to the delta equivalent of the portfolio to that risk factor.

Using this convenient notation, we can now express the vector of delta equivalents as

$$\mathbf{d}_t = \mathrm{diag}(\mathbf{S}_t)\Delta_t\mathbf{x}$$

Since each of the risk factors is assumed to be lognormal, the portfolio returns, too, are normal.

Once we have aggregated the exposures to the risk factors, we can use the variance-covariance matrix of the risk factor returns to measure portfolio risk. Letting Σ now denote an estimate of the covariance matrix, the τ-period P&L variance in dollars is estimated as

$$\tau\mathbf{d}_t'\Sigma\mathbf{d}_t$$

and the P&L volatility in dollars as

$$\sqrt{\tau}\sqrt{\mathbf{d}_t'\Sigma\mathbf{d}_t}$$

At this point, the simplifying assumption of treating returns as arithmetic rather than logarithmic comes into play: This simple matrix expression isn't possible if we measure P&L shocks exponentially. The VaR is

$$\mathrm{VaR}_t(\alpha,\tau)(\mathbf{x}) = -z_*\sqrt{\tau}\sqrt{\mathbf{d}_t'\Sigma\mathbf{d}_t}$$

This is the same expression as in Equation (5.1), for the case of one security with multiple risk factors. What has changed here is only the way we compute the vector of delta equivalents.

In the case of two securities, each exposed to one risk factor, we have

$$\mathbf{d}_t = \begin{pmatrix} x_1 S_{1t}\delta_{11t} \\ x_2 S_{2t}\delta_{22t} \end{pmatrix}$$

Just as a matter of notation, we have security m mapped to risk factor n, $m, n = 1, 2$. The VaR is then

$$\mathrm{VaR}_t(\alpha,\tau)(\mathbf{x}) = -z_*\sqrt{\tau}\sqrt{\begin{pmatrix} x_1 S_{1t}\delta_{11t} \\ x_2 S_{2t}\delta_{22t} \end{pmatrix}' \begin{pmatrix} \sigma_1^2 & \sigma_1\sigma_2\rho_{12} \\ \sigma_1\sigma_2\rho_{12} & \sigma_2^2 \end{pmatrix} \begin{pmatrix} x_1 S_{1t}\delta_{11t} \\ x_2 S_{2t}\delta_{22t} \end{pmatrix}}$$

$$= -z_*\sqrt{\tau}\sqrt{(x_1 S_{1t}\delta_{11t})^2\sigma_1^2 + (x_2 S_{2t}\delta_{22t})^2\sigma_2^2 + 2x_1 x_2 S_{1t} S_{2t}\delta_{11t}\delta_{22t}\sigma_1\sigma_2\rho_{12}}$$

If all the delta equivalents are positive, it can helpful to express VaR as a percent of portfolio value. For example, if $\delta_{11t} = \delta_{22t} = 1$, we can divide by $x_1 S_{1t} + x_2 S_{2t}$ to express VaR as

$$\text{VaR}_t(\alpha, \tau)(\mathbf{x}) = -z_* \sqrt{\tau} \sqrt{\omega_1^2 \sigma_1^2 + \omega_2^2 \sigma_2^2 + 2\omega_1^2 \sigma_1 \omega_2 \sigma_1 \sigma_2 \rho_{12}}$$

$$= -z_* \sqrt{\tau} \sigma_p$$

where the ω_m are the shares of $x_m S_{mt}$ in V_t, $m = 1, 2$, with $\omega_1 + \omega_2 = 1$, and

$$\sigma_p = \sqrt{\omega_1^2 \sigma_1^2 + \omega_2^2 \sigma_2^2 + 2\omega_1 \omega_2 \sigma_1 \sigma_2 \rho}$$

is the volatility of portfolio returns as a percent of initial market value.

Example 5.3 (A Portfolio Example of the Delta-Normal Approach) We'll calculate VaR results for a portfolio of five securities. The securities and the risk factors they are mapped to are listed in Table 5.1. We have already encountered two of the securities and three of the risk factors in our earlier examples of the delta-normal approach.

The portfolio is assumed to be U.S.–dollar-based, hence risk is measured in dollar terms. Each position has a market value of $1,000,000. The risk factors are identified by their Bloomberg tickers. The number of shares or units of each security is

$$\mathbf{x} = \frac{1,000,000}{f(S_t)} = \begin{pmatrix} 777,424 \\ -117,410,029 \\ -726 \\ 1,000,000 \\ 36,565,786 \end{pmatrix}$$

The matrix of deltas is

$$\Delta_t = \begin{bmatrix} 1 & 0 & 0 & 0 & 0 \\ 0 & 1 & 0 & 0 & 0 \\ 0 & 0 & 1 & 0 & 0 \\ 0 & 0 & 0 & -7.8 & 0 \\ 0 & 0 & 0 & 0 & 6.90132 \times 10^{-7} \\ 0 & 0 & 0 & 0 & 39627.2 \end{bmatrix}$$

TABLE 5.1 Portfolio Description

			Securities
m	Description	$f(S_t)$	Detailed Description
1	long EUR	S_{1t}	Long spot EUR vs. USD
2	short JPY	S_{2t}	Short spot JPY vs. USD
3	short SPX	S_{3t}	Short S&P 500 via futures; mapped to SPX Index
4	long GT10	$p(S_{4t}) = 1.0000$	Price of a long on-the-run U.S. 10-year Treasury note with a duration of 7.8; duration mapping applied
5	long ISE 100	$S_{5t}S_{6t}$	Long Istanbul Stock Exchange 100 Index via futures, with no currency hedge; mapped to XU100 Index

			Risk Factors
	Ticker	Last Price	Description
S_{1t}	EUR Crncy	1.2863	Spot price of EUR 1 in USD
S_{2t}	JPY–USD Crncy	0.008517	Spot price of JPY 1 in USD
S_{3t}	SPX Index	1376.91	Closing price of S&P 500 Index
S_{4t}	GT10 Govt	0.0458	Yield of on-the-run U.S. 10-year note
S_{5t}	XU100 Index	39627.2	Closing price of Istanbul Stock Exchange 100 Index
S_{6t}	TRL Crncy	6.90132×10^{-7}	Spot price of 1 (old) TRL in USD

with the m-th column representing the exposure of security m to each risk factor. The vector of delta equivalents is therefore:

$$\mathbf{d}_t = \text{diag}(\mathbf{S}_t)\Delta_t\mathbf{x} = \begin{pmatrix} 1{,}000{,}000 \\ -1{,}000{,}000 \\ -1{,}000{,}000 \\ -357{,}240 \\ 1{,}000{,}000 \\ 1{,}000{,}000 \end{pmatrix}$$

The delta equivalent exposure of the bond position to the yield risk factor per dollar's worth of bond is equal to minus one, times the yield as a decimal, times the bond's modified duration, or -0.0458×7.8.

Next, we need the statistical properties of the risk factors. In the delta-normal approach, these are the volatilities and correlations, which we calculate using the EWMA/RiskMetrics approach with a decay factor of 0.94. But the delta-normal approach can be used together with any other estimator of these parameters. The vector of annualized volatility estimates is

Position	σ_n
EUR	0.0570
JPY	0.0644
SPX	0.0780
GT10	0.1477
XU100	0.2018
TRL	0.1236

and the estimated correlation matrix is

	EUR	JPY	SPX	GT10	XU100
JPY	0.75				
SPX	−0.08	−0.05			
GT10	−0.58	−0.68	−0.09		
XU100	0.25	0.26	0.25	−0.22	
TRL	0.13	−0.09	0.00	0.18	0.51

The estimated covariance matrix is then

$$
\Sigma = \text{diag}
\begin{pmatrix}
0.0570 \\
0.0644 \\
0.0780 \\
0.1477 \\
0.2018 \\
0.1236
\end{pmatrix}
\begin{pmatrix}
1.00 & 0.75 & -0.08 & -0.58 & 0.25 & 0.13 \\
0.75 & 1.00 & -0.05 & -0.68 & 0.26 & -0.09 \\
-0.08 & -0.05 & 1.00 & -0.09 & 0.25 & 0.00 \\
-0.58 & -0.68 & -0.09 & 1.00 & -0.22 & 0.18 \\
0.25 & 0.26 & 0.25 & -0.22 & 1.00 & 0.51 \\
0.13 & -0.09 & 0.00 & 0.18 & 0.51 & 1.00
\end{pmatrix}
\text{diag}
\begin{pmatrix}
0.0570 \\
0.0644 \\
0.0780 \\
0.1477 \\
0.2018 \\
0.1236
\end{pmatrix}
$$

$$
=
\begin{pmatrix}
0.003246 & 0.002751 & -0.000343 & -0.004863 & 0.002887 & 0.000931 \\
0.002751 & 0.004148 & -0.000249 & -0.006456 & 0.003415 & -0.000741 \\
-0.000343 & -0.000249 & 0.006088 & -0.001081 & 0.003876 & 0.000018 \\
-0.004863 & -0.006456 & -0.001081 & 0.021823 & -0.006609 & 0.003223 \\
0.002887 & 0.003415 & 0.003876 & -0.006609 & 0.040738 & 0.012635 \\
0.000931 & -0.000741 & 0.000018 & 0.003223 & 0.012635 & 0.015269
\end{pmatrix}
$$

Finally, substituing the values of $\mathbf{d}_t$ and Σ, the VaR of the portfolio is $43,285:

$$
\text{VaR}_t\left(0.99, \frac{1}{252}\right)(\mathbf{x}) = 2.33\sqrt{\frac{1}{252}}\sqrt{\mathbf{d}_t'\Sigma\mathbf{d}_t} = 43{,}285
$$

In Chapter 13, we further analyze this portfolio to identify the main drivers of risk.

5.4 PORTFOLIO VAR VIA MONTE CARLO SIMULATION

We can also compute VaR via Monte Carlo or historical simulation. The process is similar to that described in Chapter 3 for a single position. The main difference is that, instead of simulating I values of a single random variable, we require I values of a multivariate random variable, each a vector with a length equal to the number of risk factors. The i-th simulation thread, for example, would use a vector random variable $(\tilde{\epsilon}_{i1}, \ldots, \tilde{\epsilon}_{iN})$, drawn from a zero-mean normal distribution with variance-covariance matrix Σ. Rather than one return shock in each simulation thread, we have a set of return shocks $\sqrt{\tau}(\tilde{\epsilon}_{i1}, \ldots, \tilde{\epsilon}_{iN})$.[1]

In parametric VaR, we are bound to treat P&L as normally distributed in order to compute the closed form expression for the annual P&L variance $d_t'\Sigma d_t$. In estimation via simulation, in contrast, we can return to the log-normal model of the P&L distribution. In each thread i of the simulation, we would then compute the vector of asset price shocks as

$$\tilde{S}_{ti} = S_0 e^{\tilde{r}_i} = e^{\sqrt{\tau}}\left(S_{0,1}e^{\tilde{\epsilon}_{i1}}, \ldots, S_{0,N}e^{\tilde{\epsilon}_{iN}}\right) \qquad i = 1, \ldots, I$$

The simulated portfolio-level P&L shocks are computed from the simulated asset price shocks by multiplying each by the vector of deltas to get $\delta'_t\tilde{S}_{t,i}$.

Table 5.2 displays the results for our sample portfolio. The VaR at the 99 percent confidence interval is the absolute value of the 10th or 11th worst portfolio outcome. The exact results are dependent on the simulations used and will vary due to simulation noise. The simulation noise can be damped to some extent by averaging the scenarios neighboring the VaR scenario, for example, by taking the average of the 10th or 11th worst outcome as the VaR. In the example, the VaR is somewhat larger computed via Monte Carlo than via parametric VaR, due to random fluctuations more than offsetting the effect of using logarithmic rather than arithmetic shocks.

---

[1]Our notation here is a bit different from that of Chapter 3. In the earlier discussion of one-factor VaR, the $\tilde{\epsilon}_i$ represented simulations from $N(0, 1)$, and were subsequently multiplied by an estimate of σ to obtain an estimate of the return shock $\sqrt{\tau}\hat{\sigma}\tilde{\epsilon}_i$. Here, $(\tilde{\epsilon}_{i1}, \ldots, \tilde{\epsilon}_{iN})$ does not need to multiplied by the volatility estimate, as it is generated using Σ.

TABLE 5.2 Example of Portfolio VaR via Monte Carlo Simulation

i	EUR	JPY	SPX	GT10	XU100	TRL	$\tilde{V}^i - V_0$
1	−0.0054	−0.0033	−0.0063	0.0113	−0.0342	−0.0198	−53,040
2	−0.0062	−0.0052	0.0038	0.0050	−0.0325	−0.0143	−52,841
3	−0.0052	−0.0024	−0.0043	0.0049	−0.0263	−0.0258	−51,648
4	0.0013	0.0032	−0.0042	0.0035	−0.0326	−0.0189	−49,778
5	−0.0041	−0.0041	0.0068	0.0049	−0.0214	−0.0196	−49,075
6	−0.0030	−0.0030	0.0057	0.0110	−0.0255	−0.0141	−48,852
7	−0.0063	−0.0039	0.0041	0.0137	−0.0264	−0.0109	−48,454
8	−0.0035	−0.0018	0.0016	0.0032	−0.0303	−0.0142	−48,247
9	−0.0029	−0.0013	0.0009	0.0094	−0.0265	−0.0160	−47,777
10	−0.0060	−0.0039	0.0025	0.0048	−0.0175	−0.0231	−46,492
11	−0.0031	−0.0014	−0.0056	0.0181	−0.0323	−0.0112	−45,508
12	−0.0010	0.0013	0.0007	0.0012	−0.0318	−0.0102	−44,901
⋮	⋮	⋮	⋮	⋮			
997	−0.0012	−0.0052	−0.0012	−0.0023	0.0313	0.0205	58,451
998	0.0028	0.0052	0.0026	−0.0079	0.0469	0.0155	61,518
999	0.0086	0.0020	−0.0018	−0.0099	0.0279	0.0219	62,363
1,000	0.0035	0.0017	0.0027	−0.0156	0.0438	0.0241	73,737

The table displays a subset of the simulation results. The second through seventh columns display the returns of each risk factor in each scenario. The rightmost column displays the simulation results for changes in portfolio value. Horizontal lines mark the VaR scenarios.

5.5 OPTION VEGA RISK

In Chapter 4, we took a first look at the risks of options. But we took into account only an option's exposure to the price of its underlying asset. In reality, most options and option strategies have significant *vega risk*, that is, exposure to changes in implied volatility. Implied volatility thus becomes an additional risk factor to changes in the underlying asset. Implied volatility often has a strong correlation to asset returns, so a portfolio approach is necessary to correctly measure the risk even of a single option position.

We'll discuss vega in two steps. First, we take a look at the behavior of implied volatility and how it differs from what standard models suggest. This is an important subject, not only in the context of option pricing and option risks, but also because of what it tells us about the behavior of the underlying asset returns. We can use implied volatilities to compute the risk-neutral probability distributions we introduced in Chapter 2, using procedures to be outlined in Chapter 10. Later in this section, in the second part of our discussion of vega, we see how we can incorporate vega risk into overall market risk measurement for options.

The differences between the empirical behavior of impled volatility and that predicted by Black-Scholes encompass the behavior of implied volatility *over time*, and the pattern of prices of options with different exercise prices and maturities *at a point in time*. We will discuss each of these, and the challenges they present to option risk measurement, in turn.

5.5.1 Vega Risk and the Black-Scholes Anomalies

We start by defining implied volatility more carefully, a concept that did not exist before the Black-Scholes model became the standard for option modeling, and options and option-like derivatives became widespread during the financial innovation wave of the 1980s (as described in Chapter 1).

Vega risk arises because option prices do not behave precisely as predicted by the Black-Scholes model. The Black-Scholes model posits the same assumption about asset price behavior as the standard asset return forecasting model described in Chapter 2. In the Black-Scholes model, there is a unique, constant, never-changing volatility for each asset. In empirical fact, implied volatilities change widely and abruptly over time. Figure 5.1 shows

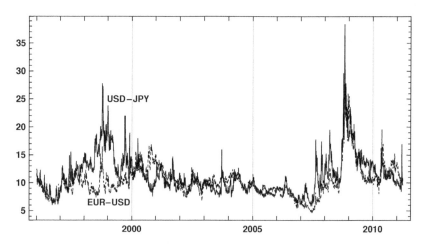

FIGURE 5.1   Time Variation of Implied Volatility
At-the-money (approximately 50δ) one-month implied volatility of the dollar-yen (solid line) and euro-dollar (dashed line) exchange rates, percent p.a., January 6, 1997, to April 1, 2011. Euro vols are for the Deutsche mark prior to January 1, 1999, and for the euro after January 1, 1999.
Source: Bloomberg Financial L.P.

one of myriad examples, the at-the-money forward implied volatilities of one-month foreign exchange options for the EUR-USD and USD-JPY exchange rates.

Let's look at a precise definition of implied volatility. Denote the quoted or market price of a European call option with maturity date T and exercise price X at time t by $c(t, T - t, X)$ and that of the congruent put by $p(t, T - t, X)$. We are using the notation $c(\cdot)$ and $p(\cdot)$ to indicate that we are focusing on observable market prices, as functions of the design parameters strike and maturity, rather than the theoretical Black-Scholes model values of Chapter 4 and Appendix A.3, $v(\cdot)$ and $w(\cdot)$. The implied volatility is the value obtained by solving

$$c(t, \tau, X) = v(S_t, \tau, X, \sigma, r, q) \tag{5.2}$$

for σ. Thus to be precise, we should refer to the *Black-Scholes* implied volatility, since it is defined by that particular model. Since we are now acknowledging the time-variation in implied volatility, we will add a time subscript to the symbol σ_t, which now stands for the value of σ that satisfies the equation in (5.2) of market to theoretical price.

Implied volatility is clearly itself volatile. What is its impact on position value? One answer is provided by the Black-Scholes option *vega*, the sensitivity of an option to changes in implied volatility. This sensitivity is analogous to the other "Greeks," those with respect to the underlying price and the time to maturity discussed in Chapter 4. The vega of a European call is:

$$v_{c,t} \equiv \frac{\partial}{\partial \sigma_t} v(S_t, \tau, X, \sigma_t, r, q)$$

Since options are often quoted in implied volatility units, vega risk can be thought of as the "own" price risk of an option position, as opposed to that of the underlying asset. Like gamma, vega is the same for European puts and calls with the same exercise price and tenor. The notion of a Black-Scholes vega is strange in the same way as the notion of a time-varying Black-Scholes implied volatility: We are using the model to define and measure a phenomenon that is incompatible with the model.

Implied volatility can be computed numerically or algebraically for European options. One needs to be careful with the units of vega. We generally have to divide $v_{c,t}$ by 100 before using it in a calculation. This is because $v_{c,t}$ is defined as the change in option value for a "unit" change in σ_t, meaning a 1 percent or 1 vol change in the level of volatility. But volatility has to be expressed as a decimal when using it in the Black-Scholes formulas.

For both puts and calls, and for any values of the other parameters, $v_{c,t} \geq 0$; higher volatility always adds value to an option. Figure 5.2 shows

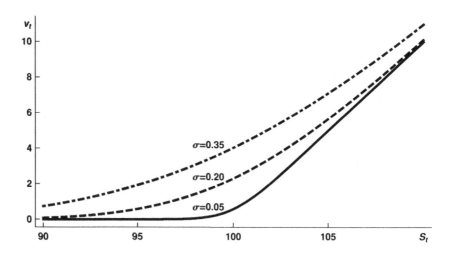

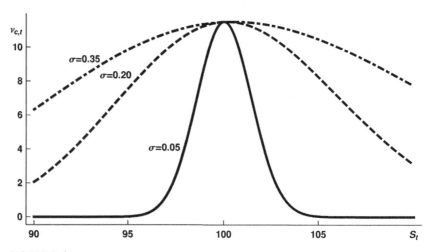

FIGURE 5.2 Option Vega

Upper panel: Black-Scholes value of a European call option as a function of underlying asset price for implied volatilities $\sigma = 0.05, 0.20, 0.35$.

Lower panel: Black-Scholes European call option vega as a function of underlying asset price for implied volatilities $\sigma = 0.05, 0.20, 0.35$.

The time to maturity is one month, and the risk-free rate and dividend rate on the underlying asset are both set to 1 percent.

two ways of looking at the impact of volatility on option value. The upper panel shows the standard hockey-stick plot of a call option's value against the underlying asset price for a low, an intermediate, and a high option price. For all values of the underlying price S_t, the option value is higher for a higher vol.

An option's value can be decomposed into two parts, *intrinsic value* and *time value*. The intrinsic value is the value the option would have if it were exercised right now. An at-the-money or out-of-the-money option has zero intrinsic value, while an in-the-money option has positive intrinsic value. The rest of the option's value is the time value derives from the possibility of ending in-the-money or deeper in-the-money. The time value is driven mainly by volatility and the remaining time to maturity; doubling the volatility, for a given τ, doubles the time value.

The curvature of the plots in the upper panel of Figure 5.2 also changes with volatility. At lower volatilities, the sensitivity of the vega—the "gamma of vega"—changes fast for changes in S_t, that is, there is a lot of curvature in the function. At higher volatilities, there is less curvature, and the sensitivity of the vega to underlying price is smaller.

The lower panel of Figure 5.2 shows the same phenomena in a different way. It plots the vega itself for different levels of implied volatility. When the option is at-the-money, the vega is the same regardless of the *level* of implied volatility. The peak vega occurs at the underlying price at which the option's *forward call delta* is 0.50, in other words, at the underlying price at which the option is "50 delta forward." The forward call delta is given by

$$\delta_{c,t}^{\text{fwd}} \equiv e^{r\tau} \frac{\partial}{\partial S_t} v(S_t, \tau, X, \sigma, r, q) = e^{r\tau} \delta_{c,t}$$

which is always on $(0, 1)$. The forward put delta is $1 - \delta_{c,t}^{\text{fwd}}$, so the peak vega for a European put occurs at the same underlying price as for a call. This price is close but not exactly equal to the current and forward prices. It is also equal to the 50th percentile of the future underlying price under the risk-neutral probability distribution, discussed in Chapter 10 and Appendix A.3.

From a risk monitoring standpoint, the implication of these properties is that at-the-money options, whether puts or calls, have the highest vega risk, and that vega risk increases with both implied volatility and time to maturity; vega risk is a function, not of σ_t alone, but of $\sigma_t\sqrt{\tau}$. In a low-volatility environment, such as that which prevailed in the early 2000s, the vega of a portfolio was likely to drop off rapidly if the market moved away from the strikes of the options. In a high-volatility environment such as that prevailing in the subprime crisis, high vega risk is more persistent.

Example 5.4 (Option Vega)   Consider a one-month at-the-money forward European call options, exercising into one share of a stock trading at \$100. The implied volatility is 20 percent, and the risk-free rate and dividend rate on the underlying asset are both set to 1 percent.

The Black-Scholes model value of the option is \$2.3011. The delta of the option is 0.511, and its vega is 11.50. If the implied volatility were to increase to 21 percent, the model value of the option would increase to \$2.4161 = \$2.3011 + 0.1150.

5.5.2 The Option Implied Volatility Surface

Apart from time variation, implied volatilities display other important departures from the Black-Scholes model's predictions. The implied volatility "biases," as these systematic disagreements between real-world behavior and the model are sometimes called, can only be defined and discussed in the context of the Black-Scholes model. Implied volatility is a Black-Scholes concept; without a model, there are only option *prices*.

The key Black-Scholes biases are:

- Options with the same exercise price but different maturities generally have different implied volatilities, giving rise to a *term structure of implied volatility*. A rising term structure indicates that market participants expect short-term implied volatility to rise or are willing to pay more to protect against longer-term return volatility.
- Out-of-the-money call options often have implied volatilities that differ from those of equally out-of-the-money puts, a pattern called the *option skew*. As we see in Chapter 10, it indicates that the market perceives the return distribution to be skewed or is willing to pay more for protection against sharp asset price moves in one direction than in the other.
- Out-of-the money options generally have higher average implied volatilities than at-the-money options, a pattern called the *volatility smile*. It indicates that the market perceives returns to be leptokurtotic or is assuming a defensive posture on large asset price moves.

The latter two phenomena are sometimes referred to collectively as the volatility smile. Figure 5.3 shows a typical example, for the S&P 500. The implied volatility of each put or call is plotted against the forward call delta corresponding to the option's exercise price. We can see that options with high call deltas, that is, low exercise prices compared to the current index level, have much higher implied volatilities than options with high strikes and low call deltas.

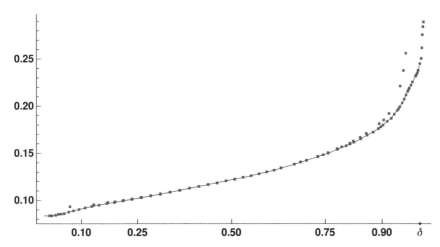

FIGURE 5.3 S&P 500 Implied Volatility Smile
June options, prices as of March 9, 2007. Exercise prices expressed as forward call deltas, annual implied volatilities expressed as decimals.

The volatility term structure and volatility smile together form the *implied volatility surface*. Figure 5.4 illustrates with the EUR-USD volatility surface for March 19, 2007. Apart from the skew in implied volatilities toward high-strike options that pay off if there is a sharp dollar depreciation, the surface also displays an upward-sloping term structure.

We can describe these observed volatility phenomena as a *volatility function* $\sigma_t(X, \tau)$ that varies both with exercise price and term to maturity, and also varies over time. Such a function is a far more realistic description of option prices than a constant, fixed volatility σ for each asset. The variation of at-the-money implied volatility over time is called the *volatility of volatility* or "vol of vol" (though the term is also sometimes used to describe the variability of historical volatility). Vol of vol is, for most portfolios containing options, the main driver of vega risk. However, the term structure and option skew also change over time, and are important additional sources of vega risk.

The exchange-traded and OTC markets have different conventions for trading options. The volatility smile has encouraged the OTC option markets to adapt the way in which they quote prices. Most of the time, most of the fluctuations in option prices are attributable to fluctuations in the underlying price. Changes in implied volatility tend to be less frequent. To make it easier to quote options, dealers in OTC option markets often quote the Black-Scholes implied volatility of an option rather than the price in

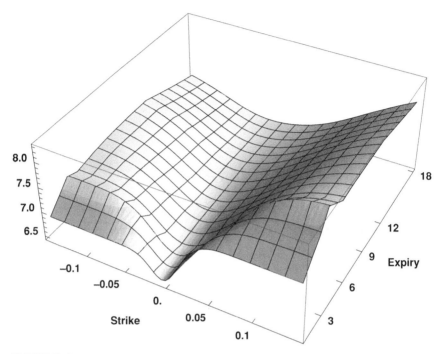

FIGURE 5.4   EUR-USD Volatility Surface
Strike expressed as decimal deviation from ATMF (at-the-money forward) strike.
Data as of March 19, 2007. Spot FX rate $1.33.

currency units. Traders use the Black-Scholes model even though they do
not believe it holds exactly, because the implied volatilities of an option with
a given maturity and strike will typically be steadier than the price in currency units. When a trade is agreed on based on implied volatility, it is easy
to ascertain the current levels of the other market inputs to the price, the
underlying price and financing rate that enter into the Black-Scholes value
of the option, and settle the trade. This enables them to revise their price
schedule only in response to less-frequent changes in $\sigma_t(X, \tau)$, rather than to
more-frequent changes in the option price in currency units.

In exchange-traded markets, option prices are quoted in currency units,
since these markets are set up to keep frequently fluctuating prices posted and
are not well set up to have a detailed conversation between counterparties
each time a trade is made. The OTC option trader first fixes a particular
value of the implied volatility for the particular exercise price and tenor of
the option on the "price schedule" $\sigma_t(X, \tau)$. That price schedule will vary, of
course, during the trading day or by date t. The trader then substitutes that

implied volatility, together with the design parameters of the option and the observable market prices into the Black-Scholes pricing function to get the option price in currency units:

$$c(t, T - t, X) = v(S_t, \tau, X, \sigma_t(X, \tau), r, q)$$

The trader's pricing process reverses the logic of Equation (5.2), which solves for an implied volatility from an option price. Information about the volatility smile is also expressed in the pricing of option combinations and spreads, such as the strangle and the risk reversal we encountered in Chapter 4. Dealers usually quote strangle prices by stating the implied volatility—the "strangle volatility"—at which they buy or sell both options. For example, the dealer might quote his selling price as 14.6 vols, meaning that he sells a 25-delta call and a 25-delta put at an implied volatility of 14.6 vols each. Dealers generally record strangle prices as the spread of the strangle volatility over the at-the-money forward volatility. If market participants were convinced that exchange rates move lognormally, the out-of-the-money options would have the same implied volatility as at-the-money options, and strangle spreads would be centered at zero. Strangles, therefore, indicate the degree of curvature of the volatility smile.

In a risk reversal, the dealer quotes the implied volatility differential at which he is prepared to exchange a 25-delta call for a 25-delta put. For example, if the dollar-yen exchange rate is strongly expected to fall (dollar depreciation), an options dealer might quote dollar-yen risk reversals as follows: "One-month 25-delta risk reversals are 0.8 at 1.2 yen calls over." This means he stands ready to pay a net premium of 0.8 vols to buy a 25-delta yen call and sell a 25-delta yen put against the dollar, and charges a net premium of 1.2 vols to sell a 25-delta yen call and buy a 25-delta yen put. The pricing thus expresses both a "yen premium" and a bid-ask spread.

5.5.3 Measuring Vega Risk

If there were time-variation in volatility, but neither a smile nor a term structure of volatility, the vol surface would be a plane parallel to the maturity and strike axes. Vega risk could then be handled precisely in the quadratic approximation framework. For now, let's assume a flat, but time-varying vol surface. If we include implied volatility as a risk factor, the approximate P&L of a call is:

$$\Delta v(S_t, \tau, X, \sigma_t, r, q) \approx \theta_{c,t} \Delta \tau + \delta_{c,t} \Delta S + \frac{1}{2} \gamma_t \Delta S^2 + v_t \Delta \sigma$$

We now have two risk factors, the underlying asset and the implied volatility. This introduces new issues and new parameters:

1. Returns on the implied volatility may behave very differently over time from those on "conventional" risk factors. If so, then simply estimating the volatility of logarithmic changes in implied volatility and treating it as an ordinary risk factor may lead to even more inaccurate VaR estimates than is the case for cash assets. As we see in Chapter 10, however, there is some evidence that the assumption of normally-distributed log returns may not be that much more inaccurate for implied volatility than for many cash assets.

2. We now also need to estimate the correlation between returns on the underlying asset and log changes in implied vol.

How significant is vega risk relative to the "delta-gamma" risk arising from fluctuations in the underlying price? Figure 5.5 provides an illustration. It incorporates a typical-size shock to the underlying price and to implied volatility for a plain-vanilla naked call. In the illustration, implied volatility causes a P&L event about one-quarter the size of that induced by the spot price. For other exercise prices or other option portfolios, however, vega risk can be more dominant, even with typical-size asset return and implied volatility shocks. For example, straddles have *de minimis* exposure to the underlying, but a great deal of exposure to vega.

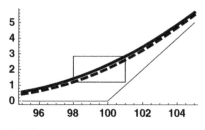 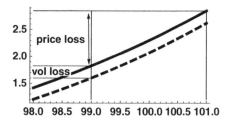

FIGURE 5.5 Impact of Vega Risk

The market value of a long position in a one-month at-the-money forward call on an asset with initial underlying price of 101.0. The time to maturity is one month, and the risk-free rate and dividend rate on the underlying asset are both set to 1 percent. The right panel is a blowup of the area in the box in the left panel. The left panel shows the option's current and intrinsic value as the current and terminal underlying asset price change. The right panel shows how much the plot of current option price against the underlying price shifts down with a decrease in implied volatility.

We'll use the delta-normal method of computing the VaR, taking vega risk into account. While other approaches to option risk measurement can be and are used in practice, the delta-normal model illustrates the issues specific to options. A single option position is treated as a portfolio containing the two risk factors, the underlying asset price and implied volatility. In this approach, we take account of the time-variation of implied volatility, but not changes in the shape of the volatility surface.

In the delta-normal approach, we have to define the exposure amounts, and measure two return volatilities and a return correlation. To avoid confusion with the implied volatility, we'll denote the underlying price volatility σ^{price} and the vol of vol σ^{vol}. As in any delta-normal approach, we have to make sure the delta equivalents are defined appropriately for the risk factors and for the way we are defining and measuring their volatilities and correlations. The delta equivalent has already been defined as $xS_t\delta_{c,t}$, where x is the number of options. Similarly, the vega exposure or "vega equivalent" is $x\sigma_t v_{c,t}$.

If we are dealing with just one option position, or a portfolio of options, all on the same underlying asset and with the same option maturity, there are two risk factors, the underlying asset return and the implied volatility. The vector of delta equivalents is

$$\mathbf{d}_t = x \begin{pmatrix} S_t\delta_{c,t} \\ \sigma_t v_{c,t} \end{pmatrix}$$

where x is the number of units of the underlying asset the option is written on. The covariance matrix of logarithmic underlying asset and volatility returns is

$$\Sigma = \begin{pmatrix} \sigma^{\text{price}} & 0 \\ 0 & \sigma^{\text{vol}} \end{pmatrix} \begin{pmatrix} 1 & \rho \\ \rho & 1 \end{pmatrix} \begin{pmatrix} \sigma^{\text{price}} & 0 \\ 0 & \sigma^{\text{vol}} \end{pmatrix}$$

where ρ is the correlation between logarithmic changes in the underlying price and implied volatility.

The portfolio may contain long or short hedge positions in the underlying asset. The number of risk factors may be greater than two if the options have different exercise prices or tenors.

Example 5.5 Consider a one-month at-the-money forward European call option on \$1,000,000 worth of euros. The option prices are denominated in U.S. dollars. We'll compute the one-day VaR at a 99-percent confidence level as of June 4, 2010. The spot and forward foreign exchange rates were

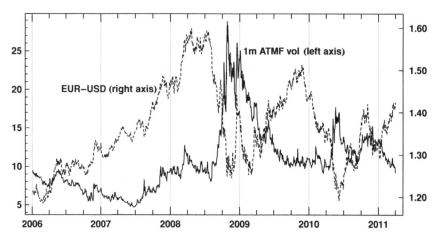

FIGURE 5.6   Euro Foreign Exchange Implied Volatilities
Spot exchange rate (dashed line) and one-month at-the-money forward implied
volatility (solid line) of the euro-dollar exchange rate, January 3, 2006, to April 1,
2010.
Source: Bloomberg Financial L.P.

1.1967 and 1.1970, the implied volatility 16.595 percent, and the U.S. and
euro money market rates 35 and 43 basis points.

As seen in Figure 5.6, the exchange rate and implied volatility have both
been quite volatile during the subprime crisis and the correlation between
their returns has also been subject to wide swings. During the first half of
2010, the correlation between underlying price and implied volatility returns
is negative: Implied vol goes up as the euro depreciates against the dollar.
The vols and correlation are

$$\Sigma = \begin{pmatrix} \sigma^{\text{price}} & 0 \\ 0 & \sigma^{\text{vol}} \end{pmatrix} \begin{pmatrix} 1 & \rho \\ \rho & 1 \end{pmatrix} \begin{pmatrix} \sigma^{\text{price}} & 0 \\ 0 & \sigma^{\text{vol}} \end{pmatrix}$$

$$= \begin{pmatrix} 0.1619 & 0 \\ 0 & 0.8785 \end{pmatrix} \begin{pmatrix} 1 & -0.3866 \\ -0.3866 & 1 \end{pmatrix} \begin{pmatrix} 0.1619 & 0 \\ 0 & 0.8785 \end{pmatrix}$$

$$= \begin{pmatrix} 0.0262 & -0.0550 \\ -0.0550 & 0.7717 \end{pmatrix}$$

The number of units of the option is $x = €\,835{,}415 = \$1{,}000{,}000 \times$
1.1967^{-1}. The vector of delta equivalents in U.S. dollars is

$$\mathbf{d}_t = x \begin{pmatrix} S_t \delta_{c,t} \\ \sigma_t \nu_{c,t} \end{pmatrix} = 835{,}415 \begin{pmatrix} 0.6099 \\ 0.0229 \end{pmatrix} = \begin{pmatrix} 509{,}553 \\ 19{,}106 \end{pmatrix}$$

We can thus quantify the exposure to vol as just under 4 percent of the total exposure to market prices via the option. The VaR is

$$\text{VaR}_t(\alpha, \tau)(x) = -z_* \sqrt{\tau} \sqrt{d_t' \Sigma d_t} = \frac{2.33}{\sqrt{252}} 74{,}570.4$$

or about \$11,366. The VaR of a long cash position in \$1,000,000 worth of euros would be slightly higher at \$12,088. That is, expressing the exposure through a long option position is slightly less risky "in the small," as there is a negative correlation between volatility and the value of the euro: As the euro declines, implied volatility tends to rise, damping the decline in the option's value. If the correlation between implied vol and the value of the euro turns positive, as during the early phase of the subprime crisis, the risk of a long euro position would be higher if expressed through options, since a decline in the value of the euro would tend to be accompanied by a decline in vol.

The delta-normal VaR estimate takes into account variability in the level of implied volatility over time, but not the variation in implied volatility along the volatility surface, and as the shape of the volatility surface changes. VaR can be made more accurate by taking account of the term structure and smile. Furthermore, the level of implied volatility is correlated with both the volatility of underlying returns and with the option skew.

To better understand these additional sources of risk, let's start with the simplest case, in which the shape of the volatility surface does not change, regardless of changes in the asset price and in the level of implied volatility. The shape of the volatility surface, however, has an impact on risk even if it doesn't change. The scenario is illustrated in Figure 5.7. The initial underlying price and implied volatility are indicated as a point on the initial smile (solid curve). Suppose implied volatilities increase across the board, so the volatility smile shifts up by 0.01 (one vol), to the dashed curve. If the asset price does not change, the initial underlying price and new implied volatility are represented by point *a*. If the cash price also experiences fluctuations, the new state might be at point *b* or *c*.[2]

The asset price has changed, while the exercise price of the option hasn't, so the option delta has changed. The increase in implied volatility may then be larger or smaller than the one-vol parallel shift in the smile, as

---

[2]The volatility smiles displayed in Figure 5.7 are interpolated by fitting a polynomial to five observed implied volatilities for call deltas equal to (0.10, 0.25, 0.50, 0.75, 0.90) using the *Mathematica* function `InterpolatingPolynomial`.

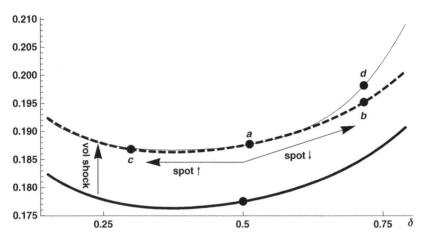

FIGURE 5.7 Vega and the Smile
The figure illustrates the sticky delta approach. The initial delta of the call option
is 0.5. The initial volatility smile is that for one-month USD-EUR options,
October 17, 2008. The shocked volatility smile represented by the dashed curve is
one vol higher for each delta. At point *a*, the spot rate is unchanged. Point *b*
corresponds to a lower spot rate and point *c* to a higher one. The thin solid curve
represents a shocked curve in which the negative put skew has increased in
addition to an increase in the level of volatility.

the market will price the option using an implied volatility appropriate to
the new delta. This is known as a *sticky delta* approach to modeling, since
implied volatilities remain "attached" to the delta of the option as underlying
prices change. It contrasts with the *sticky strike* approach, in which implied
volatilities do not adjust to the changed moneyness of the option, but rather
remain "attached" to the exercise price. The sticky delta approach is more
realistic, especially in periods of higher volatility.

In the example illustrated in Figure 5.7, if the asset price declines, the
call delta increases, and the new implied volatility is given by point *b* on the
shocked volatility smile, resulting in an additional increase in the implied
volatility along the smile. If the asset price increases, so that the call delta
decreases, the new implied volatility is given by point *c*, resulting in almost
no change in implied volatility along the smile. Thus, even if the shape of
the smile does not change, fluctuations in the underlying asset price can
induce significant changes in implied volatility—and thus P&L—along the
volatility smile.[3]

---

[3]We are ignoring the shortening of the option's time to maturity and any changes in
money market rates in this analysis.

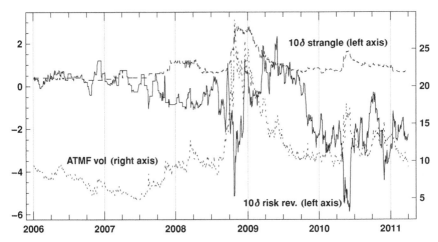

FIGURE 5.8 Euro Implied Volatilities, Risk Reversals, and Strangle Prices
One-month at-the-money forward implied volatility (dotted line) and prices in vols
of 10-delta risk reversals (solid line) and strangle prices (dashed line) for the
euro-dollar exchange rate, January 3, 2006, to April 1, 2011.
Source: Bloomberg Financial L.P.

The preceding paragraphs examined the case of a parallel shift in the volatility surface. Generally, however, the shape of the volatility surface will change
when there are shocks to implied volatility, especially if those shocks are
large. The correlation between the option skew and the level of vol can
change rapidly, as seen for EUR-USD in Figure 5.8. During the subprime
crisis, for example, rising implied volatility was typically accompanied by a
more pronounced skew toward euro depreciation. This reflected an investor
bias in favor of the U.S. dollar and was part of the "flight to safety" markets
exhibited during the financial crisis. But at times, such as during the first
half of 2009, this correlation was positive.

Such changes in the shape of the volatility surface can have an important
impact on option P&L. Imagine a short position in an out-of-the-money
EUR-USD put option in a high-volatility environment. The option may have
been sold to express a view that the underlying price will rise, or at least not
fall. In an adverse case, a sharp move up in implied volatility and lower in the
underlying price might be accompanied by an increase in the negative skew.
This is illustrated by the thin solid curve in Figure 5.7. The new state might
be a point such as d, adding to the losses to the short put option position
caused by the underlying price decline and the increase in vol caused by the
change in delta.

FURTHER READING

Factor models are discussed in Fama and French (1992, 1993) and Zangari (2003).

See Malz (2000, 2001b) for a more detailed discussion of the material on vega risk. Dumas, Fleming, and (1997), Gatheral (2006), Daglish, Hull, and (2007) are good starting points on implied volatility behavior. Cont and da Fonseca (2002) discusses factor model approaches to the behavior of implied volatility surfaces over time. "Sticky" strikes and deltas are discussed in Derman (1999). See also the Further Reading sections at the end of Chapters 10 and 14.

CHAPTER 6

Credit and Counterparty Risk

To understand credit risk and how to measure it, we need both a set of analytical tools and an understanding of such financial institutions as banks and rating agencies. In this chapter

- We define credit risk and its elements, such as the likelihood that a company goes bankrupt, or the amount the investor loses if it happens.
- A great deal of effort goes into assessing the credit risk posed by borrowers. This is, in fact, one of the oldest activities of banks. We will look at different ways this is done, including both time-sanctioned, relatively non-quantitative techniques and more recently developed modeling approaches.
- As with market risk, we sometimes want to summarize credit risk in one number, such as credit Value at Risk, so we will also look at quantitative approaches to measuring credit risk.

This is the first, covering basic concepts, in a sequence of chapters on credit risk. One way credit risk is expressed is through the spread, or the difference between credit-risky and risk-free interest rates. Since the market generally demands to be compensated for credit risk, credit-risky securities are priced differently from securities that promise the same cash flows without credit risk. They are discounted by a credit risk premium that varies with the perceived credit risk and market participants' desire to bear or avoid credit risk. When measured in terms of the interest rate paid on a debt security, this premium is part of the *credit spread*. In the next chapter, we will extend Section 4.2's discussion of interest-rate analytics and risk measurement to credit-risky securities.

In practice, very few investors or financial institutions have exposure to only one credit-risky security. The present chapter also sets up the concepts we need to study portfolios of credit-risky securities in Chapter 8. Finally, we apply the techniques of portfolio credit risk measurement to the valuation and risk measurement of structured credit products in Chapter 9.

6.1 DEFINING CREDIT RISK

Let's begin by defining some terms. *Credit* is an economic obligation to an "outsider," an entity that doesn't own equity in the firm. *Credit risk* is the risk of economic loss from *default* or changes in ratings or other *credit events*.

Credit-risky securities include:

Corporate debt securities are the only type that can default in the narrowest sense of the word. The most common members of this group are fixed and floating rate bonds, and bank loans.

Sovereign debt is denominated either in the local currency of the sovereign entity or in foreign currency. It may be issued by the central government or by a state-owned or state-controlled enterprise. State or provincial and local governments also issue debt. In the United States, such issues are called *municipal bonds*. We discussed credit risk issues around sovereign debt in Chapter 2 and have more to say in the context of financial crises in Chapter 14.

Credit derivatives are contracts whose payoffs are functions of the payoffs on credit-risky securities. The most important and widespread are credit default swaps (CDS), which we introduced in Chapter 2 and discuss in more detail in Chapter 7.

Structured credit products are bonds backed by pools of mortgage, student, and credit card loans to individuals, by commercial mortgages and other business loans, and by other types of collateral. They are often not defaultable in the narrow sense that the issuer can file for bankruptcy. They are, however, credit risky in the sense that, when enough loans in the collateral pool default, at least some of the liabilities issued against the collateral must be written down, that is, the creditor takes a loss.

All of these types have in common that their interest rates include a credit spread; interest rates on these securities are higher than credit risk-free securities with the same promised future cash flows.

6.2 CREDIT-RISKY SECURITIES

6.2.1 The Economic Balance Sheet of the Firm

We start with an *economic balance sheet* for the firm:

Assets	Liabilities
Value of the firm (A_t)	Equity (E_t)
	Debt (D_t)

While this looks familiar, it differs from the *accounting* balance sheet in that asset values are not entered at book or accounting values, but at market values, or at some other value, such as an option delta equivalent, that is more closely related to the market and credit risk generated by the asset. In Chapter 12, we use this concept to create more accurate measures of the firm's indebtedness. Here, we will use an economic balance sheet to more accurately value the firm's equity, that is, the part of the value of the assets belonging to the owners of the firm once the debt has been deducted.

The assets of the firm, equal to A_t at current market prices, produce cash flows, and, hopefully, profits.[1] These assets are financed by:

Debt obligations are contractually bound to pay fixed amounts of money. Occasionally, debt may be repaid in the form of securities, as in the case of pay-in-kind (PIK) bonds, discussed just below. A debtor or issuer of debt securities is called the *obligor*.

Equity is the *capital* invested by the firm's owners. Once the creditors—the owners of the firm's debt securities—are paid any interest and principal they are owed in full, the firm's owners can keep any remaining cash flow, either as a *dividend* they permanently extract from the firm, or to be added to their equity capital and reinvested in the firm. Equity capital absorbs any losses fully until it is exhausted. Only then does debt take a loss.

The ratio of equity to assets $\frac{E_t}{A_t}$ is called the *equity ratio*. The ratio of assets to equity $\frac{A_t}{E_t}$ is (often) called the *leverage ratio*. We discuss leverage in more detail in Chapter 12.

---

[1] The asset value of the firm is greater than its *enterprise value* by the value of its cash and cash equivalent assets.

6.2.2 Capital Structure

So far, we've presented a simplified version of the firm's balance sheet that distinguishes only between equity and debt. Equity receives the *last* free cash flow, and suffers the *first* loss. Within the capital structure of a firm, however, different securities have different rights. These rights determine their *seniority* or *priority* within the capital structure.

Debt seniority refers to the order in which obligations to creditors are repaid. *Senior debt* is paid first, while *subordinated* or *junior debt* is repaid only if and when the senior debt is paid.

Many corporate debt securities combine characteristics of equity and debt. The issues raised have become particularly important for financial firms in the context of regulatory policy:

Preferred stock or "pref shares" are similar to bonds in that they pay a fixed dividend or coupon if and only if all other debt obligations of the firm are satisfied. However, they often do not have a fixed maturity date (*perpetual preferred stock*), and failure of the pref shares to pay their dividend does not usually constitute an event of default. Rather, if the shares are *cumulative*, the dividends cumulate, and must be paid out later before the common shares receive a dividend. The pref shares may then also receive voting rights, which they do not generally have.

Pref shares have a priority between that of equity and bonds; in the event of default, preferred stock bears losses before the bonds but after common equity is wiped out. In spite of the name, they behave for the most part like highly subordinated bonds with a distant maturity date.

Convertible bonds are bonds that can be converted into common shares. They therefore have some characteristics of options, such as option time value and risk sensitivity to the implied volatility of the issuer's stock price. But they retain, as well, characteristics of corporate bonds, such as risk sensitivity to interest rates and credit risk.

Conventional, or "plain-vanilla" convertible bonds, act broadly speaking like bonds with equity options attached. Some varieties of convertible bonds, however, act almost entirely like options or like bonds:

Mandatory convertible bonds are bonds that must be converted into equity at a future date, and pay a fixed coupon during that period. They generally have terms to maturity of about three years, so the present value of the coupon payment is not generally a large part of the value. Rather, their values are close to that of a portfolio consisting of a long out-of-the money call option and a short out-of-the-money put option.

Convertible preferred shares are pref shares that are convertible into common stock.

Payment in Kind (PIK) bonds do not pay interest in cash, but rather in the form of additional par value of bonds. The amount of bonds issued thus rises over time. They are typically issued by borrowers who do not have sufficient cash flow to meet cash interest obligations and have historically typically been issued by purchasers of entire companies with borrowed money. In these *leveraged buyouts*, which we discussed in Chapter 1, the purchasing firm may have a high debt ratio and seeks *ab initio*, rather than conditionally on encountering financial difficulties, to defer cash interest payments as long as possible.

Such bonds are usually much riskier than bonds paying regular cash interest, since they increase the firm's indebtedness over time, and have higher nominal interest rates. If PIK bonds are not the most junior in the capital structure, they also have an adverse effect on the credit quality of any bonds to which they are senior. The PIK feature may also be an option, to be exercised by the company if it has concerns about its future cash flow (*PIK toggle notes*).

6.2.3 Security, Collateral, and Priority

One of the major problems in engaging in credit transactions is to ensure performance by the obligor. Over the many centuries during which credit transactions have been developed, a number of mechanisms have been developed for providing greater assurance to lenders. These mechanisms benefit both parties, since, by reducing the expected value of credit losses, they reduce the cost of providing credit.

Credit obligation may be *unsecured* or *secured*. These are treated differently in the event of default. Unsecured obligations have a general claim on the firm's assets in bankruptcy. Secured obligations have a claim on specific assets, called *collateral*, in bankruptcy. A claim on collateral is called a *lien* on the property. A lien permits the creditor to seize specific collateral and sell it, but the proceeds from the sale must be used only to discharge the specific debt collateralized by the property. Any proceeds left over are returned to the owner. They cannot be used by the creditor even to repay other debt owed to him by the owner of the collateral.

Most liens are on real estate, but bonds, subsidiaries of large firms, a specific factory, or even personal property can also serve as collateral. A pawnbroker, for example, has a lien on the goods pledged or pawned; if the debt is not discharged within the 30 days typically set as the term for a pawnshop loan, the pawnbroker can sell the goods to discharge the debt.

In collateralized lending, a *haircut* ensures that the full value of the collateral is not lent. As the market value of the collateral fluctuates, the haircut may be increased or lowered. The increment or reduction in haircut is called *variation margin*, in contrast to the *initial haircut* or *margin*.

Secured loans can be with or without *recourse*. The proceeds from the sale of the property collateralizing a loan may not suffice to cover the entire loan. In a non-recourse or *limited liability* loan, the lender has no further claim against the borrower, even if he has not been made whole by the sale of the collateral. If the loan is with recourse, the lender can continue to pursue a claim against the borrower for the rest of what is owed.

Secured debt is said to have *priority* over unsecured debt in the event of bankruptcy. Even within these classes, there may be priority distinctions. Secured claims may have a first, second, or even third lien on the collateral. The claims of a second-lien obligation cannot be met until those of the first lien are fully satisfied. Similarly, unsecured debt may be senior or junior. A *debenture*, for example, is a junior claim on the assets that are left after all the secured claims and all the senior unsecured claims have been satisfied.

6.2.4 Credit Derivatives

Credit risk can be assumed not only in the form of the *cash securities*—bonds, notes, and other forms of corporate debt—but also in the form of derivatives contracts written on an underlying cash security. The most common type of credit derivative are CDS, in which one party makes fixed payments each period to the other party unless a specified firm goes bankrupt. In case of bankruptcy, the other party to the contract will pay the value of the underlying firm's bonds. We describe CDS in more detail in the next chapter.

Derivatives can be written not only on the obligations of individual firms, but also on portfolios. We describe some common types of portfolio credit derivatives in our discussions of structured credit in Chapter 9, and of model risk in Chapter 11.

6.3 TRANSACTION COST PROBLEMS IN CREDIT CONTRACTS

Credit contracts have a number of problems that can be subsumed under the concepts of *transaction costs* and *frictions*. Credit contracts are rife with conflicts of interest between the contracting parties. Many of these conflicts arise from information problems that are inherent in credit transactions and are costly to overcome. Acquiring information about a borrower's condition is costly, and harmonizing the actions of market participants involves negotiation, also costly. In understanding credit risk, it is helpful to be familiar with concepts from economics that help in identifying and analyzing these conflicts:

Asymmetric information describes a situation in which one party has different information than another. In credit contracts, the borrower generally has more information than the lender about the project the loan proceeds have been applied to, and thus about his ability to repay. Information disparities can be mitigated through *monitoring* by the lender and reporting by the borrower, but only incompletely and at some cost.

Principal-agent problems arise because it is costly to align incentives when a principal employs an agent, and the latter has better information about the task at hand. A common example is investment management; the manager, though employed as the investor's agent, may maximize his own fee and trading income rather than the investor's returns. Another is *delegated monitoring*, which arises for depositors and other creditors of banks. Bank managers are charged with monitoring, on behalf of the bank's depositors and other creditors, how bank loan proceeds are being used. Apart from banking, as we see in Chapter 9, principal-agent problems are particularly difficult to address in structured credit products, since managers of the underlying loans may also own the securities.

Risk shifting can occur when there is an asymmetry between the risks and rewards of market participants who have different positions in the capital structure of the firm or different contracts with a firm's managers. The classic example is the conflict between equity investors and lenders. Increasing risk to the firm's assets can benefit the equity investor, since their potential loss is limited to their equity investment, while their potential return is unlimited. Debt holders have no benefit from increased risk, since their return is fixed, only the increased risk of loss. Increasing risk therefore shifts risk from equity to bondholders.

The problem of risk shifting, however, also occurs in the context of regulation of financial intermediaries, and in particular, the problem of "too-big-to-fail." If at least some positions in the capital structure, such as the senior unsecured debt, will be protected in the event of a failure of the firm, then increasing the risk to the firm's assets may shift risk to the public rather than to bondholders. Bondholders then will not need to be compensated for the increased risk. We discuss these and related issues in more detail in Chapter 15.

Moral hazard is an old term, originating in economic analysis of the insurance business. The problem it describes is that buying insurance reduces the incentives of the insured to avoid the insurable event. Moral hazard describes a situation in which (a) the insured party has some ability to mitigate the risk of occurrence of the event against which he is insured, (b) the insurer cannot monitor the action the insured does or doesn't take to avert the event, and (c) mitigating the risk is costly for the insured. For example, a person insuring a residence against fire might not buy costly smoke detectors that could reduce the risk of fire damage, or a person with medical insurance might take less care of himself, or use more medical services, than someone without health insurance.

In finance, it arises in the propensity of financial firms that can expect to be rescued from bankruptcy by public policy actions to take greater risks than otherwise. Moral hazard arises in many financial contracts aside from insurance. It can occur whenever one party to a contract has incentives to act in a way that does harm or diminishes economic benefit to another party in a way the other party can't easily see or find out about.

Adverse selection or the "lemons problem" also occurs when transaction parties possess asymmetric information. This issue arises in all trading of financial assets. The fact that a seller is bringing an asset to market is a bit of evidence that he knows something negative about the asset that is not yet incorporated into its price. It may or may not be true that the seller has negative information, but even a low probability that such is the case must lower the price the buyer is prepared to pay. In models of liquidity, this phenomenon is one of the fundamental explanations of the bid-ask spreads (see Chapter 12).

An example is the sale by a bank of loans or securities into the secondary markets or into a structured credit product. A bank is expected to be well-informed and exercise care about the credit quality of its assets, especially that of loans it has originated. The incentive to do so may be diminished if it plans to sell the assets shortly after originating them. We discuss this phenomenon and its effects in Chapter 9.

Externalities are benefits or costs that the actions of one actor cause another without the ability to exact compensation via a market transaction. A common example arises in short-term lending markets, where the excessive risk-taking of one or a small number of borrowers can raise borrowing costs for prudent borrowers, as potential lenders are uncertain about the risk-taking of each individual firm. Lenders have less information than borrowers about how much risk each is taking, and asymmetric information generates the externality.

Collective action problems or *coordination failures* are situations in which all would benefit from all taking a course of action that is not to the individual's benefit if he alone takes it. The classic example studied in game theory is the Prisoner's Dilemma. Another important example is the "tragedy of the commons," in which a limited resource is depleted by overuse.

Examples of coordination failure in finance occur when creditors of a particular class cannot come to agreement with one another and are made worse off in corporate bankruptcy as a result. A typical way in which this occurs is a restructuring plan in which junior creditors receive equity in the reorganized company. This class of creditors will be worse off if the company is liquidated and the assets sold. But any single holdout among them will be better off if all the rest accept the reorganization plan and they keep their credit claim against the company. The collective action problem is to induce them all to agree to accept the less-valuable equity claims.

Another example from financial crises are bank runs (see Chapters 12 and 14), which can be modeled as resulting from a collective action problem among bank depositors.

These information problems do not just increase the costs of credit transactions. To the extent they involve externalities, they may also introduce problems of public policy that are difficult and costly to mitigate.

Conflicts of interest may be resolvable thorough pricing. Conflicts between creditors with claims of different priorities, for example, can be resolved *ex ante* through the pricing of different securities.

6.4 DEFAULT AND RECOVERY: ANALYTIC CONCEPTS

In this section, we introduce some basic analytical concepts around credit events. We use these concepts extensively in credit risk modeling.

6.4.1 Default

Default is failure to pay on a financial obligation. Default events include *distressed exchanges*, in which the creditor receives securities with lower value or an amount of cash less than par in exchange for the original debt. An alternative definition of default is based on the firm's balance sheet: Default occurs when the value of the assets is smaller than that of the debt, that is, the equity is reduced to zero or a negative quantity. *Impairment* is a somewhat weaker accounting concept, stated from the standpoint of the lender; a credit can be impaired without default, in which case it is permissible to write down its value and reduce reported earnings by that amount.

Example 6.1 (Distressed Exchange)   CIT Group Inc. is a specialty finance company that lent primarily to small businesses, and fell into financial distress during the subprime crisis. On August 17, 2009, it obtained agreement from bondholders via a tender offer to repurchase debt that was to mature that day, at a price of 87.5 cents on the dollar. The company stated that, had it been obliged to redeem the bonds at par, it would have been forced to file for bankruptcy protection. CIT Group was downgraded to selective default status as a result.

Bankruptcy is a legal procedure in which a person or firm "seeks relief" from its creditors to either reorganize and restructure its balance sheet and operations (Chapter 11 in the United States), or liquidate and go out of business in an orderly way (Chapter 7). During the first half of the nineteenth century, limited liability of corporations in the United Kingdom and the United States became generally recognized, paving the way for public trading in their securities. Creditors of limited liability corporations and partnerships do not have recourse to property of shareholders or partners apart from the latter's invested capital.

In practice, firms generally file for bankruptcy protection well before their equity is reduced to zero. During bankruptcy, the creditors are prevented from suing the bankrupt debtor to collect what is owed them, and the obligor is allowed to continue business. At the end of the bankruptcy process, the debt is extinguished or *discharged*. There are a very few exceptions. For example, many student loans cannot be discharged through personal bankruptcy.

6.4.2 Probability of Default

In formal models, the *probability of default* is defined over a given time horizon τ, for instance, one year. Each credit has a random default time t^*. The probability of default π is the probability of the event $t^* \leq \tau$. Later in this chapter, we discuss various models and empirical approaches to estimating π.

Three points of time need to be distinguished in thinking about default modeling, default timing, and default probabilities. Incorporating these time dimensions into default analytics is a potential source of confusion:

1. The time t from which we are viewing default: The point of view is usually "now," that is, $t = 0$, but in some contexts we need to think about default probabilities viewed from a future date. The "point of view" or "perspective" time is important because it determines the amount of information we have. In the language of economics, the perspective time determines the information set; in the language of finance, it determines the filtration.
2. The time interval over which default probabilities are measured: If the perspective time is $t = 0$, this interval begins at the present time and ends at some future date T, with $\tau = T - 0 = T$ the length of the time interval. But it may also be a future time interval, with a beginning time T_1 and ending time T_2, so $\tau = T_1 - T_2$. The probability of default will depend on the length of the time horizon as well as on the perspective time.
3. The time t^* at which default occurs. In modeling, this is a random variable, rather than a parameter that we choose.

6.4.3 Credit Exposure

The *exposure at default* is the amount of money the lender can potentially lose in a default. This may be a straightforward amount, such as the par or market value of a bond, or a more difficult amount to ascertain, such as the net present value (NPV) of an interest-rate swap contract.

For derivatives, exposure depends in part on whether the contract is linear. As noted in Chapter 4, linear derivatives such as futures have zero NPV at initiation, while nonlinear derivatives such as options have a positive or negative NPV at (nearly) all times.

6.4.4 Loss Given Default

If a default occurs, the creditor does not, in general, lose the entire amount of his exposure. The firm will likely still have assets that have some value. The firm may be unwound, and the assets sold off, or the firm may be reorganized, so that its assets continue to operate. Either way, there is likely to be some *recovery* for the investor that is greater than zero, but less than 100 percent of the exposure. The *loss given default* (LGD) is the amount the creditor loses in the event of a default. The two sum to the exposure:

$$\text{exposure} = \text{recovery} + \text{LGD}$$

The *recovery amount* is the part of the money owed that the creditors receive in the event of bankruptcy. It depends on debt seniority, the value of the assets at the time of default, and general business conditions. Typical recovery rates for senior secured bank debt are in excess of 75 percent, while for junior unsecured bonds, it can be much closer to zero. In credit modeling, recovery is often conventionally assumed to be 40 percent. As we see in a moment, it can also be assumed to be a random variable, or linked to the *ex ante* default probability.

Recovery is usually expressed as a *recovery rate R*, a decimal value on [0, 1]:

$$R = \frac{\text{recovery}}{\text{exposure}}$$

We have

$$R = 1 - \frac{\text{LGD}}{\text{exposure}}$$

LGD and recovery are in principle *random* quantities. They are not not known for certain in advance of default. This raises two very important issues. First, the uncertainty about LGD makes it more difficult to estimate credit risk. Second, because it is random, the LGD may be correlated with the default probability, adding an additional layer of modeling difficulty. There is a large body of recovery research, primarily conducted by the rating agencies, focusing on the distribution of losses if default occurs. In many applications, however, the expected LGD is treated as a *known* parameter.

The recovery rate can be defined as a percent of the current value of an equivalent risk-free bond (*recovery of Treasury*), of the market value (*recovery of market*), or of the face value (*recovery of face*) of the obligation. In modeling, assumptions about recovery are made for modeling tractability as well as to stay close to empirical behavior of recovery rates.

6.4.5 Expected Loss

The *expected loss* (EL) is the expected value of the credit loss. From a balance sheet point of view, it is the portion of the loss for which the creditor should be provisioning, that is, treating as an expense item in the income statement and accumulating as a reserve against loss on the liability side of the balance sheet.

If the only possible credit event is default, that is, we are disregarding the potential for changes in ratings (referred to as *credit migration*), then the expected loss is equal to

$$\text{EL} = \pi \times (1 - R) \times \text{exposure} = \pi \times \text{LGD}$$

If credit migration as well as default are possible, the expected loss is equal to the probability-weighted sum of the changes in value that occur under the various migration scenarios.

LGD and recovery are *conditional* expectations. The LGD has therefore been "divided" by the default probability:

$$E\left[\text{loss}|\text{default}\right] = \text{LGD} = \frac{\text{EL}}{P\left[\text{default}\right]} = \frac{\text{EL}}{\pi}$$

Thus, the LGD can be large, even if the expected loss is small.

Example 6.2 (Recovery and Loss Given Default) Suppose our exposure is $1,000,000, and we know with certainty that the LGD is $400,000. The recovery is then $600,000, and we have $R = 0.60$.

Next, suppose the default probability is 1 percent. The expected loss is then $0.01 \times 400,000 = \$4,000$.

Why would an investor hold a security that has an expected loss? Because the investor believes that the credit spread more than compensates for the expected loss. Suppose an investor compares a defaultable one-year bond that pays an annual coupon of $r + z$ percent with a risk-free bond that pays a coupon of r. The coupon spread z is the compensation for default risk. If z is large enough, the expected future value of the defaultable bond will be greater than the expected future value of a riskless bond.

For simplicity, suppose the credit-risky bond can only default in exactly one year, just before it is scheduled to pay the coupon, if it defaults as all. The probability of default is π, and if it occurs, the recovery value is a decimal fraction R of the par value. There are two possible payoffs on the credit risky bond:

1. With probability $1 - \pi$, the investor receives $1 + r + z$.
2. With probability π, the investor receives R.

The future value of the risk-free bond is $1 + r$ with certainty. Therefore, if the expected value of the risky bond

$$(1 - \pi)(1 + r + z) + \pi R > 1 + r$$

the investor *may* find the credit-risky bond preferable. The expected loss is $\pi(1 - R)$. In the event of default, the unexpected loss is $(1 - \pi)(1 - R)$.

6.4.6   Credit Risk and Market Risk

A common source of confusion in discussions of fixed-income risks is the distinction between credit risk and market risk. There is no universally accepted distinction between the two. *Market risk* is the risk of economic loss from change in market prices, *including fluctuations in market prices of credit-risky securities*.

An example of a pure credit event is this: A previously AAA-rated company downgraded to AA, but no change in AAA spreads or in risk-free rates. An example of a pure market event is a widening spread between AAA and risk-free rates, or a rise in risk-free rates.

There is some ambiguity in the distinction between credit and market risk. Spreads may change even in the absence of a default or migration, because the likelihood of the event, as perceived by the market has changed, or because of a change in risk premiums. But migration generally results in a change in market value, and may oblige the lender to write the credit up or down, that is, record a higher or lower value in its balance sheet. A change in market perception of a firm's credit quality, even if it does not result in migration, may cause a change in spreads. In the credit risk context, this is called *mark-to-market* risk, as opposed to default risk.

6.5   ASSESSING CREDITWORTHINESS

Lenders and investors in credit-risky securities need a way to assess the creditworthiness of borrowers. This takes place in a variety of ways. All are "quantitative," at least in the sense of relying on balance sheet and other business data of the firm as well as data on the state of the economy or the firm's industry. Some approaches are based on more formal mathematical or statistical modeling.

6.5.1   Credit Ratings and Rating Migration

A *credit rating* is an alphanumeric grade that summarizes the creditworthiness of a security or a corporate entity. Credit ratings are generally assigned by *credit rating agencies* that specialize in credit assessment. The most prominent in the United States are Standard and Poor's (S&P), Moody's, Fitch Ratings, and Duff and Phelps. Along with a handful of others, they have been granted special recognition by the Securities and Exchange Commission (SEC). Their ratings are used as part of the bank and securities markets' regulatory system, though the 2010 Dodd-Frank Act mandates a reduction of the regulatory role of ratings in the United States (see

TABLE 6.1 The S&P and Moody's Long-Term Rating Systems

Investment grade		Speculative grade	
S&P	Moody's	S&P	Moody's
AAA	Aaa	BB+	Ba1
AA+	Aa1	BB	Ba2
AA	Aa2	BB-	Ba3
AA-	Aa3	B+	B1
A+	A1	B	B2
A	A2	B-	B3
A-	A3	CCC+	Caa1
BBB+	Baa1	CCC	Caa2
BBB	Baa2	CCC-	Caa3
BBB-	Baa3	CC	Ca
		C	C

These ratings apply to debt with an original term to maturity of one year or longer. There is a comparable system applied to short-term securities such as commercial paper.

Chapter 14). For example, a high rating from one of these *Nationally Recognized Statistical Rating Organization* (NRSRO) can reduce the compliance burden in issuing a security or the regulatory capital requirement for owning it. Table 6.1 lists the rating categories of the two largest NRSROs.

Rating agencies also assess the probability of default for companies based on their letter ratings. These probabilities can be compared with the annual rates at which firms with different ratings actually default, plotted in Figure 6.1. Rating agencies assess not only the probability of default, but also of rating migration, or change in letter rating, which occurs when one or more of the rating revises the rating of a firm (or a government) or its debt securities. These probability estimates are summarized in *transition matrices*, which show the estimated likelihood of a company with any starting rating ending a period, say, one year, with a different rating or in default.

Typically, the diagonal elements in a transition matrix, which show the probability of finishing the year with an unchanged rating, are the largest elements (see Table 6.2). Also typically, the probability of ending in default rises monotonically as the letter rating quality falls. Finally, note that there is no transition *from* default to another rating; default is a terminal state.

The ratings business provides a good example of conflicts of interest in credit markets. Since the advent of photocopy technology, ratings agencies have generally been compensated for ratings by bond issuers rather than by sale of ratings data to investors. In this so-called *issuer-pays model*, a

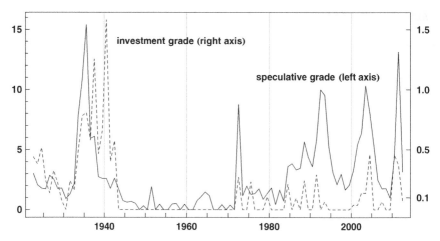

FIGURE 6.1 Default Rates 1920–2010

Issuer-weighted default rates, that is, the fraction of rated issuers defaulting each year, in percent. For recent years, Moody's also reports *volume-weighted* default rates, that is, rates based on the notional value outstanding of each issuer's debt. Solid line plots speculative defaults and dashed line plots investment grade defaults. *Source:* Moody's Investor Service (2011), Exhibit 31.

potential conflict arises between investors in rated bonds, who expect ratings to be based on objective methodologies, and issuers of bonds. This conflict has been identified by some observers as having played a material role in causing the subprime crisis. Structured product ratings are said to have been more permissive than appropriate because of rating agencies' competition for issuers' business. We discuss this problem further in Chapter 15.

TABLE 6.2 One-Year Ratings Transition Matrix

	AAA	AA	A	BBB	BB	B	CCC/C	Default
AAA	91.42	7.92	0.51	0.09	0.06	0.00	0.00	0.00
AA	0.61	90.68	7.91	0.61	0.05	0.11	0.02	0.01
A	0.05	1.99	91.43	5.86	0.43	0.16	0.03	0.04
BBB	0.02	0.17	4.08	89.94	4.55	0.79	0.18	0.27
BB	0.04	0.05	0.27	5.79	83.61	8.06	0.99	1.20
B	0.00	0.06	0.22	0.35	6.21	82.49	4.76	5.91
CCC/C	0.00	0.00	0.32	0.48	1.45	12.63	54.71	30.41

One-year ratings transitions, based on ratings history of 11,605 global S&P-rated companies 1981–2005, adjusted for withdrawn ratings. *Source:* Standard & Poor's (2006), p. 17.

6.5.2 Internal Ratings

Ratings provide third-party assessments of the credit quality of a borrower. Many firms also carry out their own assessments of credit quality. Such assessments are used in making decisions about whether to buy a debt security or extend credit, and are in some ways similar to the work of equity analysts. Credit analysis includes detailed attention to the legal documentation accompanying debt contracts.

In larger firms, credit analysis may be formalized into *internal ratings*. In such firms, internal ratings can play a role in setting regulatory capital, as we see in Chapter 15. Internal credit assessments may use quantitative techniques such as *credit scoring*, in which a numerical ranking is a function of balance-sheet or other firm data.

6.5.3 Credit Risk Models

A widely used approach to estimating credit risk is via formal credit risk models. There are two broad approaches to assessing the credit risk of a single company or other issuer of debt.

> *Reduced-form models* are, in a sense, not risk models at all. Rather than producing, as a model output, an estimate of the default probability or LGD, they take these quantities as inputs. The models are most often used to simulate default times as one step in portfolio credit risk measurement. We study how to estimate such models in the next chapter, and apply them in Chapters 8 and 9.
>
> *Structural models* derive measures of credit risk from fundamental data, particularly elements of the firm's balance sheet such as the volumes of assets and debt.

A third type of model, *factor models*, falls somewhere in between; they are "informed" by company, industry, and economy-wide fundamentals, but in a highly schematized way that lends itself to portfolio risk modeling.

Credit risk models may also be distinguished by whether they take into account credit migration, in which case the model is said to operate in *migration mode*, or only default, in which case the model is said to operate in *default mode*.

6.6 COUNTERPARTY RISK

Counterparty risk is a special form of credit risk. It arises whenever *two* conditions both need to be fulfilled in order for a market participant to profit from an investment: The investment must be profitable, and another party must fulfil a contractual obligation to him.

Every credit transaction is, of course, a contractual relationship between two counterparties. But the term "counterparty risk" is not typically applied to situations in which credit risk is "one-way," that is, in which only one of the counterparties can incur a loss due to default or impairment. Only the lender bears the credit risk of a loan or bond, not the borrower. Counterparty risk is "two-way," and it is often not clear who is the borrower and who the lender. It typically arises in two contexts:

OTC *derivatives trading.* Every derivatives contract has two sides. Depending on how asset prices evolve, either party may end up owing money to the other. Just as in their impact on leverage, which we discuss in Chapter 12, there is a difference in this regard between swaps and other linear derivatives on the one hand, and options on the other. Swaps can have a positive net present value for either counterparty, so both counterparties are potentially exposed to counterparty risk. Only the purchaser of an option is exposed to counterparty risk, since his obligation to the option-selling counterparty is limited to payment of the premium.

The issue of counterparty risk arises particularly for OTC derivatives, since these are purely bilateral contracts between two private counterparties. Exchange-traded futures and options have far less counterparty risk, since the exchanges interpose a *clearinghouse* as a counterparty to every trade. The clearinghouses historically have been well capitalized, since each clearing member is obliged to put up *clearing margin,* and clearinghouse failure is quite rare. No individual customer is exposed to another individual counterparty. Rather, each is matched up against the clearinghouse.

Title VII of the Dodd-Frank Act of 2011 (see Chapter 15) requires exchange clearing of OTC derivatives, but also permits many exemptions. Rules specifying what types of OTC derivatives and what types of counterparties will be subject to "mandatory clearing" have not yet been adopted.

Brokerage relationships. The financing of positions has been increasingly closely related to intermediation and trading services, particularly with the increase in hedge fund trading and concomitant expansion of the prime brokerage business (see Section 12.2). Brokerage clients often assume significant counterparty risk to their brokers. Prior to the subprime crisis, the presumption had been that the broker, but not the client, had credit exposure. The crisis experience, in which clients experienced losses on exposures to failed brokerages such as Lehman, but broker losses on client exposures remained comparatively rare, changed this presumption.

6.6.1 Netting and Clearinghouses

It is very natural in derivatives trading for contracts to proliferate. Consider a single forward commodities contract with a single maturity date. A dealer might buy and sell various quantities of the same contract in the course of a trading day. Two dealers might find they have traded with one another at various prices, obliging each one to deliver a large amount of the commodity to the other in exchange for a large amount of money. *Netting* their contracts is an obvious efficiency gain for both dealers. It is easy to carry out *bilateral netting* by having one of the dealers owe the other only a net amount of the commodity, against a net amount of money determined by the prices at which the contracts were struck. For example, if traders A and B made three trades with each other, each obliging one to deliver 100,000 bushels of wheat to the other, with trader A having gone long at $100 and $110, and short at $105, either of his long contracts can be netted against the short. If the $100 contract is netted out, trader A will receive $5 from B, and only remain long the $110 contract. If the $110 contract is netted out, trader A will pay $5 to B, and only remain long the $100 contract.

Multilateral netting, or netting among many counterparties, is far more complicated, but brings the same efficiencies. Netting, as well as settlement services, are among the reasons clearinghouses were introduced in U.S. futures markets in the latter half of the nineteenth century. Clearinghouses and clearing associations were also important features of U.S. banking in the nineteenth and early twentieth centuries.

6.6.2 Measuring Counterparty Risk for Derivatives Positions

The counterparty risk of a derivatives position is closely related to, but distinct from, its market risk. Market risk is the risk that the market factors underlying the position will move against the trader, so that the NPV of the position is negative. Counterparty risk is the risk that the NPV is positive, but the counterparty fails to perform, so that no gain is reaped. Counterparty risk is thus a conditional risk. In order to realize a counterparty loss, the NPV of the contract must be positive. The amount at risk from a counterparty default will be quite close to the amount at risk from market moves. Adjustments may be made to the fair NPV to account for counterparty risk. Such an adjustment is called a *counterparty valuation adjustment* (CVA).

A key mechanism in protecting against counterparty risk in derivatives trading is *margin*, a form of collateralization in which one or both counterparties set aside a cash amount to cover losses in the event of counterparty default. We will return to the subject in Chapter 12's discussion of leverage in securities markets. Initial margin, as noted above, is the amount of cash collateral set aside when a trade is intiated. Initial margin tends to be relatively small on most derivatives transactions, though, as we see in Chapter 14, margins generally rose rapidly during the subprime crisis. The bulk of margin on derivatives, once enough time has elapsed since initiation, is therefore the NPV of swap contracts. Generally, as prices and NPVs fluctuate, changes in NPV are remitted daily as variation margin, that is, as increments to collateral rather than as settlement, by that day's losing counterparty to the gaining counterparty. This is a general practice, however, rather than an ironclad rule.

In some cases, initial margin on swaps can be relatively large. Examples are CDS, CDS indexes, and structured-credit CDS such as the ABX and CMBX—credit derivatives that provide exposure to subprime mortgage and commercial real estate loans—and synthetic CDO tranches, when these products are trading in *points upfront*, or "points up." In these cases, the counterparty selling protection receives an initial payment equal to the points up. The points upfront serve the function of initial margin. We further discuss point upfront and other CDS refinements in Chapter 7.

The treatment of the counterparty exposure and the scope for netting is often governed by legal agreements called *master agreements* or "ISDAs" (after the International Swap Dealer Association that drafted the templates for these contracts). As is the case for margin on cash securities, the net exposure at any moment is determined by the effect of the netting agreements and the collateral exchanged up to that point in time.

Derivatives dealers have historically had a privileged role in this process, much like that of brokers vis-à-vis their clients. They may be in a position to demand initial margin from their customers on both the long and short protection sides of a swap. The dealer, but not the client, might reasonably consider making CVAs to OTC derivatives' position values. This presumption proved faulty during the Lehman bankruptcy. In the wake of the Lehman bankruptcy, many of its swap counterparties suffered losses because Lehman held margin. Any collateral Lehman held became part of the bankruptcy estate, and its counterparties became general unsecured creditors of Lehman. In some cases, counterparties of Lehman such as hedge funds suffered losses on derivatives contracts in which Lehman held margin from them although the NPV of the contract was positive for the hedge fund. The counterparty would then become an unsecured general creditor of the Lehman bankruptcy estate both for the margin it had paid to Lehman and the claim arising from the derivatives contract. The details of any netting depended in part on the netting and cross-margining agreements in place and with which entities of the bankrupt broker these transactions had been carried out.

6.6.3 Double Default Risk

Double default risk arises from the possibility that the counterparty of a credit derivative such as a CDS that protects you against the default of a third party will default at the same time as that third party. This type of risk is both a counterparty risk and a form of credit correlation risk.

An important example of double default risk was prominent during the subprime crisis. It involved the counterparty exposures of American International Group (AIG), an internationally active insurance company with large property and casualty as well as life insurance businesses. AIG was a well-capitalized firm with an AAA rating, and was therefore an attractive counterparty for firms, especially banks and broker-dealers, looking to buy protection on a wide range of credit exposures via CDS. Because of AIG's strong capital base, the financial intermediaries were able to hedge their credit exposures while incurring only minimal apparent counterparty risk.

AIG's protection-selling activity was housed mainly within a subsidiary called AIG Financial Products (AIGFP), and one of its focuses was the most highly-rated tranches of structured credit products, particularly mortgage-backed securities. It was implicitly long a very large quantity of senior CDO tranches. Its counterparties had been long these exposures, and had now substituted counterparty risk for their initial long exposures. If AIGFP proved unable to meet its obligations under the CDS contracts at the same time that the bonds they owned suffered a material impairment, they would lose their hedges. This scenario became far likelier during the subprime crisis.

Another, similar, example of double default risk is the "wrap" business carried on by *monoline insurers*. In this business, an insurance company with a strong capital base and an AAA rating guarantees payment on a debt security issued by a company, another customer, or a municipality in exchange for an annual fee. The guarantee, called the "wrap," raises the creditworthiness of the bond sufficiently for rating agencies to grant it a higher rating. A number of monoline insurers suffered large losses during the subprime crisis, as the bonds they had guaranteed suffered credit downgrades or impairments, increasing the risk they would not have sufficient capital to make good on the guarantees they had written.

6.6.4 Custodial Risk

Securities in the contemporary financial system almost invariably exist in electronic, rather than paper form. *Bearer securities* have virtually disappeared. Even so, securities have to be "kept somewhere," dividends and interest have to be collected, and the securities have to be available for delivery if they are sold, lent, or transfered to another account. These services are called *custodial services*.

In margin lending and prime brokerage relationships, customers of large intermediaries such as banks and broker-dealers typically keep much of their securities in *margin accounts*, where the intermediary providing financing also has custody of the securities. These securities are collateral against the financing, and are said to be in "street name." In the event the borrower defaults on the financing, securities in street name can be sold immediately in order to protect the lender against credit losses.

Many retail brokerage accounts are also margin accounts, and are subject to much the same risks. Securities in cash or nonmargin accounts are in customer name. If the broker defaults, the retail customer's ownership of the security is not called into question. Securities in margin accounts, that is, in street name, are subject to custodial risk.

Many brokers perform custodial as well as credit intermediation services for their clients. The customers keep securities in custody with the broker that may at times be pledged as collateral and at other times be "in the box." The broker can *rehypothecate* pledged securities to fund its own operations. That is, the broker can itself employ, as collateral to borrow money, the very securities it holds as collateral against money it has lent to customers. The customer securities can also be lent to generate fee and interest income. The rules governing rehypothecation differ in important ways internationally.

These arrangements pose a counterparty risk to the broker's customers that was not widely noted until it was realized during the Lehman bankruptcy in September 2008. Customers of the firm's U.K. subsidiary were particularly badly situated, as even their unpledged assets were typically not segregated, but might be subject to rehypothecation. If the customer's securities are rehypothecated by the broker, the customer becomes a creditor of the broker. If the broker files for bankruptcy protection, the customer might not receive the securities back, but instead be treated as an unsecured lender of the broker-dealer. The amount of the unsecured exposure is then equal to the amount arrived at by netting the customer's margin across all exposures, including equity in margin loans and the positive NPV in his derivatives contracts.

6.6.5 Mitigation of Counterparty Risk

The ideal approach to mitigating counterparty risk would be to accurately measure exposures, maintain assessments of the credit condition of counterparty, maintain a diverse set of counterparties, and promptly limit exposure to weaker counterparties. For large firms with many counterparties, this can be a complex undertaking requiring considerable staff and systems investment. Exposure to specific counterparties can be reduced by reducing the volume of OTC contracts with them or by increasing the amount of collateral held against them. One difficulty in managing counterparty risk in CDS trades is that typically CDS trades are not netted or cancelled. Rather, an offsetting trade with another counterparty is initiated, a process called *novation*.

One tool for limiting counterparty risk is therefore CDS *compression*, or reducing the volume of redundant contracts with the same reference entity. A firm might put on long and short protection positions on the same name as it varies the size of its position. Compression reduces the set of CDS to a single net long or short position, thus eliminating a certain amount of nominal exposure and counterparty risk. There are many practical difficulties in carrying out compression trades, since in general the contracts will not be identical as to counterparty, premium, and maturity.

Individual firms have less control over systemic counterparty risk, that is, the risk that all counterparties become weaker in a systemic risk event, other than to keep overall counterparty exposure low.

6.7 THE MERTON MODEL

In the rest of this and the next chapter, we will focus on *single-obligor credit risk models*, that is, models of a single issuer of debt obligations. In Chapter 8, we will extend our discussion to *portfolio credit risk models*, which treat the credit risk of portfolios containing obligations of several obligors. The specific additional problem that portfolio credit models deal with is that of the correlation between credit events of different obligors.

In structural credit risk models, the evolution of the firm's balance sheet drives credit risk. The approach is sometimes called the *Merton model*. It applies the Black-Scholes option pricing model to value credit-risky corporate debt.

The setup for a simple variety of the Merton structural model combines a set of assumptions we need so that we can apply the Black-Scholes option pricing model, with a set of additional assumptions that tailor the model to our credit-risk valuation context. We'll set out the model assumptions, and then use the model to derive the firm's default probability:

- The value of the firm's assets A_t is assumed to follow a geometric Brownian motion:

$$dA_t = \mu A_t dt + \sigma_A A_t dW_t$$

Two of the parameters, the market value of the assets A_t and the expected return μ, are related to one another. In equilibrium, if r is the riskless continuously compounded interest rate for the same maturity as the firm's debt, the market's assessment of the asset value will be such that, given investors' risk appetites and the distribution of returns they expect, the risk premium $\mu - r$ on the assets is a sufficient, but not too generous, reward.

■ The balance sheet of the firm is simple:

$$A_t = E_t + D_t$$

The debt consists entirely of one issue, a zero-coupon bond with a nominal payment of D, maturing at time T. The notation D, with no subscript, is a constant referring to the par value of the debt. The notation D_t, with a time subscript, refers to the value of the debt at that point in time. In reality, most firms with tradeable debt have different types of issues, with different maturities and different degrees of seniority. In this model, the firm can default only on the maturity date of the bond. Similarly, we also assume the entire equity consists of common shares.

■ Limited liability holds, so if the equity is wiped out, the debtholders have no recourse to any other assets.

■ Contracts are strictly enforced, so the equity owners cannot extract any value from the firm until the debtholders are paid in full. In reality, when a firm is expected to reorganize rather than liquidate in bankruptcy, there is usually a negotiation around how the remaining value of the firm is distributed to debtholders and equity owners, and all classes may have to lose a little in order to maximize the value with which they all emerge from bankruptcy.

■ There is trading in the assets of the firm, not just in its equity and debt securities, and it is possible to establish both long and short positions. This rules out intangible assets such as goodwill.

■ The remaining assumptions are required to "enforce" limited liability: The firm can default only on the maturity date of the bond. There are no cash flows prior to the maturity of the debt; in particular, there are no dividends.

Default takes place if and only if, at time T, the firms assets are less than its debt repayment obligation:

$$A_T < D$$

The probability of default over the next T years is therefore the probability that the Brownian motion A_t hits the level D within the interval $(0, T_0)$. The quantity $A_T - D$ is called the *distance to default*. In this setup, we can view both the debt and equity securities as European options on the value of the firm's assets, maturing at the same time T as the firm's zero-coupon debt. We can value the options using the Black-Scholes formulas of Appendix A.3. The model will then help us obtain estimates of the probability of default and other default and recovery parameters.

However, in contrast to the way in which option pricing models are usually applied in finance, we are interested, in the credit risk context, in *both* risk-neutral and "physical" or true quantities, so we will have to be careful to identify clearly which one we are talking about, and we have to use the correct formulas.

We are also making some unrealistic assumptions about what parameters we know. In particular, it is unrealistic to imagine we will know at every point in time what exactly is the current market value of the firm's assets. It is even less likely we will know their volatility.

With these assumptions, we can use option-pricing theory to compute the equity and debt values. These in turn will lead us to the default probability:

> *Equity value of the firm.* For expositional purposes, we treat the current value of the firm's assets A_t and the volatility of the assets σ_A as known quantities. The equity can then be treated as a call option on the assets of the firm A_t with an exercise price equal to the face value of the debt D. If, at the maturity date T of the bond, the asset value A_T exceeds the nominal value of the debt D, the firm will pay the debt. If, in contrast, we have $A_T < D$, the owners of the firm will be wiped out, and the assets will not suffice to pay the debt timely and in full.
>
> The equity value at maturity is therefore
>
> $$E_T = \max(A_T - D, 0)$$
>
> Denoting $\tau = T - t$, and the Black-Scholes value of a τ-year European call struck at D by $v(A_t, D, \tau, \sigma_T, r, 0)$—remember that we assume no dividends—can value the firm's equity as a call on its assets, struck at the value of the debt:
>
> $$E_t = v(A_t, D, \tau, \sigma, r, 0)$$
>
> *Market value of the debt.* We can also apply option theory from the point of view of the lenders. We can treat the debt of the firm as a portfolio consisting of a risk-free bond with par value D *plus* a short position in a put option on the assets of the firm A_t with exercise

price D. In other words, if the bondholders received, as a gift, a put option on the firm's assets struck at the par value of the debt, with, crucially, no counterparty risk, they would be indifferent between that portfolio and a risk-free bond.

The present value of the risk-free bond is $De^{-r\tau}$. We can state the future value of the debt as

$$D_T = D - \max(D - A_T, 0)$$

Denoting the Black-Scholes value of a European put $w(A_t, D, \tau, \sigma_A, r, 0)$, we have the current value of the bond, as adjusted for risk by the market:

$$D_t = e^{-r\tau}D - w(A_t, D, \tau, \sigma_A, r, 0)$$

Firm balance sheet. The firm's balance sheet now also expresses put-call parity:

$$A_t = E_t + D_t$$
$$= v(A_t, D, \tau, \sigma_A, r, 0) + e^{-r\tau}D - w(A_t, D, \tau, \sigma_A, r, 0)$$

This means that the firm's assets are equal in value to a portfolio consisting of a risk-free discount bond in the nominal amount of the firm's debt, plus a long call and a short put, each struck at the nominal value of the debt.

Leverage. As a simple consequence of the balance sheet quantities, we can also compute balance sheet ratios. The leverage of the firm, expressed as the equity ratio at market prices, is

$$1 - \frac{e^{-r\tau}D - w(A_t, D, \tau, \sigma_A, r, 0)}{A_t}$$

We could specify the leverage ratio and the principal amount of the debt, and deduce the level of assets. In fact, we can specify any two of the three quantities—assets, debt principal, or leverage—and solve for the remaining quantity.

Default probabilities. The probability of default is identical to the probability of exercise of the put and call options we have been describing. However, we now have to distinguish between the true, actuarial or "physical" probability of exercise, and the risk-neutral probability.

The actuarial probability of default can be computed from the stochastic process followed by the firm's assets, provided we know or have a plausible estimate of the return on assets μ. The firm's assets are then lognormally distributed with parameters μ and σ_A. The probability of default is equal to

$$\mathbf{P}[A_T < D] = \Phi\left[-\frac{\log\left(\frac{A_t}{D}\right) + \left(\mu - \frac{1}{2}\sigma_A^2\right)\tau}{\sigma_A\sqrt{\tau}}\right]$$

The default probability estimated this way has in common with the rating agencies' estimates that it is an estimate of the true probability. It is different from agencies' estimates in that it is not a "through the cycle" rating, but rather a short-term estimate over the term of the debt.

In the Black-Scholes model, the risk-neutral probability of exercise is given by

$$\frac{\partial}{\partial D}v(A_t, D, \tau, \sigma, r, 0) = \Phi\left[-\frac{\log\left(\frac{A_t}{D}\right) + \left(r - \frac{1}{2}\sigma_A^2\right)\sigma_A^2\tau}{\sigma_A\sqrt{\tau}}\right]$$

Since this is a non–dividend paying stock (an inessential assumption), we can switch from true to risk-neutral by changing the asset return to the risk-free rate.

Credit spread. We now have enough information to compute the yield to maturity and the credit spread of the firm's debt. The yield to maturity y_t solves

$$D_t e^{y_t\tau} = D$$

Substituting the current market value of the debt, we have

$$[e^{-r\tau}D - w(A_t, D, \tau, \sigma_A, r, 0)]e^{y_t\tau} = D$$

so after taking logarithms, we have

$$y_t = \frac{1}{\tau}\log[(1 - e^{-r\tau})D + w(A_t, D, \tau, \sigma_A, r, 0)]$$

The credit spread is

$$y_t - r = \frac{1}{\tau} \log[(1 - e^{-r\tau})D + w(A_t, D, \tau, \sigma_A, r, 0)] - r$$

Loss given default. The LGD in the Merton model is a *random* quantity. It depends on how far short of the par value of the debt the firm's assets fall on the maturity date, if the firm defaults at all.

The default loss is equal to $\max(D - A_T, 0)$, which, of course, is the value *at expiry* of the "virtual" put option we are using to price the debt. However, the actuarial expected default loss is *not* equal to the current market value of the put option. The put option value is the risk-neutral value of protection against default in the Black-Scholes world of perfect and costless hedging via trading in the firm's assets. In computing its expected value, we use the risk-neutral, not the physical probability distribution that takes the growth rate of the assets μ into account. The value of the put option is greater than the actuarial expected loss, because there is compensation to the put writer for taking on the risk as well as the expected cost of providing the default protection.

To get the actuarial expected loss, we need to compute the expected value of $\max(D - A_T, 0)$, conditional on $A_T < D$

$$\text{expected loss} = \mathbf{E}\,[A_T | A_T < D]\,\mathbf{P}\,[A_T < D] - D\mathbf{P}\,[A_T < D]$$

Fortunately, we don't need to compute this; rather, we can use the Black-Scholes formula, but with μ in place of r and taking the future rather than the present value of the payoff:

$$\mathbf{E}\,[\text{LGD}] = e^{r\tau} w(A_t, D, \tau, \sigma_A, \mu, 0)$$

$$= D\Phi\left[-\frac{\log\left(\frac{A_t}{D}\right) + \left(\mu - \frac{1}{2}\sigma_A^2\right)\tau}{\sigma_A\sqrt{\tau}} \right]$$

$$-e^{r\tau} A_t \Phi\left[-\frac{\log\left(\frac{A_t}{D}\right) + \left(\mu + \frac{1}{2}\sigma_A^2\right)\tau}{\sigma_A\sqrt{\tau}} \right]$$

Dividing this by the actuarial default probability conditions the expected loss on the occurrence of default and gives us the expected LGD: that is, the amount the debtholder can expect to lose in the event of default.

$$\text{expected LGD} = \frac{e^{r\tau} w(A_t, D, \tau, \sigma_A, \mu, 0)}{\mathbf{P}[A_T < D]}$$

We can use this expression to compute the recovery rate on the debt, or to be precise, the *expected* recovery rate. The LGD is a conditional quantity, that is, the loss *if* default occurs. So to find it, we divide the expected value of the loss by the probability of its occurrence to get the conditional expected value of default loss. We can then state the expected value of the recovery rate as

$$R = 1 - \frac{1}{D} \frac{e^{r\tau} w(A_t, D, \tau, \sigma_A, \mu, 0)}{\mathbf{P}[A_T < D]}$$

Figure 6.2 illustrates the idea behind the Merton model using the parameters of Example 6.3.

Example 6.3 (Merton Model) We apply the model to a firm that has an asset value of \$140. We'll assume the firm's sole debt issue is a bond, with one 6 percent coupon left, to be paid in one year along with the principal at the maturity of the bond. This is effectively a zero-coupon bond with a par value of 106, but looking at the debt this way conveniently centers current debt prices near 100 percent of par.

The parameters for the example are:

Firm's current asset value	A_t	140
Nominal value of debt	D	100
Coupon on debt	c	0.06
Asset volatility	σ_A	0.25
Debt maturity in years	$\tau = T - t$	1
Risk-free rate	r	0.05
Return on firm's assets	a	0.10

The market value of the debt is equivalent to a portfolio consisting of the present value of the debt, discounted at the risk-free rate, plus a short put on the assets. The put has a value of

$$w(A_t, D, \tau, \sigma, r, 0) = w(140, 106, 1, 0.25, 0.05, 0) = 1.3088$$

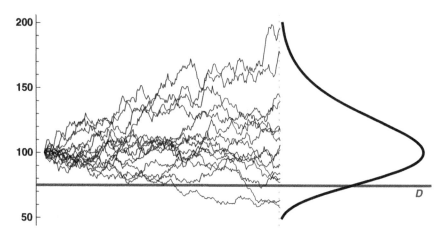

FIGURE 6.2   Merton Model
To the left, the graph displays 15 daily-frequency sample paths of the geometric
Brownian motion process.

$$dA_t = \mu A_t dt + \sigma_A A_t dW_t$$

with parameters as stated in the example. To the right, the graph displays the
probability density of the firm's assets on the maturity date of the debt. The grid
line represents the debt's par value D.

The bonds must be priced so as to incorporate the cost of insuring the
bondholders against a default, so the current market value of the debt is:

$$De^{-r\tau} - w(A_t, D, \tau, \sigma, r, 0) = 106 \times 0.9512 - 1.3088 = 99.5215$$

We can now calculate the fair market value of the firm's equity:

$$A_t - [De^{-r\tau} - p(A_t, D, \tau, \sigma, r, 0)] = 140 - 99.5215 = 40.4785$$

which put-call parity tells us is also equal to the value today of a European
call on the future residual value of the firm's assets over and above the par
value of the debt. The economic balance sheet of the firm is:

Assets	Liabilities
	Equity $E_t = 40.4785$
Value of the firm $A_t = 140$	Debt $D_t = 99.5215$

So the leverage (defined as the reciprocal of the equity ratio) is 3.4586.
The physical probability of default is

$$\Phi\left[-\frac{\log\left(\frac{140}{106}\right)+\left(0.05-\frac{1}{2}0.25^2\right)\cdot 1}{0.25\cdot\sqrt{1}}\right]=0.0826$$

or 8.3 percent, while the risk-neutral probability is somewhat higher at

$$\Phi\left[-\frac{\log\left(\frac{140}{106}\right)+\left(0.10-\frac{1}{2}0.25^2\right)\cdot 1}{0.25\cdot\sqrt{1}}\right]=0.1175$$

or 11.8 percent.

The expected value of default losses is represented by the future value of the "actuarial default put,"

$$e^{r\tau}w(A_t, D, \tau, \sigma, \mu, 0) = e^{0.05}w(140, 106, 1, 0.25, 0.05, 0)$$
$$= 1.05127 \times 0.8199$$

This value, of course, is lower than the risk-neutral default put value.

To arrive at the LGD and recovery rate, we convert the loss to a conditional expected loss in the event of default

$$\frac{e^{r\tau}w(A_t, D, \tau, \sigma, \mu, 0)}{P[A_T < D]} = \frac{1.05127 \times 0.8575}{0.0826} = 10.4349$$

The conditional expected recovery rate is

$$1 - \frac{1}{106}10.4349 = 0.9016$$

We can now summarize our results:

Discount factor	0.9512
Exposure	106.0000
Present value of exposure	100.8303
Put value	1.3088
Current market value of debt	99.5215
Current market price of debt	0.9952
Current market value of equity	40.4785
Leverage: Equity ratio	0.2891
Leverage: Reciprocal of equity ratio	3.4586
Actuarial default probability	0.0826
Risk-neutral default probability	0.1175
Fair yield to maturity	0.0631
Fair credit spread	0.0131
Actuarial expected loss	0.8619
Risk-neutral expected loss	1.3759
Expected LGD	10.4349
Expected recovery	95.5651
Expected recovery rate	0.9016

One drawback of the Merton model becomes clearer from this example. Leverage of nearly $3\frac{1}{2}$ times is quite high, at least for a nonfinancial company. Yet the default probability is low, at 8.3 percent, and the recovery rate is very high at 90 percent. Companies with such high leverage would typically have ratings that imply higher default probabilities, and recovery would be expected to be considerably lower.

We've laid out the basic structure of the Merton model, and along the way we have flagged some of its features that lack realism. The model has been adapted in commercial applications, particularly Moody's *KMV* and RiskMetrics' *CreditGrades*. These applications also attempt to address the two main respects in which the basic Merton model differs "too much" from reality. First, the capital structure of a typical firm is much more complex, particularly in its debt structure, than we have assumed. Second, in contrast to other applications of Black-Scholes, the underlying asset value A_t and the volatility σ_A, whether implied or historical, are not directly observable.

6.8 CREDIT FACTOR MODELS

Factor models can be seen as a type of structural model, since they try to relate the risk of credit loss to fundamental economic quantities. In contrast to other structural models, however, the fundamental factors have their impact directly on asset returns, rather than working through the elements of the firm's balance sheet.

A simple but widely used type is the *single-factor model*. The model is designed to represent the main motivating idea of the Merton model—a random asset value, below which the firm defaults—while lending itself well to portfolio analytics.

The horizon of the model is fixed at a future date $T = t + \tau$. The logarithmic asset return is

$$a_T = \log\left(\frac{A_T - A_t}{A_t}\right)$$

so the event that $A_T < D$ is identical to the event that

$$a_T < \log\left(\frac{D - A_t}{A_t}\right) = -\log\left(\frac{E_t}{A_t}\right) = -\log(\text{equity ratio})$$

or, in terms of financial ratios, that the asset return is negative and greater in absolute value than the initial equity ratio.[2] The horizon is constant, so to keep the notation from cluttering, we suppress the time subscript from here on.

The firm's asset return is represented as a function of two random variables: the return on a "market factor" m that captures the correlation between default and the general state of the economy, and a shock ϵ_i capturing idiosyncratic risk. However, the fundamental factor is not explicitly modeled: It is *latent*, meaning that its impact is modeled indirectly via the model parameters. We can write the model as:

$$a_T = \beta m + \sqrt{1 - \beta^2}\epsilon$$

We assume that m and ϵ are standard normal variates, and are not correlated with one another:

$$m \sim N(0, 1)$$

$$\epsilon \sim N(0, 1)$$

$$\text{Cov}[m, \epsilon] = 0$$

---

[2]We have expressed the model in terms of the asset return. Some presentations in the literature are done in terms of the level of asset value. Because of the way the model is set up, this doesn't matter. As long as the statistical behavior of the latent and idiosyncratic factors are as we have specified, the results are the same.

Under these assumptions, a is a standard normal variate. Since both the market factor and the idiosyncratic shocks are assumed to have unit variance (since they're standard normals), the beta of the firm's asset return to the market factor is equal to β:

$$\mathrm{E}\,[a_T] = 0$$
$$\mathrm{Var}[a_T] = \beta^2 + 1 - \beta^2 = 1$$

The role of σ_A in the Merton model is taken in the single-factor model by $\sqrt{1 - \beta^2}$. Figure 6.3 illustrates the role of the latent factor, the market index, and of the correlation, in driving asset returns.

The β in this model is related, but not identical, to a firm's equity beta. In this model, β captures comovement with an unobservable index of market conditions, rather than with an observable stock index. Also, β here relates the firm's asset, rather than equity, return to the market index. Still, they are related, because cyclical firms—that is, firms that do well when the economy overall is doing well—have high equity betas and will also have a higher β in the credit single-factor model. Defensive stocks will have low equity betas and low β.

Typically, in applications, we have an estimate of the default probability π, derived externally to the model, either market-implied or fundamentals/ratings-based. We can then use this probability to "calibrate" the model, that is, to determine values for the parameters. Rather than an output, as in the Merton model, the default probability is an input in the single-factor model. The default probability calibrates the default threshold asset value. Since under our assumptions a_T is a standard normal variate, the following holds

$$\pi = \mathbf{P}\,[a_T \leq k] \Leftrightarrow k = \Phi^{-1}(\pi)$$

where $\Phi^{-1}(\cdot)$ is the quantile function of the standard normal distribution and $\Phi^{-1}(\pi)$ is the π-th quantile of a_T (see Appendix A.2). The firm defaults if $a_T \leq k$, the logarithmic distance to the default asset value, measured in standard deviations. The asset return could bump into the default threshold via an infinite number of combinations of market factor realizations and idiosyncratic shocks, but the probability is π.

Example 6.4 (Single-Factor Model) For what value of β do systematic and idiosyncratic risk contribute equally to total risk of a credit, as measured by

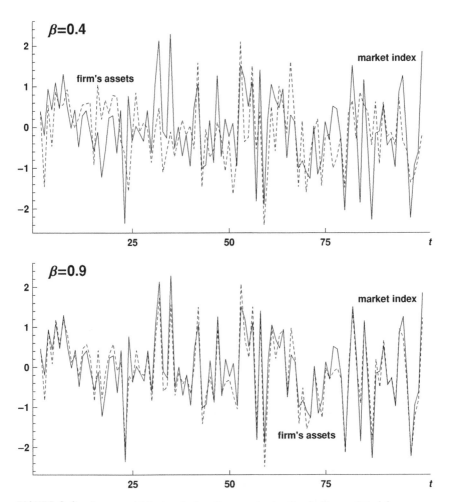

FIGURE 6.3 Asset and Market Index Returns in the Single-Factor Model
Each panel shows a sequence of 100 simulations from the single-factor model for
the indicated value of beta. The solid line plots the returns on the market index (a
sequence of $N(0, 1)$ realizations). The dashed line plots the corresponding returns
on a firm's assets with the specified β to the market, generated as $\beta m + \sqrt{1 - \beta^2}\epsilon$
using a second independent set of $N(0, 1)$ realizations.

its asset return variance? It is the β for which

$$\beta^2 = 1 - \beta^2 = \frac{1}{2} \quad \Rightarrow \quad \beta = \frac{1}{\sqrt{2}}$$

In sum, the single-factor model has two parameters, β and k. In applications, β and k may be estimated using the firm's balance-sheet and stock price data, or using the firm's rating and rating agency transition matrices. The mapping from default probability to default threshold is just that from standard normal cumulative probabilities to the associated z-values, for example:

π	k
0.05	−1.65
0.01	−2.33
0.001	−3.09

The parameters can be set independently, since a firm with a high default probability may be cyclical or defensive.

One of the main motivations of the single-factor model is to model portfolio credit risk, and we spend more time with it in Chapter 8.

6.9 CREDIT RISK MEASURES

The models we have sketched help us estimate corporate default probabilities and recovery rates. The next step is to use these models to estimate a risk statistic. The most common credit risk statistics, unexpected loss and credit VaR, are closely related, in that they incorporate the notion of potential loss at a future time horizon with a stated probability.

But the concepts are not quite identical, and, as we will see, they have different implications for how banks and investors should determine the appropriate amount of capital to set aside as a buffer against losses. These issues arise because

- The typical time horizon for measuring credit risk is much longer, on the order of one year, than for measuring market risk, where time horizons are almost always between one day and one month. An immediate consequence is that expected credit returns, the credit "drift," cannot be assumed to be immaterial, as the drift is for market risk. This in turn creates additional issues, involving the treatment of promised coupon payments and the cost of funding positions, which do not arise in the same form in the market risk context.

■ A second set of issues is driven by the extreme skewness of credit return distributions. For most unleveraged individual credit-risky securities and credit portfolios, the overwhelming likelihood is that returns will be relatively small in magnitude, driven by interest payments made on time or by ratings migrations. But on the rare occasions of defaults or clusters of defaults, returns are large and negative. This contrasts with market risk in most cases, although similar market risk skewness can be seen in option portfolios.

Because of the skewness of credit portfolios, the confidence level for credit VaR measures tend to be somewhat higher than for market risk; 95 percent confidence levels appear less frequently, 99.9 percent more so.

As an example of the skewness of credit returns, consider the distribution of future bond value in our Merton model Example 6.3, illustrated in Figure 6.4. Most of the probability mass is located at a single point, $D = 106$. The rest is distributed smoothly below D.

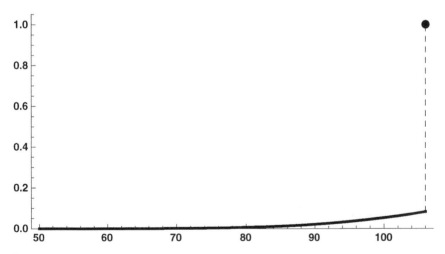

FIGURE 6.4 Distribution of Bond Value in the Merton Model
Cumulative probability distribution of bond value in the Merton model. The parameters are as set out in the text.

6.9.1 Expected and Unexpected Loss

Credit losses can be decomposed into three components: expected loss, unexpected loss, and the loss "in the tail," that is, beyond the unexpected.

Unexpected loss (UL) is a quantile of the credit loss in excess of the expected loss. It is sometimes defined as the standard deviation, and sometimes as the 99th or 99.9th percentile of the loss in excess of the expected loss. The standard definition of *credit Value-at-Risk* is cast in terms of UL: It is the worst case loss on a portfolio with a specific confidence level over a specific holding period, minus the expected loss.

This is quite different from the standard definition of VaR for market risk. The market risk VaR is defined in terms of P&L. It therefore compares a future value with a current value. The credit risk VaR is defined in terms of differences from EL. It therefore compares two future values.

To make this concept clearer, let's continue the Merton model example. The results are illustrated in Figure 6.5, the probability density function of the bond's future value.

Example 6.5 (Credit VaR in the Merton Model)   Figure 6.5 displays a portion of the density corresponding to the cumulative distribution of Figure 6.4, to the left of the default threshold. The graph shows how outcomes for the future value of the debt are decomposed into expected and unexpected

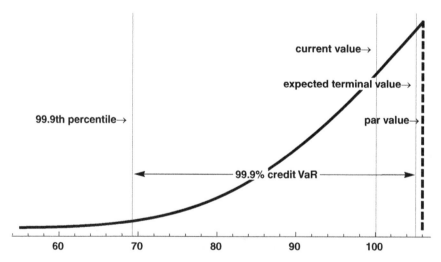

FIGURE 6.5   Credit VaR in the Merton Model
Probability density function of bond future value in the Merton model. The parameters are as set out in the text.

loss, and how the unexpected loss is decomposed into the credit VaR and losses beyond the credit VaR. The expected loss is the small gap between the par value and the expected future value of the bond, taking account of the default probability and recovery.

Actuarial expected loss	0.8619
Expected future value of debt	105.1381
0.001 quantile of bond value	69.2577
Credit VaR at the 99.9 confidence level	35.8804

6.9.2 Jump-to-Default Risk

Jump-to-default risk is an estimate of the loss that would be realized if a position, were to default instantly. It is based on the market value of the position or that of the underlying credit if the trade is expressed through derivatives. The jump-to-default value of a position consisting of x units of a bond with a value p is xpR.

Jump-to-default risk can be computed without using a probability of default. It is a form of stress testing, in that it realizes a worst-case scenario (see Section 13.3). It is a valuable tool for assessing the size and risk of individual positions. However, it can be misleading for portfolios. If there are long and short positions in a portfolio, the jump-to-default value of the portfolio is a net value that is likely to be small, even if the portfolio has significant risk. If the portfolio is large and consists entirely of long positions, the jump-to-default value will be misleadingly large, since it does not take diversification into account, that is, the fact that the probability of all the positions defaulting is lower than the typical probability of a single position defaulting. We discuss more precise ways of measuring credit risk for portfolios in the next chapter.

FURTHER READING

Duffie and Singleton (2003), Schönbucher (2003), and Lando (2004) are textbook introductions to credit risk models.

Although it has a focus on distressed rather than general corporate debt investing, Moyer (2005) is a good source on legal and quantitative credit analysis, and on capital structure issues. Baskin and Miranti (1997) discuss the historical development of limited liability. A classic paper on credit scoring is Altman (1968). Default rate histories are provided by Moody's Investors Service (2011) and Standard and Poor's (2010). See Duffie and Singleton (1999) on definitions of recovery in default, and Altman and Kishore (1996) on empirical recovery research. Frye (2000, 2001) discuss the relationship between recovery and default, and its impact on the use of credit risk models.

Williamson (1985), Chapters 1 and 2, gives an overview of information cost problems in contracts. Gertler (1988), p. 568ff, and Mehran and Stulz (2007) provides applications to financial intermediation. Jensen and Meckling (1976) is a seminal text explaining the typical debt-equity capital structure of a firm as a response to the problem of agency costs. The term "moral hazard" was introduced into economics in Arrow (1963). The classic paper on adverse selection is Akerlof (1970).

Segoviano Basurto and Singh (2008) provide an overview of counterparty credit risk. Williams (1986) discusses the development of clearinghouses for futures markets. Timberlake (1984) and Kroszner (2000) discuss bank clearinghouses. The Lehman episode is described in Aragon and Strahan (2009). See also the Further Reading sections of Chapters 12 and 14.

Basel Committee on Banking Supervision (1999) and Task Force of the Market Operations Committee of the European System of Central Banks (2007) are surveys of credit risk models. O'Kane and Schloegl (2001) and Crouhy, Mark, and Galai (2000a) provide surveys focusing on commercial applications. Gupton, Finger, and Bhatia (2007) focus on the CreditMetrics methodology while providing a great deal of credit modeling background.

The original presentation of the Merton model is Merton (1974). Finger (2002) describes the *CreditGrades* variant on the Merton model. Credit factor models are presented in Finger (2001) and Gordy (2003). See Kupiec (2002) on issues in the definition of credit VaR.

CHAPTER **7**

Spread Risk and Default Intensity Models

This chapter discusses credit spreads, the difference between risk-free and default-risky interest rates, and estimates of default probabilities based on credit spreads. Credit spreads are the compensation the market offers for bearing default risk. They are not pure expressions of default risk, though. Apart from the probability of default over the life of the security, credit spreads also contain compensation for risk. The spread must induce investors to put up not only with the uncertainty of credit returns, but also liquidity risk, the extremeness of loss in the event of default, for the uncertainty of the timing and extent of recovery payments, and in many cases also for legal risks: Insolvency and default are messy.

Most of this chapter is devoted to understanding the relationship between credit spreads and default probabilities. We provide a detail example of how to estimate a risk neutral default curve from a set of credit spreads. The final section discusses spread risk and spread volatility.

7.1 CREDIT SPREADS

Just as risk-free rates can be represented in a number of ways—spot rates, forward rates, and discount factors—credit spreads can be represented in a number of equivalent ways. Some are used only in analytical contexts, while others serve as units for quoting prices. All of them attempt to decompose bond interest into the part of the interest rate that is compensation for credit and liquidity risk and the part that is compensation for the time value of money:

> *Yield spread* is the difference between the yield to maturity of a credit-risky bond and that of a benchmark government bond with the

same or approximately the same maturity. The yield spread is used more often in price quotes than in fixed-income analysis.

i-spread. The benchmark government bond, or a freshly initiated plain vanilla interest-rate swap, almost never has the same maturity as a particular credit-risky bond. Sometimes the maturities can be quite different. The *i*- (or interpolated) spread is the difference between the yield of the credit-risky bond and the linearly interpolated yield between the two benchmark government bonds or swap rates with maturities flanking that of the credit-risky bond. Like yield spread, it is used mainly for quoting purposes.

z-spread. The *z*- (or zero-coupon) spread builds on the zero-coupon Libor curve, which we discussed in Section 4.2. It is generally defined as the spread that must be added to the Libor spot curve to arrive at the market price of the bond, but may also be measured relative to a government bond curve; it is good practice to specify the risk-free curve being used. Occasionally the *z*-spread is defined using the forward curve.

If the price of a τ-year credit-risky bond with a coupon of c and a payment frequency of h (measured as a fraction of a year) is $p_{\tau,h}(c)$, the *z*-spread is the constant z that satisfies

$$p_{\tau,h}(c) = ch \sum_{i=1}^{\frac{\tau}{h}} e^{-(r_{ih}+z)ih} + e^{-(r_\tau+z)\tau}$$

ignoring refinements due to day count conventions.

Asset-swap spread is the spread or quoted margin on the floating leg of an asset swap on a bond.

Credit default swap spread is the market premium, expressed in basis points, of a CDS on similar bonds of the same issuer.

Option-adjusted spread (OAS) is a version of the *z*-spread that takes account of options embedded in the bonds. If the bond contains no options, OAS is identical to the *z*-spread.

Discount margin is a spread concept applied to floating rate notes. It is the fixed spread over the current (one- or three-month) Libor rate that prices the bond precisely. The discount margin is thus the floating-rate note analogue of the yield spread for fixed-rate bonds. It is sometimes called the *quoted margin*.

Example 7.1 (Credit Spread Concepts) Let's illustrate and compare some of these definitions of credit spread using the example of a U.S. dollar-denominated bullet bond issued by Citigroup in 2003, the $4\frac{7}{8}$ percent fixed-rate bond maturing May 7, 2015. As of October 16, 2009, this (approximately) $5\frac{200}{360}$-year bond had a semiannual pay frequency, no embedded options, and at the time of writing was rated Baa1 by Moody's and A– by S&P. These analytics are provided by Bloomberg's YAS screen.

Its yield was 6.36, and with the nearest-maturity on-the-run Treasury note trading at a yield of 2.35 percent, the yield spread was 401 bps.

The i-spread to the swap curve can be calculated from the five- and six-year swap rates, 2.7385 and 3.0021 percent, respectively. The interpolated $5\frac{200}{360}$-year swap rate is 2.8849 percent, so the i-spread is 347.5 bps.

The z-spread, finally, is computed as the parallel shift to the fitted swap spot curve required to arrive at a discount curve consistent with the observed price, and is equal to 351.8 bps.

To see exactly how the z-spread is computed, let's look at a more stylized example, with a round-number time to maturity and pay frequency, and no accrued interest.

Example 7.2 (Computing the z-Spread) We compute the z-spread for a five-year bullet bond with semiannual fixed-rate coupon payments of 7 percent per annum, and trading at a dollar price of 95.00. To compute the z-spread, we need a swap zero-coupon curve, and to keep things simple, we assume the swap curve is flat at 3.5 percent per annum. The spot rate is then equal to a constant 3.470 percent for all maturities, as we saw in Section 4.2.

The yield to maturity of this bond is 8.075 percent, so the i-spread to swaps is $8.075 - 3.50 = 4.575$ percent. The z-spread is the constant z that satisfies

$$0.95 = \frac{0.07}{2}\sum_{i=1}^{5\cdot2} e^{-(0.03470+z)\frac{1}{2}} + e^{-(0.03470+z)5}$$

This equation can be solved numerically to obtain $z = 460.5$ bps.

7.1.1 Spread Mark-to-Market

In Chapter 4.2, we studied the concept of DV01, the mark-to-market gain on a bond for a one basis point change in interest rates. There is an analogous concept for credit spreads, the "spread01," sometimes called DVCS, which measures the change in the value of a credit-risky bond for a one basis point change in spread.

For a credit-risky bond, we can measure the change in market value corresponding to a one basis point change in the z-spread. We can compute the spread01 the same way as the DV01: Increase and decrease the z-spread by 0.5 basis points, reprice the bond for each of these shocks, and compute the difference.

Example 7.3 (Computing the Spread01)   Continuing the earlier example, we start by finding the bond values for a 0.5-bps move up and down in the z-spread. The bond prices are expressed per \$100 of par value:

$$\frac{0.07}{2}\sum_{i=1}^{5\cdot2}e^{-(0.03470+0.04605-0.00005)\frac{1}{2}}+e^{-(0.03470+0.04605-0.00005)5}=0.950203$$

$$\frac{0.07}{2}\sum_{i=1}^{5\cdot2}e^{-(0.03470+0.04605+0.00005)\frac{1}{2}}+e^{-(0.03470+0.04605+0.00005)5}=0.949797$$

The difference is $95.0203 - 94.9797 = 0.040682$ dollars per basis point per \$100 of par value. This would typically be expressed as \$406.82 per \$1,000,000 of par value. The procedure is illustrated in Figure 7.1.

The spread01 of a fixed-rate bond depends on the initial level of the spread, which in turn is determined by the level and shape of the swap curve, the coupon, and other design features of the bond. The "typical" spread01 for a five-year bond (or CDS) is about \$400 per \$1,000,000 of

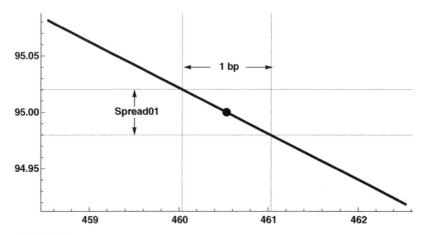

FIGURE 7.1   Computing Spread01 for a Fixed-Rate Bond
The graph shows how spread01 is computed in Example 7.3 by shocking the z-spread up and down by 0.5 bps. The plot displays the value of the bond for a range of z-spreads. The point represents the initial bond price and corresponding z-spread. The vertical grid lines represent the 1 bps spread shock. The horizontal distance between the points on the plot where the vertical grid lines cross is equal to the spread01 per \$100 par value.

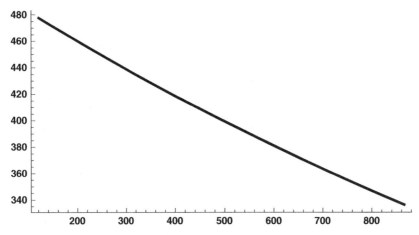

FIGURE 7.2 Spread01 a Declining Function of Spread Level
The graph shows how spread01, measured in dollars per $1,000,000 of bond par value, varies with the spread level. The bond is a five-year bond making semiannual fixed-rate payments at an annual rate of 7 percent. The graph is constructed by permitting the price of the bond to vary between 80 and 110 dollars, and computing the z-spread and spread01 at each bond price, holding the swap curve at a constant flat 3.5 percent annual rate.

bond par value (or notional underlying amount). At very low or high spread levels, however, as seen in Figure 7.2, the spread01 can fall well above or below $400.

The intuition is that, as the spread increases and the bond price decreases, the discount factor applied to cash flows that are further in the future declines. The spread-price relationship exhibits convexity; any increase or decrease in spread has a smaller impact on the bond's value when spreads are higher and discount factor is lower. The extent to which the impact of a spread *change* is attenuated by the high *level* of the spread depends primarily on the bond maturity and the level and shape of the swap or risk-free curve.

Just as there is a duration measure for interest rates that gives the proportional impact of a change in rates on bond value, the *spread duration* gives the proportional impact of a spread change on the price of a credit-risky bond. Like duration, spread duration is defined as the ratio of the spread01 to the bond price.

7.2 DEFAULT CURVE ANALYTICS

Reduced-form or *intensity models* of credit risk focus on the analytics of default timing. These models are generally focused on practical applications such as pricing derivatives using arbitrage arguments and the prices of other securities, and lead to simulation-friendly pricing and risk measurement techniques. In this section, we lay out the basics of these analytics. Reduced form models typically operate in default mode, disregarding ratings migration and the possibility of restructuring the firm's balance sheet.

Reduced-form models, like the single-factor model of credit risk, rely on estimates of default probability that come from "somewhere else." The default probabilities can be derived from internal or rating agency ratings, or from structural credit models. But reduced form models are most often based on market prices or spreads. These *risk-neutral estimates of default probabilities* can be extracted from the prices of credit-risky bonds or loans, or from credit derivatives such as credit default swaps (CDS). In the next section, we show how to use the default curve analytics to extract default probabilities from credit spread data. In Chapter 8, we use the resulting default probability estimates as an input to models of credit portfolio risk.

Default risk for a single company can be represented as a *Bernoulli trial*. Over some fixed time horizon $\tau = T_2 - T_1$, there are just two outcomes for the firm: Default occurs with probability π, and the firm remains solvent with probability $1 - \pi$. If we assign the values 1 and 0 to the default and solvency outcomes over the time interval $(T_1, T_2]$, we define a random variable that follows a *Bernoulli distribution*. The time interval $(T_1, T_2]$ is important: The Bernoulli trial doesn't ask "does the firm ever default?," but rather, "does the firm default over the next year?"

The mean and variance of a Bernoulli-distributed variate are easy to compute. The expected value of default on $(T_1, T_2]$ is equal to the default probability π, and the variance of default is $\pi(1 - \pi)$.

The Bernoulli trial can be repeated during successive time intervals $(T_2, T_3], (T_3, T_4], \ldots$. We can set each time interval to have the same length τ, and stipulate that the probability of default occurring during each of these time intervals is a constant value π. If the firm defaults during any of these time intervals, it remains defaulted forever, and the sequence of trials comes to an end. But so long as the firm remains solvent, we can imagine the firm surviving "indefinitely," but not "forever."

This model implies that the Bernoulli trials are *conditionally independent*, that is, that the event of default over each future interval $(T_j, T_{j+1}]$ is independent of the event of default over any earlier $(j > i)$ interval $(T_i, T_{i+1}]$. This notion of independence is a potential source of confusion. It means that, from the current perspective, if you are told that the firm will survive up to time T_j, but have no idea when thereafter the firm will default, you "restart the clock" from the perspective of time T_j. You have no more or less information bearing on the survival of the firm over $(T_j, T_j + \tau]$ than you did at an earlier time T_i about survival over $(T_i, T_i + \tau]$. This property is also called *memorylessness*, and is similar to the martingale property we noted for geometrical Brownian motion in Chapter 2.

In this model, the probability of default over some longer interval can be computed from the binomial distribution. For example, if τ is set equal to one year, the probability of survival over the next decade is equal $(1 - \pi)^{10}$, the probability of getting a sequence of 10 zeros in 10 independent Bernoulli trials.

It is inconvenient, though, to use a discrete distribution such as the binomial to model default over time, since the computation of probabilities can get tedious. An alternative is to model the random time at which a default occurs as the first arrival time—the time at which the modeled event occurs—of a *Poisson process*. In a Poisson process, the number of events in any time interval is *Poisson-distributed*. The time to the next arrival of a Poisson-distributed event is described by the *exponential distribution*. So our approach is equivalent to modeling the time to default as an exponentially distributed random variate. This leads to the a simple algebra describing default-time distributions, illustrated in Figure 7.3.

In describing the algebra of default time distributions, we set $t = 0$ as "now," the point in time from which we are considering different time horizons.

7.2.1 The Hazard Rate

The *hazard rate*, also called the *default intensity*, denoted λ, is the parameter driving default. It has a time dimension, which we will assume is annual.[1] For each future time, the probability of a default over the tiny time interval dt is then

$$\lambda dt$$

and the probability that no default occurs over the time interval dt is

$$1 - \lambda dt$$

In this section, we assume that the hazard rate is a constant, in order to focus on defining default concepts. In the next section, where we explore how to derive risk-neutral default probabilities from market data, we'll relax this assumption and let the hazard rate vary for different time horizons.

---

[1]In life insurance, the equivalent concept applied to the likelihood of death rather than default is called the *force of mortality*.

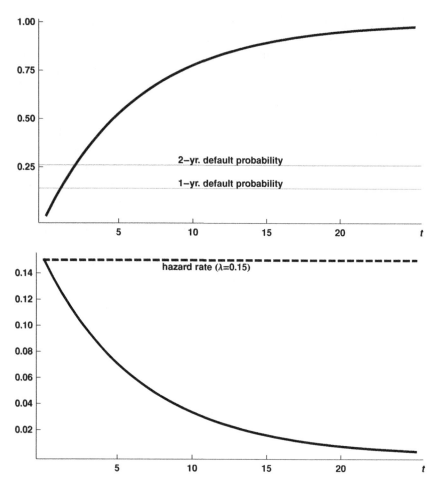

FIGURE 7.3 Intensity Model of Default Timing

The graphs are plotted from the perspective of time 0 and assume a value $\lambda = 0.15$, as in Example 7.4.

Upper panel: Cumulative default time distribution $1 - e^{-\lambda t}$. The ordinate of each point on the plot represents the probability of a default between time 0 and the time t represented by the abscissa.

Lower panel: Hazard rate λ and marginal default probability $\lambda e^{-\lambda t}$. The ordinate of each point on the plot represents the annual rate at which the probability of a default between time 0 and the time t is changing. The marginal default probability is decreasing, indicating that the one-year probability of default is falling over time.

7.2.2 Default Time Distribution Function

The *default time distribution function* or *cumulative default time distribution* $F(\tau)$ is the probability of default sometime between now and time t:

$$P[t^* < t] \equiv F(t) = 1 - e^{-\lambda t}$$

The survival and default probabilities must sum to exactly 1 at every instant t, so the probability of *no* default sometime between now and time t, called the *survival time distribution*, is

$$P[t^* \geq t] = 1 - P[t^* < t] = 1 - F(t) = e^{-\lambda t}$$

The survival probability converges to 0 and the default probability converges to 1 as t grows very large: in the intensity model, even a "bullet-proof" AAA-rated company will default eventually. This remains true even when we let the hazard rate vary over time.

7.2.3 Default Time Density Function

The *default time density function* or *marginal default probability* is the derivative of the default time distribution w.r.t. t:

$$\frac{\partial}{\partial t} P[t^* < t] = F'(t) = \lambda e^{-\lambda t}$$

This is always a positive number, since default risk "accumulates"; that is, the probability of default increases for longer horizons. If λ is small, it will increase at a very slow pace. The survival probability, in contrast, is declining over time:

$$\frac{\partial}{\partial t} P[t^* \geq t] = -F'(t) = -\lambda e^{-\lambda t} < 0$$

With a *constant* hazard rate, the marginal default probability is positive but declining, as seen in the lower panel of Figure 7.3. This means that, although the firm is likelier to default the further out in time we look, the rate at which default probability accumulates is declining. This is not necessarily true when the hazard rate can change over time. The default time density is still always positive, but if the hazard rate is rising fast enough with the time horizon, the cumulative default probability may increase at an increasing rather than at a decreasing rate.

7.2.4 Conditional Default Probability

So far, we have computed the probability of default over some time horizon $(0, t)$. If instead we ask, what is the probability of default over some horizon $(t, t + \tau)$ given that there has been no default prior to time t, we are asking about a *conditional default probability*. By the definition of conditional probability, it can be expressed as

$$\mathbf{P}\left[t^* < t + \tau | t^* > t\right] = \frac{\mathbf{P}\left[t^* > t \cap t^* < t + \tau\right]}{\mathbf{P}\left[t^* > t\right]}$$

that is, as the ratio of the probability of the joint event of survival up to time t and default over some horizon $(t, t + \tau)$, to the probability of survival up to time t.

That joint event of survival up to time t and default over $(t, t + \tau)$ is simply the event of defaulting during the discrete interval between two future dates t and $t + \tau$. In the constant hazard rate model, the probability $\mathbf{P}\left[t^* > t \cap t^* < t + \tau\right]$ of surviving to time t and then defaulting between t and $t + \tau$ is

$$
\begin{aligned}
\mathbf{P}\left[t^* > t \cap t^* < t + \tau\right] &= F(t + \tau) - F(t) \\
&= 1 - e^{-\lambda(t+\tau)} - \left(1 - e^{-\lambda t}\right) \\
&= e^{-\lambda t}\left(1 - e^{-\lambda \tau}\right) \\
&= [1 - F(t)]F(\tau) \\
&= \mathbf{P}\left[t^* > t\right]\mathbf{P}\left[t^* < t + \tau | t^* > t\right]
\end{aligned}
$$

We also see that

$$F(\tau) = \mathbf{P}\left[t^* < t + \tau | t^* > t\right]$$

which is equal to the unconditional τ-year default probability. We can interpret it as the probability of default over τ years, if we started the clock at zero at time t. This useful result is a further consequence of the memorylessness of the default process.

If the hazard rate is constant over a very short interval $(t, t + \tau)$, then the probability the security will default over the interval, given that it has not yet defaulted up until time t, is

$$\lim_{\substack{\tau \to 0 \\ \tau > 0}} P\,[t < t^* < t + \tau | t^* > t] = \frac{F'(t)\tau}{1 - F(t)} = \lambda \tau$$

The hazard rate can therefore now be interpreted as the instantaneous conditional default probability.

Example 7.4 (Hazard Rate and Default Probability) Suppose $\lambda = 0.15$. The unconditional one-year default probability is $1 - e^{-\lambda} = 0.1393$, and the survival probability is $e^{-\lambda} = 0.8607$. This would correspond to a low speculative-grade credit.

The unconditional two-year default probability is $1 - e^{-2\lambda} = 0.2592$. In the upper panel of Figure 7.3, horizontal grid lines mark the one- and two-year default probabilities. The difference between the two- and one-year default probabilities—the probability of the joint event of survival through the first year and default in the second—is 0.11989. The conditional one-year default probability, given survival through the first year, is the difference between the two probabilities (0.11989), divided by the one-year survival probability 0.8607:

$$\frac{0.11989}{0.8607} = 0.1393$$

which is equal, in this constant hazard rate example, to the unconditional one-year default probability.

7.3 RISK-NEUTRAL ESTIMATES OF DEFAULT PROBABILITIES

Our goal in this section is to see how default probabilities can be extracted from market prices with the help of the default algebra laid out in the previous section. As noted, these probabilities are risk neutral, that is, they include compensation for both the loss given default and bearing the risk of default and its associated uncertainties. The default intensity model gives us a handy way of representing spreads. We denote the spread over the risk-free rate on a defaultable bond with a maturity of T by z_T. The constant risk-neutral hazard rate at time T is λ_T^*. If we line up the defaultable securities by maturity, we can define a *spread curve*, that is, a function that relates the credit spread to the maturity of the bond.

7.3.1 Basic Analytics of Risk-Neutral Default Rates

There are two main types of securities that lend themselves to estimating default probabilities, bonds and credit default swaps (CDS). We start by describing the estimation process using the simplest possible security, a credit-risky zero-coupon corporate bond.

Let's first summarize the notation of this section:

p_τ	Current price of a default-free τ-year zero-coupon bond
p_τ^{corp}	Current price of a defaultable τ-year zero-coupon bond,
r_τ	Continuously compounded discount rate on the default free bond
z_τ	Continuously compounded spread on the defaultable bond
R	Recovery rate
λ_τ^*	τ-year risk neutral hazard rate
$1 - e^{-\lambda_\tau^*}$	Annualized risk neutral default probability

We assume that there are both defaultable and default-free zero-coupon bonds with the same maturity dates. The issuer's credit risk is then expressed by the discount or price concession at which it has to issue bonds, compared to the that on government bonds, rather than the coupon it has to pay to get the bonds sold. We'll assume there is only one issue of defaultable bonds, so that we don't have to pay attention to seniority, that is, the place of the bonds in the capital structure.

We'll denote the price of the defaultable discount bond maturing in τ years by p_τ^{corp}, measured as a decimal. The default-free bond is denoted p_τ. The continuously compounded discount rate on the default-free bond is the spot rate r_τ of Chapter 4, defined by

$$p_\tau = e^{-r_\tau \tau}$$

A corporate bond bears default risk, so it must be cheaper than a risk-free bond with the same future cash flows on the same dates, in this case $1 per bond in τ years:

$$p_\tau \geq p_\tau^{\text{corp}}$$

The continuously compounded τ-year spread on a zero coupon corporate is defined as the difference between the rates on the corporate and default-free bonds and satisfies:

$$p_\tau^{\text{corp}} = e^{-(r_\tau + z_\tau)\tau} = p_\tau e^{-z_\tau \tau}$$

Since $p_\tau^{\text{corp}} \leq p_\tau$, we have $z_\tau \geq 0$.

The credit spread has the same time dimensions as the spot rate r_τ. It is the constant exponential rate at which, if there is no default, the price difference between a risky and risk-free bond shrinks to zero over the next τ years.

To compute hazard rates, we need to make some assumptions about default and recovery:

- The issuer can default any time over the next τ years.
- In the event of default, the creditors will receive a deterministic and known recovery payment, but only at the maturity date, regardless of when default occurs. Recovery is a known fraction R of the par amount of the bond (recovery of face).

We'll put all of this together to estimate λ_τ^*, the risk-neutral constant hazard rate over the next τ years. The risk-neutral τ-year default probability is thus $1 - e^{-\lambda_\tau^* \tau}$. Later on, we will introduce the possibility of a time-varying hazard rate and learn how to estimate a term structure from bond or CDS data in which the spreads and default probabilities may vary with the time horizon. The time dimensions of λ_τ^* are the same as those of the spot rate and the spread. It is the conditional default probability over $(0, T)$, that is, the constant annualized probability that the firm defaults over a tiny time interval $t + \Delta t$, given that it has not already defaulted by time t, with $0 < t < T$.

The risk-neutral (and physical) hazard rates have an exponential form. The probability of defaulting over the next instant is a constant, and the probability of defaulting over a discrete time interval is an exponential function of the length of the time interval.

For the moment, let's simplify the setup even more, and let the recovery rate $R = 0$. An investor in a defaultable bond receives either \$1 or zero in τ years. The expected value of the two payoffs is

$$e^{-\lambda_\tau^* \tau} \cdot 1 + (1 - e^{-\lambda_\tau^* \tau}) \cdot 0$$

The expected present value of the two payoffs is

$$e^{-r_\tau \tau}[e^{-\lambda_\tau^* \tau} \cdot 1 + (1 - e^{-\lambda_\tau^* \tau}) \cdot 0]$$

Discounting at the risk-free rate is appropriate because we want to estimate λ_τ^*, the risk-neutral hazard rate. To the extent that the credit-risky bond price and z_τ reflect a risk premium as well as an estimate of the true default probability, the risk premium will be embedded in λ_τ^*, so we don't have to discount by a risky rate.

The risk-neutral hazard rate sets the expected present value of the two payoffs equal to the price of the defaultable bond. In other words, if market prices have adjusted to eliminate the potential for arbitrage, we can solve Equation (7.1) for λ_τ^*:

$$e^{-(r_\tau + z_\tau)\tau} = e^{-r_\tau \tau}[e^{-\lambda_\tau^* \tau} \cdot 1 + (1 - e^{-\lambda_\tau^* \tau}) \cdot 0] \tag{7.1}$$

to get our first simple rule of thumb: If recovery is zero, then

$$\lambda_\tau^* = z_\tau$$

that is, the hazard rate is equal to the spread. Since for small values of x we can use the approximation $e^x \approx 1 + x$, we also can say that the spread $z_\tau \approx 1 - e^{-\lambda_\tau^*}$, the default probability.

Example 7.5 Suppose a company's securities have a five-year spread of 300 bps over the Libor curve. Then the risk-neutral annual hazard rate over the next five years is 3 percent, and the annualized default probability is approximately 3 percent. The exact annualized default probability is 2.96 percent, and the five-year default probability is 13.9 percent.

Now let the recovery rate R be a positive number on $(0, 1)$. The owner of the bond will receive one of two payments at the maturity date. Either the issuer does not default, and the creditor receives par (\$1), or there is a default, and the creditor receives R. Setting the expected present value of these payments equal to the bond price, we have

$$e^{-(r_\tau + z_\tau)\tau} = e^{-r_\tau \tau}[e^{-\lambda_\tau^* \tau} + (1 - e^{-\lambda_\tau^* \tau})R]$$

or

$$e^{-z_\tau \tau} = e^{-\lambda_\tau^* \tau} + (1 - e^{-\lambda_\tau^* \tau})R = 1 - (1 - e^{-\lambda_\tau^* \tau})(1 - R)$$

giving us our next rule of thumb: The additional credit-risk discount on the defaultable bond, divided by the LGD, is equal to the τ-year default probability:

$$1 - e^{-\lambda_\tau^* \tau} = \frac{1 - e^{-z_\tau \tau}}{1 - R}$$

We can get one more simple rule of thumb by taking logs in Equation (7.1):

$$-(r_\tau + z_\tau)\tau = -r_\tau \tau + \log[e^{-\lambda_\tau^* \tau} + (1 - e^{-\lambda_\tau^* \tau})R]$$

or

$$z_\tau \tau = -\log[e^{-\lambda_\tau^* \tau} + (1 - e^{-\lambda_\tau^* \tau})R]$$

This expression can be solved numerically for λ_τ^*, or we can use the approximations $e^x \approx 1 + x$ and $\log(1 + x) \approx x$, so $e^{-\lambda_\tau^* \tau} + (1 - e^{-\lambda_\tau^* \tau})R \approx 1 - \lambda_\tau^* \tau + \lambda_\tau^* \tau R = 1 - \lambda_\tau^* \tau (1 - R)$. Therefore,

$$\log[1 - \lambda_\tau^* \tau (1 - R)] \approx -\lambda_\tau^* \tau (1 - R)$$

Putting these results together, we have

$$z_\tau \tau \approx \lambda_\tau^* \tau (1 - R) \Rightarrow \lambda_\tau^* \approx \frac{z_\tau}{1 - R}$$

The spread is approximately equal to the default probability times the LGD. The approximation works well when spreads or risk-neutral default probabilities are not too large.

Example 7.6 Continuing the example of a company with a five-year spread of 300 bps, with a recovery rate $R = 0.40$, we have a hazard rate of

$$\lambda_\tau^* \approx \frac{0.0300}{1 - 0.4} = 0.05$$

or 5 percent.

So far, we have defined spot hazard rates, which are implied by prices of risky and riskless bonds over different time intervals. But just as we can define spot and forward risk-free rates, we can define spot and forward hazard rates. A forward hazard rate from time T_1 to T_2 is the constant hazard rate over that interval. If $T_1 = 0$, it is identical to the spot hazard rate over $(0, T_2)$.

7.3.2 Time Scaling of Default Probabilities

We typically don't start our analysis with an estimate of the hazard rate. Rather, we start with an estimate of the probability of default π over a given time horizon, based on either the probability of default provided by a rating agency—the rightmost column of the transition matrix illustrated in Table 6.2—or a model, or on a market credit spread.

These estimates of π have a specific time horizon. The default probabilities provided by rating agencies for corporate debt typically have a horizon of one year. Default probabilities based on credit spreads have a time horizon equal to the time to maturity of the security from which they are derived. The time horizon of the estimated default probability may not match the time horizon we are interested in. For example, we may have a default probability based on a one-year transition matrix, but need a five-year default probability in the context of a longer-term risk analysis.

We can always convert a default probability from one time horizon to another by applying the algebra of hazard rates. But we can also use a default probability with one time horizon directly to estimate default probabilities with longer or shorter time horizons. Suppose, for example, we have an estimate of the one-year default probability π_1. From the definition of a constant hazard rate,

$$\pi_1 = 1 - e^{-\lambda}$$

we have

$$\lambda = \log(1 - \pi_1)$$

This gives us an identity

$$\pi_1 = 1 - e^{-\log(1-\pi_1)}$$

We can then approximate

$$\pi_t = 1 - (1 - \pi_1)^t$$

7.3.3 Credit Default Swaps

So far, we have derived one constant hazard rate using the prices of default-free and defaultable discount bonds. This is a good way to introduce the analytics of risk-neutral hazard rates, but a bit unrealistic, because corporations do not issue many zero-coupon bonds. Most corporate zero-coupon issues are commercial paper, which have a typical maturity under one year, and are issued by only a small number of highly rated "blue chip" companies. Commercial paper even has a distinct rating system.

In practice, hazard rates are usually estimated from the prices of CDS. These have a few advantages:

> *Standardization.* In contrast to most developed-country central governments, private companies do not issue bonds with the same cash flow structure and the same seniority in the firm's capital structure

at fixed calendar intervals. For many companies, however, CDS trading occurs regularly in standardized maturities of 1, 3, 5, 7, and 10 years, with the five-year point generally the most liquid.

Coverage. The universe of firms on which CDS are issued is large. Markit Partners, the largest collector and purveyor of CDS data, provides curves on about 2,000 corporate issuers globally, of which about 800 are domiciled in the United States.

Liquidity. When CDS on a company's bonds exist, they generally trade more heavily and with a tighter bid-offer spread than bond issues. The liquidity of CDS with different maturities usually differs less than that of bonds of a given issuer.

Figure 7.4 displays a few examples of CDS credit curves.

Hazard rates are typically obtained from CDS curves via a bootstrapping procedure. We'll see how it works using a detailed example. We first need more detail on how CDS contracts work. We also need to extend our discussion of the default probability function to include the possibility of time-varying hazard rates. CDS contracts with different terms to maturity can have quite different prices or spreads.

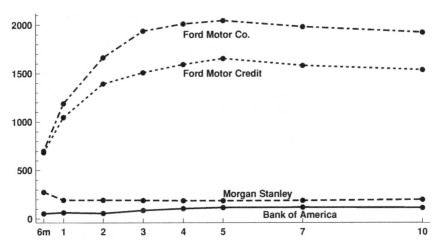

FIGURE 7.4 CDS Curves
CDS on senior unsecured debt as a function of tenor, expressed as an annualized CDS premium in basis points, July 1, 2008.
Source: Bloomberg Financial L.P.

To start, recall that in our simplified example above, the hazard rate was found by solving for the default probability that set the expected present value of the credit spread payments equal to the expected present value of the default loss. Similarly, to find the default probability function using CDS, we set the expected present value of the spread payments by the protection buyer equal to the expected present value of the protection seller's payments in the event of default.

The CDS contract is written on a specific *reference entity*, typically a firm or a government. The contract defines an event of default for the reference entity. In the event of default, the contract obliges the protection seller to pay the protection buyer the par amount of a deliverable bond of the reference entity; the protection buyer delivers the bond. The CDS contract specifies which of the reference entity's bonds are "deliverable," that is, are covered by the CDS.

In our discussion, we will focus on single-name corporate CDS, which create exposure to bankruptcy events of a single issuer of bonds such as a company or a sovereign entity. Most, but not all, of what we will say about how CDS work also applies to other types, such as CDS on credit indexes.

CDS are traded in spread terms. That is, when two traders make a deal, the price is expressed in terms of the spread premium the counterparty buying protection is to pay to the counterparty selling protection. CDS may trade "on spread" or "on basis." When the spread premium would otherwise be high, CDS trade points upfront, that is, the protection buyer pays the seller a market-determined percentage of the notional at the time of the trade, and the spread premium is set to 100 or 500 bps, called "100 running." Prior to the so-called "Big Bang" reform of CDS trading conventions that took place on March 13, 2009, only CDS on issuers with wide spreads traded "points up." The running spread was, in those cases, typically 500 bps. The reformed convention has all CDS trading points up, but with some paying 100 and others 500 bps running.

A CDS is a swap, and as such

- Generally, no principal or other cash flows change hands at the initiation of the contract. However, when CDS trade points upfront, a percent of the principal is paid by the protection buyer. This has an impact primarily on the counterparty credit risk of the contract rather than on its pricing, since there is always a spread premium, with no points up front paid, that is equivalent economically to any given market-adjusted number of points upfront plus a running spread.

There are generally exchanges of collateral when a CDS contract is created.

■ Under the terms of a CDS, there are agreed future cash flows. The protection buyer undertakes to make spread payments, called the *fee leg*, each quarter until the maturity date of the contract, unless and until there is a default event pertaining to the underlying name on which the CDS is written. The protection seller makes a payment, called the *contingent leg*, only if there is a default. It is equal to the estimated loss given default, that is, the notional less the recovery on the underlying bond.[2]

■ The pricing of the CDS, that is, the market-adjusted spread premium, is set so that the expected net present value of the CDS contract is zero. In other words, on the initiation date, the expected present value of the fee leg is equal to that of the contingent leg. If market prices change, the net present value becomes positive for one counterparty and negative for the other; that is, there is a mark-to-market gain and loss.

The CDS contract specifies whether the contract protects the senior or the subordinated debt of the underlying name. For companies that have issued both senior and subordinated debt, there may be CDS contracts of both kinds.

Often, risk-neutral hazard rates are calculated using the conventional assumption about recovery rates that $R = 0.40$. An estimate based on fundamental credit analysis of the specific firm can also be used. In some cases, a risk-neutral estimate is available based on the price of a *recovery swap* on the credit. A recovery swap is a contract in which, in the event of a default, one counterparty will pay the actual recovery as determined by the settlement procedure on the corresponding CDS, while the other counterparty will pay a fixed amount determined at initiation of the contract. Subject to counterparty risk, the counterparty promising that fixed amount is thus able to substitute a fixed recovery rate for an uncertain one. When those recovery swap prices can be observed, the fixed rate can be used as a risk-neutral recovery rate in building default probability distributions.

---

[2]There is a procedure for cash settlement of the protection seller's contingent obligations, standard since April 2009 as part of the "Big Bang," in which the recovery amount is determined by an auction mechanism. The seller may instead pay the buyer the notional underlying amount, while the buyer delivers a bond, from a list of acceptable or "deliverable" bonds issued by the underlying name rather than make a cash payment. In that case, it is up to the seller to gain the recovery value either through the bankruptcy process or in the marketplace.

7.3.4 Building Default Probability Curves

Next, let's extend our earlier analysis of hazard rates and default probability distributions to accommodate hazard rates that vary over time. We will add a time argument to our notation to indicate the time horizon to which it pertains. The conditional default probability at time t, the probability that the company will default over the next instant, given that it has survived up until time t, is denoted $\lambda(t)$, $t \in [0, \infty)$.

The default time distribution function is now expressed in terms of an integral in hazard rates. The probability of default over the interval $[0, t)$ is

$$\pi_t = 1 - e^{\int_0^t \lambda(s)ds} \tag{7.2}$$

If the hazard rate is constant, $\lambda(t) = \lambda$, $t \in [0, \infty)$, then Equation (7.2) reduces to our earlier expression $\pi_t = 1 - e^{\lambda t}$. In practice, we will be estimating and using hazard rates that are not constant, but also don't vary each instant. Rather, since we generally have the standard CDS maturities of 1, 3, 5, 7, and 10 years available, we will extract 5 piecewise constant hazard rates from the data:

$$\lambda(t) = \begin{Bmatrix} \lambda_1 \\ \lambda_2 \\ \lambda_3 \\ \lambda_4 \\ \lambda_5 \end{Bmatrix} \quad \text{for} \quad \begin{Bmatrix} 0 < t \le 1 \\ 1 < t \le 3 \\ 3 < t \le 5 \\ 5 < t \le 7 \\ 7 < t \end{Bmatrix}$$

The integral from which default probabilities are calculated via Equation (7.2) is then

$$\int_0^t \lambda(s)ds = \begin{Bmatrix} \lambda_1 t \\ \lambda_1 + (t-1)\lambda_2 \\ \lambda_1 + 2\lambda_2 + (t-3)\lambda_3 \\ \lambda_1 + 2\lambda_2 + 2\lambda_3 + (t-5)\lambda_4 \\ \lambda_1 + 2\lambda_2 + 2\lambda_3 + 3\lambda_4 + (t-7)\lambda_5 \end{Bmatrix} \quad \text{for} \quad \begin{Bmatrix} 0 < t \le 1 \\ 1 < t \le 3 \\ 3 < t \le 5 \\ 5 < t \le 7 \\ 7 < t \end{Bmatrix}$$

Now, let's look at the expected present value of each CDS leg. Denote by s_τ the spread premium on a τ-year CDS on a particular company. The protection buyer will pay the spread in quarterly installments if and only if the credit is still alive on the payment date. The probability of survival up to date t is π_t, so we can express this expected present value, in dollars per dollar of underlying notional, as

$$\frac{1}{4 \times 10^3} s_\tau \sum_{u=1}^{4\tau} p_{0.25u} \left(1 - \pi_{0.25u}\right)$$

where p_t is the price of a risk-free zero-coupon bond maturing at time t. We will use a discount curve based on interest-rate swaps. The summation index u takes on integer values, but since we are adding up the present values of quarterly cash flows, we divide u by 4 to get back to time measured in years.

There is one more wrinkle in the fee leg. In the event of default, the protection buyer must pay the portion of the spread premium that accrued between the time of the last quarterly payment and the default date. This payment isn't included in the summation above. The amount and timing is uncertain, but the convention is to approximate it as half the quarterly premium, payable on the first payment date following default. The implicit assumption is that the default, if it occurs at all, occurs midway through the quarter. The probability of having to make this payment on date t is equal to $\pi_{t-0.25} - \pi_t$, the probability of default during the interval $(t - \frac{1}{4}, t]$. This probability is equal to the probability of surviving to time $(t - \frac{1}{4}]$ minus the smaller probability of surviving to time t.

Taking this so-called fee accrual term into account, the expected present value of the fee leg becomes

$$\frac{1}{4 \times 10^4} s_\tau \sum_{u=1}^{4\tau} p_{0.25u} \left[(1 - \pi_{0.25u}) + \frac{1}{2} \left(\pi_{0.25(u-1)} - \pi_{0.25u} \right) \right]$$

Next, we calculate the expected present value of the contingent leg. If a default occurs during the quarter ending at time t, the present value of the contingent payment is $(1 - R)p_t$ per dollar of notional. We assume that the contingent payment is made on the quarterly cash flow date following the default. The expected present value of this payment is obtained by multiplying this present value by the probability of default during the quarter:

$$(1 - R)p_t \left(\pi_{t-0.25} - \pi_t \right)$$

The expected present value of the contingent leg is therefore equal to the sum of these expected present values over the life of the CDS contract:

$$(1 - R) \sum_{u=1}^{4\tau} p_{0.25u} \left(\pi_{0.25(u-1)} - \pi_{0.25u} \right)$$

The fair market CDS spread is the number s_τ that equalizes these two payment streams, that is, solves

$$\frac{1}{4 \times 10^4} \sum_{u=1}^{4\tau} p_{0.25u} \left[(1 - \pi_{0.25u}) + \frac{1}{2} \left(\pi_{0.25(u-1)} - \pi_{0.25u} \right) \right]$$

$$= (1 - R) \sum_{u=1}^{4\tau} p_{0.25u} \left(\pi_{0.25(u-1)} - \pi_{0.25u} \right) \qquad (7.3)$$

Now we're ready to estimate the default probability distribution. To solve Equation (7.3), the market must "have in its mind" an estimate of the default curve, that is the π_t. Of course, it doesn't: The s_τ are found by supply and demand. But once we observe the spreads set by the market, we can infer the π_t by backing them out of Equation (7.3) via a bootstrapping procedure, which we now describe.

The data we require are swap curve interest data, so that we can estimate a swap discount curve, and a set of CDS spreads s_τ on the same name and with the same seniority, but with different terms to maturity. We learned in Chapter 4 how to generate a swap curve from observation on money-market and swap rates, so we will assume that we can substitute specific numbers for all the discount factors p_t.

Let's start by finding the default curve for a company for which we have only a single CDS spread, for a term, say, of five years. This will result in a single hazard rate estimate. We need default probabilities for the quarterly dates $t = 0.25, 0.50, \ldots, 5$. They are a function of the as-yet unknown hazard rate λ: $\pi_t = e^{-\lambda t}, t > 0$. Substituting this, the five-year CDS spread, the recovery rate and the discount factors into the CDS valuation function (7.3) gives us

$$\frac{1}{4 \times 10^4} s_\tau \sum_{u=1}^{4\tau} p_{0.25u} \left[e^{-\lambda \frac{u}{4}} + \frac{1}{2} \left(e^{-\lambda \frac{u-1}{4}} - e^{-\lambda \frac{u}{4}} \right) \right]$$

$$= (1 - R) \sum_{u=1}^{4\tau} p_{0.25u} \left(e^{-\lambda \frac{u-1}{4}} - e^{-\lambda \frac{u}{4}} \right)$$

with $\tau = 5$. This is an equation in one unknown variable that can be solved numerically for λ.

Example 7.7 We compute a constant hazard rate for Merrill Lynch as of October 1, 2008, using the closing five-year CDS spread of 445 bps. We assume a recovery rate $R = 0.40$. To simplify matters, we also assume a flat swap curve, with a continuously compounded spot rate of 4.5 percent for all maturities, so the discount factor for a cash flow t years in the future is $e^{0.045t}$. As long as this constant swap rate is reasonably close to the actual swap rate prevailing on October 1, 2008, this has only a small effect on the numerical results.

With $\tau = 5, s_\tau = 445, R = 0.40$, we have

$$\frac{445}{4 \times 10^4} \sum_{u=1}^{4 \cdot 5} e^{0.045\frac{u}{4}} \left[e^{-\lambda\frac{u}{4}} + \frac{1}{2} \left(e^{-\lambda\frac{u-1}{4}} - e^{-\lambda\frac{u}{4}} \right) \right]$$

$$= 0.60 \sum_{u=1}^{4 \cdot 5} e^{0.045\frac{u}{4}} \left(e^{-\lambda\frac{u-1}{4}} - e^{-\lambda\frac{u}{4}} \right)$$

This equation can be solved numerically to obtain $\lambda = 0.0741688$.

The bootstrapping procedure is a bit more complicated, since it involves a sequence of steps. But each step is similar to the calculation we just carried out for a single CDS spread and a single hazard rate. The best way to explain it is with an example.

Example 7.8 We will compute the default probability curve for Merrill Lynch as of October 1, 2008. The closing CDS spreads on that date for each CDS maturity were

i	τ_i(yrs)	s_{τ_i}(bps/yr)	λ_i
1	1	576	0.09600
2	3	490	0.07303
3	5	445	0.05915
4	7	395	0.03571
5	10	355	0.03416

The table above also displays the estimated forward hazard rates, the extraction of which we now describe in detail. We continue to assume a recovery rate $R = 0.40$ and a flat swap curve, with the discount function $p_t = e^{0.045t}$.

At each step i, we need quarterly default probabilities over the interval $(0, \tau_i], i = 1, \ldots, 5$, some or all of which will still be unknown when we carry out that step. We progressively "fill in" the integral in Equation (7.2) as the bootstrapping process moves out the curve. In the first step, we find

$$\pi_t = 1 - e^{\lambda_1 t} \qquad t \in (0, \tau_1]$$

We start by solving for the first hazard rate λ_1. We need the discount factors for the quarterly dates $t = \frac{1}{4}, \frac{1}{2}, \frac{3}{4}, 1$, and the CDS spread with the shortest maturity, τ_1. We solve this equation in one unknown for λ_1:

$$\frac{1}{4 \times 10^3} s_{\tau_1} \sum_{u=1}^{4\tau_1} p_{0.25u} \left[e^{-\lambda_1 \frac{u}{4}} + \frac{1}{2} \left(e^{-\lambda_1 \frac{u-1}{4}} - e^{-\lambda_1 \frac{u}{4}} \right) \right]$$

$$= (1 - R) \sum_{u=1}^{4\tau_1} p_{0.25u} \left(e^{-\lambda_1 \frac{u-1}{4}} - e^{-\lambda_1 \frac{u}{4}} \right)$$

With $\tau_1 = 1$, $s_{\tau_1} = 576$, and $R = 0.40$, this becomes

$$\frac{576}{4 \times 10^3} \sum_{u=1}^{4} e^{0.045 \frac{u}{4}} \left[e^{-\lambda_1 \frac{u}{4}} + \frac{1}{2} \left(e^{-\lambda_1 \frac{u-1}{4}} - e^{-\lambda_1 \frac{u}{4}} \right) \right]$$

$$= 0.60 \sum_{u=1}^{4} e^{0.045 \frac{u}{4}} \left(e^{-\lambda_1 \frac{u-1}{4}} - e^{-\lambda_1 \frac{u}{4}} \right)$$

which we can solve numerically for λ_1, obtaining $\lambda_1 = 0.0960046$. Once the default probabilities are substituted back in, the fee and the contingent legs of the swap are found to each have a fair value of \$0.0534231 per dollar of notional principal protection.

In the next step, we extract λ_2 from the data, again by setting up an equation that we can solve numerically for λ_2. We now need quarterly default probabilities and discount factors over the interval $(0, \tau_2] = (0, 3]$. For any t in this interval,

$$\pi_t = e^{-\int_0^t \lambda(s)ds} = \left\{ \begin{array}{l} e^{-\lambda_1 t} \\ e^{-[\lambda_1 + (t-1)\lambda_2]} \end{array} \right\} \quad \text{for} \quad \left\{ \begin{array}{l} 0 < t \leq 1 \\ 1 < t \leq 3 \end{array} \right\}$$

The default probabilities for $t \leq \tau_1 = 1$ are known, since they use only λ_1.

Substitute these probabilities, as well as the discount factors, recovery rate, and the three-year CDS spread into the expression for CDS fair value to get:

$$\frac{1}{4 \times 10^3} s_{\tau_2} \sum_{u=1}^{4\tau_1} p_{0.25u} \left[e^{-\lambda_1 \frac{u}{4}} + \frac{1}{2} \left(e^{-\lambda_1 \frac{u-1}{4}} - e^{-\lambda_1 \frac{u}{4}} \right) \right]$$

$$+ \frac{1}{4 \times 10^3} s_{\tau_2} e^{-\lambda_1 \tau_1} \sum_{u=4\tau_1+1}^{4\tau_2} p_{0.25u} \left[e^{-\lambda_2\left(\frac{u}{4}-\tau_1\right)} + \frac{1}{2} \left(e^{\lambda_2\left[\frac{u-1}{4}-\tau_1\right]} - e^{\lambda_2\left(\frac{u}{4}-\tau_1\right)} \right) \right]$$

$$= (1-R) \sum_{u=1}^{4\tau_1} p_{0.25u} \left(e^{-\lambda_1 \frac{u-1}{4}} - e^{-\lambda_1 \frac{u}{4}} \right)$$

$$+ (1-R)e^{-\lambda_1 \tau_1} \sum_{u=4\tau_1+1}^{4\tau_2} p_{0.25u} \left(e^{-\lambda_2\left[\frac{u-1}{4}-\tau_1\right]} - e^{-\lambda_2\left(\frac{u}{4}-\tau_1\right)} \right)$$

and solve numerically for λ_2.

Notice that the first term on each side of the above equation is a known number at this point in the bootstrapping process, since the default probabilities for horizons of one year or less are known. Once we substitute the known quantities into the above equation, we have

$$\frac{490}{4 \times 10^3} \sum_{u=1}^{4} e^{0.045\frac{u}{4}} \left[e^{-0.0960046\frac{u}{4}} + \frac{1}{2} \left(e^{-0.0960046\frac{u-1}{4}} - e^{-0.0960046\frac{u}{4}} \right) \right]$$

$$+ \frac{490}{4 \times 10^3} e^{-0.0960046} \sum_{u=5}^{4\cdot3} e^{0.045\frac{u}{4}} \left\{ e^{-\lambda_2\left(\frac{u}{4}-1\right)} + \frac{1}{2} \left[e^{\lambda_2\left(\frac{u-1}{4}-1\right)} - e^{\lambda_2\left(\frac{u}{4}-1\right)} \right] \right\}$$

$$= 0.04545$$

$$+ \frac{490}{4 \times 10^3} e^{-0.0960046} \sum_{u=5}^{4\cdot3} e^{0.045\frac{u}{4}} \left\{ e^{-\lambda_2\left(\frac{u}{4}-1\right)} + \frac{1}{2} \left[e^{\lambda_2\left(\frac{u-1}{4}-1\right)} - e^{\lambda_2\left(\frac{u}{4}-1\right)} \right] \right\}$$

$$= 0.60 \sum_{u=1}^{4} e^{0.045\frac{u}{4}} \left(e^{-0.0960046\frac{u-1}{4}} - e^{-0.0960046\frac{u}{4}} \right)$$

$$+ 0.60 \sum_{u=5}^{4\cdot3} e^{0.045\frac{u}{4}} \left[e^{\lambda_2\left(\frac{u-1}{4}-1\right)} - e^{\lambda_2\left(\frac{u}{4}-1\right)} \right]$$

$$= 0.05342 + 0.60 \sum_{u=5}^{4\cdot3} e^{0.045\frac{u}{4}} \left[e^{\lambda_2\left(\frac{u-1}{4}-1\right)} - e^{\lambda_2\left(\frac{u}{4}-1\right)} \right]$$

which can be solved numerically to obtain $\lambda_2 = 0.0730279$.

Let's spell out one more step explicitly and extract λ_3 from the data. The quarterly default probabilities and discount factors we now need cover the interval $(0, \tau_3) = (0, 5)$. For any t in this interval,

$$\pi_t = e^{-\int_0^t \lambda(s)ds} = \left\{ \begin{array}{l} e^{-\lambda_1 t} \\ e^{-[\lambda_1 + (t-1)\lambda_2]} \\ e^{-[\lambda_1 + 2\lambda_2 + (t-3)\lambda_3]} \end{array} \right\} \quad \text{for} \quad \left\{ \begin{array}{l} 0 < t \le 1 \\ 1 < t \le 3 \\ 3 < t \le 5 \end{array} \right\}$$

The default probabilities for $t \le \tau_2 = 3$ are known, since they are functions of λ_1 and λ_2 alone, which are known after the second step.

Now we use the five-year CDS spread in the expression for CDS fair value to set up:

$$\frac{s_{\tau_3}}{4 \times 10^3} \sum_{u=1}^{4\tau_1} p_{0.25u} \left[e^{-\lambda_1 \frac{u}{4}} + \frac{1}{2} \left(e^{-\lambda_1 \frac{u-1}{4}} - e^{-\lambda_1 \frac{u}{4}} \right) \right]$$

$$+ \frac{s_{\tau_3}}{4 \times 10^3} e^{-\lambda_1 \tau_1} \sum_{u=4\tau_1+1}^{4\tau_2} p_{0.25u} \left[e^{-\lambda_2 \frac{u}{4}} + \frac{1}{2} \left(e^{-\lambda_2 \frac{u-1}{4}} - e^{-\lambda_2 \frac{u}{4}} \right) \right]$$

$$+ \frac{s_{\tau_3}}{4 \times 10^3} e^{-[\lambda_1 \tau_1 + \lambda_2 (\tau_2 - \tau_1)]} \sum_{u=4\tau_2+1}^{4\tau_3} p_{0.25u} \left[e^{-\lambda_3 \frac{u}{4}} + \frac{1}{2} \left(e^{\lambda_3 \frac{u-1}{4}} - e^{\lambda_3 \frac{u}{4}} \right) \right]$$

$$= (1 - R) \sum_{u=1}^{4\tau_1} p_{0.25u} \left(e^{-\lambda_1 \frac{u-1}{4}} - e^{-\lambda_1 \frac{u}{4}} \right)$$

$$+ (1 - R) e^{-\lambda_1 \tau_1} \sum_{u=4\tau_1+1}^{4\tau_2} p_{0.25u} \left(e^{-\lambda_2 \frac{u-1}{4}} - e^{-\lambda_2 \frac{u}{4}} \right)$$

$$+ (1 - R) e^{-[\lambda_1 \tau_1 + \lambda_2 (\tau_2 - \tau_1)]} \sum_{u=4\tau_2+1}^{4\tau_3} p_{0.25u} \left(e^{\lambda_3 \frac{u-1}{4}} - e^{\lambda_3 \frac{u}{4}} \right)$$

Once again, at this point in the bootstrapping process, since the default probabilities for horizons of three years or less are known, the first two terms on each side of the equals sign are known quantities. And once we have substituted them, we have

$$0.10974$$

$$+ \frac{445}{4 \times 10^3} e^{-[\lambda_1 + 2\lambda_2]} \sum_{u=4\tau_2+1}^{4\tau_3} p_{0.25u} \left\{ e^{-\lambda_3\left(\frac{u}{4}-1\right)} + \frac{1}{2}\left[e^{\lambda_3\left(\frac{u-1}{4}-1\right)} - e^{\lambda_3\left(\frac{u}{4}-1\right)} \right] \right\}$$

$$= 0.12083 + 0.60 \sum_{u=4\tau_2+1}^{4\tau_3} p_{0.25u} \left[e^{\lambda_3\left(\frac{u-1}{4}-1\right)} - e^{\lambda_3\left(\frac{u}{4}-1\right)} \right]$$

which can be solved numerically to obtain $\lambda_3 = 0.05915$.

The induction process should now be clear. It is illustrated in Figure 7.4. With our run of five CDS maturities, we repeat the process twice more. The intermediate results are tabulated by step in the table below. Each row in the table displays the present expected value of either leg of the CDS after finding the contemporaneous hazard rate, and the values of the fee and contingent legs up until that step. Note that last period's value of either leg becomes the next period's value of contingent leg payments in previous periods:

i	Either leg → τ_i	Fee leg → τ_{i-1}	Contingent leg → τ_{i-1}
1	0.05342	0.00000	0.00000
2	0.12083	0.04545	0.05342
3	0.16453	0.10974	0.12083
4	0.18645	0.14605	0.16453
5	0.21224	0.16757	0.18645

The CDS in our example did not trade points up, in contrast to the standard convention since 2009. However, Equation (7.3) also provides an easy conversion between pure spread quotes and points up quotes on CDS.

To keep things simple, suppose that both the swap and the hazard rate curves are flat. The swap rate is a continuously compounded r for any term to maturity, and the hazard rate is λ for any horizon. Suppose further that the running spread is 500 bps. The fair market CDS spread will then be a constant s for any term τ. From Equation (7.3), the expected present value of all the payments by the protection buyer must equal the expected present

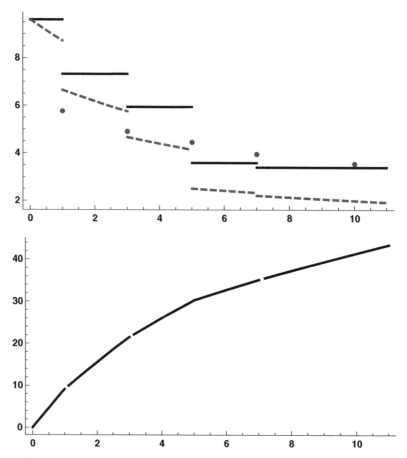

FIGURE 7.5   Estimation of Default Curves
Upper panel shows the CDS spreads from which the hazard rates are computed as dots, the estimated hazard rates as a step function (solid plot). The default density is shown as a dashed plot.
Lower panel shows the default distribution. Notice the discontinuities of slope as we move from one hazard rate to the next.

value of loss given default, so the points upfront and the constant hazard rate must satisfy

$$\frac{\text{points upfront}}{100} = (1 - R) \sum_{u=1}^{4\tau} e^{-r\frac{u}{4}} \left(e^{-\lambda \frac{u-1}{4}} - e^{-\lambda \frac{u}{4}} \right)$$

$$- \frac{500}{4 \times 10^4} \sum_{u=1}^{4\tau} e^{-r\frac{u}{4}} \left[e^{-\lambda \frac{u}{4}} + \frac{1}{2} \left(e^{-\lambda \frac{u-1}{4}} - e^{-\lambda \frac{u}{4}} \right) \right] \quad (7.4)$$

Once we have a hazard rate, we can solve Equation (7.4) for the spread from the points upfront, and vice versa.

7.3.5 The Slope of Default Probability Curves

Spread curves, and thus hazard curves, may be upward- or downward-sloping. An upward-sloping spread curve leads to a default distribution that has a relatively flat slope for shorter horizons, but a steeper slope for more distant ones. The intuition is that the credit has a better risk-neutral chance of surviving the next few years, since its hazard rate and thus unconditional default probability has a relatively low starting point. But even so, its marginal default probability, that is, the conditional probability of defaulting in future years, will fall less quickly or even rise for some horizons.

A downward-sloping curve, in contrast, has a relatively steep slope at short horizons, but flattens out more quickly at longer horizons. The intuition here is that, if the firm survives the early, "dangerous" years, it has a good chance of surviving for a long time.

An example is shown in Figure 7.6. Both the upward- and downward-sloping spread curves have a five-year spread of 400 basis points. The downward-sloping curve corresponds to an unconditional default probability that is higher than that of the upward-sloping curve for short horizons, but significantly lower than that of the upward-sloping curve for longer horizons.

Spread curves are typically gently upward sloping. If the market believes that a firm has a stable, low default probability that is unlikely to change for the foreseeable future, the firm's spread curve would be flat if it reflected default expectations only. However, spreads also reflect some compensation for risk. For longer horizons, there is a greater likelihood of an unforeseen and unforeseeable change in the firm's situation and a rise in its default probability. The increased spread for longer horizons is in part a risk premium that compensates for this possibility.

Downward-sloping spread curves are unusual, a sign that the market views a credit as distressed, but became prevalent during the subprime crisis. Figure 7.7 displays an example typical for financial intermediaries, that of Morgan Stanley (ticker MS), one of the five large broker-dealers not associated with a large commercial bank within a bank holding company during the period preceding the crisis. (The other large broker-dealers were Bear Stearns, Lehman Brothers, Merrill Lynch, and Goldman Sachs.) Before the crisis, the MS spread curve was upward-sloping. The level of spreads was, in retrospect, remarkably low; the five-year CDS spread on Sep. 25, 2006 was a mere 21 basis points, suggesting the market considered a Morgan Stanley bankruptcy a highly unlikely event.

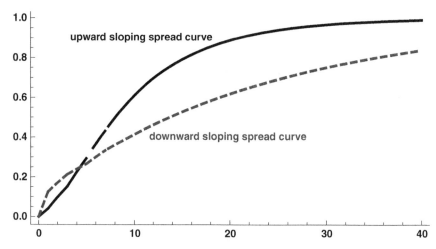

Graph displays cumulative default distributions computed from these CDS curves, in basis points:

Term	Upward	Downward
1	250	800
3	325	500
5	400	400
7	450	375
10	500	350

A constant swap rate of 4.5 percent and a recovery rate of 40 percent were used in extracting hazard rates.

FIGURE 7.6   Spread Curve Slope and Default Distribution

     The bankruptcy of Lehman Brothers cast doubt on the ability of any of the remaining broker-dealers to survive, and also showed that it was entirely possible that senior creditors of these institutions would suffer severe credit losses. Morgan Stanley in particular among the remaining broker-dealers looked very vulnerable. Bear Stearns had already disappeared; Merrill Lynch appeared likely to be acquired by a large commercial bank, Bank of America; and Goldman Sachs had received some fresh capital and was considered less exposed to credit losses than its peers.

     By September 25, 2008, the five-year CDS spread on MS senior unsecured debt had risen to 769 basis points. Its 6-month CDS spread was more than 500 basis points higher at 1,325 bps. At a recovery rate of 40 percent, this corresponded to about a 12 percent probability of bankruptcy over the

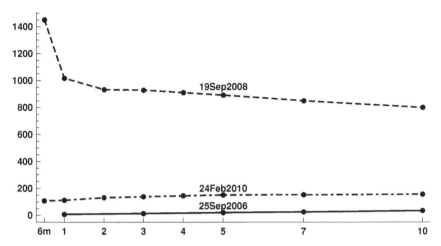

FIGURE 7.7 Morgan Stanley CDS Curves, select dates
Morgan Stanley senior unsecured CDS spreads, basis points.
Source: Bloomberg Financial L.P.

next half-year. The one-year spread was over 150 times larger than two years earlier. Short selling of MS common equity was also widely reported, even after the company announced on September 25 that the Federal Reserve Board had approved its application to become a bank holding company.

One year later, the level of spreads had declined significantly, though they remained much higher than before the crisis. On Feb. 24, 2010, the MS five-year senior unsecured CDS spread was 147 basis points, and the curve was gently upward-sloping again.

7.4 SPREAD RISK

Spread risk is the risk of loss from changes in the pricing of credit-risky securities. Although it only affects credit portfolios, it is closer in nature to market than to credit risk, since it is generated by changes in prices rather than changes in the credit state of the securities.

7.4.1 Mark-to-Market of a CDS

We can use the analytics of the previous section to compute the effect on the mark-to-market value of a CDS of a change in the market-clearing premium. At initiation, the mark-to-market value of the CDS is zero; neither counterparty owes the other anything. If the spread increases, the premium paid by the fixed-leg counterparty increases. This causes a gain to existing fixed-leg payers, who in retrospect got into their positions cheap, and a loss to the contingent-leg parties, who are receiving less premium than if they had entered the position after the spread widening. This mark-to-market effect is the spread01 of the CDS.

To compute the mark-to-market, we carry out the same steps needed to compute the spread01 of a fixed-rate bond. In this case, however, rather than increasing and decreasing one spread number, the z-spread, by 0.5 bps, we carry out a parallel shift up and down of the entire CDS curve by 0.5 bps. This is similar to the procedure we carried out in computing DV01 for a default-free bond, in which we shifted the entire spot curve up or down by 0.5 bps.

For each shift of the CDS curve away from its initial level, we recompute the hazard rate curve, and with the shocked hazard rate curve we then recompute the value of the CDS. The difference between the two shocked values is the spread01 of the CDS.

7.4.2 Spread Volatility

Fluctuations in the prices of credit-risky bonds due to the market assessment of the value of default and credit transition risk, as opposed to changes in risk-free rates, are expressed in changes in credit spreads. Spread risk therefore encompasses both the market's expectations of credit risk events and the credit spread it requires in equilibrium to put up with credit risk. The most common way of measuring spread risk is via the *spread volatility* or "spread vol," the degree to which spreads fluctuate over time. Spread vol is the standard deviation—historical or expected—of changes in spread, generally measured in basis points per day.

Figure 7.8 illustrates the calculations with the spread volatility of five-year CDS on Citigroup senior U.S. dollar-denominated bonds. We return to the example of Citigroup debt in our discussions of asset price behavior during financial crises in Chapter 14. The enormous range of variation and potential for extreme spread volatility is clear from the top panel, which plots the spread levels in basis points. The center panel shows daily spread changes (also in bps). The largest changes occur in the late summer and early autumn of 2008, as the collapses of Fannie Mae and Freddie Mac, and then of Lehman, shook confidence in the solvency of large intermediaries, and Citigroup in particular. Many of the spread changes during this period are extreme outliers from the average—as measured by the root mean square—over the entire period from 2006 to 2010.

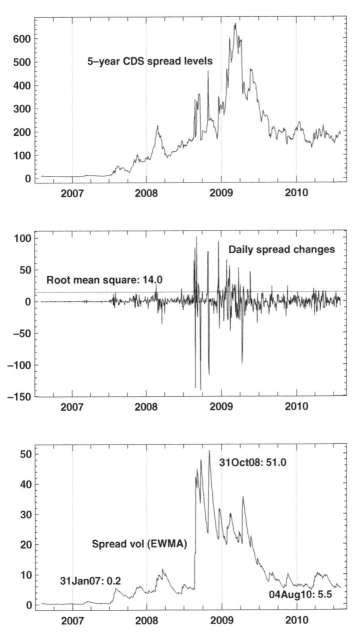

FIGURE 7.8   Measuring Spread Volatility: Citigroup Spreads 2006–2010
Citigroup 5-year CDS spreads, August 2, 2006, to September 2, 2010. All data
expressed in bps.
Source: Bloomberg Financial L.P.
Upper panel: Spread levels.
Center panel: Daily spread changes.
Lower panel: Daily EWMA estimate of spread volatility at a daily rate.

The bottom panel plots a rolling daily spread volatility estimate, using the EWMA weighting scheme of Chapter 3. The calculations are carried out using the recursive form Equation (3.2), with the root mean square of the first 200 observations of spread changes as the starting point. The volatility is expressed in basis points per day. A spread volatility of, say, 10 bps, means that, if you believe spread changes are normally distributed, you would assign a probability of about 2 out of 3 to the event that tomorrow's spread level is within ±10 bps of today's level. For the early part of the period, the spread volatility is close to zero, a mere quarter of a basis point, but spiked to over 50 bps in the fall of 2008.

FURTHER READING

Klugman, Panjer, and Willmot (2008) provides an accessible introduction to hazard rate models. Litterman and Iben (1991); Berd, Mashal, and Wang (2003); and O'Kane and Sen (2004) apply hazard rate models to extract default probabilities. Schönbucher (2003), Chapters 4–5 and 7, is a clear exposition of the algebra.

Duffie (1999), Hull and White (2000), and O'Kane and Turnbull (2003) provide overviews of CDS pricing. Houweling and Vorst (2005) is an empirical study that finds hazard rate models to be reasonably accurate.

See Markit Partners (2009) and Senior Supervisors Group (2009a) on the 2009 change in CDS conventions.

CHAPTER 8

Portfolio Credit Risk

I n this chapter, we extend the study of credit risk to portfolios containing several credit-risky securities. We begin by introducing the most important additional concept we need in this context, default correlation, and then discuss approaches to measuring portfolio credit risk.

A portfolio of credit-risky securities may contain bonds, commercial paper, off-balance-sheet exposures such as guarantees, as well as positions in credit derivatives such as credit default swaps (CDS). A typical portfolio may contain many different obligors, but may also contain exposures to different parts of one obligor's capital structure, such as preferred shares and senior debt. All of these distinctions can be of great importance in accurately measuring portfolio credit risk, even if the models we present here abstract from many of them.

In this chapter, we focus on two approaches to measuring portfolio credit risk. The first employs the factor model developed in Chapter 6, the key feature of which is latent factors with normally distributed returns. Conditional on the values taken on by that set of factors, defaults are independent. There is a single future time horizon for the analysis. We will specialize the model even further to include only default events, and not credit migration, and only a single factor. In the CreditMetrics approach, this model is used to compute the distribution of credit migrations as well as default. One could therefore label the approach described in this chapter as "default-mode CreditMetrics." An advantage of this model is that factors can be related to real-world phenomena, such as equity prices, providing an empirical anchor for the model. The model is also tractable.

The second approach we take in this chapter uses simulation, together with the intensity models developed in Chapters 6 and 7, to measure credit portfolio risk. We sketch the theoretical basis for the approach, which employs a mathematical structure called a copula, and offer a simple example. Chapter 9 provides a full-blown application of the approach to valuation and risk measurement of securitizations.

8.1 DEFAULT CORRELATION

In modeling a single credit-risky position, the elements of risk and return that we can take into consideration are

- The probability of default
- The loss given default (LGD), the complement of the value of recovery in the event of default
- The probability and severity of rating migration (nondefault credit deterioration)
- Spread risk, the risk of changes in market spreads for a given rating
- For distressed debt, the possibility of restructuring the firm's debt, either by negotiation among the owners of the firm and of its liabilities, or through the bankruptcy process. Restructuring opens the possibility of losses to owners of particular classes of debt as a result of a negotiated settlement or a judicial ruling

To understand credit portfolio risk, we introduce the additional concept of *default correlation*, which drives the likelihood of having multiple defaults in a portfolio of debt issued by several obligors. To focus on the issue of default correlation, we'll take default probabilities and recovery rates as given and ignore the other sources of return just listed.

8.1.1 Defining Default Correlation

The simplest framework for understanding default correlation is to think of

- Two firms (or countries, if we have positions in sovereign debt)
- With probabilities of default (or restructuring) π_1 and π_2
- Over some time horizon τ
- And a joint default probability—the probability that both default over τ—equal to π_{12}

This can be thought of as the distribution of the product of two Bernoulli-distributed random variables x_i, with four possible outcomes. We must, as in the single-firm case, be careful to define the Bernoulli trials as default or solvency over a specific time interval τ. In a portfolio credit model, that time interval is the same for all the credits in the book.

We have a new parameter π_{12} in addition to the single-name default probabilities. And it is a genuinely new parameter, a primitive: It is what it is, and isn't computed from π_1 and π_2, *unless* we specify it by positing that defaults are independent.

Since the value 1 corresponds to the occurrence of default, the product of the two Bernoulli variables equals 0 for three of the outcomes—those included in the event that at most one firm defaults—and 1 for the joint default event:

Outcome	x_1	x_2	$x_1 x_2$	Probability
No default	0	0	0	$1 - \pi_1 - \pi_2 + \pi_{12}$
Firm 1 only defaults	1	0	0	$\pi_1 - \pi_{12}$
Firm 2 only defaults	0	1	0	$\pi_2 - \pi_{12}$
Both firms default	1	1	1	π_{12}

These are proper outcomes; they are distinct, and their probabilities add up to 1. The probability of the event that at least one firm defaults can be found as either 1 minus the probability of the first outcome, or the sum of the probabilities of the last three outcomes.

$$\mathbf{P}\left[\text{Firm 1 or Firm 2 or both default}\right] = \pi_1 + \pi_2 - \pi_{12}$$

We can compute the moments of the Bernoulli variates:

- The means of the two Bernoulli-distributed default processes are

$$\mathbf{E}\left[x_i\right] = \pi_i, \qquad i = 1, 2$$

- The expected value of the product—representing joint default—is $\mathbf{E}\left[x_1 x_2\right] = \pi_{12}$.
- The variances are

$$\mathbf{E}\left[x_i\right]^2 - \left(\mathbf{E}\left[x_i\right]\right)^2 = \pi_i(1 - \pi_i) \qquad i = 1, 2$$

- The covariance is

$$\mathbf{E}\left[x_1 x_2\right] - \mathbf{E}\left[x_1\right]\mathbf{E}\left[x_2\right] = \pi_{12} - \pi_1 \pi_2$$

- The default correlation, finally, is

$$\rho_{12} = \frac{\pi_{12} - \pi_1 \pi_2}{\sqrt{\pi_1(1 - \pi_1)}\sqrt{\pi_2(1 - \pi_2)}} \tag{8.1}$$

We can treat the default correlation, rather than joint default probability, as the primitive parameter and use it to find the joint default probability:

$$\pi_{12} = \rho_{12}\sqrt{\pi_1(1-\pi_1)}\sqrt{\pi_2(1-\pi_2)} + \pi_1\pi_2$$

The joint default probability if the two default events are independent is $\pi_{12} = \pi_1\pi_2$, and the default correlation is $\rho_{12} = 0$. If $\rho_{12} \neq 0$, there is a linear relationship between the probability of joint default and the default correlation: The larger the "excess" of π_{12} over the joint default probability under independence, $\pi_1\pi_2$, the higher the correlation. Once we specify or estimate the π_i, we can nail down the joint default probability either directly or by specifying the default correlation. Most models, including those set out in this chapter, specify a default correlation rather than a joint default probability.

Example 8.1 (Default Correlation)   Consider a pair of credits, one BBB+ and the other BBB-rated, with $\pi_1 = 0.0025$ and $\pi_2 = 0.0125$. If the defaults are uncorrelated, then $\pi_{12} = 0.000031$, less than a third of a basis point. If, however, the default correlation is 5 percent, then $\pi_{12} = 0.000309$, nearly 10 times as great, and at 3 basis points, no longer negligible.

In a portfolio containing more than two credits, we have more than one joint default probability and default correlation. And, in contrast to the two-credit portfolio, we cannot specify the full distribution of defaults based just on the default probabilities and the pairwise correlations or joint default probabilities. To specify all the possible outcomes in a three-credit portfolio, we need the three single-default probabilities, the three two-default probabilities, and the no-default and three-default probabilities, a total of eight. But we have only seven conditions: the three single-default probabilities, three pairwise correlations, and the constraint that all the probabilities add up to unity. It's the latter constraint that ties out the probabilities when there are only two credits. With a number of credits $n > 2$, we have 2^n different events, but only $n + 1 + \frac{n(n-1)}{2}$ conditions:

n	2^n	$n + 1 + \frac{n(n-1)}{2}$
2	4	4
3	8	7
4	16	11
10	1,024	56

We can't therefore build an entire credit portfolio model solely on default correlations. But doing so is a pragmatic alternative to estimating or stipulating, say, the 1,024 probabilities required to fully specify the distribution of a portfolio of 10 credits.

Even if all the requisite parameters could be identified, the number would be quite large, since we would have to define a potentially large number of pairwise correlations. If there are N credits in the portfolio, we need to define N default probabilities and N recovery rates. In addition, we require $N(N-1)$ pairwise correlations. In modeling credit risk, we often set all of the pairwise correlations equal to a single parameter. But that parameter must then be non-negative, in order to avoid correlation matrices that are not positive-definite and results that make no sense: Not all the firms' event of default can be negatively correlated with one another.

Example 8.2 Consider a portfolio containing five positions:

1. A five-year senior secured bond issued by Ford Motor Company
2. A five-year subordinate unsecured bond issued by Ford Motor Company
3. Long protection in a five-year CDS on Ford Motor Credit Company
4. A five-year senior bond issued by General Motors Company
5. A 10-year syndicated term loan to Starwood Resorts

If we set a horizon for measuring credit risk of $\tau = 1$ year, we need to have four default probabilities and 12 pairwise default correlations, since there are only four distinct corporate entities represented in the portfolio. However, since the two Ford Motor Company bonds are at two different places in the capital structure, they will have two different recovery rates.

This example has omitted certain types of positions that will certainly often occur in real-world portfolios. Some of their features don't fit well into the portfolio credit risk framework we are developing:

- Guarantees, revolving credit agreements, and other contingent liabilities behave much like credit options.
- CDS basis trades are not essentially market- or credit-risk–oriented, although both market and credit risk play a very important role in their profitability. Rather, they may be driven by "technical factors," that is, transitory disruptions in the typical positioning of various market participants.

  A dramatic example, which we discuss in Chapter 13, occurred during the subprime crisis. The CDS basis widened sharply as a result of the dire lack of funding liquidity.
- Convertible bonds are both market- and credit-risk oriented. Equity and equity vega risk can be as important in convertible bond portfolios as credit risk.

8.1.2 The Order of Magnitude of Default Correlation

For most companies that issue debt, most of the time, default is a relatively rare event. This has two important implications:

1. Default correlation is hard to measure or estimate using historical default data. Most studies have arrived at one-year correlations on the order of 0.05. However, estimated correlations vary widely for different time periods, industry groups, and domiciles, and are often negative.
2. Default correlations are small in magnitude.

In other contexts, for example, thinking about whether a regression result indicates that a particular explanatory value is important, we get used to thinking of, say, 0.05 as a "small" or insignificant correlation and 0.5 as a large or significant one. The situation is different for default correlations because probabilities of default tend to be small—on the order of 1 percent—for all but the handful of CCC and below firms. The probability of any particular pair of credits defaulting is therefore also small, so an "optically" small correlation can have a large impact, as we saw in Example 8.1.

8.2 CREDIT PORTFOLIO RISK MEASUREMENT

To measure credit portfolio risk, we need to model default, default correlation, and loss given default. In more elaborate models, we can also include ratings migration. We restrict ourselves here to default mode. But in practice, and in such commercial models as Moody's KMV and CreditMetrics, models operate in migration mode; that is, credit migrations as well as default can occur.

8.2.1 Granularity and Portfolio Credit Value-at-Risk

Portfolio credit VaR is defined similarly to the VaR of a single credit. It is a quantile of the credit loss, minus the expected loss of the portfolio.

Default correlation has a tremendous impact on portfolio risk. But it affects the volatility and extreme quantiles of loss rather than the expected loss. If default correlation in a portfolio of credits is equal to 1, then the portfolio behaves as if it consisted of just one credit. No credit diversification is achieved. If default correlation is equal to 0, then the number of defaults in the portfolio is a binomially distributed random variable. Significant credit diversification may be achieved.

To see how this works, let's look at diversified and undiversified portfolios, at the two extremes of default correlation, 0 and 1. Imagine a portfolio of n credits, each with a default probability of π percent and a recovery rate of zero percent. Let the total value of the portfolio be $1,000,000,000. We will set n to different values, thus dividing the portfolio into larger or smaller individual positions. If $n = 50$, say, each position has a value of $20,000,000. Next, assume each credit is in the same place in the capital structure and that the recovery rate is zero; in the event of default, the position is wiped out. We'll assume each position is an obligation of a different obligor; if two positions were debts of the same obligor, they would be equivalent to one large position. We can either ignore the time value of money, which won't play a role in the example, or think of all of these quantities as future values.

Now we'll set the default correlation to either 0 or 1.

- If the default correlation is equal to 1, then either the entire portfolio defaults, with a probability of π, or none of the portfolio defaults. In other words, with a default correlation of 1, regardless of the value of n, the portfolio behaves as though $n = 1$.

    We can therefore continue the analysis by assuming all of the portfolio is invested in one credit. The expected loss is equal to $\pi \times 1,000,000,000$. But with only one credit, there are only the two all-or-nothing outcomes. The credit loss is equal to 0 with probability $1 - \pi$. The default correlation doesn't matter.

    The extreme loss given default is equal to $1,000,000,000, since we've assumed recovery is zero. If π is greater than the confidence level of the credit VaR, then the VaR is equal to the entire $1,000,000,000, less the expected loss. If π is less than the confidence level, then the VaR is less than zero, because we always subtract the expected from the extreme loss. If, for example, the default probability is $\pi = 0.02$, the credit VaR at a confidence level of 95 percent is negative (i.e., a gain), since there is a 98 percent probability that the credit loss in the portfolio will be zero. Subtracting from that the expected loss of $\pi \times 1,000,000,000 = 20,000,000$ gives us a VaR of $-$20,000,000. The credit VaR in the case of a single credit with binary risk is well-defined and can be computed, but not terribly informative.

- If the default correlation is equal to 0, the number of defaults is binomially distributed with parameters n and π. We then have many intermediate outcomes between the all-or-nothing extremes.

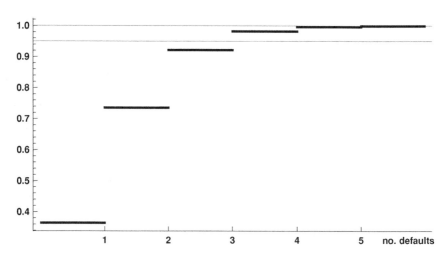

FIGURE 8.1 Distribution of Defaults in an Uncorrelated Credit Portfolio
Cumulative probability distribution function of the number of defaults in a
portfolio of 50 independent credits with a default probability of 2 percent.

Suppose there are 50 credits in the portfolio, so each position has
a future value, if it doesn't default, of $20,000,000. The expected loss
is the same as with one credit: $\pi \times 1,000,000,000$. But now the extreme
outcomes are less extreme. Suppose again that $\pi = 0.02$. The number
of defaults is then binomially distributed with parameters 50 and 0.02.
The 95th percentile of the number of defaults is 3, as seen in Figure 8.1;
the probability of two defaults or less is 0.92 and the probability of
three defaults or less is 0.98. With three defaults, the credit loss is
$60,000,000. Subtracting the expected loss of $20,000,000, which
is the same as for the single-credit portfolio, we get a credit VaR of
$40,000,000.

As we continue to increase the number of positions and decrease
their size, keeping the total value of the portfolio constant, we decrease
the variance of portfolio values. For $n = 1,000$, the 95th percentile of
defaults is 28, and the 95th percentile of credit loss is $28,000,000, so
the credit VaR is $8,000,000.

We summarize the results for $n = 1, 50, 1,000$, for default probabilities
$\pi = 0.005, 0.02, 0.05$, and at confidence levels of 95 and 99 percent in
Table 8.1 and in Figure 8.2.

TABLE 8.1 Credit VaR of an Uncorrelated Credit Portfolio

	$\pi = 0.005$	$\pi = 0.02$	$\pi = 0.05$
Expected loss	5,000,000	20,000,000	50,000,000
	$n = 1$		
	95 percent confidence level		
Number of defaults	0	0	0
Proportion of defaults	0.000	0.000	0.000
Credit Value-at-Risk	−5,000,000	−20,000,000	−50,000,000
	99 percent confidence level		
Number of defaults	0	1	1
Proportion of defaults	0.000	1.000	1.000
Credit Value-at-Risk	−5,000,000	980,000,000	950,000,000
	$n = 50$		
	95 percent confidence level		
Number of defaults	1	3	5
Proportion of defaults	0.020	0.060	0.100
Credit Value-at-Risk	15,000,000	40,000,000	50,000,000
	99 percent confidence level		
Number of defaults	2	4	7
Proportion of defaults	0.040	0.080	0.140
Credit Value-at-Risk	35,000,000	60,000,000	90,000,000
	$n = 1000$		
	95 percent confidence level		
Number of defaults	9	28	62
Proportion of defaults	0.009	0.028	0.062
Credit Value-at-Risk	4,000,000	8,000,000	12,000,000
	99 percent confidence level		
Number of defaults	11	31	67
Proportion of defaults	0.011	0.031	0.067
Credit Value-at-Risk	6,000,000	11,000,000	17,000,000

What is happening as the portfolio becomes more *granular*, that is, contains more independent credits, each of which is a smaller fraction of the portfolio? The credit VaR is, naturally, higher for a higher probability of default, given the portfolio size. But it decreases as the credit portfolio becomes more granular for a given default probability. The convergence is more drastic with a high default probability. But that has an important converse: It is harder to reduce VaR by making the portfolio more granular, if the default probability is low.

Eventually, for a credit portfolio containing a very large number of independent small positions, the probability converges to 100 percent that

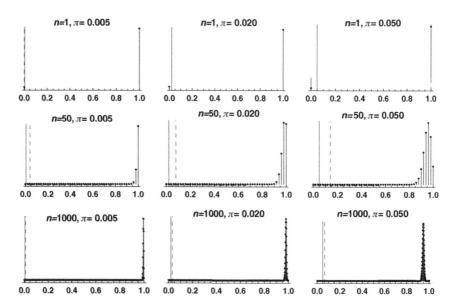

FIGURE 8.2   Distribution of Losses in an Uncorrelated Credit Portfolio
The graph displays the probability density of losses for each combination of a number of equally sized credits and default probabilities. The initial future value of the portfolio is $1,000,000,000. The values on the x-axis can be interpreted as the fraction of credit losses or as the dollar value of loss in billions. The dashed grid line marks the 99th percentile of loss. The solid grid line marks the expected loss and is the same in each panel.

the credit loss will equal the expected loss. While the single-credit portfolio experiences no loss with probability $1 - \pi$ and a total loss with probability π, the granular portfolio experiences a loss of 100π percent "almost certainly." The portfolio then has zero volatility of credit loss, and the credit VaR is zero.

In the rest of this chapter, we show how models of portfolio credit risk take default correlation into account, focusing on two models in particular:

1. The single-factor model, since it is a structural model, emphasizes the correlation between the fundamental driver of default of different firms. Default correlation in that model depends on how closely firms are tied to the broader economy.
2. Intensity models emphasize the timing of defaults. Default correlation depends on how many firms default within a given timeframe. It is driven by how default simulation exercises are set up and parameterized.

8.3 DEFAULT DISTRIBUTIONS AND CREDIT VAR WITH THE SINGLE-FACTOR MODEL

In the example of the last section, we set default correlation only to the extreme values of 0 and 1, and did not take account of idiosyncratic credit risk. In the rest of this chapter, we permit default correlation to take values anywhere on $(0, 1)$. We took a first look at the single-factor model, along with other structural credit models, in Chapter 6. The single-factor model enables us to vary default correlation through the credit's beta to the market factor and lets idiosyncratic risk play a role.

8.3.1 Conditional Default Distributions

To use the single-factor model to measure portfolio credit risk, we start by imagining a number of firms $i = 1, 2, \ldots$, each with its own correlation β_i to the market factor, its own standard deviation of idiosyncratic risk $\sqrt{1 - \beta_i^2}$, and its own idiosyncratic shock ϵ_i. Firm i's return on assets is

$$a_i = \beta_i m + \sqrt{1 - \beta_i^2}\epsilon_i \qquad i = 1, 2, \ldots$$

As in Chapter 6, we assume that m and ϵ_i are standard normal variates, and are not correlated with one another. We now in addition assume the ϵ_i are not correlated with one another:

$$m \sim N(0, 1)$$

$$\epsilon_i \sim N(0, 1) \quad i = 1, 2, \ldots$$

$$\mathrm{Cov}[m, \epsilon_i] = 0 \quad i = 1, 2, \ldots$$

$$\mathrm{Cov}[\epsilon_i, \epsilon_j] = 0 \quad i, j = 1, 2, \ldots$$

Under these assumptions, each a_i is a standard normal variate. Since both the market factor and the idiosyncratic shocks are assumed to have unit variance, the beta of each credit i to the market factor is equal to β_i. The correlation between the asset returns of any pair of firms i and j is $\beta_i\beta_j$:

$$\mathrm{E}\,[a_i] = 0 \quad i = 1, 2, \ldots$$

$$\mathrm{Var}[a_i] = \beta_i^2 + 1 - \beta_i^2 = 1 \quad i = 1, 2, \ldots$$

$$\mathrm{Cov}[a_i, a_j] = E\left[\left(\beta_i m + \sqrt{1 - \beta_i^2}\epsilon_i\right)\left(\beta_j m + \sqrt{1 - \beta_j^2}\epsilon_j\right)\right]$$

$$= \beta_i\beta_j \quad i, j = 1, 2, \ldots$$

Just as in the single-credit version of the model, firm i defaults if $a_i \leq k_i$, the logarithmic distance to the default asset value, measured in standard deviations.

Example 8.3 (Correlation and Beta in Credit Single-Factor Model) Suppose firm 1 is "cyclical" and has $\beta_1 = 0.5$, while firm 2 is "defensive" and has $\beta_2 = 0.1$. The asset return correlation of the two firms is then $\beta_1 \beta_2 = 0.5 \times 0.1 = 0.05$.

The single-factor model has a feature that makes it an especially handy way to estimate portfolio credit risk: conditional independence, the property that once a particular value of the market factor is realized, the asset returns—and hence default risks—are independent of one another. Conditional independence is a result of the model assumption that the firms' returns are correlated only via their relationship to the market factor.

To see this, let m take on a particular value $\bar{m}$. The distance to default—the asset return—increases or decreases, and now has only one random driver ϵ_i, the idiosyncratic shock:

$$a_i - \beta_i \bar{m} = \sqrt{1 - \beta_i^2}\, \epsilon_i \qquad i = 1, 2, \ldots$$

The mean of the default distribution shifts for any $\beta_i > 0$ when the market factor takes on a specific value. The variance of the default distribution is reduced from 1 to $\sqrt{1 - \beta_i^2}$, even though the default threshold k_i has not changed. The change in the distribution that results from conditioning is illustrated in Figure 8.3.

Example 8.4 (Default Probability and Default Threshold) Suppose a firm has $\beta_i = 0.4$ and $k_i = -2.33$, it is a middling credit, but cyclical (relatively high β_i). Its unconditional probability of default is $\Phi(-2.33) = 0.01$. If we enter a modest economic downturn, with $\bar{m} = -1.0$, the conditional asset return distribution is $N(-0.4, \sqrt{1 - 0.40^2})$ or $N(-0.4, 0.9165)$, and the conditional default probability is found by computing the probability that this distribution takes on the value -2.33. That probability is 1.78 percent.

If we were in a stable economy with $m = 0$, we would need a shock of -2.33 standard deviations for the firm to die. But with the firm's return already 0.4 in the hole because of an economy-wide recession, it takes only a 1.93 standard deviation *additional* shock to kill it.

Now suppose we have a more severe economic downturn, with $\bar{m} = -2.33$. The firm's conditional asset return distribution is $N(-0.932, 0.9165)$

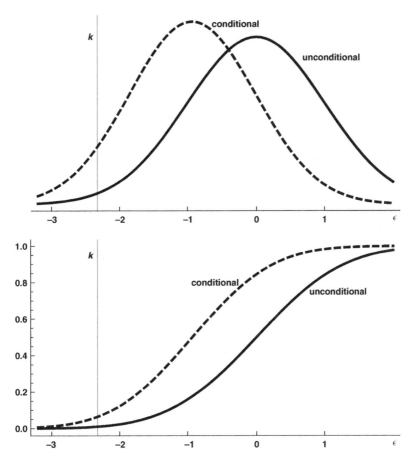

FIGURE 8.3 Default Probabilities in the Single-Factor Model
The graph assumes $\beta_i = 0.4$, $k_i = -2.33 (\Leftrightarrow \pi_i = 0.01)$, and $\bar{m} = -2.33$. The unconditional default distribution is a standard normal distribution, while the conditional default distribution is $N(\beta_i \bar{m}, \sqrt{1 - \beta_i^2}) = N(-0.4, 0.9165)$.
Upper panel: Unconditional and conditional probability density of default. Note that the mean as well as the volatility of the conditional distribution are lower.
Lower panel: Unconditional and conditional cumulative default distribution function.

and the conditional default probability is 6.4 percent. A 0.93 standard deviation shock ($\epsilon_i \leq -0.93$) will now trigger default.

To summarize, specifying a realization $m = \bar{m}$ does three things:

1. The conditional probability of default is greater or smaller than the unconditional probability of default, unless either $\bar{m} = 0$ or $\beta_i = 0$, that

is, either the market factor shock happens to be zero, or the firm's returns are independent of the state of the economy.

There is also no longer an infinite number of combinations of market and idiosyncratic shocks that would trigger a firm i default. Given $\bar{m}$, a realization of ϵ_i less than or equal to

$$k_i - \beta_i \bar{m} \qquad i = 1, 2, \ldots$$

triggers default. This expression is linear and downward sloping in $\bar{m}$: As we let $\bar{m}$ vary from high (strong economy) to low (weak economy) values, a smaller (less negative) idiosyncratic shock will suffice to trigger default.

2. The conditional variance of the default distribution is $1 - \beta_i^2$, so the conditional variance is reduced from the unconditional variance of 1.

3. It makes the asset returns of different firms *independent*. The ϵ_i are independent, so the conditional returns $\sqrt{1 - \beta_i^2}\epsilon_i$ and $\sqrt{1 - \beta_j^2}\epsilon_j$ and thus the default outcomes for two different firms i and j are independent.

Putting this all together, while the unconditional default distribution is a standard normal, the conditional distribution can be represented as a normal with a mean of $-\beta_i \bar{m}$ and a standard deviation of $\sqrt{1 - \beta_i^2}$.

The *conditional cumulative default probability function* can now be represented as a function of m:

$$p(m) = \Phi\left(\frac{k_i - \beta_i m}{\sqrt{1 - \beta_i^2}}\right) \qquad i = 1, 2, \ldots$$

It is plotted in the lower panel of Figure 8.4 for different correlations. This function is the standard normal distribution function of a random variable that has been standardized in a specific way. The mean, or "number of standard deviations," is set to the new distance to default, given the realization of the market factor, while the standard deviation itself is set to its value $\sqrt{1 - \beta_i^2}$ under conditional independence. The intuition is that, for a given value of the market factor, the probability of default depends on how many standard deviations below its mean of 0 is the realization of ϵ_i. The density function corresponding to the cumulative default function is plotted in the upper panel of Figure 8.4.

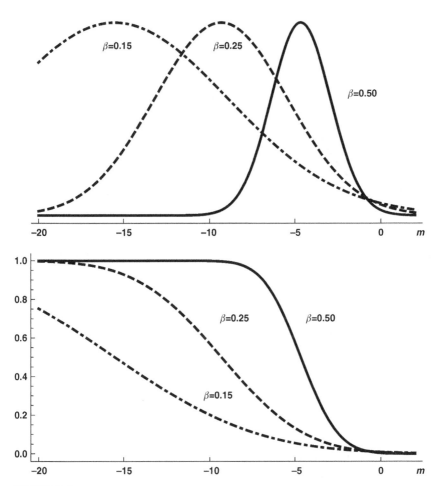

FIGURE 8.4 Single-Factor Default Probability Distribution
Probability of default of a single obligor, conditional on the realization of m
(x-axis). The default probability is set to 1 percent ($k = -2.33$), and the default
correlation is set to different values as specified by the plot labels.
Upper panel: Conditional default density function, that is, the density function
corresponding to $p(m)$.
Lower panel: Conditional cumulative distribution function of default $p(m)$.

8.3.2 Asset and Default Correlation

We began earlier to discuss the difference between the asset return and the
default correlation. Let's look for a moment at the relationship between the
two.

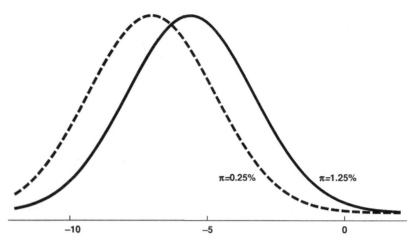

FIGURE 8.5 Conditional Default Density Function in the Single-Factor Model
Both plots take $\beta = 0.40$. For a given correlation, the probability of default
changes the location of the default distribution, but not its variance.

In the single-factor model, the cumulative return distribution of any pair
of credits i and j is a bivariate standard normal with a correlation coefficient
equal to $\beta_i \beta_j$:

$$\begin{pmatrix} a_i \\ a_j \end{pmatrix} \sim N\left[\begin{pmatrix} 0 \\ 0 \end{pmatrix} \begin{pmatrix} 1 & \beta_i \beta_j \\ \beta_i \beta_j & 1 \end{pmatrix} \right]$$

Its cumulative distribution function is $\Phi\begin{pmatrix} a_i \\ a_j \end{pmatrix}$. The probability of a joint default is then equal to the probability that the realized value is in the region
$\{-\infty \leq a_i \leq k_i, -\infty \leq a_j \leq k_j\}$:

$$\Phi\begin{pmatrix} k_i \\ k_j \end{pmatrix} = \mathbf{P}\left[-\infty \leq a_i \leq k_i, -\infty \leq a_j \leq k_j \right]$$

To get the default correlation for this model, we substitute $\pi_{ij} = \Phi\begin{pmatrix} k_i \\ k_j \end{pmatrix}$
into Equation (8.1), the expression for the linear correlation:

$$\rho_{ij} = \frac{\Phi\begin{pmatrix} k_i \\ k_j \end{pmatrix} - \pi_i \pi_j}{\sqrt{\pi_i(1 - \pi_i)}\sqrt{\pi_j(1 - \pi_j)}}$$

From here on, let's assume that the parameters are the same for all firms; that is, $\beta_i = \beta$, $k_i = k$, and $\pi_i = \pi, i = 1, 2, \ldots$ The pairwise asset return correlation for any two firms is then β^2. The probability of a joint default for any two firms for this model is

$$\Phi\binom{k}{k} = P\left[-\infty \leq a \leq k, -\infty \leq a \leq k\right]$$

and the default correlation between any pair of firms is

$$\rho = \frac{\Phi\binom{k}{k} - \pi^2}{\pi(1 - \pi)}$$

Example 8.5 (Default Correlation and Beta) What β corresponds to a "typical" low investment-grade default probability of 0.01 and a default correlation of 0.05? We need to use a numerical procedure to find the parameter β that solves

$$\rho = 0.05 = \frac{\Phi\binom{k}{k} - \pi^2}{\pi(1 - \pi)}$$

With $\pi = 0.01$, the results are $\beta = 0.561$, the asset correlation $\beta^2 = 0.315$, and a joint default probability of 0.0006, or 6 basis points. Similarly, starting with $\beta = 0.50$ ($\beta^2 = 0.25$), we find a joint default probability of 4.3 basis points and a default correlation of 0.034.

8.3.3 Credit VaR Using the Single-Factor Model

In this section, we show how to use the single-factor model to estimate the credit VaR of a "granular," homogeneous portfolio. Let n represent the number of firms in the portfolio, and assume n is a large number. We will assume the loss given default is \$1 for each of the n firms. Each credit is only a small fraction of the portfolio and idiosyncratic risk is de minimis.

Conditional Default Probability and Loss Level Recall that, for a given realization of the market factor, the asset returns of the various credits are independent standard normals. That, in turn, means that we can apply the law of large numbers to the portfolio. For each level of the market factor, the *loss level* $x(m)$, that is, the fraction of the portfolio that defaults, converges to the *conditional probability* that a single credit defaults, given for any credit by

$$p(m) = \Phi\left(\frac{k - \beta m}{\sqrt{1 - \beta^2}}\right) \tag{8.2}$$

So we have

$$\lim_{N \to \infty} x(m) = p(m) \qquad \forall m \in \mathbb{R}$$

The intuition is that, if we know the realization of the market factor return, we know the level of losses realized. This in turn means that, given the model's two parameters, the default probability and correlation, portfolio returns are driven by the market factor.

Unconditional Default Probability and Loss Level   We are ultimately interested in the unconditional, not the conditional, distribution of credit losses. The unconditional probability of a particular loss level is equal to the probability that the the market factor return that leads to that loss level is realized. The procedure for finding the unconditional distribution is thus:

1. Treat the loss level as a random variable X with realizations x. We don't simulate x, but rather work through the model analytically for each value of x between 0 (no loss) and 1 (total loss).
2. For each level of loss x, find the realization of the market factor at which, for a single credit, default has a probability equal to the stated loss level. The loss level and the market factor return are related by

$$x(m) = p(m) = \Phi\left(\frac{k - \beta m}{\sqrt{1 - \beta^2}}\right)$$

So we can solve for $\bar{m}$, the market factor return corresponding to a given loss level $\bar{x}$:

$$\Phi^{-1}(\bar{x}) = \frac{k - \beta \bar{m}}{\sqrt{1 - \beta^2}}$$

or

$$\bar{m} = \frac{k - \sqrt{1 - \beta^2}\,\Phi^{-1}(\bar{x})}{\beta}$$

3. The probability of the loss level is equal to the probability of this market factor return. But by assumption, the market factor is a standard normal:

$$P[X \leq \bar{x}] = \Phi(\bar{m}) = \Phi \left(\frac{k - \sqrt{1 - \beta^2} \Phi^{-1}(\bar{x})}{\beta} \right)$$

4. Repeat this procedure for each loss level to obtain the probability distribution of X.

Another way of describing this procedure is: Set a loss level/conditional default probability x and solve the conditional cumulative default probability function, Equation (8.2), for $\bar{m}$ such that:

$$\bar{m} = \frac{k - \sqrt{1 - \beta^2} \Phi^{-1}(x)}{\beta}$$

The loss distribution function is thus

$$P[X \leq x] = \Phi \left(\frac{k - \sqrt{1 - \beta^2} \Phi^{-1}(x)}{\beta} \right)$$

Example 8.6 (Loss Level and Market Level)   A loss of 0.01 or worse occurs when—converges to the event that—the argument of $p(m)$ is at or below the value such that $p(m) = 0.01$.

$$p(\bar{m}) = 0.01 = \Phi \left(\frac{k - \beta \bar{m}}{\sqrt{1 - \beta^2}} \right)$$

The value $\bar{m}$ at which this occurs is found by solving

$$\Phi^{-1}(0.01) \approx -2.33 = p^{-1}(\bar{m}) = \frac{k - \beta \bar{m}}{\sqrt{1 - \beta^2}}$$

for $\bar{m}$. This is nothing more than solving for the $\bar{m}$ that gives you a specific quantile of the standard normal distribution.

With a default probability $\pi = 0.01$ and correlation $\beta^2 = 0.50^2 = 0.25$, the solution is $\bar{m} = -0.6233$. The probability that the market factor ends up at -0.6233 or less is $\Phi(-0.6233) = 0.2665$.

As simple as the model is, we have several parameters to work with:

■ The probability of default π sets the unconditional expected value of defaults in the portfolio.
■ The correlation to the market β^2 determines how spread out the defaults are over the range of the market factor. When the correlation is high, then, for any probability of default, defaults mount rapidly as business conditions deteriorate. When the correlation is low, it takes an extremely bad economic scenario to push the probability of default high.

To understand the impact of the correlation parameter, start with the extreme cases:

■ $\beta \to 1$ (perfect correlation). Recall that we have constructed a portfolio with no idiosyncratic risk. If the correlation to the market factor is close to unity, there are two possible outcomes. Either $m \leq k$, in which case nearly all the credits default, and the loss rate is equal to 1, or $m > k$, in which case almost none default, and the loss rate is equal to 0.
■ $\beta \to 0$ (zero correlation). If there is no statistical relationship to the market factor, so idiosyncratic risk is nil, then the loss rate will very likely be very close to the default probability p.

In less extreme cases, a higher correlation leads to a higher probability of either very few or very many defaults, and a lower probability of intermediate outcomes. This can be seen in Figure 8.6 in the cumulative loss distribution and loss density functions, which converge to an L-shape. The loss density converges to a ray over the default probability as the correlation goes to zero, that is, the volatility goes to zero. Figure 8.7 compares loss densities for a given correlation and different default probabilities.

8.4 USING SIMULATION AND COPULAS TO ESTIMATE PORTFOLIO CREDIT RISK

The big problem with which portfolio credit risk models grapple is the likelihood of joint default. The single-factor model introduces a latent factor that drives joint default. Factor models make sense, because they link the probability of joint default with our intuition that default is driven by the state of the economy and perhaps an industry sector, that is common to all or to a group of credits, as well as to a company's unique situation.

An alternative approach is more agnostic about the fundamental forces driving defaults. It relies on simulations, and ties the simulations together

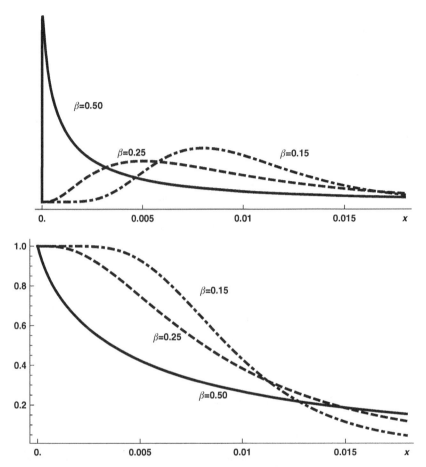

FIGURE 8.6 Distribution of Losses in the Single-Factor Model
Homogeneous and completely diversified portfolio; default probability
1.0 percent.
Upper panel: Density function of the loss rate. Note that the mean as well as the
volatility of the conditional distribution are lower.
Lower panel: Cumulative distribution function of the loss rate.

using a "light" modeling structure. This approach uses a particular mathematical trick, the *copula*, to correlate defaults.

 We assume in this section that we have a default time distribution for
each of the credits in the portfolio, either by risk-neutral estimation from
bond or CDS prices, or using ratings, or from a structural model. The rest

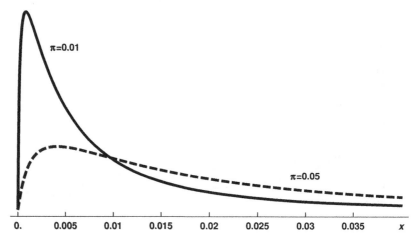

FIGURE 8.7   Density Function of Portfolio Losses in the Single-Factor Model
$\beta = 0.40$.

of this chapter thus builds on Chapter 7, in which we defined the concept
of a default time distribution and showed how to estimate it from market
data. We will also assume that credit spreads, recovery rates, and risk-free
interest rates are deterministic, and focus on default risk.

8.4.1   Simulating Single-Credit Risk

To explain how this approach works, we first describe how to estimate the
default risk of a single credit via simulation. Simulation is not really necessary
to estimate single-credit risk, and we are going to describe a needlessly
complicated way to do so. We're taking this trouble in order to build up to
portfolio credit risk estimation.

To see why simulation is not required, imagine we have a portfolio
consisting of a bond issued by a single-B credit with an estimated one-year
default probability of 0.05. The portfolio has a probability of 0.95 of being
worth a known future market value and a probability of 0.05 of being worth
only its recovery value in one year. If we assume that yield and credit curves
are flat (so that we do not roll up a curve as we move the maturity date
closer), the portfolio credit VaR at a confidence level of 0.95 or more is
equal to the recovery value less the expected loss.

Let's begin by describing a simple technique for simulating default distributions for a single credit. We use the cumulative default time distribution,
which we defined and derived from credit spread data in Chapter 7.

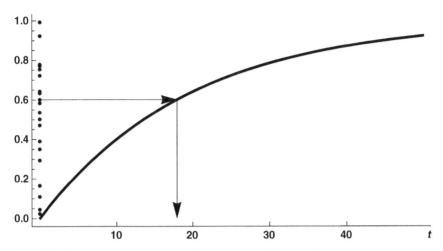

FIGURE 8.8 Estimated Single-Credit Default Risk by Simulation
The graph shows the cumulative default time distribution for a credit with a one-year default probability of 0.05. The hazard rate is 0.0513. The points represent 20 simulated values of the uniform distribution.

Figure 8.8 illustrates the procedure using a default time distribution similar to that illustrated in Figure 7.3. The points parallel to the y-axis represent simulated values of the uniform distribution. For each of the uniform simulations, we can find the default time with a probability equal to the uniform variate. For example, the arrows trace one of the simulation threads, with a value of about 0.6. The probability of a default within the next 18 years or so is about 0.6. So that simulation thread leads to the simulated result of default in about 18 years.

We can repeat this process for a large number of simulated uniform variates. We will find that very close to 5 percent of our simulations lead to default times of one year or less; we can get arbitrarily close to about 5 percent defaulting within one year by taking enough simulations. This does not add anything to what we already knew, since the one-year 5 percent default probability was our starting point.

Now we make the simulation procedure even more complicated by transforming the cumulative default time distribution function. Up to now, we've worked with a mapping from a future date or elapsed time to a probability. We now transform it into a mapping from a future date to a standard normal z value.

This procedure will seem to add needless complexity, but it is a crucial part of applying copula techniques to measuring portfolio credit risk. It enables us to use the joint normal distribution to simulate credit returns for

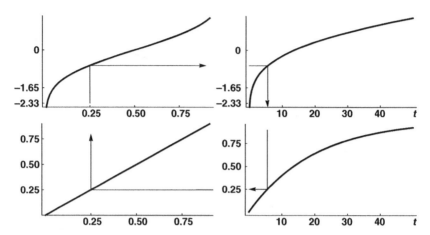

FIGURE 8.9 Shifting from Uniform to Normal Distribution Simulations
Starting in the lower right panel, the graph traces how to change one thread of a
uniform simulation to a normal simulation. The lower right panel shows the
default time distribution for a single-B credit with a one-year default probability
of 5 percent.

portfolios containing more than one credit. The procedure is illustrated in
Figure 8.9 for our single-B credit with a one-year default probability of 0.05.

We can move from simulations of the uniform distribution to simulations of the univariate normal distribution using the *transformation principle*, explained in Appendix A.5:

- We start with an arbitrary default time, say, 5.61 years. The probability
  of a default over the next 5.61 years is 0.25, as illustrated in the lower
  right panel of Figure 8.9.
- The second step is to find, in the upper left panel, the corresponding standard normal distribution value, -0.675. That is, $\Phi(-0.675) = 0.25$.
- The final step closes the loop by mapping the normal distribution value
  to the default time with a probability of 0.25. This step is illustrated in
  the two right panels of Figure 8.9.
- The upper right panel displays the result, a function mapping from
  default times to standard normal values.

8.4.2 Simulating Joint Defaults with a Copula

Next, we simulate joint defaults. To do so, we need a multivariate default
time distribution. But the default time distributions that we have are univariate, covering one issuer at a time. We don't have a statistical theory that
tells us how these distributions might be associated with one another.

We could model default times as multivariate normal, a distribution with which we are very familiar. The problem with that is that the marginal distributions would then also be normal, and as different as can be from the default time distributions we have been using. We would, for example, have default times that are potentially negative. The problem would not be solved by using an alternative to the normal, since the alternative distribution, too, would have marginal distributions that bear no resemblance to our default time distributions.

To summarize, the problem is this: We have a set of univariate default time distributions that we believe in, or are at least willing to stipulate are realistic. But we do not know how to connect them with one another to derive the behavior of portfolios of credits. On the other hand, we are familiar with a few families of multivariate distributions, but none of them have marginal distributions we feel are appropriate for the analysis of default risk.

A now-standard solution to problems such as this is the use of copulas. The great benefit of a copula for our purposes is that it permits us to separate the issue of the default-time distribution of a single credit from the issue of the dependence of default times for a portfolio of credits, that is, their propensity or lack of propensity to default at the same time.

We can then combine the default-time distributions we believe in with a distribution that makes talking about joint events easier, namely, the multivariate normal distribution. One of the reasons the copula approach has become so popular is that it exploits the familiarity of multivariate normal distributions and the ease of simulation using them, without having to accept a multivariate normal model of defaults.

We will spend a little time sketching the theory that justifies this approach, and then illustrate by continuing the example of the previous section. Mathematically, a copula has these properties:

- It is a function $c : \{[0, 1]^n\} \mapsto [0, 1]$. That is, it maps from the Cartesian product of $[0, 1]$, repeated n times, to $[0, 1]$.
- It is therefore an n-dimensional distribution function; that is, it takes as its argument n uniformly $[0, 1]$ distributed random variables and returns a probability.
- The marginal distributions are all uniformly distributed on $[0, 1]$.

Formally, our problem is this: Suppose we have a portfolio with securities of n issuers. We have estimated or specified single-issuer default-time distributions $F_1(t_1), \ldots, F_n(t_n)$. We do not know the joint distribution $F(t_1, \ldots, t_n)$. We can, however, somewhat arbitrarily specify a copula function $c(F(t_1, \ldots, t_n))$, stipulating that

$$c(F_1(t_1), \ldots, F_n(t_n)) = F(t_1, \ldots, t_n)$$

Since $c(F_1(t_1), \ldots, F_n(t_n))$ is a copula, its marginal distributions are the single-issuer default-time distributions $F_1(t_1), \ldots, F_n(t_n)$. For any multivariate distribution, we can always find a copula.

Let's reduce the level of generality and consider a portfolio consisting of two credits, one single-B and one CCC-rated, each with a known/stipulated hazard rate λ_B or λ_{CCC}. The default-time distribution functions are

$$
\begin{aligned}
F(t_B) &= 1 - e^{\lambda_B t_B} & t_B &\in [0, \infty) \\
F(t_{CCC}) &= 1 - e^{\lambda_{CCC} t_{CCC}} & t_{CCC} &\in [0, \infty)
\end{aligned}
$$

and we can use them to define corresponding uniform-[0, 1] random variates

$$
\begin{aligned}
u_B &= F(t_B) \\
u_{CCC} &= F(t_{CCC})
\end{aligned}
$$

as well as corresponding quantile functions

$$
\begin{aligned}
t_B &= F^{-1}(u_B) &= -\tfrac{1}{\lambda_{B_\cdot}} \log(1 - u_B) & u_B &\in [0, 1] \\
t_{CCC} &= F^{-1}(u_{CCC}) &= -\tfrac{1}{\lambda_{CCC}} \log(1 - u_{CCC}) & u_{CCC} &\in [0, 1]
\end{aligned}
$$

The transformation principle (see Appendix A.5) tells us that u_B and u_{CCC}, which are ranges of distribution functions, are uniform-[0, 1]. In the last section, we saw how to move back and forth between distribution and quantile functions. We can do this in a multivariate context, too. We do not know the joint default-time distribution function $F(t_B, t_{CCC})$. But by virtue of being a distribution function,

$$
\begin{aligned}
F(t_B, t_{CCC}) &= \mathbf{P}\left[\tilde{t}_B \leq t_B \wedge \tilde{t}_{CCC} \leq t_{CCC}\right] \\
&= \mathbf{P}\left[F^{-1}(\tilde{u}_B) \leq t_B \wedge F^{-1}(\tilde{u}_{CCC}) \leq t_{CCC}\right] \\
&= \mathbf{P}\left[\tilde{u}_B \leq F(t_B) \wedge \tilde{u}_{CCC} \leq F(t_{CCC})\right] \\
&= \mathbf{P}\left[\tilde{u}_B \leq u_B \wedge \tilde{u}_{CCC} \leq u_{CCC}\right] \\
&= c(u_B, u_{CCC})
\end{aligned}
$$

The tildes identify the symbols representing the random times and their probabilities. The first line follows from the definition of a distribution function, while the last line follows from the copula theorem, known as *Sklar's theorem*, which tells us *some* copula must exist.

So far, all we have done is define a type of mathematical object called a copula and seen how it can be related to the "known" (or at least stipulated) single-issuer default-time distributions $F_1(t_1), \ldots, F_n(t_n)$ and the "unknown" joint distribution $F(t_1, \ldots, t_n)$. How do we compute a credit VaR? There are four steps:

1. Specify the copula function that we'll use.
2. Simulate the default times.
3. Apply the default times to the portfolio to get the market values and P&Ls in each scenario.
4. Add results to get portfolio distribution statistics.

So next we need to actually specify a copula. The most common type or family of copulas is the *normal copula*. The user provides the $F_1(t_1), \ldots, F_n(t_n)$ and an estimate of a multivariate normal correlation matrix Σ.

In our bivariate example, the normal copula is

$$c(u_B, u_{\text{CCC}}) = \Phi\left(\Phi^{-1}[F(t_B)],\ \Phi^{-1}[F(t_{\text{CCC}})]; 0, \Sigma\right)$$
$$= \Phi\left(\Phi^{-1}(u_B),\ \Phi^{-1}(u_{\text{CCC}}); 0, \Sigma\right)$$

with

$$\Sigma = \begin{pmatrix} 1 & \rho \\ \rho & 1 \end{pmatrix}$$

Once we have chosen this copula function and have set the parameter ρ, we can use it to simulate joint defaults. Figure 8.10 illustrates the procedure for our two-credit portfolio.

The starting point is a simulation of the joint standard normal distribution $N(0, \Sigma)$, as seen in the lower left panel of Figure 8.10. Each of these pairs can be mapped to the standard normal quantile function to get the pair

$$(\Phi^{-1}(z_B^{(i)}),\ \Phi^{-1}(z_{\text{CCC}}^{(i)})) \qquad i = 1, \ldots, I$$

with I the number of simulations. Each of the latter is a pair in $[0, 1]^2$.

Next, map the first element of each of these pairs to the single-B default time that has the probability $\Phi^{-1}\left(z_B^{(j)}\right)$ and the second element of each of these pairs to the CCC default time that has the probability $\Phi^{-1}\left(z_{\text{CCC}}^{(j)}\right)$.

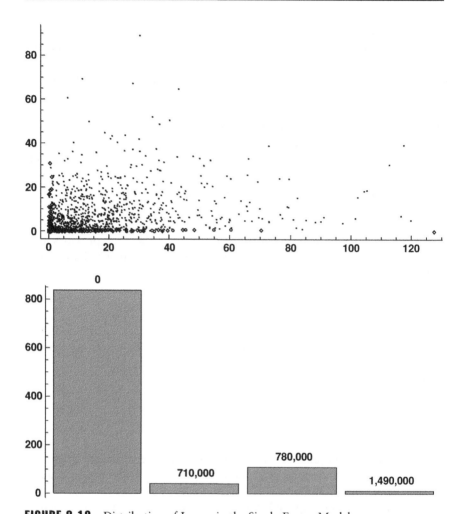

FIGURE 8.10 Distribution of Losses in the Single-Factor Model

Estimate of credit VaR for a portfolio consisting of two credit-risky securities based on 1,000 simulations.

Upper panel: Simulated default times. The simulation trials are partitioned and marked as follows:

- * trials leading to losses in the 0.01 quantile
- ○ trials leading to losses in the 0.05 quantile, but smaller than the 0.01 quantile
- ◇ trials leading to losses in the 1-s.d. quantile, but smaller than the 0.05 quantile
- · trials leading to losses smaller than the 1-s.d. quantile

Lower panel: Histogram of loss levels. Each bar is labelled by the portfolio loss realized in the number of simulation trials indicated on the *y*-axis.

This step is illustrated by the arrows drawn from the lower left panel to the upper left and lower right panels.

Each of these pairs is then plotted to the upper-right panel of Figure 8.10. We now have our correlated joint default-time simulation.

Two features of this procedure seem arbitrary. First, we chose a normal copula; there are alternatives. Second, how do we estimate or otherwise assign the correlation parameter ρ, or in a more general context, the correlation matrix? One answer is provided by the prices of credit derivatives written on credit indexes, which we will study in the next chapter.

We next give a detailed example of the procedure for a portfolio consisting of just two speculative-grade credits, each with a current notional and market value of $1,000,000. As we saw above, for a two-credit portfolio, if we have the default probabilities of each credit and their default correlation, we can determine the entire credit distribution of the portfolio, so we are carrying out this example for illustrative purposes. We imagine the credits to have single-B and CCC ratings and assume:

	p	λ	Notional	Coupon	Spread
CCC	0.10	0.1054	1,000,000	0.18	0.13
Single-B	0.05	0.0513	1,000,000	0.11	0.06

We assume a recovery rate of 40 percent. The horizon of the credit VaR is one year.

There are four possible outcomes over the next year: no default, only the single-B loan defaults, only the CCC loan defaults, and both default. To keep things simple, we ignore the distinction between expected and unexpected credit loss, assuming, in effect, that the lender does not set aside any provision for credit losses. If there is a default, we assume the coupon is not paid. The credit losses then consist of forgone principal and coupon, mitigated by a recovery amount paid one year hence. The losses for each of the four scenarios are:

	Default time realization	Terminal value	Loss
No default	$(\tau_{B,i} > 1, \tau_{CCC,i} > 1)$	2,290,000	0
Single-B default	$(\tau_{B,i} \leq 1, \tau_{CCC,i})$	1,580,000	710,000
CCC default	$(\tau_{B,i} > 1, \tau_{CCC,i} \leq 1)$	1,510,000	780,000
Both default	$(\tau_{B,i} \leq 1, \tau_{CCC,i} \leq 1)$	800,000	1,490,000

To estimate the VaR, we first simulate correlated default times using the normal copula. We apply a correlation of 0.25. Following the procedure outlined above, the results are

■ We first generate 1,000 realizations of the bivariate standard normal distribution using a correlation coefficient $\rho = 0.25$, giving us 1,000 pairs of real numbers.

■ Each of these 2,000 real numbers is mapped to its standard univariate normal quantile, giving us 1,000 pairs of numbers in $(0, 1)$.

■ The first element of each pair is mapped to the single-B default time with that probability. The second element of each pair is mapped to the CCC default time with that probability. We now have 1,000 pairs of simulated default times $(\tau_{B,i}, \tau_{CCC,i})$. These are illustrated in the upper right panel of Figure 8.10.

■ Each default time is either greater than, less than, or equal to the one-year horizon of the credit VaR. We can accordingly assign a terminal value to each loan in each simulation, sum across the two loans, and subtract the sum from the no-default future value to get the loss. There are four distinct possible values for each simulation trial. In the upper panel of Figure 8.11, each trial is marked by its pair of default times.

■ Finally, we tally up the number of simulation trials resulting in each loss level. This is displayed as a histogram in the lower panel of Figure 8.10.

The credit VaR estimates (in dollars) are:

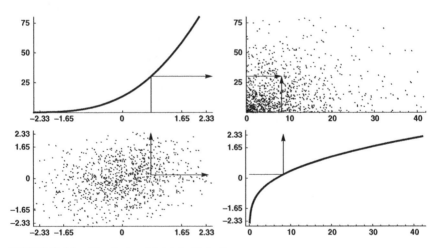

FIGURE 8.11 Simulating Multiple Defaults
Starting in the lower right panel, the graph traces how to change one thread of a uniform simulation to a normal simulation. The lower right panel shows the default time distribution for a single-B credit with a one-year default probability of 5 percent.

Confidence level	VaR
99 percent	1,490,000
95 percent	780,000
1 s.d. (84.135 percent)	710,000

Copulas are a very attractive modeling technique, since they permit the model to generate quite detailed results—the entire probability distribution of portfolio credit outcomes—with a very light theoretical apparatus and requiring the estimation of only one additional parameter, the correlation, beyond those used in single-credit modeling. However, the copula approach also has a number of pitfalls. Most important among these is that the choice of copula is arbitrary and that we simply do not know enough to reliably estimate the copula correlation. It is difficult enough to estimate default correlations, and the copula correlation is only related to, not identical to it. Yet once a parameter value is assigned, the temptation to rely on the wide range of model results that can then be generated is enormous. Reliance on a poorly understood and hard-to-estimate parameter in a simplified model is dangerous. This particular example was important in the subprime crisis. We explore model risk further in Chapter 11.

Copula techniques are widely used in the valuation and risk management of credit portfolios. The most frequent application, however, is in modeling portfolio credit products, such as securitizations and credit index products. We describe these in more detail in Chapter 9. Variants of the model let default intensity vary over time stochastically, or correlate the intensities of different firms with one another.

The models presented in this chapter focus on default, but ratings migration, of course, is also an important driver of credit risk. The Gaussian single-factor approach can be applied in migration mode as well as default mode. In addition to a default probability and a corresponding default threshold, the model requires a set of migration or transition probabilities, for example those contained in the transition matrices described in Chapter 6.

FURTHER READING

Lucas (1995) provides a definition of default correlation and an overview of its role in credit models. See also Hull and White (2001).

Credit Suisse First Boston (2004) and Lehman Brothers (2003) are introductions by practitioners. Zhou (2001) presents an approach to modeling correlated defaults based on the Merton firm value, rather than the factor-model approach.

The application of the single-factor model to credit portfolios is laid out in Finger (1999) and Vasicek (1991). Accessible introduction to copula theory are Frees and Valdez (1998) and in Klugman, Panjer, and Willmot (2008). The application to credit portfolio models and the equivalence to Gaussian CreditMetrics is presented in Li (2000).

The correlated intensities approach to modeling credit portfolio risk, as well as other alternatives to the Gaussian single-factor approach presented here, are described in Schönbucher (2003), Chapter 10, and Lando (2004), Chapter 5.

CHAPTER 9

Structured Credit Risk

This chapter focuses on a class of credit-risky securities called *securitizations* and *structured credit products*. These securities play an important role in contemporary finance, and had a major role in the subprime crisis of 2007 and after. As described in Chapter 1, these securities have been in existence for some time, and their issuance and trading volumes were quite large up until the onset of the crisis. They have also had a crucial impact on the development of the financial system, particularly on the formation of the market-based or "shadow banking system" of financial intermediation.

In this chapter, we look at structured products in more detail, with the goal of understanding both the challenges they present to risk management by traders and investors, and their impact on the financial system before and during the crisis. These products are complex, so we'll employ an extended example to convey how they work. They are also issued in many variations, so the example will differ from any extant structured product, but capture the key features that recur across all variants. A grasp of structured credit products will also help readers understand the story, told in Chapters 12, 14 and 15, of the growth of leverage in the financial system and its role in the subprime crisis.

9.1 STRUCTURED CREDIT BASICS

We begin by sketching the major types of securitizations and structured credit products, sometimes collectively called *portfolio credit products*. These are vehicles that create bonds or credit derivatives backed by a pool of loans or other claims. This broad definition can't do justice to the bewildering variety of structured credit products, and the equally bewildering terminology associated with their construction.

First, let's put structured credit products into the context of other securities based on pooled loans. Not surprisingly, this hierarchy with respect to complexity of structure corresponds roughly to the historical development of structured products that we summarized in Chapter 1:

Covered bonds are issued mainly by European banks, mainly in Germany and Denmark. In a covered bond structure, mortgage loans are aggregated into a *cover pool*, by which a bond issue is secured. The cover pool stays on the balance sheet of the bank, rather than being sold off-balance-sheet, but is segregated from other assets of the bank in the event the bank defaults. The pool assets would be used to make the covered bond owners whole before they could be applied to repay general creditors of the bank. Because the underlying assets remain on the issuer's balance sheet, covered bonds are not considered full-fledged securitizations. Also, the principal and interest on the secured bond issue are paid out of the general cash flows of the issuer, rather than out of the cash flows generated by the cover pool. Finally, apart from the security of the cover pool, the covered bonds are backed by the issuer's obligation to pay.

Mortgage pass-through securities are true securitizations or structured products, since the cash flows paid out by the bonds, and the credit risk to which they are exposed, are more completely dependent on the cash flows and credit risks generated by the pool of underlying loans. Mortgage pass-throughs are backed by a pool of mortgage loans, removed from the mortgage originators' balance sheets, and administered by a *servicer*, who collects principal and interest from the underlying loans and distributes them to the bondholders. Most pass-throughs are *agency MBS*, issued under an explicit or implicit U.S. federal guarantee of the performance of the underlying loans, so there is little default risk. But the principal and interest on the bonds are "passed through" from the loans, so the cash flows depend not only on amortization, but also voluntary prepayments by the mortgagor. The bonds are repaid slowly over time, but at an uncertain pace, in contrast to bullet bonds, which receive full repayment of principal on one date. Bondholders are therefore exposed to prepayment risk.

Collateralized mortgage obligations were developed partly as a means of coping with prepayment risk, but also as a way to create both longer- and shorter-term bonds out of a pool of mortgage loans. Such loans amortize over time, creating cash flow streams that diminish over time. CMOs are "sliced," or tranched into bonds or *tranches*, that are paid down on a specified schedule. The simplest structure is *sequential pay*, in which the tranches are ordered, with "Class A" receiving all principal repayments from the loan until it is retired, then "Class B," and so on. The higher tranches in the sequence have less prepayment risk than a pass-through, while the lower ones bear more.

Structured credit products introduce one more innovation, namely the sequential distribution of credit losses. Structured products are backed by credit-risky loans or bonds. The tranching focuses on creating bonds that have different degrees of credit risk. As losses occur, the tranches are gradually written down. Junior tranches are written down first, and more senior tranches only begin to bear credit losses once the junior tranches have been written down to zero.

This basic credit tranching feature can be combined with other features to create, in some cases, extremely complex security structures. The bottom-up treatment of credit losses can be combined with the sequential payment technology introduced with CMOs. Cash flows and credit risk arising from certain constituents of the underlying asset pool may be directed to specific bonds.

Securitization is one approach to financing pools of loans and other receivables developed over the past two decades. An important alternative and complement to securitization are entities set up to issue *asset-backed commercial paper* (ABCP) against the receivables, or against securitization bonds themselves. We describe these in greater detail in Chapter 12.

A structured product can be thought of as a "robot" corporate entity with a balance sheet, but no other business. In fact, structured products are usually set up as *special purpose entities* (SPE) or *vehicles* (SPV), also known as a *trust*. This arrangement is intended to legally separate the assets and liabilities of the structured product from those of the original creditors and of the company that manages the payments. That is, it makes the SPE *bankruptcy remote*. This permits investors to focus on the credit quality of the loans themselves rather than that of the original lenders in assessing the credit quality of the securitization. The underlying debt instruments in the SPV are the robot entity's assets, and the structured credit products built on it are its liabilities.

Securitizations are, depending on the type of underlying assets, often generically called *asset-* (ABS) or *mortgage-backed securities* (MBS), or *collateralized loan obligations* (CLOs). Securitizations that repackage other securitizations are called *collateralized debt obligations* (CDOs, issuing bonds against a collateral pool consisting of ABS, MBS, or CLOs), *collateralized mortgage obligations* (CMOs), or *collateralized bond obligations* (CBOs). There even exist third-level securitizations, in which the collateral pool consists of CDO liabilities, which themselves consist of bonds backed by a collateral pool, called *CDO-squareds.*

There are several other dimensions along which we can classify the great variety of structured credit products:

Underlying asset classes. Every structured product is based on a set of underlying loans, receivables, or other claims. If you drill down far enough into a structured product, you will get to a set of relatively conventional debt instruments that constitute the *collateral* or *loan pool.* The collateral is typically composed of residential or commercial real estate loans, consumer debt such as credit cards balances and auto and student loans, and corporate bonds. But many other types of debt, and even nondebt assets such as recurring fee income, can also be packaged into securitizations. The credit quality and prepayment behavior of the underlying risks is, of course, critical in assessing the risks of the structured products built upon them.

Type of structure. Structured products are tools for redirecting the cash flows and credit losses generated by the underlying debt instruments. The latter each make contractually stipulated coupon or other payments. But rather than being made directly to debt holders, they are split up and channeled to the structured products in specified ways. A key dimension is tranching, the number and size of the bonds carved out of the liability side of the securitization. Another is how many levels of securitization are involved, that is, whether the collateral pool consists entirely of loans or liabilities of other securitizations.

How much the pool changes over time. We can distinguish here among three different approaches, tending to coincide with asset class. Each type of pool has its own risk management challenges:

Static pools are amortizing pools in which a fixed set of loans is placed in the trust. As the loans amortize, are repaid, or default, the deal, and the bonds it issues, gradually wind down. Static pools are common for such asset types as auto loans and residential mortgages, which generally themselves have a fixed and relatively long term at origination but pay down over time.

Revolving pools specify an overall level of assets that is to be maintained during a *revolving period.* As underlying loans are repaid, the size of the pool is maintained by introducing additional loans from the balance sheet of the originator. Revolving pools are common for bonds backed by credit card debt, which is not issued in a fixed amount, but can within limits be drawn upon and repaid by the borrower at his own discretion and without notification. Once the revolving period ends, the loan pool becomes fixed, and the deal winds down gradually as debts are repaid or become delinquent and are charged off.

Managed pools are pools in which the manager of the structured product has discretion to remove individual loans from the pool, sell them, and replace them with others. Managed pools have typically been seen in CLOs. Managers of CLOs are hired in part for skill in identifying loans with higher spreads than warranted by their credit quality. They can, in theory, also see credit problems arising at an early stage, and trade out of loans they believe are more likely to default. There is a secondary market for syndicated loans that permits them to do so, at least in many cases. Also, syndicated loans are typically repaid in lump sum, well ahead of their legal final maturity, but with random timing, so a managed pool permits the manager to maintain the level of assets in the pool.

The number of debt instruments in pools depends on asset type and on the size of the securitization; some, for example CLO and commercial mortgage-backed securities (CMBS) pools, may contain around 100 different loans, each with an initial par value of several million dollars, while a large residential mortgage-backed security (RMBS) may have several tens of thousands of mortgage loans in its pool, with an average loan amount of $200,000.

The assets of some structured products are not cash debt instruments, but rather credit derivatives, most frequently CDS. These are called *synthetic* securitizations, in contrast to *cash* or *cash-flow* securitizations. The set of underlying cash debt instruments on which a synthetic securitization is based generally consists of securitization liabilities rather than loans, and is called the *reference portfolio*.

Each structured product is defined by the cash flows thrown off by assets and the way they are distributed to the liabilities. Next, we examine the mechanisms by which they are distributed: the capital structure or tranching, the waterfall, and overcollateralization.

9.1.1 Capital Structure and Credit Losses in a Securitization

Tranching refers to how the liabilities of the securitization SPV are split into a capital structure. Each type of bond or note within the capital structure has its own coupon or spread, and depending on its place in the capital structure, its own priority or seniority with respect to losses. The general principle of tranching is that more senior tranches have priority, or the first right, to payments of principal and interest, while more junior tranches must be written down first when credit losses occur in the collateral pool. There may be many dozen, or only a small handful of tranches in a securitization, but they can be categorized into three groups:

Equity. The equity tranche is so called because it typically receives no fixed coupon payment, but is fully exposed to defaults in the collateral pool. It takes the form of a note with a specified notional value that is entitled to the residual cash flows after all the other obligations of the SPE have been satisfied. The notional value is typically small compared to the market value of the collateral; that is, it is a "thin" tranche.

Junior debt earns a relatively high fixed coupon or spread, but if the equity tranche is exhausted by defaults in the collateral pool, it is next in line to suffer default losses. Junior bonds are also called *mezzanine tranches* and are typically also thin.

Senior debt earns a relatively low fixed coupon or spread, but is protected by both the equity and mezzanine tranches from default losses. Senior bonds are typically the bulk of the liabilities in a securitization. This is a crucial feature of securitization economics, as we will see later. If the underlying collateral cannot be financed primarily by low-yielding senior debt, a securitization is generally not viable.

The capital structure is sometimes called the "capital stack," with senior bonds at the "top of the stack." Most securitizations also feature securities with different maturities but the same seniority, a technique similar to sequential-pay CMOs for coping with variation in the term to maturity and prepayment behavior of the underlying loans, while catering to the desire of different investors for bonds with different durations.

The example of the next few sections of this chapter features three tranches, a simple structure that can be summarized in this balance sheet:

Assets	Liabilities
Underlying debt instruments	Equity Mezzanine debt Senior debt

The boundary between two tranches, expressed as a percentage of the total of the liabilities, is called the *attachment point* of the more senior tranche and *detachment point* of the more junior tranche. The equity tranche only has a detachment point, and the most senior only has an attachment point.

The part of the capital structure below a bond tranche is called its *subordination* or *credit enhancement*. It is the fraction of the collateral pool that must be lost before the bond takes any loss. It is greater for more senior bonds in the structure. The credit enhancement may decline over time as the collateral experiences default losses, or increase as *excess spread*, the interest from the collateral that is not paid out to the liabilities or as fees and expenses, accumulates in the trust.

A securitization can be thought of as a mechanism for securing long-term financing for the collateral pool. To create this mechanism, the senior tranche must be a large portion of the capital structure, and it must have a low coupon compared to the collateral pool. In order to create such a liability, its credit risk must be low enough that it can be marketed. To this end, additional features can be introduced into the cash flow structure. The most important is *overcollateralization*; that is, selling a par amount of bonds that is smaller than the par amount of underlying collateral. Overcollateralization provides credit enhancement for all of the bond tranches of a securitization.

There are typically reserves within the capital structure that must be filled and kept at certain levels before junior and equity notes can receive money. These reserves can be filled from two sources: gradually, from the excess spread, or quickly via overcollateralization. These approaches are often used in combination. The latter is sometimes called *hard credit enhancement*, in contrast to the *soft credit enhancement* of excess spread, which accrues gradually over time and is not present at initiation of the securitization. Deals with revolving pools generally have an *early amortization trigger* that terminates the replenishment of the pool with fresh debt if a default trigger is breached.

Typically, the collateral pool contains assets with different maturities, or that amortize over time. Loan maturities are uncertain because the loans can be prepaid prior to maturity, possibly after an initial *lockout period* has elapsed. The senior liabilities in particular are therefore generally amortized over time as the underlying loans amortize or mature; while they may have legal final maturity dates that are quite far in the future, their durations are uncertain and much shorter. Risk analysis therefore generally focuses on the *weighted average life* (WAL) of a securitization, the weighted average of the number of years each dollar of par value of the bond will remain outstanding before it is repaid or amortized. A WAL is associated with a particular prepayment assumption, and standard assumptions are set for some asset classes by convention.

As noted above, the sequential-pay technology can be combined with credit tranching in securitizations. This creates multiple senior bonds with different WALs, to better adapt the maturity structure of the liabilities to that of the collateral pool. This feature is called *time tranching* to distinguish it from the seniority tranching related to credit priority in the capital structure. The example presented in the rest of this chapter abstracts from this important feature. Thus, in addition to the credit risk that is the focus of this chapter, securitizations also pose prepayment and *extension risk* arising from loans either prepaying faster or slower than anticipated, or being extended past their maturity in response to financial distress.

In any securitization, there is a possibility that at the maturity date, even if the coupons have been paid timely all along, there may not be enough principal left in the collateral pool to redeem the junior and/or senior debt at par unless loans can be refinanced. The bonds are therefore exposed to the *refinancing risk* of the loans in the collateral pool. If some principal cash flows are paid out to the equity note along the way, refinancing risk is greater. Time tranching of the senior bonds, and their gradual retirement through amortization, is one way securitizations cope with this risk.

The tranche structure of a securitization leads to a somewhat different definition of a default event from that pertaining to individual, corporate, and sovereign debt. Losses to the bonds in securitizations are determined by losses in the collateral pool together with the waterfall. Losses may be severe enough to cause some credit loss to a bond, but only a small one. For example, if a senior ABS bond has 20 percent credit enhancement, and the collateral pool has credit losses of 21 percent, the credit loss or writedown to the bond will be approximately $\frac{1}{100-20}$ or 1.25 percent, since the bond is 80 percent of the balance sheet of the trust. The LGD of a securitization can therefore take on a very wide range, and is driven by the realization of defaults and recoveries in the collateral pool.

For a corporate or sovereign bond, default is a binary event; if interest and/or principal cannot be paid, bankruptcy or restructuring ensues. Corporate debt typically has a "hard" maturity date, while securitizations have a distant maturity date that is rarely the occasion for a default. For these reasons, default events in securitizations are often referred to as *material impairment* to distinguish them from defaults. A common definition of material impairment is either missed interest payments that go uncured for more than a few months, or a deterioration of collateral pool performance so severe that interest or principal payments are likely to stop in the future.

9.1.2 Waterfall

The *waterfall* refers to the rules about how the cash flows from the collateral are distributed to the various securities in the capital structure. The term "waterfall" arose because generally the capital structure is paid in sequence, "top down," with the senior debt receiving all of its promised payments before any lower tranche receives any monies. In addition to the coupons and other payments promised to the bonds, there are fees and other costs to be paid, which typically take priority over coupons.

A typical structured credit product begins life with a certain amount of hard overcollateralization, since part of the capital structure is an equity note, and the debt tranches are less than 100 percent of the deal. Soft overcollateralization mechanisms may begin to pay down the senior debt over time with part of the collateral pool interest, or divert part of it into a reserve that provides additional credit enhancement for the senior tranches. That way, additional credit enhancement is built up at the beginning of the life of the product, when collateral cash flows are strongest. Typically, there is a detailed set of *overcollateralization triggers* that state the conditions under which excess spread is to be diverted into various reserves.

To clarify these concepts and introduce a few more, let's develop our simple example. Imagine a CLO, the underlying assets of which are 100 identical leveraged loans, with a par value of $1,000,000 each, and priced at par. The loans are floating rate obligations that pay a fixed spread of 3.5 percent over one-month Libor. We'll assume there are no upfront, management, or trustee fees. The capital structure consists of equity, and a junior and a senior bond, as displayed in this schematic balance sheet:

Assets	Liabilities
Underlying debt instruments:	Equity note $5 million Mezzanine debt $10 million coupon: Libor+500 bps
$100 million coupon: L+350 bps	Senior debt $85 million coupon: Libor+50 bps

For the mezzanine debt in our example, the initial credit enhancement is equal to the initial size of the equity tranche. For the senior bond, it is equal to the sum of the equity and mezzanine tranches. There is initially no overcollateralization.

The junior bond has a much wider spread than that of the senior, and much less credit enhancement; the mezzanine attachment point is

5 percent, and the senior attachment point is 15 percent. We assume that, at these prices, the bonds will price at par when they are issued. In the further development of this example, we will explore the risk analysis that a potential investor might consider undertaking. The weighted average spread on the debt tranches is 97.4 basis points.

The loans in the collateral pool and the liabilities are assumed to have a maturity of five years. All coupons and loan interest payments are annual, and occur at year-end.

We assume the swap curve ("Libor") is flat at 5 percent. If there are *no* defaults in the collateral pool, the annual cash flows are

	Libor+spread	×	Principal amount	=	Annual interest
Collateral	(0.050 + 0.0350)	×	100,000,000	=	$8,500,000
Mezzanine	(0.050 + 0.0500)	×	10,000,000	=	$1,000,000
Senior	(0.050 + 0.0050)	×	85,000,000	=	$4,675,000

The excess spread if there are no defaults, the difference between the collateral cash flows coming into the trust and the tranche coupon payments flowing out, is $2,825,000.

The assumption that all the loans and bonds have precisely the same maturity date is a great simplification in several respects. Although one of the major motivations of securitization is to obtain term financing of a pool of underlying loans, such perfect *maturity matching* is unusual in constructing a securitization. The problem of maturity transformation in financial markets is pervasive and important; we discuss it in Chapter 12.

The example so far has assumed no defaults. Of course, there may well be at least some defaults in a pool of 100 loans, even in a benign economic environment. If defaults occur at a constant rate, and defaulted collateral is not replaced, the annual number of defaults will fall over time as the pool shrinks due to defaults that have already occurred. The cumulative number of defaults will grow at a progressively slower rate. Suppose, for example, the default rate is expected to be 5 percent annually. The number of defaults in a pool of 100 loans is then likely to be an integer close to 5. After four years, if only 80 loans are still performing and we still expect 5 percent to default, the expected number of defaults is 4.

Regardless of whether the default rate is constant, default losses accumulate, so for any default rate, cash flows from any collateral pool will be larger early in the life of a structured credit product, from interest and amortization of surviving loans and recovery from defaulted loans, than later.

The example also illustrates a crucial characteristic of securitizations: the *timing* of defaults has an enormous influence on the returns to different tranches. If the timing of defaults is uneven, the risk of inadequate principal at the end may be enhanced or dampened. If defaults are accelerating, the risk to the bond tranches will increase, and vice versa. Other things being equal, the equity tranche benefits relative to more senior debt tranches if defaults occur later in the life of the structured product deal.

9.1.3 Issuance Process

The process of creating a securitized credit product is best explained by describing some of the players in the cast of characters that bring it to market. As we do so, we note some of the conflicts of interest that pose risk management problems to investors.

Loan Originator The loan originator is the original lender who creates the debt obligations in the collateral pool. This is often a bank, for example, when the underlying collateral consists of bank loans or credit card receivables. But it can also be a specialty finance company or mortgage lender. If most of the loans have been originated by a single intermediary, the originator may be called the *sponsor* or *seller*.

Underwriter The *underwriter* or *arranger* is often, but not always, a large financial intermediary. Typically, the underwriter aggregates the underlying loans, designs the securitization structure and markets the liabilities. In this capacity, the underwriter is also the *issuer* of the securities. A somewhat technical legal term, *depositor*, is also used to describe the issuer.

During this aggregation phase, the underwriter bears *warehousing risk*, the risk that the deal will not be completed and the value of the accumulated collateral still on its balance sheet falls. Warehousing risk became important in the early days of the subprime crisis, as the market grew aware of the volumes of "hung loans" on intermediaries' balance sheets. Underwriting in the narrow sense is a "classical" broker-dealer function, namely, to hold the finished securitization liabilities until investors purchase them, and to take the risk that not all the securities can be sold at par.

Rating Agencies Rating agencies are engaged to assess the credit quality of the liabilities and assign ratings to them. An important part of this process is determining attachment points and credit subordination. In contrast to corporate bonds, in which rating agencies opine on creditworthiness, but have little influence over it, ratings of securitizations involve the agencies in decisions about structure.

As noted in Chapter 6, rating agencies are typically compensated by issuers, creating a potential conflict of interest between their desire to gain rating assignments and expand their business, and their duty to provide an objective assessment. The potential conflict is exacerbated by the rating agencies' inherent role in determining the structure. The rating agency may tell the issuer how much enhancement is required, given the composition of the pool and other features of the deal, to gain an investment-grade rating for the top of the capital stack. These seniormost bonds have lower spreads and a wider investor audience, and are therefore uniquely important in the economics of securitizations. Or the issuer may guess at what the rating agency will require before submitting the deal to the agency for review. Either way, the rating agency has an incentive to require less enhancement, permitting the issuer to create a larger set of investment-grade tranches. Investors can cope with the potential conflict by either demanding a wider spread or carrying out their own credit review of the deal.

Ratings may be based solely on the credit quality of the pool and the liability structure. In many cases, however, bonds have higher ratings because of the provision of a guarantee, or *wrap*, by a third party. These guarantees, as noted in Chapter 6, are typically provided by *monoline insurance companies*. Monolines have high corporate ratings of their own and ample capital, and can use these to earn guarantee fees. Such guarantees were quite common until the subprime crisis caused large losses and widespread downgrades among monoline insurers.

Servicers and Managers The servicer collects principal and interest from the loans in the collateral pool and disburses principal and interest to the liability holders, as well as fees to the underwriter and itself. The servicer may be called upon to make advances to the securitization liabilities if loans in the trust are in arrears. Servicers may also be tasked with managing underlying loans in distress, determining, for example, whether they should be resolved by extending or refinancing the loan, or by foreclosing. Servicers are thereby often involved in conflicts of interest between themselves and bondholders, or between different classes of bondholders.

One example arises in CMBS. If one distressed loan is resolved by foreclosure, the senior bonds are unlikely to suffer a credit writedown, but rather will receive an earlier-than-anticipated repayment of principal, even if the property is sold at a loss. The junior bond, however, may suffer an immediate credit writedown. If, in contrast, the loan is extended, the junior bond avoids the immediate loss, and has at least a small positive probability of a recovery of value. The senior bond, in contrast, faces the risk that the loss on the property will be even greater, eroding the credit enhancement and increasing the riskiness of the bond. The servicer is obliged to maximize the total present value of the loan, but no matter what he does, he will take an action that is better aligned with the interests of some bonds than of others.

Managers of actively managed loan pools may also be involved in conflicts of interest. As is the case with bankers, investors delegate the task of monitoring the credit quality of pools to the managers, and require mechanisms to align incentives. One such mechanism that has been applied to managed as well as static pools is to require the manager to own a first-loss portion of the deal. As we see in Chapter 15, this mechanism has been enshrined in the Dodd-Frank Act changes to financial regulatory policy. Such conflicts can be more severe for asset types, especially mortgages, in which servicing is not necessarily carried out by the loan originator. Third-party servicing also adds an entity whose soundness must be verified by investors in the bonds.

Among the economically minor players are the *trustee* and *custodian*, who are tasked with keeping records, verifying documentation, and moving cash flows among deal accounts and paying noteholders.

9.2 CREDIT SCENARIO ANALYSIS OF A SECURITIZATION

The next step in understanding how a securitization works is to put together the various elements we've just defined—collateral, the liability structure, and the waterfall—and see how the cash flows behave over time and in different default scenarios. We'll continue to use our three-tranche example to lay these issues out. We'll do this in two parts, first analyzing the cash flows prior to maturity, and then the cash flows in the final year of the illustrative securitization's life, which are very different.

Let's take as a base assumption an annual expected default rate of 2 percent. As we will see, the securitization is "designed" the securitization for that default rate, in the sense that if defaults prove to be much higher, the bond tranches may experience credit losses. If the default rate proves much lower, the equity tranche will be extremely valuable, and probably more valuable than the market requires to coax investors to hold the position at par.

9.2.1 Tracking the Interim Cash Flows

Let's introduce a simple overcollateralization mechanism into our example. Instead of letting all the excess spread flow to the equity note, we divert up to $1,750,000 per year to a reserve account, which we will call the "overcollateralization account," where it will earn the financing/money market rate of 5 percent. This is a bit of a misnomer, since the funds in the account represent soft rather than hard credit enhancement. If excess spread is less than $1,750,000, that smaller amount is diverted to the overcollateralization account. If excess spread is greater than $1,750,000, the amount that exceeds $1,750,000 is paid out to the equity.

The funds in the overcollateralization account will be used to pay interest on the bonds if there is not enough interest flowing from the loans in the collateral pool during that period. Any remaining funds in the account will be released to the equity tranche only at maturity. It is not a robust mechanism for protecting the senior bonds, but at least has the virtue that, unless defaults are very high early in the deal's life, the overcollateralization account is likely to accumulate funds while cumulative defaults are low.

We assume that the loans in the collateral pay no interest if they have defaulted any time during the prior year. There is no partial interest; interest is paid at the end of the year by surviving loans only.

We also have to make an assumption about recovery value if a loan defaults. We will assume that in the event of default, the recovery rate is 40 percent, and that the recovery amount is paid into the overcollateralization account, where it is also invested at the financing/money market rate. We have to treat recovery this way in order to protect the senior bond; if the recovery amounts flowed through the waterfall, the equity would perversely benefit from defaults. In a typical real-world securitization, the recovery would flow to the senior bonds, and eventually the mezzanine bond tranche, until they are paid off. Time-tranching would endeavor to have recoveries that occur early in the life of the deal flow to short-duration bonds and later recoveries to long-duration bonds. To keep our example simple, we "escrow" the recovery and defer writedowns until the maturity of the securitization.

We need some notation to help us track cash flows in more detail for different default scenarios. We'll assign these symbols to the cash flows and account values:

N	Number of loans in initial collateral pool; here $N = 100$
d_t	Number of defaults in the course of year t
L_t	Aggregate loan interest received by the trust at the end of year t
B	Bond coupon interest due to both the junior and senior bonds (a constant for all t; here \$5,675,000).
K	Maximum amount diverted annually from excess spread into the overcollateralization account; here \$1,750,000
OC_t	Amount actually diverted from excess spread into the overcollateralization account at the end of year t
R_t	Recovery amount deposited into the overcollateralization account at the end of year t
r	Money market or swap rate, assumed to be constant over time and for all maturities; here $r = 0.05$

Once we take defaults into account, the loan interest flowing from the surviving collateral at the end of year t is

$$L_t = (0.050 + 0.035) \times \left(N - \sum_{\tau=1}^{t} d_\tau \right) \times 1000000 \qquad t = 1, \ldots, T-1$$

Let's tabulate the interim cash flows for three scenarios, with default rates of 1.5, 5.25, and 9.0 percent annually. As noted, the cash flows during the first four years of our five-year securitization are different from the terminal cash flows, so we tabulate them separately a bit further on.

Interest equal to $5,675,000 is due to the bondholders. The excess spread is $L_t - B$. The excess spread will turn negative if defaults have been high. In that case, bond interest can't be paid out of the collateral cash flow, but must come in whole or in part out of the overcollateralizaton account.

The amount diverted from the excess spread to the overcollateralization account is

$$\max[\min(L_t - B, K), 0] \qquad t = 1, \ldots, T-1$$

If the excess spread is negative, any bond interest shortfall will be paid out of the overcollateralization account. Also, additional funds equal to

$$R_t = 0.4 d_t \times 1,000,000 \qquad t = 1, \ldots, T-1$$

will flow into the overcollateralization account from default recovery. Thus the value of the overcollateralization account at the end of year t, including the cash flows from recovery and interest paid on the value of the account at the end of the prior year, is

$$R_t + OC_t + \sum_{\tau=1}^{t-1} (1+r)^{t-\tau} OC_\tau \qquad t = 1, \ldots, T-1$$

This value is not fully determined until we know OC_t. And as simple as this securitization structure is, there are a few tests that the custodian must go through to determine the overcollateralization cash flow. These rules can be thought of as a two-step decision tree, each step having two branches. The test is carried out at the end of each year. In the first step, the custodian tests whether the excess spread is positive; that is, is $L_t - B > 0$?

- If $L_t - B \geq 0$, the next test determines whether the excess spread is great enough to cover K; that is, is $L_t - B \geq K$?

- If $L_t - B \geq K$, then K flows into the overcollateralization account, and there may be some excess spread left over for the equity, unless $L_t - B = K$.
- If $L_t - B < K$, then the entire amount $L_t - B$ flows into the overcollateralization account, and there is no excess spread left over for the equity. If $L_t - B = 0$, then there is exactly enough excess spread to cover bond payments and nothing flows into the overcollateralization account.

- If the excess spread is negative ($L_t - B < 0$), the custodian tests whether there are enough funds in the overcollateralization account, plus proceeds from recovery on defaults over the past year, to cover the shortfall. The funds in the overcollateralization account from prior years amount to $\sum_{\tau=1}^{t-1}(1 + r)^{t-\tau} OC_\tau$ and current year recoveries are R_t, so the test is

$$\sum_{\tau=1}^{t-1}(1 + r)^{t-\tau} OC_\tau + R_t \geq B - L_t$$

- If the shortfall can be covered, then the entire amount $B - L_t$ flows out of the overcollateralization account.
- If not, that is, if

$$\sum_{\tau=1}^{t-1}(1 + r)^{t-\tau} OC_\tau + R_t < B - L_t$$

then $\sum_{\tau=1}^{t-1}(1 + r)^{t-\tau} OC_\tau + R_t$ flows out of the overcollateralization account, leaving it entirely depleted.

The amount to be diverted can be written

$$OC_t = \left\{ \begin{array}{c} \min(L_t - B, K) \\ \max[L_t - B, -(\sum_{\tau=1}^{t-1}(1 + r)^{t-\tau} OC_\tau + R_t)] \end{array} \right\} \quad \text{for} \quad \left\{ \begin{array}{c} L_t \geq B \\ L_t < B \end{array} \right\}$$

Once we know how much excess spread, if any, flows into the overcollateralization account at the end of year t, we can determine how much cash flows to the equity noteholders at the end of year t. The equity cash flow is

$$\max(L_t - B - OC_t, 0) \qquad t = 1, \ldots, T - 1$$

Obviously, there is no cash flow to the equity prior to maturity unless there is positive excess spread.

The results for our example can be presented in a cash flow table, presented as Table 9.1, that shows the cash flows in detail, as specified by

TABLE 9.1 Interim Cash Flow Table for the CLO

(1) t	(2) Def	(3) Cum	(4) Srv	(5) Loan int	(6) Exc spr	(7) OC	(8) Recov	(9) OC+Recov	(10) Eq flow	(11) Results	(12) OC a/c
Default rate 2.0 percent											
1	2	2	98	8,330,000	2,655,000	1,750,000	800,000	2,550,000	905,000	Y	2,550,000
2	2	4	96	8,160,000	2,485,000	1,750,000	800,000	2,550,000	735,000	Y	5,227,500
3	2	6	94	7,990,000	2,315,000	1,750,000	800,000	2,550,000	565,000	Y	8,038,875
4	2	8	92	7,820,000	2,145,000	1,750,000	800,000	2,550,000	395,000	Y	10,990,819
Default rate 7.5 percent											
1	8	8	92	7,820,000	2,145,000	1,750,000	3,200,000	4,950,000	395,000	Y	4,950,000
2	7	15	85	7,225,000	1,550,000	1,550,000	2,800,000	4,350,000	0	Y	9,547,500
3	6	21	79	6,715,000	1,040,000	1,040,000	2,400,000	3,440,000	0	Y	13,464,875
4	6	27	73	6,205,000	530,000	530,000	2,400,000	2,930,000	0	Y	17,068,119
Default rate 10.0 percent											
1	10	10	90	7,650,000	1,975,000	1,750,000	4,000,000	5,750,000	225,000	Y	5,750,000
2	9	19	81	6,885,000	1,210,000	1,210,000	3,600,000	4,810,000	0	Y	10,847,500
3	8	27	73	6,205,000	530,000	530,000	3,200,000	3,730,000	0	Y	15,119,875
4	7	34	66	5,610,000	−65,000	−65,000	2,800,000	2,735,000	0	Y	18,610,869

Key to columns:
(1) Year index
(2) Number of defaults during year t
(3) Cumulative number of defaults $\sum_{\tau=1}^{t} d_\tau$ at the end of year t
(4) Number of surviving loans $N - \sum_{\tau=1}^{t} d_\tau$ at the end of year t
(5) Loan interest
(6) Excess spread
(7) Overcollateralization increment
(8) Recovery amount R_t
(9) Aggregate flow into overcollateralization account $OC_t + R_t$
(10) Interim cash flow to the equity at the end of year t.
(11) Results of a test to see if interest on the bonds can be paid in full at the end of year t.
(12) The value of the overcollateralization account at time t.

the waterfall, in each period. There is a panel in the cash flow table for each default scenario.

We can now summarize the results. The excess spread declines over time in all scenarios as defaults pile up, as one would expect. For the high-default scenarios, the loan interest in later years is not sufficient to cover the bond interest and the excess spread turns negative.

The overcollateralization amount is capped at $1,750,000, and when the default rate is 2.0 percent that amount can be paid into the overcollateralization account in full every year. For higher default rates, the cap kicks in early on. For the highest default rate, in which the excess spread in the later years turns negative, not only is no additional overcollateralization diverted away from the equity, but rather funds must be paid out of the overcollateralization account to cover the bond interest.

The most dramatic differences between the default scenarios are in the equity cash flows, the last cash flows to be determined. For the lowest default rate, the equity continues to receive at least some cash almost throughout the life of the securitization. In the higher default scenarios, interim cash flows to the equity terminate much earlier.

Because the recovery amounts are held back rather than used to partially redeem the bonds prior to maturity, and because, in addition, even in a very high default scenario, there are enough funds available to pay the coupons on the bond tranches, the bonds cannot "break" before maturity. In real-world securitizations, trust agreements are written so that in an extreme scenario, the securitization can be unwound early, thus protecting the bond tranches from further loss.

9.2.2 Tracking the Final-Year Cash Flows

To complete the cash flow analysis, we need to examine the final-year payment streams. Our securitization has an anticipated maturity of five years, and we have tabulated cash flows for the first four. Next, we examine the terminal, year 5, cash flows. There are four sources of funds at the end of year 5:

1. Loan interest from the surviving loans paid at the end of year 5, equal to

$$\left(N - \sum_{t=1}^{T} d_t\right) \times (0.05 + 0.035) \times 1,000,000$$

2. Proceeds from redemptions at par of the surviving loans:

$$\left(N - \sum_{t=1}^{T} d_t\right) \times 1,000,000$$

3. The recovery from loans defaulting in year 5:

$$R_T = 0.4 \times d_T \times 1,000,000$$

4. The value of the overcollateralization account at the end of year 5, equal to $1 + r$ times the value displayed, for each default rate, in the last row of the last column of Table 9.1:

$$\sum_{\tau=1}^{T}(1+r)^{t-\tau} OC_\tau$$

There is no longer any need to divert funds to overcollateralization, so all funds are to be used to pay the final coupon and redemption proceeds to the bondholders, in order of priority and to the extent possible. There is also no longer any need to carry out an overcollateralization test.

Next, we add all the terminal cash flows and compare their sum with the amount due to the bondholders. If too many loans have defaulted, then one or both bonds may not receive its stipulated final payments in full. The terminal available funds are:

$$F = \sum_{t=1}^{T-1}(1+r)^{t-\tau} OC_\tau + \left[\left(N - \sum_{t=1}^{T} d_t\right)1.085 + 0.4d_T\right] \times 1,000,000$$

If this amount is greater than the \$100,675,000 due to the bondholders, the equity note receives a final payment. If it is less, at least one of the bonds will default. The custodian therefore must perform a sequence of two shortfall tests. The first tests if the senior note can be paid in full:

$$F \begin{Bmatrix} \geq \\ < \end{Bmatrix} 89,675,000$$

If this test is passed, the senior bond is money good. If not, we subtract the shortfall from its par value. The senior bond value then experiences a credit loss or writedown of \$89,675,000 − F. We can express the loss as $\max(89,675,000 - F, 0)$.

Since the senior bond must be paid first, the default test for the junior bond is

$$F - 89,675,000 \begin{Bmatrix} \geq \\ < \end{Bmatrix} 11,000,000$$

which is the amount due the mezzanine note holders. If there is a shortfall, the credit loss of the mezzanine is $\max[11,000,000 - (F - 89,675,000), 0]$.

The credit risk to the bonds is of a shortfall of interest and, potentially, even principal. What about the equity? The equity is not "owed" anything, so is there a meaningful measure of its credit risk? One approach is to compute the equity tranche's *internal rate of return* (IRR) in different scenarios. Credit losses in excess of expectations will bring the rate of return down, possibly below zero, if not even the par value the equity investor advanced is recovered over time. The equity investor will typically have a target rate of return, or *hurdle rate*, representing an appropriate compensation for risk, given the possible alternative uses of capital. Even if the rate of return is non-negative, it may fall below this hurdle rate and represent a loss. We could use a posited hurdle rate to discount cash flows and arrive at an equity dollar price. While the results would be somewhat dependent on the choice of hurdle rate, we can speak of the equity's value more or less interchangeably in terms of price or IRR.

To compute the equity IRR, we first need to assemble all the cash flows to the equity tranche. The initial outlay for the equity tranche is $5,000,000. If the equity tranche owner is both the originator of the underlying loans and the sponsor of the securitization, this amount represents the difference between the amount lent and the amount funded at term via the bond tranches. If the equity tranche owner is a different party, we assume that party bought the equity "at par." Recall that we've assumed that the bond and underlying loan interest rates are market-clearing, equilibrium rates. We similarly assume the equity has a market-clearing expected return at par.

We saw earlier that the interim cash flows to the equity, that is, those in the first 4 years, are $\max(L_t - B - OC_t, 0), t = 1, \ldots, 4$. The terminal cash flow to the equity is $\max(F - 100,675,000, 0)$, since the bond tranches have a prior claim to any available funds in the final period. Thus the IRR is the value of x that satisfies

$$0 = -5,000,000 + \sum_{t=1}^{T-1}(1 + x)^{-t}\max(L_t - B - OC_t, 0)$$
$$+(1 + x)^{-T}\max(F - 100,675,000, 0)$$

To complete the scenario analysis, we display these values for the three default scenarios in Table 9.2. The first three rows of data display the final-year default count, and the cumulative number of defaulted and surviving loans. The next five rows of data show the terminal available funds and how they are generated—loan interest, redemption proceeds, and recovery. The main driver is, not surprisingly, redemption proceeds from surviving loans. The next row of data is the amount owed to the bondholders at time T, the same, of course, in all default scenarios.

We can see that in the low default scenario, the bonds will be paid in full and the equity tranche will get a large final payment. At higher default

TABLE 9.2 Terminal Cash Flows of the CDO

	2.0	7.5	10.0
Default rate	2.0	7.5	10.0
Time T default counts:			
Final period current default count	2	5	7
Final period cumulative default count	10	32	41
Final period surviving loan count	90	68	59
Available funds at time T:			
Final period loan interest	7,650,000	5,780,000	5,015,000
Loan redemption proceeds	90,000,000	68,000,000	59,000,000
Final period recovery amount	800,000	2,000,000	2,800,000
Ending balance of overcollateralization account	11,540,360	17,921,525	19,541,412
Total terminal available funds	109,990,360	93,701,525	86,356,412
Owed to bond tranches	100,675,000	100,675,000	100,675,000
Equity returns:			
Equity terminal cash flow	9,315,360	0	0
Equity internal rate of return (%)	23.0	−92.1	−95.5
Bond writedowns:			
Total terminal bond shortfall	0	6,973,475	14,318,588
Terminal mezzanine shortfall	0	6,973,475	11,000,000
Terminal senior shortfall	0	0	3,318,588

rates, the equity receives no residual payment, and one or both of the bonds cannot be paid in full.

For the expected default rate of 2 percent, the equity IRR is 23 percent. At high default rates, the IRR approaches minus 100 percent. At a default rate of 10 percent, for example, the equity receives an early payment out of excess spread, but nothing subsequently, so the equity tranche owner is "out" nearly the entire $5,000,000 initial investment.

The final rows of the table show credit losses, if any, on the bond tranches. At a default rate of 2 percent, both bonds are repaid in full. At a default rate of 7.5 percent, the junior bond loses its final coupon payment and a portion of principal. At a default rate of 10 percent, even the senior bond cannot be paid off in full, but loses part of its final coupon payment.

The table shows extreme loss levels that will "break" the bonds and essentially wipe out the equity tranche. We have focused here on explaining how to take account of the structure and waterfall of the securitization in determining losses, while making broad-brush assumptions about the performance of the collateral pool. Another equally important task in scenario analysis is to determine what are reasonable scenarios about pool losses. How we interpret the results for a 10 percent collateral pool default rate depends on how likely we consider that outcome to be. As explained in

Chapter 10, it is difficult to estimate the probabilities of such extreme events precisely. But we can make sound judgements about whether they are highly unlikely but possible, or close to impossible.

For structured credit products, such judgments are based on two assessments. The first is a credit risk assessment of the underlying loans, to determine how the distribution of defaults will vary under different economic conditions, requiring expertise and models pertinent to the type of credit in the pool, say, consumer credit or commercial real estate loans. The second is a judgement about how adverse an economic environment to take into account. The latter is based on both economic analysis and the risk appetite of the investor. We discuss the issues arising in designing appropriate stress tests in Chapter 13.

9.3 MEASURING STRUCTURED CREDIT RISK VIA SIMULATION

Up until now, we have analyzed losses in the securitization for specific default scenarios. But this approach ignores default correlation, that is, the propensity of defaults to coincide. Once we take default correlation into account, we can estimate the entire probability distribution of losses for each tranche into account. The loss distributions provide us with insights into valuation as well as risk.

Chapter 8 introduced two approaches to taking account of default correlation in a credit portfolio, one based on the single-factor model and the other on simulation via a copula model. We'll apply the simulation/copula approach to the loan portfolio that constitutes the securitization trust's collateral pool. While in Chapter 8, we applied the simulation approach to a portfolio of two credit-risky securities, here we apply it to a case in which the underlying collateral contains many loans. This simulation-based analysis of the risk of a securitization, by taking into account the default correlation, unlocks the entire distribution of outcomes, not just particular outcomes.

9.3.1 The Simulation Procedure and the Role of Correlation

The simulation process can be summarized in these steps:

Estimate parameters. First we need to determine the parameters for the valuation, in particular, the default probabilities or default distribution of each individual security in the collateral pool, and the correlation used to tie the individual default distributions together.

Generate default time simulations. Using the estimated parameters and the copula approach, we simulate the default times of each security (here, the underlying loans) in the collateral pool. With the default times in hand, we can next identify, for each simulation thread and each security, whether it defaults within the life of the securitization, and if so, in what period.

Compute the credit losses. The default times can be used to generate a sequence of cash flows from the collateral pool in each period, for each simulation thread. This part of the procedure is the same as the cash flow analysis of the previous section. The difference is only that in the simulation approach, the number of defaults each period is dictated by the results of the simulation rather than assumed. The securitization capital structure and waterfall allocate the cash flows over time, for each simulation thread, to the securitization tranches. For each simulation thread, the credit loss, if any, to each liability and the residual cash flow, if any, to the equity tranche can then be computed. This gives us the entire distribution of losses for the bonds and of IRRs for the equity. The distributions can be used to compute credit statistics such as credit VaR for each tranche.

The default probability parameters can, as usual, be estimated in two ways, either as a physical or, if comparable spread data is available, as a risk-neutral probability. We have N (in our example, 100) pieces of collateral in the pool, so we need up to N distinct default probabilities $\pi_n, n = 1, \ldots, N$. If we want to use time-varying hazard rates, we also need a term structure of default probabilities. For our securitization example, we assume, as in Chapter 8, that we have obtained a one-year physical default probability π_n from an internal or external rating. We convert this to a hazard rate using the formula

$$\pi_n = 1 - e^{-\lambda_n} \quad \Leftrightarrow \quad \lambda_n = -\log(1 - \pi_n) \quad n = 1, \ldots, N$$

We'll assume each loan has the same probability of default, so $\pi_n = \pi, n = 1, \ldots, 100$.

The correlations $\rho_{m,n}, m, n = 1, \ldots, N$ between the elements of the collateral pool are more difficult to obtain, since the copula correlation, as we have seen, is not a natural or intuitive quantity, and there is not much market or financial data with which to estimate it. We'll put only one restriction on the correlation assumption: that $\rho_{m,n} \geq 0, m, n = 1, \ldots, N$.

In our example we assume the correlations are pairwise constant, so $\rho_{mn} = \rho, m, n = 1, \ldots, 100$. We will want to see the effects of different assumptions about default probability and correlation, so, for both the default probability and correlation parameter, we'll compare results for different pairs of π and ρ. Our posited loan default probabilities range from $\pi = 0.075$ to $\pi = 0.975$, in increments of 0.075, and we apply correlation parameters between $\rho = 0$ and $\rho = 0.9$, in increments of 0.3. This gives us a total of 52 pairs of default probability and correlation parameter settings to study.

Once we have the parameters, we can begin to simulate. Since we are dealing with an N-security portfolio, each simulation thread must have N elements. Let I be the number of simulations we propose to do. In our example, we set the number of simulations at $I = 1,000$. The first step is to generate a set of I draws from an N-dimensional joint standard normal distribution. This is an N-dimensional random variable in which each element is normally distributed with a mean of zero and a standard deviation equal to unity, and in which each pair of elements m and n has a correlation coefficient of $\rho_{m,n}$.

The result of this step is a matrix

$$
\tilde{z} = \begin{pmatrix}
\tilde{z}_{11} & \tilde{z}_{12} & \cdots & \tilde{z}_{1N} \\
\tilde{z}_{21} & \tilde{z}_{22} & \cdots & \tilde{z}_{2N} \\
\vdots & \vdots & \ddots & \vdots \\
\tilde{z}_{I1} & \tilde{z}_{I2} & \cdots & \tilde{z}_{IN}
\end{pmatrix}
$$

Each row of $\tilde{z}$ is one simulation thread of an N-dimensional standard normal variate with a covariance matrix equal to

$$
\Sigma = \begin{pmatrix}
1 & \rho_{12} & \cdots & \rho_{1N} \\
\rho_{12} & 1 & \cdots & \rho_{2N} \\
\vdots & \vdots & \ddots & \vdots \\
\rho_{1N} & \rho_{2N} & \cdots & 1
\end{pmatrix}
$$

For example, suppose we take the correlations coefficient to be a constant $\rho = 0.30$. We can generate 1,000 correlated normals. The result of this step is a matrix

$$
\tilde{z} = \begin{pmatrix}
\tilde{z}_{1,1} & \cdots & \tilde{z}_{1,100} \\
\vdots & \ddots & \vdots \\
\tilde{z}_{1000,1} & \cdots & \tilde{z}_{1000,100}
\end{pmatrix}
$$

with each row representing one simulation thread of a 100-dimensional standard normal variate with a mean of zero and a covariance matrix equal to

$$
\begin{pmatrix} 1 & \cdots & \rho \\ \vdots & \ddots & \vdots \\ \rho & \cdots & 1 \end{pmatrix} = \begin{pmatrix} 1 & \cdots & 0.3 \\ \vdots & \ddots & \vdots \\ 0.3 & \cdots & 1 \end{pmatrix}
$$

In the implementation used in the example, the upper left 4×4 submatrix of the matrix $\tilde{z}$ is

$$
\begin{pmatrix}
-1.2625 & -0.3968 & -0.4285 & -1.0258 & \cdots \\
-0.3778 & -0.1544 & -1.5535 & -0.4684 & \cdots \\
0.2319 & -0.1779 & -0.4377 & -0.5282 & \cdots \\
-0.6915 & -0.5754 & -0.3939 & -0.1683 & \cdots \\
\vdots & \vdots & \vdots & \vdots & \ddots
\end{pmatrix}
$$

The actual numerical values would depend on the random number generation technique being used and random variation in the simulation results, as outlined in Appendix A.5. For our example, we generate four such matrices $\tilde{z}$, one for each of our correlation assumptions.

The next step is to map each element of $\tilde{z}$ to a default time $\tilde{t}_{ni}, n = 1, \ldots, N, i = 1, \ldots, I$. If we have one hazard rate λ_n for each security, we carry out the mapping via the formula

$$
\tilde{t}_{ni} = -\frac{\log[1 - \Phi(\tilde{z}_{ni})]}{\lambda_n} \qquad n = 1, \ldots, N; i = 1, \ldots, I
$$

giving us a matrix $\tilde{t}$ of default times. We can now count off the number of defaults, and the cumulative number, occurring in each period within the term of the securitization liabilities. Note that we need a distinct matrix of simulated standard normals for each correlation assumption, but not for each default probability assumption.

In our example, we use a constant hazard rate across loans:

$$
\tilde{t}_{ni} = -\frac{\log[1 - \Phi(\tilde{z}_{ni})]}{\lambda} \qquad n = 1, \ldots, 100; i = 1, \ldots, 1000
$$

For $\pi = 0.0225$, for example, we have $\lambda = -\log(1 - \pi) = -\log(0.9775) = 0.022757$. Together with the assumption $\rho = 0.30$, this results in another $1,000 \times 100$ matrix. In our simulation example, it has upper left 4×4 submatrix

$$\begin{pmatrix} 4.7951 & 18.6433 & 17.8702 & 7.2705 & \cdots \\ 19.1194 & 25.3727 & 2.7262 & 16.9309 & \cdots \\ 39.3599 & 24.6542 & 17.6515 & 15.5915 & \cdots \\ 12.3274 & 14.5882 & 18.7161 & 24.9461 & \cdots \\ \vdots & \vdots & \vdots & \vdots & \ddots \end{pmatrix}$$

We generate as many such matrices of simulated default times as we have pairs of default time-correlation parameter assumptions, namely 52. For example, focusing on element (1,1) of the submatrix of correlated normal simulations of the previous page, we compute the corresponding element (1,1) of the matrix of default times as

$$-\frac{\log[1 - \Phi(-1.2625)]}{-\log(1 - 0.0225)} = 4.7951$$

Note that there are two defaults (default times less than 5.0) within the five-year term of the securitization for these first four loans in the first four threads of the simulation for the parameter pair $\pi = 0.0225$, $\rho = 0.30$. Again, we have 52 such matrices, one for each parameter pair, each of dimension $1,000 \times 100$.

This completes the process of generating simulations of default times. The next step is to turn the simulated default times $\tilde{t}$ into vectors of year-by-year defaults and cumulative defaults, similar to columns (2) and (3) of the cash flow Table 9.1, and the row of final year defaults in Table 9.2. To do this, we count, for each of the 1,000 rows, how many of the 100 simulated default times fall into each of the intervals $(t - 1, t], t = 1, \ldots, T$. The result in our example is a set of 1,000 vectors of length $T = 5$, each containing the number of defaults occurring in each ρ of the five years of the CLO. The cumulative sum of each of these vectors is the cumulative default count, also a five-element vector.

The full first row of $\tilde{t}$ for the parameter pair $\pi = 0.0225$, $\rho = 0.30$, for example, is

4.80	18.64	17.87	7.27	3.86	18.39	3.89	5.85	11.37	25.80
22.39	5.35	17.60	20.62	0.84	4.27	39.38	11.22	30.37	3.44
6.70	10.21	29.41	26.93	8.79	36.20	24.55	48.12	2.48	0.55
11.89	4.55	12.81	69.02	24.22	7.99	16.70	4.94	12.36	7.48
2.55	8.12	4.75	91.37	32.10	35.34	25.53	0.39	3.55	10.55
1.83	2.80	0.79	1.26	5.72	2.69	1.12	0.91	3.94	32.04
2.69	2.94	12.66	9.80	2.40	40.70	7.47	0.46	15.31	16.72
5.31	5.85	0.14	5.89	25.30	9.80	13.96	8.73	5.73	48.27
26.22	7.39	5.25	3.13	0.68	4.51	1.88	3.31	39.46	8.38
42.29	0.73	4.53	11.38	15.70	0.99	0.91	22.43	1.94	12.41

It gives us the simulated default times in the first simulation thread of each of the 100 pieces of collateral. The associated current default count vector is

$$(11, 5, 7, 7, 7)$$

since there are 11 elements in the first row of $\tilde{t}$ that are less than or equal to 1, 4 elements in the range $(1, 2)$, and so on. The corresponding cumulative default count vector is

$$(11, 16, 23, 30, 37)$$

Thus, in that first simulation thread, there is a cumulative total of 37 defaults by the end of year 5. (This is, incidentally, one of the grimmer simulation threads for this parameter pair.) We generate 1,000 such cumulative default count vectors, one for each simulation thread, for this parameter pair.

We want to see the effects of different assumptions, so we repeat this procedure for all 52 pairs of default probabilities $\pi = 0.0075$, $0.0150, \ldots, 0.0975$ and correlations $\rho = 0.00, 0.30, 0.60, 0.90$. One of the advantages of this approach is that, if we want to see the effects of changing distributional parameters, or characteristics of the collateral or liability structure, such as the recovery rate or the interest paid by the collateral, we don't have to do a fresh set of simulations. We only change the way the simulations are processed. We would need to do new simulations only if we want to increase the number of threads I for greater simulation accuracy, or we change the number of loans in the collateral pool, or we introduce new correlation settings not included in the set $\{0.00, 0.30, 0.60, 0.90\}$.

The final step is to pass these loan-loss results, scenario by scenario, through the waterfall. To accomplish this, we repeat, for each simulation, the process we laid out for scenario analysis. For each simulation, we use the current and cumulative default count vectors to generate the cash flows, distribute them through the waterfall, and tabulate the cash flows for each security.

9.3.2 Means of the Distributions

We can now describe the distributions of the results. We'll begin with the means.

The results for the equity tranche are displayed in the next table. Each value is the *mean* IRR over all the simulations for the parameter pair displayed in the row and column headers. For low default rates, the mean equity IRRs are over 30 percent per annum, while for high default rates

and low correlations, the equity tranche is effectively wiped out in many
simulation threads.

	Equity IRR (percent)			
π	$\rho = 0.00$	$\rho = 0.30$	$\rho = 0.60$	$\rho = 0.90$
0.0075	33.9	32.4	30.8	32.2
0.0225	20.6	13.3	14.2	19.8
0.0375	−2.8	−8.1	−0.9	10.5
0.0525	−46.9	−26.3	−13.8	1.5
0.0675	−79.3	−41.2	−24.0	−6.5
0.0825	−89.7	−53.5	−33.3	−13.8
0.0975	−93.8	−63.1	−41.1	−20.3

In order to compute risk statistics such as VaR, we use dollar values rather
than IRRs. To do so, we make a somewhat arbitrary parameter assignment,
namely, that the equity hurdle rate is 25 percent. Some assumption on
hurdle rates is required in order to identify the IRR at which a loss occurs,
and is similar to our setting the market-clearing bond coupons as part of the
example. This hurdle rate more or less prices the equity tranche at its par
value of \$5,000,000 for $\pi = 2.25$ percent and $\rho = 0.30$. We use this hurdle
rate to discount to the present the future cash flows to the equity tranche in
each simulation scenario. The sum of these present values is the equity value
in that scenario. A present value is computed for each simulation as:

$$\sum_{t=1}^{T-1} (1.25)^{-t} \max(L_t - B - OC_t, 0) + (1.25)^{-T} \max(F - 100675000, 0)$$

Averaging these present values over all 1,000 simulations gives us the estimated equity value for each (π, ρ) pair. Table 9.3 tabulates the means of the
simulated equity values and the bond credit writedowns. We display them
graphically in Figure 9.1. Each result is the mean over the 1,000 simulations
of the IRR or credit loss. The bond writedowns are expressed as a percent
of the par value of the bond, rather than in millions of dollars to make comparison of the results for the mezzanine and senior bonds more meaningful.

The means of the mezzanine and senior bond writedowns don't "add
up," even though the results add up simulation by simulation. Consider,
for example, the parameter pair $\pi = 0.0225$ and $\rho = 0.30$. There are small
losses for both the senior and junior bonds. How can there be losses to the
senior at all, if the junior losses are small? The reason is that the senior loss

TABLE 9.3 Mean Equity Values and Bond Credit Losses

	Equity value ($ million)			
π	$\rho = 0.00$	$\rho = 0.30$	$\rho = 0.60$	$\rho = 0.90$
0.0075	6.59	6.72	6.85	7.14
0.0225	4.44	4.98	5.61	6.33
0.0375	2.47	3.69	4.64	5.69
0.0525	1.06	2.75	3.90	5.08
0.0675	0.51	2.07	3.32	4.56
0.0825	0.33	1.57	2.84	4.13
0.0975	0.22	1.23	2.44	3.74
	Mezzanine bond writedown (percent of tranche par value)			
π	$\rho = 0.00$	$\rho = 0.30$	$\rho = 0.60$	$\rho = 0.90$
0.0075	0.00	1.11	3.36	4.84
0.0225	0.00	7.35	12.82	15.49
0.0375	1.03	19.30	23.97	23.14
0.0525	14.81	33.90	33.75	31.32
0.0675	49.86	46.45	43.82	39.64
0.0825	85.74	58.60	51.54	46.40
0.0975	103.92	69.58	58.68	52.87
	Senior bond writedown (percent of tranche par value)			
π	$\rho = 0.00$	$\rho = 0.30$	$\rho = 0.60$	$\rho = 0.90$
0.0075	0.00	0.05	0.41	1.31
0.0225	0.00	0.52	2.14	5.05
0.0375	0.00	1.44	4.36	8.81
0.0525	0.00	2.96	6.96	12.08
0.0675	0.12	5.17	9.71	15.49
0.0825	1.07	7.78	12.75	18.96
0.0975	4.02	10.64	15.92	22.29

of 0.05 percent of par stems from six simulation threads out of the 1,000 in which, of course, the junior tranche is entirely wiped out. However, there are only 19 threads in which the junior tranche experiences a loss at all, so the average loss for the parameter pair is low.

There are several important patterns in the results we see in the example, particularly with respect to the interaction between correlation and default probability:

Increases in the default rate increase bond losses and decrease the equity IRR for all correlation assumptions. In other words, for any given correlation, an increase in the default rate will hurt all of the tranches. This is an unsurprising result, in contrast to the next two.

Increases in correlation can have a very different effect, depending on the level of defaults. At low default rates, the impact of an increase

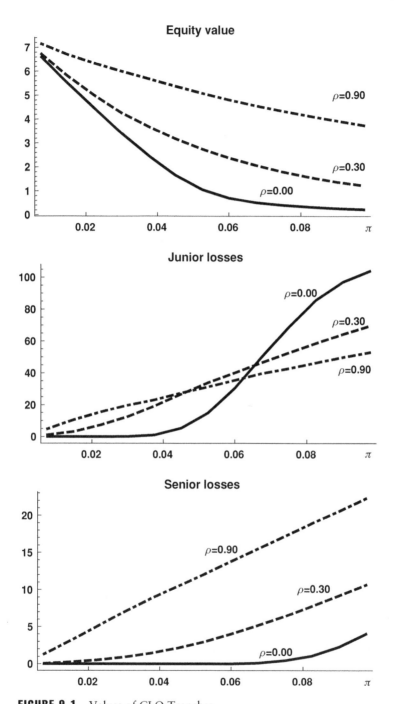

FIGURE 9.1   Values of CLO Tranches

Equity value and bond losses in millions of $ as a function of default probabilities for different constant pairwise correlations. The equity is valued using a discount factor of 25 percent per annum. Bond losses are in percent of par value.

in correlation is relatively low. But when default rates are relatively high, an increase in correlation can materially *increase* the IRR of the equity tranche, but also *increase* the losses to the senior bond tranche. In other words, the equity benefits from high correlation, while the senior bond is hurt by it. We will discuss this important result in more detail in a moment.

The effect on the mezzanine bond is more complicated. At low default rates, an increase in correlation increases losses on the mezzanine bond, but decreases losses for high default rates. In other words, the mezzanine bond behaves more like a senior bond at low default rates, when it is unlikely that losses will approach its attachment point and the bond will be broken, and behaves more like the equity tranche when default rates are high and a breach of the attachment point appears likelier.

Convexity. At low correlations, the equity value is substantially *positively convex* in default rates. That is, the equity tranche loses value rapidly as default rates increase from a low level. But as default rates increase, the responsiveness of the equity value to further increases in the default rate drops off. In other words, you can't beat a dead horse: If you are long the equity tranche, once you've lost most of your investment due to increases in default rates, you will lose a bit less from the next increase in default rates.

For low correlations, the senior bond tranche has *negative convexity* in default rates; its losses accelerate as defaults rise. The mezzanine tranche, again, is ambiguous. It has negative convexity for low default rates, but is positively convex for high default rates. At high correlations, all the tranches are less convex; that is, they respond more nearly linearly to changes in default rates.

9.3.3 Distribution of Losses and Credit VaR

Table 9.3 and Figure 9.1 display the means over all the simulations for each parameter pair. We can gain additional insights into the risk characteristics of each tranche by examining the entire distribution of outcomes for different parameter pairs; the patterns we see differ across tranches.

Characteristics of the Distributions Figures 9.2 through 9.4 present histograms of all 1,000 simulated values of each of the three CLO tranches for a subset of our 52 (π, ρ) assumption pairs. Each histogram is labeled by its (π, ρ) assumption. The expected value of the tranche for the (π, ρ)

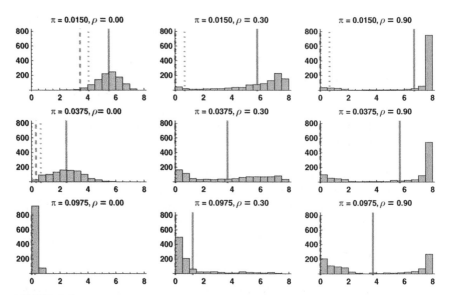

FIGURE 9.2 Distribution of Simulated Equity Tranche Values
Histograms of simulated values of equity tranche, in millions of $. Each histogram
is labeled by its default probability and correlation assumption. Values are
computed using a discounting rate of 25 percent. The solid grid line marks the
mean value over the 1,000 simulations. The dashed and dotted grid lines mark the
0.01 and 0.05 quantile values.

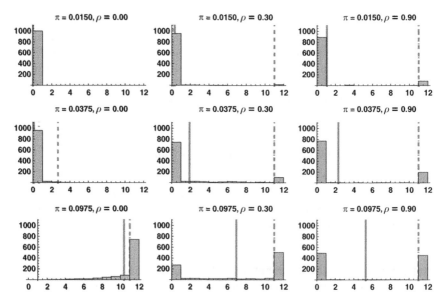

FIGURE 9.3 Distribution of Simulated Mezzanine Bond Tranche Losses
Histograms of simulated losses of mezzanine bond, in millions of $. Each histogram
is labeled by its default probability and correlation assumption. The solid grid line
marks the mean loss over the 1,000 simulations. The dashed and dotted grid lines
mark the 0.99 and 0.95 quantiles of the loss.

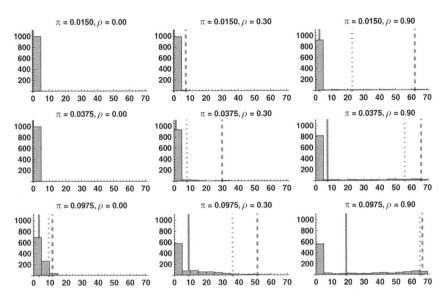

FIGURE 9.4 Distribution of Simulated Senior Bond Tranche Losses
Histograms of simulated losses of senior bonds, in millions of $. Each histogram is labeled by its default probability and correlation assumption. The solid grid line marks the mean loss over the 1,000 simulations. The dashed and dotted grid lines mark the 0.99 and 0.95 quantiles of the loss.

assumption is marked by a solid grid line. The 0.01-(0.05)-quantile of the value distribution is marked by a dashed (dotted) grid line.

The distribution plots help us more fully understand the behavior of the mean values or writedowns of the different tranches. Before we look at each tranche in detail, let's recall how correlation affects the pattern of defaults. When correlation is high, defaults tend to arrive in clusters. Averaged over all of the simulations, the number of defaults will be approximately equal to the default probability. But the defaults will not be evenly spread over the simulation. Some simulations will experience unusually many and some unusually few defaults for any default probability. The higher the correlation, the more such extreme simulation results there will be.

> *Equity tranche.* The results for the equity tranche (Figure 9.2) are plotted as dollar values, with the cash flows discounted at our stipulated IRR of 25 percent. The most obvious feature of the histograms is that for low correlations, the simulated values form a bell curve. The center of the bell curve is higher for lower default probabilities. For high enough default rates, the bell curve is squeezed up against the lower bound of zero value, as it is wiped out in most scenarios

before it can receive much cash flow. In a low correlation environment, the equity note value is close to what you would expect based on the default probability. It is high for a low default rate and vice versa.

The surprising results are for high correlations. The distribution is U-shaped; extreme outcomes, good or bad, for the equity value are more likely than for low correlations. In a scenario with unusually many defaults, given the default probability, the equity is more likely to be wiped out, while in low-default scenarios, the equity will keep receiving cash flows for a surprisingly long time.

The equity note thus behaves like a lottery ticket in a high-correlation environment. If defaults are low, the high correlation induces a higher probability of a high-default state, reducing the equity note's value. If defaults are high, the high correlation induces a higher probability of a low-default state, raising the equity note's value.

If, in contrast, the correlation is low, some defaults will occur in almost every simulation thread. Since the equity tranche takes the first loss, this means that at least some equity losses are highly likely even in a relatively low-default environment. Therefore low correlation is bad for the equity. Correlation is more decisive for equity risk and value than default probability.

This behavior is related to the convexity of the mean equity values we see in Figure 9.1. At a low correlation, equity values have fewer extremes and are bunched closer to what you would expect based on the default probability, much like the results we obtained using default scenario analysis above. But there is only so much damage you can do to the equity tranche; as it gets closer to being wiped out, a higher default rate has less incremental impact.

Bond tranches. The bond tranche distributions (Figures 9.3 and 9.4) are plotted as dollar amounts of credit losses. They appear quite different from those of the equity; even for low correlations, they are not usually bell-curve–shaped. Rather, in contrast to the equity, the credit subordination concentrates the simulated losses close to zero, but with a long tail of loss scenarios. For the senior bond, this is particularly clear, as almost all simulation outcomes show a zero or small loss, unless both default probability and correlation are quite high.

But the distributions have one characteristic in common with the equity. The distribution of simulated loss tends towards a U shape for higher default probabilities and higher correlations. This tendency is much stronger for the mezzanine, which, as we have seen, behaves like the equity at high correlations and default probabilities.

For low correlations and high default probabilities, finally, we see an important contrast between the mezzanine and senior bonds. The mezzanine is a relatively thin tranche, so a small increase in default rates shifts the center of gravity of the distribution from par to a total loss. We can see this clearly by comparing the histograms for ($\pi = 0.0375$, $\rho = 0.00$) with that for ($\pi = 0.0975$, $\rho = 0.00$).

Credit VaR of the Tranches We can, finally, compute the credit VaR. To do so, we need to sort the simulated values for each tranche by size. For the equity tranche, we measure the credit VaR at a confidence level of 99 (or 95) percent as the difference between the 10th (or 50th) lowest sorted simulation value and the par value of \$5,000,000. The latter value, as noted, is close to the mean present value of the cash flows with $\pi = 2.25$ percent and $\rho = 0.30$. For the bonds, we measure the VaR as the difference between the expected loss and the 10th (or 50th) highest loss in the simulations.

The results at a 99 percent confidence level are displayed in Table 9.4. To make it easier to interpret the table, we have also marked with grid lines the 99th (dashed) and 95th (dotted) percentiles in Figures 9.2 through 9.4. The 99-percent credit VaR can then be read graphically as the horizontal distance between the dashed and solid grid lines. To summarize the results:

Equity tranche. The equity VaR actually falls for higher default probabilities and correlations, because the expected loss is so high at those parameter levels. Although the mean values of the equity tranche increase with correlation, so also does its risk.

Mezzanine bond. The junior bond again shows risk characteristics similar to those of the equity at higher default rates and correlation and to those of the senior bond for lower ones.

The mezzanine, like the equity tranche, is thin. One consequence is that, particularly for higher (π, ρ) pairs, the credit VaRs at the 95 and 99 percent confidence levels are very close together. This means that, conditional on the bond suffering a loss at all, the loss is likely to be very large relative to its par value.

Senior bond. We see once again that correlation is bad for the senior bond. At high correlations, the 99 percent credit VaR of the senior bond is on the order of one-half the par value, while if defaults are uncorrelated, the bond is virtually risk-free even at high default probabilities.

TABLE 9.4 CLO Tranche Credit VaR at a 99 Percent
Confidence Level

	Equity VaR ($ million)			
π	$\rho = 0.00$	$\rho = 0.30$	$\rho = 0.60$	$\rho = 0.90$
0.0075	1.62	6.33	6.85	7.14
0.0225	2.53	4.98	5.61	6.33
0.0375	2.16	3.69	4.64	5.69
0.0525	0.95	2.75	3.90	5.08
0.0675	0.51	2.07	3.32	4.56
0.0825	0.33	1.57	2.84	4.13
0.0975	0.22	1.23	2.44	3.74
	Mezzanine bond VaR ($ million)			
π	$\rho = 0.00$	$\rho = 0.30$	$\rho = 0.60$	$\rho = 0.90$
0.0075	0.00	3.79	10.66	10.52
0.0225	0.00	10.26	9.72	9.45
0.0375	2.59	9.07	8.60	8.69
0.0525	7.09	7.61	7.63	7.87
0.0675	6.01	6.36	6.62	7.04
0.0825	2.43	5.14	5.85	6.36
0.0975	0.61	4.04	5.13	5.71
	Senior bond VaR ($ million)			
π	$\rho = 0.00$	$\rho = 0.30$	$\rho = 0.60$	$\rho = 0.90$
0.0075	0.00	−0.04	11.23	48.30
0.0225	0.00	17.77	41.43	59.99
0.0375	0.00	28.82	49.76	58.61
0.0525	0.00	35.74	52.66	56.23
0.0675	2.85	39.89	52.75	53.57
0.0825	7.03	41.61	51.88	50.62
0.0975	8.33	42.60	50.25	47.79

For a correlation of 0.90, the risk of the senior bond at a 99 percent confidence level varies surprisingly little with default probability. The reason is that at a high correlation, clusters of defaults in a handful of simulations guarantee that at least 1 percent of the simulations will show extremely high losses.

Note that there is one entry, for the senior bond with $(\pi, \rho) = (0.0075, 0.30)$, for which the VaR is negative. This odd result is an artifact of the simulation procedure, and provides an illustration of the difficulties of simulation for a credit portfolio. For this assumption pair, almost all the simulation results value the senior bond at par, *including* the 10th ordered simulation result. There are, however, seven threads in which the senior bond has a loss.

So the expected loss is in this odd case actually higher than the 0.01-quantile loss, and the VaR scenario is a gain.

The anomaly would disappear if we measured VaR at the 99.5 or 99.9 percent confidence level. However, the higher the confidence level, the more simulations we have to perform to be reasonably sure the results are not distorted by simulation error.

9.3.4 Default Sensitivities of the Tranches

The analysis thus far has shown that the securitization tranches have very different sensitivities to default rates. Equity values always fall and bond losses always rise as default probabilities rise, but the response varies for different default correlations and as default rates change. This has important implications for risk management of tranche exposures. In this section, we examine these default sensitivities more closely.

To do so, we develop a measure of the responsiveness of equity value or bond loss to small changes in default probabilities. The "default01" measures the impact of an increase of 1 basis point in the default probability. It is analogous to the DV01 we studied in Chapter 4 and the spread01 we studied in Chapter 7 and is calculated numerically in a similar way.

To compute the default01, we increase and decrease default probability 10bps and revalue each tranche at these new values of π. This requires repeating, twice, the entire valuation procedure from the point onward at which we generate simulated default times. We can reuse our correlated normal simulations $\tilde{z}$. In fact, we should, in order to avoid a change of random seed and the attendant introduction of additional simulation noise. But we have to recompute $\tilde{t}$, the list of vectors of default counts for each simulation, and all the subsequent cash flow analysis, valuation, and computation of losses. The default01 sensitivity of each tranche is then computed as

$$\frac{1}{20}[(\text{mean value/loss for } \pi + 0.0010) - (\text{mean value/loss for } \pi - 0.0010)]$$

We compute this default01 for each combination of π and ρ. The results are displayed in Table 9.5 and Figure 9.5. Each default01 is expressed as a positive number and expresses the decline in value or increase in loss resulting from a 1-basis point rise in default probability.

For all tranches, in all cases, default01 is positive, as expected, regardless of the initial value of π and ρ, since equity and bond values decrease monotonically as the default probability rises. The default01 sensitivity converges to zero for all the tranches for very high default rates (though we are not displaying high enough default probabilities to see this for the senior

TABLE 9.5 CLO Tranche Default Sensitivities

	Equity loss (\$ million per bp)			
π	$\rho = 0.00$	$\rho = 0.30$	$\rho = 0.60$	$\rho = 0.90$
0.0075	0.0144	0.0129	0.0094	0.0069
0.0225	0.0140	0.0104	0.0076	0.0046
0.0375	0.0116	0.0076	0.0056	0.0039
0.0525	0.0065	0.0052	0.0038	0.0035
0.0675	0.0021	0.0039	0.0036	0.0030
0.0825	0.0009	0.0026	0.0032	0.0030
0.0975	0.0006	0.0021	0.0025	0.0024
	Mezzanine bond loss (Percent of par per bp)			
π	$\rho = 0.00$	$\rho = 0.30$	$\rho = 0.60$	$\rho = 0.90$
0.0075	0.0000	0.0231	0.0572	0.0843
0.0225	0.0000	0.0655	0.0658	0.0687
0.0375	0.0317	0.0924	0.0659	0.0436
0.0525	0.1660	0.0863	0.0658	0.0595
0.0675	0.2593	0.0753	0.0605	0.0498
0.0825	0.1939	0.0778	0.0478	0.0465
0.0975	0.0723	0.0664	0.0458	0.0403
	Senior bond loss (Percent of par per bp)			
π	$\rho = 0.00$	$\rho = 0.30$	$\rho = 0.60$	$\rho = 0.90$
0.0075	0.0000	0.0018	0.0084	0.0190
0.0225	0.0000	0.0041	0.0140	0.0255
0.0375	0.0000	0.0081	0.0152	0.0229
0.0525	0.0000	0.0127	0.0170	0.0226
0.0675	0.0027	0.0159	0.0194	0.0228
0.0825	0.0117	0.0176	0.0220	0.0228
0.0975	0.0243	0.0198	0.0217	0.0220

bond). Once losses are extremely high, the incremental impact of additional defaults is low.

The default01 varies most as a function of default probability when correlation is low. With $\rho = 0$, the default01 changes sharply in a certain range of default probabilities, and then tapers off as the tranche losses become very large. The differences in the patterns for the different tranches are related to the locations of their attachment points. For each tranche, the range of greatest sensitivity to an increase in defaults, that is, the largest-magnitude default01, begins at a default rate that brings losses in the collateral pool near that tranche's attachment point. Thus the peak default01 is at a default probability of zero for the equity tranche, and occurs at a lower default rate for the mezzanine than for the senior tranche because it has a lower attachment point. As we see in Chapter 11, this introduces additional risk when

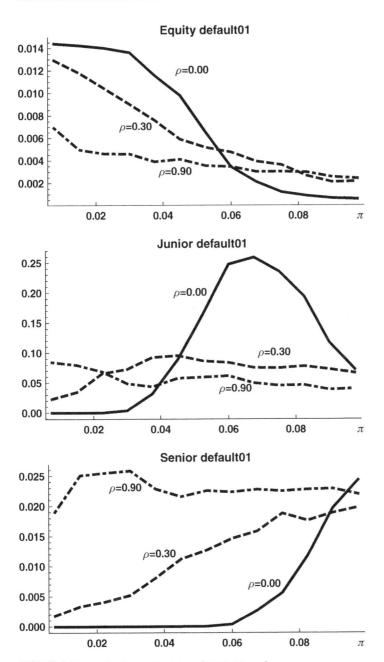

FIGURE 9.5 Default Sensitivities of CLO Tranches
Default01 as a function of default probability for different constant pairwise
correlations. Equity in $ million per bp, bonds in percent of par per bp.

structured credit exposures are put on in a low-correlation environment, or correlation is underestimated. Underestimation of default correlation in structured credit products was an important factor in the origins of the subprime crisis.

Note that some of the default01 plots are not smooth curves, providing us with two related insights. The first is about the difficulty or "expense" of estimating the value and risk of credit portfolios using simulation methods. The number of defaults at each t in each simulation thread must be an integer. Even with 100 loans in the collateral pool, the distribution of value is so skewed and fat-tailed that simulation noise amounting to one or two defaults can make a material difference in the average of the simulation results. The curves could be smoothed out further by substantially increasing the number of simulations used in the estimation procedure. This would be costly in computing time and storage of interim results.

We have enough simulations that the fair value plots are reasonably smooth, but not so all the default01 plots. The lumpiness shows up particularly in the plots of the senior bond default01 plots and those for higher correlations for all tranches. The reason is intuitive. At higher correlations, the defaults tend to come in clusters, amplifying the lumpiness. A chance variation in the number of default clusters in a few simulation threads can materially change the average over all the threads.

The second insight is that because of the fat-tailed distribution of losses, it is difficult to diversify a credit portfolio and reduce idiosyncratic risk. Even in a portfolio of 100 credits, defaults remain "lumpy" events.

9.3.5 Summary of Tranche Risks

We've now examined the risk of the securitization liabilities in several different ways: mean values, the distribution of values and credit VaR, and the sensitivities of the values to changes in default behavior, all measured for varying default probabilities and correlations. As in the scenario analysis of the previous section, we've focused on the securitization's liability structure and waterfall, and less on the equally crucial credit analysis of the underlying loans.

On the basis of the example, we can make a few generalizations about structured credit product risk. In Chapter 14, we see that neglect of these risks played an important role during the subprime crisis, in its propagation and in the losses suffered by individual institutions.

Systematic risk. Structured credit products can have a great deal of systematic risk, even when the collateral pools are well-diversified. In our example, the systematic risk shows up in the equity values and bond losses when default correlation is high. High default correlation is one way of expressing high systematic risk, since it means that there is a low but material probability of a state of the world in which an unusually large number of defaults occurs.

Most notably, even if the collateral is well-diversified, the senior bond has a risk of loss, and potentially a large loss, if correlation is high. While its expected loss may be lower than that of the underlying loan pool, the tail of the loss and the credit VaR are high, as seen in the rightmost column of plots in Figure 9.4. In other words, they are very exposed to systematic risk. The degree of exposure depends heavily on the credit quality of the underlying collateral and the credit enhancement.

Tranche thinness. Another way in which the senior bond's exposure to systematic risk is revealed is in the declining difference between the senior bond's credit VaRs at the 99 and 95 percent confidence levels as default probabilities rise for high default correlations. For the mezzanine bond, the difference between credit VaR at the 99 and 95 percent confidence levels is small for most values of π and ρ, as seen in Figure 9.3. The reason is that tranche is relatively thin. The consequence of tranche thinness is that, conditional on the tranche suffering a loss at all, the size of the loss is likely to be large.

Granularity can significantly diminish securitization risks. In Chapter 8, we saw that a portfolio of large loans has greater risk than a portfolio with equal par value of smaller loans, each of which has the same default probability, recovery rate, and default correlation to other loans. Similarly, "lumpy" pools of collateral have greater risk of extreme outliers than granular ones. A securitization with a more granular collateral pool can have a somewhat larger senior tranche with no increase in credit VaR. A good example of securitizations that are not typically granular are the many CMBS deals in which the pool consists of relative few mortgage loans on large properties, or so-called *fusion* deals in which a fairly granular pool of smaller loans is combined with a few large loans. When the asset pool is not granular, and/or correlation is high, the securitization is said to have high *concentration risk*.

9.4 STANDARD TRANCHES AND IMPLIED CREDIT CORRELATION

Structured credit products are claims on cash flows of credit portfolios. Their prices therefore contain information about how the market values certain characteristics of those portfolios, among them default correlation. In the previous section, we have seen how to use an estimate of the default correlation to estimate model values of securitization tranches. Next, we see how we can reverse engineer the modeling process, applying the model to observed market prices of structured credit products to estimate a default correlation. The correlation obtained in this way is called an *implied credit or implied default correlation*. It is a risk-neutral parameter that we can estimate whenever we observe prices of portfolio credit products. In Chapter 11, we will discuss an example of the risk management challenges presented by implied correlation. In Chapter 14 (see especially Figure 14.21), we discuss the use of implied credit correlation as an indicator of market sentiment regarding systemic risk.

9.4.1 Credit Index Default Swaps and Standard Tranches

We begin by introducing an important class of securitized credit products that trades in relatively liquid markets. In Chapter 7, we studied CDS, the basic credit derivative, and earlier in this chapter we noted that CDS are often building blocks in synthetic structured products. *Credit index default swaps* or CDS indexes are a variant of CDS in which the underlying security is a portfolio of CDS on individual companies, rather than a single company's debt obligations. Two groups of CDS indexes are particularly frequently traded:

CDX (or CDX.NA) are index CDS on North American companies.

iTraxx are index CDS on European and Asian companies.

Both groups are managed by Markit, a company specializing in credit-derivatives pricing and administration. There are, in addition, customized credit index default swaps on sets of companies chosen by a client or financial intermediary.

CDX and iTraxx come in series, initiated semiannually, and indexed by a series number. For example, series CDX.NA.IG.10 was introduced in March 2008. Each series has a number of index products, which can be classified by

Maturity. The standard maturities, as with single-name CDS, are 1, 3, 5, 7, and 10 years. The maturity dates are fixed calendar dates.

Credit quality. In addition to the investment grade CDX.NA.IG, there is a high-yield group (CDX.NA.HY), and subsets of IG and HY that focus on narrower ranges of credit quality.

We'll focus on investment grade CDX (CDX.NA.IG); the iTraxx are analogous. Each IG series has an underlying basket consisting of equal notional amounts of CDS on 125 investment-grade companies. Thus a notional amount $125,000,000 of the CDX contains $1,000,000 notional of CDS on each of the 125 names. The list of 125 names changes from series to series as firms lose or obtain investment-grade ratings, and merge with or spin off from other firms.

Cash flows and defaults are treated similarly to those of a single-name CDS credit event. Given the CDS spread premiums on the individual names in the index, there is a fair market CDS spread premium on the CDX. One difference from single-name CDS is that the spread premium is fixed on the initiation date, so subsequent trading is CDX of a particular series generally involves the exchange of net present value. The buyer of CDX protection pays the fixed spread premium to the seller. If credit spreads have widened since the initiation date, the buyer of protection on CDX will pay an amount to the seller of protection.

In the event of default of a constituent of the CDX, the company is removed from the index. In general, there is cash settlement, with an auction to determine the value of recovery on the defaulting company's debt. The dollar amount of spread premium and the notional amount of the CDX contract are reduced by 0.8 percent (since there are 125 equally weighted constituents), and the CDX protection seller pays 0.8 percent of the notional, minus the recovery amount, to the protection buyer.

The constituents of a CDX series can be used as the reference portfolio of a synthetic CDO. The resulting CDO is then economically similar to a cash CLO or CDO with a collateral pool consisting of equal par amounts of bonds issued by the 125 firms in the index. There is a standard capital structure for such synthetic CDOs based on CDX:

Assets	Liabilities
$1 million notional long protection on each constituent of CDX.NA.IG, total $125 million notional	Equity 0–3% Junior mezzanine 3–7% Senior mezzanine 7–10% Senior 10–15% Super senior 15–30%

The liabilities in this structure are called the *standard tranches*. They are fairly liquid and widely traded, in contrast to *bespoke tranches*, generally issued "to order" for a client that wishes to hedge or take on exposures to a specific set of credits, with a specific maturity, and at a specific point in the capital structure. Similar products exist for the iTraxx, with a somewhat different tranching. The fair market value or spread of each tranche is tied to those of the constituent CDS by arbitrage.

The equity tranche, which is exposed to the first loss, is completely wiped out when the loss reaches 3 percent of the notional value. The weight of each constituent is the same, and if we assume default recovery is the same 40 percent for each constituent, then 9 or 10 defaults will suffice: 9 defaults will leave just a small sliver of the equity tranche, and 10 defaults will entirely wipe it out and begin to eat into the junior mezzanine tranche.

9.4.2 Implied Correlation

The values, sensitivities, and other risk characteristics of a standard tranche can be computed using the copula techniques described in this and Chapter 8, but with one important difference. In the previous section, the key inputs to the valuation were estimates of default probabilities and default correlation. But the constituents of the collateral pools of the standard tranches are the 125 single-name CDS in the IG index, relatively liquid products whose spreads can be observed daily, or even at higher frequency. Rather than using the default probabilities of the underlying firms to value the constituents of the IG index, as in our CLO example in this chapter, we use their market CDS spreads, as in Chapter 7, to obtain risk-neutral default probabilities. In many cases, there is not only an observation of the most liquid five-year CDS, but of spreads on other CDS along the term structure. There may also be a risk-neutral estimate of the recovery rate from recovery swaps. CDS indexes and their standard tranches are therefore typically valued, and their risks analyzed, using risk-neutral estimates of default probabilities.

The remaining key input into the valuation, using the copula technique of this and the last chapter, is the constant pairwise correlation. While the copula correlation is not observable, it can be inferred from the market values of the tranches themselves, once the risk-neutral probabilities implied by the single-name CDS are accounted for. Not only the underlying CDS, but the tranches themselves, are relatively liquid products for which daily market prices can be observed. Given these market prices, and the risk-neutral default curves, a risk-neutral *implied correlation* can be computed for each tranche. Typically, the correlation computed in this fashion is called a *base correlation*, since it is associated with the attachment point of a specific tranche. Correlations generally vary by tranche, a phenomenon called *correlation skew*.

Since the implied correlation is computed using risk-neutral parameter inputs, the calculation uses risk-free rates rather than the fair market discount rates of the tranches. To compute the equity base correlation, we require the market equity tranche price (or compute it from the points upfront and running spread), and the spreads of the constituent CDS. Next, we compute the risk-neutral default probabilities of each of the underlying

125 CDS. Given these default probabilities, and a copula correlation, we can simulate the cash flows to the equity tranche. There will be one unique correlation for which the present value of the cash flows matches the market price of the equity tranche. That unique value is the implied correlation.

The CLO example of the previous section can be used to illustrate these computations. Suppose the observed market price of the equity is $5 million, and that we obtain a CDS-based risk-neutral default probability of the underlying loans equal to 2 percent. In the top panel of Table 9.3, we can see that a constant pairwise correlation of 0.3 "matches" the equity price to the default probability. If we were to observe the equity price rising to $5.6 million, with no change in the risk-neutral default probability, we would conclude that the implied correlation had risen to 0.6, reflecting an increase in the market's assessment of the systematic risk of the underlying loans.

Implied credit correlation is as much a market-risk as a credit-risk concept. The value of each tranche has a distinct risk-neutral partial spread01, rather than a default01, that is, sensitivities to each of the constituents of the IG 125. The spread01 measures a market, rather than a credit risk, though it will be influenced by changing market assessments of each firm's creditworthiness. Each of these sensitivities is a function, *inter alia*, of the implied correlation. Conversely, the implied correlation varies in its own right, as well as with the constituent and index credit spreads. For the cash CLO example in this chapter, changes in default rates and correlation result in changes in expected cash flows and credit losses to the CLO tranches, that is, changes in fundamental value. For the standard tranches, changes in risk-neutral probabilities and correlations bring about mark-to-market changes in tranche values. Chapter 11 explores the correlation and other market risks of synthetic CDOs in more detail.

9.4.3 Summary of Default Correlation Concepts

In discussing credit risk, we have used the term "correlation" in several different ways. This is a potential source of confusion, so let's review and summarize these correlation concepts:

Default correlation is the correlation concept most directly related to portfolio credit risk. We formally defined the default correlation of two firms over a given future time period in Section 8.1 as the correlation coefficient of the two random variables describing the firms' default behavior over a given time period.

Asset return correlation is the correlation of logarithmic changes in two firms' asset values. In practice, portfolio credit risk measurement of corporate obligations often relies on asset return correlations. Although this is in a sense the "wrong" correlation concept, since it isn't default correlation, it can be appropriate in the right type of model. For example, in a Merton-type credit risk model, the occurrence of default is a function of the firm's asset value. The asset return correlation in a factor model is driven by each firm's factor loading.

Equity return correlation is the correlation of logarithmic changes in the market value of two firms' equity prices. The asset correlation is not directly unobservable, so in practice, asset correlations are often proxied by equity correlations.

Copula correlations are the values entered into the off-diagonal cells of the correlation matrix of the distribution used in the copula approach to measuring credit portfolio risk. Unlike the other correlation concepts, the copula correlations have no direct economic interpretation. They depend on which family of statistical distributions is used in the copula-based risk estimate. However, the correlation of a Gaussian copula is identical to the correlation of a Gaussian single-factor factor models.

The normal copula has become something of a standard in credit risk. The values of certain types of securities, such as the standard CDS index equity tranches, as we just noted, depend as heavily on default correlation as on the levels of the spreads in the index. The values of these securities can therefore be expressed in terms of the implied correlation.

Spread correlation is the correlation of changes, generally in basis points, in the spreads on two firms' comparable debt obligations. It is a mark-to-market rather than credit risk concept.

Implied credit correlation is an estimate of the copula correlation derived from market prices. It is not a distinct "theoretical" concept from the copula correlation, but is arrived at differently. Rather than estimating or guessing at it, we infer it from market prices. Like spread correlation, it is a market, rather than credit risk concept.

9.5   ISSUER AND INVESTOR MOTIVATIONS FOR STRUCTURED CREDIT

To better understand why securitizations are created, we need to identify the incentives of the loan originators, who sell the underlying loans into the trust in order create a securitization, and of the investors, who buy the equity and bonds. These motivations are also key to understanding the regulatory issues raised by securitization and the role it played in the subprime crisis, themes we return to in Chapters 12, 14 and 15.

9.5.1 Incentives of Issuers

An important motive for securitization is that it provides a technology for maturity matching, that is, for providing term funding for the underlying loans.[1] There are two aspects to this motive: first, whether lower cost of funding can be achieved via securitization, and, second, whether, in the absence of securitization, the loan originator would have to sell the loans into the secondary market or would be able to retain them on his balance sheet. The securitization "exit" is attractive for lenders only if the cost of funding via securitization is lower than the next-best alternative. If the loans are retained, the loan originator may be able to fund the loans via unsecured borrowing. But doing so is generally costlier than secured borrowing via securitization.

Securitizations undertaken primarily to capture the spread between the underlying loan interest and the coupon rates of the liabilities are sometimes called *arbitrage CDOs*, while securitizations motivated largely for balance sheet relief are termed *balance-sheet CDOs*. However, while the motivations are conceptually distinct, it is hard to distinguish securitizations this way.

Among the factors that tend to lower the spreads on securitization liabilities are loan pool diversification and an originator's reputation for high underwriting standards. Originators that have issued securitization deals with less-than-stellar performance may be obliged by the market to pay higher spreads on future deals. Issuer spread differentials are quite persistent. These factors also enable the issuer to lower the credit enhancement levels of the senior bonds that have the narrowest spreads, increasing the proceeds the issuer can borrow through securitization and decreasing the weighted-average financing cost.

Idiosyncratic credit risk can be hard to expunge entirely from credit portfolios, limiting the funding advantage securitization can achieve for some lending sectors. This limitation is important for sectors such as credit card and auto loans, where a high degree of granularity in loan pools can be achieved. As noted, commercial mortgage pools are particularly hard to diversify. Residential mortgage pools can be quite granular, but both commercial and residential mortgage loans have a degree of systematic risk

---

[1] The discussion in Chapter 12 provides a fuller appreciation of these issues.

that many market participants and regulators vastly underestimated prior to the subprime crisis.

The interest rates on the underlying loans, the default rate, the potential credit subordination level, and the spreads on the bonds interact to determine if securitization is economically superior to the alternatives. If, as is often the case, the issuer retains the servicing rights for the loans, and enjoys significant economies of scale in servicing, securitization permits him to increase servicing profits, raising the threshold interest rates on the liabilities at which securitization becomes attractive.

Looking now at the originator's alternative of selling the loans after origination, secondary trading markets exist for large corporate and commercial real estate loans, in which purchasers take an ongoing monitoring role. It is more difficult to sell most consumer loans to another financial intermediary. One of the impediments to secondary-market loan sales is the twin problem of monitoring and asymmetric information. The credit quality of loans is hard to assess and monitor over the life of the loan. The mere fact that the originator is selling a loan may indicate he possesses information suggesting the loan is of poorer quality than indicated by the securitization disclosures—the "lemons" problem (see Chapter 6). The originator's superior information on the loan and the borrower often puts him in the best position to monitor the loan and take mitigating action if the borrower has trouble making payments.

These problems can be mitigated if equity or other subordinated tranches, or parts of the underlying loans themselves, are either retained by the loan originator or by a firm with the capability to monitor the underlying collateral. Their first-loss position then provides an incentive to exercise care in asset selection, monitoring and pool management that protects the interests of senior tranches as well. As discussed in Chapter 15, *risk retention* has been viewed as a panacea for the conflicts of interest inherent in securitization and has been in enshrined in the Dodd-Frank regulatory changes. Rules embodying the legislation have not yet been promulgated but will likely bar issuers of most securitizations from selling all tranches in their entirety. Other mitigants include legal representations by the loan seller regarding the underwriting standards and quality of the loans.

The loan purchaser has legal rights against the seller if these representations are violated, for example, by applying lower underwriting standards than represented. In the wake of the subprime crisis, a number of legal actions have been brought by purchasers of loans as well as structured credit investors on these grounds. These mitigants suggest the difficulty of economically separating originators from loans, that is, of achieving genuine *credit risk transfer*, regardless of how legally robust is the sale of the loans into the securitization trust. The ambiguities of credit risk transfer also arise in credit derivatives transactions and in the creation of off-balance sheet vehicles by intermediaries, and contribute to financial instability by making it harder for market participants to discern issuers' asset volume and leverage.

9.5.2 Incentives of Investors

To understand why securitizations take place, we also need to understand the incentives of investors. Securitization enables capital markets investors to participate in diversified loan pools in sectors that would otherwise be the province of banks alone, such as mortgages, credit card, and auto loans.

Tranching technology provides additional means of risk sharing over and above diversification. Investors, not issuers, motivate credit tranching beyond the issuers' retained interests. Issuers' needs are met by pooling and securitization—they don't require the tranching. Tranching enables investors to obtain return distributions better-tailored to their desired risk profile. A pass-through security provides only the benefit of diversification.

Introducing tranching and structure can reduce default risk for higher tranches, though at the price of potentially greater exposure to systematic risk. Thinner subordinate tranches draw investors desiring higher risk and returns. Some securitization tranches provide *embedded leverage*, which we discuss further in Chapter 12. Thicker senior tranches draw investors seeking lower-risk bonds in most states of the economy, but potentially severe losses in extremely bad states, and willing to take that type of risk in exchange for additional yield.

However, these features are useful to investors only if they carry out the due diligence needed to understand the return distribution accurately. Some institutional investors, particularly pension funds, have high demand for high-quality fixed-income securities that pay even a modest premium over risk-free or high-grade corporate bonds. This phenomenon, often called "searching" or "reaching for yield," arises because institutional investors deploy large sums of capital, while being required to reach particular return targets. Securitization is founded to a large extent on institutional demand for senior bonds. In the presence of regulatory safe harbors and imperfect governance mechanisms, this can lead to inadequate due diligence of the systematic risks of securitized credit products.

Mezzanine tranches, as we have seen, are an odd duck. Depending on the default probability, correlation, and tranche size, they may may behave much like a senior tranche. That is, they have a low probability of loss, but high systematic risk; expected loss in the event of impairment is high, and impairment is likeliest in an adverse scenario for the economy as a whole. They may, in a different structure and environment, behave more like an equity tranche, with a high probability of impairment, but a respectable probability of a low loss. A mezzanine tranche may also switch from one behavior to another. In consequence, mezzanine tranches have less of a natural investor base than other securitized credit products. One result was that many mezzanine tranches were sold into CDOs, the senior tranches of which could be sold to yield-seeking investors uncritically buying structured products on the basis of yield and rating.

Fees also provide incentives to loan originators and issuers to create securitizations. A financial intermediary may earn a higher return from originating and, possibly, servicing loans than from retaining them and earning the loan interest. Securitization then provides a way for the intermediary to remove the loans from its balance sheet after origination. This motivation is related to *regulatory arbitrage*, discussed further in Chapter 15. For example, an intermediary may be able to retain some of the risk exposure and return from a loan pool while drastically reducing the regulatory capital required through securitization.

Off-balance sheet vehicles, and thus, ultimately, money market mutual funds, were also important investors in securitizations. We return to these in Chapter 12 on liquidity risk and Chapter 15 on financial regulation.

FURTHER READING

Rutledge and Raynes (2010) is a quirky, but comprehensive overview of structured finance, with particularly useful material on legal and structure issues. Textbook introductions to structured credit products include the somewhat untimely-titled Kothari (2006) and (2009), and Mounfield (2009). Meissner (2008) is a useful collection of articles on structured credit. Many of the references following Chapters 1, 7 and 8, 14, and 15 are also useful here.

Gibson (2004) provides a similar analysis to that this chapter of a structured credit product, but focusing on synthetic CDOs and carrying out the analysis using the single-factor model. Duffie and Gârleanu (2001) is an introduction to structured product valuation. Schwarcz (1994) is an introduction from a legal standpoint, which is important in all matters pertaining to credit and particularly so where securitization is concerned.

Gibson (2004) and Coval, Jurek, and Stafford (2009) discuss the embedded leverage in structured products and the motivations of investors. Zimmerman (2007), Ashcraft and Schuermann (2008) and Gorton (2008) provide thorough discussions of the securitization markets for subprime residential mortgages. Ashcraft and Schuermann (2008) also provide a detailed accounting of the information cost, monitoring, and other conflict-of-interest issues arising at different stages of the securitization. The discussion is useful both for the risk analysis of securitizations and as an illustration of the role of information cost issues in credit transactions generally. Benmelech and Dlugosz (2009) describes the ratings process for a class of structured products,

Li (2000) was an early application of copula theory to structured credit modeling. Tranche sensitivities are explained in Schloegl and Greenberg (2003).

Belsham, Vause, and Wells (2005); and Amato and Gyntelberg (2005) are introductions to credit correlation concepts. O'Kane and Livesey (2004), Kakodkar, Martin, and Galiani (2003), and Kakodkar, Galiani, and Shchetkovskiy (2004) are introductions by trading desk strategists to structured credit correlations. Amato and Remolona (2005) discusses the difficulty, compared with equities, of reducing idiosyncratic risk in credit portfolios and applies this finding to the risk of structured credit.

Alternatives to the Standard Market Risk Model

I n Chapters 2 through 5, we got pretty far using the standard model of jointly normally distributed asset or risk factor returns. It treats the main-body risks of a portfolio fairly accurately. We now need to take account of the fact that the model is not perfectly accurate. In particular, very large-magnitude returns occur much more frequently than the standard return model predicts, leading to far greater tail risk than the standard risk model acknowledges. The entire distribution of returns, not just the expected return and return volatility, is important to investors.

In this chapter, we look at the behavior of asset prices and alternative models to the joint normal model that might better explain return behavior. We will also see how market prices, especially of options, reflect these alternatives. In Chapter 13, we discuss stress tests, an approach to risk measurement that takes account of the prevalence of extreme returns. Tools such as VaR can help measure the risk of losses that, while large and unpleasant, will be a recurrent cost of doing business. The models described in this chapter and stress testing attempt to measure risks that are life-threatening to a financial firm.

10.1   REAL-WORLD ASSET PRICE BEHAVIOR

We start by comparing the standard model, in which asset prices or risk factors are lognormally distributed, to actual market price behavior, as evidenced by the time-series behavior of their returns. We then provide a few statistical measures of deviations from the normal and a visual tool that summarizes how far asset prices are from normal.

Deviations from the normal model can be summarized under three headings:

Kurtosis (or *leptokurtosis*, literally, "fat tails") is the phenomenon that large returns occur more frequently than is consistent with a normal distribution. The coefficient of kurtosis is the fourth standardized moment of a distribution and provides a statistical measure of the frequency of large positive or negative asset returns. The kurtosis of the normal distribution is precisely 3, so the *kurtosis excess* is defined as the kurtosis coefficient minus 3.

High kurtosis means that returns far above or below the mean occur relatively often, regardless of sign. Since that implies that fewer returns are in the center of the distribution, kurtotic distributions are "peakier" than nonkurtotic ones. If there is enough displacement of probability mass out to the tails, the distribution may exhibit multiple modes or peaks.

The upper panel of Figure 10.1 compares a kurtotic distribution to a normal with same mean and standard deviation.

Skewness. Large moves in asset prices are not necessarily symmetrically distributed; rather, large moves in one direction occur more frequently than in the other. The *skewness coefficient* of a distribution is its third standardized moment and provides a statistical measure of the tendency of large returns, when they occur, to have a particular sign. The normal distribution is symmetrical, that is, its coefficient of skewness is exactly zero. So a high positive or negative skewness coefficient in a return time series is inconsistent with the assumption that returns are normal.

The mean and median of a symmetrical distribution are equal. For a skewed distribution, they are not. The mean is lower than the median for a negatively skewed distribution, that is, one skewed to the left, or having a "fat" left tail. Like kurtosis, skewness can manifest itself in multiple modes in the distribution. The mean is higher than the median for a distribution that is skewed to the right, that is, has unusually large positive returns more often than negative ones.

The lower panel of Figure 10.1 compares a distribution with negative skewness to a normal with same mean and standard deviation. The mean of the skewed distribution is below its median.

Time variation. Asset return distributions are not identical over time. Return volatilities in particular vary, as we noted in introducing volatility estimators in Chapter 3. The variation in volatility behavior is only partly captured by the EWMA/RiskMetrics volatility estimator we described there. In particular, EWMA does not capture "regime changes" and other dramatic and lasting changes in behavior.

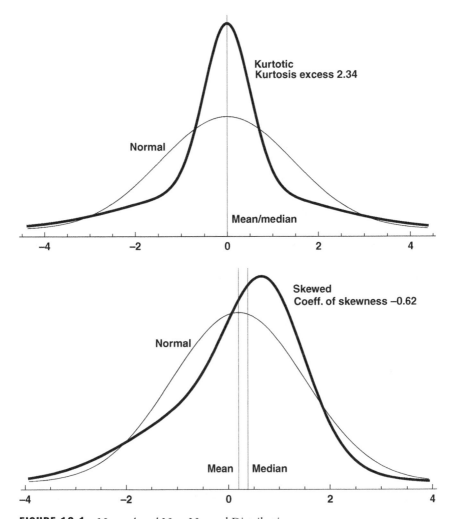

FIGURE 10.1 Normal and Non-Normal Distributions
Upper panel: Kurtotic and normal distributions, both zero mean and with identical variances. The kurtotic distribution is a mixture of two normals, with distributions $N(0, 2.0)$ and $N(0, 0.5)$, each with a probability of 50 percent of being realized.
Lower panel: Skewed and normal distributions with identical means and variances. The kurtotic distribution is a mixture of two normals, with distributions $N(-0.35, 1.5)$ and $N(0.75, 0.75)$, each with a probability of 50 percent of being realized.

These stylized facts are interrelated. For example, a negative correlation between returns and volatility has been noted; large negative returns for stocks and stock indexes, for example, are more reliably followed by an increase in return volatility than positive returns. This phenomenon is called the *leverage effect*, since it is thought to be related to the use of borrowed funds in establishing positions. We discuss leverage and its impact on financial markets in detail in Chapters 12 and 14.

The anomalies we have just cited are closely related to the implied volatility smile and other departures from the Black-Scholes model predictions of option price patterns described in Chapter 5. The option skew is related to return skewness and to the leverage effect. The volatility smile is related to kurtosis. The term structure of implied volatility is related to the time-variation of volatility. But all the departures from normality in historical return behavior jointly influence the so-called implied volatility biases. Later in this chapter we discuss how to extract the information in option prices about future return behavior more precisely.

It would be easy to assemble a large menagerie of historical asset price return plots that evidence highly non-normal behavior. Let's focus on just three assets that illustrate departures from, as well as very approximate adherence to, the normal model. We'll start with a detailed long-run view of the S&P 500, an important asset in its own right, since it has a very large market value, represents the core asset class of equity securities, and is often used to represent the market portfolio, the universe of all risky assets. It also illustrates many typical features of asset returns. We'll also look at two currency pairs, the exchange rates of the dollar against the euro and the Turkish lira.

Figure 10.2 displays daily returns on the S&P index for the past 83 years.[1] The solid lines are the 99 percent confidence interval for the one-day return, using the EWMA approach of Chapter 3 to update the estimates for each date. Extreme outliers (also called "upcrossings" or "exceedances") lying outside the 99.8 and 99.98 percent confidence intervals, are marked by x's and o's.[2]

---

[1]The S&P 500 index was introduced in 1957. Prior to 1957, data are for the various forerunner indexes published by Standard & Poor's.

[2]The term "exceedance" is typically used in the context of extreme moves in financial returns. "Exceedance" is not found in the online version of the *Oxford English Dictionary*. The term "excession" is typically used in the context of VaR testing, as in the next chapter, to describe returns greater than the VaR shock or losses greater than the VaR. The *Oxford English Dictionary* defines it as "[a] going out or forth," and helpfully provides a usage example from the seventeenth century.

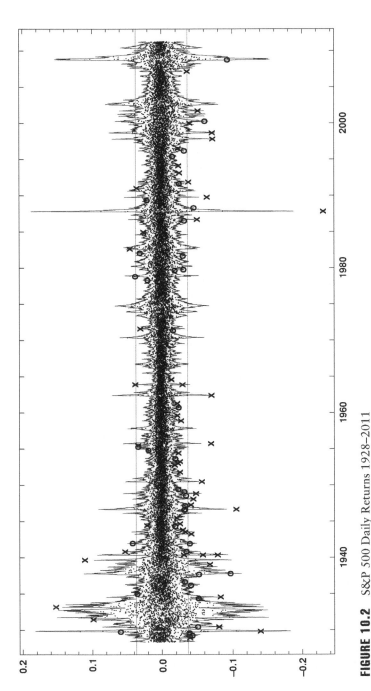

FIGURE 10.2 S&P 500 Daily Returns 1928–2011

The return data cover the interval from Jan. 3, 1928 to Apr. 14, 2011 and are represented by tiny dots. The thin solid plots represent the ±3.09 standard deviation or 9.8 percent forecast confidence interval, based on the EWMA method using 90 days of data and with the standard decay factor of 0.94. Next-day returns outside the 99.98 percent forecast confidence interval are marked by o's. Next-day returns outside the 99.98 percent forecast confidence interval are marked by x's. The horizontal grid lines mark the 99.98 percent forecast confidence interval for returns using the unconditional daily standard deviation of the entire historical sample.

Data source: Bloomberg Financial L.P.

The distribution displays kurtosis—the number of outliers is greater than one would expect if S&P returns were time-varying, but conditionally normally distributed. The excess kurtosis is quite substantial at 19.2. If the distribution were in fact conditionally normal, the "surprise" at observing "too many" exceedances becomes much greater, the higher the confidence level. Suppose daily returns are a normal random variable with a constant volatility. At the 95 percent confidence level, one should expect about one exceedance per month. But the S&P 500 time series exhibits about 30 percent "too many." At the 99.999 percent confidence level, one should expect to see an exceedance only once in a few centuries, but there are 211 times the expected number for the 80 years we observe.

The outliers are not evenly divided between positive and negative returns, as would be expected for a symmetric conditional return distribution. Rather, the distribution of S&P returns is skewed, with a coefficient of skewness of −0.48. Large negative returns are predominant, and this disparity also increases with the confidence level, up to a very high confidence level of 99.99 percent. The latter phenomenon reflects the sharp positive returns that often occur after the S&P index has had sustained and sharp negative returns.

Table 10.1 summarizes the results of this exercise, which can be thought of as a test of the accuracy of VaR of the type to be discussed in Chapter 11. The lower limit of the confidence interval plotted in Figure 10.1 can be thought of as the one day VaR at the specified confidence level, expressed as a return, of a long unleveraged S&P 500 position.

Apart from the high-frequency variations in volatility captured by the EWMA confidence-interval limits, the S&P 500 also displays low-frequency changes in volatility that can persist for years. Two periods of extremely high volatility commence in 1929, when the Great Depression began, and in 1937, when a severe unanticipated relapse occurred. They are separated by

TABLE 10.1 Extreme returns in the S&P 500 Index 1928–2011

Confidence level	0.95	0.99	0.9999	0.99999
Number of exceedances	1331	453	77	44
No. negative exceedances	738	288	62	35
No. positive exceedances	593	165	15	9
Ratio negative/positive	1.2445	1.7455	4.1333	3.8889
Rel. frequency of exceedances	0.0639	0.0217	0.0037	0.0021
Expected no. exceedances	1014.5	208.3	2.1	0.2
Actual/expected no. exceedances	1.3	2.2	37.0	211.2

Daily S&P 500 index returns falling outside a confidence interval with the stated confidence level, based on a prior-day EWMA estimate of volatility. Return data are those of Figure 10.1. EWMA estimates use 90 days of data and a decay factor of 0.94.

two years of relatively low volatility. Similarly, volatility was much higher beginning in the late 1990s through 2003 than during the subsequent three years. This unusually low level of volatility, as we see in Chapter 14, was an important feature of the run-up to the subprime crisis.

Figure 10.3 displays similar time-series return plots for the euro and dollar-Turkish lira exchange rates over an approximately 15-year period. These assets display a number of similarities and contrasts to the S&P 500. The euro return history, in the upper panel, is among the return distributions of widely-traded assets that are closest to the normal. While the volatility varies over time, the variations are not dramatic, apart from the increase in volatility coinciding with the subprime crisis. The exceedances from the conditional 99 percent confidence interval are not particularly frequent, nor are exceedances in one direction more frequent than in the other. So the kurtosis and skewness appear low under visual inspection.

The Turkish lira return plot presents a sharp contrast. Its most note-worthy feature is one extremely sharp move, a decline in the lira against the dollar of about 30 percent occurring on February 22, 2001. The lira depreciation was occasioned by Turkey's abandonment of its exchange-rate peg against the dollar. Such currency crashes are not unusual, and are discussed further in Chapter 14. The lira episode is a good illustration of *regime switching*, a shift from one set of statistical parameters governing asset return behavior to another. In the Turkish lira case, the switch is one of both the official exchange-rate regime administered by Turkey as well as a shift in return behavior.

Regime-switching models have been applied using a range of techniques and for a range of assets. One approach, for example, is to model the asset return distribution as a mixture of two normal distributions, as are the distributions displayed in Figure 10.1. One normal distribution describes the behavioral regime currently in place, while the second, perhaps higher-volatility, distribution comes into effect with a probability equal to the mixing parameter.

In foreign exchange, the problem of capturing large moves is called the *peso problem*, since it was first identified in the context of Mexican peso exchange rate behavior in the late 1970s and early 1980s. Forward exchange rates persistently predicted greater peso depreciation against the U.S. dollar than actually took place. This bias could be explained by the occasional drastic depreciations that took place when Mexico carried out a devaluation.

Apart from extreme time variation in return volatility, the Turkish lira also illustrates a high degree of kurtosis and skewness. The statistics describing these phenomena are dominated by the lira's return behavior around exchange-rate regime switches.

However, both examples show that the normal return model with volatility forecast using predominantly recent information is not a bad first

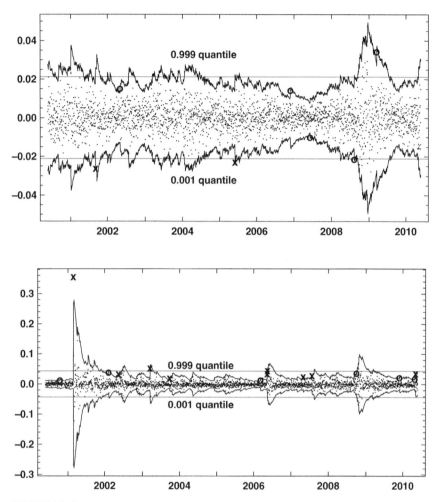

FIGURE 10.3   Statistical Properties of Exchange Rates
Each panel shows the daily return history from Jan. 2, 2000 to June 16, 2010, with
the 99.8% confidence interval computed two ways, one using the volatility over the
entire observation interval (horizontal grid lines), and the other using the
time-varying EWMA volatility estimate. Next-day returns outside the 99.98
percent forecast confidence interval are marked by o's. Next-day returns outside
the 99.998 percent forecast confidence interval are marked by x's.
Upper panel: EUR-USD: U.S. dollar price of the foreign currency, so a positive
return is a dollar depreciation.
Lower panel: USD-TRY: Foreign currency price of the U.S. dollar, so a positive
return is a lira depreciation.
Source: Bloomberg Financial L.P.

approximation to short-term return behavior, as long as it is not used to draw inferences about extreme tail behavior. Only the one wildly extreme lira observation is very far outside the forecast interval. The standard model describes the typical variations in asset values quite well. The shortcoming of the model is its failure to forecast returns that are extremely large and extremely rare.

The anomalies we have just observed are also evident for other assets. Table 10.2 displays the statistical properties of returns on a number of assets in various asset classes. These are based on the unconditional distributions of the asset returns, with volatilities represented by the root means squared (RMS). We use the RMS rather than the standard deviation in the spirit of the zero-mean assumption of Chapter 3. However, mean daily returns are very small for most assets most of the time, so the difference is small.

The VIX, an implied volatility index, has the highest return volatility. Among cash asset classes, equity indexes have the highest volatilities, as seen in both the ranges of returns and the root means squared. The Turkish lira range is very high relative to its volatility, partly due to the influence of the two large devaluation outliers.

Most of the asset returns display at least some distinctly non-normal characteristics. Normality can also be tested formally, for example, via the *Jarque-Bera* test. All the asset returns series of Table 10.2 have very high Jarque-Bera statistics (not displayed) that lead to rejection of the normality hypothesis even for very high confidence levels. Distributional hypotheses generally can be tested via the *Kolmogorov-Smirnov goodness-of-fit test*. The latter test is based on the idea that if a set of observations are generated by a specific distribution, then the largest outlier from that distribution is unlikely to exceed a specified amount.

Kurtosis appears to be universal; even the euro displays mild kurtosis. The Turkish lira has exceptionally high kurtosis. As we see in Chapter 14, currencies are among the few asset prices routinely subjected to price controls. Consequently, they display some of the largest-magnitude returns when authorities are obliged to lift these controls.

Skewness is characteristic of most of these assets. Equity markets exhibit mild downward skewness, while commodities and currencies differ one from the other. Fixed-income futures are skewed toward lower rates. The direction of skewness might well be different in a different observation interval or for a different sample of assets. However, the prevalence of skewness is well-attested.

There are several useful analytical and graphical tools for comparing the distribution of historical returns with a benchmark or model probability distribution. The *kernel estimator* is a technique for estimating the probability density function from a sample of the data it generates. It can

TABLE 10.2 Statistical Properties of Selected Asset Returns

	EUR	JPY	TRY	SPX	IBOV	CL1	GOLDS	CRB	TY1	ED1	VIX
Mean return (bps)	0.04	−0.98	13.49	2.34	33.35	2.50	2.35	1.02	0.41	0.16	0.77
Median return (bps)	0.00	0.00	0.00	5.65	24.23	4.60	0.00	1.05	1.38	0.00	−33.46
Minimum return (%)	−3.38	−6.95	−14.07	−9.47	−39.30	−40.05	−7.24	−6.01	−11.87	−0.81	−35.06
Maximum return (%)	3.47	5.50	35.69	10.96	34.21	22.80	10.24	5.93	3.54	0.93	49.60
Root mean square (% p.a.)	10.60	11.70	22.00	19.04	52.71	41.26	16.50	7.15	7.25	0.98	96.47
Skewness coefficient	0.00	−0.37	5.92	−0.18	0.12	−0.69	0.06	−0.36	−3.87	0.14	0.67
Kurtosis excess	1.78	5.08	137.02	8.38	19.31	16.75	8.90	16.58	96.14	48.71	3.79

Key to columns:
EUR Curncy: Euro spot
JPY Curncy: Japanese yen spot
TRY Curncy New Turkish lira spot
SPX Index: S&P 500 index
IBOV Index: Brazil Bovespa index

CL1 Comdty:generic 1st oil futures
GOLDS Index: Gold spot $/oz.
CRB Index: Commodity Research Bureau/Reuters index
TY1 Comdty: generic 1st 10-year note futures
ED1 Comdty: generic 1st eurodollar futures
VIX Index: CBOE SPX Volatility Index

Data from Jan. 2, 1900, to June 17, 2010.
Data source: Bloomberg Financial L.P.

be thought of as a method of constructing a histogram of the data, but with useful properties such as smoothness and continuity that a histogram lacks. A kernel estimator of a return time series $r_t, t = i, \ldots, T$ can be expressed as

$$\hat{f}(r) = \frac{1}{Th} \sum_{t}^{T} K \left(\frac{r - r_t}{h} \right)$$

To implement the kernel estimator, we need to specify K, the *kernel function*, and h, the *bandwidth*, which controls the smoothness of the kernel estimate. In typical applications, the standard normal density $\phi(\cdot)$ is employed as a kernel function, together with the so-called *optimal bandwidth*

$$h = \frac{1.06\hat{\sigma}}{(T - 1)^{\frac{1}{5}}}$$

where $\hat{\sigma}$ is the sample standard deviation of the return time series. Specified this way, the kernel estimator can be viewed as creating a "histogram" in which each observation has a bar to itself. But instead of a bar, the estimator places a small normal density over each observation. Using very tight normal distributions this way would, in aggregate, produce a jagged distribution for the sample as a whole, potentially with many modes. Normals with very high standard deviation would produce a smooth distribution for the whole sample, but would obscure individual data points. The optimal bandwidth takes the sample standard deviation into account in finding a middle ground between these extremes.

In addition to intuitiveness, the kernel estimator has the virtue of being quite easy to implement. Figure 10.4 displays an important example, the VIX implied volatility index, that is pertinent to the discussion of option risk measurement in Chapter 5. Together with the sample moments displayed above, this example provides the useful insight that the VIX does not differ more than many cash assets from the normal distribution. It has significant, but not extreme kurtosis, and a noticeable positive skew; that is, large changes in implied volatility tend to be increases. This provides some support for using implied volatility returns as a risk factor in an option portfolio VaR estimate based on lognormal returns.

Another useful graphical tool for comparing historical returns to a benchmark distribution, such as the normal, is the *QQ plot*, short for "quantile quantile" plot, in which the quantiles of the historical and benchmark distributions are plotted against one another.

To generate a QQ plot, we need two things. First, we need the *order statistics* of the historical return series; that is, we order the returns in

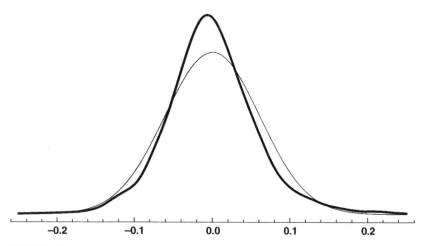

FIGURE 10.4   Kernel Estimate of the Distribution of VIX Returns
The thick plot is the kernel estimate of logarithmic changes in the VIX index,
January 2, 1900, to June 17, 2010, using an optimal bandwidth. The thin plot is a
normal distribution with mean and variance equal to the sample mean and
variance of the data.
Data source: Bloomberg Financial L.P.

ascending order by size rather than by date. Second, we need a benchmark
probability distribution, that is, the distribution against which we will compare the historical return distribution at hand. Typically, we use the normal
distribution as a benchmark for historical asset returns, but we could also
use another specific alternative distribution to the normal.

Suppose we have $T + 1$ data points in our risk factor time series and
therefore T return data points. The fraction $\frac{i}{T}$ is the relative place of the
i-th order statistic in the return series. Based solely on the data sample, we
would say that the probability of the return having a realized value less than
or equal to the i-th order statistic is $\frac{i}{T}$. The likelihood of a return less than
or equal to the smallest (most negative) return (the first-order statistic) is
estimated at $\frac{1}{T}$, while that of a return less than or equal to the largest return
is estimated at 1.

The abscissa of the i-th point on a QQ plot is thus the i-th order
statistic. The ordinate of the i-th point is the $\frac{i}{T}$-quantile of the benchmark
distribution. For example, if $T = 1,000$, about four years of daily data, the
10th smallest return should be close to the first percentile of the benchmark
distribution. If the benchmark distribution is, say, $N(0, \sigma)$, with σ equal to
the historical daily volatility of the time series, then the pair consisting of
the 10th order statistic of the return series and the 0.01 quantile of $N(0, \sigma)$
constitute one point on the QQ plot. If the historical returns are, in fact,

drawn from the benchmark distribution, the two values are likely to be close together. The QQ-plot will then lie close to a 45-degree line through the origin.

What if the two distributions are dissimilar? Let's answer using the normal distribution, the usual benchmark for financial return behavior. The plot may take on a variety of shapes, depending on what kinds of deviations from the benchmark the historical returns display:

- Kurtosis manifests itself in an S-shaped plot. The extreme values occur more frequently than one would expect in a normal distribution, so the largest-magnitude negative historical returns will be smaller (more negative) than normal returns with the same expected frequency. The largest positive historical returns will be bigger than normal returns with the same expected frequency.

   The QQ plot will consequently lie *above* the 45°-line left of the origin, and *below* the 45°-line right of the origin. The QQ plot has to cross the 45°-line somewhere in between, hence the S shape.
- Suppose positive skewness, that is, to the right tail, is present in a historical return distribution, so large positive returns occur more frequently than negative ones. Then the largest historical returns will exceed normal returns with the same expected frequency. This manifests itself in a QQ plot that is below the 45° line to the right of the origin, but not as far above it to the left. The graph will be asymmetrical.
- If the historical return distribution evidences both skewness and kurtosis, the shape depends on which influence is more powerful. Kurtosis will impose a symmetrical S shape, while skewness will drag one arm further above or below the 45° line than the other.
- If the mean of the historical returns is higher than that of the benchmark, the QQ plot will be shifted, and lie to the left or right of the 45° line, rather than intersecting it at the origin. If the variance of the historical returns is higher than that of the benchmark, the QQ plot will be flatter and closer to a straight line.

There is a small problem in constructing a QQ plot using the tabulated quantiles of the benchmark distribution. The relative frequency of the T-th order statistic is 1, but the normal quantile of 1 is infinite. We therefore use the order statistics of a set of T random numbers generated by the benchmark distribution instead of the theoretical quantiles. This introduces some simulation noise (less, the more observations we have), but permits us to plot even the extreme returns in the historical data and is.

We illustrate these patterns in Figure 10.5 with two QQ plots of the currency returns displayed in Figure 10.3. The two plots contrast sharply in some ways, and are similar in others. The QQ plot for the EUR-USD

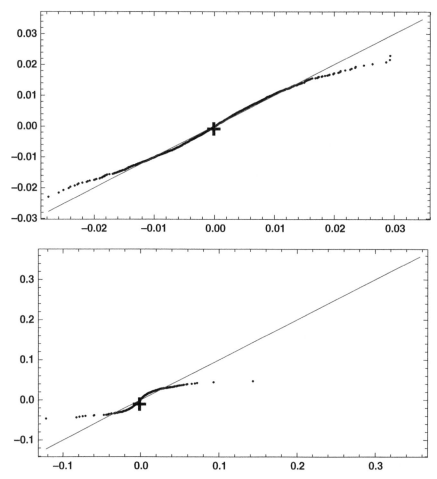

FIGURE 10.5 QQ Plot of USD Exchange Rates against the Euro and Turkish Lira Quantiles of daily returns, Jan. 2, 2000 to June 16, 2010, plotted against simulations from a normal distribution with mean zero and standard deviation equal to the historical volatility at a daily rate. The cross marks the origin.
Upper panel: EUR-USD exchange rate (USD per EUR). Standard deviation equal to 0.61 percent. Positive returns correspond to dollar depreciation.
Lower panel: USD-TRY exchange rate (TRY per USD). Standard deviation equal to 1.17 percent. Positive returns correspond to lira depreciation.
Source: Bloomberg Financial L.P.

exchange rate appears to be close to normally distributed. It lies reasonably close to the 45° line, though there appear to be some extreme negative and positive returns compared to the normal. This is consistent with the modest kurtosis excess we saw in the statistical summary. The USD-TRY plot in the lower panel shows very high kurtosis and considerable skewness. For example, the point corresponding to the largest USD-TRY return in the sample is further below the 45° line than the smallest return is above it. Both plots show only small deviations from the zero-mean return assumption. Overall, the appearance of both QQ plots is consistent with the statistical analysis presented earlier and summarized in Table 10.2.

10.2 ALTERNATIVE MODELING APPROACHES

A great variety of alternatives to the standard model have been put forward to better account for and forecast asset return behavior. In this section, we provide a few examples that are suggestive of the range of approaches: a specific alternative hypothesis to the stochastic process followed by asset prices, and a set of models focusing on forecasts of extreme returns.

10.2.1 Jump-Diffusion Models

Alternative models of the stochastic process that asset returns follow may more fully capture their behavior than the standard model. One such alternative, the *jump-diffusion model*, builds on the standard model of geometric Brownian motion. The jump-diffusion combines geometric Brownian motion with a second process, in which the asset price makes discontinuous moves at random times. This *jump process* is similar to the model we used to study defaults in Chapter 7. The major difference is that in default modeling, only one default event can occur; the default time is modeled as the first—and one and only—arrival time of a Poisson-distributed event, in that case default. A jump-diffusion process permits more than one jump to occur.

The stochastic process thus imagines the asset price following a diffusion punctuated by large moves at random, Poisson-distributed times. To help compare it to geometric Brownian motion, we can write the stochastic differential equation (SDE) of an asset price S_t following a jump-diffusion as

$$dS_t = \left(\mu + \frac{1}{2}\sigma^2 - \lambda \mathrm{E}\left[k_t\right]\right) S_t dt + \sigma S_t dW_t + k_t S_t dq_t$$

This differs from geometric Brownian motion, defined by Equation (2.1), by the addition of the jump term $k_t S_t dq_t$, and the corresponding

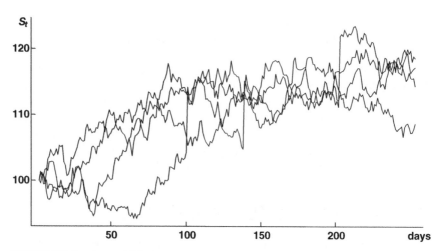

FIGURE 10.6 Jump-Diffusion Process: Asset Price Level
Four simulations of the price level over time S_t of an asset following a
jump-diffusion process with $\mu = 0$ and $\sigma = 0.12$ (12 percent) at an annual rate.
Jumps are Poisson distributed with frequency parameter $\lambda = \frac{1}{252}$ and a
nonstochastic jump size $k = 0.10$ (10 percent). The initial price of the asset is
$S_0 = 100$.

adjustment of the mean increment to the asset price by the expected value
of the jump size $\lambda E\,[k_t]\,S_t$. The size of the jump may be modeled as random
or deterministic. The (possibly random) jump size at time t is given by k_t,
measured as a percent of the current asset price S_t. The jump probability
is driven by a parameter λ, which plays a similar role to the hazard rate of
Chapter 7; dq_t is an increment to a Poisson process with

$$dq_t = \begin{Bmatrix} 1 \\ 0 \end{Bmatrix} \quad \text{with probability} \quad \begin{Bmatrix} \lambda dt \\ 1 - \lambda dt \end{Bmatrix}$$

Figure 10.6 displays four realizations of a jump-diffusion in which the
jumps are modeled as deterministic 10 percent increases in the asset price.
Figure 10.7 displays a simulation of a time series of returns from the same
jump-diffusion process. Figures 10.6 and 10.7 correspond to Figures 2.5 and
2.6 illustrating the behavior of a pure diffusion or random walk process.

With smaller, more frequent jumps that are hard to discern visually,
the jump-diffusion model can mimic a wide variety of asset-price behaviors.
The model can generate return time series that exhibit kurtosis as well as
skewness. The jumps per se generate kurtosis; if the jumps are modeled so
that they are not zero on average, they generate skewness.

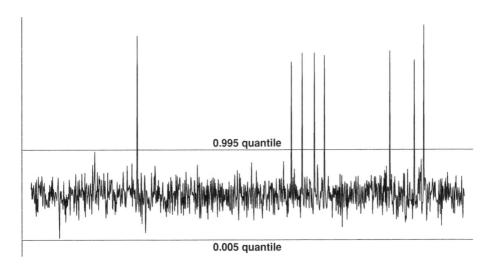

FIGURE 10.7 Jump-Diffusion: Daily Returns
Simulation of 1,000 sequential steps of a jump-diffusion process with $\mu = 0$ and $\sigma = 0.12$ (12 percent) at an annual rate. The y-axis displays returns in percent. Jumps are Poisson distributed with frequency parameter $\lambda = \frac{1}{252}$ and a nonstochastic jump size $k = 0.10$ (10 percent). The horizontal grid lines mark the 99 percent confidence interval.

With larger, less frequent jumps, the jump-diffusion model can mimic assets that are subject to sudden, large moves. One example is currency crises, which we have illustrated here with the Turkish lira and discuss further in Chapter 14. Another category of asset prices subject to sudden, drastic breaks in behavior, and well-described by the jump-diffusion model, are certain equities. For example, pharmaceutical and biotechnology companies are often highly dependent on one product or patent. Figure 10.8 displays an example, the stock price of Elan Corporation, a pharmaceutical company focused on diseases of the brain. Elan is highly dependent on a very small number of drugs for future revenue. On five occasions in the past decade, the firm has lost 50 percent or more of its market value in a single day, due to failure to obtain regulatory approval for a drug, a drastic swing in reported earnings, or reports of side effects from one of its key products. Its kurtosis excess is over 122, rivaling that of the Turkish lira exchange rate, and its skewness coefficient is an extremely large-magnitude –7.7.

10.2.2 Extreme Value Theory

A branch of statistics called *extreme value theory* (EVT) provides a somewhat different approach. Rather than looking for a parametric family of

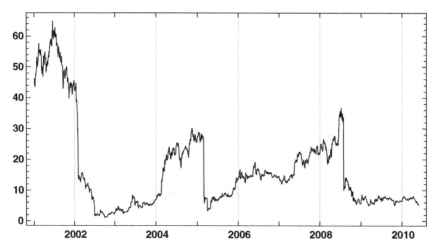

FIGURE 10.8   Elan Corporation Stock Price
Price of Elan Corporation PLC common shares, Jan. 2, 2001 to May 28, 2010.
Source: Bloomberg Financial L.P.

distributions or stochastic processes that can better explain observed returns than does the normal, it looks for techniques that can summarize and,
hopefully, forecast extreme returns from a wide range of distributions. EVT
concerns itself with the distribution of tail events, rather than with the distribution of main-body returns. Corresponding to this more data-focused
approach, the user of these tools often has to make judgements about what
constitutes extreme returns in a time series.

We'll illustrate these concepts using the long time series of S&P 500
returns underlying Figure 10.2. We start by presenting, in the table below,
and in Figure 10.9, the long-term characteristics of the return series, as we
did for the past two decades in Table 10.2. The returns display considerable
kurtosis, and some negative skewness.

Long-term statistical properties of daily S&P 500 returns

Number of observations (*NOBS*)	20,921
Mean return (bps)	2.06
Median return (bps)	4.63
Minimum return (%)	−22.90
Maximum return (%)	15.37
Root mean square (%, annual)	18.96
Skewness coefficient	−0.46
Kurtosis excess	19.20

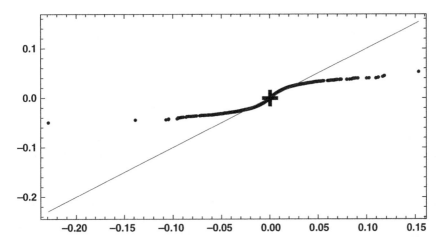

FIGURE 10.9 QQ Plot of the S&P 500

Quantiles of daily returns of the S&P 500 index, 1929–2011, plotted against simulations from a normal distribution with mean zero and a standard deviation equal to 1.2 percent, the daily historical volatility of the S&P 500 series over the full sample. The data are those plotted in Figure 10.2.

Data source: Bloomberg Financial L.P.

In finance applications, EVT focuses on two ways of defining extreme returns:

1. The maximum or minimum of a return stream
2. The size and probability of outliers, that is, returns larger or smaller than some large-magnitude threshold

A set of statistical tools has been developed to characterize these types of extreme events. The starting point for both is a set of independently and identically distributed (i.i.d.) returns $r_1, \ldots, r_t$. Nothing else is said at the outset about their distribution function, which we denote $F(r_t)$. The largest return (or, if we multiply the entire series by -1, the largest loss) is denoted m_t. The order statistics of the data set are denoted $r_{1,t}, \ldots, r_{t,t}$.

For the fat-tailed distributions typically encountered in finance, the distribution of the normalized maximum return $\frac{m_t - a_t}{b_t}$ converges to the *Frechèt distribution*:

$$P\left[\frac{m_t - a_t}{b_t} \leq x\right] \to \exp\left[-\left(\frac{x}{\alpha}\right)^{-\alpha}\right] \quad \text{for} \quad t \to \infty \quad x > 0, \alpha > 0$$

where a_t and b_t are sequences of normalizing constants, playing the same role as the mean and standard deviation in standardizing a normal random variable. The Frechèt is an example of an *extreme value distribution*. (An analogous asymptotic distribution exists for thin-tailed distributions.) Under a few additional technical conditions, outliers in a Frechèt-distributed return series follow a *power law*, that is, if r_t is a large return, then

$$\mathbf{P}\left[r_t \geq x\right] = 1 - F(r_t) = -x^{-\alpha} \quad x, \alpha > 0$$

We call α the *tail index*. The tail index of the normal distribution is $\alpha = 2$. For fat-tailed financial security returns, we expect to see a tail index in excess of 2.

It's worth reflecting for a moment on how remarkable these statements are. We've said nothing about the distribution of the r_t, beyond their being independent and identically distributed (i.i.d.) and having a fat-tailed distribution. But we've been able to state distribution functions for the largest return in the series and for large returns generally, just as the central limit theorem tells us that the distributions of suitably normalized means of i.i.d. random variables converge to the normal distribution. Still, the power law is not a magic bullet; the i.i.d. assumption, for example, is not valid for returns that display stochastic volatility and other time-varying return properties.

A simple estimator for the tail index is called *Hill's estimator*. We set a standard of extreme return, somewhat arbitrarily, by identifying them with the k largest returns in the data set. The estimate is then

$$\hat{\alpha} = \left[\frac{1}{k}\sum_{t=1}^{k}\log(r_{i,t}) - \log(r_{k,t})\right]^{-1}$$

A problem with this simple estimator is that it can vary quite a bit with the threshold for defining extreme returns. If the threshold, which we'll denote u, is low, then k is high, and the estimate may include many observations that are from the main body rather than the tail of the distribution. That will bias $\hat{\alpha}$ downward. If the threshold is high and k is a small number, there may be too few observations to accurately estimate α. We can see this tendency in the estimates in the next example.

Example 10.1 (Hill's Estimator) Each row of the next table shows the Hill estimate $\hat{\alpha}$ applied to S&P 500 returns that are below the threshold in the first column. The negative return threshold is converted to a positive one by multiplying the entire return time series by -1. The second column displays the number of observations k that are included in the estimate for each return threshold u, the third column displays their relative frequency in the time series, and the fourth column displays the Hill estimate.

But although $\hat{\alpha}$ varies widely as k changes, there is some consolation in the example, too. The estimates appear to be converging toward a value of about 4.5, consistent with the pronounced, but not extreme degree of kurtosis visible in Figure 10.9 and reflected in the coefficient of kurtosis excess.

u	k	$k \times NOBS^{-1}$ (%)	$\hat{\alpha}$
−0.020	751	3.590	2.334
−0.030	329	1.573	2.937
−0.050	79	0.378	3.447
−0.075	22	0.105	4.474
−0.100	5	0.024	4.559

Next, we give an example of how EVT can be used to provide not only a characterization of the return distribution, but also risk measures. We needed to select a return threshold that defined extreme returns in order to estimate the tail index. Similarly, we need to specify a threshold in order to estimate the probability that we will observe a return that is even larger than the threshold by a given amount. The amount by which a particular return exceeds a predefined standard of extremeness is called an *exceedance* or *peak over threshold* (so the approach is sometimes fetchingly referred to as POT modeling).

The probability of a return in excess of a threshold u is $1 - F(u)$, where $F(\cdot)$, again, is the distribution function of the r_t, about which little has had to be said. The probability of a return r_t that exceeds u by $y_t = r_t - u$ (the exceedance over threshold) is $1 - F(u + y_t)$, and the probability of realizing a return r_t between u and $u + y_t$ is $F(u + y_t) - F(u)$. Therefore, the conditional probability of a return between u and $u + y_t$ given that $r_t > u$ is

$$\mathbf{P}\left[r_t - u | r_t > u\right] = \frac{F(u + y_t) - F(u)}{1 - F(u)}$$

For i.i.d. fat-tailed returns, exceedances over thresholds follow a *generalized Pareto distribution* (GPD), with cumulative distribution function $G(y_t; \alpha, \beta, u)$:

$$\mathbf{P}\left[r_t - u | r_t > u\right] = G(y_t; \alpha, \beta, u) = 1 - \left(1 + \frac{y_t}{\alpha\beta}\right)^{-\alpha} \quad 0 < \alpha < \infty$$

where α is the tail index and β is a normalizing constant associated with the standard deviation. The parameters α and β can be estimated from data via maximum likelihood.

The estimation procedure starts by obtaining the density of the GPD $g(y_t; \alpha, \beta, u)$ by differentiating $G(\cdot)$ w.r.t. y_t:

$$g(y_t; \alpha, \beta, u) = \left[\frac{1}{\beta} \left(1 + \frac{y_t}{\alpha\beta} \right) \right]^{-(1+\alpha)}$$

The log-likelihood function is therefore

$$\sum_i^k \log \left\{ \left[\frac{1}{\beta} \left(1 + \frac{y_{(i,t)}}{\alpha\beta} \right) \right]^{-(1+\alpha)} \right\}$$

where k is the number of exceedances corresponding to u and $y_{(i,t)} = |r_{(i,t)}| - u$, $i = 1, \ldots, k$ is the set of exceedances in the data. To estimate the parameters α and β, we numerically find the values $\hat{\alpha}$ and $\hat{\beta}$ that maximize the log-likelihood function. The estimate of $G(y_t; \alpha, \beta, u)$ is then

$$G(y_t; \hat{\alpha}, \hat{\beta}, u) = 1 - \left(1 + \frac{y_t}{\hat{\alpha}\hat{\beta}} \right)^{-\hat{\alpha}}$$

We can combine this with the definition of the *conditional* probability distribution of exceedances to estimate the tail return distribution. The natural estimate of the probability $1 - F(u)$ of the conditioning event—a return less than or equal to the threshold u—is $\frac{k}{NOBS}$, the frequency of returns less than u in the sample. Our estimate of the conditional probability of an exceedance over u less than or equal to y_t is $G(y_t; \hat{\alpha}, \hat{\beta}, u)$, so the conditional probability of an exceedance greater than y_t is

$$1 - G(y_t; \hat{\alpha}, \hat{\beta}, u) = \left(1 + \frac{y_t}{\hat{\alpha}\hat{\beta}} \right)^{-\hat{\alpha}}$$

The *unconditional* probability of a return r_t in excess of u is therefore

$$\frac{k}{NOBS} \left(1 + \frac{r_t - u}{\hat{\alpha}\hat{\beta}} \right)^{-\hat{\alpha}}$$

We can use this probability distribution to calculate the probability of a very low return, or to find the VaR, that is, a low-return quantile. The next example illustrates.

Example 10.2 (Estimating VaR with EVT) Continuing the S&P 500 example, let's set a threshold of −7.5 percent. The 22 days on which returns were that low or lower are tabulated here, together with the order statistics of the corresponding exceedances $y_{(i,t)}$. The exceedance column of data will be entered into the log-likelihood function.

i	Date	$r_{(i,t)}$	$y_{(i,t)}$
1	24Sep1931	−0.0757	0.0007
2	31May1932	−0.0775	0.0025
3	14May1940	−0.0776	0.0026
4	09Oct2008	−0.0792	0.0042
5	16Jun1930	−0.0794	0.0044
6	26Jul1934	−0.0815	0.0065
7	12Aug1932	−0.0836	0.0086
8	05Oct1932	−0.0855	0.0105
9	26Oct1987	−0.0864	0.0114
10	10Oct1932	−0.0893	0.0143
11	21Jul1933	−0.0911	0.0161
12	29Sep2008	−0.0920	0.0170
13	20Jul1933	−0.0930	0.0180
14	01Dec2008	−0.0935	0.0185
15	15Oct2008	−0.0947	0.0197
16	05Oct1931	−0.0951	0.0201
17	18Oct1937	−0.0956	0.0206
18	03Sep1946	−0.1044	0.0294
19	06Nov1929	−0.1045	0.0295
20	29Oct1929	−0.1071	0.0321
21	28Oct1929	−0.1386	0.0636
22	19Oct1987	−0.2290	0.1540

Our estimated parameters are $\hat{\alpha} = 4.514$, not far from the Hill estimate of the tail index, and $\hat{\beta} = 0.0177$, higher, but not by much, than the full-sample standard deviation of returns. They are obtained numerically as the values that maximize the likelihood function.

We have $k = 22$ and $NOBS = 20{,}921$. Our estimate of the probability of a return less than −7.5 percent is $22 \times 20{,}921^{-1} = 0.001052$. The estimated probability of a return of, say, −10 percent is therefore

$$0.000307 = 0.001052 \left(1 + \frac{0.10 - 0.075}{4.514 \times 0.0177} \right)^{-4.514}$$

or 3.1 basis points. The actual frequency of returns of −10 percent or less in the sample is 2.4 basis points.

The VaR shock at a confidence level of, say, 99.99 percent is the number r that satisfies

$$0.00001 = 0.001052 \left(1 + \frac{r - 0.075}{4.514 \times 0.0177} \right)^{-4.514}$$

or 12.96 percent. In other words, using our estimated extreme value distribution, we would expect to see a one-day decline of about 13 percent or worse roughly once in 40 years. This is not a surprising estimate in view of the two observations of such large outliers in our 80-odd years of daily data.

10.3   THE EVIDENCE ON NON-NORMALITY IN DERIVATIVES PRICES

In Chapter 2, we defined a risk-neutral probability distribution, the probability distribution of the future asset price that is implied by current market prices of assets. The risk-neutral distribution is contrasted with the real-life, "subjective" or "physical" probability distribution. The term "subjective" focuses on the fact that it is the distribution that "the market" or the representative agent believes in when assessing future returns and making investment decisions. The term "physical," particularly in the context of a specific model, focuses on the fact that it is the distribution the model posits is true.

We can use risk-neutral distributions to obtain information about what the market—that is, the consensus expressed in prices—thinks about the distribution of asset returns. Option prices contain a great deal of information about market perceptions of the distribution of future asset prices, and they adjust to take account of the deviations from the standard model we noted at the beginning of this chapter. The information is expressed through the implied volatility smile, but is masked in two ways. First, it is embedded in option prices and needs to be extracted, via techniques we describe shortly. Second, the information is on risk-neutral rather than physical probability distributions, and is therefore blended with information about market preferences concerning risk. In this section, we see how to use option prices to derive risk-neutral distributions.

10.3.1   Option-Based Risk-Neutral Distributions

Chapter 5 introduced the so-called Black-Scholes option biases or anomalies, the important ways in which actually observed option prices differ from the predictions of the model. We also saw examples of one aspect of this phenomenon, the implied volatility smile: the cross-section, at a point in time, of the implied volatilities of European call or put options on the same underlying and with the same maturity, but different exercise prices. Chapter 5 was focused on identifying sources of option risk and applying appropriate measures of that risk. But the option biases and the volatility smile also have great significance for the study of the real-world behavior of asset returns.

The Black-Scholes model is similar to the standard risk-management model of conditionally normal returns. The models differ mainly in that in the Black-Scholes model does not allow for variation in volatility over time. The option biases are driven by market perceptions and expectations of future returns as well as by deviations of realized return behavior from the standard model. The volatility smile results from kurtosis in returns, and the expectation that it will persist in the future. Option skew expresses an expectation that large-magnitude returns in a particular direction will predominate.

Risk appetites and the desire to hedge against rare events play the key role here. Some option biases, such as the equity market put skew—the tendency for low-strike options to be expensive relative to high-strike options—have been remarkably persistent. The put skew manifested itself through many years in which the actual behavior of equity returns was much closer to the normal model. Only with the subprime crisis did the "crash insurance" it seems to have captured appear fully warranted. The persistent put skew is similar in this respect to the peso problem in currency forward prices, discussed earlier in this chapter.

The techniques of this section build on the asset pricing model of Chapter 2. There, we saw that risk-neutral probabilities are equal to the present values of elementary claims that provide a payoff of $1 in one specific future state, and 0 otherwise. The value of an elementary claim is related to the state of the world—feast or famine—it is associated with, and the representative agent's, that is, the market's, desire to hedge against low-consumption states.

Chapter 2 is a finite-state setting, with discrete states. In a continuous-state setting, we have a probability density function, rather than a set of discrete probabilities. To understand how to actually estimate the risk-neutral distribution using option prices, we reframe the discussion in terms of a continuous risk-neutral density function $\tilde{\pi}(S_T)$, where S_T is the future asset price. But we return to the finite-state to describe practical procedures for estimating risk-neutral probabilities.

In a number of areas of applied finance, as noted, a market index, typically the S&P 500, is a proxy for the state of the economy, and its future random value is an index of the future state. "States" are modeled as "realizations of future price." Taking that analogy a step further, if we can estimate the risk-neutral density of the S&P 500 at some future date, we have a proxy for the state price density.

Option Prices and Risk-Neutral Distributions   We start by presenting an important result, known as the *Breeden-Litzenberger formula*, about the relationship between prices of European call options and the risk-neutral density. Specifically, the mathematical first derivative of the call option's value with respect to the strike price is closely related to the risk-neutral probability that the future asset price will be no higher than the strike price.

The payoff at maturity to a European call option maturing at time T, with an exercise price X, is $\max(S_T - X, 0)$. The observed market value at time t of a European call option is therefore the present expected value of that payoff under the risk-neutral distribution.[3] In the Black-Scholes model, in which perfect delta hedging is possible, that expected value is evaluated using the risk-free rate, rather than a discount factor that includes a risk premium. For our purposes, since we are trying to extract a risk-neutral, rather than the subjective probability, it is appropriate to use the risk-free rate even without the Black-Scholes model assumptions. We are not formulating an alternative or independent model to the market of what the asset price ought to be. Rather, we can describe what we are trying to do in two complementary ways:

1. Find a probability distribution that matches up with the market value, thus blending the risk premiums embedded in observable asset prices into probabilities assigned to various outcomes
2. Find the subjective probability distribution that a representative agent would have to have in his head, if he were indifferent to risk and market prices were as we find them

Matching the option price to the risk-neutral present expected value of that payoff gives us

$$c(t, \tau, X) = e^{-r\tau}\tilde{\mathbf{E}}\left[\max(S_T - X, 0)\right] = e^{-r\tau}\int_X^\infty (s - X)\tilde{\pi}(s)ds$$

where
$\qquad S_T$ = terminal, or time-T, asset price
$\qquad X$ = exercise price
$\qquad \tau \equiv T - t$ = time to maturity
$\qquad c(t, \tau, X)$ = observed time-t price of an option struck at X and maturing at time T
$\qquad \tilde{\mathbf{E}}[\cdot]$ = an expectation taken under the risk-neutral probability measure
$\qquad \tilde{\pi}(\cdot)$ = risk-neutral probability density of S_T, conditional on S_t
$\qquad r$ = continuously compounded risk-free rate, assumed constant over both time and the term structure of interest rates

---

[3]We specify European options since they have a fixed maturity date on which they can be exercised. American options, which can be exercised at any time prior to maturity, are not associated with one fixed forecast horizon, and consequently don't lend themselves as well to estimating fixed-horizon risk-neutral distributions. Most exchange-traded options and options on futures have American-style exercise.

We're assuming for simplicity that the asset pays no dividend or other cash flow. Taking the integral over the interval $[X, \infty]$ lets us substitute out the max($\cdot$) function in the expression for the expected value of the payoff, the difference between S_T and X, given that S_T is greater.

We define the risk-neutral probabilities by matching them up with the option prices. There is an important assumption behind this, as we saw in Chapter 2: the absence of arbitrage opportunities. The risk-neutral probabilities may be quite far from the physical probabilities market participants actually believe in. But the market prices cannot contain opportunities to make money without risk; otherwise the risk-neutral probabilities would not be well-defined. Another assumption is that there are observable call prices for any strike price X. The sparser the option price data, the more difficult is the empirical estimation process.

Differentiating the no-arbitrage market call price with respect to the exercise price X, we have

$$\frac{\partial}{\partial X}c(t, \tau, X) = e^{-r\tau}\frac{\partial}{\partial X}\int_X^\infty (s - X)\tilde{\pi}(s)ds$$

$$= -e^{-r\tau}\int_X^\infty \tilde{\pi}(s)ds$$

$$= -e^{-r\tau}\left[\int_{-\infty}^\infty \tilde{\pi}(s)ds - \int_{-\infty}^X \tilde{\pi}(s)ds\right]$$

$$= e^{-r\tau}\left[\int_0^X \tilde{\pi}(s)ds - 1\right]$$

In the second line of this derivation, we used Leibniz's Rule to differentiate with respect to an integration limit. In the third line, we recognized that the lower limit of integration can't be less than zero, because asset prices can't be negative. We also split the integral into the difference of two integrals. In the fourth line, we recognized that $\int_{-\infty}^\infty \tilde{\pi}(s)ds = 1$, because $\tilde{\pi}(\cdot)$ is a probability density function and, again, that $\int_{-\infty}^X \tilde{\pi}(s)ds = \int_0^X \tilde{\pi}(s)ds$.

This result implies that the risk-neutral cumulative distribution function of the future asset price is equal to one plus the future value of the "exercise price delta" of the market price of a European call:

$$\tilde{\Pi}(X) \equiv \int_0^X \tilde{\pi}(s)ds = 1 + e^{r\tau}\frac{\partial}{\partial X}c(t, \tau, X)$$

Differentiate again to see that the risk-neutral probability density function is the future value of the second derivative of the call price with respect to the exercise price:

$$\tilde{\pi}(X) = e^{r\tau} \frac{\partial^2}{\partial X^2} c(t, \tau, X)$$

Extracting the risk-neutral density from option prices preserves an important property of asset prices, namely, that the expected value of the future asset price under the risk-neutral probability distribution equals the current forward asset price. To see this, consider a call option with an exercise price of zero:

$$c(t, \tau, 0) = e^{-r\tau} \int_0^\infty s\tilde{\pi}(s)ds$$
$$= e^{-r\tau} \tilde{E}[S_T]$$
$$= e^{-r\tau} F_{t,T}$$

where $F_{t,T}$ is the forward price. The last line of this derivation holds by virtue of the definition of a forward price.

Using call prices is a slightly convoluted path to the risk-neutral cumulative distribution function. Put prices are more direct: The first derivative of the price of a European put $p(t, \tau, X)$ with respect to the exercise price is the future value of the risk-free cumulative distribution function itself. The payoff at maturity of a put with an exercise price X, maturing at time T, is $\max(X - S_T, 0)$. The current value of a put is therefore

$$p(t, \tau, X) = e^{-r\tau} \tilde{E}[\max(X - S_T, 0)] = e^{-r\tau} \int_0^X (X - s)\tilde{\pi}(s)ds$$

and its first derivative with respect to X is

$$\frac{\partial}{\partial X} p(t, \tau, X) = e^{-r\tau} \int_0^X \tilde{\pi}(s)ds$$
$$= e^{-r\tau} \tilde{\Pi}(S_T)$$

The second derivative with respect to the exercise price is identical to that of a call.

Pricing Elementary Claims from Options Now let's return to the finite-state setup for more intuition on these results and to actually estimate risk-neutral distributions. We start by setting out a discretized version of our option-based estimate of the risk-neutral cumulative probability distribution and density functions. The "exercise price delta" and thus the CDF can be approximated by

$$\tilde{\Pi}(X) \approx 1 + e^{r\tau} \frac{1}{\Delta} \left[c\left(t, \tau, X + \frac{\Delta}{2}\right) - c\left(t, \tau, X - \frac{\Delta}{2}\right) \right]$$

As $\Delta \to 0$, this should get very close to the CDF. Similarly, the PDF can be approximated as

$$\begin{aligned}
\tilde{\pi}(X) &\approx \frac{1}{\Delta} \left[\tilde{\Pi}\left(X + \frac{\Delta}{2}\right) - \tilde{\Pi}\left(X - \frac{\Delta}{2}\right) \right] \\
&= \frac{1}{\Delta} \left\{ 1 + e^{r\tau} \frac{1}{\Delta} [c(t, \tau, X + \Delta) - c(t, \tau, X)] \right\} \\
&\quad - \frac{1}{\Delta} \left\{ 1 + e^{r\tau} \frac{1}{\Delta} [c(t, \tau, X) - c(t, \tau, X - \Delta)] \right\} \\
&= e^{r\tau} \frac{1}{\Delta^2} [c(t, \tau, X + \Delta) + c(t, \tau, X - \Delta) - 2c(t, \tau, X)]
\end{aligned}$$

In Chapter 5, we discussed option spreads and combinations, option portfolios that combine puts and calls, such as straddles. That discussion was in the context of vega risk, and we saw how these combinations embed information about the volatility smile and how to take the smile into account in order to accurately measure vega risk. In the present context, we will use the volatility smile to estimate risk-neutral distributions.

For the next bit of analysis, we rely on an option spread called a *butterfly*, which consists of long positions in two calls with different exercise prices, and a short position in a call with an exercise price midway between those of the long calls. Figure 10.10 shows the payoff profile of a butterfly with exercise prices 99, 100, and 101, and centered at 100. It corresponds to $X = 100$ and $\Delta = 1$.

Butterflies can be used to construct claims on an asset that pay off if the realized future asset price falls in a narrow range. A butterfly must be priced as if it were a lottery ticket paying off if that particular range for the future asset prices is realized. If the calls we are scrutinizing are options on a broad index such as the S&P 500, which is often taken as the price of a claim on future consumption, then the prices of butterflies are proxies for elementary

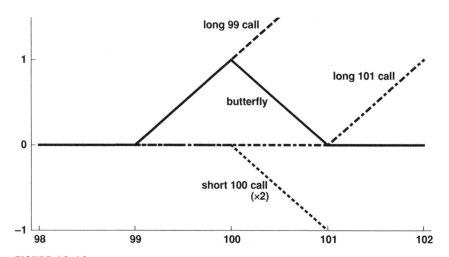

FIGURE 10.10   Constructing a Long Butterfly
The butterfly is constructed by combining long positions of one call option in each of the "flanking" strikes ($X = 99$ and $X = 101$) and a short position in two call options struck at the "center" of the butterfly ($X = 100$).

claims and, as we saw in Chapter 2, for a probability measure on the future asset price.

Suppose the future values of the asset can take on only integer values, that is, the state space is not only countable, but also doesn't have many elements. A long butterfly centered at 100 will pay exactly \$1 if the future index level is 100 and zero otherwise. Absence of arbitrage implies that the price of the butterfly must equal the price of an elementary claim that pays \$1 if the future price is 100 and zero otherwise. The value of the butterfly is

$$c(t, \tau, 99) + c(t, \tau, 101) - 2c(t, \tau, 100)$$

Let's now imagine that we "undiscretize" the state space by letting the future index take on noninteger values, say, at quarter-point intervals. We can still create a butterfly that pays \$1 conditional on $S_T = 100$, but its value is now

$$\frac{1}{0.25} [c(t, \tau, 99.75) + c(t, \tau, 100.25) - 2c(t, \tau, 100)]$$

For any level of the terminal price $S_T = X$, and any price interval Δ, we have

$$\frac{1}{\Delta} [c(t, \tau, X - \Delta) + c(t, \tau, X + \Delta) - 2c(t, \tau, X)]$$

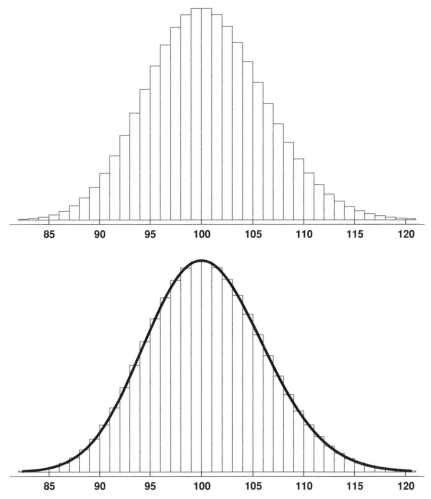

FIGURE 10.11 State Prices and the Risk Neutral Density
Upper panel: State prices along the price axis. The state prices are computed by assuming a specific risk neutral distribution for the future value of the index.
Lower panel: State prices and the risk neutral density.

The expression above gives the value of the elementary claim itself. These are equal to the *areas* of the rectangles in the upper panel of Figure 10.11. The *height* of each of these rectangles is approximately equal to the present value of the risk-neutral density of S_T, evaluated at X:

$$\frac{1}{\Delta^2} \left[c(t, \tau, X - \Delta) + c(t, \tau, X + \Delta) - 2c(t, \tau, X) \right]$$

Finally, taking $\Delta \rightarrow 0$, we get the expression for a continuous risk-neutral density derived above. This gives us some intuition on the Breeden-Litzenberger formula, and shows us the way to actually estimate a risk-neutral density.

We've mentioned that finding enough option prices is one of the challenges in estimating $\bar{\pi}(S_T)$. The expression above spells out exactly what we need to estimate it at one specific point X: We need prices of three options, with exercise prices X, $X + \Delta$, and $X - \Delta$, all with the same maturity and all observed at the same time. Since there generally aren't that many different options trading on a single underlying asset, we will have to interpolate between the handful of observable option prices.

10.3.2   Risk-Neutral Asset Price Probability Distributions

Implementing this approach is difficult because it requires, in principle, a set of options with exercise prices closely spaced, in increments of Δ, on the asset price axis. In practice, not enough option contracts, with different exercise prices on a given asset with a given maturity, trade simultaneously. The option price data must also be of good quality; since we take second differences of the European call price as a function of strike to approximate the risk-neutral density, even small errors, such as rounding prices to the nearest tick, can lead to large anomalies in the estimated density. Carrying out these techniques therefore requires intensive data preparation to eliminate or correct flawed prices, and techniques for extracting information efficiently from the prices that remain after filtering.

Apart from lack of high-quality data, but also as a result of it, risk-neutral densities extracted from options can display violations of no-arbitrage conditions. Two in particular are worth mentioning:

1. The value of a call or put must be a convex function of the exercise price. Observed option prices interpolated ones can violate this no-arbitrage condition in a minor way over small intervals on the exercise price axis. This leads to computation of negative probability densities over the interval.
2. The mean of the risk-neutral density may not exactly equal the forward or futures price of the underlying asset.

A number of techniques have been developed to estimate risk-neutral densities from the generally sparse available data. We'll give a few examples of the results, based on a simple approach to estimation. It starts with the option data themselves. In order to have a European call price function that is as smooth as possible, it helps to begin with option-implied volatilities as a function of the Black-Scholes call option delta rather than of exercise price. We'll denote the date-t implied volatility of a European option on a given underlying asset, maturing at time $T = t + \tau$, and with a delta δ, by $\sigma(t, \tau, \delta)$.

In the foreign exchange markets, options actually trade in these terms. In Chapter 5, we described combinations of options called risk reversals and strangles. These combinations can be readily converted into prices of individual options with specified deltas. For example, consider a 25-delta one-month strangle. Its price is quoted as the difference between the average implied vols of the 25-delta put and call, and the at-the-money forward (ATMF) put or call vol $\sigma(t, \tau, 0.50)$:

$$\text{strangle price} = \frac{1}{2}[\sigma(t, \tau, 0.25) + \sigma(t, \tau, 0.75)] - \sigma(t, \tau, 0.50)$$

This is equivalent to the implied vol of a butterfly set at the 25- and 75-delta strikes. The risk reversal quote is the implied vol spread between the two "wing" options:

$$\text{risk reversal price} = \sigma(t, \tau, 0.25) - \sigma(t, \tau, 0.75)$$

Note that strangle and risk reversal are quoted as vol spreads, while the ATMF is a vol level.[4] Using these definitions, the vol levels of options with different deltas can be recovered from the strangle, risk reversal, and ATMF quotes:

$$\sigma(t, \tau, 0.25) = \sigma(t, \tau, 0.50) + \text{strangle price} + \frac{1}{2} \times \text{risk reversal price}$$

$$\sigma(t, \tau, 0.75) = \sigma(t, \tau, 0.50) + \text{strangle price} - \frac{1}{2} \times \text{risk reversal price}$$

We can carry out the same operations for the 10-delta risk reversal and strangle. For most major currency pairs, these prices can all be readily obtained, for a wide range of tenors from overnight to several years.

Once we have a set of implied volatilities for different deltas, we can interpolate between them. There are a number of ways to do this, including the parametric approach of least-squares fitting and the nonparametric

---

[4]Note also as a minor detail that the ATM or ATMF option will have a delta close to but not exactly equal to 0.50.

approaches of applying a spline or an interpolating polynomial. However we go about it, the result is a function $\sigma(t, \tau, \delta)$, defined for any call delta $0 < \delta < 1$.

The next step is to find the exercise price X corresponding to $\sigma(t, \tau, \delta)$ for each delta. The quotation convention for implied volatilities is the Black-Scholes model, even though markets are perfectly aware the model is not accurate; it merely provides a set of units. The delta corresponding to an implied volatility is therefore the Black-Scholes delta, rather than the "true" sensitivity of the option value to changes in the underlying asset value. The Black-Scholes delta is

$$e^{-r^*\tau}\Phi\left[\frac{\ln\left(\frac{S_t}{X}\right) + \left(r - r^* + \frac{\sigma^2}{2}\right)\tau}{\sigma\sqrt{\tau}}\right]$$

where r^* is the continuously compounded dividend, interest rate, or cost of carry of the underlying asset. For any particular value of the delta δ°, we can solve

$$\delta^\circ = e^{-r^*\tau}\Phi\left[\frac{\ln\left(\frac{S_t}{X}\right) + \left(r - r^* + \frac{\sigma(t, \tau, \delta^\circ)^2}{2}\right)\tau}{\sigma(t, \tau, \delta^\circ)\sqrt{\tau}}\right]$$

numerically for X to derive a volatility function $\sigma(t, \tau, X)$. The search algorithm would do so by finding the pair (σ, X) that lies on the interpolated volatility smile $\sigma(t, \tau, \delta)$ at the point δ°, and also returns δ° when substituted into the Black-Scholes delta.

The last step is to calculate the risk-neutral distribution. We substitute the volatility function $\sigma(t, \tau, X)$ into the Black-Scholes formula for the value of a European call option $v(S_t, \tau, X, \sigma, r, q)$ to obtain $v[S_t, \tau, X, \sigma(t, \tau, X), r, q]$. The volatility function $\sigma(t, \tau, X)$ is an estimate of the Black-Scholes implied volatility, that is, the volatility that, for exercise price X, would match the Black-Scholes formula to the market option price. So $v[S_t, \tau, X, \sigma(t, \tau, X), r, q]$ is an estimate of the market price of a call option with any X. In other words, we set

$$c(t, \tau, X) = v[S_t, \tau, X, \sigma(t, \tau, X), r, q]$$

Although we can differentiate $v(S_t, \tau, X, \sigma, r, q)$ algebraically, we generally will have to differentiate $v[S_t, \sigma(t, \tau, X, \tau, X), r, q]$ numerically. The cumulative probability distribution of the asset price is estimated by

$$\tilde{\Pi}(X) \approx 1 + e^{r\tau} \frac{1}{\Delta} \left\{ v \left[S_t, \tau, X + \frac{\Delta}{2}, \sigma \left(t, \tau, X + \frac{\Delta}{2} \right), r, q \right] \right.$$
$$\left. - v \left[S_t, \tau, X - \frac{\Delta}{2}, \sigma \left(t, \tau, X - \frac{\Delta}{2} \right), r, q \right] \right\}$$

and the density by

$$\tilde{\pi}(X) \approx e^{r\tau} \frac{1}{\Delta^2} \{ v[S_t, \tau, X + \Delta, \sigma(t, \tau, X + \Delta), r, q]$$
$$+ v[S_t, \tau, X - \Delta, \sigma(t, \tau, X - \Delta), r, q] - 2v[S_t, \tau, X, \sigma(t, \tau, X), r, q] \}$$

We don't have to believe in the validity or perfect accuracy of the Black-Scholes model at all to use it this way. All we need is our estimates of observed volatilities and the Breeden-Litzenberger relationship.

Example 10.3 Let's look at an example of how a risk-neutral distribution is constructed for the S&P index. The data used are displayed in the following table:

	September 29, 2008	May 27, 2010
Index	1,106.39	1,103.06
Risk-free rate	0.06	0.15
Dividend rate	2.72	1.99
10-δ call vol	44.08	20.03
25-δ call vol	46.29	21.52
40-δ call vol	48.79	23.30
50-δ call vol	50.62	24.67
60-δ call vol	52.65	26.38
75-δ call vol	56.39	29.95
90-δ call vol	61.88	37.20

Index: S&P index closing index level; risk-free rate: one month U.S. Treasury bill rate. All volatilities are of 1-month options, annualized and expressed in percent.

Figure 10.12 displays $\sigma(t, \tau, \delta)$ and $\sigma(t, \tau, X)$, the two versions of the interpolated volatility smile. The curve on the left, $\sigma(t, \tau, \delta)$, interpolates

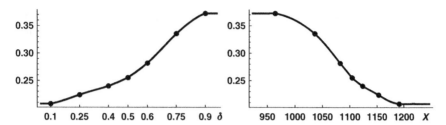

FIGURE 10.12   Fitted Implied Volatility Smile
The left panel displays the volatility smile in delta-vol space, the right panel in
strike-vol space, one month options on the S&P index, May 27, 2010. The points
represent actually observed implied volatilities, expressed as decimals.
Data source: Bloomberg Financial L.P.

between the volatility levels derived from the option quotes displayed in the
table above. The curve on the right is $\sigma(t, \tau, X)$, the one required for the next
step in obtaining a risk-neutral distribution, in which we estimate the probabilities and the probability density as first and second differences in the call
option value. Note that the high implied volatilities are those for options
with high call deltas, corresponding to low strikes in index terms and low
put deltas.

The volatility smiles displayed in Figure 10.12 are interpolated by fitting
a cubic spline to seven observed implied volatilities for call deltas equal
to (0.10, 0.25, 0.40, 0.50, 0.60, 0.75, 0.90). The spline is "clamped" at the
endpoints by imposing the condition that the first derivative, that is, the
slope of the volatility smile, is equal to zero at $\sigma(t, \tau, 0.10)$ and $\sigma(t, \tau, 0.90)$,
the endpoint implied volatilities.[5]

The resulting risk-neutral densities for the two dates are displayed in
Figure 10.13. Each plot represents the probability density of the S&P index
one month in the future. The index levels on these two dates happen to
be very close to one another, just above 1,100, but the distributions of the
future exchange rate implied by options are very different.[6] The density on
September 29, 2008, is drawn from a high-volatility regime, just after the
Lehman bankruptcy. It is very dispersed around the mean and has high
skew and kurtosis. On May 27, 2010, in contrast, the distribution has a
much lower variance, in spite of the European debt crisis then currently in

---

[5]For more detail on how to compute cubic splines and clamped cubic splines, see
Stoer and Bulirsch (1993) and Klugman, Panjer, and Willmot (2008).
[6]The technique used is similar to that of Malz (1997). The main difference is to
employ a cubic spline rather than polynomial interpolation through the observed
volatilities to represent the volatility smile.

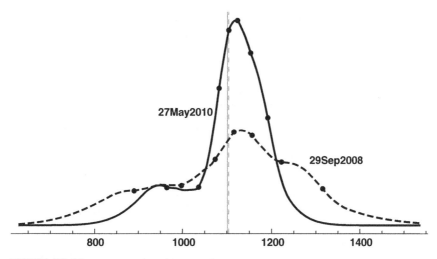

FIGURE 10.13 Estimated Risk-Neutral Densities
One-month risk-neutral density functions for the S&P index, May 27, 2010, and September 29, 2008. The vertical grid lines represent the forward stock index level for each date. The points correspond to the exercise prices for which implied volatilities are directly observed.
Data source: Bloomberg Financial L.P.

full blossom, making the skew even more apparent to the eye. Both show a pronounced negative skew toward lower index levels.

One way to compare the two distributions is to compute the risk-neutral probability of shocks of different sizes. The table below summarizes the risk-neutral probabilities of arithmetic returns in percent on the index over the month following the observation date. Thus we see that the risk-neutral probability that the index would fall by 25 percent over the subsequent month was over 4 times higher just after the Lehman bankruptcy as in the spring of 2010.

Shock	May 27, 2010	September 29, 2008
−33.3	0.23	2.03
−25.0	1.48	6.18
−10.0	9.36	23.69
0.0	41.50	46.80
10.0	95.53	74.57
25.0	99.99	96.56
33.3	100.00	99.10

Another way to compare the distributions is through its quantiles. The next table displays the first and fifth percentiles of the risk-neutral distribution on the two dates:

		0.01 Quantile		0.05 Quantile	
	SPX close	SPX level	loss (%)	SPX level	loss (%)
May 27, 2010	1,103.06	852	22.6	917	16.7
September 29, 2008	1,106.39	716	35.1	809	26.7

The September 29, 2008, distribution attributes a probability of 1 percent to a one-month decline in excess of 35.1 percent in the index, to a level of 716. The later distribution states that a smaller decline, of only 22.6 percent or more, has a 1 percent likelihood of occurring.

Risk-neutral distributions are useful in several ways. A straightforward application is to draw inferences about the probabilities being assigned by the market, in its collective wisdom, to the realization of different asset price levels or events. For a broad index, such as the S&P 500, the probability that a low future index level is realized can be interpreted as the probability of an adverse state of the economy.

A fair critique of such inferences is that the probabilities obtained in this way are risk-neutral rather than physical, so treating them as straightforward forecasts is unwarranted. However, they nonetheless contain valuable information. Consider the S&P example. We cannot discern whether the dramatic fall in the risk-neutral probability of a massive decline in the index reflects a change in the market's belief in or fear of a market crash, but we know it must be some combination of the two, and the fact of the change is important to both traders and policy makers. The increased risk-neutral probability can also be interpreted as a large increase in the market's willingness to pay up to hedge against that event. That might indicate that some market participants with sensitivity to mark-to-market losses have long positions they are uncomfortable with.

Another important application of risk-neutral distributions is in estimating risk aversion. If we can obtain a reliable estimate of the physical probability distribution of a representative index such as the S&P 500, the differences from the risk-neutral distribution permit us to draw inferences about risk premiums. The physical distribution might, for example, be based on historical volatility estimates such as those presented in Chapter 3. One such approach, called *implied binomial trees*, has become important in developing tools for pricing exotic derivatives. It extracts not only the risk-neutral distribution of returns at one future point in time, but also the stochastic process followed by returns over time.

10.3.3 Implied Correlations

Risk-neutral probability distributions are one of several types of information about asset return distributions contained in market prices. Chapter 1 used data on nominal and inflation-protected bond yields to obtain risk-neutral estimates of future inflation rates (see Figure 1.14). In Chapters 7 and 8, we saw how to obtain risk-neutral estimates of default probabilities and correlations from credit derivatives prices. In this section, we extract data on return correlations among individual stocks, called the *risk-neutral implied equity correlation*, using the implied volatilities of individual stocks in an index and the implied volatility of the index itself. We describe how equity implied correlation is computed and see how it has behaved in recent years.

An equity index is a weighted sum of the constituent stocks. Its returns can be expressed as:

$$r_{\text{index},t} = \sum_{n}^{N} \omega_{nt} r_{nt}$$

where $r_{\text{index},t}$ represents the time-t index return, and ω_{nt} and r_{nt} the time-t weights and returns on the $n = 1, \ldots, N$ constituent stocks. The index return volatility $\sigma_{\text{index},t}^2$ is related to the N volatilities of individual stock returns by

$$\sigma_{\text{index},t}^2 = \sum_{i} \omega_{nt}^2 \sigma_{nt}^2 + 2 \sum_{n} \sum_{m<n} \omega_{mt} \omega_{nt} \sigma_{mt} \sigma_{nt} \rho_{mn,t}$$

where $\rho_{mn,t}$ is the time-t correlation between returns on stocks m and n. Note that the index volatility cannot exceed the average individual stock volatility; there cannot be negative diversification in the index as a whole.

Let's make a simplifying assumption, that the pairwise correlation $\rho_{mn,t} = \rho_t, \forall m, n$. This is analogous to the assumption that a single copula correlation or a single beta drives the pairwise default correlations in a portfolio credit model. We can then estimate an implied correlation by using the relationship

$$\rho_t = \frac{\sigma_{\text{index},t}^2 - \sum_{i} \omega_{nt}^2 \sigma_{nt}^2}{2 \sum_{i} \sum_{m<n} \omega_{mt} \omega_{nt} \sigma_{mt} \sigma_{nt}}$$

and substituting the index and individual stock implied volatilities for σ_t and $\sigma_{n,t}$.

As with any risk-neutral quantity, the implied correlation will differ from the actual implied correlation by an unobservable risk premium. The risk premium will be driven by the estimated correlations and the urgency of hedging individual stock exposures. For a given expected correlation, the implied correlation or the risk premium will be higher when market participants are less eager to have undiversified individual equity exposures or are more averse to bearing systematic risk.

To get some additional intuition into this relationship, suppose all the stocks in the index are identical and the index is equally weighted, that is, $\sigma_{nt} = \sigma_t$ and $\omega_{nt} = 1/N, \forall n$. Then

$$
\begin{aligned}
\rho_t &= \frac{\sigma_{\text{index},t}^2 - NN^{-2}\sigma_t^2}{2N^{-2}\dfrac{N(N-1)}{2}\sigma_t^2} \\
&= \frac{\sigma_{\text{index},t}^2 - N^{-1}\sigma_t^2}{(N-1)N^{-1}\sigma_t^2} \\
&\approx \left(\frac{\sigma_{\text{index},t}}{\sigma_t}\right)^2
\end{aligned}
$$

In this simplification, the implied correlation is close to zero (unity) when the index volatility is small (large) relative to the typical individual stock volatility. During financial crises, index as well as single-stock volatilities rise sharply, but index volatility rises faster, as market participants flee systematic risk, driving implied correlation higher.

Just as the option skew can be interpreted as an indicator of the market's perception or fear of large asset returns, implied equity correlation can be interpreted as an indicator of the perceptions or fear of systemic risk. Figure 10.14 shows that implied correlation peaks at times of market stress. At the worst point of the subprime crisis, it drew close to its maximum possible value of 1.

Implied correlation is also a market risk factor. Just as with volatility, traders can take positions on the difference between the current and anticipated implied equity correlation over some future horizon. There are several ways to execute such *dispersion trades*. There can also be hard-to-detect implied correlation risk in any equity option portfolio hedged using index options, even if the trade is not focused on implied correlation. The primary motivation for such trades can include profiting from long gamma, from the difference between implied and realized volatility, or from individual option vega. Some examples of portfolios exposed to implied correlation include:

- Some traders hold portfolios of individual options. These may be arbitrage portfolios taking long positions in options considered overpriced and short positions in options considered underpriced, or as part of

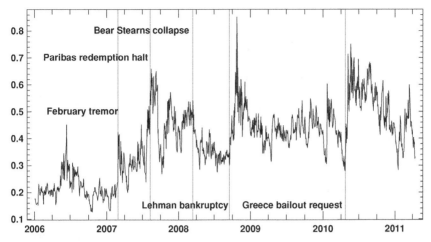

FIGURE 10.14 Risk-Neutral Implied Equity Correlation
Implied correlation of the S&P 500 index, using the largest 193 stocks and
market-capitalization weights and constituents as of Apr. 15, 2011. The included
stocks account for about 80 percent of the total market capitalization of the index.
Data source: Bloomberg Financial L.P.

long-short equity portfolios. The net long or short exposure of such
a portfolio is generally hedged with index options. A portfolio with a
substantial long individual option "overhang," hedged with short index options, will experience losses if implied correlation rises in a stress
environment.

■ *Variance swaps* are OTC derivatives contracts in which one party pays a
fixed premium and receives the squared returns on a stock or on a basket
of stocks. They can be used for hedging or to take advantage of the fact
that implied volatility generally exceeds realized volatility. Arbitrage positions in variance swaps on individual stocks are generally hedged with
variance swaps on equity indexes. When implied correlation increases,
such portfolios are overhedged. The short position in index variance
swaps has losses that may exceed the gains on the single-stock variance
swaps.

■ Consider a portfolio of convertible bonds in which the credit exposure
is hedged with long protection positions in credit default swaps on the
convertible bond issuers, the risk-free curve risk is hedged with payer
swaps or short government bond positions, the option risk is delta
hedged, and the vega risk is hedged via index options. Such a portfolio
has risks quite similar to a correlation portfolio of individual equity
options hedged with equity index options.

Another important implied correlation that can be extracted from option prices is that between two currency pairs, for example, the correlation between the exchange rates of the U.S. dollar against the euro and the Japanese yen, or that between pound sterling's exchange rates against the euro and the U.S. dollar. This implied correlation can be extracted using prices of the three distinct European options on the three currency pairs involved. For example, to estimate the correlation between EUR-USD and USD-JPY, we would require options on the two major currency pairs, and, in addition, prices of options on the EUR-JPY exchange rate.

FURTHER READING

Two classic postwar papers studying asset return distributions are Fama (1965) and Mandelbrot (1963). Cont (2001) is a more recent summary of asset return behavior; de Vries (1994) summarizes the statistical properties of foreign exchange rates. Glosten, Jagannathan, and Runkle (1993) discusses the asymmetric impact of positive and negative returns on volatility.

Duffie and Pan (1997); Hull and White (1998); and Glasserman, Heidelberger, and Shahabuddin (2002) discuss fat-tailed return distributions and alternatives to the standard model in the context of VaR modeling. An adaptation of VaR to encompass extreme returns is applied to the Asian crisis of 1997 in Pownall and Koedijk (1999). See also Rosenberg and Schuermann (2006). The term "peso problem" was introduced in Krasker (1980). See Evans (1996) for a survey of the earlier literature on the peso problem.

Kernel density estimators are discussed in Silverman (1986) and Klugman, Panjer, and Willmot (2008).

The classic discussion of jump-diffusions and their properties is Merton (1976). Empirical applications include Ball and Torous (1985), Jorion (1988), and Akgiray and Booth (1988).

Gabaix (2009) discusses finance applications of power laws. An early empirical application in finance was to currency pegs; see, for example, Nieuwland, Verschoor and Wolff (1994). On Hill's estimator, see Bangia, Diebold, Schuermann, and Stroughair (1999). Embrechts, Klüppelberg, and Mikosch (2004) is the standard work on extreme value theory, and while advanced, has a number of accessible introductory sections. Klugman, Panjer, and Willmot (2008) includes an introduction to extreme value distributions. Introductions to extreme value theory are also provided by Longin (2000) and Neftci (2000).

Surveys of techniques for extracting risk-neutral distributions from option prices include Jackwerth (1999, 2004), Mandler (2003), and Bliss and

Panigirtzoglou (2002). The Breeden-Litzenberger theorem was first stated in Breeden and Litzenberger (1978). Examples of the use of these techniques include Bates (1991), Shimko (1993), and Malz (1996, 1997). Examples of central bank use of these techniques in drawing inferences about market sentiment include Bahra (1996) and Clews, Panigirtzoglou, and Proudman (2000).

Amin and Ng (1997) and Christensen and Prabhala (1998) discuss "second-moment efficiency," the question of whether implied volatility is an accurate forecast of future realized volatility. The relationship between risk-neutral and physical distributions is studied in Aït-Sahalia and Lo (2000), Rosenberg and Engle (2002), and Bliss and Panigirtzoglou (2004). See Rubinstein (1994) and Derman and Kani (1994) on the implied binomial tree approach.

Implied correlations between exchange rates are studied in Campa and Chang (1998) and Lopez and Walter (2000).

CHAPTER 11

Assessing the Quality of Risk Measures

VaR has been subjected to much criticism. In the previous chapter, we reviewed the sharpest critique: that the standard normal return model underpinning most VaR estimation procedures is simply wrong. But there are other lines of attack on VaR that are relevant even if VaR estimates are not based on the standard model. This chapter discusses three of these viewpoints:

1. The devil is in the details: Subtle and not-so-subtle differences in how VaR is computed can lead to large differences in the estimates.
2. VaR cannot provide powerful tests of its own accuracy.
3. VaR is "philosophically" incoherent: It cannot do what it purports to be able to do, namely, rank portfolios in order of riskiness.

We will also discuss a pervasive basic problem with all models, including risk models: The fact that they can err or be used inappropriately. A further major critique, the putative potential for VaR to exacerbate systemic risk, is discussed in Chapter 14.

11.1 MODEL RISK

In Chapter 10, we focused on the basic modeling problem facing VaR, that the actual distribution of returns doesn't conform to the model assumption of normality under which VaR is often computed. Using a VaR implementation that relies on normality without appreciating the deviations of the model from reality is an example of *model risk*. Models are used in risk measurement as well as in other parts of the trading and investment process. The term "model risk" describes the possibility of making incorrect trading or risk management decisions because of errors in models and how they are applied. Model risk can manifest itself and cause losses in a number of ways. The *consequences* of model error can be trading losses, as well as adverse legal, reputational, accounting, and regulatory results.

All social science models are "wrong," in the sense that model assumptions are always more or less crude approximations to reality. In Friedman's (1953) view on the methodology of economics, deviation from reality is a virtue in a model, because the model then more readily generates testable hypotheses that can be falsified empirically, adding to knowledge. We encountered an example of this in the previous chapter. The so-called Black-Scholes biases provide very useful insights into return behavior, and yet are defined as violations of the model predictions. A model may, however, be inherently wrong, in that it is based on an incorrect overall view of reality. The data inputs can be inaccurate, or may be inappropriate to the application.

Error can be introduced into models in any number of ways. A seemingly trivial channel, but one that can have large consequences, is that the programming of a model algorithm can contain bugs. An example occurred in the ratings process for structured credit products, and was revealed during the subprime crisis. The press reported in May 2008 that Moody's had incorrectly, given their own ratings methodology, assigned AAA ratings to certain structured credit products using materially flawed programming. Another example occurred when AXA Rosenberg Group LLC, an asset-management subsidiary of the French insurance company AXA, using a quantitative investment approach, discovered a programming error in its models that had likely induced losses for some investors.[1]

These episodes also provide examples of the linkages between different types of risk. In the Moody's case, the model risk was closely linked to the reputational and liquidity risks faced by Moody's. The error had been discovered by Moody's before being reported in the press, but had coincided with changes in the ratings methodology for the affected products, and had not resulted in changes in ratings while still known only within the firm. Moody's therefore, once the bugs became public knowledge, came under suspicion of having tailored the ratings model to the desired ratings, tarnishing its reputation as an objective ratings provider. Within a few days of the episode being reported, S&P placed Moody's-issued commercial paper on negative watch, illustrating the economic costs that reputational risk events can cause. In the AXA Rosenberg episode, the discovery of the error had not been communicated in a timely fashion to investors, resulting in

---

[1]On Moody's, see Sam Jones, Gillian Tett, and Paul J. Davies, "CPDOs expose ratings flaw at Moody's," *Financial Times*, May 20, 2008. On AXA Rosenberg, see Jean Eaglesham and Jenny Strasburg, "Big Fine Over Bug in 'Quant' Program," Wall Street Journal, Feb. 4, 2011.

loss of assets under management, an SEC fine, and considerable overall reputational damage.

Even when software is correctly programmed, it can be used in a way that is inconsistent with the model that was intended to be implemented in the software. One type of inconsistency that arises quite frequently concerns the mapping of positions to risk factors, which we'll discuss in a moment. Such inconsistencies can contribute to differences in VaR results.

11.1.1 Valuation Risk

Model errors can occur in the valuation of securities or in hedging. Errors in valuation can result in losses that are hidden within the firm or from external stakeholders. A portfolio can be more exposed to one or more risk factors than the portfolio manager realizes because of hedging errors.

Valuation errors due to inaccurate models are examples of market risk as well as of operational risk. As a market risk phenomenon, they lead, for example, to buying securities that are thought to be cheaply priced in the market, but are in fact fairly priced or overpriced. As an operational risk phenomenon, the difficulty of valuing some securities accurately makes it possible to record positions or trades as profitable that have in fact lost money.

Model errors can, in principle, be avoided and valuation risk reduced, by relying on market prices rather than model prices. There are several problems with this approach of always marking-to-market and never *marking-to-model*. Some types of positions, such as longer-term bank commercial loans, have always been difficult to market-to-market because they do not trade frequently or at all, and because their value is determined by a complex internal process of monitoring by the lender. Accounting and regulatory standards mandating marking such positions to market have been held responsible by some for exacerbating financial instability, an issue we discuss in Chapter 14.

11.1.2 Variability of VaR Estimates

VaR also faces a wide range of practical problems. To understand these better, we'll first briefly sketch the implementation process for risk computation. This entire process and its results are sometimes referred to as the firm's "VaR model." We'll then discuss how implementation decisions can lead to differences in VaR results.

Risk management is generally carried out with the aid of computer systems that automate to some extent the process of combining data and computations, and generating reports. Risk-measurement systems are available commercially. Vendor systems are generally used by smaller financial firms. Large firms generally build their own risk-measurement systems, but may purchase some components commercially.

One particular challenge of implementing risk-measurement systems is that of data preparation. Three types of data are involved:

Market data are time series data on asset prices or other data that we can use to forecast the distribution of future portfolio returns. Obtaining appropriate time series, purging them of erroneous data points, and establishing procedures for handling missing data, are costly but essential for avoiding gross inaccuracies in risk measurement. Even with the best efforts, appropriate market data for some exposures may be unobtainable.

Security master data include descriptive data on securities, such as maturity dates, currency, and units. Corporate securities such as equities and, especially, debt securities present particular challenges in setting up security master databases. To name but one, issuer hierarchy data record which entity within a large holding company a transaction is with. Such databases are difficult to build and maintain, but are extremely important from a credit risk management point of view. Netting arrangements, for example, may differ for trades with different entities. Such issues become crucial if counterparties file for bankruptcy. Chapter 6 discussed one important example from the subprime crisis: Recovery by Lehman's counterparties depended in part on which Lehman subsidiary they had faced in the transactions.

Position data must be verified to match the firm's books and records. Position data may have to be collected from many trading systems and across a number of geographical locations within a firm.

To compute a risk measure, software is needed to correctly match up this data, and present it to a calculation engine. The engine incorporates all the formulas or computation procedures that will be used, calling them from libraries of stored procedures. The calculations have to be combined with the data appropriately. Results, finally, must be conveyed to a reporting layer that manufactures documents and tables that human managers can read. All of these steps can be carried out in myriad ways. We focus on two issues, the variability of the resulting measures, and the problem of using data appropriately.

The computation process we've just described applies to any risk measure, not just to VaR, but for concreteness, we focus on VaR. The risk manager has a great deal of discretion in actually computing a VaR. The VaR techniques we described in Chapter 3—modes of computation and the user-defined parameters—can be mixed and matched in different ways. Within each mode of computation, there are major variants, for example, the so-called "hybrid" approach of using historical simulation with exponentially weighted return observations. This freedom is a mixed blessing. On the one hand, the risk manager has the flexibility to adapt the way he is calculating VaR to the needs of the firm, its investors, or the nature of the portfolio. On the other hand, it leads to two problems with the use of VaR in practice:

1. There is not much uniformity of practice as to confidence interval and time horizon; as a result, intuition on what constitutes a large or small VaR is underdeveloped.
2. Different ways of measuring VaR would lead to different results, even if there were standardization of confidence interval and time horizon. There are a number of computational and modeling decisions that can greatly influence VaR results, such as
   - Length of time series used for historical simulation or to estimate moments
   - Technique for estimating moments
   - Mapping techniques and the choice of risk factors, for example, maturity bucketing
   - Decay factor if applying EWMA
   - In Monte Carlo simulation, randomization technique and the number of simulations

Dramatic changes in VaR can be obtained by varying these parameters. In one well-known study (Beder, 1995), the VaRs of relatively simple portfolios consisting of Treasury bonds and S&P 500 index options were computed using different combinations of these parameters, all of them well within standard practice. For example, 100 or 250 days of historical data might be used to compute VaR via historical simulation, or Monte Carlo VaR might be computed using different correlation estimates. For a given time horizon and confidence level, VaR computations differed by a factor of six or seven times. Other oddities included VaR estimates that were higher for shorter time horizons.

A number of large banks publish VaR estimates for certain of their portfolios in their annual reports, generally accompanied by backtesting results. These VaR estimates are generated for regulatory purposes, as discussed in Chapter 15. Perusing these annual reports gives a sense of how different the VaR models can be, as they use inconsistent parameters and cannot be readily compared.

11.1.3 Mapping Issues

Mapping, the assignment of risk factors to positions, can also have a large impact on VaR results. We discussed mapping, and the broad choices risk managers can make, in Chapter 5. Some decisions about mapping are prag-matic choices among alternatives that each have their pros and cons. An example is the choice between cash flow versus duration-convexity mapping for fixed-income. Cash flow mappings are potentially more accurate than duration mappings, since, in the former, each cash flow is mapped to a fixed income security with a roughly equal discount factor, to which the latter is clearly only an approximation. But cash flow mapping requires using many more risk factors and more complex computations, which are potentially more expensive and entail risks of data errors and other model risks.

In other cases, it may be difficult to find data that address certain risk factors. Such mapping problems may merely mirror the real-world difficul-ties of hedging or expressing some trade ideas. An example is the practice, said to be widespread prior to the subprime crisis, of mapping residential mortgage-backed securities (RMBS) and other securitized credit products to time series for corporate credit spreads with the same rating. Market data on securitization spreads generally is sparse, available only for very generic types of bonds and hard to update regularly from observed market prices. Figure 14.14 and the discussion in Chapter 14 illustrate how misleading such a mapping to a proxy risk factor could be. Prior to the crisis, the spread volatility of investment-grade securitizations was lower than those of corporate bonds with similar credit ratings. Yet during the financial crisis, spreads on securitizations widened, at least relatively, far more than corpo-rate spreads. This episode illustrates not only the model risks attendant on proxy mapping, but also the inefficacy of VaR estimates in capturing large moves in market prices and the importance of stress testing.

Another example is convertible bond trading. As we saw in Chapter 10, convertible bonds can be mapped to a set of risk factors including, among others, implied volatilities, interest rates, and credit spreads. Such mappings are based on the theoretical price of a convertible bond, which is arrived at using its replicating portfolio. However, at times theoretical and market prices of converts can diverge dramatically, as can be seen in Figure 12.2. These divergences are liquidity risk events that are hard to capture with market data, so VaR based on the replicating portfolio alone can drastically understate risk. This problem can be mitigated through stress testing, which is discussed in Chapter 13.

In some cases, a position and its hedge might be mapped to the same risk factor or set of risk factors. The mapping might be justified on the grounds that the available data do not make it possible to discern between the two closely related positions. The result, however, will be a measured VaR of zero, even though there is a significant *basis risk*; that is, risk that the hedge will not provide the expected protection. Risk modeling of securitization exposures provides a pertinent example of basis risk, too. Securitizations are often hedged with similarly-rated corporate CDS indexes. If both the underlying exposure and its CDX hedge are mapped to a corporate spread time series, the measured risk disappears. We discuss basis risk further in Chapter 13.

For some strategies, VaR can be misleading for reasons over and above the distribution of returns and VaR's dependence on specific modeling choices. For some strategies, outcomes are close to binary. One example is *event-driven* strategies, a broad class of strategies that includes trades that depend on the occurrence of terms of a corporate acquisition or merger, the outcome of bankruptcy proceedings, or of lawsuits. For many such trades, there is no historical time series of return data that would shed light on the range of results. Another example are dynamic strategies, in which the risk is generated by the trading strategy over time rather than the set of positions at a point in time. We present some tools for treating the risks of such strategies in Chapter 13.

11.1.4 Case Study: The 2005 Credit Correlation Episode

An episode of volatility in the credit markets that occurred in the late spring of 2005 provides a case study of model risk stemming from misinterpretation and misapplication of models. Some traders suffered large losses in a portfolio credit trade in which one dimension of risk was hedged in accordance with a model, while another dimension of risk was neglected. We start by reviewing the mechanics of the trade, which involved credit derivatives based on CDX.NA.IG, the investment grade CDS index.

Description of the Trade and Its Motivation A widespread trade among hedge funds, as well as proprietary trading desks of banks and brokerages, was to sell protection on the equity tranche and buy protection on the junior mezzanine tranche of the CDX.NA.IG. The trade was thus long credit and credit-spread risk through the equity tranche and short credit and credit-spread risk through the mezzanine. It was executed using several CDX.NA.IG series, particularly the IG3 introduced in September 2004 and the IG4 introduced in March 2005.

The trade was designed to be default-risk-neutral at initiation, by sizing the two legs of the trade so that their credit spread sensitivities were equal. The motivation of the trade was not to profit from a view on credit or credit spreads, though it was primarily oriented toward market risk. Rather, it was intended to achieve a positively convex payoff profile. The portfolio of two positions would then benefit from credit spread volatility. In addition, the portfolio had positive carry; that is, it earned a positive net spread. Such trades are highly prized by traders, for whom they are akin to delta-hedged long option portfolios in which the trader receives rather than paying away time value. Compare this to the situation depicted in Figure 4.3. As we'll see, the trade was also a short credit dispersion trade, analogous to the equity dispersion trades discussed in the last chapter.

To understand the trade and its risks, we can draw on the tools we developed in Chapter 9. The securities in the extened example of that chapter are similar enough in structure to the standard tranches of the CDX.NA.IG that we can mimic the trade and understand what went wrong. Let's set up a trade in tranches of Chapter 9's illustrative CLO that is similar in structure and motivation to the standard tranche trade we have been describing. The trade takes a long credit risk position in the equity tranche and an offsetting short credit position in the mezzanine bond. Bear in mind that we would unlikely be able, in actual practice, to take a short position in a cash securitization, since the bond would be difficult to locate and borrow. We might be able to buy protection on the mezzanine tranche through a CDS, but the dealer writing it would probably charge a high spread to compensate for the illiquidity of the product and the difficulty of hedging it, in addition to the default and correlation risk. The standard tranches are synthetic CDS and their collateral pools also consist of CDS. They are generally more liquid than most other structured products, so it is easier to take short as well as long positions in them.

To determine the hedge ratio, that is, the amount of the mezzanine we are to short, we use the default sensitivities, the default01s. These are credit-risk sensitivities, while the 2005 CDX trade employed market-risk sensitivities, the spread01s. But the mechanics of hedging are similar. We assume that, at the time the trade is initiated, the expected default rate and implied correlation are $\pi = 0.03$ and $\rho = 0.30$. The default01 of a \$1,000,000 notional position in the equity is $-\$6,880$. The default01 of the mezzanine is -0.07212 times the notional value, so the default01 of a \$1,000,000 notional position is $-\$721$. These values can be read off of Figure 9.5 or Table 9.5. With a hedge ratio of about 9.54—that is, by shorting \$9,540,000 of par value of the mezzanine for every \$1,000,000 notional of long equity—we create a portfolio that, at the margin, is default-risk neutral.

Figure 11.1 illustrates how the trade was set up. At a default rate of 0.003, the portfolio has zero sensitivity to a small rise or decline in defaults. But the trade has positive convexity. The equity cheapens at a declining rate in response to spread widening. A noteworthy feature is that, because at low default rates, the mezzanine tranche has *negative* convexity, the short position *adds* positive convexity to the portfolio. The trade benefits from changes in the default rate in either direction. The actual CDX trade benefitted from large credit spread changes. It behaved, in essence, like an option

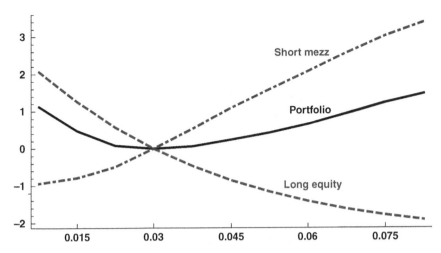

FIGURE 11.1 Convexity of CLO Liabilities

The graph plots the P&L, for varying default rates, of a portfolio consisting of (1) a long credit position in the equity tranche of the CLO described in Chapter 9 with a notional amount of $1,000,000, and (2) a short credit position in the mezzanine tranche of the same CLO with a notional amount of $1,000,000 times the hedge ratio of 9.54, that is, a par value of $9,540,000. The P&Ls of the constituent positions are also plotted. The default rates vary in the graph, but the correlation is fixed at 0.30. That is, the hedge ratio is set at a default rate of 3 percent, and a correlation of 0.30, but only the default rate is permitted to vary in the plot. The default rates are measured on the horizontal axis as decimals. The P&L is expressed on the vertical axis in millions of dollars.

straddle on credit spreads. In contrast to a typical option, however, this option, when expressed using the CDX standard tranches at the market prices prevailing in early 2005, paid a premium to its owner, rather than having negative net carry.

In the actual standard tranche trade, the mechanics were slightly different. Since the securities were synthetic CDO liabilities, traders used spread sensitivities; that is, spread01s or risk-neutral default01s, rather than actuarial default01s. The sensitivities used were not to the spreads of the underlying constituents of the CDX.NA.IG, but to the tranche spread. The hedge ratio in the actual trade was the ratio of the P&L impact of a 1bp widening of CDX.NA.IG on the equity and on the junior mezzanine tranches. The hedge ratio was between 1.5 and 2 at the beginning of 2005, lower than our example's 9.54, and at the prevailing tranche spreads, resulted in a net flow of spread income to the long equity/short mezz trade. However, the trade was set up at a particular value of implied correlation. As we will see, this was the critical error in the trade.

One additional risk should be highlighted, although it did not in the end play a crucial role in the episode we are describing: The recovery amount was at risk. In the event of a default on one or more of the names in the index, the recovery amount was not fixed but a random variable.

The Credit Environment in Early 2005   In the spring of 2005, the credit markets came under pressure, focused on the automobile industry, but not limited to it. The three large U.S.-domiciled original equipment manufacturers (OEMs), Ford, General Motors (GM), and Chrysler, had long been troubled. For decades, the OEMs had been among the most important companies in the U.S. investment-grade bond market, both in their share of issuance and in their benchmark status. The possibility of their being downgraded to junk was new and disorienting to investors. They had never been constituents of the CDX.NA.IG, but two "captive finance" companies, General Motors Acceptance Co. (GMAC) and Ford Motor Credit Co. (FMCC), were.

A third set of companies at the core of the automotive industries were the auto parts manufacturers. Delphi Corp. had been a constituent of IG3, but had been removed in consequence of its downgrade below investment grade. American Axle Co. had been added to IG4.

From a financial standpoint, the immediate priority of the OEMs had been to obtain relief from the UAW auto workers union from commitments to pay health benefits to retired workers. The "hot" part of the 2005 crisis began with two events in mid-April, the inability of GM and the UAW to reach an accord on benefits, and the announcement by GM of large losses. On May 5, GM and Ford were downgraded to junk by S&P. Moody's did the same soon after. The immediate consequence was a sharp widening of some corporate spreads, including GMAC and FMCC and other automotive industry names. Collins and Aikman, a major parts manufacturer, filed for Chapter 11 protection from creditors in May. Delphi and Visteon, another large parts manufacturer, filed later in 2005.

The two captive finance arms and the two auto parts manufacturers American Axle and Lear together constituted 4 out of the 125 constituents of the IG4. The market now contemplated the possibility of experiencing several defaults in the IG3 and IG4. The probability of extreme losses in the IG3 and IG4 standard equity tranches had appeared to be remote; it now seemed a distinct possibility. Other credit products also displayed sharp widening; the convertible bond market, in particular, was experiencing one of its periodic selloffs, as seen in Figure 12.2.

The automotive and certain other single-name spreads widened sharply, among them GMAC and FMCC. The IG indexes widened in line with the widening in their constituents, many of which did not widen at all. The pricing of the standard tranches, however, experienced much larger changes, brought about by the panicky unwinding of the equity-mezzanine tranche trade. Figure 11.3 shows the behavior of credit spreads and the price of the standard equity tranche during the episode.

- The mark-to-market value of the equity tranche dropped sharply. This can be seen in the increase in points upfront that buyers of protection had to pay.
- The implied correlation of the equity tranche dropped sharply. Stated equivalently, its mark-to-market value dropped more and its points upfront rose more sharply than the widening of the IG 4 spread alone would have dictated.
- The junior mezzanine tranche experienced a small widening, and at times even some tightening, as market participants sought to cover positions by selling protection on the tranche, that is, taking on long credit exposures via the tranche.
- The relative value trade as a whole experienced large losses.

The implied correlation fell for two reasons. The automotive parts supplier bankruptcies had a direct effect. All were in the IG4, which meant that about 10 percent of that portfolio was now near a default state. But the correlation fell also because the widening of the IG 4 itself was constrained by hedging. The short-credit position via the equity tranche could be hedged by selling protection on a modest multiple of the mezzanine tranche, or a large multiple of the IG4 index. Although spreads were widening and the credit environment was deteriorating, at least some buyers of protection on the IG4 index found willing sellers among traders long protection in the equity tranche who were covering the short leg via the index as well as via the mezzanine tranche itself.

Modeling Issues in the Setup of the Trade The relative value trade was set up in the framework of the standard copula model, using the analytics described in Chapter 9. These analytics were simulation-based, using risk-neutral default probabilities or hazard-rate curves derived from single-name CDS. The timing of individual defaults was well modeled. Traders generally used a normal copula. The correlation assumption might have been based on the relative frequencies of different numbers of joint defaults, or, more likely, on equity return correlations or prevailing equity implied correlations, as described at the end of Chapter 10.

In any event, the correlation assumption was static. This was the critical flaw, rather than using the "wrong" copula function, or even the "wrong" value of the correlation. The deltas used to set the proportions of the trade were partial derivatives that did not account for changing correlation. Changing correlation drastically altered the hedge ratio between the

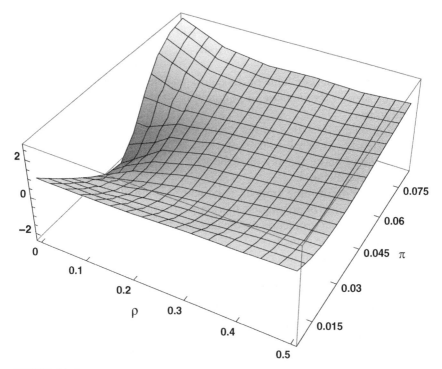

FIGURE 11.2   Correlation Risk of the Convexity Trade
The graph plots the P&L of the convexity trade for default rates from 0.0075 to
0.0825 per annum and constant pairwise Gaussian copula correlations from 0.0 to
0.5. The P&L is expressed on the vertical (z) axis in millions of dollars.

equity and mezzanine tranches, which more or less doubled to nearly 4 by
July 2005. In other words, traders needed to sell protection on nearly twice
the notional value of the mezzanine tranche in order to maintain spread
neutrality in the portfolio.

Figure 11.2 displays the P&L profile of the trade for different spreads
and correlations, again using the CLO example of Chapter 9. The portfolio P&L plotted as a solid line in Figure 11.1 is a cross-section through
Figure 11.2 at a correlation of 0.30. Figure 11.2 shows that the trade was
profitable for a wide range of spreads, but only if correlation did not fall. If
correlation fell abruptly, and spreads did not widen enough, the trade would
become highly unprofitable.

The model did not ignore correlation, but the trade thesis focused on
anticipated gains from convexity. The flaw in the model could have been
readily corrected if it had been recognized. The trade was put on at a time

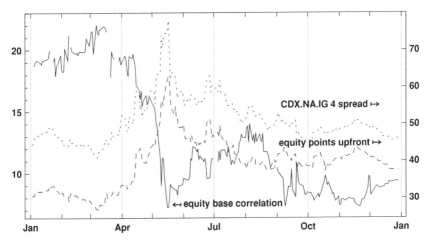

FIGURE 11.3 Implied Correlation in the 2005 Credit Episode
The graph plots the implied or base correlation of the equity (0–3 percent) tranche (solid line, percent, left axis), the price of the equity tranche (dashed line, points upfront, right axis), and the CDX IG 4 spread (dotted line, basis points, right axis). *Source:* JPMorgan Chase.

when copula models and the concept of implied correlation generally had only recently been introduced into discussions among traders, who had not yet become sensitized to the potential losses from changes in correlation. Stress testing correlation would have revealed the risk. The trade could also have been hedged against correlation risk by employing an overlay hedge: that is, by going long single-name protection in high default-probability names. In this sense, the "arbitrage" could not be captured via a two-leg trade, but required more components.

11.1.5 Case Study: Subprime Default Models

Among the costliest model risk episodes was the failure of subprime residential mortgage-based security (RMBS) valuation and risk models. These models were employed by credit-rating agencies to assign ratings to bonds, by traders and investors to value the bonds, and by issuers to structure them. While the models varied widely, two widespread defects were particularly important:

■ In general, the models assumed positive future house price appreciation rates. In the stress case, house prices might fail to rise, but would not actually drop. The assumption was based on historical data, which was sparse, but suggested there had been no extended periods of falling house prices on a large scale in any relevant historical period. As can be seen in Figure 15.1, house prices did in fact drop very severely starting in 2007. Since the credit quality of the loans depended on the borrowers' ability to refinance the loans without additional infusions of equity, the incorrect assumption on house price appreciation led to a severe underestimate of the potential default rates in underlying loan pools in an adverse economic scenario.

- Correlations among regional housing markets were assumed to be low. Bonds based on pools of loans from different geographical regions were therefore considered well-diversified. In the event, while house prices fell more severely in some regions than others, they fell—and loan defaults were much higher than expected in a stress scenario—in nearly all.

Together, these model errors or inappropriate parameters led to a substantial underestimation of the degree of systematic risk in subprime RMBS returns. Once the higher-than-expected default rates began to materialize, the rating agencies were obliged to downgrade most RMBS. The large-scale downgrades of AAA RMBS were particularly shocking to the markets, as it was precisely these that revealed the extent to which systemic risk had been underestimated and mispriced. As of the end of 2009, about 45 percent of U.S. RMBS with original ratings of AAA had been downgraded by Moody's.[2]

The inaccuracy of rating agency models for subprime RMBS is a complex phenomenon with a number of roots. As noted in Chapter 6, some observers have identified the potential conflict of interest arising from compensation of rating agencies by bond issuers as a factor in driving ratings standards lower. Others have focused on reaching for yield and the high demand for highly rated bonds with even modestly higher yields.

As we saw earlier in this chapter, a number of instances of mapping problems, contributing to seriously misleading risk measurement results, arose in securitization and structured credit products. Up until relatively recently, little time-series data was available covering securitized credit products. Highly rated securitized products were often mapped to time series of highly rated corporate bond spread indexes in risk measurement systems, or, less frequently, to the ABX index family, introduced in 2006. VaR measured using such mappings would have indicated that the bonds were unlikely under any circumstances to lose more than a few points of value. As can, however, be seen in Figure 11.4, the ABX index of the most highly rated RMBS lost 70 percent of their value during the subprime crisis. Somewhat lower, but

---

[2]See Moody's Investors Service (2010), p. 19.

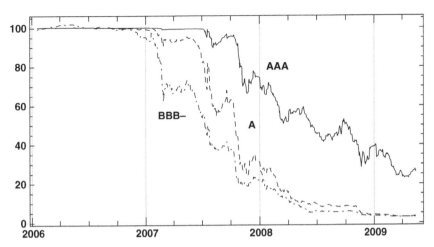

FIGURE 11.4 ABX Index of RMBS Prices
Rolling indexes of AAA, A, and BBB– ABX. For each index, the graph displays the
most recent vintage.
Source: JPMorgan Chase.

still investment-grade RMBS lost almost all their value. As we will see in
Chapter 14, securitizations suffered far greater losses than corporate bonds.
Losses varied greatly by asset class, the year in which they were issued, or
"vintage," and position in the capital structure. The corporate-bond and
ABX mappings were highly misleading and would have understated po-
tential losses by several orders of magnitude for investment-grade bonds.
Similar issues arose for CMBS, and their relationship to the ratings curves
and the CMBX, an index of CMBS prices analogous to the ABX.

11.2 BACKTESTING OF VAR

Assessing the accuracy of VaR estimates is important not only because firms
may rely on it to assess risk, but also because, as we describe in more detail
in Chapter 15, the international regulatory framework relies on it to set
bank capital requirements, and to assess how accurately banks assess risk.
We discuss the role of VaR in the regulatory framework in that chapter. For
now, we set out some of the issues involved in assessing VaR accuracy and
give some examples of the statistical techniques used.

   We focus on the standard model, in which the portfolio return is normally distributed with a mean of zero. We can test VaR estimates from two
points of view:

1. The first is to test the estimated standard deviation of the portfolio return, treating it as a type of parameter test. This approach is relevant only if we have estimated a parametric or Monte Carlo VaR. If we have estimated VaR by historical simulation, there is no return volatility to test.

   Statistically, setting the mean return to zero is a strong assumption, but it allows one to focus on the well-known problem of putting a confidence interval around a standard deviation estimate, rather than the much less well-known problem of jointly testing estimates of the mean and standard deviation of a distribution.

2. The second approach to assessing VaR accuracy studies the performance of the VaR rather than the accuracy of the parameters. This *backtesting* approach focuses on how often the portfolio return falls below the VaR. Such an event is often called an *excession.* The backtesting approach focuses on the VaR model itself, rather than its constituent hypotheses. In this context, "VaR model" doesn't mean the distributional hypothesis underpinning the VaR, say, normally distributed returns. Rather, it refers to the entire process, described earlier, from data gathering and position capture to implementation and reporting. Backtesting is therefore applicable to VaR estimates derived using historical as well as Monte Carlo simulation.

Several standard backtests are available. They are developed in the context of classical statistical hypothesis testing, summarized in Appendix A.4. In our context, the null hypothesis is a specific statement about the statistical distribution of excessions. The null hypothesis underpinning most backtesting, and the regulatory framework, is based on the idea that, if the model is accurate, then the proportion of excessions should be approximately equal to one minus the confidence level of the VaR.

Suppose we have a VaR estimation procedure that produces τ-period VaR estimates with a confidence level α. To simplify, we'll set $\tau = \frac{1}{\sqrt{252}}$, that is, a one-day VaR. We also assume that the VaR estimates are being generated in such a way that the estimates made in different periods are independent draws from the same distribution. That is, we assume not only an unchanging distribution of risk factor returns, but also that we're not changing the VaR estimation procedure in a way that would change the distribution of results. Excessions are then binomially distributed. The confidence level parameter α takes on the role of the event probability.

If the VaR model is accurate, then, by definition, the probability p of an excession in each period is equal to $1 - \alpha$, where α is the confidence level of the VaR, say, 99 percent. Therefore, if the VaR model is accurate, the probability of observing x excessions in T periods, given by the binomial distribution, is

$$\binom{T}{x}(1-\alpha)^x \alpha^{T-x}$$

and one would expect the proportion of exceedances in the sequence of VaR estimates to equal $1 - \alpha$:

$$\frac{x}{T} \approx 1 - \alpha = p$$

A formal test takes as the null hypothesis $\mathfrak{H}_0 : p = 1 - \alpha$. The log likelihood ratio test statistic is

$$2\left\{\log\left[\left(\frac{x}{T}\right)^x \left(1 - \frac{x}{T}\right)^{T-x}\right] - \log\left[(1-\alpha)^x \alpha^{T-x}\right]\right\}$$

What does this expression mean? If the null hypothesis is true, then, on the one hand, we expect $\frac{x}{T}$ to be fairly close to $1 - \alpha$ and the test statistic to be fairly close to zero. On the other hand, we recognize that because of random error, it's very unlikely for $\frac{x}{T}$ to be exactly $1 - \alpha$. Under the null hypothesis, this test statistic is asymptotically distributed as a χ^2-variate with one degree of freedom (for the one parameter α). This distribution has most of its weight near zero, but a long right tail, as can be seen in Figure 11.5; increasing the degrees of freedom even moderately pushes the distribution away from zero. Using this distribution to carry out the test is intuitive, since a fraction of excessions different from the expected value, equal to one minus the confidence level, pushes our test statistic away from zero.

Some examples of specific interesting questions we can try to answer in this framework are:

- We can set a specific probability of a *Type I error* (false positive), that is, rejecting $\mathfrak{H}_0$ even though it is true, and determine an acceptance/non-rejection region for x, the number of excessions we observe. The probability of a Type I error is set to a level "we can live with." The acceptance region will depend on the sample size, that is the number of periods we observe the VaR model at work. The region has to be a range of integers.

    For example, if $\alpha = 0.99$, and we observe the VaR for 1,000 trading days, we would expect to see about 10 excessions. If we set the probability of a Type I error at 5 percent, the acceptance region for $\mathfrak{H}_0$ is $x \in (4, 17)$.

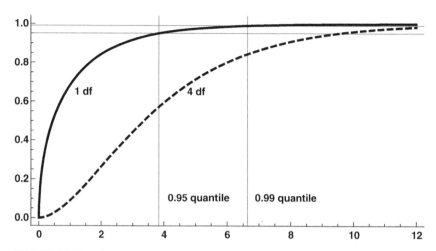

FIGURE 11.5 Chi-Square Distribution
Cumulative distribution functions of chi-square distributions with 1 and 4 degrees
of freedom. The grid lines mark the 95th and 99th percentiles of the chi-square
distribution with 1 df, equal to 3.841 and 6.635.

   If instead we set $\alpha = 0.95$ and $T = 1,000$, but keep the probability
of a Type I error at 5 percent, the acceptance region for $\mathfrak{H}_0$ is $x \in$
$(37, 65)$. We expect to see a higher fraction of excessions—days on
which trading losses exceed the VaR—at a lower VaR confidence level,
but the range within which we feel comfortable concluding that the null
has not been rejected is also wider.

- We can assess the probability of a *Type II error* (false negative), that is,
  nonrejection of $\mathfrak{H}_0$ even though a specific alternative hypothesis $\mathfrak{H}_1$ is
  true. This test will be a function of the probability of a Type I error, α, T,
  and the alternative hypothesis. For example, if the probability of a Type
  I error is fixed at 5 percent, $\alpha = 0.99$, $T = 1,000$, and $\mathfrak{H}_1 : p = 0.02$,
  then there is a 21.8 percent probability of a Type II error.

   These examples show how inaccurate VaR can be. Setting $T = 1,000$
corresponds to almost four years of data. And after four years, we cannot
reject the accuracy of a 99 percent daily VaR (Type I error) even if we
observe as few as 60 percent less or as many as 70 percent more than the
expected 10 excessions. And if the true probability of an excession is 2
percent, there is still over a 20 percent chance of mistakenly accepting the
lower probability (Type II error), even after watching our VaR model in
action for four years.

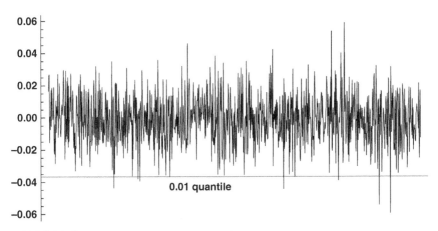

FIGURE 11.6 Backtest of a Normal Distribution
Simulation of 1,000 sequential steps of a geometric Brownian motion process with
$\mu = 0$ and $\sigma = 0.25$ at an annual rate. The horizontal grid line marks the 0.01
quantile. There should be about 10 occurrences of returns below the grid lines. In
this simulation, there are nine.

To provide more intuition on this test, let's look at two examples.
In both examples, we look at the return series rather than a VaR, but
this is just a convenient simplification: It would be trivial to multiply each
return series by the number of units of a linear asset to get a VaR. In the
terminology of Chapter 3, we are looking here at the VaR shock rather than
the VaR.

The first example is a normal distribution. We know for this distribution that the null hypothesis is true. Figure 11.6 shows 1,000 simulation
from a normal distribution with mean zero and an annual volatility of
25 percent. There happen to be nine outliers. The value of the likelihood
ratio test statistic is 0.105, quite close to zero and well below either the 95th
or 99th percentiles of the χ^2 distribution. We therefore do not reject the null
hypothesis that the probability of a loss exceeding the VaR shock equals the
confidence level of the VaR. If there had been 20 excessions, the test statistic
would equal 7.827, well in excess of the critical values, and we would reject
the null.

The second example is a VaR estimated using the historical simulation
approach and time series data for the dollar-yen exchange rate and the S&P
500. We compute VaR shocks for each return series on its own, not as a
portfolio. We use daily return data from January 2, 1996, through November 10, 2006, so the number of VaR observations is 2,744. Figure 11.7

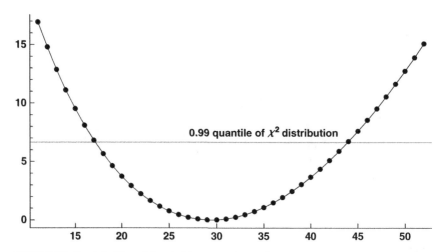

FIGURE 11.7   Likelihood-Ratio Test
Value of the likelihood ratio test statistic for the null hypothesis $\mathfrak{H}_0 : p = 0.01$ and with $T = 2{,}744$. The horizontal gridline marks the 0.99 quantile of the χ^2 distribution with one degree of freedom, denoted $\chi^2_{1,0.01} = 6.635$. It intersects the plot of the test statistic at the critical values for tests of the null at a confidence level of 99 percent.

plots the log likelihood ratio test statistic as a function of the number of excessions for $T = 2{,}744$. The number of excessions can only take on non-negative integer values, so the possible values of the test statistic are marked by dots. The horizontal grid lines mark the critical region for the 99 percent confidence level.

Figure 11.8 illustrates the tests at a confidence level of 99 percent. We can see that the S&P estimate fails the backtest (rejection of $\mathfrak{H}_0$), since there are 49 excessions. The value of the test statistic is 13.89, exceeding the upper critical value of 6.635. However, at the 95 percent confidence level, there are 141 excessions of the 0.05 quantile (not shown in Figure 11.8). Of course, these are more numerous than excessions of the 0.01 quantile, but they amount to 5.14 percent of the observations, close to the expected 5 percent if the null hypothesis is true. The test statistic is 0.113, and the critical value is 3.84, so we don't reject at the 95 percent confidence level.

For USD-JPY, we have 35 excessions and a test statistic value of 1.941, so we do not reject $\mathfrak{H}_0$ at a 99 percent confidence level. There are 130 excessions of the 0.05 quantile, or 4.74 percent of the observations. The test statistic is 0.399, and the critical value is 3.84, so we don't reject at the 95 percent confidence level, either.

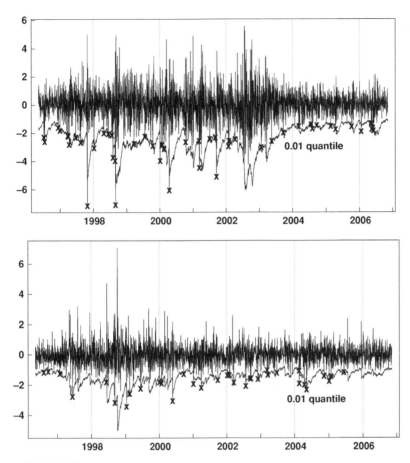

FIGURE 11.8 Historical Backtesting
Upper panel: S&P 500 index. There are 49 excessions or 1.79 percent of the sample size. The null is rejected at the 99 percent confidence level.
Lower panel: USD-JPY exchange rate. There are 35 excessions or 1.28 percent of the sample size. The null is not rejected at the 99 percent confidence level. Both panels display return data from January 2, 1996, through November 10, 2006.
Source: Bloomberg Financial L.P.

There are a number of related tests that are discussed in the references at the end of the chapter. One similar test, for example, is based on the same model but exploiting the fact that in the model, the time to the first excession is a random variable with a known distribution.

11.3   COHERENCE OF VAR ESTIMATES

VaR has been criticized on the grounds that it cannot be grounded axiomat-ically and therefore lacks scientific underpinning. This is often stated as the notion that VaR is not a *coherent* risk measure.

To explain what coherence means, we need to explain the general idea of a *risk measure* as a function. As in other areas of finance theory, we start by defining a finite set Ω of I possible future states of the world. We can think of the return on a portfolio as a random variable X defined on Ω and call the set of all possible random returns X the *risk set*, denoted $\mathfrak{G}$. We can think of the X as portfolio returns; the important point here is that each $X \in \mathfrak{G}$ is a random variable with I possible outcomes. Now we can define a risk measure $\rho : \mathfrak{G} \to \mathbb{R}$ as a particular method for assigning a "single-number" measure of risk to a portfolio.

The risk measure ρ is called coherent if it has the following properties:

Monotonicity. If $X, Y \in \mathfrak{G}$, $X \geq Y$, then

$$\rho(X) \leq \rho(Y)$$

The notation $X \geq Y$ means that the value of X is at least as great as that of Y in every state $\omega \in \Omega$. The property means that if one portfolio never has a smaller return than another, it must have a smaller risk measure.

Homogeneity of degree one. For any $X \in \mathfrak{G}$ and any positive number h, we have

$$\rho(hX) = h\rho(X)$$

If you just double all the positions in a portfolio, or double the return for each outcome, the risk measure of the new portfolio must also double. Appendix A.6 explains what homogeneous functions are. We use this property in defining risk capital measures in Chapter 13.

Subadditivity. $X, Y, X + Y \in \mathfrak{G} \Rightarrow \rho(X + Y) \leq \rho(X) + \rho(Y)$

A portfolio consisting of two subportfolios can have a risk measure no greater, and possibly lower, than the sum of the risk measures of the two subportfolios. In other words, you can't reduce the risk by breaking a portfolio into pieces and measuring them separately.

Translation invariance. Let r represent the risk-free return, and let a be an amount invested in the risk-free security. Then for $X \in \mho$, $a \in \mathbb{R}$ we have

$$\rho(X + a \cdot r) = \rho(X) - a$$

This property means that adding a risk-free return equal to $a \cdot r$ to every possible outcome for a portfolio reduces its risk by a. In other words, adding cash to a portfolio doesn't essentially change its risk measure; it does, however, add a capital buffer against losses and reduces the risk measure by that amount.

An additional axiom is not part of the definition of coherence of a risk measure:

Relevance. If $X \in \mho$, $X \leq 0$, then

$$\rho(X) > 0$$

This property says that if a portfolio's return is never positive, and is negative in at least one state $\omega \in \Omega$, the risk measure must be positive. It guarantees that really bad portfolios have a large risk measure.

VaR does not have the subadditivity property. There are cases in which the VaR of a portfolio is greater than the sum of the VaRs of the individual securities in the portfolio. We provide a market risk and a credit risk example.

Example 11.1 (Failure of Subadditivity of VaR) A classic counterexample to subadditivity is a portfolio consisting of two one-day options: a short out-of-the-money put and a short out-of-the-money call. We assume logarithmic returns on the underlying security are normally distributed with a known drift and volatility.

The options expire tomorrow, so the P&L of each is equal to the accrual of a one-day option premium less tomorrow's intrinsic value if the option expires in-the-money. The options are so short-dated that there is no trading P&L from vega. We set the exercise price of each option so that its overnight, 99 percent VaR is barely zero. To do so, we need to set the exercise prices so there is a 1 percent probability of ending slightly in-the-money or better. Then the terminal intrinsic value lost exactly offsets or exceeds the option premium or time decay earned. For the put we find the exercise price X_1

such that

$$P[S_{t+\tau} \leq X_1 - p(S_t, \tau, X_1, \sigma, r_t, q_t)] = 0.01$$

and for the call we set X_2 such that

$$P[S_{t+\tau} \leq X_2 + c(S_t, \tau, X_2, \sigma, r_t, q_t)] = 0.99$$

The notation and parameters for the example are

Initial underlying price	$S_t = 100$
VaR confidence level is set at 99 percent	$z_* = -2.33$
Time horizon of the VaR and the option maturity	$\tau = \frac{1}{252}$
Underlying security's volatility	$\sigma = 0.30$
Overnight risk-free rate	$r_t = 0.03$
Underlying security's dividend or cash-flow rate	$q_t = 0.00$
Put exercise price	$X_1 = 95.6993$
Call exercise price	$X_2 = 104.4810$
Put fair value at time t	$p(S_t, \tau, X_1, \sigma, r_t, q_t) = 0.00615$
Call fair value at time t	$c(S_t, \tau, X_2, \sigma, r_t, q_t) = 0.00680$

The premium of the options is negligible, since they are so far out-of-the-money and close to expiry. If the put (call) exercise price were any lower (higher), the VaR would be zero at a higher confidence level.

Now consider the portfolio consisting of *both* options. The probability that at least one of the options will end in-the-money enough to incur a loss is close to 2 percent, so the 99 percent VaR of the portfolio is not zero, but a positive number. Figure 11.9 illustrates. The two-tailed 99 percent confidence interval for the portfolio has endpoints that are considerably deeper in-the-money than the one-tailed VaR of each option. There is a 1 percent probability, for the portfolio, of an outcome at one of these endpoints or worse.

This example shows that cases in which VaR is not subadditive are uncommon, but not pathological. One would not expect to observe violations of subadditivity frequently, but they do crop up.

The practical effect of a phenomenon like this is that it creates an avenue for market participants to game a system of *VaR limits*, position size limits that are based on VaR. A bank in which proprietary option trading is carried out could reduce the VaR it reports, and thus its regulatory capital, by separating the two options into two different "departments" and adding them, rather than reporting the higher consolidated VaR. But in practice, it

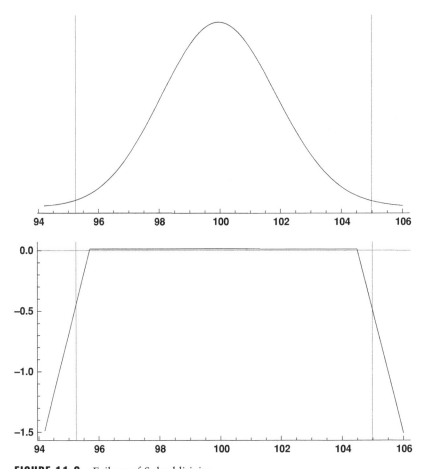

FIGURE 11.9   Failure of Subadditivity
The initial underlying price is 100.
Upper panel: One-day probability distribution of the underlying asset price.
Lower panel: Terminal P&L of the option portfolio. The intersection of the
horizontal grid line at 0 with the P&L function shows the exercise prices at which
each option individually breaks even with a probability of 1 percent.
The vertical grid lines mark the 99 percent confidence interval.

is unlikely that enough such anomalies could be found to have a meaningful
impact.

While VaR as a measure of diversification appears unambiguously misleading in the option example, it may make more sense in others. Let's look
at the apparently similar example of a credit portfolio.

Example 11.2 (Non-Subadditivity of Credit VaR) Suppose we have a set of one-year corporate bonds that pay a credit spread of 200 basis points. Let the risk-free rate be close enough to zero that it has little effect. The bonds will trade at approximately $S_t = 0.98$ dollars per dollar of par value. Let the issuers each have a default probability just under 1 percent, say, 99 basis points; defaults are independent. If there is no default, the bonds are redeemed at par, and if a default occurs, recovery is zero.

We'll look at the one year, 99 percent credit VaR of three possible portfolios, each with a current market value of $98:

1. $98 invested in one bond. The distribution of one-year net returns, in dollars, on this portfolio is

$$\left\{ \begin{array}{c} 100 - 98 \\ 0 - 98 \end{array} \right\} = \left\{ \begin{array}{c} 2 \\ -98 \end{array} \right\} \quad \text{w.p.} \quad \left\{ \begin{array}{c} 0.9901 \\ 0.0099 \end{array} \right\}$$

   Since a capital loss occurs with a probability less than 1 percent, the 99 percent VaR is zero.

2. $49 invested in each of two different bonds. The distribution of returns on this portfolio is

$$\left\{ \begin{array}{c} 100 - 98 \\ 50 - 98 \\ 0 - 98 \end{array} \right\} = \left\{ \begin{array}{c} 2 \\ -48 \\ -98 \end{array} \right\} \quad \text{w.p.} \quad \left\{ \begin{array}{c} 0.980298 \\ 0.019604 \\ 0.000098 \end{array} \right\}$$

   The 99 percent VaR is $48.

3. A highly granular portfolio consisting of tiny amounts invested in each of very many bonds with independent defaults, totalling $98. There is no material risk in this portfolio. It has a virtually certain return of $1.01, and its VaR is zero.

Subadditivity is violated, because diversifying the portfolio from one to two bonds increases the VaR massively.

But there is more to this example than meets the eye. Is the second portfolio really better for the investor? Suppose the investor is a pension fund and will be unable to meet its pension liabilities if it suffers a capital loss of $48 or more. It is actually worse off with the second, "diversified" portfolio, because there is nearly a 2 percent probability of such a loss, even though the probability of a $98 loss is now less than 1 basis point. With the single-bond portfolio, the probability of a catastrophic loss is only 99 basis points.

Some investors may have good reasons to be concerned with the probability as well as the size of a catastrophic loss.

FURTHER READING

Model risk is defined and discussed in Derman (1996, 2009). Crouhy, Mark, and Galai (2000b) is a textbook with an extensive treatment of model risk. See Plosser (2009) for discussion of some recent model risk episodes.

Important critiques of VaR include Danielsson (2002, 2008). Studies of variation in the implementation of VaR estimates include Beder (1995) and Marshall and Siegel (1997). Pritsker (1997) is worth reading as a survey of VaR techniques, as a study of the variability of VaR estimates, and as an approach to accuracy and backtesting of VaR.

Correlation trading is discussed in Collin-Dufresne (2009). See Coudert and Gex (2010) and Finger (2005) on the 2005 credit market episode. The references on credit correlation concepts at the end of Chapter 9 are also germane here.

Backtesting of VaR is discussed in Kupiec (1995b), Jorion (1996b), and Lopez (1999). Berkowitz (2001) proposes an approach to model testing that takes fat-tailed distributions and the potential for large losses into account. Kuester, Mittnik and Paolella (2006) employs backtesting of VaR as a means of testing volatility forecasting models. Berkowitz and O'Brien (2002) use supervisory data on bank P&L, rather than specified portfolios, to test the performance of VaR models empirically. See also Hendricks (1996).

Artzner, Delbaen, and Heath (1999) and Acerbi and Tasche (2002) discuss the concept of coherent risk measures.

CHAPTER 12

Liquidity and Leverage

One of the most important aspects of the subprime crisis was the sudden reluctance of financial institutions to lend money, and the increased reluctance to borrow on the part of financial as well as nonfinancial businesses and households, a development called "The Great Deleveraging." It contributed to the rapid decline in the market prices of risky assets and was self-perpetuating. In this chapter, we try to disentangle the concepts of liquidity and leverage. We give definitions of each, showing how they are related, and, in Chapter 14, explain their role in financial crises.

The term "liquidity" has been defined in myriad ways that ultimately boil down to two properties, *transactions liquidity*, a property of assets or markets, and *funding liquidity*, which is more closely related to credit-worthiness. Transaction liquidity is the property of an asset being easy to exchange for other assets. Most financial institutions are heavily leveraged; that is, they borrow heavily to finance their assets, compared to the typical nonfinancial firm. Funding liquidity is the ability to finance assets continuously at an acceptable borrowing rate. For financial firms, many of those assets include short positions and derivatives.

As with "liquidity," the term "liquidity risk" is used to describe several distinct but related phenomena:

Transaction liquidity risk is the risk of moving the price of an asset adversely in the act of buying or selling it. Transaction liquidity risk is low if assets can be liquidated or a position can be covered quickly, cheaply, and without moving the price "too much." An asset is said to be liquid if it is "near" or a good substitute for cash. An asset is said to have a *liquidity premium* if its price is lower and expected return higher because it isn't perfectly liquid. A market is said to be liquid if market participants can put on or unwind positions quickly, without excessive transactions costs and without excessive price deterioration.

Balance sheet risk or funding liquidity risk. Funding liquidity risk is the risk that creditors either withdraw credit or change the terms on which it is granted in such a way that the positions have to be unwound and/or are no longer profitable. Funding liquidity can be put at risk because the borrower's credit quality is, or at least perceived to be, deteriorating, but also because financial conditions as a whole are deteriorating.

Systemic risk refers to the risk of a general impairment of the financial system. In situations of severe financial stress, the ability of the financial system to allocate credit, support markets in financial assets, and even administer payments and settle financial transactions may be impaired.

These types of liquidity risk interact. For example, if a counterparty increases collateral requirements or otherwise raises the cost of financing a long position in a security, the trader may have to unwind it before the expected return is fully realized. By shrinking the horizon of the trade, the deterioration of funding liquidity also increases the transaction liquidity risk. The interaction also works the other way. If a leveraged market participant is perceived to have illiquid assets on its books, its funding will be in greater jeopardy.

We begin our discussion of liquidity risk by discussing its credit aspect, funding liquidity risk, and the ways in which this risk can manifest itself, in more detail. Later sections discuss transactions liquidity. The discussion of liquidity risk will provide important background for understanding financial panics, the subject of Chapter 14.

12.1 FUNDING LIQUIDITY RISK

12.1.1 Maturity Transformation

Funding liquidity risk arises for market participants who borrow at short term to finance investments that require a longer time to become profitable. Many traders and investors, such as banks, securities firms, and hedge funds, are largely short-term borrowers, so their capacity to maintain long-term positions and their flexibility when circumstances or expectations change is limited. The balance-sheet situation of a market participant funding a longer-term asset with a shorter-term liability is called a *maturity mismatch*.

Managing maturity mismatches is a core function of banks and other financial intermediaries. All financial and economic investment projects take time, in some cases a very long time, to come to fruition. To provide the needed capital, financial intermediaries effect a *maturity transformation* and possibly also a *liquidity transformation*; they obtain shorter-term funding and provide longer-term funding to finance projects. Funding longer-term assets with longer-term debt is called *matched funding*.

Intermediaries engage in maturity mismatch because it is generally profitable. Every market participant has a *cost of capital*, the rate of return on all its liabilities, including equity. The most "expensive" capital is equity, because it takes the most risk; it has no contractually stipulated remuneration and is the first liability to bear losses. To convince providers of capital to place equity with a firm, they must be promised a high expected return. At the other end of the spectrum, short-term debt instruments generally have lower required returns and contribute less to the cost of capital, as long as the borrower's credit risk is perceived to be low.

The spread between the interest intermediaries pay—their funding cost—and the interest they earn is called the *net interest margin*. Yield curves are typically upward sloping. Intermediaries therefore have a powerful incentive to introduce maturity mismatches into their balance sheets. In the aftermath of economic downturns and financial crises, the yield curve typically has a sharper upward slope, increasing net interest margin, which becomes an important part of banks' rebuilding following the downturn.

Because short-term rates are generally lower than long-term rates, there is a powerful incentive to borrow short-term if possible. Funding long-term assets with short-term debt exposes an intermediary to *rollover risk*, the risk that the short-term debt cannot be refinanced, or can be refinanced only on highly disadvantageous terms. In a rollover risk event, cash flow can become negative. For example, an investor may be financing bonds with short-term borrowing at a positive spread. If the debt cannot be refinanced at an interest rate below the bond yield, negative cash flow and losses result.

Funding conditions can change rapidly. A firm or investor can, after a long period of short-term funding with positive cash flow, suddenly find himself in a negative cash flow situation from which there is no obvious escape if short-term funding is suddenly closed to him or its costs escalate. Because of this binary character, rollover risk is sometimes called "cliff risk." The liquidity condition of a market participant relying heavily on short-term funding can reach a state of distress very quickly.

12.1.2 Liquidity Transformation

Intermediaries earn net interest margin from maturity transformation because short-term debt generally carries lower interest than longer-term debt. Very short-term yields—money-market rates—are almost invariably lower. But the short-term funding of an intermediary is the short-term asset of the lender, and may provide liquidity and payment services to the investor as well as a flow of interest payments. Money-market instruments such as short-term interbank loans to sound banks, commercial paper of creditworthy issuers, repos with adequate haircuts, and government bills, are not generally classified as money, but have certain characteristics of money. They can be readily exchanged for cash, and roll off into cash within a short time. Short-term yields are lower because short-term debt partially satisfies the need for liquidity as well as having far less interest-rate risk, as we saw in Chapter 4.

The major exception to this general observation are short-term interest rates on currencies in imminent danger of devaluation (see Chapter 14). Because a discrete depreciation causes an instantaneous capital loss to market participants long the currency, short-term yields of currencies under pressure can rise to extremely high levels, limited only by uncertainty about whether and when the depreciation will take place.

Some forms of very short-term debt serve the means-of-payment function of money, particularly those forms that are checkable, that is, can be very easily transferred to a third party: demand deposits and money market mutual fund (MMMF) liabilities. These types of debt have even lower yields than can be explained by their short maturities because of their usefulness as means of payment and settling debts. Providing liquidity and payment services contributes to intermediaries' net interest margin. The liquidity transformation bundled with maturity transformation has long made banks more efficient intermediaries.

The process by which financial intermediaries use their balance sheets to create assets that can be used as money goes back to the origins of banking. Prior to the mid-1970s, this activity was the almost exclusive province of commercial banks. Nowadays, the money supply is defined to include certain nonbank liabilities such as those of MMMFs, as well as banknotes and bank deposits. They have in common that, in contrast to other short-term debt instruments, their values don't depend on interest rates, and they can be used to buy both goods and assets. To the extent that an asset has the characteristics of *immediacy* and certainty, they resemble money and are said to be liquid.

Deposit liabilities of banks were at one time the main form of money not created by central banks. In the contemporary financial system, the core banking functions of maturity and liquidity transformation are increasingly carried out by other means and other institutions, such as the commercial paper markets and MMMFs. With the introduction and growth of money market funds, an important new type of short-term assets that could be used as money was created. In the United States, retail MMMF balances are included in the M2 measure of the money supply, accounting for roughly 10 percent of the total. Institutional MMMF balances are about twice as large as retail, but are not included in U.S. monetary aggregates.

Market participants hold money to conduct transactions and for speculative reasons. In Keynes' well-known explanation of the demand for money, balances held for the purpose of conducting transactions include a portion attributable to uncertainty about the timing and volume of cash flows. But market participants also hold money out of a *speculative motive* which is a function of current asset prices, especially interest rates, uncertainty about future asset prices, and risk preferences. Keynes denoted this motive as "speculative" because of his focus on one of the key phenomena in financial crises, namely, asset-price spirals in which market participants want to hold cash because they expect asset prices to be lower in the future, thus driving prices lower in fact (see Chapter 14).[1]

Uncertainty of value is a property even of assets that have minimal credit risk, but mature in the future, such as U.S. Treasury bills, because their values depend on interest rates. Interest rates fluctuate, and affect the price even of short-term T-bills; hence T-bills are not money. However, if, like T-bills, their interest-rate risk is very low, and they also have little or no credit risk, they are viewed as relatively liquid and thus close in character to money.

Keynes's term for the demand for money, *liquidity preference*, has become particularly pertinent during the subprime crisis. In normal times, the desire for liquidity is counterbalanced by the zero or low yields earned by cash and liquid assets. In crises, risk-aversion and uncertainty are high, so market participants wish to hold a much larger fraction of their assets in liquid form, and are relatively indifferent to the yield. In the terminology of economics, the *velocity of money* declines drastically. Market participants desire larger liquidity portfolios, they prefer cash to money-market instruments, and become abruptly more sensitive to even the relatively low credit and counterparty risk of instruments other than government bills.[2]

12.1.3 Bank Liquidity

The core function of a commercial bank is to take deposits and provide commercial and industrial loans to nonfinancial firms. In doing so, it carries out a liquidity and maturity, as well as a credit, transformation. It transforms long-term illiquid assets—loans to businesses—into short-term liquid ones, including deposits and other liabilities that can be used as money.

---

[1]In his typically memorable phrasing, these motives were the answer to the question, "Why should anyone outside a lunatic asylum wish to use money as a store of wealth?" (Keynes [1937], p. 216).

[2]In the older economics literature, this urge is called *hoarding*.

Liquidity Transformation by Banks Banks carry out their functions through operations on both sides of the balance sheet. Prior to the advent of shadow banking and the incursion of commercial banks into investment banking, depository institutions generally earned most of their revenues from net interest margin. In contemporary finance, banks earn a higher proportion of revenues from origination, investment banking, and other fees. They also have important revenues from market making, that is, earning the bid-ask spread on transactions executed for customers, and proprietary trading, taking risky positions in assets with their own capital. But net interest margin remains a crucial source of revenues.

The balance sheet of a "classic bank," that is, one chiefly reliant on deposits for funding, might look like this:

Assets	Liabilities
Cash and government bonds $15	Common equity $10
5-year corporate loans $85	Deposits $90

Banks and similar intermediaries are *depository institutions*, that is, institutions that borrow from the public in the form of liabilities that must be repaid in full on demand, instantly, in cash, on a first-come first-served basis. This aspect of the deposit contract is called the *sequential service constraint*, and contrasts sharply with bankruptcy, in which claims are paid pro rata. Deposits pay zero or relatively low rates of interest, though one of the main areas of financial innovation over the past few decades has been in making it possible for lenders to earn interest while still enjoying such benefits of liquidity as check-writing, for example, in MMMFs.

Banks can also tap the broader capital markets and raise funds by issuing bonds, commercial paper, and other forms of debt. These sources of *wholesale funding* are, on the one hand, generally of longer term than deposits, which can be redeemed at short notice. However, deposits are considered "sticky." Depositors tend to remain with a bank unless impelled to switch by a life change such as moving house; bankers joke that depositors are more apt to divorce than remove deposits. Depositors are also a naturally diversified set of counterparties, so a large deposit base reduces reliance on a small number of lenders.

Shorter-term forms of wholesale funding such as commercial paper are less reliable and potentially more concentrated sources of longer-term liquidity than a solid deposit base. These funding decisions are nowadays also heavily influenced by regulatory capital requirements (see Chapter 15), which can favor or disfavor particular types of assets and thus influence their funding costs as liabilities.

The borrowing firms invest the loan proceeds in physical and other capital. A span of time and many stages are needed, in addition to the capital resources, before these projects produce goods and services that can be sold to repay the loans that finance them. Until then, the invested capital can be sold only at a loss, so the firms cannot in general repay the loans in full prior to maturity.

The bank could borrow at a longer term to match the maturity of its assets, but this would reduce its net interest margin. The bank would still be rewarded for another important set of banking functions, namely selecting worthy projects thats are likely to repay loans fully and timely, and monitoring borrowers' financial condition and timely payment of principal and interest. And to the extent that the banks' *delegated monitoring* function does not produce added value, borrowers could turn directly to the bond markets themselves.

The investments on the asset side of the bank's balance sheet not only have longer terms to maturity than their liabilities, they are also less liquid; deposits in contrast are very close substitutes for cash. The liquidity transformation function of banks has been described as "turning illiquid assets into liquid ones." However, this transformation depends on confidence in the bank's solvency.

How, then, can the liquidity and maturity transformations be made to work? Only a small fraction of deposits and other short-term funding are expected to be redeemed at any one time. Banks engage in *asset-liability management* (ALM). This is a technique for aligning available cash and short-term assets with expected requirements. A well-managed bank leaves an ample buffer of cash and highly liquid assets for unexpected redemptions of deposits and other funding.

Fragility of Commercial Banking   The classic depository institution we have been describing is a *fractional-reserve* bank, that is a bank that lends deposits. The alternative to a fractional-reserve bank is a 100 percent reserve bank, which lends only its own capital, or funds raised in capital markets, and keeps a reserve of cash and highly liquid securities equal to its entire deposit base. Throughout the history of banking, almost all banks have been fractional-reserve banks. Banking originated in the Low Countries, and a bit later in Italy, in the thirteenth century. In its earlier stages, customers of banks deposited money in the form of gold and silver coin for safekeeping. The warehouse receipts the bank issued as evidence of a deposit could be used as money, as long as the bank was trusted to return the coin on demand, and receipts were easier and safer to transport and exchange.

As long as warehouse receipts were issued only against the coin brought to the bank for safekeeping, commercial loans could only be made with the owners' equity or with capital-market borrowing. Eventually, banks discovered that they could issue warehouse receipts, and later private banknotes, in a greater volume than the amount of coin deposited with them; that is, loans were made by issuing banknotes. In a fractional-reserve banking system, if depositors wish to make withdrawals in excess of a bank's reserves, and the bank cannot liquidate enough loans or other assets to meet the demand immediately, it is forced into *suspension of convertibility*; that is, it will not be able to convert its deposits and notes into money immediately.

At the extreme, all or a large number of depositors may ask for the return of their money simultaneously, an event called a *bank run*. Depositors and other short-term creditors are aware the banks cannot meet large-scale redemption requests. If they are concerned about banks' liquidity, they will endeavor to redeem before other depositors and lenders.

No asset-liability management system can protect a fractional-reserve bank against a general loss of confidence in its ability to pay out depositors. As long as the bank carries out a liquidity and maturity transformation, and has liabilities it is obligated to repay at par and on demand, no degree of liquidity that a bank can achieve can protect it completely against a run. Fragility can be mitigated through higher capital, which reduces depositors' concern about solvency, the typical trigger of a run, and higher reserves, which reduces concern about liquidity. Historically, banks have also protected themselves against runs through individual mechanisms such as temporary suspension of convertibility, and collective mechanisms such as clearing-houses.

Because banking is fragile, there have from time to time been calls to abolish traditional, deposit-dependent commercial banking, and replace it with a more robust type of financial institution. An alternative view is that depository institutions must be restricted in their activities and closely supervised to prevent them from taking risks that could jeopardize their ability to meet withdrawals. Under the rubric "Volcker Rule," it has been incorporated in the regulatory restructuring mandated by the 2010 Dodd-Frank Act. We discuss these issues particularly in the context of deposit insurance and the lender of last resort function of central banks in Chapter 15.

Apart from deposits, banks are generally dependent on short-term financing, exposing them to rollover risk events that, while less extreme than runs, can be costly or increase fragility. Commercial banks' main source of funding is deposits; in the United States, deposits account for about 60 percent of banks' liabilities. Banks rely on capital markets for much of the rest of their funding. Commercial paper is an important component and accounts for roughly 1.5 percent of U.S. banks' liabilities.

The commercial paper market in the immediate aftermath of the Lehman bankruptcy provides an example of how quickly funding conditions can change, and of the fragility of bank funding. The upper panel of Figure 12.1 displays the volume outstanding of commercial paper by AA-rated financial firms, a category comprised mostly of banks, but also including nonbank intermediaries such as GE Capital. Financial firms' issuance of commercial paper had grown rapidly between 2004 and the end of 2007, as their leverage and balance-sheet expansion increased. The amount borrowed via commercial paper became more volatile, but continued to grow, as banks sought to finance previously off-balance-sheet assets and credit lines they granted earlier were drawn upon. Commercial paper borrowing declined precipitously following the Lehman bankruptcy, as it could no longer be placed.

The lower panel displays the shares in total issuance of shorter- and longer-term commercial paper. With the onset of the subprime crisis, financial firms attempted to reduce the volume of both, and to "term out" the issuance, that is, increase the average term of the smaller total. The share of very short-term paper in total issuance declined from about 80 to about 60 percent during the 18 months preceding the Lehman bankruptcy. After the Lehman event, banks faced difficulty in rolling over longer-term commercial paper, and more generally in obtaining funding with maturities of more than a few weeks. The share of very short-term issuance rose dramatically, to near 90 percent, as financial firms had few other alternatives. The European debt crisis had a similar, but more muted, impact in the spring of 2010. The funding difficulty was reflected also in the Libor-OIS spread, as can be seen in Figure 14.10.

The Federal Reserve intervened following the Lehman bankruptcy and amid subsequent fears of a run on MMMFs to support liquidity via the Commercial Paper Funding Facility (CPFF), which purchased commercial paper from issuers unable to roll paper over, and the Asset-Backed Commercial Paper Money Market Mutual Fund Liquidity Facility (AMLF), which lent to financial institutions purchasing ABCP from MMMFs.

12.1.4 Structured Credit and Off-Balance-Sheet Funding

Structured credit products *per se* do not face funding liquidity problems, as they are maturity matched. Asset-backed securities (ABS), mortgage-based securities (MBS), and commercial mortgage-based securities (CMBS) themselves primarily carry out a credit and liquidity, rather than a maturity transformation. They can be viewed as providing matched funding for the assets in the collateral pool. The securities issued typically include at least some longer-term bonds.

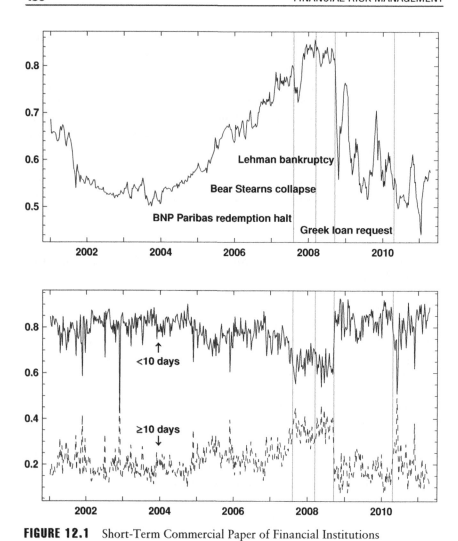

FIGURE 12.1 Short-Term Commercial Paper of Financial Institutions
Upper panel: Amount outstanding of AA financial commercial paper, weekly,
beginning of 2001 to end-April, 2011, trillions of US$.
Lower panel: Shares (summing to 1) of total dollar amount issued of AA financial
commercial paper with original maturities between 1 and 9 days (solid line,
marked "<10 days") and maturities of 10 days or more (dashed line, marked
"≥10 days"), weekly.
Source: Federal Reserve Board, available at www.federalreserve.gov/releases/cp/.

The way the securitization liabilities themselves are financed by investors can, however, introduce liquidity risk. The difficulties experienced by securitization have been related not only to the questionable credit quality of underlying assets such as real estate loans. Prior to mid-2008, the liabilities were held substantially by investors relying on short-term financing, increasing the fragility of the financial system.

The short-term financing of securitizations played a crucial role in the subprime crisis and in the opaque increase in financial system leverage prior to the subprime crisis. There were two major forms of such financing, *securities lending*, the use of structured credit products as collateral for short-term loans, which we discuss in detail later in this chapter, and off–balance-sheet vehicles.

Like securitizations themselves, off-balance-sheet vehicles are "robot companies" or special-purpose vehicles (SPVs) that are defined by their assets and liabilities. They issue asset-backed commercial paper (ABCP), which, in contrast to most commercial paper, is secured rather than unsecured debt. The two major types are:

1. *Asset-backed commercial paper conduits* purchase various types of assets, including securities as well as whole loans and leases, and finance the assets by issuing ABCP. They typically enjoy explicit credit and liquidity support from the sponsors in the form of credit guarantees and liquidity support should the conduit be unable to roll over the debt. Because of the guarantees, ABCP conduits generally have little equity.
2. *Structured investment vehicles* (SIVs) are similar to ABCP conduits in some respects, but differ in the crucial matter of credit and liquidity support. SIVs typically did not enjoy full explicit support by sponsors. They invested primarily in highly rated securitized credit products, and to a lesser extent in whole loans. Their funding mix was also generally somewhat different from that of ABCP conduits. In addition to ABCP, many SIVs issued medium-term notes (MTNs), which are at least somewhat less vulnerable to rollover risk. They also typically had larger equity cushions.

In spite of their differences, the two types were economically similar in many ways. Both types of vehicles profited from the spread between the asset yields and the funding cost. Another similarity is their economic function of maturity and liquidity transformation. The assets in the vehicles have longer, and possibly much longer, maturities than the commercial paper with which they are funded. This is typical for a bank; indeed, this maturity intermediation is the essence of what a bank does. However, instead of carrying out this function on its own balance sheet, the sponsoring bank has been able to reduce its balance sheet and its regulatory capital, while still deriving the economic benefits.

The vehicles also carried out liquidity transformation, creating ABCP, which is not only a much shorter-term, but, until the subprime crisis, was a more liquid asset than the underlying assets in the conduit or SIV. The final step in the liquidity transformation was the purchase of ABCP and money-substitute creation by MMMFs.

These financial innovations were accompanied and enabled by changes in regulatory capital and accounting rules that permitted firms to hold less capital against given levels of economic risk. The use of these vehicles did not lead to bona fide risk transfer. Even in the absence of explicit guarantees, sponsors that were large intermediaries felt obliged to provide support or assume the assets onto their balance sheets when the ABCP could no longer be rolled over. In spite of the fact that the vehicles were off-balance-sheet from an accounting and regulatory perspective, they contributed greatly to the leverage and fragility of the sponsors, largely banks.

12.1.5 Funding Liquidity of Other Intermediaries

Depository institutions and MMMFs are at an extreme position, because they must repay depositors instantly on demand. But other types of financial intermediaries face similar problems. These examples focus on the liquidity risk events they experienced during the subprime crisis.

Securities Firms   Securities firms hold inventories of securities for sale, and finance them by borrowing at short term. The collapse of Bear Stearns in March 2008 was an extreme case of a securities firm's lenders abruptly withdrawing credit. Bear Stearns, like other large broker-dealers, had relied to a large extent on short-term borrowing. Bear was particularly dependent on free cash deposits of the firm's large base of brokerage and clearing customers, including many hedge funds. These cash deposits were often collateralized, but generally not by better-quality collateral. Hedge funds withdrew deposits—and their business—rapidly towards the end of Bear's existence, in what was essentially a run. Bear also issued MTNs and commercial paper to fund its activities. We discuss these forms of borrowing in more detail later in this chapter, and discuss the Bear Stearns episode in more detail in Chapter 14.

Money Market Mutual Funds   MMMFs provide instant liquidity for their investors by giving them the ability to draw on their accounts via checks and electronic bank transfers. MMMFs are designed to invest in money market securities of high credit quality with just a few weeks or months to maturity. In this design, the market and credit risks of the assets are low, but still material. The assets can fluctuate in value, so the ability to offer unlimited instantaneous withdrawals is potentially limited if asset values fall. They are thus similar to banks in that their investments are less liquid than their liabilities. The liabilities of a MMMF are, however, quite different from those of banks. The account holders' claims are not first-priority unsecured debt, like those of bank depositors, but rather equity. A further structural feature is therefore required for these liabilities to become money substitutes.

MMMFs are similar in many ways to other mutual funds, which are organized in the United States under the Investment Company Act of 1940. This permits the instantaneous withdrawal of equity. But in contrast to other mutual funds, equity is not added or withdrawn at a fluctuating market-determined net asset value (NAV). Under the U.S. Securities and Exchange Commission's (SEC) Rule 2a-7, they are permitted to use a form of accounting, the "amortized cost method," that further reduces the tension—in normal times—between instant withdrawal and fluctuating asset value. The rule permits MMMFs to use the historical or acquisition cost of the money-market paper they purchase, plus any accrual gains. The reasoning is that, as long as the short-term debt is expected to be redeemed at par within a short time, it is not necessary to revalue it in response to fluctuations in interest rates and credit spreads. Because the paper is short-term, these fluctuations are likely in any case to be relatively small.

Other mutual funds must mark assets to market each day. This daily NAV is the price at which investors can contribute and withdraw equity. MMMFs, in contrast, are able to set a notional value of each share equal to exactly $1.00, rather than an amount that fluctuates daily. The residual claim represented by the shares is paid the net yield of the money market assets, less fees and other costs. MMMF shares thereby become claims on a fixed nominal value of units, rather than proportional shares of an asset pool. Their equity nature is absorbed within limits by fluctuations in the net yield.

This structure only works if market, credit, and liquidity risks are managed well. Some losses cannot be disregarded under the amortized cost method, particularly credit writedowns. These losses can cause the net asset value to fall below $1.00, a phenomenon called "breaking the buck."

Liquidity risk can also jeopardize the ability of a MMMF to maintain a $1.00 net asset value. In this respect, it is much like a classic commercial bank, and similarly vulnerable to runs. If a high proportion of shareholders attempt to redeem their shares simultaneously under adverse market conditions, the fund may have to liquidate money market paper at a loss, forceing writedowns and potentially breaking the buck. An episode of this kind involving credit writedowns by a MMMF, the Reserve Fund, was an important event in the subprime crisis, as we see in Chapter 14.

Hedge Funds Hedge funds face liquidity risk all through their capital structures. In contrast to the equity capital of corporations, which may be traded but not withdrawn, but much like mutual fund investments, hedge fund capital can be redeemed. Hedge funds permit investors to withdraw their funds at agreed intervals. Quarterly withdrawals are the rule, though some funds have annual and a very small number of monthly withdrawals. These withdrawal terms, colloquially called the "liquidity" of the fund, are subject in general to additional restrictions called "gates," that permit a suspension or limitation of withdrawal rights if investors collectively request redemptions in excess of some limit.[3]

The potential extent of liquidity demands by investors is shown in the decline in assets under management by hedge funds during the subprime crisis, displayed in Figure 1.7; the decline in assets was a result of both investment losses and redemptions of capital. These redemptions hit not only those hedge funds experiencing or expected to experience large losses. Redemption requests were submitted also to hedge funds that were profitable or had low losses. Investors sought at the onset of the crisis to marshal cash balances from all possible sources, among which were intact hedge fund investments. Hedge funds were obliged to liquidate assets, or impose barriers to redemptions so far as offering documents permitted. Hedge funds were in essence being asked to become liquidity providers to investors, a function for which they are not well-designed and were never intended, rather than to the markets.

Like other intermediaries, hedge funds also face short-term funding risk on their assets. Hedge funds typically have no access to wholesale funding and rely entirely on collateral markets, short positions, derivatives, and other mechanisms we describe below to take on leverage.

12.1.6 Systematic Funding Liquidity Risk

Funding liquidity is a latent risk factor in major corporate financial transactions. A dramatic example are leveraged buyouts (LBOs), which we discussed in Chapter 1. LBOs are generally financed by large loans, called *leveraged*

---

[3]Similar mechanisms have been used by commercial banks; for example in eighteenth-century Scotland, to limit the impact of bank runs by depositors in the absence of public-sector deposit insurance.

loans. As LBOs and private equity funds grew, leveraged loans became the dominant type, by volume, of *syndicated loans*, originated by banks, but distributed to other investors and traded in secondary markets. Many leveraged loans became part of CLO pools, and tranches of CLOs were important in CDO pools. The shadow banking system and the "CDO machine" were important providers of funding to private equity and LBOs. Other corporate events, such as mergers and acquisitions, are also dependent on financing.

The funding liquidity risk in corporate transactions is both idiosyncratic and systematic. Funding for a particular LBO or merger might fall through, even if the deal would otherwise have been consummated. But funding conditions generally can change adversely. This occurred in mid-2007 as the subprime crisis took hold. Many LBO and merger deals fell apart as financing came to a halt. Banks also incurred losses on inventories of syndicated loans, called "hung loans," that had not yet been distributed to other investors or into completed securitizations, as noted in Chapter 9. As risk aversion and demand for liquidity increased, the appetite for these loans dried up, and their prices fell sharply.

Apart from providers of financing, other participants in these transactions, such as hedge funds involved in *merger arbitrage*, also experienced losses. Mergers typically result in an increase in the target acquisition price, though not usually all the way to the announced acquisition price, and in a decrease in the acquirer's price, since the acquirer often takes on additional debt to finance the acquisition. Merger arbitrage exploits the remaining gap between the current and announced prices. The risk arises from uncertainty as to whether the transactions will be closed. In the early stages of the subprime crisis, merger arbitrage strategies generated large losses as merger plans were abandoned for lack of financing.

Investors taking on exposure to such transactions are therefore exposed not only to the idiosyncratic risk of the deal, but to the systematic risk posed by credit and funding conditions generally. This risk factor is hard to relate to any particular time series of asset returns. Rather, it is a "soft factor," on which information must be gathered from disparate sources ranging from credit and liquidity spreads to quantitative and anecdotal data on credit availability. We look at such data more closely in Chapter 14.

Systematic funding liquidity risk is pervasive. Other asset types or strategies that are good examples of sensitivity to the "latent" factor of economy-wide financing conditions include real estate, convertible bonds, and statistical arbitrage. Real estate is one of the longest-lived assets. Mortgages—loans collateralized by real estate—are therefore traditionally and most frequently originated as long-term, amortizing, fixed-rate loans. The typical home mortgage, for example, is a 30-year amortizing, fixed-rate loan. When lending practice departs from this standard and shorter-term loans predominate, lenders and borrowers both face funding liquidity risk, as borrowers are unlikely to be in a position to repay unless they can refinance. This risk is primarily systematic, as it is likely to affect all borrowers and lenders at the same time.

Convertible bond prices are generally only slightly lower than their theoretical prices based on the replicating portfolio of plain-vanilla equity options and bonds that should mimic convert bonds' values. Traders, many of them at hedge funds and dependent on credit extended by broker-dealers, take advantage of this gap to earn excess returns. The strategy is only attractive with leverage, as it has relatively low unlevered returns, but is generally also relatively low-risk given the arbitrage relationship between the convert bonds and the replicating portfolio.

Convert returns do, however, have a systematic extreme-loss risk. When the financing becomes unavailable because of credit conditions in the economy, converts cheapen dramatically. This effect is compounded by redemptions from convertible-bond funds, compounding the funding liquidity problem with a market liquidity problem.

These episodes of convert bond illiquidity also illustrate the effect of concentrated positions. Convertible bonds have a limited "clientele" among investors. When the existing clientele develops an aversion to the product during a period of market stress, it is difficult to move the product smoothly into new hands without large price declines.

Figure 12.2 displays a measure of arbitrage opportunities in the convertible bond market: the cheapness of bonds to their theoretical replicating portfolios. At the height of the pre-crisis boom, the gap had not only disappeared, but became negative. In a sense, investors were overpaying for the package in their search for yield. As the subprime crisis evolved, the positive discount to theoretical was first reestablished, and eventually widened to an unprecedented extent. Viewed from a different angle, under conditions of severe liquidity stress, even a large gap between convert prices and their replicating portfolio did not bring arbitrage capital into the market.

A similar problem occurred for securitized credit products in the fall of 2008. The clientele for the bonds had relied to a large extent on short-term finance via repo, SIVs, and other mechanisms. When financing for the SIVs disappeared, a new investor base for the bonds could not be established quickly, and spreads on securitized credit products widened dramatically. Figure 14.14 displays the impact on structured product credit spreads.

A final example is statistical arbitrage, which we discussed briefly in Chapter 1. Like convert arbitrage, statistical arbitrage requires some degree of leverage for profitability. In August 2007, as the subprime crisis got underway, one of its first effects was on statistical arbitrage strategies. Curtailing the liquidity of these strategies caused losses and return volatility

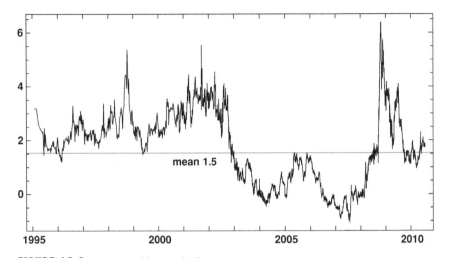

FIGURE 12.2 Convertible Bond Cheapness
Difference between theoretical and market prices of convertible bonds in the
Merrill Lynch All U.S. Convertibles Index (VXA0), weekly through 1997 and daily
through July 2010, in percent. The theoretical price is the value of the replicating
portfolio, taking the credit, risk-free rates, and the embedded option into account.
Source: Bank of America Corp.

that were extremely far outside the range of historical experience. In fact,
this episode was one of the first overt signs of how severe the crisis could
potentially become.

12.2 MARKETS FOR COLLATERAL

Markets for collateral are formed when securities are used as collateral
to obtain secured loans of cash or other securities. The loans are used to
finance securities holdings or otherwise invest, often as part of a larger trade.
Securities used as collateral "circulate," since the borrower of securities
can typically lend them to another, a practice called *rehypothecation* or
repledging of collateral we described in Chapter 6. In this way, the supply of
securities that can be used as collateral is an important element in facilitating
leverage in the financial system.

Collateral has always played an important role in credit transactions by
providing security for lenders and thus ensuring the availability of credit to
borrowers. The role of collateral has changed and expanded in contemporary
finance, hand in hand with the development of securitization, but also with
the growing volume and transactions liquidity of securities trading.

The obvious and direct effect of securitization is to remove credit intermediation from the balance sheets of financial intermediaries. However, it also creates securities that can be pledged as collateral in further credit transactions. Securities have additional economic value to the extent that they not only throw off cash flows and may appreciate in value, but can be used as collateral to obtain credit.

Collateral markets are an important institutional element supporting the growth of nonbank intermediation. Participants in these markets include:

- Firms such as life insurance companies may own portfolios of high-quality securities that can be used as collateral to borrow cash at the low interest rates applicable to well-collateralized loans. The motivation is to borrow cash at a low rate, which it can then reinvest, earning a spread.
- Firms such as hedge funds have inventories of securities that they finance by pledging the securities as collateral. The motivation is to obtain financing of the portfolio at a lower rate than unsecured borrowing, if the latter is available at all.
- Firms may have excess cash that they are willing to lend out at a low interest rate, as long as they are appropriately secured by collateral.

The securitization process relied heavily on rating agencies to create bonds "with the highest credit rating," which could then be lent, repoed out, or pledged as collateral by their owners.

12.2.1 Structure of Markets for Collateral

Firms can borrow or lend collateral against cash or other securities. A *haircut* ensures that the full value of the collateral is not lent. A haircut of 10 percent, for example, means that if the borrower of cash wants to buy $100 of a security, he can borrow only $90 from the broker and must put $10 of his own funds in the margin account by the time the trade is settled. Similarly, the lender of cash will be prepared to lend $90 against $100 of collateral.

Borrowing may be at short term, such as overnight, or for longer terms. Overnight borrowing may be extended automatically until terminated. As the market value of the collateral fluctuates, variation margin may be paid. Most collateralized borrowing arrangements provide for such *remargining*. The total margin at any point in time, if adequate, provides a liquidation cushion to the lender. If, for example, the loan has a maturity of (or cannot be remargined for the duration of) one week, a 10 percent haircut ensures that the value of the securities held as collateral can fall 10 percent and still leave the loan fully collateralized. The variation margin protects the lender of cash against fluctuations in the value of the collateral.

Markets for collateral have existed for a long time in three basic forms that are economically very similar, although they differ in legal form and market practice.

Margin Loans *Margin lending* is lending for the purpose of financing a security transaction in which the loan is collateralized by the security. It is generally provided by the broker intermediating the trade, who is also acting as a lender. Margin lending is generally short term, but rolled over automatically unless terminated by one of the counterparties.

Collateralization for the loan is achieved by having the broker retain custody of the securities in a separate customer account, but in "street name," that is, registered in the name of the broker rather than in the name of the owner. This simplifies the process of seizing the securities and selling them to cover the margin loan if it is not repaid timely. But registration in street name also lets the broker use the securities for other purposes, for example, lending the securities to other customers who want to execute a short sale.

In practice, the most important purpose for which the broker is likely to use the customer's collateral is to borrow money in the secured money market to obtain the funds it lends to margin customers. The repledged securities become the collateral for a margin loan to the broker, and the collateral is moved to the broker's customer account with its creditor. Collateral may, however, also be repledged in order to borrow another security rather than cash collateral. This will typically be done in order to short the borrowed security or to facilitate a client's short position. In extreme market conditions, such as the subprime crisis, the practice of rehypothecation of securities can become quite important, as it introduces additional risk for the broker's customers. We saw a dramatic example as part of our discussion of counterparty risk in Chapter 6.

In the United States, initial haircuts on equity purchases are set at 50 percent by the Federal Reserve Board's Regulation T ("Reg T"), but, as we will see, derivatives can be used to increase the amount implicitly borrowed. Many transactions occur outside U.S. jurisdiction in order to obtain lower haircuts.

Reg T governs initial margin for common stock and other listed securities. After a position is established, the margin will be adjusted as the value of the security fluctuates. As the market value of a long position declines, the broker loses the protection the collateral provides against the customer defaulting on the margin loan, so he will issue a *margin call* to the customer. Most customers have portfolios of long and short positions in cash securities, so *cross-margining agreements* are put in place to govern the net margin assessed.

Repurchase Agreements   *Repurchase agreements* or *repos* are matched pairs of the spot sale and forward repurchase of a security. Both the spot and forward price are agreed now, and the difference between them implies an interest rate. The collateralization of the loan is achieved by selling the security temporarily to the lender. The collateralization is adjusted for the riskiness of the security through the haircut.

Repos are also a fairly old form of finance, but have grown significantly in recent decades. More significantly, the range of collateral underlying repos has widened. At one time, repo lending could be secured only by securities with no or de minimis credit risk. A few decades ago, repo began to encompass high-yield bonds and whole loans, and more recently, structured credit products. It has been a linchpin of the ability of large banks and brokerages to finance inventories of structured credit products, facilitated also by extending high investment-grade ratings to the senior tranches of structured credit products such as ABS and CDOs.

The mechanics of repo lending are similar to margin loans. Like margin lending, repo creates a straightforward liability on the economic balance sheet. However, under certain circumstances, such as back-to-back security lending and borrowing for customers, transactions can be combined so as to permit the gross economic exposure to remain off-balance-sheet.

Securities Lending   In a *securities lending* transaction, one party lends a security to another in exchange for a fee, generally called a *rebate*. The security lender, rather than the borrower, continues to receive dividend and interest cash flows from the security. A common type of securities lending is stock lending, in which shares of stock are borrowed.

As in repo transactions, the "perfection" of the lien on the collateral is enhanced by structuring the transaction as a sale, so that the lender holding the collateral can rehypothecate it or, in the event that the loan is not repaid, sell it with minimal delay and transactions costs.

There are a few typical patterns of securities lending:

■ In a stock lending transaction, the source of the securities is a large institutional investor in equities or a hedge fund. The investor makes the equities available for lending by holding them at the custodian or prime broker in "street name," so that they can be rehypothecated to a trader who wishes to sell the securities short. The owner receives a rebate in exchange. A securities lending transaction is generally "born" on the broker's balance sheet; that is, the securities are already in a margin account when a customer indicates a desire to go short.

■ A typical fixed-income securities lending transaction aims to earn a spread between less- and more-risky bonds. The transaction would again typically start with an institutional investor in, say, U.S. Treasury or agency bonds that can be used as collateral for a short-term loan at a rate lower than other money-market rates, and a low haircut. The investor receives *cash collateral* in exchange for the loan of the Treasury bonds. The cash can then be used to invest in other, higher-yielding securities.

Much securities lending is carried out via *agency securities lending* programs, whereby a third party, usually a large broker-dealer, or a custodial bank with many institutional clients (e.g. State Street), intermediates between the lender and borrower of securities.

Total Return Swaps The ability to short equities depends on the ability to borrow and lend stock. An important instrument of many short stock trades are *total return swaps* (TRS), in which one party pays a fixed fee and receives the total return on a specified equity position on the other. TRS are OTC derivatives in which one counterparty, usually a bank, broker-dealer or prime broker, takes on an economic position similar to that of a stock lender, enabling the other counterparty, often a hedge fund, to establish a synthetic short stock position, economically similar to that of a borrower of stock. The broker then needs either to lay off the risk via a congruent opposite TRS, or to hedge by establishing a short position in the cash market.

12.2.2 Economic Function of Markets for Collateral

There are two main purposes served by collateral markets. First, they create the ability to establish leveraged long and short positions in securities. Without these markets, there would be no way to short a cash security; short positions could only be created synthetically.

Second, collateral markets enhance the ability of firms to borrow money. In collateral markets, cash is just another—and not necessarily the primary—asset to be borrowed and lent, alongside securities of all types, hence the term "cash collateral."

It helps in understanding the risks of securities lending and its role in the financial system to flesh out how it is embedded in and has supported a number of important activities in finance. Repo and securities lending are mechanically distinct, but economically similar. They both enable market participants to finance assets with borrowed funds using the assets as collateral. They are both structured in such a way that the party investing in the assets appears to have "borrowed" the assets, though economically having bought them. However, in a repo transaction, the assets are financed directly, while in a securities lending transaction, the investor starts off owning liquid assets that are "good currency" and can be used to obtain cash collateral with a relatively low haircut. The investor can then step forward as a lender of cash against the securities in which he wants to invest, or as an outright buyer, rather than, as would be the case in a repo, as a borrower of cash to purchase the securities.

Fixed-income securities lending, like repo programs, has historically functioned primarily as a source of short-term financing for financial firms, and as an additional source of revenue for institutional investors and insurance companies. In more recent years, it has been an important element facilitating credit creation in the bank and nonbank intermediation systems. It supported the "manufacturing system" for securitized credit products. The ability to finance positions in securitized credit products via securities lending made the bonds more marketable and increased their value, that is, decreased their required credit spreads. These programs also provided a channel through which firms using cash collateral to invest in higher-risk bonds could increase leverage and returns.

Different forms of collateral markets serve different trading motivations, but these forms are economically so similar that no hard-and-fast distinctions can be drawn:

- Margin lending, the simplest form of a market for collateral, is primarily used by investors wishing to take leveraged *long* positions in securities, most often equities.
- Reverse repo transactions are similar, in that they are often used to finance long positions in securities, typically bonds. Repo transactions, in contrast, are usually intended to borrow cash by owners of bonds.

    However, in some instances, a repo or reverse repo transaction is focused on the need of one counterparty to establish a long position in a particular security. An important example is the U.S. Treasury *specials* market, in which a scarcity arises of a particular bond. The mechanism by which the market is cleared is a drop in the implied interest rate for loans against a bond "on special," which can become zero or even negative. Recently issued U.S. Treasury notes typically go on special when dealers sell them to customers prior to the issue date on a when-issued basis, and have underestimated the demand. Following the next

U.S. government bond auction, when the bond is issued, the dealer must borrow it to deliver to the customer at a penalty rate, expressed in the cheap rate at which the dealer must lend cash collateral to borrow the security.

■ Securities lending has typically been focused on the securities rather than the cash collateral, typically to establish short positions. In recent years, the focus of their use has shifted to borrowing cash collateral.

High-quality bonds that can be readily used as collateral command higher prices than bonds that cannot be used in this way. This creates additional demand for high-quality collateral; their utility as collateral adds to the value of securitized credit products, and provided an additional incentive to create them.

Collateral markets bring owners of securities, such as institutional investors and insurance companies, into the financing markets. They lend their securities to earn extra return. Whether through repo or securities lending, they earn an extra return by making their securities available for other market participants to use as collateral.

A crucial element in permitting bonds to serve as collateral is their credit quality. Credit-rating agencies are important participants in collateral markets because of the need for highly rated bonds. Conversely, awarding high ratings to lower-quality bonds added a large volume of collateral to these markets that evaporated almost overnight during the subprime crisis.

These markets grew tremendously in volume in the years preceding the subprime crisis, as the range and amount of collateral that could be lent expanded. Figure 12.3 shows net repo market borrowing by U.S. broker-dealers. The volumes displayed in the graph are likely much smaller than the gross amounts. Reported balance sheet volumes understate the volume of repo lending and the amount of leverage introduced into the financial system by excluding transactions in which a dealer hypothecates one security in order to borrow a different security. Broker-dealers carry out a large volume of such transaction on behalf of customers. Net repo use more than tripled between mid-2004 and its peak in mid-2007. During the subprime crisis, net repo liabilities contracted by about two-thirds. The three-year spike is likely due in large part to the expansion in use of non-Treasury securities as collateral and the growth in hedge fund funding business, which we now briefly discuss.

12.2.3 Prime Brokerage and Hedge Funds

Much of the growth in volume in collateral markets is intermediated through *prime brokers*, subsidiaries of large banks and broker dealers that have

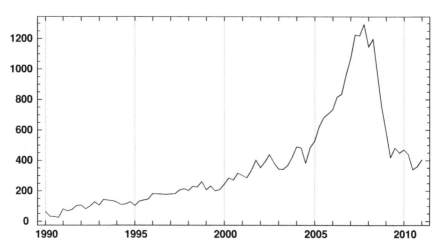

FIGURE 12.3   U.S. Broker-Dealer Repo 1980–2011
Net liabilities under security repurchase agreements of U.S. broker-dealers, billions
of dollars.
Source: Federal Reserve Board, Flow of Funds Accounts of the United States (Z.1),
Table L.129.

emerged as important service providers to the hedge fund industry. They
serve as a single point of service that provides trading, clearing, custody,
financing, and other services. In some cases, prime brokers have been involved in the hedge fund business itself through "capital introduction," that
is, arranging contact between funds and potential investors.

Hedge funds often maintain portfolios of long and short positions. For
both the hedge fund and the prime broker providing the financing, the net
value may be quite small compare to the gross volume of lending. Within a
firm's account with a broker, margin lending may be extended on a portfolio
basis. This may be as simple as reducing the margin for offsetting long and
short trades in the same security. Margin may also be reduced for less
direct portfolio effects. Some brokers use risk models such as VaR to help
determine the appropriate margin for an account.

Prime brokerage businesses have been valuable to large intermediaries
not only because of the fees and spreads they earn on the services and
lending they provide. As noted above in discussing the run on Bear Stearns,
the intermediaries also benefit from the cash balances the hedge funds hold.
Typically, even highly leveraged hedge funds maintain cash balances with
prime brokers, so the prime brokerage business becomes an important funding source, akin to retail deposits, but far less "sticky." The cash balances

at prime brokers are part of the intermediaries' general liquidity pool. They are available to finance any of the intermediaries' other activities. Short positions also generate cash, not all of which can be freely devoted to making additional investments.

The interest rates paid on these cash balances are generally somewhat higher than the funds could obtain from alternative money market investments, such as Treasury bills, commercial paper, and money market mutual funds. They are also, from the standpoint of the funds, riskier than the alternatives, as they are unsecured claims against the intermediary, or are secured by possibly inadequate collateral. Conversely, prime brokers are important intake points for banks and broker-dealers to gather collateral and cash that can be used to finance their activities. Earlier in this chapter, we observed that hedge funds were drawn on as sources of liquidity by their investors during the subprime crisis. Their prime brokerage relationships are an equally counterintuitive instance of the "peacetime" role of hedge funds as liquidity providers.

12.2.4 Risks in Markets for Collateral

The risks in markets for collateral are similar to those of other leveraged positions. They comprise market, credit, and counterparty risks. There are some risks in common for the borrower and lender of securities, and some that are unique to only one side of the transaction. The risks vary widely, depending on the motivation of the trade, what type of collateral is involved, and how the cash generated is deployed. For example, the market risk of reversing in a bond is a rise in long-term interest rates. A trader selling borrowed equities short will gain if the stock price falls.

Prior to the subprime crisis, many institutional investors and mutual funds maintained large securities lending programs, in which they lent high-quality securities and received cash collateral, which they invested in higher-yielding bonds. These "sec-lending" programs invested heavily in structured credit products, as they had AAA ratings, thus satisfying investment mandates, but had somewhat higher yields than the bonds lent. These programs were intended to earn a narrow but steady interest margin, but had severe losses during the crisis, as securitized product prices collapsed.

Another major market risk in markets for collateral is changes in lending rates or other terms of margin, repo, or securities loans. The loans themselves are generally short-term, so losses to a borrower of securities in a decline in rates are generally small. However, the transactions liquidity risk can be high. We have already discussed one important example, the Treasury specials market.

Another example is the phenomenon of *hard-to-borrow* securities in equity markets. In order to establish a short position, even one expressed via TRS, stock must be located and borrowed. Smaller stocks and stocks under price pressure can be difficult to borrow, as many owners will not be willing to lend.

Collateral markets permit owners of high-quality collateral—or collateral perceived by the market as high-quality—to borrow or to finance positions in high-quality collateral at low interest rates. The upper panel of Figure 12.4 displays the overnight repo rate at which market participants can borrow against collateral consisting of U.S. Treasury obligations, the highest-quality collateral available even after the S&P downgrade of the U.S. long-term credit rating. In normal times, the repo rate is very close to the yield of T-bills or other short-term lending rates, and the spread between them is close to zero. However, when times are not normal, for example during the subprime crisis, rates on loans collateralized by the highest-quality securities drop even faster than interest rates generally. Having the very best collateral in a stressed market is almost as good as having cash, because you can then borrow cash at a low or even zero rate using such collateral. Lenders will provide cash at a low rate to gain custody of such collateral. This is evident in the upper panel, where one can see downward spikes in the Treasury repo rate following the inception of each phase of the subprime crisis.

The center and lower panels of Figure 12.4 display the spread between overnight Treasury repo and interbank rates (center panel), and the spread between Treasury repo and repo rates for loans collateralized by a different type of collateral, agency MBS (lower panel). Agency MBS are also highly creditworthy, but not quite as unquestionably so as Treasuries, and are also not as liquid. In times of stress, rates on loans with agency MBS collateral will not fall quite as low as for the very best collateral. Both spreads are close to zero in normal times, widening and becoming highly volatile during the crisis. Questions about the solvency of the issuers of agency bonds, the government-sponsored enterprices (GSEs), exacerbated the size and volatility of these spreads. The data illustrate a key point regarding funding liquidity risk: The higher the quality of the securities a market participant owns unencumbered, the more liquid he is.

The owner of high-quality collateral who uses it to finance a position in lower-quality bonds can maintain a highly leveraged position, since haircuts on the collateral lent are typically small. When the subprime crisis began, and values of low-quality collateral began to fall, investors engaged in this trade suffered large losses via forced sales. The lenders demanded variation margin in cash as specified in margin agreements. If the investor was unable or unwilling to meet that demand, positions had to be liquidated.

The size and structure of collateral markets also contributes to systemic risk. Owners of lower-quality collateral may suddenly have their loans

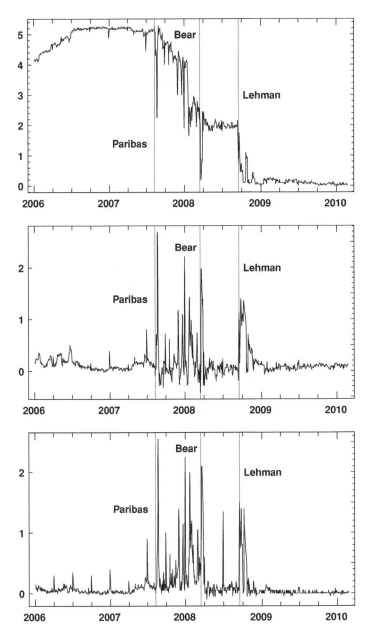

FIGURE 12.4 Repo Rates and Spreads 2006–2010
Upper panel: Overnight repo rates collateralized by U.S. Treasury securities, daily.
Center panel: Spread between one month OIS and overnight Treasury repo rates
(OIS minus Treasury repo), daily.
Lower panel: Spread between overnight repo rates collateralized by U.S. Treasury
securities and by agency MBS (agency repo minus Treasury repo), daily.
Source: Bloomberg Financial L.P.

terminated, or have the loans be subjected to sudden and large increases in
the margin demanded by lenders of cash. Drastic remargining is tantamount
to drastically decreasing the loan proceeds available to the borrower on the
strength of the collateral. The owners of the collateral may then be forced
to liquidate the assets. In a distressed market, this contributes to the rapid
decline in asset prices.

Calling and remargining loans collateralized by securities gives rise to a
phenomenon similar to classic bank runs, but involving nonbank intermediaries as well as banks, and focused on wholesale funding rather than deposits. One instance was the March 2008 collapse of Bear Stearns. Bear had
large exposures to subprime residential mortgage debt in a number of forms,
and its vulnerability in this respect had become clear in mid-2007 when several hedge funds that it sponsored collapsed. Once its solvency was called
into question, providers of funding began to withdraw. As noted above,
these included commercial paper lenders and hedge funds with free cash
balances at Bear as part of its clearing and prime brokerage businesses. We
study these and similar self-reinforcing mechanisms in crises in Chapter 14.

12.3 LEVERAGE AND FORMS OF CREDIT IN CONTEMPORARY FINANCE

12.3.1 Defining and Measuring Leverage

So far in this chapter, we have seen how pervasive leverage is in the financial
system, and some of the new forms it takes. Next, we look at the mechanics
of leverage, particularly via the economic, as opposed to the accounting,
balance sheet of the firm. In Chapter 6, we presented the standard definition
of leverage as the ratio of the firm's assets to its equity. The schematic
balance sheet of the firm is

Assets	Liabilities
	Equity (E)
Value of the firm (A)	Debt (D)

The leverage ratio is defined as[4]

$$L = \frac{A}{E} = \frac{E + D}{E} = 1 + \frac{D}{E}$$

[4]The leverage ratio is sometimes defined as the debt-to-equity ratio $\frac{D}{E}$.

The lowest possible value of leverage is 1, if there is no debt. For a single collateralized loan, such as a mortgage or repo, leverage is the reciprocal of one minus the *loan-to-value ratio* (LTV). The borrower's equity in the position is one minus the LTV. The equity at the time a collateralized trade is initiated is the initial margin. For a firm, equity is also referred to as *net worth*.

Leverage is important because it provides an opportunity to increase returns to equity investors, the so-called *leverage effect*, which can be exploited whenever the return on the firm's assets is expected to exceed the cost of debt capital. The leverage effect is the increase in equity returns that results from increasing leverage and is equal to the difference between the returns on the assets and cost of funding.

The leverage effect can be seen by writing out the relationship between asset returns r^a, equity returns r^e, and the cost of debt r^d:

$$r^e = Lr^a - (L-1)r^d$$

The effect of increasing leverage is

$$\frac{\partial r^e}{\partial L} = r^a - r^d$$

Increasing leverage by one "turn," that is, increasing assets and taking on an equal amount of additional debt that increases leverage from an initial value L_0 to $L_0 + 1$ increases equity returns by $r^a - r^d$. By the same token, leverage will amplify losses should the asset return prove lower than the cost of debt.

In foreign exchange trading, leveraged trades, called *carry trades*, involve borrowing (going short) a low-interest rate currency, and using the proceeds to buy (go long) a higher-interest rate currency. The *net carry* is $r_a - r_d$, with r_a representing the higher and r_d the lower interest rate. Carry trades lose money when the low-yielding currency appreciates enough to more than offset the net carry.

The equity denominator of the leverage measure depends on what type of entity we are looking at and the purpose of the analysis. For an intermediary such as a bank or broker-dealer, the equity might be the book or market value of the firm. These firms also issue *hybrid capital*, securities such as subordinated preference shares that combine characteristics of debt and equity. Hybrid capital can be included or excluded from the denominator of a leverage ratio depending on the purpose of the analysis. As we see in Chapter 15, regulators have invested considerable effort in ascertaining the capacity to absorb losses and thus nearness to pure equity of these securities.

For a hedge fund, the appropriate equity denominator is the net asset value (NAV) of the fund, the current value of the investors' capital. For any investment firm or investment vehicle, the leverage of individual positions or of subportfolios can be calculated using the haircut, margin, or risk capital, which we study in the next chapter, as the equity denominator.

An alternative definition often used in fundamental credit analysis relates the debt, not to the assets of the firm, but to its cash flows. The cash flow measure typically used is earnings before interest, taxes, depreciation, and amortization (EBITDA). This measure of cash flow captures the net revenues of the firm, while excluding costs that are particularly heavily influenced by accounting techniques. It also excludes interest, which is determined less by the firm's business activities than by its choice of capital structure. Leverage is then defined as the ratio of debt to EBITDA.

Example 12.1 (Leverage and the Leverage Effect)   Suppose the firm's return on assets is fixed at $r^a = 0.10$, while its cost of debt is $r^d = 0.05$, and initially has this balance sheet:

Assets	Liabilities
Value of the firm $A = 2$	Equity $E = 1$
	Debt $D = 1$

Its leverage is then 2 and its return on equity is

$$2 \cdot 0.10 - 0.05 = 0.15$$

Adding a turn of leverage, that is, borrowing an additional unit of funds and investing it in an additional unit of assets, changes the balance sheet to

Assets	Liabilities
Value of the firm $A = 3$	Equity $E = 1$
	Debt $D = 2$

and increases the equity return to 0.20.

In reality, of course, asset returns are not fixed, but risky. What if asset returns end up a disappointing 0 percent? The equity return with leverage of 2 will be a loss of 5 percent, and with leverage of 3, a loss of 10 percent.

The effect of leverage depends as much on the cost of funding as on the asset return. Investors sometimes choose a degree of leverage based on the return they need to achieve. For a given cost of debt, and a given asset return, there is a unique leverage ratio that will permit the equity owners to "break even," in the sense of reaching a given hurdle rate, or required rate of return on equity. This orientation has surfaced in the debates on bank regulatory capital (see Chapter 15), in which some bankers and observers have stated that increased capital requirements will oblige banks to reduce their return-on-equity (ROE) targets.

Example 12.2 (Leverage and Required Returns) Continuing the previous example, suppose the firm's return on assets is $r^a = 0.10$, while its cost of debt is $r^d = 0.05$. If the hurdle rate or return on equity is 15 percent, the firm will choose leverage of 2. If the hurdle rate, however, is 25 percent, then the firm will choose a leverage ratio of 4:

$$4 \cdot 0.10 - 3 \cdot 0.05 = 0.25$$

Many leveraged fixed-income trades involve spreads. If a fixed-income security has a coupon rate higher than the borrowing rate on a loan collateralized by the security, for example via a repo transaction, the rate of return to a leveraged purchase is limited only by the haircut. To see this, denote the coupon rate by c, the haircut by h, and the repo rate by r, and assume $c > r$ (all in percent). The coupon and repo rates have a time dimension; the haircut does not. For every \$100 of par value, the investor puts up capital of h, earns a coupon of c, and pays $(1 - h)r$ in repo interest. The leverage is equal to $\frac{1}{h}$. The leveraged return, measured as a decimal fraction of the investor's equity capital, is

$$\frac{c - (1 - h)r}{h} = c + \frac{1 - h}{h}(c - r)$$

As h decreases, the levered return rises. The increase in returns as the debt-to-equity ratio $\frac{1-h}{h}$ rises is proportional to the spread $c - r$. Conversely, the increase in returns as the spread $c - r$ rises is proportional to the debt-to-equity ratio $\frac{1-h}{h}$.

The tension between required returns and leverage played an important role in creating the conditions of the subprime crisis, in an environment in which prospective asset returns were falling more rapidly than funding costs; the decline in credit spreads in the years just prior to the subprime crisis, displayed in Figure 14.14 is one example. Higher leverage is needed to achieve a given required rate of return on capital as the spread $c - r$ contracts, and mechanisms were found to achieve it. For example, the net spreads earned by the off-balance-sheet vehicles described earlier in this chapter, ABCP conduits and SIVs, were extremely tight, often under 10 bps. But with sufficient leverage, it could be turned into a substantial return stream.

The use of leverage applies not only to financial intermediaries, but also to households able to borrow to finance asset purchases. Most households that own homes, for example, have borrowed at least part of the purchase price by means of a mortgage loan. The down payment is the household's equity and is a form of haircut. The leverage is the ratio of the value of the house to the down payment (and inversely related to the LTV). During the decade preceding the subprime crisis, the terms on which mortgage credit was granted were loosened to permit higher leverage and low initial interest rates, which amplified the impact of the prevailing low-interest rate environment. As discussed in Chapter 11, analysis of credit risk in residential mortgage loans assumed rising house prices. For households, equally confident that house prices would rise, or at least not fall, easy credit terms created strong incentives to make leveraged investments in housing, as shown in Example 12.3.

Example 12.3 (Leveraged Returns to Housing)   Suppose house values are expected to rise 10 percent a year, including, for simplicity, rental income and net of property maintenance costs. The following table shows the resulting annual rate of return to the homeowner for different down payments and loan rates (all data in percent):

Down payment	Loan rate	
	5.5	8.0
10	50.5	28.0
20	28.0	18.0

The returns are calculated as

$$100 \frac{\text{House price appreciation} - (1 - \text{Down payment})\text{Loan rate}}{\text{Down payment}}$$

Lowering the lending rate and the down payment or haircut increases the leveraged return from 18 to over 50 percent per annum. We return to the phenomenon of leveraged investment in housing in discussing asset price targeting in Chapter 15.

Leverage ratios can amplify sensitivity to changes in cash flow. If the net cash flow on a leveraged trade or of a leveraged firm is positive, but small, a small change in interest rates can make the cash flow negative.

These relationships show why firms or investors employ leverage. It also illustrates why leverage is often used as a measure of risk, and why leverage is sometimes considered to be an independent source of risk. These last two ideas can be misleading. Leverage is not a well-defined risk measure. Part of the difficulty is that financial accounting standards have been developed with a view to solving a completely different set of problems, for example, accurately recognizing profits, or accurately capturing the explicit liabilities of the firm.

Although it is difficult to state an unambiguous definition of leverage, it is an important concept. Most severe losses suffered by financial intermediaries involve leverage in some way, and it is important to understand the extent to which borrowing is being used, implicitly or explicitly, to boost returns. To do so, we can construct an economic balance sheet for a firm or an investor that captures the implicit or *embedded leverage* in short positions, swaps, and options. This can at least provide a reasonable answer to the question of how much he has borrowed to finance positions.

We've reviewed some of the financial instruments by which credit is extended outside the traditional bank lending and bond markets in our discussion of collateral markets earlier in this chapter, in our discussion of financial innovation in Chapter 1, and in our introduction to credit risk concepts in Chapter 6. Here, we show, using T-accounts, the great extent to which a financial firm can use them to take on leverage. Some of these forms of credit are by no means new, but their volume has grown enormously in recent decades with the rise in the volume of trading in securities and OTC derivatives. Among the reasons for their growth are:

- They have lower transactions costs than traditional bank or capital markets debt. Originating a bank loan or security is a cumbersome, slow, and expensive process. It requires underwriting, syndication, and distribution by banks or securities firms. Most of the forms of credit discussed here require only a counterparty. But along with that cost saving, counterparty risk has become more prevalent.
- The granting of credit is an inherent part of trading in the assets being financed, and the amount of credit granted adjusts naturally to the size of the position being financed.
- Collateralization of the loan and adjustments to the amount lent occur naturally as part of trading and brokering trades.

These forms of borrowing are generally collateralized in some way, which also affects the economic leverage. When borrowing is explicit, as for example through taking loans or deposits, or issuing bonds, the impact on leverage is straightforward. In other forms of borrowing, some analysis is required to measure leverage. For each of these forms, we see how to determine the amount of borrowing or leverage implicit in the position.

12.3.2 Margin Loans and Leverage

Margin lending has a straightforward impact on leverage. The haircut determines the amount of the loan that is made: at a haircut of h percent, $1 - h$ is lent against a given market value of margin collateral, and h percent of the position's market value is the borrower's equity in the position. The leverage on a position with a haircut of h percent is $\frac{1}{h}$.

Haircut (%)	Amount borrowed (%)	Leverage
10	90	10
50	50	2
90	10	$\frac{1}{0.9}$

Example 12.4 (Leverage and Margin Loans)   We take as the starting point of this and the remaining examples in this section a firm with $100 in cash, corresponding to an initial placement of $100 in equity by its owners. For concreteness, we imagine a hedge fund account, Lever Brothers Multistrategy Master Fund LP, with this economic balance sheet on opening day:

Assets	Liabilities
Cash	Equity $100
$100	Debt $0

Assume Lever Brothers finances a long position in $100 worth of an equity at the Reg T margin requirement of 50 percent. It invests $50 of its own funds and borrows $50 from the broker. Immediately following the trade, its margin account has $50 in equity and a $50 loan from the broker:

Assets	Liabilities
Stock value $100	Equity $50
	Margin loan $50

The broker retains custody of the stock as collateral for the loan. Lever Brothers' full economic balance sheet, including the entries in its margin account, is now

Assets	Liabilities
Cash $50	Equity $100
Stock value $100	Margin loan $50

The firm's leverage has risen from 1 to 1.5.

12.3.3 Short Positions

Short positions lengthen the balance sheet, since both the value of the borrowed short securities and the cash generated by their sale appear on the balance sheet. They therefore increase leverage, which looks at the gross amount of assets, that is, longs plus the absolute value of short positions.

Example 12.5 (Leverage and Short Positions)   Our starting point, as in Example 12.4, is a hedge fund with $100 in cash, corresponding to an initial placement of $100 in equity by its owners.

To create a short position in a stock, Lever Brothers borrows $100 of the security and sells it. It has thus created a liability equal to the value of the borrowed stock, and an asset, equal in value, consisting of the cash proceeds from the short sale. The cash cannot be used to fund other investments, as it is collateral; the broker uses it to ensure that the short stock can be repurchased and returned to the stock lender. It remains in a segregated short account, offset by the value of the borrowed stock. The stock might rise in price, in which case the $100 of proceeds would not suffice to cover its return to the borrower. Lever Brothers must therefore in addition put up margin of $50.

Immediately following this trade, Lever Brothers' margin and short accounts have $50 in equity and a $50 loan from the broker:

Assets	Liabilities
$150 Due from broker:	Equity $50
$50 Margin	Borrowed stock $100
$100 Short sale proceeds	

Lever Brothers' full economic balance sheet is

Assets	Liabilities
$50 Cash	Equity $100
$150 Due from broker	Borrowed stock $100

The firm has gone from leverage of 1 to 2. Notice that the leverage in this example is higher than in the example of a long position via margin lending. The reason is that in establishing a short position, the securities must be borrowed; leverage is inherent in short positions, but is a choice for long positions. In the example of the long position, only half the value of the purchased stock was borrowed, so the leverage was 1.5. Here, the entire stock position must be borrowed to execute the short. The fund could reduce its overall leverage by reducing its borrowing to finance long positions, but cannot reduce leverage in the short position itself.

Gross and Net Leverage   Although, like any other risk asset, short positions generate leverage, they reduce risk if there are long positions with which they are positively correlated, or other short positions with which they are negatively correlated. If short positions play a hedging role in the portfolio, leverage will overstate the risk, since adding the short positions increases leverage, but reduces market risk.

This leads to a distinction between *gross* and *net leverage*. Gross leverage is defined as the sum of all the asset values, including cash generated by shorts or assets acquired with that cash, divided by capital. It can be thought of as the total "length" of the balance sheet divided by the capital. Net leverage is computed as the ratio of the difference between the market values of the long and short positions to the capital.

The balance sheet alone will not tell the risk manager whether the short positions are risk-augmenting or -reducing. Other information in addition to the long and short leverage, such as VaR and stress test reports, or a qualitative examination, are needed. For this reason, in reporting leverage, long positions and short positions should be reported separately. Leverage reporting is important, but far from a complete view of the risks of a portfolio.

12.3.4 Derivatives

Derivative securities are a means to gain an economic exposure to some asset or risk factor without buying or selling it outright. One motivation for market participants to use derivatives is as a means of increasing leverage. Leveraged ETFs are an example of an investment product that uses derivatives in order to create the economics of leveraged investment in, say, an equity index.

Although derivatives are generally off-balance-sheet items in standard accounting practice, they belong on the economic balance sheet, since they may have a large impact on returns. Each side of a derivatives contract is synthetically long or short an asset or risk factor. But the market values of derivative securities are not equal to the value of the underlying asset, or the riskiness of the positions. Therefore, their market values or NPVs are generally not the best values to represent them. Rather, for purposes of measuring economic leverage, we wish to find, for each type of derivative, a *cash-equivalent market value*. As with most issues around the measurement and interpretation of leverage, as much judgment as science is involved.

As we discussed in Chapter 4, there are two basic types of derivatives, futures, forwards, and swaps on the one hand, and options on the other. Their use has a very different impact on leverage:

> *Futures, forwards, and swaps* are linear and symmetric in the underlying asset price and can be hedged statically. Therefore, the amount of the underlying that the derivatives contract represents is set once and for all at the initiation of the contract, even though the net present value (NPV) may vary over time. The cash-equivalent market value of futures, forwards, and swaps can be represented on an economic balance sheet by the market value of the underlying security, rather than the NPV.

> *Options* have a nonlinear relationship to the underlying asset price and must be hedged dynamically. Therefore, the amount of the underlying that the derivatives contract represents varies over time. It can be fixed approximately at any point in time by the option delta, or by a delta-gamma approximation. In general, volatility is important in the value of an option, so option contracts cannot generally have a zero NPV at initiation. Rather, it has a market value that can be decomposed into an *intrinsic value*, which may be zero, and a *time value*, which is rarely zero.
>
> The cash-equivalent market value of options can be represented on an economic balance sheet by their delta equivalents rather than their market values. As the underlying price varies, the amount of the economic balance sheet exposure, and the leverage, will vary. Measured this way, the cash-equivalent market value doesn't take the time value and volatility of the option into account, except insofar as it influences the option delta.

Like margin arrangements, derivatives also generate counterparty credit risk. If the derivative creates a synthetic long (short) position, the economic balance sheet entries mimic those of a cash long (short) position. The implicit assets and liabilities created on the economic balance sheet are vis-à-vis the derivatives counterparties.

In the rest of this section, we illustrate these principles of how best to represent derivatives positions for purposes of computing leverage.

Example 12.6 (Leverage and Derivatives) We again take as the starting point a hedge fund account with $100 in cash, corresponding to an initial placement of $100 in equity by investors. Suppose Lever Brothers now adds:

- A one month currency forward, in which Lever Brothers is short $100 against the euro
- An at-the-money (currently 50-delta) three month long call option on S&P 500 equity index futures, with an underlying index value of $100
- A short equity position expressed via a three-month equity total return swap (TRS), in which Lever Brothers pays the total return on $100 market value of Intel and the short rebate, or cost of borrowing Intel stock
- Short protection on Ford Motor Co. via a five year credit default swap, with a notional amount of $100

We assume that the nonoption positions are initiated at market-adjusted prices and spreads, and therefore have zero NPV. We'll also assume that the counterparty is the same for all the positions, namely the prime broker or broker-dealer with which they are executed.

Let's look at the economic balance sheet for each position, assuming there is no initial margin. Then we'll consolidate the positions and add a margin requirement to find Lever Brothers' overall leverage, as if margin were being assessed by a single broker or counterparty on a portfolio basis.

We start with the currency forward, which is implicitly a pair of money market positions, a long one-month euro-denominated bank deposit with a value of $100, financed by borrowing $100 for one month. Assuming the one month forward exchange rate is $1.20 per euro, we have:

Assets	Liabilities
$100 equivalent of € 80 bank deposit	$100 broker loan

The equity option, with a delta of 50 percent, is equivalent to having bought $50 worth of the S&P 500 index with a broker loan of $50:

Assets	Liabilities
$50 long S&P 500 position	$50 broker loan

The Intel TRS is equivalent to a short position in Intel stock (ticker INTC), established with no initial margin. If the price of INTC is $20, we have:

Assets	Liabilities
$100 due from broker (short sale proceeds)	Borrowed stock (5 sh INTC)

The short CDS protection position, finally, is equivalent to a long position in a par-value five year Ford floating-rate note (FRN), financed by borrowing at a floating rate at five years' term. We assume that the financing can be terminated early without penalty if there is a credit event. Its economic balance sheet is

Assets	Liabilities
$100 Ford FRN	$100 term loan

Note that the leverage in each of these transactions, if there is no initial margin requirement, is infinite.

Now let's put these positions together to get Lever Brothers' complete balance sheet. Recall that the account starts with $100 placed by investors. We make the additional assumption that the initial margin on the portfolio of these derivatives positions is $50.

Assets	Liabilities
Cash $50	Equity $100
$150 due from broker	
$50 margin	$150 short-term
$100 short sale proceeds	broker loan
$100 equivalent of	$100 term loan
€ 80 bank deposit	Borrowed stock
$50 long S&P 500 position	(5 sh INTC)
$100 Ford FRN	

The fund has attained leverage in its long positions of 3.5, plus a short position with a magnitude equal to its NAV. It has thus gained economic exposure to securities valued at $450, using only $50 in cash.

These examples illustrate a serious issue in computing and interpreting leverage ratios, which we alluded to in the context of gross and net leverage: how to treat routine hedges such as currency hedges for foreign currency-denominated positions, and risk-free rate hedges for credit-risky fixed-income positions. In general, these currency and rate exposures can be neutralized quite accurately and reliably. The currency and rate hedges, however, are of the same order of magnitude as the underlying exposures themselves, and if carried on the economic balance sheet will bloat it, distort the resulting leverage reports, and obscure the more material risks in the portfolio.

12.3.5 Structured Credit

Structured credit also provides embedded leverage. As we saw in the securitization example of Chapter 9, the bond tranches take losses only in more extreme default and correlation scenarios. The mezzanine tranche is relatively thin, so while it takes an extreme default scenario to cause any loss at all to the mezzanine tranche, if a loss occurs, it is likely to be large. This property of thin subordinated securitization tranches is called "cuspiness," since it materializes when the attachment point of the bond is at the cusp of default losses in the pool.

The equity note bears most of the risk of loss in the securitization example of Chapter 9. It has, however, a notional amount of only $5,000,000, while the underlying collateral pool is $100,000,000, financed long-term through the bond tranches. Implicitly, the balance-sheet leverage used is a bit less than 20 turns, once we take account of the residual risk borne by the bonds. If the equity note itself is financed in the repo markets, with, say, an 80 percent haircut, the economic leverage could easily reach 100.

12.3.6 Asset Volatility and Leverage

Investing in assets with a higher return volatility is economically quite similar to leverage. Ignoring the potential reputational risk, losses beyond the investor's equity in a trade don't matter to him. An asset with more volatile returns provides a higher probability of higher leveraged returns to the investor, but also a higher probability of losses to the provider of credit. The upside adds to the investor's expected return, but the downside doesn't diminish it. In other words, leverage adds optionality or convexity to the return profile. Examples of the impact of the convexity inherent in leveraged returns include:

1. An investor in assets financed with margin loans can systematically favor more-volatile over less-volatile assets within a class with the same haircut. This behavior is also an example of adverse selection.
2. Equity holders may favor greater risk-taking by a firm than do its creditors because of the risk-shifting incentives discussed in Chapter 6. Public risk policy that leads creditors of financial intermediaries to believe that they will be made whole in the event of a systematic risk event ("too-big-to-fail") reduces credit risk premiums and makes leverage

more economically appealing to equity holders, compounding the effect. We discuss this phenomenon further in the context of financial stability policies in Chapter 15.

Leverage ratios do not capture the effect of volatility on convexity, which amplifies leverage economics and can make it more attractive. At the same time, volatility estimates do not capture the funding risk of a portfolio. Both are needed for genuine insight into the risk of a portfolio.

12.4 TRANSACTIONS LIQUIDITY RISK

Next, we turn to market or transactions liquidity risk. We begin by describing what is meant when we say an asset, as opposed to a market or a market participant, is "liquid." An asset is liquid if it resembles money, in that it can be exchanged without delay for other goods and assets, and in that its value is certain.[5] Most assets other than money do not completely share these characteristics of immediacy and certainty. They cannot be exchanged directly for other goods and assets, because we don't live in a barter economy; only money can do that. Nonmoney assets must be sold or liquidated before they can be exchanged for other goods or assets. This takes at least some time, and the proceeds from the sale are uncertain to at least some extent.

Transactions liquidity includes the ability to buy or sell an asset without moving its price. An order to buy an asset increases demand and causes its price to increase. The effect is usually small, but can be large when the order causes a large transitory imbalance between the demand and supply of the asset at the initial price. A market participant can thereby be locked into a losing position by lack of market liquidity.

12.4.1 Causes of Transactions Liquidity Risk

Transaction liquidity risk is ultimately due to the cost of searching for a counterparty, to the market institutions that assist in search, and to the cost of inducing someone else to hold a position. We can classify these *market microstructure* fundamentals as follows:

> *Cost of trade processing.* Facilitating transactions, like any economic activity, has fixed and variable costs of processing, clearing,

---

[5]This is true even if there is inflation. At any moment, the holder of money knows exactly how many *nominal* units he has, even if he can't be quite sure what the *real* value of his money balances is.

and settling trades, apart from the cost of finding a counterparty and providing immediacy. These costs are tied partly to the state of technology and partly to the organization of markets. While processing may be a significant part of transaction costs, it is unlikely to contribute materially to liquidity risk. An exception is natural or man-made disasters that affect the trading infrastructure.

Inventory management by dealers. The role of dealers is to provide trade immediacy to other market participants, including other dealers. In order to provide this service, dealers must be prepared to estimate the equilibrium or market-clearing price, and to hold long or short inventories of the asset. Holding inventories exposes dealers to price risk, for which they must be compensated by price concessions. The dealers' inventory risk is fundamentally a volatility exposure and is analogous to short-term option risk.

Adverse selection. Some traders may be better informed than others, that is, better situated to forecast the equilibrium price. Dealers and market participants cannot distinguish perfectly between offers to trade arising from the counterparty's wish to reallocate into or out of cash, or responses to non-fundamental signals such as recent returns ("liquidity" or "noise" traders) from those who recognize that the prevailing price is wrong ("information" traders). A dealer cannot be sure for which of these reasons he is being shown a trade and therefore needs to be adequately compensated for this "lemons" risk through the bid-ask spread. A dealer does, however, have the advantage of superior information about the flow of trading activity, and learns early if there is a surge in buy or sell orders, or in requests for two-way prices.

Differences of opinion. Investors generally disagree about the "correct" price of an asset, or about how to interpret new information, or even about whether new information is important in assessing current prices. Investors who agree have less reason to trade with one another than investors who disagree. When agreement predominates, for example, when important and surprising information is first made public, or during times of financial stress, it is more difficult to find a counterparty.

These fundamentals take different forms in different types of market organization:

■ In a *quote-driven system*, certain intermediaries, who may be dealers, market makers, or specialists, are obliged to publicly post two-way prices or quotes and to buy or sell the asset at those prices within known transaction size limits. These intermediaries must be prepared to hold long or short inventories of the asset and typically trade heavily among themselves and with the "buy side" in order to redistribute inventories of securities and reduce them overall. Quote-driven systems are typically found in OTC markets.

■ *Order-driven* systems come closest to the perfectly competitive auction model. In this type of market clearing, market participants transmit orders to an aggregation facility, for example, a broker, specialist, or electronic trading system. In some cases, a call auction is held in which the price is gradually adjusted until the volumes of bids and offers forthcoming at that price are equated. More typically, a continuous auction is conducted in which the best bids and offers are matched, where possible, throughout the trading session. Order-driven systems are typically found on organized exchanges.

12.4.2 Characteristics of Market Liquidity

A standard set of characteristics of market liquidity, focusing primarily on asset liquidity, helps to understand the causes of illiquidity:

> *Tightness* refers to the cost of a round-trip transaction, and is typically measured by the bid-ask spread and brokers' commissions.
>
> *Depth* describes how large an order it takes to move the market adversely.
>
> *Resiliency* is the length of time for which a lumpy order moves the market away from the equilibrium price.

The latter two characteristics of markets are closely related to immediacy, the speed with which a market participant can execute a transaction.

Lack of liquidity manifests itself in these observable, if hard-to-measure ways:

> *Bid-ask spread.* If the bid-ask spread were a constant, then going long at the offer and short at the bid would be a predictable cost of doing the trade. However, the bid-ask spread can fluctuate widely, introducing a risk.
>
> *Adverse price impact* is the impact on the equilibrium price of the trader's own activity.
>
> *Slippage* is the deterioration in the market price induced by the amount of time it takes to get a trade done. If prices are trending, the market can go against the trader, even if the order is not large enough to influence the market.

These characteristics, and particularly the latter two, are hard to measure, making empirical work on market liquidity difficult. Data useful for the study of market microstructure, especially at high-frequency, are generally sparse. Bid-ask spreads are available for at least some markets, while transactions volume data is more readily available for exchange-traded than for OTC securities.

12.5 LIQUIDITY RISK MEASUREMENT

12.5.1 Measuring Funding Liquidity Risk

Asset-Liability Management Remaining liquid in the sense of reducing funding liquidity risk is part of the traditional asset-liability management function in banks. This process includes measures such as

- Tracking and forecasting available cash and sources of funding on the one hand, and cash needs on the other
- Keeping certain ratios of ready cash and readily marketable securities to meet unusual demands by depositors and other short-term lenders for the return of their money

Example 12.7 (Goldman Sachs Global Core Excess) Goldman Sachs, for example, describes its liquidity risk management policy as maintaining a "Global Core Excess"

> to pre-fund what we estimate will be our likely cash needs during a liquidity crisis and hold such excess liquidity in the form of un-encumbered, highly liquid securities that may be sold or pledged to provide same-day liquidity . . . to allow us to meet immediate obligations without needing to sell other assets or depend on additional funding from credit-sensitive markets.

The liquidity buffer accounts for about 20 percent of the balance sheet. It includes cash and a portfolio of securities that can be pledged as collateral rather than sold.[6]

Apart from cash, liquidity portfolios can contain cash equivalents, defined in the International Accounting Standards as "short-term, highly liquid

---

[6]See Goldman Sachs Group, Inc. (2010).

investments that are readily convertible to known amounts of cash and which are subject to an insignificant risk of changes in value."

Funding Liquidity Management for Hedge Funds Hedge funds, even if only moderately leveraged, are vulnerable to the withdrawal of liquidity, either by counterparties or through withdrawals of investor capital. Both have the same effect of potentially obliging the fund manager to unwind positions rapidly and generating exposure to transactions liquidity risk. When this happens to many funds at the same time, it can contribute to "fire sales," a financial crisis phenomenon we discuss in Chapter 14.

Hedge funds have a number of sources of liquidity that can be monitored as part of overall risk management:

Cash provides unfettered liquidity. It can be held in the form of money market accounts or Treasury bills. Excess cash balances with brokers and money market accounts are not entirely riskless and therefore are not perfectly liquid. Broker balances carry with them the counterparty risk of the broker; in the event the broker fails, the cash balances will be immobilized for a time and only a fraction may ultimately be paid out. Money market funds, as was demonstrated during the subprime crisis, may suspend redemptions or "break the buck" and pay out at less than 100 percent of par.

Unpledged assets (or assets "in the box") are unencumbered assets not currently used as collateral. They are generally also held with a broker, who in this case is acting only as a custodian and not as a credit provider.

This source of liquidity is limited by the price volatility of the assets and the ability to use the assets as collateral. In a financial crisis, only U.S. Treasuries, particularly short-term Treasuries, will be liquid enough to serve as near-cash assets. Other high-credit quality assets, such as U.S. agency bonds, that is, bonds issued by Fannie Mae and Freddie Mac, were less reliable stores of value during the subprime crisis. The usefulness of bonds other than Treasuries and agencies to serve as collateral and the ability to obtain funding by pledging them was also impaired during the crisis, as seen for agency debt in Figure 12.4 above. Haircuts on such debt were reportedly also rising.

Assets can be sold rather than pledged. This alternative route to liquidity is limited by the likely proceeds from a sale. In a distressed market, these may be far lower than recent market prices or a model-based fair value. Thus, as a source of funding liquidity, unpledged assets are subject not only to fluctuations in the amount of borrowing they can support, but also to transactions liquidity risk.

Unused borrowing capacity on pledged assets can be used to finance additional positions. Like unpledged assets, this form of liquidity is not unfettered. Rather, it is subject to revocation by counterparties, who may raise haircuts or decline to accept the securities as collateral when the time comes to roll over a collateralized securities loan. Since most of these collateralized loans are very short term, credit can disappear rapidly. This occurred for many lower-quality forms of collateral during the subprime crisis.

However, a systemic risk event, in which hedge fund investments are regarded as potential sources of liquidity by investors, will be a challenge even for most effective liquidity risk management. We referred to this phenomenon earlier in this chapter: Many hedge funds that had not experienced large losses received redemption requests for precisely that reason from investors who were themselves seeking liquidity.

12.5.2 Measuring Transactions Liquidity Risk

There are two major types of quantitative liquidity risk measures. They focus on the available data that are pertinent to liquidity risk:

- Bid-ask data
- Transaction or turnover volume data
- Data on the size outstanding of securities issues

Quantitative measures of transactions liquidity risk are not as widely used as funding liquidity risk measures, and quantitative liquidity risk measurement is generally less widely practiced than quantitative market and credit risk. Partly, this is because they have not been incorporated into the regulatory framework to the same extent as have standard models of market and credit risk measurement. As we see in Chapter 15, regulators have focused more intently on banks' liquidity risk since the onset of the subprime crisis. Partly, it is due to the measurement challenges alluded to above.

Transaction Cost Liquidity Risk These measures focus on the risk of variation in transactions costs. The starting point is a distributional hypothesis regarding the future bid-ask spread.

Daily changes in the relative bid-ask spread, that is, the spread as a fraction of the price, can be assumed as a starting point to be normally distributed with a mean of zero and a constant variance (estimated by the sample variance of the spread σ_s). The zero-mean assumption at least is unobjectionable, since bid-ask spreads cannot rise indefinitely or shrink to zero. The expected transactions cost is the half-spread or mid-to-bid spread

$$E[P_{t+1}]\frac{\bar{s}}{2}$$

where

$$s = 2\frac{\text{ask price} - \text{bid price}}{\text{ask price} + \text{bid price}} = \frac{\text{ask price} - \text{bid price}}{\text{midprice}}$$

$\bar{s}$ is an estimate of the expected or typical bid-ask spread, and P is the asset midprice.

Under the zero-mean normality hypothesis, we set $\bar{s} = s$, the most recent observation on the relative spread. The 99 percent confidence interval on the transactions cost, in dollars per unit of the asset, is then

$$\pm \bar{P}\frac{1}{2}(\bar{s} + 2.33\sigma_s)$$

where $\bar{P}$ is an estimate of the next-day asset midprice. We typically set $\bar{P} = P$, the most recent observation on price. We refer to $\frac{1}{2}(\bar{s} + 2.33\sigma_s)$ as the 99 percent *spread risk factor*.

The transactions cost risk at a 99 percent confidence level is then measured by the current value of the spread risk factor, that is, by the 99th percentile of the actual proportional daily changes in the half-spread over a given historical period, say, the past two years. It represents the worst case, at a 99 percent confidence level, of the bid-ask spread cost of changing a position.

Measuring the Risk of Adverse Price Impact   A tool for measuring the risk of adverse price impact is *liquidity-adjusted VaR*. The starting point is an estimate of the number of trading days, T, required for the orderly liquidation of a position. If the position is liquidated in equal parts at the end of each day, the trader faces a one-day holding period on the entire position, a two-day holding period on a fraction $\frac{T-1}{T}$ of the position, a three-day holding period on a fraction $\frac{T-2}{T}$ of the position, and so forth if he wishes to liquidate the position with no adverse price impact.

The next step is to arrive at an estimate of the one-day position VaR. Suppose the entire position X were being held for T days. The T-day VaR would be estimated by the familiar square-root-of-time rule:

$$\text{VaR}_t\left(\alpha, \frac{1}{252}\right)(X) \times \sqrt{1^2 + 1^2 + \cdots + 1^2} = \text{VaR}_t(\alpha, \tau)(X) \times \sqrt{T}$$

However, this would be an overstatement of the VaR; the VaR has to be greater than the one-day position VaR, but less than the one-day position VaR$\times\sqrt{T}$. We will be holding a sequence of position sizes $1, \frac{T-1}{T}, \frac{T-2}{T}, \ldots, \frac{T-2}{T}$, rather than $1, 1, \ldots, 1$, all with the same variance. The VaR is therefore

$$
\mathrm{VaR}_t\left(\alpha, \frac{1}{252}\right)(X) \times \sqrt{1 + \left(\frac{T-1}{T}\right)^2 + \left(\frac{T-2}{T}\right)^2 + \cdots + \left(\frac{1}{T}\right)^2}
$$

$$
= \mathrm{VaR}_t\left(\alpha, \frac{1}{252}\right)(X) \times \sqrt{\sum_{t=1}^{T}\left(1 - \frac{t-1}{T}\right)^2}
$$

which simplifies to

$$
\mathrm{VaR}_t\left(\alpha, \frac{1}{252}\right)(X) \times \sqrt{\frac{(1 + T)(1 + 2T)}{6T}}
$$

For example, suppose the trader estimates that a position can be liquidated in $T = 5$ trading days. The adjustment to the overnight VaR of the position is then 1.48324, that is, we increase the VaR by 48 percent. For $T \approx 10$, the liquidity risk adjustment doubles the overnight VaR of the position. These adjustments are large by comparison with the transaction cost liquidity risk measures of the previous section. Estimates of the time to liquidate or "time to escape" are usually based on a comparison of the position size with the daily transactions volume.

In extreme cases, or during financial crises, there may be several constraints on liquidation decisions. There may be trade-offs among adverse price impact, funding liquidity, and solvency. An example is that of a hedge fund facing redemptions. It must liquidate some positions to meet redemptions. Suppose it liquidates those with the smallest adverse price impact first, but redemptions continue. The fund may face collapse because it can not meet the ongoing withdrawals by quickly selling the remaining, relatively illiquid positions. If, on the other hand, it sells the least liquid positions first, it will incur losses due to adverse price impact, and likely post NAV losses earlier on, which may accelerate redemptions.

Liquidation decisions may also interact with the incentive structure of credit markets. An example of this is the "sellers' strike" observed early in the subprime crisis, in which banks were reluctant to reduce leverage by selling certain positions, often referred to as "toxic assets," primarily structured credit products and mortgage loans. However, prices for these products were falling rapidly, and the banks were reluctant to realize losses at market valuations many considered to be well below fundamental value. The paradox of this phenomenon is that it was stronger banks that were the most active sellers, while the weaker banks were more inclined to hold back. By avoiding sales, weak banks increased the probability of illiquidity and possibly failure in the short run, but increased the potential profit from these assets in the long run once their prices recovered. In other words, they had an option-like position in the assets. The longer-term profit was conditional on the banks' survival through the crisis and on the fundamental values of the assets proving to be higher than their current market prices.

12.6 LIQUIDITY AND SYSTEMIC RISK

Systemic risk, the risk of severe, widespread financial stress and intermediary failure, possibly including disruption of payment systems, is a function among other things of economy-wide liquidity.

Systemic risk can be thought of as resulting from *external costs* in the production of financial services, analogous to pollution or traffic jams. Market participants, in this approach, incur risks that are partially shifted to the market as a whole. These collectively borne risks are generated by correlation between the impact of market events on different market participants. When general market conditions deteriorate, many borrowers are affected in the same way at the same time. One way this happens is when the value of collateral declines, or lenders become more concerned about the transactions liquidity risk of certain types of collateral. Another way many borrowers can be affected at once is when the market becomes more reluctant to finance certain types of trades or lend to certain types of institutions. Finally, asset price declines may contribute to the simultaneous deterioration of different market participants' financial positions.

Liquidity is ephemeral for many securities. It tends to become impaired at precisely the moments when market participants most need it. Liquidity is a result of network effects and mutually reinforcing expectations that are hard to capture quantitatively. A well-functioning market can depend on whether the market will "all hold hands," or not, and on whether enough market makers will make two-way prices they would be willing to honor in actual transactions.

12.6.1 Funding Liquidity and Solvency

Liquidity is the ability to meet immediate demand for cash. Solvency is having a positive amount of equity capital, that is, assets exceeding liabilities. Liquidity and solvency are closely related, since both pertain to the ability to repay debts. But a firm can be insolvent, yet able to continue for some time to roll over its debts, or may funded largely by long-term debt, and thus not face illiquidity. A firm may be solvent, that is, able to pay its long-term debt, because its assets will ultimately be worth more than its liabilities, but illiquid, since it cannot roll over short-term debt or raise enough cash to repay it timely. Liquidity and solvency are linked by asset values; large changes in the mark-to-market value of assets can expose a solvent financial intermediary to illiquidity.

Illiquidity can become insolvency if it is extreme enough, as a debtor can become unable to either borrow or realize the funds required to meet debt obligations by selling assets. Because intermediaries are not transparent—the asymmetric information problem of Chapter 6—liquidity and solvency are also linked by market perceptions about the state of intermediaries. The suspicion by market participants that a financial firm is insolvent can lead to that firm becoming illiquid. At the time of the bankruptcies of Bear Stearns and Lehman Brothers, and to this day, there was a great deal of debate of whether one or both firms were insolvent, or merely illiquid.

During the financial crisis, both illiquidity and insolvency played a role in causing the collapse of financial institutions. Schematically, the sequence of events in the collapse of an intermediary can be described this way:

- Reports of losses at the intermediary, or even losses to other institutions, raise questions about the firm's solvency. Actual losses at the intermediary are not necessary to set the process in motion.
- All firms, financial intermediaries as well as nonfinancial firms, become more reluctant to lend to the intermediary. The reluctance is reflected not only in higher credit spreads, but more importantly, in an inability of the affected firm to obtain the previous volume of loan proceeds.
- The intermediary is forced to raise cash by liquidating assets. In a distressed market, the firm is likely to realize losses by doing so.
- Lenders are aware that the intermediary's problems are now being compounded by realized mark-to-market losses, further reducing their willingness to extend credit.
- The process now accelerates, becoming a run. Lenders to the intermediary act out of the belief that it is insolvent and that they will be repaid in full only if they are repaid early. The intermediary cannot instantly liquidate its remaining assets for the full amount it owes. Within a very few days, the intermediary will be unable to meet the demand for cash.

It is the drain of cash, not defaults, that destroy the firm. But it is questionable whether a pure liquidity event, unaccompanied by even the shadow of a doubt about its solvency, can occur for one firm in isolation. We look at the mechanics of runs, and the role they play in financial crises, in Chapter 14.

We discuss the regulatory approach to the distinction between liquidity and solvency in Chapter 15 in our treatment of capital and reserve requirements and minimum liquidity ratios.

12.6.2 Funding and Market Liquidity

A key mechanism linking funding and market liquidity is leverage. A market participant with a long position for which it can no longer obtain funding is forced to sell. If funding has become tight in the market as a whole, the set of potential holders of the asset will be reduced. This mechanism depresses the asset price, regardless of its expected future cash flows. The effect may only be transitory, but "transitory" may be a relatively long time, and may affect the solvency of the initial holder of the asset during that period. This mechanism becomes most evident during financial crises. Rapid deleveraging causes a "debt-deflation crisis," which we discuss in more detail in Chapter 14.

Mark-to-market risk combines aspects of market and credit risk. It is often the case that the holding period of an asset, or the time horizon of a trade, is quite long. The investor or trader, however, may be required to report frequently the values of assets and liabilities.

Market liquidity can constrain funding liquidity. As we saw just above in describing the liquidation dilemma of a hedge fund facing redemptions, a market participant obliged to sell assets in order to raise cash faces a choice about what assets to sell first: those with the greatest or the least market liquidity. Such situations are most liable to arise during times of heightened financial fragility and distress, when there are many other traders in a similar situation, and possibly with a similar portfolio. The key trade-off is that by selling the most liquid assets first, the market participant incurs the smallest adverse impact, but left with a more illiquid portfolio with which to face any continuing funding liquidity pressure. If, instead, he sells illiquid assets first, the realized losses increase the real or perceived risk of insolvency, and may therefore worsen the funding liquidity pressure.

12.6.3 Systemic Risk and the "Plumbing"

An important channel through which liquidity risk events can become systemic risk events is through problems in the payments, clearing, and settlements systems. Disruptions in these systems, often called the "plumbing" of the financial system, can be systemic risk events in their own right, or amplify an initial market or credit risk event into a systemic problem. These systems, called *financial market infrastructures* or *utilities* in contemporary regulatory parlance, include securities exchanges, clearinghouses, securities depositories and settlement systems, and payment systems. A disruption of any of these can impact many market participants simultaneously, and illiquidity or insolvency of one counterparty can have downstream effects on others through these systems.

The *tri-party repo system* is a relatively recently developed infrastructure that has rapidly gained in importance in the past decade. It differs from conventional repo in that securities are held in custody by a third party, almost always one of two major *clearing banks*, Bank of New York Mellon (BNY) and JPMorgan Chase. In the tri-party repo cycle, the counterparty borrowing cash collateralized by securities deposits the securities with the custodian, while the counterparty lending cash deposits the funds with the custodian. The custodian sees to it that the funds are made available to the borrower and maintains the securities in a segregated account so that they can be seized without delay by the lender should the borrower default.

Most tri-party repo transactions are short-term, often overnight. However, they are typically renewed regularly at maturity, so they become a part of the longer-term financing mix of the borrower. Tri-party repo is typically used by securities firms to finance securities portfolios. Funding, that is, cash collateral, is typically provided by money market mutual funds, insurance companies, and other institutional investors.

Tri-party repo has grown enormously over the past two decades, along with repo markets in general, as seen in Figure 12.3, reaching a volume of $2.8 trillion of securities financed by early 2008, encompassing a wide range of security types as collateral. Two reasons for this growth are economies of scale in clearing, which are generated in part by the greater scope for book-entry transactions rather than delivering securities, and the desirability of third-party custody of securities.

However, the mechanics of tri-party repo also involve liquidity risks. Like most repo contracts, much tri-party repo has a one-day term. Regardless of the term of the repo, each transaction is unwound daily. The clearing bank returns the securities to the account of the securities lender/borrower of cash, generally a large broker-dealer, and the cash to the account of the securities borrower/lender of cash. The clearing bank in effect finances the dealer, generally a broker-dealer financing its securities inventory, by permitting a *daylight overdraft*. Thus, apart from clearing and custody services, the custodial bank provides intraday credit to the borrower of cash, collateralized by the securities. The custodial bank thereby assumes an exposure to the cash borrower; that is, the counterparty credit risk that the value of the collateral, if liquidated, will not be enough to cover the debt.

A number of funding liquidity risks are inherent in this process. A clearing bank might decline credit to one of its customers, provoking or amplifying a rollover risk event for the customer. The lenders of cash might decline to leave cash with a clearing bank, or might withdraw from the repo market generally. Tri-party repo is not only large, but concentrated; three dealers accounted for 38 percent of outstanding tri-party repo in early 2010. The default of a large dealer would likely trigger the immediate sale of the securities in its account that collateralize its intraday overdraft. The mere possibility that the dealer's account is undercollateralized would also call the clearing bank's liquidity and solvency into question. While these systemic risk events have not materialized, the risks were among the background factors in the Federal Reserve's introduction the Primary Dealer Credit Facility (PDCF) on March 17, 2008, during the run on Bear Stearns. The PDCF provided primary dealers with access to collateralized overnight funding.

12.6.4 "Interconnectedness"

Credit transactions, as we have now seen, take myriad forms. The set of market participants involved as either borrowers or lenders in at least some credit transactions includes most adults and every firm, including nonfinancial firms, even in less-developed economies. Credit relationships form a network in which each entity is a creditor and debtor of numerous other entities. Each entity's creditworthiness depends, therefore, in part on the creditworthiness of its obligors. If debts owed to a firm become uncollectible, it may become unable to pay its own creditors.

Financial intermediaries are the most enmeshed entities in this network, since they specialize in intermediating savings between lenders and borrowers and have leveraged balance sheets in which the bulk of the assets are debt of another entity. We have discussed the counterparty risks that arise from these networks, focusing on the standpoint of an individual firm managing these risks. Counterparty risk also has an important systemic risk aspect; a decline in the creditworthiness of its borrowers imperils the financial intermediaries' own creditworthiness.

Another aspect of interconnectedness is the prevalence in contemporary finance of long intermediation chains involving securitization, off-balance sheet vehicles, and MMMFs, in addition to traditional intermediaries. Some observers view these chains as proliferating potential points of failure in the financial system. The complexity of intermediation can make itself known in surprising ways, drawing attention to vulnerabilities that had not previously been widely identified, such as the hedge fund losses on securities in custody with Lehman during its bankruptcy. The web of credit thereby makes credit risk a matter of public policy and concern, as we see in Chapter 15, as well as a phenomenon for firms to cope with.

FURTHER READING

Greenbaum and Thakor (2007) provides a textbook introduction to financial intermediation by banks and other institutions. Much of the literature on intermediation tries to explain why commercial banks are so prominent in the financial landscape. Diamond and Dybvig (1983) and Diamond (1984) are classic papers on depository institutions. Diamond (1984) explains banks' prominence in intermediation from an information cost viewpoint. Diamond and Dybvig (1983) focuses on random fluctuations in households' need for cash to explain the susceptibility of banks to panics and runs. Diamond (1996, 2007) are accessible presentations of the theory in these papers. A counterpoint is provided by Calomiris and Kahn (1991) and Randall (1993), which argue that uninsured depositors also provide some restraint on excessive risk-taking by banks. Acharya, Gale, and Yorulmazer (2009) presents a model of rollover risk and an application to the subprime crisis. Goodhart (1990), 89ff., and Cowen and Kroszner (1990) discuss payment services provided by mutual funds with varying market values as an alternative to deposit banking based on par-value redemption.

Allen and Santomero (1997), and Dowd (1992) are critical surveys of this literature, testing its relevance against the evolution of finance from a banking-focused to a market-focused system.

The treatment of money as an asset among others in explaining the demand for money—or, in any event, the term "liquidity preference—goes back at least to Keynes (1936). Haberler (1958) is a history, by a participant, in the debates on the theory of money in their relationship to business cycles, up to and including Keynes. The classic "modern" exposition is Tobin (1958).

Developments in the commercial paper market leading up to and during the subprime crisis are discussed in Anderson and Gascon (2009), and in Adrian, Kimbrough, and Marchioni (2010). Pozsar, Adrian, Ashcraft, and Boesky (2010); Covitz, Liang, and Suarez (2009); Arteta, Carey, Correa, and Kotter (2010); and Acharya and Schnabl (forthcoming) provide details on leverage through ABCP conduits and SIVs and examples of specific vehicles. These papers also chronicle the unraveling of these vehicles during the subprime crisis and their contribution to its intensification.

Examples of the role of liquidity in the impact of the subprime crisis on specific investment strategies can be studied in Mitchell, Pedersen, and Pulvino (2007) (convertible bond arbitrage) and Khandani and Lo (2008) (statistical arbitrage). Case studies of the relationship of payments, clearing, and settlements system to systemic risk include Bernanke (1990) and Copeland, Martin, and Walker (2010).

The development of collateral markets and their role in financial developments leading up to the subprime crisis are reviewed in a series of papers including Gorton (2008, 2009), and Gorton and Metrick (2010). The role of rehypothecation in financial markets is emphasized in Singh and Aitken (2010). Shin (2009*b*) discusses the impact of the supply of securitizations on the volume of credit and of aggregate leverage.

Institutional aspects of collateral markets, particularly the mechanics of shorting and lending stock, are discussed in Weiss (2006) and D'Avolio (2002). Institutional and legal aspects of rehypothecation are discussed in Johnson (1997).

Breuer (2002) discusses the measurement of derivatives leverage. Carry trades in currency markets are discussed in Brunnermeier, Nagel, and Pedersen (2009), and in Clarida, Davis, and Pedersen (2009). Adrian and Shin (2009*a*, 2009*b*), and King (2008) discuss the increase in broker-dealer leverage during the years leading up to the subprime crisis. King (2008) in particular, explains how these transactions can be kept off-balance sheet, and provides a guide to extracting additional information on repo exposures from the footnotes to broker-dealer disclosures other than the balance sheet.

Introductions to market microstructure are provided by Stoll (2003) and O'Hara (1995). Demsetz (1968), Kyle (1985), and Amihud and Mendelson (1986) are important early papers on transactions liquidity. See Black (1986) and Shleifer and Summers (1990) on noise versus information trading. Madhavan (2000) and Madhavan (2002) are good starting points for the institutional background of transactions liquidity. Amihud, Mendelson, and Pedersen (2005) is an extensive survey focusing on transactions liquidity. Chordia, Roll, and Subrahmanyam (2001) focuses on volume data. Committee on the Global Financial System (1999*b*) is an introductory survey and review of policy issues, while Basel Committee on Banking Supervision (2000) presents recommendations on liquidity risk management.

Several papers, for example, Almgren and Chriss (2000, 2001), discuss trading and investment in the presence of market liquidity risk. Duffie and Ziegler (2003) treat the problem of whether to liquidate more- or less-liquid assets first in a liquidity risk event. Diamond and Rajan (2010) discuss the 2008 sellers strike. See also Acerbi and Finger (2010).

Hicks (1962) is an early treatment of the relationship between funding and market liquidity. Brunnermeier and Pedersen (2009) present a model of their interaction in stress scenarios. Brunnermeier, Nagel, and Pedersen (2009) discusses funding liquidity, together with fat-tailed returns, as an explanation of the option biases discussed in Chapter 10.

See Morgan Guaranty Trust Company (1996) and Marrison (2002) for a discussion of asset-liability management. Senior Supervisors Group (2009*b*) discusses liquidity risk management lessons from the subprime crisis.

CHAPTER **13**

Risk Control and Mitigation

he purpose of having accurate risk measurement tools is to benefit traders
and investors. In this chapter, we tie together the modeling tools we have
developed and see how to move from risk measurement to risk management.
Ultimately, the benefits of risk measurement come from putting investors in
a better position to make tradeoffs between risk and return, and between different aspects of risk. Some investors may be more tolerant of volatility, but
quite sensitive to the risk of large losses. If adequately compensated, other
investors may prefer exposure to large losses, but remain averse to volatility,
a risk profile characterizing some option portfolios and senior securitized
credit products. Metaphorically, one can imagine investors choosing distributions of returns they prefer over distributions that are inferior from their
point of view. It is only a metaphor, in view of the problems in maintaining a distributional hypothesis on returns that we've encountered in earlier
chapters. Among the risk management objectives market participants might
have are:

Reduce volatility of portfolio returns, including any hedges.

Diversification. Risk measurement tools can be used to ensure the portfolio does not contain any undesired concentrations and to identify
exposures to extreme economic scenarios.

Left-tail truncation. Identifying extreme-loss scenarios and the positions that contribute to them can guide investors to reducing the
extreme losses with only a small sacrifice of—or even an increase
in—expected return.

Groping towards optimum. Risk management tools can help investors
quantify risk-reward trade-offs and identify trades that improve
their return distributions.

Sizing of trades in accordance with the risk takers' goals. As we have
seen in Chapter 2 and will explore further here, the size of a position
is not linearly related to its impact on the risk of a portfolio.

477

Selection of risk factors in accordance with the risk takers' goals. Hedging can reduce or eliminate undesired exposures you don't want, such as foreign-exchange risk in a global equity portfolio.

The improvement in investment results that can be achieved through risk management is sometimes called the "risk management alpha."

Risk measurement can help in several ways that are related to the allocation of *risk capital* or to hedging. The concept of risk capital is central to the *risk budgeting* approach to asset management, in which a desired risk level is chosen for a fund or portfolio, and allocated to a set of asset managers, or to the risk factors or positions to which the portfolio is exposed.

13.1 DEFINING RISK CAPITAL

The term "capital" has a number of meanings in business and economics. In economic theory, it refers to intermediate goods, natural resources that have been combined with labor and are capable of producing consumption goods or other intermediate goods. The consumption goods have utility, so capital goods have value "stored" within them. In accounting theory, capital can refer to all of the resources marshalled by a firm, including both liabilities and owners' equity, or only the latter. Owners' equity is the share of a firm's assets that belongs to the firm's owners. It is defined as a residual, once the liabilities to outside parties are accounted for.

In finance generally, "capital" sometimes refers to assets that generate income by being invested and placed at risk. In this sense, it is closer to the economists' definition. In other contexts, "capital" refers to a stock of assets that buffer a business against bankruptcy, a sense that is closer to the accountants' definition of equity. For large complex financial intermediaries, it can be difficult to distinguish between pure liabilities and owners' equity or the buffer stock, as some hybrid securities, such as preferred shares, have characteristics both of debt (fixed obligations to outsiders) and equity (residual interests of owners).

For hedge funds and other pooled investment vehicles such as mutual funds and ETFs, the notion of equity capital is unambiguous: It is the net asset value (NAV) of the funds placed with the fund's management by investors. The NAV is the amount available to be withdrawn in cash by investors, at the most recent valuation of the positions.[1]

The notion of risk capital has elements of all these definitions. We define it as an asset reserve earmarked to cover the largest acceptable loss with a given confidence level: that is, a quantile of the portfolio's or firm's

---

[1]Investors actually withdrawing funds will have to do so within the agreed restrictions placed on withdrawals by the hedge fund, and net of fees.

loss distribution. This definition is closely related to the definition of VaR as the largest loss possible at a given confidence level. Similarly to VaR, other things being equal, imposing a higher confidence level implies that a higher loss level can be tolerated. However, the notion of risk capital, like that of VaR, is not tied to any specific distributional hypothesis, or to a view that VaR can be reliably measured.

In financial firms, equity capital plays a particularly important role, because their balance sheets are part of the production process of intermediation and payment services. A financial firm may lose its ability to raise debt or be seized by regulators long before it becomes bankrupt, or its equity value reaches zero, so a purely bankruptcy-oriented definition of risk capital is not adequate. Most financial firms have far higher leverage than the typical nonfinancial firm, so capital must be carefully managed.

Risk capital is a tool for translating loss measures into equity terms. Acquiring assets puts capital at risk, all the more so when acquired by using borrowed funds. Measuring the risk to equity capital is thus a different approach to measuring risk that is directly related to profitability and the ability to continue the business.

The risk capital approach doesn't necessary take an accounting measure of equity as a starting point. It can rely on a "shadow" measure of equity attributed to a portfolio or other activity, rather than on a balance sheet quantity. It can thereby be applied to entities that don't have an individual corporate existence. The risk capital of a portfolio or an activity is the amount of capital needed to absorb a given loss. It is defined so that, even in an extreme event, the firm, strategy, or account will not lose 100 percent of its capital. A risk capital framework thus requires us to set a loss tolerance, a time horizon for the loss to occur, and a probability or confidence interval with which the loss will not be exceeded over the time horizon. A higher confidence level then requires that we hold more risk capital, so we can be more certain that it will be greater than potential losses.

"Acceptable" can mean very different things to different types of investors or intermediaries. For a nonfinancial corporation, it may mean the largest loss that falls short of triggering insolvency. For a bank or other financial intermediary, it may mean a loss that falls well short of triggering bankruptcy, seizure by bank supervisors, large-scale depositor runs, or investor redemptions. An unacceptable loss may thus be one with implications for liquidity as well as solvency (see Chapter 12). For a pension fund, it might mean the largest loss that still leaves the fund overwhelmingly likely to be able to meet its pension obligations in the future. However, all of these firms have in common that there is some level of loss that would mean the end of their business or would be in some other respect catastrophic.

The first task of risk capital measurement is thus to define that level of loss and to construct a portfolio for which the likelihood of its occurrence is less than the confidence level. Every investor faces the task, in some form, of quantifying the threshold at which loss becomes catastrophic, and having a portfolio that has at least enough "safe" investments or is constructed in such a way as to avoid it.

Risk capital can also be defined for subportfolios and individual positions as their largest acceptable loss, as well as at the level of a firm or an entire portfolio. One of the issues we discuss in this chapter is how a total pool of risk capital can be allocated to individual investments. It hinges on how we measure the impact on the total risk capital of a single investment or subportfolio. In other words, how much of the total risk capital does it "use up"? To answer this, we need to understand the diversification impact of adding to or subtracting from the position or subportfolio.

This leads to the second key task of risk capital measurement: how the parts relate to the whole. How can we set risk capital in such a way that the risk capital allocations to individual positions, subportfolios, or activities are sensible, but also add up to the total risk capital of the firm? These are large questions, and we endeavor in this chapter to answer them in a small way, within the framework of the standard market risk model developed in Chapters 2 through 5.

13.2   RISK CONTRIBUTIONS

We begin with the second task, finding how much of the total risk in a portfolio is contributed by one position. For example, if a portfolio manager is told to reduce his risk, he needs to know how much risk, if any, he can take off by unwinding a given amount of a specific position. In some cases, risk at the portfolio level could actually be increased by the position reduction. Similarly, an asset manager may want to know how and how much the risk of the portfolio will change if he changes the allocation.

We'll define *risk contributions*, starting with the simplest case, a long-only asset manager who allocates assets to two types of security, stocks and bonds. There are a number of ways to define a risk contribution, depending on which standard-model risk measure we use, for example, the portfolio variance, volatility, or VaR. It also depends on how we vary the exposure: Do we increase it by a little bit, or do we remove it entirely from the portfolio? Two useful formal concepts here are:

- **Incremental VaR**, the contribution of an entire position to the total VaR: How much does the portfolio risk change if I add or unwind an entire position?
- **Marginal VaR**, the derivative of the VaR with respect to the size of a position; what happens to risk if I increase or reduce a position by a small amount?

13.2.1   Risk Contributions in a Long-Only Portfolio

In a two-asset allocation problem, assuming asset-class returns are jointly normally distributed, the variance of portfolio returns as a percent of initial market value is given by

$$\sigma_p^2 = \omega_1^2\sigma_1^2 + \omega_2^2\sigma_2^2 + 2\omega_1\omega_2\sigma_1\sigma_2\rho \qquad (13.1)$$

The portfolio shares invested in stocks ($m = 1$) and bonds ($m = 2$) are denoted ω_m, with $\omega_1 + \omega_2 = 1$. Stock and bond returns have volatilities σ_1 and σ_2, and a correlation ρ, and the portfolio volatility is σ_p. We assume that only long positions are taken, so $\omega_m \geq 0, m = 1, 2$. This expression should be familiar from our discussion of diversification in Chapter 2 and of portfolio VaR in Chapter 5. The τ-period VaR at a confidence level of α is given by

$$\text{VaR}(\alpha, \tau) = -z_*\sqrt{\tau}\sigma_p$$

where z_* is the ordinate of $N(0, 1)$ corresponding to the selected confidence level α. This expression employs the arithmetic approximation of the delta-normal approach, as in Equation (3.3) or (5.1). For the rest of this section, we simplify the notation by setting the time horizon to one year, so the square-root-of-time term drops out.

The *marginal variance* is found by differentiating Equation (13.1) with respect to the ω_m:

$$\frac{\partial\sigma_p^2}{\partial\omega_m} = 2\omega_m\sigma_m^2 + 2\omega_n\sigma_1\sigma_2\rho \qquad m \neq n; m, n = 1, 2$$

We can find the change in portfolio volatility by applying the chain rule of calculus. With f and g proper functions of a (possibly) vector-valued argument x, the chain rule states

$$\frac{d}{dx}f[g(x)] = f'(g(x))g'(x)$$

Setting

$$g(x) = \sigma_p^2$$

a function of $\boldsymbol{\omega} = (\omega_1, \omega_2)$, and

$$f(g) = \sqrt{g} \quad \Rightarrow \quad f'(g) = \frac{1}{2}\frac{1}{\sqrt{g}}$$

In other words, the volatility is treated as a function of the variance in computing the derivative, to get the volatility contribution defined as the *marginal volatility*, the contribution of position m to the standard deviation of portfolio returns, measured in dollars:

$$\frac{\partial \sigma_p}{\partial \omega_m} = \frac{1}{2}\frac{1}{\sqrt{\sigma_p^2}}\frac{\partial \sigma_p^2}{\partial \omega_i}$$

$$= \frac{1}{\sigma_p}(\omega_m\sigma_m^2 + \omega_n\sigma_1\sigma_2\rho) \qquad m \neq n; m,n = 1,2$$

So far, we have defined risk contribution as the marginal impact on portfolio variance or volatility. We can however, also define a marginal contribution to VaR by simply taking a different quantile than the one-sigma quantile. The *marginal VaR* is:

$$\frac{\partial \text{VaR}(\alpha,\tau)}{\partial \omega_m} = -z_*\frac{1}{\sigma_p}(\omega_m\sigma_m^2 + \omega_n\sigma_1\sigma_2\rho) \qquad m \neq n; m,n = 1,2$$

The marginal VaR or volatility is the rate at which an increase in allocation to position m increases VaR or volatility. The analogues to the risk contribution metrics presented here can all be computed for expected shortfall as well as for variance, volatility, and VaR. These quantities can also be computed in a simulation as opposed to an analytic/algebraic framework.

The marginal risk contributions have a very useful property, which we will exploit in our discussion of risk capital. As we saw in Chapter 11, VaR is a *homogeneous function* of the investment amounts in the portfolio. As it happens, the portfolio variance and volatility are homogeneous functions of the allocations $\{\omega_2, \omega_1\}$, too.[2]

Specifically, the portfolio variance is homogeneous of degree 2, and the volatility and VaR are linearly homogeneous; if all the allocations double, that is, the total investment rises from x to $2x$, and the fractions allocated to stocks and bonds are not altered, the variance will quadruple, while the dollar volatility and the VaR will double. The marginal variance, volatility, and VaR therefore have the convenient *Euler property*:

- The sum of the marginal variances of the bond and stock allocations, each multiplied by its allocation, is equal to twice the portfolio variance:

$$\sum_{1,2}\omega_m\frac{\partial \sigma_p^2}{\partial \omega_m} = 2\left(\sum_{1,2}\omega_m^2\sigma_m^2 + 2\omega_m\omega_n\sigma_1\sigma_2\rho\right)$$

$$= 2\sigma_p^2$$

[2]Appendix A.6 provides formal statements and proofs of these properties.

- The sum of the marginal volatilities of the bond and stock allocations, each multiplied by its allocation, is equal to the portfolio volatility:

$$\sum_{1,2} \omega_m \frac{\partial \sigma_p}{\partial \omega_m} = \frac{1}{\sigma_p} \sum_{1,2} \omega_m \left(\omega_m \sigma_m^2 + \omega_n \sigma_1 \sigma_2 \rho \right)$$

$$= \frac{1}{\sigma_p} \left(\omega_1^2 \sigma_1^2 + \omega_2^2 \sigma_2^2 + 2\omega_1 \omega_2 \sigma_1 \sigma_2 \rho \right)$$

$$= \sigma_p$$

These allocation-weighted risk contributions are sometimes called the *component* variances, volatilities, and VaR. The component VaR or volatility turns the marginal rate per additional dollar or percent allocated into an amount in dollars.

- The sum of the marginal VaRs of the bond and stock allocations is equal to the portfolio VaR, $z_* \sigma_p$. This is obvious, since the volatility contributions are just the marginal VaRs for $\alpha = 0.8413$, the confidence level at which $z_* = -1.0$.

A final property of the risk contributions can be seen by dividing each component risk contribution by the total risk to get the shares of each risk contribution to the total risk, as measured by variance, volatility, or VaR. The sum of these for the variance is 2, while the sum for the volatility and VaR is 1. We can see this by simply dividing the expressions above through by the respective total risk measure:

$$\frac{1}{\sigma_p^2} \sum_{1,2} \omega_m \frac{\partial \sigma_p^2}{\partial \omega_m} = 2 \qquad \text{(variance)}$$

$$\frac{1}{\sigma_p} \sum_{1,2} \omega_m \frac{\partial \sigma_p}{\partial \omega_m} = 1 \qquad \text{(volatility)}$$

$$\frac{1}{\text{VaR}(\alpha, \tau)} \sum_{1,2} \omega_m \frac{\partial \, \text{VaR}(\alpha, \tau)}{\partial \omega_m} = 1 \qquad \text{(VaR)}$$

In economics, these shares would be called *elasticities*, since they are the product of a mathematical first derivative times the ratio of the function argument with respect to which it being differentiated. The volatility and

VaR elasticities are identical. The fact that they sum to 100 percent is quite useful.[3]

The following example shows how these measures of risk contribution are calculated.

Example 13.1 (Risk Contributions in a Long-Only Portfolio) Let the stock and bond return volatilities be $\sigma = (\sigma_1, \sigma_2) = (0.10, 0.18)$, and let the correlation between the two asset classes be $\rho = 0.40$. The return covariance matrix, as in Chapter 5, is then

$$\text{diag}\begin{pmatrix} 0.10 \\ 0.18 \end{pmatrix} \begin{pmatrix} 1 & 0.40 \\ 0.40 & 1 \end{pmatrix} \text{diag}\begin{pmatrix} 0.10 \\ 0.18 \end{pmatrix} = \begin{pmatrix} 0.0100 & 0.0072 \\ 0.0072 & 0.0324 \end{pmatrix}$$

with variances and covariances expressed at an annual rate as decimals. Thus the covariance between stock and bond returns is 72 bps per annum.

Suppose the portfolio has a market value of $300, of which $100 is invested in bonds and $200 in stocks. The portfolio variance is then $1,684 and the volatility is $41.04.

Next, let's compute the VaR and marginal VaRs of the portfolio. The annual VaR at a 99 percent confidence level is $95.47. The risk contributions are

	Bonds	Stocks	Total
Variance			
Portfolio variance			1,684.00
Marginal variance	4.88	14.40	
Component variance	488.00	2,880.00	3,368.00
Variance elasticities	0.29	1.71	2.00
Volatility			
Portfolio volatility			41.04
Marginal volatility	0.06	0.18	
Component volatility	5.95	35.09	41.04
Volatility elasticities	0.14	0.86	1.00
VaR			
Portfolio VaR			95.47
Marginal VaR	0.14	0.41	
Component VaR	13.83	81.63	95.47
Variance elasticities	0.14	0.86	1.00

[3]We run into some terminological confusion here. The RiskMetrics documentation reverses the definitions, so that incremental VaR is the continuous and marginal VaR, the discrete amount concept. The use of "marginal" to describe economic concepts that have differential calculus definitions, such as marginal utility and marginal product, is ingrained in economics, though, and preferable. RiskMetrics labels the *component*, not marginal VaR, as "incremental VaR."

Note that although bonds are $\frac{1}{3}$ of the portfolio by market value, at the margin they contribute only 14.5 percent of the volatility.

The volatility contributions of the two asset classes are very sensitive to all of the parameters—the volatilities, correlation, and relative sizes of the stock and bond allocations. Let's look at these sensitivities a bit more closely. Figure 13.1 illustrates a few key points, which were foreshadowed in Chapter 2's discussion of diversification. Each panel shows how risk contributions change with correlation for a given allocation to stocks and bonds.

■ When the correlation between the two asset classes are relatively high, the total portfolio volatility is higher, and each asset class tends to be more of a risk amplifier than a risk mitigator. When the correlation is low or negative, the total portfolio volatility is lower, and the risk contributions of the two asset classes diverge more and more. In the baseline Example 13.1, the bond allocation had a positive risk contribution. But as seen in the upper panel of Figure 13.1, if the correlation is low enough, bonds can become a "diversifier," that is, have a negative risk contribution, without any change in allocation or in the stock or bond return volatilities. This is related to the result we saw in Figure 2.10 of Chapter 2: Correlations don't have to be negative for a diversification benefit to be present.
■ The relative allocations matter a lot. The lower panel of Figure 13.1 shows how the risk contributions vary with correlation if we shift the allocation towards bonds. With a larger bond allocation, bonds never become a diversifier. At a very low correlation near -1, and with the lower allocation, stocks "overcome" their high volatility and become a diversifier.
■ Size and volatility work together. Notice, in the lower panel of Figure 13.1, that for correlations that are not very low, say above -0.4, the bond and stock allocations have about the same volatility contribution. The large bond allocation, with its lower volatility, has the same impact on portfolio volatility as the smaller stock allocation with its high volatility. In fact, there is a trade-off curve, shown in Figure 13.2, along which we can increase volatility and decrease allocation without changing the risk contribution of the asset class.

13.2.2 Risk Contributions Using Delta Equivalents

We next want to generalize in two ways, by extending the analysis to more than one asset, and by introducing negative allocations, that is short positions with respect to a risk factor. Let's start with a simple extension

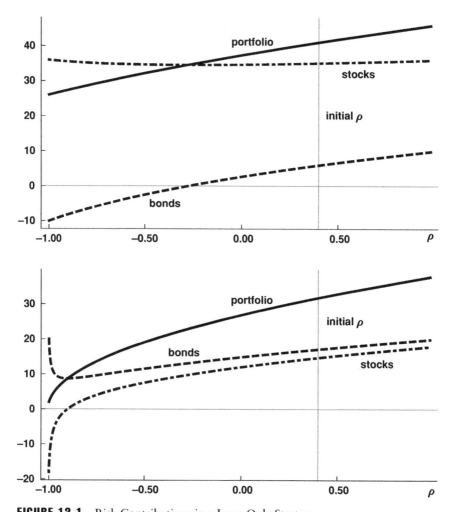

FIGURE 13.1 Risk Contributions in a Long-Only Strategy
Volatility contributions of the stock and bond allocations as correlation from -1
(complete diversification) to $+1$ (no diversification). The values on the y-axis are the
component volatilities for stocks and bonds and the portfolio volatility. The stock
and bond volatilities are $(\sigma_1, \sigma_2) = (0.10, 0.18)$. The market value of the portfolio is
$300.
Upper panel: Allocations $100 to bonds and $200 to stocks.
Lower panel: Allocations $200 to bonds and $100 to stocks.

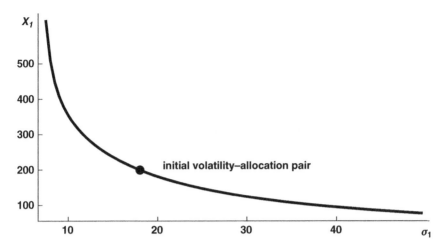

FIGURE 13.2 Allocation, Volatility, and Constant Risk Contribution
The plot shows how much the stock allocation needs to increase as the volatility
decreases in order to keep the risk contribution constant. Note that as the volatility
becomes quite low, the allocation must increase at an increasing rate per volatility
point. Note also that, at a stock allocation greater than 300, we must have a short
position in bonds.

of the previous long-only example. Imagine a portfolio consisting entirely
of stocks, but long some stocks and short others. Hedge fund managers
following an *equity market-neutral or long-short strategy*, rather than traditional asset managers, might have such a portfolio. We'll elaborate with an
example.

Example 13.2 (Volatility Contribution in a Long-Short Strategy) We now
consider an allocation to two different stock portfolios. The long stock portfolio has a market value d_l, and the long stock portfolio has a market value
d_s, with $(d_l, d_s) = (500, -500)$, measured in millions of dollars. The two
subportfolios have identical return volatilities $\sigma = 0.20$, and the correlation
between the two subportfolios returns is high, $\rho = 0.75$. We would expect
such a high correlation, unless the stocks have exceptionally low betas, because most of the risk in both subportfolios is systematic stock market risk.
    The return covariance matrix is then

$$\text{diag}\begin{pmatrix} 0.20 \\ 0.20 \end{pmatrix}\begin{pmatrix} 1 & 0.75 \\ 0.75 & 1 \end{pmatrix}\text{diag}\begin{pmatrix} 0.20 \\ 0.20 \end{pmatrix} = \begin{pmatrix} 0.04 & 0.03 \\ 0.03 & 0.04 \end{pmatrix}$$

with variances and covariances expressed at an annual rate as decimals.

The risk contributions are

	Longs	Shorts	Total
Variance			
Portfolio variance			5,000.00
Marginal variance	10.00	−10.00	
Component variance	5,000.00	5,000.00	10,000.00
Variance elasticities	1.00	1.00	2.00
Volatility			
Portfolio volatility			70.71
Marginal volatility	0.07	−0.07	
Component volatility	35.36	35.36	70.71
Volatility elasticities	0.50	0.50	1.00
VaR			
Portfolio VaR			164.50
Marginal VaR	0.16	−0.16	
Component VaR	82.25	82.25	164.50
Variance elasticities	0.50	0.50	1.00

In this example, the short stock portfolio has a negative marginal contribution, equal in magnitude to the positive contribution of the long portfolio. It is a diversifier, so increasing the short portfolio by a small amount would, at the margin, offset the risk impact of an increase in the long portfolio. But both the longs and the shorts make an equal and positive contribution to risk, as seen in the component contributions. The negative marginal contribution is multiplied by a negative portfolio allocation to get a positive contribution for the short portfolio. That guarantees that growing the entire portfolio, while keeping equal long and short shares, would grow the risk proportionally.

We can generalize this to a larger portfolio with many positive and negative delta equivalents. From here on, let's focus exclusively on the marginal VaRs. As we know by now, the marginal volatilities are closely related to them, while the marginal variances are, in the end, less interesting because their elasticities add up to 200 rather than 100 percent of the portfolio variance.

To express the marginal VaR formally for a portfolio, we need the following rule from matrix algebra. For any proper matrix Σ and conformable vector d,

$$\frac{\partial}{\partial \mathbf{d}} \mathbf{d}' \mathbf{\Sigma} \mathbf{d} = 2 \mathbf{\Sigma} \mathbf{d} = 2 \begin{pmatrix} \sum_m^M d_m \sigma_{1m} \\ \sum_m^M d_m \sigma_{2m} \\ \vdots \\ \sum_m^M d_m \sigma_{Nm} \end{pmatrix}$$

Using the chain rule, we get

$$\frac{\partial}{\partial \mathbf{d}} \sqrt{\mathbf{d}' \mathbf{\Sigma} \mathbf{d}} = \frac{\mathbf{\Sigma} \mathbf{d}}{\sqrt{\mathbf{d}' \mathbf{\Sigma} \mathbf{d}}}$$

We can now use these facts from matrix algebra to define the important marginal concepts and derive some of their properties. The derivative of the variance with respect to position m is defined as

$$\frac{\partial}{\partial d_m} \mathbf{d}' \mathbf{\Sigma} \mathbf{d}$$

that is, the increase in variance resulting from an increase in the delta equivalent of position m by \$1.

The marginal VaR is

$$\mathrm{MVaR}_{mt}(\alpha, \tau) \equiv d_m \frac{\partial}{\partial d_m} \mathrm{VaR}_t(\alpha, \tau)$$

$$= -z_* \sqrt{\tau} d_m \frac{\partial}{\partial d_m} \sqrt{\mathbf{d}' \mathbf{\Sigma} \mathbf{d}}$$

$$= -z_* \sqrt{\tau} d_m \frac{\mathbf{\Sigma} \mathbf{d}}{\sqrt{\mathbf{d}' \mathbf{\Sigma} \mathbf{d}}}$$

The vector of marginal VaRs is then

$$\mathrm{MVaR}_t(\alpha, \tau) = -z_* \sqrt{\tau} \frac{\mathbf{d}' \mathbf{\Sigma} \mathbf{d}}{\sqrt{\mathbf{d}' \mathbf{\Sigma} \mathbf{d}}}$$

We can now confirm the Euler property—the sum of the marginal VaRs is equal to the VaR—for general portfolios:

$$\sum_m \text{MVaR}_{mt}(\alpha, \tau) = -z_* \sqrt{\tau} \sum_m d_m \frac{\Sigma d}{\sqrt{d'\Sigma d}}$$

$$= \frac{z_*^2 \tau \sum_m d_m \Sigma \delta}{\text{VaR}_t(\alpha, \tau)}$$

$$= \frac{z_*^2 \tau d'\Sigma d}{\text{VaR}_t(\alpha, \tau)}$$

$$= \frac{\text{VaR}_t(\alpha, \tau)^2}{\text{VaR}_t(\alpha, \tau)}$$

$$= \text{VaR}_t(\alpha, \tau)$$

The *incremental VaR* is computed as the difference between the VaR with and without a particular position or subportfolio:

$$\text{IVaR}_{mt}(\alpha, \tau) \equiv \text{VaR}_t(\alpha, \tau)(\text{entire portfolio}) - \text{VaR}_t(\alpha, \tau)(\text{partial portfolio})$$

Both measures have in common that a position that reduces risk by either diversifying or hedging the portfolio will have a low or even negative marginal and/or incremental VaR.

13.2.3 Risk Capital Measurement for Quantitative Strategies

For some investments and some investment companies, especially hedge funds, it can be difficult to define the size or "amount" of the position, or the level of the activity, in a way that accomodates the VaR contribution calculations we have just outlined. We first describe a few examples of strategies for which the delta equivalents of the positions in the portfolio at a point in time don't capture the exposure sizes appropriately. We can, however, use risk capital calculations to provide an alternative way to measure the level of activity of these strategies and capture the size at which they are being run.

Examples of such strategies include statistical arbitrage, equity and credit correlation trading, and gamma trading and other systematic option strategies. Such strategies are typically *market-neutral*, meaning there are both long and short positions, intended to eliminate net exposure to the stock market or credit spreads, or that the portfolio has zero net market value, that is, the market value of the long positions is close to that of the short positions. Each position in such strategies may have a well-defined delta, but returns on the strategy as a whole have a very different distribution—in particular, the potential losses may be far greater—than a delta-based VaR would predict.

These strategies are generally leveraged; the financing is provided by counterparties or by an exchange clearing house. The strategies often in addition have embedded leverage, and involve short positions. The cash investment in such strategies is generally used to put up margin requirements and may have little relation to the volatility of returns relative to the cash invested. If the cash requirements are low, a prudent portfolio manager may hold a cash reserve, as a risk management tool, in order to increase his equity in the strategy. Risk capital calculations can be a useful tool to determine the appropriate level of such additional cash buffers. The additional cash buffer is then set so that the total equity against the strategy is adequate risk capital.

We have briefly encountered some of these strategies in Chapter 1, in describing the growth of hedge funds and other large capital pools, in Chapter 10, in describing correlation trading, and in Chapter 12, describing the range of techniques for increasing leverage in trading strategies. To help understand the example we'll provide in a moment, let's further describe some of these quantitative strategies:

Statistical arbitrage attempts to profit from transitory differences between actual prices and the fair market or forecast value according to a model. The word "arbitrage" is of course a misnomer, since market prices may not converge to their model values quickly or at all. There are two general orientations for such models, which are typically applied in equity and futures markets. They may rely on price forecasts from a fundamental-data model extrapolation from time-series, or technical trading models, to arrive at short-term asset price forecasts. These strategies rely on or "use" market liquidity, that is, the ability to buy and sell without materially affecting prices.

Or they may attempt to detect and exploit transitory imbalances in order flow, acting as liquidity providers at a very granular level of the price discovery process. Such models, called *high-frequency* or *algorithmic trading*, are also most frequently applied to assets traded on organized exchanges, such as equities and futures, where there is strong, but fluctuating, two-way order flow in most stocks. High-frequency trading uses computing power to rapidly detect these imbalances and enter orders on the "other side." If not filled, the orders are rapidly withdrawn. While generally acting as liquidity providers, the strategies have come under scrutiny following the May 6, 2010 "flash crash," in which stock prices experienced extremely high intraday volatility. Some observers held high frequency traders responsible for the volatility by placing large automated sell orders or by withdrawing entirely from trading.

The trading frequency of such strategies varies very widely, from fractions of a second to several weeks, as measured by the average length of time a dollar's worth of stock resides in the portfolio. The portfolios are typically adjusted so that the net market exposure is close to zero. For this reason, the cash investment can be relatively small. For equity portfolios, the cash requirements will be greater than for exchange-traded derivatives strategies.

Gamma trading attempts to exploit the tendency of option implied volatilities to exceed realized volatility over the life of the option. The trader sells an option, typically at-the-money with a short time to maturity, and delta hedges. The option hedge is adjusted frequently, at least daily. If the underlying asset price moves significantly less than predicted by the implied volatility, the time decay on the short option position will exceed the trading costs, and the effect of the asset price move on the option value will be offset nearly exactly by that on the asset position itself. Such strategies can be carried out for a variety of asset types, such as currencies, equities, money markets, and fixed-income securities, and in a number of ways, such as exchange-traded futures and options, OTC options, or variance swaps. The cash requirements of the strategy can be quite low.

Convertible bond trading is a long version of the gamma trading strategy. It can be profitable when the options embedded in the bonds are cheap relative to exchange-traded and OTC options on the underlying stock, and realized volatility is high. Convertible bond trading is also typically levered, but not extremely so.

Even if the risk contributions of other strategies the hedge fund pursues would otherwise be straightforward, the presence of one or more of these quantitative strategies will make it hard to compute them, since all the risk contributions depend on all of the allocations in the portfolio. This makes sizing any of the strategies more difficult.

Typically, however, portfolio managers work with some measure of the size or level at which the strategy is being carried out. There are a few such rule-of-thumb approaches to measuring the size of the strategy. The first is to measure the activity level of the strategy by the amount of cash used, all of which is generally devoted to margin requirements with exchanges, intermediaries, or counterparties. As noted, since some of these strategies can be levered up quite a bit, and also may have considerable embedded leverage, this is potentially quite misleading. A strategy may appear "small" measured by the cash it employs, but very large measured by its potential losses, implying that an appropriate risk capital is higher than the rule of thumb states.

The second frequently encountered rule-of-thumb is to use some measure of long market exposure. For example, the size at which a credit correlation strategy is run may be stated as the notional amount or market value on each side, or as a delta or spread01 on each side, neither of which is closely related to potential loss.

Especially for strategies that can be highly leveraged, the size of the strategy may be more accurately measured by the risk capital the trader imputes to the strategy. In effect, this approach sets an equity measure for the strategy that is distinct from the out-of-pocket cost of implementation. The trader implicitly sets aside a cash reserve in addition to the required margin in order to run the strategy at a prudent level, given the amount of capital he has. This is a means of reducing the probability of "bankrupting" the strategy, or of forcing it to be unwound immediately. The trader can meet margin calls out of the cash reserve rather than being forced out of positions immediately at a loss. Another strategy might have cash funding requirements that are high relative to the risk of the strategy. It can then be viewed as freeing up risk capital that is then available for other strategies.

Once measures of each quantitative strategy's size are established, they can be treated as deltas in a portfolio of assets with correlated returns. The return volatility and covariances with respect to other strategies can be computed using the dollar returns and the risk capital measure. An important assumption in this approach is that the level of the fund's own activity does not affect returns in the market via adverse price impact or other market liquidity effects. For example, if the fund doubles the level at which it operates the strategy, we assume it doesn't lower the rate of return by causing the arbitrage opportunity to disappear or haircuts to increase. This is consistent with the assumption typically underpinning these strategies, that market and funding liquidity are adequate to support them. The subprime crisis revealed how unreliable this assumption can be.

In this approach, just scaling the strategy up or down won't affect risk measurement. To see this, imagine doubling the measured risk capital of one strategy arbitrarily. This means that the return volatility and all of the covariances with that strategy must be halved, since the dollar returns haven't changed. This has no effect on either the portfolio volatility or the marginal risk contributions.

In the rest of this section, we set out an example of this approach, showing how risk capital computations can be used to appropriately size and assess capital charges for quantitative strategies. We imagine a hedge fund operating two quantitative strategies, which we'll call gamma trading and

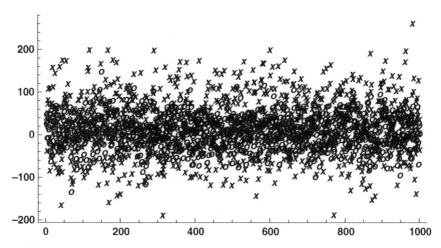

FIGURE 13.3   Simulated Hedge Fund Strategy Returns
The plot shows the P&L, in millions of dollars, for the two strategies. The gamma
trading dollar returns are marked by small circles, and the stat arb returns by x's.

statistical arbitrage for concreteness. The fund is able to accurately estimate
the strategies' expected returns, and return variances and covariances. It may
do so by actually running the strategies at a specified size and observing daily
P&L over some period, or it may have backtested the models on historical
data, so the P&L time series is based on "paper trading." An example of
what such results might look like for one year is displayed in Figure 13.3. For
concreteness, we assume that the strategies' sizes are initially measured by
the amount of cash they require, one of the sizing rules-of-thumb mentioned
above, so returns are measured as each day's dollar P&L divided by the cash
employed in the strategy. For the gamma strategy, the margin is $50, and
for stat arb, $200.

Based on these results of the backtest, the fund estimates the returns and
volatilities of the two strategies as

	Gamma ($m = 1$)	Stat arb ($m = 2$)
Mean annual excess return (μ_m, %)	15.0	10.0
Annual volatility (σ_m, %)	75.0	35.0

The correlation is estimated as 0.40.

We also assume that the hedge fund operates no other strategies, and
that there are no investor redemptions and subscriptions, so the fund NAV is
affected only by P&L. The gross dollar return to the fund's investors equals
the sum of the dollar returns or P&L of the two strategies, and the rate of

return is equal to the dollar return divided by the NAV of the fund. We ignore the "level-changing" effect of the fund's P&L, which reduces returns when returns have been positive, and vice versa.

Next, suppose that the fund manager wishes to increase the risk capital supporting each strategy by holding a cash reserve against it, over and above the cash required for financing. We look at this first from the point of view of the individual strategies, as though each were run in a dedicated single-strategy fund of its own, and then from the point of view of the fund as a whole. Essentially, the manager is reducing the VaR or the volatility of each strategy to a target level by setting aside extra cash. Framed in terms of volatility, the portfolio manager might want to reduce the annual return volatility to say, 25 percent. To reduce the probability of exhausting equity and "bankrupting" the strategy. The additional cash is used as additional equity, not as a liquidity reserve.

Denote the *share* of the additional cash in the total risk capital of strategy m by χ_m, $m = 1, 2$. For a target volatility of, say, 0.25, χ_m is

$$\chi_m = 1 - \frac{0.25}{\sigma_m} \qquad m = 1, 2$$

If, for example, the target volatility is half the strategy's actual return volatility, the risk capital doubles, since the appropriate additional cash buffer is then half the total risk capital. If the target volatility happens to equal the strategy's volatility, then no additional risk capital is set aside. In our example, for each dollar of required margin, setting aside additional equity capital, held in a liquid, risk-free form, of $2.00 for the gamma trading strategy and $0.40 for statistical arbitrage, will reduce the volatility of each strategy to 25 percent. The dollar amount of additional cash required to achieve this suppression of volatility is $\frac{\chi_m}{1-\chi_m}$ times the required margin. Returns are reduced by the same proportion as volatility, to $\mu_m(1 - \chi_m)$. (We assume the return on the additional cash is zero.) In our example, we have:

	Gamma	Stat arb
χ_m	0.667	0.286
Additional risk capital ($)	100	80
Total risk capital ($)	150	280
Return on risk capital ($\mu_m(1 - \chi_m)$, %)	5.00	7.14
Volatility on risk capital ($\sigma_m(1 - \chi_m)$, %)	25.0	25.0

Returns are diluted in the same proportion as the volatility.

So far, we have viewed each strategy in isolation. That is, these results are applied to each strategy as if it were a standalone fund. Next, we use our definition of component VaR (or volatility) and VaR elasticities to attribute the fund's NAV to the two strategies, that is, to determine the amount of risk capital each strategy is using. Imagine investors have placed $500 with the fund; that is, it starts with an NAV of $500. Initially, the fund manager operates the two strategies using no additional cash buffer, and allocates 20 percent of the fund to gamma and 80 percent to stat arb. Applying the algebra developed earlier in this chapter, the risk contributions are

	Gamma	Stat arb	Fund
Variance ($, ann.)			
Portfolio variance			33,625.00
Marginal variance	196.50	119.00	
Component variance	19,650.00	47,600.00	67,250.00
Variance elasticities	58.44	141.56	200.00
Volatility (%)			
Portfolio volatility (%, ann.)			36.67
Marginal volatility	53.58	32.45	
Component volatility	10.72	25.96	36.67
Volatility elasticities	29.22	70.78	100.00
VaR			
Portfolio VaR ($, $\tau = \frac{1}{12}, \alpha = 0.99$)			123.14
Marginal VaR	0.36	0.22	
Component VaR	35.98	87.16	123.14
VaR elasticities	29.22	70.78	100.00

Although the gamma strategy uses only $\frac{1}{6}$ of the cash invested, its risk contribution is nearly 30 percent.

We can use risk contributions to make a risk-based allocation of the fund's resources. Suppose the fund manager wants to allocate 25 percent of its risk capital to the gamma strategy and 75 percent to statistical arbitrage. Further, it has a target volatility of 25 percent per annum for the fund as a whole, which is exceeded by its return volatility of 36.67 with the current allocation of 20 percent gamma, 80 percent stat arb, and no cash buffer. The fund needs to determine the level at which to operate each strategy and the total additional cash reserve needed to achieve its target volatility and risk capital allocation. It can then attribute the additional cash as risk capital to the two strategies. By solving this problem, the fund manager links the risk tolerance of the fund, expressed through its target volatility, and the strategy size or allocation decision.

To solve this problem, we first find the "cash allocation" shares: ω_1 for the gamma trading strategy, ω_2 for stat arb, and χ the cash buffer, expressed as fractions of the fund's initial $500 NAV. The ω_m are the shares of the fund's initial cash resources used to fund the strategies and are equal to the cash margin required for each, divided by the initial NAV. These shares plus the cash buffer share must sum to unity. Once the cash buffer χ required to achieve the target volatility is determined, it is allocated to the two strategies consistently with the total risk capital allocation. This second step is carried out within the fund; it is an internal reckoning, not a transaction with the market.

The desired risk capital allocation can be most simply expressed using the volatility elasticities

$$\omega_m \frac{\omega_m \sigma_m^2 + \omega_n \sigma_1 \sigma_2 \rho}{\omega' \Sigma \omega} \quad m, n = 1, 2, m \neq n$$

where $\omega' = (\omega_1, \omega_2)$. The fund manager must solve the following equations for the ω_m and χ:

$$\omega_1 + \omega_2 + \chi = 1$$

$$\omega_1 \frac{\omega_1 \sigma_1^2 + \omega_2 \sigma_1 \sigma_2 \rho}{\omega' \Sigma \omega} = 0.25 \tag{13.2}$$

$$\sigma_p = \sqrt{\omega' \Sigma \omega} = 0.25$$

The elasticities and the portfolio volatility are nonlinear functions of the ω_m and of the volatility and correlation parameters, so a numerical search procedure must be used to obtain the solution.[4]

The first condition in the optimization problem (13.2) is the "budget constraint," and limits the manager to the funds placed by investors. The second condition expresses the fund manager's decision to set the risk capital allocation of the gamma strategy to 25 percent. No additional condition is required to impose the risk capital allocation of stat arb to 75 percent, because the volatility elasticities, like the cash allocation shares, sum to unity. The third and last condition sets the fund's return volatility to 25 percent, its overall risk limit.

The results are

	Gamma	Stat arb	Cash buffer
Allocation of cash (%)	12.18	56.86	30.96
Required margin ($)	60.92	284.29	154.79
Attribution of risk capital ($)	125.00	375.00	
Attribution of cash buffer ($)	64.08	90.71	

---

[4]The results in the examples were computed using *Mathematica*'s `FindRoot` algorithm.

Although the fund maintains a cash reserve of nearly $155, a bit more than 30 percent of the funds placed by investors, it is "fully invested" from a risk standpoint, since it is at its desired volatility ceiling. Of this additional cash, $64.08 is attributed to the gamma and $90.71 to the stat arb strategy. In contrast to the tripling of the capital attributed to the gamma strategy as a standalone strategy, as part of this portfolio, the gamma strategy's risk capital is merely doubled. The reason is that its marginal volatility is already reduced by the diversification benefit it enjoys as a relatively small allocation within the fund. The required margin is the capital actually invested in the strategy; additional cash is attributed from the reserve to fill out the risk capital. Expected fund returns are 37.57 percent.

This approach also provides a basis on which to assess traders a risk capital charge. It would be based on the risk capital allocations of $125 and $375, rather than on the amounts of cash actually used in the strategies.

In this example, both strategies have risk capital that is higher than the required margin. If we relax the target volatility constraint to 35 percent, setting $\sigma_p = 0.35$ in the numerical search problem that solves the set of equations (13.2), we get a contrasting result. The results are now

	Gamma	Stat arb	Cash buffer
Allocation of cash (%)	17.06	79.60	3.34
Required margin ($)	85.29	398.00	16.71
Attribution of risk capital ($)	125.00	375.00	
Attribution of cash buffer ($)	39.71	−23.00	

Expected returns, of course, are higher at 52.59 percent. The additional cash reserve is much lower, $16.71. The interesting feature in this example is that the additional risk capital of $39.71 is funded mainly by the excess capital in the stat arb strategy. Stat arb is less highly levered in the sense that a given cash outlay provides a less volatile return, so it frees up risk capital for gamma when a higher level of risk is desired. It would be assessed a capital charge corresponding to less cash than it actually uses.

Note also that the risk capital allocation works here because of the low required cash margin of the gamma strategy. If the gamma strategy used cash equal to its required risk capital, it couldn't be ramped up to attain a higher risk/volatility target. If the market doesn't provide enough "slack" in its margin requirements, or if the manager sets the fund's risk tolerance high enough, he fund manager can't use the discrepancies between market and model risk assessments to increase leverage.

This approach can be extended to any number of strategies to determine the level at which to operate each strategy consistently with the desired risk allocation. The examples focused on quantitative strategies; the disparity between the cash investment made in quantitative strategies and their actual risks tends to be large, making a risk capital approach to allocation particularly apt. But it can be applied as readily to conventional strategies, and provides an example of how risk analysis can be integrated into the investment process.

The approach sketched here has important limitations. It is based on portfolio and marginal volatility. But as we have seen, volatility as a measure of risk is inadequate if returns don't follow the standard model. But our example is suggestive of the ways in which quantitative risk data can aid investors in achieving a risk and return profile that is closer to their objectives.

In the quantitative strategy example above, and in the risk budgeting approach generally, the fund manager may assess a capital charge for the risk capital allocated. This is sometimes called a *transfer pricing* problem, as it shares characteristics with the problem of pricing transfers of goods within a nonfinancial firm that don't pass through a market pricing process. Among the reasons for risk capital charges is to create incentives for portfolio managers to identify risk-minimizing investment approaches, and as a part of compensation mechanisms in which portfolio managers are rewarded for excess returns only, rather than for the absolute level of returns.

Capital charges are generally based on an estimate of the cost of capital. There are two bases for such cost calculations:

1. The cost of equity capital is the minimum expected return on equity that will induce investors to put their own capital behind an investment. That is, the cost of capital is the hurdle rate required for the fund to retain capital. Because equity is the riskiest position in the capital structure, expected returns on equity generally must be high to induce investment.
2. The cost of debt financing is the blended rate paid for different types of debt. It depends on interest rates on long- and short-term, and secured and unsecured debt. A firm or investor can make choices among these sources of funding to arrive at a funding blend that works best for it. The cost of debt is lower than that of equity, so a blended cost of financing will be lower than an equity hurdle rate. Capital charges based on borrowing costs can be viewed as a "cost-recovery" approach.

13.3 STRESS TESTING

Stress testing is an approach to risk measurement that attempts to grapple with the difficulties of modeling returns statistically. It posits the size of shocks directly, or with a "light" modeling apparatus. It is also sometimes called *scenario analysis*, since it asks the question, "what happens to our firm (or portfolio) if the following asset price changes take place." In spite— or because—of its light modeling infrastructure, stress testing has become a very widespread approach to risk measurement. While only indirectly related to internal risk management by banks, an important example were the supervisory stress testing procedures carried out in the United States in early 2009 and in Europe in mid-2010. The U.S. exercise, repeated in 2011 and to be conducted regularly thereafter, helped authorities determine which banks would be obliged to raise additional equity capital or prevented from paying out dividends.

In a stress test, we compute the losses resulting from sharp adverse price moves, or from an adverse macroeconomic scenario. The challenge of stress testing is to design scenarios that are extreme enough to constitute a fair test of severe potential loss, but are still plausible and could realistically take place. One can distinguish two schools of thought on stress testing by the extent to which macroeconomic design, as opposed to statistical analysis of risk-factor behavior, enters into scenario design.

Another purpose of stress testing is to examine scenarios in which market prices behave in a way unlikely in the classical normal-return model. To a large extent, increasing reliance on stress testing is a response to the many drawbacks of the market and credit risk modeling approaches we have been studying in Chapters 2 through 9. We have reviewed some critiques of these models in Chapters 10 and 11. One possible response to the drawbacks of the standard statistical models is to develop better statistical models or techniques, and much valuable discussion has explored the potential advantages of, say, extreme value theory (EVT) techniques, or the use of implied volatility data. However, these discussions have not led to a definitive and widely shared conclusion about a superior alternative to the standard model. Another potential response is agnosticism about the capacity of risk managers to make useful quantitative statements about tail events and their impact on the firm's or investor's returns. But pure agnosticism does not yield practical tools that firms and investors can use to manage risk day to day. Stress testing is a third type of response. Rather than relying entirely on the results of a model to obtain a "likely worst case," stress testing skirts the modeling issues by placing the scenario itself, rather than the model, in the forefront.

Stress testing has also become more important over time because it is easier to communicate stress test results than model results to most audiences. Most investors and financial firm executives do not have specialized training in statistical modeling. It is remarkable that VaR, a fairly sophisticated risk measure involving quantiles and distributional hypotheses, as well as a good understanding of its limitations, have extended as far into mainstream financial discussion as they have. Even if better statistical models could provide the solution to the limitations of the normal distribution, it is unlikely that the necessary fluency in the statistical issues would keep up. To be useful, and to having an impact on decision making, risk measures have to be understandable. It is therefore appropriate to develop risk measures that can be understood and acted on without extensive quantitative training.

Stress testing need not stand in opposition to statistical modeling. As noted, some approaches to stress testing build on the results of return models. Depending on one's view of the standard models, stress testing can be considered a supplement or a substitute for the joint normally distribution and other non-normal model-based approaches. We may use historical data, or human judgment, or both, to create likely worst-case scenarios.

13.3.1 An Example of Stress Testing

Consider the sample portfolio we studied in Chapter 5. The second column of Table 13.1 displays the volatilities of the risk factors, computed using the EWMA approach, as in Chapter 5. The parametric estimates of the annualized marginal volatility for each of the six risk factors are displayed

TABLE 13.1 Volatility and Shocks

Factor	Vol	MVol	VaR Shocks		Stress Test Shocks		Price Units
			% Shock	Δ Price	% Shock	Δ Price	
EUR	5.70	2.16	0.42	−5.42	−5.0	−64.32	USD ticks
JPY	6.44	1.30	0.25	−21.51	−5.0	−425.86	$10^6 \times \Delta$ USD price of yen)
SPX	7.80	−0.64	−0.13	1.73	−10.0	−137.69	points
GT10	14.77	−2.88	−0.56	0.20	−10.0	3.49	bond points
XU100	20.18	17.38	3.38	−1,340.61	−15.0	−5,944.08	points
TRL	12.36	9.62	1.87	−12.92	−7.5	−51.76	$10^9 \times \Delta$ (USD price of TRL)

"Vol" represents the volatility of each risk factor at an annual rate. For GT10, the vol is the yield vol. "MVol" represents the marginal volatility contribution as defined above, again, as a yield vol for GT10. The VaR shock is 3.09 times the MVol, expressed at a daily rate. The stress shock is the risk factor return stipulated by the scenario. Both the VaR and stress shocks are therefore expressed as a percent change in the risk factor. The volatilities and shocks are all expressed in percent. The "Δ price" corresponding to the VaR and stress scenarios states the price units, as detailed in the last column.

in the third column. Recall that the marginal volatility, like the marginal VaR, takes into account not only the return volatilities of the risk factors, but also their return correlations and the portfolio weights.

The VaR shock is the percentage change in the risk factor in the VaR scenario and is related to the marginal volatility by

$$\text{VaR shock} = -z_* \times \text{marginal volatility}$$

where z_* is the ordinate of $N(0, 1)$ corresponding to the selected confidence level α. In a portfolio context, the VaR shock depends not only on the the asset return volatility, but also on the correlation to other returns and thus on the composition of the portfolio. It is displayed for each risk factor in the next two columns of Table 13.1. The change in the value of the risk factor—the risk factor return—is the VaR shock times the current level of the risk factor. To facilitate comparison to the stress scenario, we set a high confidence level $\alpha = 0.999$, so $z_* = 3.09$. That corresponds to a loss size, which, within the model, could be expected to occur on about one trading day in four years.

The stress shocks are displayed in the next column. While the VaR shocks are outputs from the statistical model used to calculate the volatilities, the stress shocks are "designed," that is, chosen to represent a highly adverse scenario. To facilitate comparison with the VaR analysis, they are to be understood as one-day returns to the risk factors. The stress shocks are set to represent a pattern frequently observed in the financial market crises of recent decades, as we discuss in Chapter 14: the U.S. dollar appreciates sharply against other currencies, while U.S. Treasury bond yields and all equity markets drop sharply. Corresponding to the decline in yields, U.S. Treasury prices rise sharply; this aspect of the scenario design is consistent with the "flight to quality" or "risk off" behavior typically seen in financial markets under stress. The same flight to quality pattern would tend to drive the dollar sharply higher, but without knowing more about the specific background of a crisis, it would be hard to predict whether the euro would appreciate against the yen, or vice versa, or neither. The drop in equity prices is large in all markets, but is even worse for emerging than for developed-country markets.

The results for the positions and the portfolio are displayed in the table below. For consistency with the VaR estimates, stress losses (gains) are represented as positive (negative) U.S. dollar amounts. There are a number of notable differences from the VaR estimates.

- The P&L estimates are much larger, of course, since the stress scenario shocks are much larger than the VaR shocks. In particular, the Turkish stock market position becomes an even more dominant driver of the aggregate risk of the portfolio.

■ The positions that would be expected to act as risk mitigants, such as the short S&P 500 position, have a much larger effect. In the VaR estimates, it is a minor risk contributor. In the stress scenario, it helps a great deal to limit portfolio losses.

■ The two major-currency positions offset one another completely rather than partially. Of course, this is an artifact of the stress scenario, which assigns identical returns to the two currencies.

■ The U.S. Treasury position, which in "normal" markets is a small risk contributor, becomes a risk mitigant in the stress scenario.

	MVaR	Stress Loss
long EUR	4,214	50,000
short JPY	−2,526	−50,000
short SPX	1,254	−100,000
long GT10	2,003	−34,937
long XU100	52,553	213,750
Portfolio	57,498	78,813

The portfolio stress loss is significantly worse than that estimated by the VaR. Partly, that is due to the fact that the VaR analysis is based on a historical observation window in which volatilities were relatively low. But it also reflects the fact that the stress scenario has been designed to take fat tails into account. The scenario is intended to reflect a risk event that occurs with a probability of about 0.1 percent, and is therefore appropriately a much larger loss than the normal return quantile in the VaR estimate.

But the stress scenario has placed not only the overall loss, but also the portfolio construction in a different light. Analyzed only with VaR tools, this looked like a fairly low-volatility portfolio, with the Turkish stock index as the one "high-octane" component, the tail wagging the portfolio dog. The stress test, if it embodies a reasonable scenario, shows that the other portfolio elements are more dynamic than the VaR analysis alone revealed, based as it is on a low-volatility sample period and a thin-tailed return model. Finally, the diversification characteristics of the portfolio look very different. Overall, because the the long U.S. Treasury and short S&P index positions have much larger gains in the stress scenario than in the VaR analysis, the entire portfolio looks better hedged for a crisis.

13.3.2 Types of Stress Tests

We have alluded to the different approaches to constructing scenarios, with one focusing more on finding empirically reasonable shocks to risk factors, while another looks more to the "story" being told by the scenario. This reflects the different purposes of stress tests. On the one hand, stress tests are designed for ensuring a firm's capital adequacy and survival through a crisis. Therefore, both risk risk appetite and economic analysis have important roles to play in determining stress scenarios. On the other hand, they are designed to take account of alternative return distribution and volatility models to the normal.

Stress tests must be formulated with a specific discrete time horizon, that is, the return scenario is posited to take place, say, over one day or one month. Unless the stress test horizon is extremely short, we need specific assumptions about what trading of positions and hedging, and at what prices, will take place within the horizon of the stress test. Some trading assumptions, such as ongoing delta hedging of option positions, are perhaps reasonable accommodations to dynamic strategies. Permitting other positions to change so as to protect against loss within a stress scenario raises the possibility that the stress test results will understate losses, since the point of a stress test is to explore potential losses given the current portfolio or book of business. More importantly, the deterioration of market and funding liquidity and impairment of market functioning is also likely to limit the amount of trading that can be done in stress conditions. Stress scenarios should therefore take current positions for the most part as unalterable.

The stress test in our example had a horizon of one day, and is consistent with a no-trading assumption. The stress test result is then just a mark-to-market P&L of the portfolio. A longer horizon may be more useful for many firms. Typically a span of one month or one calendar quarter is needed for even a relatively contained financial crisis to play out. But a longer horizon than one quarter is unrealistic if a no-trading assumption is imposed.

Stress tests have been classified into several types. *Historical stress tests* apply shocks that have actually been realized in a historical crisis to the portfolio. Table 1.1 of Chapter 1 provides some examples of episodes that could be incorporated into a historical stress test. Several ambiguities need to be resolved in carrying out a historical stress test. For example, the worst loss for a particular risk factor, say the dollar-Mexican peso exchange rate, might have been realized one week into a crisis involving Mexican markets, while the worst loss for the Mexican stock market might not have been realized until several weeks later. The stress loss for a portfolio will be greater if the worst losses are bundled together as an instantaneous mark-to-market P&L than if a particular historical interval is chosen.

Historical stress tests are important and valuable as a point of reference, but history never repeats itself. An alternative approach is based on possible future events though it may be informed by history. Most stress tests in practice are of this type. But if history is no longer a rigid guide, how do we design the scenarios? One important principle is to identify portfolio vulnerabilities and see to it that they are properly stressed. VaR analysis can be a useful complement to stress testing, as it has a capacity to identify subtle vulnerabilities in a complex portfolio that are not obvious when looking at line-item positions. Discussion with traders is also important in identifying potential stresses.

Other approaches to stress testing are less dependent on judgment and rely more on algorithms for evaluating the portfolio in different scenarios. Such approaches capture both the interaction of multiple risk factors in generating losses, such as occurs in option positions, as well as the susceptibility of the specific portfolio to particular combinations of factor returns. In the *factor-push approach*, many combinations of risk factor returns are tested, and the stress loss is taken as the largest portfolio loss that occurs. The highest and lowest returns for each risk factor are set at some reasonably large potential range, resulting in a grid of shocks. The stress test result is the largest portfolio loss resulting from this grid of stresses. An example is the Chicago Mercantile Exchange's (CME) Standard Portfolio Analysis of Risk (SPAN) system, used in establishing net margin requirements for futures positions. Such approaches can have many dimensions, since there are potentially many combinations of risk factors to search over, and the portfolio must be revalued in each one. A class of tools for limiting the range of risk factor combinations using distributional assumptions is called the *maximum loss* approach.

An example of the potential usefulness of factor-push approaches is the Amaranth hedge fund collapse of September 2006. Amaranth had put on large positions in the calendar spread between natural gas futures with different expiries. The capital at risk from this one set of positions was comparable in magnitude to the entire NAV of the fund. A large bet on a tightening of these spreads to historical norms went awry as spreads widened instead. Historical data on natural gas calendar spreads and their volatility would have underestimated the potential loss to the trade. A stress test based on a wide enough range of possible values of the calendar spreads involved might have identified the potential loss. It is, of course, unknown what degree of awareness the Amaranth fund managers possessed of the potential loss, and thus, whether the risk had been consciously taken on.

In many cases, we are interested in shocking only some risk factors in a portfolio. This raises the issue of how to treat the remaining risk factors. One approach is to use their last-observed values, that is, set their returns to zero, in computing portfolio losses in the stress scenario. This may lead to unrealistic scenarios. Another approach, sometimes called *predictive stress testing*, is to use their conditional expected values. The expected values are conditioned on the values taken by the stressed risk factors, using the estimated correlation matrix of all the risk factors. This in turn raises a final issue in the treatment of the risk factor correlations; correlations between many risk factor returns are higher during periods of financial stress. We discuss the behavior of correlation in financial crises in more detail in Chapter 14.

In spite of its difficulties, stress testing has taken on great importance relative to VaR in recent years. At one point, stress testing was discussed as a complement to VaR and in the context of VaR modeling, but the emphasis has now shifted, and the results of VaR analysis are now apt to be reported as a stress scenario among others. Stress testing should be carried out regularly, as a regular part of the risk reporting cycle. The scenario design should be varied as portfolio concentrations and market conditions evolve.

13.4 SIZING POSITIONS

Determining the appropriate size of positions is one of the major decisions investors and traders must make, alongside choosing which trade ideas to adopt and to discard, and determining hedging policy. They need to avoid excessive position concentration and achieve diversification. In investment management, this is the allocation decision.

Risk capital calculations can be helpful in determining position size. Identifying large risk contributions provides a more reliable guide to concentration than notional size. In this section, we compare a number of tools used to identify concentrations and guide the search for diversification.

13.4.1 Diversification

We have discussed diversification in a number of contexts. Here, we provide some quantitative measures for market and credit risk.

A common method for measuring the degree of diversification from a market risk standpoint is to compare the VaR of a portfolio to the sum of the VaRs of the individual positions. Let $\mathbf{x} = (x_1, \ldots, x_M)'$ denote a portfolio. The *diversification benefit* is defined as difference between the sum of the single-position VaRs and the portfolio VaR:

$$\sum_{m=1}^{M} \text{VaR}_t(\alpha, \tau)(x_m) - \text{VaR}_t(\alpha, \tau)(\mathbf{x})$$

This quantity is expected to be non-negative. But there are cases, uncommon but not pathological, in which the diversification effect is negative. VaR consequently violates the axiom of subadditivity, as discussed in Chapter 11). In almost all cases, however, the diversification benefit will be positive and make sense.

For credit risk, a common measure of diversification is the *Herfindahl index*. It is equal to the sum of the squares of the share of each credit in the portfolio. If there is only one credit, the index is equal to unity. If there are n credits, each with an equal share, the index is equal to n^{-1}.

Another diversification measure for credit risk is the *diversity score*. In Chapter 8, we saw that dividing a credit portfolio with a fixed par value into smaller pieces with uncorrelated defaults, but the same default rate, progressively reduces the fraction of the portfolio that defaults, and thus the credit VaR, up to a limit determined by the uniform default rate. The diversity score provides a comparison between such a granular portfolio and a congruent one with correlated defaults. The portfolio of correlated credits will have a high diversity score if its credit risk is closer to that of the granular, uncorrelated one and a low diversity score if its credit risk is closer to that of a single large credit. As noted earlier, because credit events are generally low-probability, so that credit returns are more fat-tailed than market returns, more granularity is required to reduce idiosyncratic risk to a desired level than for an equity portfolio.

13.4.2 Optimization and Implied Views

Reverse optimization or *implied views* is another tool, emerging from the risk capital framework, to help portolio managers decide whether to invest more or less in particular assets. Recall from Chapter 2 that in an efficient portfolio, the expected excess return of each of the M assets is equal to its beta to the portfolio, multiplied by the excess return of the portfolio. This condition was expressed in Equation (2.3), reproduced here:

$$\mu_m - r_f = \beta_m(\mu_p - r_f) \qquad m = 1, \ldots, M$$

Each of the β_m is the ratio of the covariance of asset-i excess return with the portfolio excess return to the portfolio excess return variance:

$$\beta_m = \frac{\sigma_{mp}}{\sigma_p^2} \qquad m = 1, \ldots, M$$

Putting these two expressions together, we conclude that, in an efficient portfolio,

$$\frac{\mu_m - r_f}{\mu_n - r_f} = \frac{\sigma_{mp}}{\sigma_{np}} = \frac{\sum_k^M \delta_k \sigma_{mk}}{\sum_k^M \delta_k \sigma_{nk}} \qquad m, n = 1, \ldots, M$$

for any pair of investments m and n in the portfolio. The second equality puts the implied view in the context of the delta-normal approach to portfolio risk measurement of Chapter 5.

This is a remarkably far-reaching result. An efficient portfolio is not necessarily optimal. Efficiency, as noted in Chapter 2, is a condition of "minimal rationality" in portfolio construction. A reallocation of the available capital that makes a nonefficient portfolio into an efficient one is not a trade-off; it is a zero-cost improvement.

The result states that, if the portfolio is efficient, if the asset returns are multivariate normal, and if we are confident that our estimates of the variances and covariances of the asset returns are accurate, then both of the following statements hold:

1. If we have estimated or know the excess return on even one investment in the portfolio, the portfolio itself implicitly reveals all the other expected excess returns.
2. Even if we have no estimates of excess return, the portfolio itself reveals the *ratios* of expected excess return of any pair of investments.

An asset manager may not have formulated an explicit excess return estimate for any of the assets in the portfolio. But he will certainly claim to have constructed an efficient portfolio. Suppose the marginal VaR of asset m is twice that of asset n. He can then step back and consider whether he really expects the return of asset m to be double that of asset n.

We can relate these implied views to our measures of risk contribution:

$$\frac{\mu_m - r_f}{\mu_n - r_f} = \frac{\sigma_{mp}}{\sigma_{np}} = \frac{\text{MVaR}_{mt}(\alpha, \tau)}{\text{MVaR}_{nt}(\alpha, \tau)} \qquad m, n = 1, \ldots, M$$

The ratio of the marginal VaRs are equal to the ratios of the expected excess returns.

13.5 RISK REPORTING

We have presented a range of risk statistics so far: risk factor sensitivities, VaR and related concepts, stress test results, and risk capital measures. In order to be of any use, they must be presented in the form of reports to portfolio managers and other decision makers, and interpreted. Chapter 11 briefly summarized the elements of a risk measurement system, which would typically include a reporting layer. Let's use the example of the portfolio delta-normal VaR computed earlier to see how we can use these statistics to better understand the portfolio.

We start with a VaR report on the portfolio by position. The first two columns of data display the marginal and incremental VaRs of the factors. The complement VaR is the VaR of the portfolio after the position has been removed or hedged completely. The standalone VaR, finally, is the VaR of the position viewed in isolation.

Position	MVaR	IVaR	Complement VaR	Standalone VaR
long EUR	3,172	2,435	40,849	8,349
short JPY	−1,902	−2,838	46,122	9,438
short SPX	944	−563	43,847	11,435
long GT10	1,508	825	42,460	7,734
long XU100	39,562	31,925	11,360	41,779
Total	43,285			78,735

The first noteworthy feature of this portfolio is that it has considerable diversification in it. This can be seen in the fact that most of the marginal VaRs are considerably smaller than the standalone VaRs. Viewed differently, the sum of the standalone VaRs at $78,735 is nearly double the portfolio VaR at $43,285. Nonetheless, most of the risk in the portfolio appears to be coming from the XU100 position even though the market values of all the positions are equal. Its marginal VaR is about 90 percent of the total, and is almost as great as its standalone VaR. The VaR report immediately reveals that there is a concentrated source of risk in the portfolio.

We can also report the risk of the portfolio by risk factor. We add a column showing the annualized volatility of each risk factor, measured using the exponentially weighted moving average (EWMA) algorithm and expressed in percent. The volatility of GT10, the 10-year Treasury note, has been converted from a yield to a price volatility so that it can be compared to the other factor volatilities.

Risk Factor	σ_n	MVaR	IVaR	Complement VaR	Standalone VaR
EUR	5.70	3,172	2,435	40,849	8,349
JPY	6.44	−1,902	−2,838	46,122	9,438
SPX	7.80	944	−563	43,847	11,435
GT10	5.28	1,508	825	42,460	7,734
XU100	20.18	25,468	19,967	23,317	29,578
TRL	12.36	14,094	11,958	31,326	18,108
Total		43,285			84,642

For the first four positions, since they are each a linear function of the risk factor in the same order in the list, the VaR results are identical to those reported by position. Note that the sum of standalone risk factor VaRs is somewhat higher, since we have broken out two of the risk factors. For the Turkish stock index (XU100) position, we can gain some intuition into how the high marginal risk is generated. The volatilities of the local currency XU100 and of the Turkish lira return are the two highest in the book. Moreover, as we saw in Chapter 5, these two returns have a fairly high positive correlation of 0.51, since sharp local-currency stock market declines tend to coincide with depreciation of the local currency against the dollar. The two risk factors do not have any large negative correlations with the other long risk factors or positive ones with the short risk factors that might offset their risk contributions. We can also see that about 40 percent of the risk of the XU100 position comes from the currency exposure it generates, and could be eliminated by hedging that risk.

To understand the portfolio better, we can group the positions into strategies, based on a trade thesis common to several positions, or on the use of a position to hedge an unwanted risk in other positions in the group. (In this example, as it happens, no positions are there as a deliberate hedge, though the short S&P index position will act as one in a stress scenario.) We can break our portfolio into three subportfolios, with VaR statistics as reported here:

Strategy	Standalone VaR	MVaR	IVaR	Complement VaR
Euro bullish/yen bearish	6,374	1,270	809	42,476
U.S. economy bearish	13,190	2,452	444	42,840
Turkish stock market	41,779	39,562	29,349	13,935

Euro bullish/yen bearish strategy (positions 1 and 2), both short the dollar against the other two major currencies. This strategy has the smallest standalone VaR. It is also the strategy with the smallest impact on the rest of the portfolio.

Some characteristics of the positions increase risk: EUR and JPY returns are positively correlated with the returns of the Istanbul Stock Exchange index (ISE 100), a long risk factor, and negatively with the 10-year U.S. government yield, a short risk factor. On the other hand, both EUR and JPY returns have relatively low volatility. Moreover, since the portfolio is long EUR risk, it contributes risk, while the short JPY position subtracts from the risk of the portfolio, as seen from its negative marginal and incremental VaR. The returns of the two positions are highly correlated with one another, and their correlations with the other risk factors in the portfolio are similar, so their risks are more or less offsetting. Together, therefore, this dollar-neutral bet on the euro-yen exchange rate has only a small net risk, viewed in isolation, as seen from the small standalone VaR, and it has only a small overall impact on the rest of the portfolio, as seen from the small incremental VaR.

U.S. economy bearish strategy (positions 3 and 4), which will both perform well if there is a material deterioration in U.S. growth prospects. The trade will also perform well if there is an increase in risk aversion, or, in the extreme, a "flight to quality" due to fear of a financial crisis. In that sense, the entire trade could be used as a portfolio hedge for a wide range of portfolios, such as the typical institutional portfolio, that are generally long risk assets.

This strategy also has a small impact on the risk of the entire portfolio (low incremental VaR). However, its standalone VaR is fairly high, since the risk factors underlying the two positions have an estimated correlation close to zero, limiting the diversification benefit. While one would expect a strong positive correlation between yields and equity indexes during a stress event, estimated correlations are often low. As we see in the next chapter, equity and bond return correlations are susceptible to rapid change during financial crises.

Turkish stock market strategy (position 5). This position's impact on the portfolio is overwhelming, primarily because the volatilities of both of its risk factors are high, and because the risk factors are positively correlated: A rise in the Turkish stock market is associated with a weakening of the lira against the dollar.

Marginal and incremental VaR, when used together with stress test results and with nonquantitative, judgmental data, can help us understand a set of positions as a portfolio, and to trace through the ways in which sets of positions within the portfolio contribute to, or mitigate, portfolio risk.

13.6   HEDGING AND BASIS RISK

There are two ways to mitigate risk: reducing positions and hedging. Risk management encompasses ensuring that exposures to all risk factors are the ones desired by the risk taker, ascertaining that hedges are effective, and seeing that risk exposures are sized in accordance with the risk taker's goals. We have discussed position sizing in the context of diversification and risk capital. In this section, we focus on problems and issues with hedging in the context of trading and investment risk. Hedging is an issue that affects not only traders, but every market participant, since all are exposed to a range of risks, and all must decide which to bear and which, if possible and cost effective, to mitigate.

There is no bright line between decisions on whether and how to hedge and other investment decisions. "Hedging" describes exposures that are not the core of a trade thesis, but are bundled with the securities through which the thesis is expressed. Hedging involves weighing risk against return, but is generally couched more in terms of the cost of hedging. Effective hedging reduces the volatility of the portfolio expressing the thesis, or eliminates an unwanted exposure that is not part of the thesis.

The term *basis risk* is generally used to describe the risk that two very similar, but not quite identical, securities will diverge or converge in price to the detriment of the investor. There is no clear standard of when two securities are similar enough to describe the relative price risk as "basis" rather than "market risk." Basis risk is one of the key risks to which a hedged portfolio is exposed. It can be thought of as the risk that a hedge position fails to fulfill its purpose.

Some important examples are:

> *The Treasury bond basis* is the difference between prices of U.S. Treasury notes and bonds in the cash market and the corresponding futures prices. Cash market prices are typically somewhat higher than futures prices because the seller of a Treasury futures acquires a *delivery option* from the futures buyer. At any point in time, several cash notes or bonds are eligible to be delivered by the futures seller to the buyer to satisfy the seller's delivery obligation. As interest rates change, the identity of the *cheapest-to-deliver* security

that is, the cheapest security among all those eligible, may change, but the futures seller may always discharge his obligation by delivering whatever note or bond is cheapest-to-deliver. The value of this option reduces the value of the futures relative to the cash market.

The bond-CDS basis. The spread over the Libor curve of a corporate bond in the cash market is typically not precisely equal to the premium of a CDS on the class of bonds of that issuer and seniority. Similar spreads exist between CDS indexes, such as the CDX, and indexes of CDS on asset-backed securities, on the one hand, and indexes of the spreads on underlying cash bonds. The difference can be positive or negative, but is typically small, since a large difference invites market participants to place trades that would profit from a reversal.

During the subprime crisis, however, the bond-CDS basis became unprecedentedly wide for many bonds, with CDS spreads much tighter than those of cash bonds. This phenomenon was driven by liquidity. Funding liquidity drove many market participants to attempt to raise cash by selling assets that had been financed in part by borrowing, usually in collateral markets, and could no longer be financed on the same terms as before the crisis, if at all. The preponderance of offers also impaired transactions liquidity. Together, these liquidity-based forces drove cash spreads wider than CDS. A market participant wishing to take advantage of this gap would have had to buy bonds in the cash market and buy CDS protection. The position would have had a positive cash flow, and, as noted in Chapter 11, such "arbitrage" trades are much-prized by traders. Very few market participants were in a position to do so, however, since buying cash bonds was a capital-intensive activity at a time of dire shortage of capital or "balance sheet."

Figure 13.4 illustrates this phenomenon with daily differences between spreads on Citigroup 10-year senior unsecured bonds and 10-year CDS spreads. The basis was close to zero prior to the subprime crisis, but reached a peak of close to 500 basis points, as Citi unsecured bond prices, like those of many other money-center banks, and liquidity in the financial-issuer bond market, reached their nadir in March of 2009. As can be seen, the basis not only widened, but also became very volatile.

Other important examples of basis risk arise in structured credit trading and became important drivers of large losses during the early phases of the subprime crisis. Traders sought to hedge the credit and market risk in investment-grade residential mortgage-based security (RMBS) by going long

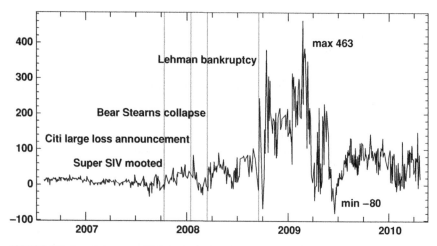

FIGURE 13.4 Citigroup CDS Basis 2007–2010
Difference between the spread over Libor (z-spread) of Citigroup Inc. bonds and the premium on Citigroup 10-year CDS on senior unsecured debt (bond spread minus CDS premium). The bond spread is blended from spreads on two senior unsecured issues: the 4.7% maturing May 29, 2015 (CUSIP 172967CY5) and the 5.85% maturing August 2, 2016 (CUSIP 172967DQ1).
Source: Bloomberg Financial L.P.

the ABX index, described in Chapter 11. But the ABX, while it captured the severe price declines in almost all RMBS over longer periods, was only very loosely tied to the performance of any particular portfolio of RMBS over any shorter time frame. As seen in Figure 11.4, the ABX indexes experienced several short-lived rallies in 2007 and 2008. Losses by some investors in lower-rated and lower-quality subprime RMBS were reportedly exacerbated by losses on ABX hedges.

In some instances, traders hedged positions in mortgage and non-mortgage structured credit with positions in the IG corporate credit indexes rather than the ABX. The corporate spread products have the virtue of relative liquidity, making it less costly to adjust hedges frequently as positions change. But as can be seen in Figure 14.14 and the table following it, such a hedge would have been disastrous during the subprime crisis. Investment-grade and high-yield corporate spreads rose by a factor of about 8 or 9 between mid-2007 and the end of 2009. Spreads on the investment-grade structured products that were to be hedged widened by a factor of about 100, in some cases considerably more.

A basis can open up almost anywhere. One might use a hedging instrument only to find that it diverges in some surprising way from the risk factor one had hoped to offset. Because of issues that can loosely be described as "basis risk," most exposures cannot be precisely hedged. There is a spectrum of hedging accuracy, ranging from simple hedges that are relatively easy to accurately gauge and vary over time, to positions that are close to unhedgable.

Some exposures can be hedged precisely enough that they can be treated as routine. Currency hedges on foreign exchange-denominated fixed-income securities, for example, are relatively easy to measure. Consider a long government bond position denominated in foreign currency. Assume the bond has no credit risk. The currency risk of the position can be hedged by selling forward the foreign-exchange proceeds of coupon and redemption payments, thus locking in the current forward foreign-exchange rates. This hedge could be combined with the initial purchase of foreign currency needed to buy the bond in a currency swap, probably executed with the dealer through which the bond is purchased. The investor now faces only the desired exposure to interest rates.

Even this currency hedge is not perfect if the security will not be held to maturity, since there is then price risk in the bond. Even if foreign risk-free rates fall, so the trade turns out well, the domestic-currency proceeds of the bond are uncertain, and the return on the investment is therefore also uncertain, particularly if the position is highly leveraged. The trader also has counterparty risk exposure through the currency swap hedge. For some currencies, there may also be liquidity risk.

If there is significant price risk in the security, the foreign-exchange risk on the profits can be material. Examples are equity or credit-risky bond positions. This risk is sometimes called *quanto risk*, after a type of exotic option introduced in the late 1980s. Quanto risk occurs when correlation risk is embedded in the price risk of a single position.

Many trade ideas require risk-free rate hedges, because the desired exposure is a credit spread, but the trade is executed through cash securities that pay a coupon and incorporate a risk-free rate as well as spread component. For example, a long investor in a U.S. fixed-coupon corporate bond may sell Treasury bonds or pay fixed in an interest-rate swap. The net cash flow then consists only of the spread at the time the trade is entered into. Such hedges can also generally be put on with high accuracy. However, even in this simple example, there is a potential for basis risk. Corporate spreads are generally set by the market relative to swap rather than Treasury rates, particularly for lower credit quality bonds. But the hedging vehicle chosen may in any event prove to be the wrong one, if the swap spread, the spread between government bond yields and swap rates, changes materially. Swap spread volatility has been extremely high at times, as can be seen in Figure 14.15.

Another issue with this type of hedge is that credit-risky securities with low spreads that trade on price can hit a "ceiling" at or slightly above par. Even if interest rates fall, the security may not appreciate in price, introducing negative convexity into its price behavior. This widens its spread, but if the clientele for the security is narrow, and the demand curve is flat at above-par prices, the widening may not generate much additional demand. One solution to this problem is to use swaptions or options on Treasury or eurodollar futures to hedge, thus matching more closely the security's convexity profile.

The most difficult types of risk to hedge are distressed and bankrupt bonds, and other securities with binary return profiles. In some cases, such as merger arbitrage, there is a natural hedge for a binary event. In general, however, hedges with continuous price behavior will not perform well.

FURTHER READING

The algebra of risk contributions is laid out in Sharpe (2002). Sharpe (2002) and Froot and Stein (1998) provide introductions to the risk capital and risk budgeting approach to investment. A general discussion of the concept of risk capital is provided by Merton and Perold (1993) and Perold (2005). See Litterman (1996) on implied views.

For an overview of stress testing, see Schachter (2010). Kupiec (1995a) and Mina and Xiao (2001) discuss issues around stress tests of subportfolios. Kim and Finger (2000) discusses stress testing techniques that take account of "regime changes" in correlation. Committee on the Global Financial System (2005) describes large banks' stress testing practices.

Breuer, Jandačka, Rheinberger, and Summer (2009) discusses systematic approaches to finding appropriate stress scenarios. See Amato and Remolona (2005) on the difficulty of achieving diversification in credit portfolios.

The supervisory stress tests conducted in the United States in 2009 are described in Hirtle, Schuermann, and Stiroh (2009), those in Europe in 2010 in Committee of European Banking Supervisors (2010). Alfaro and Drehmann's (2009) discussion of the difficulty of designing stress tests focuses on supervisory stress tests, but applies in large part to internal risk management.

Fung and Hsieh (1997, 2001) discuss dynamic strategies. Hedge fund risk management is discussed by Lo (2001), Asness, Liew, and Krail (2001), and Lhabitant (2001). Burghardt and Belton (2005) discuss the Treasury basis.

CHAPTER 14

Financial Crises

For financial market participants, financial crises are very difficult to anticipate and plan for, yet extremely destructive when they occur. From the standpoint of public policy, there is insufficient agreement on how to prevent or cope with crises. For researchers, financial crises remain a diffuse area, with poor problem definition, yet intense controversy. Crisis episodes present the most dramatic departures from the standard model of asset price behavior. The subprime crisis, by some measures, is the most severe financial crisis since the Great Depression of the 1930s, and will drastically change the financial system in ways not yet known.

Financial crises can be summarized as episodes displaying some or all of these symptoms or observable hallmarks:

Asset prices change sharply. The changes in asset prices are often a large multiple of the recently observed volatility, and thus would be judged extremely low-probability by the standard model.

Return moments change sharply. Volatility increases for almost all assets. Correlations "break down," that is, change from previous values, drawing much closer to ± 1, or to 0, or changing sign.

Aggregate credit shrinks drastically. Balance sheets shrink rapidly as assets lose value, lenders seek to reduce leverage, the credit intermediation mechanism is impaired, and borrowers are forced to curtail activity.

Market liquidity conditions deteriorate and liquidity impasses arise. Transaction volumes for many assets spike briefly, and then decline and remain low.

Payments systems integrity may be impaired. The "plumbing" of financial markets is intertwined with credit intermediation, as seen in Chapter 12, and may be dependent on the financial viability and creditworthiness of a small number of firms. Payment systems can therefore be affected by credit and liquidity problems.

Systemic risk increases; while ill-defined, it is part and parcel of a crisis.

Contagion: Dysfunction can spread to related and unrelated markets, via sentiment, hedging, and sharing the same or similar fundamentals.

Market functioning is impaired, that is, the price mechanism—security prices, interest rates, and credit spreads—cease to be the chief mechanism by which capital is allocated. Rather, various types of credit rationing come to the fore.

Economic activity, output and employment decline sharply.

Duration: These shocks and the credit contraction can last a long time. The depression following the initial financial panic of 1873, for example, lasted nearly a quarter-century.

Financial crises commonly break out openly upon a severe decline in some asset prices, a major default by a government or large financial intermediary, disruption of currency markets, or all three. But crises are the manifestation of longer-standing and less-visible problems. The causes of credit and currency market disruptions go to some of the oldest and deepest controversies in economics. In this chapter, we will discuss crises in the context of actual episodes, with special attention to the still ongoing subprime crisis.

Financial crisis is not a precisely defined technical term, but rather loosely describes certain historical episodes. Crises vary widely in severity and in the nature of the disruptions. One difficulty in studying crises is that the most severe crises are quite rare. There is, of course, disagreement as to which episodes of the past few centuries qualify as truly extreme, but, prior to the subprime crisis, the crises and associated depressions that began in 1793, 1825, 1873, and 1929 are often cited. Data on all but the last are far sketchier than that available for recent decades, making generalizations more difficult.

The paradigmatic financial crisis, at least prior to the subprime crisis, was the Great Depression, which lasted several years beginning in 1929—by some accounts over a decade—and led to tremendous suffering over large parts of the world. But the term "crisis" is also applied to events such as the breaking of the European Monetary System in 1992–1993, which had relatively limited consequences. The term "extreme events" is often used in the context of financial crises. We reserve the term "crisis" for more general and widespread episodes of distress, and describe episodes that were contained to just a few markets or a short period of time, such as the stock market crash of October 1987, as extreme events.

Our discussion starts with some "stylized facts" about the behavior of financial markets during crises, drawn from episodes of the past few decades. We then discuss theories about the causes and prevention of crises. We also see how researchers have defined and classified crises, and distinguished them from other extreme events in financial markets. We then turn to the issue most directly relevant for risk managers: Can crises be anticipated?

14.1 PANICS, RUNS, AND CRASHES

Two of the most characteristic features of financial crises are the

Credit crunch, a pervasive withdrawal of credit and decline in willingness to lend. Wojnilower (1985) defines a credit crunch as a "blockage in the supply of credit—a sudden and unanticipated intensification of nonprice rationing" (p. 351). At the time the term was introduced, it referred largely to bank lending, but fairly describes the behavior of nonbank intermediation as well.

Liquidity crunch, an intense increase in liquidity preference and the desire to exchange other financial assets for money. In the most extreme cases, all but the closest money substitutes are rejected in favor of cash or precious metals.

In this section, we describe these and other typical overt manifestations of crises. In the next section, we focus on specific self-propagating mechanisms by which financial crises take hold and worsen.

14.1.1 Monetary and Credit Contraction

A sudden decline or even a collapse in measures of financial activity is a universal hallmark of severe crises. But from a welfare point of view, the decline in real economic activity is the most important manifestation of a crisis. Unemployment rises, economic growth slows or becomes negative, and output declines, causing widespread suffering. The deterioration in business conditions tends to be worse and longer-lasting, the more badly the financial system is impacted.

Credit Expansion and Contraction A severe contraction in monetary and credit aggregates is often the most salient characteristic of a crisis. The period before the onset of a crisis typically sees strong credit expansion. In a commercial bank dominated financial system, that meant an expansion of bank lending and balance sheets. In a financial system in which capital markets and securitization play a large role in addition to that of banks, much of the credit expansion takes place through growth in the outstanding volume of securities. A crisis may occur when credit expansion abruptly slows, or it may deepen when a crisis that has begun for other reasons is exacerbated by a sharp reduction in the pace of credit expansion.

Credit growth during expansions is generally smooth and gradual, apart from recoveries immediately following credit crunches. Credit contractions are quite abrupt. The subprime crisis led to an extraordinarily sharp contraction in credit. Figure 14.1 displays net borrowing in credit markets, a measure of changes in the total volume of credit extension in the United States. It turned negative in 2009 for the first time since the end of 1946, but this time because of a sharp decline in the volume of intermediation by the

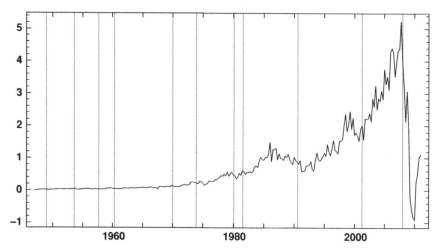

FIGURE 14.1 Net Borrowing in U.S. Credit Markets 1946–2010
All sectors, seasonally adjusted, quarterly, Q4 1946 to Q4 2010, trillions of dollars. This time series is a flow concept summarizing the net creation of credit in the United States. The vertical grid lines represent the dates of business cycle peaks, when contractions begin, as determined by the National Bureau of Economic Research (NBER).
Source: Federal Reserve Board, Flow of Funds Accounts of the United States (Z.1), Table F.1, line 1.

financial sector, rather than because of the cessation of federal government borrowing to finance World War II.

Contraction of Bank Lending Regulatory restrictions aside, bank lending is profitable as long as the interest on loans, adjusted for credit risk, exceeds the cost of capital. At times, however, banks face additional balance-sheet constraints on lending. Funding constraints occur when banks have difficulty borrowing from depositors or longer-term lenders. They may be unable to borrow at all, or the interest rates at which they can borrow rise suddenly and drastically. Balance-sheet constraints can become binding when banks are eager to preserve capital and decrease leverage, because they anticipate higher default or mark-to-market losses, or feel insecure about maintaining short-term funding as it rolls off. Regardless of net interest margin or prospective return on capital, at such times, they prefer at the margin to reduce lending and husband equity. These "non-price," i.e. non-interest rate constraints on lending distinguish credit crunches.

Figure 14.2 illustrates the behavior of bank lending, including business lending as well as mortgages and consumer loans, during economic downturns. Over the course of a credit cycle, the annual rate of growth of lending fluctuates widely, with high growth rates well in excess of 10 percent

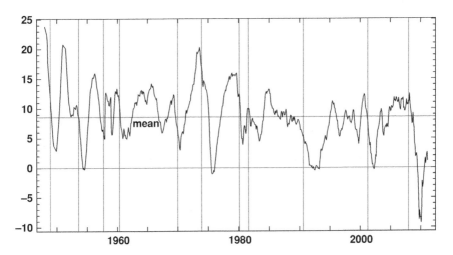

FIGURE 14.2 Growth in U.S. Bank Credit 1947–2011
Annual growth rate of loans and leases in bank credit of all commercial banks, seasonally adjusted, monthly data. Each point represents the logarithmic change, in percent, over the prior year. Vertical grid lines represent the dates of NBER business cycle peaks.
Data source: Federal Reserve Board, H.8 data release.

and an average just over $7\frac{1}{2}$ percent. In recent years, the growth rate has been somewhat lower, as capital markets and securitization accounted for much of the incremental growth in credit in the financial system as a whole.

Contractions in bank credit extension took place on five occasions during the last 65 years. By far the most severe—a decline of nearly 10 percent—occurred as the subprime crisis entered its intense phase following the Lehman bankruptcy. The overall contraction in credit was even more severe than Figure 14.2 indicates, since there was also a complete halt in credit intermediation through securitization from the fall of 2008. As we will see in a moment, the recorded decline in bank credit was somewhat attenuated by an "involuntary," but transitory, return of intermediation to the banking system.

A credit crunch can be amplified by liquidity concerns similar to those provoking a bank run. During a crisis, even financial intermediaries that are in no immediate danger of collapse become concerned about the potential demands on them for liquidity and about how their creditworthiness will be perceived. They therefore become eager to accumulate liquidity reserves of cash and highly marketable securities such as Treasury bills and notes, and reluctant to put money to work by lending.

Credit crunches are often "capital crunches," a term that describes one motivation for a credit crunch. Banks become more reluctant to extend credit, not in the first instance because they have become more concerned about the creditworthiness of the borrower or the use of the funds, but because they are concerned that their equity capital is insufficient. This was the case following large bank loan losses in the wake of the S&L crisis of the late 1980s, which led to the large recession of 1990–1991. It was very much the case during the subprime crisis, driven by the possibility of large future losses, over and above any losses that had already been realized. Uncertainty about the value of investment-grade securitized credit products, of which some banks had large holdings, was one major factor. Another was uncertainty about how long and severe the economic downturn would be and how severe the consequent loan losses would be.

Apart from a sharp decline in the volume of credit extended, a credit crunch is also characterized by a change in the terms on which credit is extended, which include not only the credit spread charged on a loan, but also the underwriting standards. In the United States, data on these terms is collected via the Federal Reserve's Senior Loan Officer Opinion Survey on Bank Lending Practices, which polls loan officers at large U.S. and foreign banks located in the United States. As seen in Figure 14.3, the reduction in credit volume was associated with a dramatic tightening of credit terms, both with respect to underwriting standards and pricing: By the end of 2008, three-quarters of respondents were tightening standards, and nearly all were

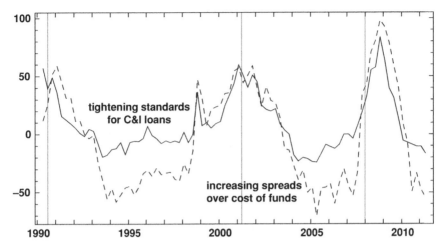

FIGURE 14.3 Tightening of Credit Terms 1990–2011
Quarterly data through Q2 2011. The solid line plots the net percentage of
respondents tightening standards for C&I loans to large and middle-market
corporate borrowers. The dotted line plots the net percentage of respondents
increasing spreads of loan rates over banks' cost of funds for such loans. "Net
percentages" equal the percentage of banks that reported tightening standards
minus the percentage of banks that reported easing standards. The vertical grid lines
represent the dates of NBER business cycle peaks.
Source: Federal Reserve Board, Senior Loan Officer Opinion Survey on Bank
Lending Practices, Table 1.

increasing credit spreads. As with all market-clearing prices and quantities,
it is difficult to establish empirically whether a contraction in the volume
of credit during a downturn is a credit crunch, that is, the result of abrupt
restriction by banks, or of lack of demand for credit brought about by bad
business conditions. The tightening of terms is evidence that the reduction
is induced by a credit crunch, and not only by lack of demand.

Figure 14.3 also illustrates the positive correlation between the pricing
of loans and underwriting standards. When funding is easy, underwriting
standards are loosened, and spreads are reduced.

The most severe form of credit contraction is caused by widespread bank
runs, which we've discussed in Chapter 12 and return to just below. A bank
run is a type of funding constraint. It occurs when all or a sizable fraction
of depositors simultaneously demand the return of the funds they've lent a
bank. Bank runs occur sporadically as isolated events even in quiet times.
But in the most serious financial crises, they can become widespread.

A bank run often leads to the failure of the impacted bank. In Chapters 1 and 12, we discussed the fragility of banks, which carry out credit

intermediation via maturity transformation, that is, by using their balance sheets to turn short-term deposits into long-term loans to firms. They also carry out a liquidity transformation, turning illiquid assets such as loans into liquid deposits. Under fractional-reserve banking, liquidity reserves may be quite small compared to a bank's deposit base, and can be quickly depleted during a run. Once this happens, the bank becomes insolvent.

Fear of banks runs, even if they do not actually occur, can also have an impact during a crisis. These fears contributed to the widening of interbank lending spreads during the subprime crisis, as seen in Figures 14.9 and 14.10.

While bank runs are a typical phenomenon of financial crises, crises can also lead to a consolidation of intermediation within the commercial banking system. Banks are fragile, but the rise of market-based lending has placed some of the most fragile parts of the financial system outside of banks. Highly leveraged transactions in structured credit products financed via short-term borrowing, for example, are even more readily disrupted than bank lending.

In addition, banks function as "lenders of second resort," a phenomenon also called "involuntary reintermediation" that describes the increase in bank lending resulting from credit implicitly or explicitly granted prior to a credit crunch. The phenomenon was quite pronounced during the subprime crisis. One visible sign was the increase in drawings on banks' lending commitments. Banks also felt obliged in many cases to assume onto their balance sheet securitization vehicles that could no longer be funded in the asset-backed commercial paper (ABCP) market, such as the ABCP conduits and structured investment vehicles (SIVs), described in Chapter 12; many of those without bank-provided backstops simply collapsed. Figure 14.4 displays the brief but sharp increase in non-mortgage bank lending to businesses in the immediate aftermath of the Lehman bankruptcy that preceded the protracted decline in lending.

Bank lending grew steadily until the panic phase of the crisis at the end of 2007. It then leveled off for several quarters. One would have expected, following the Lehman bankruptcy and the beginning of the most intense phase of the crisis, that bank lending would immediately contract sharply. The contraction did indeed occur, but not for another quarter. In fact, the immediate effect was a sharp increase in bank lending in October 2008, as borrowers dependent on access to securities markets drew on bank-based sources of financing such as credit lines and revolving credit agreements, and banks provided on-balance-sheet funding for off-balance-sheet vehicles that could no longer be financed in the capital markets. Only once these explicit and implicit guarantees by banks to extend credit had been fully met, could banks begin to effect a decrease in their lending assets.

Another example of the "lender of second resort" phenomenon that appeared during the subprime crisis is displayed in Figure 1.6 of Chapter 1.

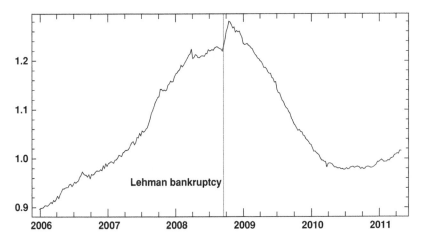

FIGURE 14.4 U.S. Bank Lending during the Subprime Crisis 2006–2011
Commercial and industrial loans, all commercial banks, seasonally adjusted,
weekly, trillions of dollars.
Source: Federal Reserve Board, H.8 data release.

With market-based intermediation paths such as securitization collapsing,
as we will see in a moment, banks took on a larger share of the remaining
intermediation activity for some types of credit. As the share of securitization via commercial mortgage-backed securities (CMBS) in commercial real
estate lending declined after its peak in 2007, for example, banks' share
grew by about the same fraction of the total.

Contraction of Securities Markets   Not only bank lending, but also other
forms of credit intermediation decline rapidly during crises. We have seen
one important example, the reduction in the volume and shortening of
the maturities of commercial paper issued by financial firms following the
Lehman bankruptcy, in Chapter 12.

Access to credit for ABCP conduits and SIVs, off-balance-sheet vehicles
set up to finance loans and structured credit products via short-term funding,
contracted even more rapidly than for financial firms during the subprime
crisis. Short-term lenders to intermediaries and ABCP conduits through the
commercial paper market responded to concerns about the creditworthiness
and liquidity of the borrowers by stepping back from the market as their
holdings rolled off. Commercial paper issuance by financial firms and ABCP
conduits together accounted at the mid-2007 peak for over 90 percent of total U.S. commercial paper issuance and declined by over 50 percent over the
subsequent three years, as seen in Figure 14.5. Part of this decline is mirrored
in the post-Lehman "involuntary reintermediation" seen in Figure 14.4.

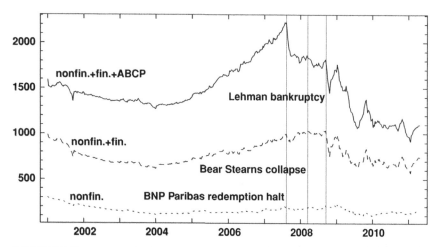

FIGURE 14.5 Outstanding Volume of Commercial Paper 2001–2011
Seasonally adjusted, billions of dollars, weekly, Jan. 10, 2001 to Apr. 20, 2011.
Source: Federal Reserve Board

Among the key investors in financial and ABCP were non–government-backed or "prime" money market mutual funds (MMMF). Institutional investors fled such funds following the Lehman bankruptcy in the MMMF equivalent of a bank run, as illustrated in Figure 14.7. Commercial paper credit spreads also rose sharply during the crisis.

Bond market issuance also declines during a crisis. This has a potentially much larger impact on real economic activity today in view of the greater importance of capital markets relative to bank lending in aggregate credit intermediation. Figure 14.6 displays bond issuance in three important sectors. The top panel displays issuance of ABS outside the real-estate sector, the center panel, issuance of residential and commercial real-estate related ABS, and the bottom panel issuance of high-yield corporate bonds. All show a drastic decline in 2008 and 2009.

The real-estate sector shows the most dramatic decline, from about $1.4 trillion in each of 2006 and 2007 to near-zero since. ABS not related to real estate and high-yield bond issuance each fell more than 50 percent in 2008. These declines mirrored a credit crunch in the nonbank sector. As the investor base for securitized loans collapsed, the capacity to originate underlying loans collapsed with it. High-yield bond issuance, however, not only recovered, but even reached a record pace in 2010. This is in part due to firms, including nonbank financial intermediaries, issuing unsecured debt rather than ABS. The underlying assets are then financed on the balance sheet rather than being moved off-balance-sheet to serve as collateral for specific

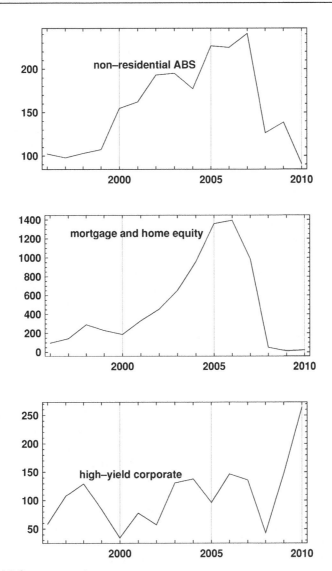

FIGURE 14.6 U.S. Bond Issuance 1996–2010
Bond issuance volume in the United States, billions of U.S. dollars, annual.
Upper panel: Issuance of ABS backed by auto loans, credit card receivables,
equipment, and student loans.
Center panel: Issuance of private-label RMBS and CMBS, and of ABS backed by
home-equity loans and manufactured housing.
Lower panel: Issuance of high-yield corporate bonds.
Data source: Securities Industry and Financial Markets Association, available at
http://www.sifma.org/ research/statistics/statistics.aspx.

bonds. But it also reflected the weakness of banks during the subprime crisis and the ability of larger firms with direct access to capital markets to find alternatives to bank lending.

14.1.2 Panics

Banks runs have been a frequent marker of financial crises for centuries since the development of fractional reserve banking. We have discussed runs as an extreme form of the contraction of credit volumes. Now we look at runs from the standpoint of the intermediaries from which funding is withdrawn. The classic form of a run is the withdrawal of deposits from commercial banks. In the modern financial system, as noted, runs also occur in other forms: Nonbanks that are relatively dependent on wholesale funding can also experience runs in the less-visible form of a withdrawal of short-term credit.

Bank Runs and Run-Like Behavior   An instance of a run that figured importantly in the early history of the subprime crisis and its spread beyond the United States was the run on Northern Rock, a British building society, or mortgage lender, which began after the lender sought emergency liquidity support from the Bank of England on September 13, 2007. The next day, the classic overt symptom of a run appeared, as depositors lined up outside the bank's branches to withdraw funds. However, what amounted essentially to a run of its wholesale funding sources had already begun. Northern Rock was exceptionally vulnerable to a run, as its leverage, measured as the ratio of assets to common stock, was close to 60 by mid-2007. A loss in the value of its assets, composed largely of mortgage loans, of even $1\frac{2}{3}$ percent would therefore have sufficed to wipe out its equity and begin to impair lenders. Under these circumstances, as soon as doubts arose as to the true value of its assets, Northern Rock was unable to roll over its short-term debt.

During the subprime crisis, runs took unusual forms not seen in the past that reflected changes in the financial system. We have seen, in Figure 12.5, the drastic reduction, over just a few weeks beginning in August 2007, in the outstanding volume of ABCP. Conduits and SIVs experienced a rollover risk event and were unable to replace ABCP borrowing as it matured. The sharp rise in draws on existing bank lines is another example of an unusual type of bank "run" by obligors. In Chapter 12, we saw that banks' and broker-dealers' prime brokerage business with hedge funds was an important source of cash funding, and of collateral that could be rehypothecated and thus used as a funding source. As doubts about Bear's and Lehman's liquidity and solvency grew in the course of 2008, they rapidly lost their hedge fund customers, and with them, access to the cash and collateral the hedge funds deposited with them.

Another unusual run-like phenomenon occurred in the credit default swap (CDS) markets. Counterparties became eager to novate outstanding CDS away from Bear and Lehman. This sent an adverse signal about market perceptions of these broker-dealers' strength, but also, to the extent novation could be achieved, deprived Bear and Lehman of the cash collateral associated with the CDS: Prior to the subprime crisis, CDS margin would have been disproportionally in the hands of large broker-dealers, rather than symmetrically in the hands of counterparties with positive net present value (NPV) positions.

Other run-like phenomena affected nontraditional intermediaries. We noted in Chapter 12 that money market mutual funds are exposed to liquidity risks similar to those of depository institutions. Immediately following the Lehman bankruptcy, a run on some MMMFs took place. It was triggered by reports that Reserve Primary Fund Class Institutional, a large and prominent MMMF, had invested a significant proportion of its assets in Lehman Brothers Holdings' commercial paper and other debt securities. There was, as noted earlier, also concern about MMMF holdings of other financial and asset-backed commercial paper.

Reserve Primary suffered massive redemptions and "broke the buck," reporting an NAV of $0.97 on September 17, 2008. Other MMMFs avoided breaking the buck, but had large redemptions, mainly by institutional investors, and reallocations by investors away from MMMFs investing mainly in commercial paper and other corporate, financial, and asset-backed issues, and into funds investing primarily in short-term government debt (see Figure 14.7). The institutional investor rejection of these assets also had important consequences for other parts of the financial system. ABCP was an important source of funding for both structured credit products, via structured investment vehicles (SIVs), and for the underlying loans, via ABCP conduits. The disappearance of the ABCP investor base thereby contributed to the shutdown of securitization markets in the fall of 2008. Part of that investor flight was indirect, through withdrawals from MMMFs.

Run-like behavior was also observed for other nonbank market participants. For example, hedge funds experienced large redemptions by investors, as discussed in Chapter 12. Some of these withdrawals were motivated by fear of losses. But in many instances, withdrawals were especially "run-like" in that they were motivated by investors' desire for liquidity and by their awareness of the sequential-service constraint on the funds. That is, they wished to retrieve liquidity from otherwise sound hedge funds before it was exhausted by other investors' redemptions.

Dealing with bank runs once they have begun is exceptionally difficult. Two drastic approaches are closing banks, as done for example during the "bank holiday" of 1933, and by guaranteeing deposits, or even banks'

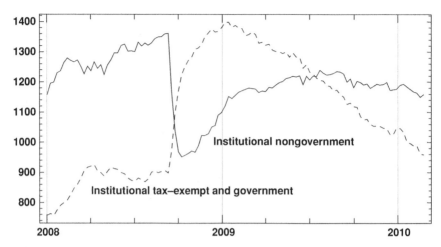

FIGURE 14.7 Institutional Investor Assets in MMMFs 2008–2010
Weekly, billions of dollars.
Source: Investment Company Institute.

debt generally. Early in the Swedish banking crisis of 1992, for example, the Swedish government guaranteed all bank debt. Ireland issued a similar guarantee in September 2008.

Liquidity Impasses and Hoarding   The Northern Rock experience of a retail depositor run was not, in fact, typical of the subprime crisis. Widespread depositor runs, the most-feared form of financial crisis historically, in which depositors, particularly retail ones, seek the immediate return of their funds, did not occur; instances, such as the run on mortgage-focused IndyMac Bancorp in late June 2008, remained isolated events. But Northern Rock's demise combined this feature of classic bank runs with a feature more typical of the subprime crisis, namely, the withdrawal of wholesale funding to the financial sector, as lenders sought to preserve their own cash balances and became extremely wary of the financial condition of intermediaries. Even where the reluctance to provide funding did not lead to the collapse of an intermediary, it led to an enormous increase in their cost of funding.

   Bank runs and run-like phenomena are, in essence, the result of many, if not all, market participants' desire to become more liquid simultaneously. They endeavor to keep their assets in the most liquid form possible, and to "term out," that is, to extend the maturity, of their short-term borrowings, in order to reduce rollover risk. They therefore become extremely reluctant to lend out their liquid assets; that is, in the language of the 1930s debates, they "hoard" them. The shift can be very rapid. From a situation in which most market participants are content to borrow short-term and invest at longer terms or in riskier assets, the markets can within days move to one in which market participants strive to borrow at longer terms and seek to drastically reduce the term and risk of their assets.

This was illustrated when the subprime crisis entered a new and more intense phase on August 9, 2007, following the announcement by BNP Paribas that it was suspending redemptions from three residential-mortgage hedge funds. This was the latest blow to market confidence, following a string of residential mortgage originator bankruptcy filings since the end of 2006, rising mortgage delinquencies on late-vintage loans, and announcements of large losses on subprime loans and securitizations by banks and by hedge funds managed by UBS and Bear Stearns. Concern about potential bank losses became more acute. The next day, the interbank money market began to clearly reflect the disturbance: Widening spreads on unsecured short-term loans to banks relative to other money market rates signaled reluctance to lend to banks. Run-like behavior affected all cash operations of intermediaries and could take unusual forms, such as the hedge fund run on prime brokers and investors' run on viable hedge funds.

In the subprime crisis, as is typical in a financial crisis, the focus of concern was the creditworthiness of banks. One source of particular worry for potential lenders to banks was the disposition of off-balance-sheet vehicles such as SIVs, the liquidity risks of which we described in Chapter 12. A number of SIVs, though by no means all, were sponsored by large banks. The vehicles invested in subprime residential securities and other structured credit products, and financed these investments by issuing a variety of debt instruments, including short-term debt. When concern emerged about the creditworthiness of the bonds the SIVs held as assets, investors grew reluctant to roll over the short-term funding they had provided. This initiated the typical "fire sale" mechanism of an asset price decline, as the SIVs were then obliged to raise capital by selling assets, compounding the price declines and accelerating withdrawals of funding. It also had features of a bank run, in that investors were eager to withdraw funds before the SIVs liquidity or access to liquidity was exhausted by other investors' withdrawals.

While banks were in general not contractually obliged to provide backstop liquidity to the SIVs they sponsored, most felt compelled to do so in order to protect their reputations and avert long-term harm to their business as a whole. This added to the considerable strain on their balance sheets. The SIVs were, even before the crisis, highly levered, so overall leverage of the bank assuming the SIV increased. Bank leverage was also increasing because the SIVs were experiencing losses, eroding the banks' capital.

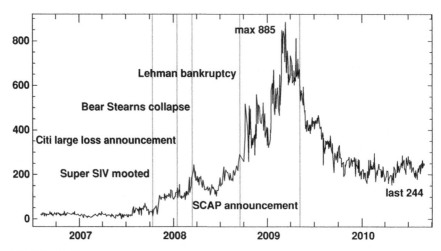

FIGURE 14.8   Citigroup Credit Spreads during the Subprime Crisis 2006–2010
Spread over Libor (z-spread) of Citigroup Inc. senior unsecured bonds with
maturities of about 10 years, daily. The construction of the data is described in the
caption to Figure 13.4.
Source: Bloomberg Financial L.P.

    Also typical of a bank run was the difficulty potential lenders to banks
had in distinguishing which intermediaries had losses great enough to cast
doubt on their ability to repay loans. The initial shock, losses on subprime
residential mortgage debt, was known to be large enough to affect a number of firms. While it was widely and firmly believed that at least some
banks had experienced serious losses that had not yet been reported, there
was considerable uncertainty as to which banks were worst affected. Potential counterparties also took into account not only the correlation of losses
brought about by the direct effect of the shock, but also correlation indirectly induced by counterparty withdrawal even from firms less affected by
subprime losses, since these could not be accurately ascertained in real time.
Rumors and adverse information on the financial health of intermediaries
play an important role in crises.

    Figure 14.8 illustrates the extent and sudden onset of distrust of banks
as borrowers. It displays the senior unsecured funding spread of Citigroup,
one of the largest banks. Prior to the onset of the crisis, it paid only a
narrow spread, often less than 20 basis points, for long-term unsecured
funding. Its debt spread began to widen in late 2007, as awareness grew of
the extent of off-balance-sheet funding it had carried out via SIVs, among
other asset-quality issues. In late 2007, the U.S. Treasury abandoned a plan
to address the problem for Citi as well as other large banks. Citi's cost of

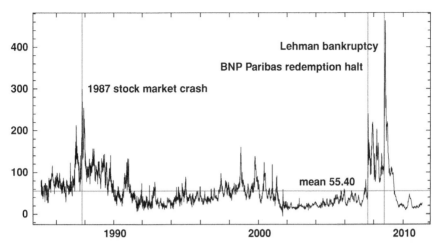

FIGURE 14.9 Three-Month TED Spread 1985–2011
Spread of three month USD BBA Libor minus the yield of the three month Treasury
bill, basis points, daily, December 6, 1984 to May 11, 2011.
Source: Bloomberg Financial L.P.

funding spiked briefly following its first announcement of extremely large
losses of over $18 billion on January 15, 2008, and then again amid the
Bear Stearns collapse. But the funding spread climbed to extreme levels in
the months following the Lehman bankruptcy, reaching a maximum near
900 basis points in mid-March 2009.

Financial crises as well as periods of less intense stress also lead to
widening of money market spreads, due to increased anxiety about credit
and liquidity risk and concern about the counterparty risk of dealing with
banks. Figure 14.9 displays one measure of this anxiety, the spread between
U.S. dollar Libor money market rates and yields on U.S. Treasury bills. This
spread is one of a class called the *TED spread*, a term originally applied to
spreads between eurodollar and Treasury bill futures. As can be seen, this
spread tends to widen sharply during stress periods, for example, following
the October 1987 stock market crash and during the subprime crisis.

As banks grew more anxious about the creditworthiness of their counterparties in mid-2007, term Libor rates increased dramatically compared
to those for short-term interbank loans. This hindered the interbank money
market in its function of distributing funds, at a price, from banks with a net
surplus liquidity position to those needing short-term funds. Figure 14.10
displays the spread between Libor and *overnight interest rate swap* (OIS)
rates, for one and three month month terms. OIS are OTC contracts in which
one counterparty pays the other the difference between a predetermined level

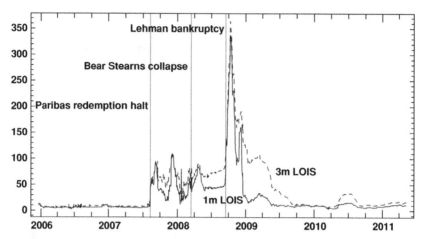

FIGURE 14.10   Libor–OIS Spread 2006–2011
Spread between three month USD BBA Libor and OIS, daily, basis points, January 2006 to May 2011. The solid (dashed) plot represents three month (one month) BBA Libor minus the price of a three month (one month) OIS swap.
Source: Bloomberg Financial L.P.

and the daily realization of the overnight money market benchmark rate over the term of the contract. The predetermined level is the quoted price, and reflects market expectations of where the overnight rate will be over the term of the OIS.

A wide spread between term Libor and OIS is unusual, since if it is costly to borrow at term, banks will prefer the overnight market, and the spread will diminish. The extreme widening of this spread in 2007 reflected the eagerness of banks with a funding need to lock up funds for longer than overnight or a few days, even if it was expensive. But it also reflected an increased desire of banks for surplus liquidity and the deep aversion of banks in a surplus liquidity position to lend at term to other banks. At the worst point of the crisis, the one-month Libor-OIS spread was nearly as wide as the three month spread. This reflected the extremity of banks' desire to shake their dependence on overnight funding. One-month funding had become almost as precious as three-month in view of the precariousness to which dependence on overnight funding had suddenly exposed them; the difference between the one- and three-month spreads was very small compared to the spread between either and the expected overnight rate.

Not only were there doubts about any particular counterparty's solvency; potential lenders also knew that the counterparty would have to find many other lenders willing to provide funding in order to remain liquid. In

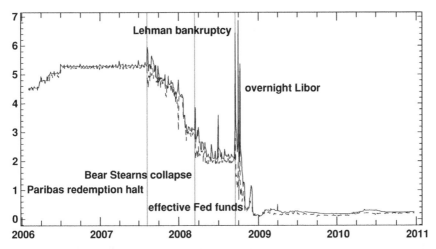

FIGURE 14.11 U.S. Dollar Overnight Rates 2006–2011
Effective Fed funds rate (dashed plot) and overnight U.S. dollar BBA Libor rates
(solid plot), percent, daily. The effective Fed funds rate is published by the New
York Fed.
Source: Bloomberg Financial L.P.

the terminology often used in the finance literature, potential lenders were
conscious of *endogenous liquidity risk.*

Another symptom of the disruption of money markets was the spread
between interbank money market rates and the federal funds market, in
which balances at Federal Reserve banks are traded. Figure 14.11 displays
the realized or "effective" Fed funds rate and the overnight Libor rate. Both
became extremely volatile, as it became more difficult for ordinary monetary
operations to bring the rate close to the target. The spread between the Fed
funds and Libor rates, although for the same term, also widened out sharply.

14.1.3 Rising Insolvencies

Financial crises are associated with an increasing incidence of insolvency.
Figure 6.1 displays corporate defaults for the past 90 years, measured by the
fraction of bond issuers defaulting in a year. Defaults by issuers of high-yield
bonds in 2009 were close to their highest level in the nearly century-long
time series, exceeded only during the Great Depression. Both high-yield and
investment grade defaults were at postwar highs in 2009.

Another measure of insolvency is the rate at which loans default. *Delinquency* occurs when borrowers stop paying interest and other debt service.

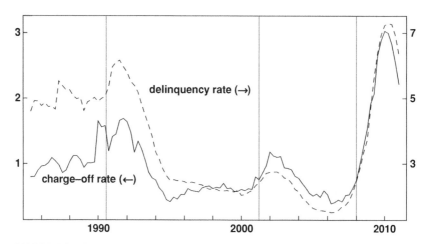

FIGURE 14.12   U.S. Commercial Bank Charge-Off and Delinquency Rates
1985–2010
Quarterly, as a percent of aggregate loan balances. Charge-offs (solid line, left
axis) are the value of loans removed from the books and charged against loss
reserves, net of recoveries. Delinquent loans (dashed line, right axis) are those
past due 30 days or more and still accruing interest as well as those in nonaccrual
status. Vertical grid lines represent the dates of NBER business cycle peaks.
Source: Federal Reserve Board.

Borrowers may resume paying later, or eventually default. Once the loan
defaults or it is determined that default is highly likely, the loan is *charged
off*, that is, a loss is taken equal to the unrecovered portion.[1] Figure 14.12
displays these measure for loans on the books of U.S. commercial banks
over the past quarter-century. The data are obtained from regular *call reports* banks submit on their financial condition. The charge-off rate was
twice as high at the end of 2009 as at its previous peak, in the aftermath of
the 1990–1991 recession. Delinquency rates were also at their record high
within the data set.

    During a financial crisis, insolvencies are more difficult to address via
restructuring, so that not only do default and bankruptcy become more
frequent, but liquidation becomes a more frequent result of insolvency.

---

[1]*Discharge* is a legal term for extinguishing a debt obligation. *Charge-off* is an
accounting term for reducing the value of the obligation on the balance sheet of its
owner.

14.1.4 Impairment of Market Functioning

Market functioning is a somewhat elusive concept that describes how smoothly markets are working to equilibrate asset supplies and demands, and to intermediate credit and liquidity. "Broken markets" are frequently observed in crises. Some symptoms of poor financial market functioning are

- Observable asset prices that fluctuate rapidly, or visibly violate no-arbitrage conditions, and at which market participants don't believe they can execute transactions in size. An example of an apparent violation of arbitrage constraints on prices took place at the auctions to determine recovery values for Fannie Mae and Freddie Mac CDS after they were placed in conservatorship by the Federal Housing Finance Agency (FHFA). The recovery rates for the subordinate debt ended higher than those for the senior debt, 99.9 percent versus 91.51 for Fannie Mae and 94 percent versus 98 for Freddie Mac. Senior Supervisors Group (2009a) attributes the result to hedging by protection sellers. A similar example is the emergence of extremely low and eventually negative swap spreads after the Lehman bankruptcy (Figure 14.15).
- Credit is always allocated in part via rationing rather than purely via prices, that is, loan rates. But in a poorly functioning credit market, rationing can become predominant.

A dramatic example of poor market functioning is the phenomenon of *settlement fails* in repo markets. A settlement fail typically occurs when a repo is not closed out as contracted via the delivery of a security. The lender of cash is the seller of the security in this closing leg. When a fail takes place, the cash collateral is also not returned to the counterparty of the failing party. The convention is not to consider the fail a default, but rather to leave the repurchase price unchanged. The securities borrower (lender of cash) is then making the economic equivalent of a zero-interest loan to the lender of the security until he delivers the security, curing the fail.

Fails can occur for a number of reasons, the last two of which were especially relevant during the subprime crisis:

1. *Operational problems and miscommunication* can arise for individual market participants. But they can also be system-wide, as occurred on September 11, 2001, in which broker offices, their personnel, records, and infrastructure were destroyed.
2. *Concern about scarcity of collateral* can motivate borrowers of securities to keep the securities and lenders of securities to step back from the market. These concerns can focus on the potential for them to be "failed to" once they enter into a new repo. When one counterparty fails to

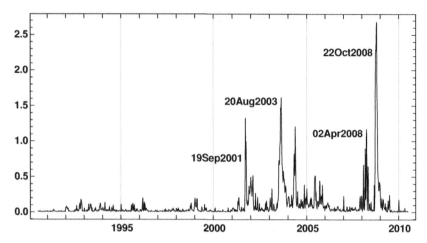

FIGURE 14.13 Settlement Fails in the Treasury Market 1990–2010
Cumulative fails to receive, weekly, trillions of dollars. Fails to receive should
equal fails to deliver, but may be reported more accurately.
Source: Federal Reserve Bank of New York.

deliver to another, the latter is more likely to fail on repos in which he
is obligated to deliver. This can lead to a cascade of connected fails, so
that a small surge in fails can easily turn into a large one.

It can also result from hoarding of high-quality collateral, particularly in an environment in which there is concern about fails, and
thus whether one will get the security back when expected, and about
counterparty risk generally.

3. *A low interest cost of failing* reduces the opportunity cost of failing. If the
interest earned by lending cash and borrowing a security is high, there
is little incentive to fail, since the securities borrower forgoes interest
for as long as a fail persists. This can happen in two ways. Specific
securities much in demand as collateral can have lending rates close to
zero. Or the money market rate itself can be low, as occurred during the
subprime crisis. Low rates reduce the incentive to avoid failing, since
foregone interest is lower.

Figure 14.13 displays data on fails reported by *primary dealers*, broker-
dealers that are authorized to conduct bond transactions with the Federal
Reserve. Four large spikes in fails are identified. The first occured after
September 11, 2001, and was induced primarily by operational issues in the
wake of the terror attack. The next, in August 2003, is related to a sharp
runup in Treasury yields during the preceding two months. We discuss this
episode in the next section as an example of "positive feedback" in financial

markets. The increase in fails was due to market participants' concern about being able to borrow Treasury securities to sell them short. Traders who had a borrow did not want to give it up.

The last two spikes occured during two acute phases of the subprime crisis, the Bear Stearns collapse and the Lehman bankruptcy. Both were due to the scarcity of collateral as well as low interest rates. One consequence was a further impairment of the interbank market. In addition to the drain of liquidity that is a typical feature of financial crises, the surge in fails showed that liquidity was not being appropriately distributed among intermediaries. Rather, intermediaries with cash or collateral that could reliably be used to raise cash were reluctant to part with it, while those short of cash and collateral found it extremely difficult to obtain it.

The drastic increase in fails during the subprime crisis is an illustration, not only of the impairment of market functioning, but also of a number of other recurrent features of financial crises, such as the operation of self-propagating mechanisms that deepen financial stress, the impact of "interconnectedness" in financial markets, and the stresses on interbank lending.

Scarcity of Collateral   During a crisis, collateral that can be used to support borrowing becomes more scarce, and high-quality collateral becomes particularly scarce via a reduction in pledging of high-quality collateral and increasing haircuts on all types. Another manifestation of scarcity of collateral is the increase in fails discussed above. Banks and other street firms reduce their own counterparty risk, a stabilizing influence, but also abruptly reduce the volume of flow of collateral. Hedge funds and other clients move their collateral from margin to cash accounts.

Scarcity of collateral is another form the contraction of securities markets; the impact is not on the volume of intermediation achieved directly through the bonds themselves, but rather on liquidity, as fewer high-quality bonds are available for rehypothecation. There is strong evidence, from the rise in fails and balance sheet reports of financial intermediaries, that collateral, like cash, was "hoarded" during the financial crisis.

The phenomenon can be seen as accentuating the demand for high-quality assets that drove yields lower prior to the crisis. But also it also led to the rejection of assets such as structured credit products that earlier had satisfied that demand.

14.2   SELF-REINFORCING MECHANISMS

In a panic, asset owners may be eager to sell, even at much lower prices than have recently been observed. This can occur for a number of reasons. They may view even the lower current price as still well above fundamental value.

They may have bought the asset during a period of rising prices, planning to sell at a higher price that now seems unattainable. They may no longer be able to fund the asset, as, for example, in the case of ABCP conduits' and SIVs' holdings of structured credit products. Or their risk aversion may have dramatically risen.

Regardless of initial motivation, the desire to sell assets becomes self-perpetuating during crises. The mechanisms by which the desire to sell reinforces and intensifies itself are sometimes called "positive feedback loops," although of course there is nothing positive about them. The result is sometimes called an asset "fire sale." Certain common mechanisms make these sales self-perpetuating.

A related concept is *contagion*, the observation that localized financial stresses very often "spread" to neighboring geographical regions or to other markets and financial institutions. A run on one bank may readily trigger runs on others. A speculative attack on one currency may lead to attacks on others. In our discussion of Citigroup's SIV-induced losses, we alluded to the distinction between contagion induced by the vulnerability of many financial firms to a common shock, that is, direct correlation of losses, and *pure contagion* induced via fear and panic, a similar concept to that of endogenous liquidity risk. A similar ecologically tinged concept is that of *herding behavior*, the observation that market participants may have strong incentives to mimic or preempt actions by others.

In this section, we discuss some of these mechanisms. A broader discussion of whether or not the financial system is inherently stable or cyclical follows later in this chapter. A closely related question is whether the financial system tends to *procyclicality*; that is, a tendency for a positive credit environment, in which both the demand for credit and eagerness to lend are growing, to create an even more positive credit environment, and vice versa, leading to booms and busts. Some of these forces, such as procyclical capital standards, may be regulatory, and are discussed in Chapter 15.

14.2.1 Net Worth and Asset Price Declines

At the start of a crisis, a firm may suffer market or credit losses that reduce its equity capital. As its net worth falls, it finds itself more highly leveraged than it was before. A financial institution that is leveraged 20-to-1 might have credit losses of 1 percent of the value of its assets, reducing its equity capital by 20 percent. Suppose, for example, the firm's starting position is:

Assets	Liabilities
$A = 20$	Equity $E = 1$
	Debt $D = 19$

If it experiences a loss of 0.2 and there is no other change in its assets, and it doesn't raise additional equity, its leverage will rise to

$$\frac{20 - 0.2}{1 - 0.2} = 24.75$$

so the loss, although accounting for only 1 percent of its assets, has increased its leverage by nearly 25 percent:

Assets	Liabilities
$A = 19.8$	Equity $E = 0.8$
	Debt $D = 19$

The firm, even if it only wishes to restore its initial leverage ratio, must either raise capital equal to 25 percent of its now-diminished equity, or sell an additional 19.2 percent of its initial assets. In its more highly leveraged state, it will find it more difficult to raise additional or even maintain its existing funding; in particular, it becomes more vulnerable to rollover risk. If the defaults are severe enough, even if the firm's equity is not wiped out by the initial losses, the induced illiquidity may eventually lead to insolvency.

The asset owner's need for cash may arise because loans against other assets are coming due or their terms are tightening. Unencumbered assets purchased for cash, without leverage, may then need to be sold to raise additional cash to continue financing those other assets.

Losses sufficient to raise questions about solvency among market participants began to manifest themselves among large banks by the end of 2007, as the subprime crisis began to impact their balance sheets. For example, Citigroup announced on January 15, 2008, that it had lost $9.83 billion during the fourth quarter of 2007. This was a loss of about 0.5 percent of its assets, but at a leverage ratio of 20-to-1, it represented about a 10 percent reduction in equity. As noted in Chapter 12, the extent of this leverage is hard to discern from firms' financial reporting, and some critical information must be estimated or painstakingly extracted from various text elements rather than simply read off the tabular balance sheet presentation. Citi's counterparties may well have attributed far higher leverage to it, and thus considered the January 15 loss as potentially jeapordizing solvency.

We can now better understand the subsequent deterioration in lending terms it faced (see Figure 14.8). The widening of spreads reflects the "capital crunch" effect of these losses. Losses cause capital to decline dollar-for-dollar with assets, reducing the capital and increasing the leverage ratio. At the same time, Citigroup, like other large banks, had felt obliged to assume the assets of off-balance-sheet vehicles such as SIVs onto its balance sheet. This increased leverage further, since no equity capital came back along with the SIVs. Moreover, the SIV assets were expected to continue to decline in value. Once back on the balance sheet, these losses, too, would increase leverage. Under these circumstances, the cost of fresh equity capital increased appreciably. Banks' willingness to extend credit plummeted in response. Rather, they sought all opportunities to reduce assets.

14.2.2 Collateral Devaluation

As noted in Chapter 12, a market participant is liquid if he holds sufficient unencumbered, high-quality assets. As asset prices and thus collateral values rise, market participants are able to borrow more and finance larger stocks of assets with a given amount of collateral. This applies generally, but is particularly important for financial intermediaries, for whom the capacity to put on leverage and to effect a liquidity transformation are the primary means of production of financial services.

The process works in reverse, but much more rapidly and disruptively, during a downturn. As intermediaries' balance sheets weaken, they must act to preserve liquidity and capital, and begin to shed assets. For market participants generally, if an asset purchase has been financed by using the asset itself as collateral, the loan may be terminated by the lender, or the loan terms may be changed adversely. The asset owner will then require cash or other still-liquid assets, either to finance the asset entirely, or to meet the changed loan terms.

One of the key loan terms that can change abruptly is the haircut. While data on haircuts, especially for lower-quality collateral, is not readily available, evidence is strong that haircuts rose drastically during the subprime crisis; Gorton and Metrick (2010) compute an index of repo haircuts that shows an increase in haircuts from near-zero in early 2007 to about 45 percent by mid-2009. Increasing haircuts are a key feature of episodes of collateral devaluation, so this self-reinforcing mechanismn is sometimes called a "haircut spiral."

The amount of top-quality, "unimpeachable" collateral, such as Treasury bonds, is limited. However, with higher haircuts, or at least greater acceptance by the market, other types of financial assets can also serve as collateral. The devaluation of collateral played a crucial role in the subprime crisis, primarily because the range of collateral had expanded so greatly during the preceding years.

By using collateral markets, banks and securities firms were able to finance purchases or borrowing of securitized credit products by investors, and then refinance themselves, that is, fund the loans to investors, by repledging the collateral obtained. For example, an insurance company or a pension fund might pledge U.S. Treasuries to a dealer, and use the cash collateral thus obtained to invest in higher-yielding, but riskier securities. The dealer can refinance itself using the pledged Treasuries. In this respect, securities firms carried out a bank-like function and increased the amount of leverage in the financial system as a whole.

Collateral devaluation also has an impact on capital and credit risk calculations by banks. Unless the dependence of recovery on the state of the economy is incorporated into the models with which banks estimate the value of loan collateral, they may overestimate recovery in stress scenarios. They may thus underestimate the extent of systematic risk to which they are exposed and the amount of risk capital required.[2]

14.2.3 Risk Triggers

Risk triggers are mechanisms by which traders are forced to unwind positions in response to rising volatility or other metrics of risk. The unwinding of positions in turn causes large changes in asset prices, amplifying the increase in volatility, and intensifying the unwinding pressure imposed by the initial risk trigger. If volatility is high enough, it may render a leveraged market participant insolvent: in the example at the beginning of this section, a drop in asset value of 5 percent would trigger insolvency, forcing a bankruptcy sale or other resolution of the firm and its assets. The phenomenon of increased measured risk inducing behavior that further increases risk is sometimes called *endogenous risk*, in analogy to endogenous liquidity.

Risk triggers can take various forms. We will look at some that are defined quantitatively. But risk triggers can also be set informally. Portfolio or risk managers may simply require traders to "lighten up" in response to a downturn in the markets, but the effect on asset prices will be the same.

VaR Triggers VaR triggers require traders to unwind positions when VaR reaches certain levels. Even in the absence of formal triggers, rising VaR may induce firms to trim positions. VaR can increase in response to higher volatility or changes in correlations, even with unchanged positions. So traders may be forced to reduce portfolios that had previously been approved as appropriately sized. Unwinding positions can add to downward pressure on asset prices and upward pressure on the prices of hedging instruments.

The impact of VaR on positions during periods of stress is the converse of its impact during periods of low volatility. As we see later in this chapter,

---

[2]See Frye (2000, 2001).

volatility can be very low for long periods but suddenly increase during a financial crisis. During the low-volatility period, VaR will naturally be quite low, regardless of how it is computed. To the extent that market participants rely on VaR either for setting formal risk limits or as an overall metric of risk, or as a basis for setting capital requirements, they will be encouraged to put on larger positions. VaR can thus contribute to greater risk taking and to the procyclical behavior of the financial system.

Potential VaR triggers include VaR-based regulatory risk capital. As discussed in Chapter 15, under the Basel capital standards, the capital required to protect against the market risk of banks' trading book portfolios may be estimated using VaR. Capital standards then rise with volatility, even with unchanged risk-weighted assets, a phenomenon called *procyclicality of capital requirements*. In Chapter 11, we reviewed several critiques of VaR. The claim that it has a potentially destabilizing influence is among the more biting because of VaR's regulatory role, akin to finding that mandatory airbags cause an increase in auto accidents.

Stop-Loss Orders   *Stop-loss orders* are buy or sell orders that are set at the time a trade is initiated, and are intended to unwind the trade in the event that prices move far enough in an adverse direction. They are attractive to portfolio manager because they appear to be automatic. Stop-loss orders are also said to align incentives appropriately, by countering the traders' typical insistence on "doubling down," that is, adding to a position rather than reducing it in response to adverse price moves. But they may prove ineffective if the orders cannot be filled in a volatile market; stop-loss orders are exposed to significant execution risk.

Stop-loss orders can add to selling pressure in declining markets. Frequently, stop-losses for an asset are set at roughly the same level, or within a narrow range, by many different traders. These bunched levels may be determined, for example, by technical trading indicators such as a previous low price. When the asset price approaches this level or range, it may quickly drop further as the stop-loss orders come into effect.

Dynamic Hedging   Dynamic hedging can amplify the momentum of asset prices. One example is the dynamic hedging of options. As the underlying price declines, the delta of a long call also falls. Sellers of calls who hedge their positions by taking a long position in the underlying asset must then sell the underlying asset, amplifying the downward pressure. Sellers of puts must increase short positions in the underlying as prices fall, increasing put deltas, also amplifying the fall. Similar dynamics hold for increases in the underlying price. Option dealers are typically short options and hedge their positions. Their hedging behavior is therefore sometimes held responsible for exacerbating price volatility.

A similar phenomenon can occur with dynamic strategies other than option hedging. Two examples are particularly noteworthy. The first is *portfolio insurance*, an approach to asset management in which the investor replicates the impact of an option hedge by selling the asset and increasing cash holdings on price declines, and vice versa. The stock market crash of 1987 has been attributed by some observers to the use of portfolio insurance.

Another example of option-induced price dynamics is the hedging of mortgage-based securities (MBS) portfolios. The interest rate risk of a long MBS position can be hedged by shorting U.S. Treasury bonds. But as discussed in Chapters 1 and 9, MBS are also exposed to prepayment risk. When interest rates decline, creditworthy homeowners will refinance their mortgages at lower rates, causing the expected duration of higher-coupon MBS to decline. The MBS therefore doesn't fully participate in the bond rally, causing a mismatch between the MBS and the Treasury hedge. The mismatch must be addressed by buying back part of the Treasury bond short position, further depressing yields.

Usually the Treasury market, one of the deepest and most liquid of asset markets, can readily absorb the fluctuation in hedging demand by MBS investors. Occasionally, however, long-term interest rates can be persistently dislodged, and some market participants can take large losses. One such episode occured in the summer of 2003, following a period in which Treasury yields had sharply declined on concern that the supply of bonds issued by the Treasury would decline. We describe this background in more detail in our discussion of swap spreads below. The end of the bond rally triggered a sharp reversal in yields. MBS durations had become very short, so Treasury hedges were small. As bond yields rose, expected MBS prepayments fell, and MBS durations lengthened. MBS investors then had to sell more Treasury bonds as a hedge, amplifying the rise in yields. The 10-year yield rose 140 basis points in the 10 weeks beginning in mid-June 2003. To get a sense of how large this move in yield was, we can apply the price-yield calculation we developed in Chapter 4; at an annual yield volatility of 15 percent, and with yields about 4 percent, this represented about a 5-standard deviation move. As noted earlier, repo fails also spiked (Figure 14.13).

Option Exercise Prices   Concentration of option exercise prices can have a similar effect to stop-loss orders. A long position in a put option with a strike equal to the stop-loss level is economically similar to a stop-loss order. As the underlying asset price approaches the exercise price, delta hedging by traders tends to press the asset price lower. Like stop-loss levels, the exercise prices may be bunched at certain key asset price levels, compounding the effect.

In some markets, such as foreign exchange, *barrier options* are relatively common. These are an exotic option type that comes into existence (*knock-ins*) or is canceled (*knock-outs*) when the underlying price touches a stated level. Like exercise prices, barrier levels may be concentrated in the set of option contracts outstanding at any point in time. Barrier options can have extremely high deltas, well outside the range $(-1, 1)$, and correspondingly high gammas. Barrier options can thereby have an amplifying effect on underlying price behavior.

Credit Ratings   Credit ratings are ubiquitous in credit portfolio management. Minimum or minimum average credit ratings are legally mandated for many institutional investors' portfolios, though, as we see in Chapter 15, the Dodd-Frank Act aims to diminish that role. They also play a critical role in regulatory capital standards. Ratings downgrades can force many investors to shed securities simultaneously. Credit ratings can therefore amplify credit cycles. Credit ratings affect the demand for bonds and credit spreads in at least three ways:

1. To the extent that ratings are perceived to provide accurate information, ratings upgrades will increase demand for an issue.
2. Some investors are restricted by law or regulation to meet ratings criteria. Downgrades of investment-grade bonds can materially decrease the audience for a bond.
3. High ratings increase the ability of a security to circulate as collateral for securitized loans, so a downgrade decreases a bond's liquidity as well as value.

All these factors tend to tighten spreads during a credit expansion. If ratings are procyclical, that is, if there is a tendency to award higher ratings during expansions, when balance sheets appear stronger and potential credit problems are less readily apparent, these influences will be intensified further.

A drastic example of the impact of ratings triggers manifested itself in mid-2007. Rating agencies began to downgrade the highest-rated tranches of subprime residential mortgage-based securities (RMBS), the largest bonds by original par value. Many banks had invested in these bonds because of their low regulatory capital requirements, and a few large banks and securities dealers had large concentrations of such paper. The downgrades forced some sales and triggered price declines, obliging some institutions to realize losses or mark their books lower, increasing the downward pressure on the bonds' prices. Apart from the self-propagating impact on asset prices, the downgrades added to uncertainty and anxiety about the extent and distribution of capital attrition among large intermediaries.

14.2.4 Accounting Triggers

Accounting rules may also reinforce asset price declines. Some market participants are obliged to publicly report the *fair market value* (FMV) of at least some positions at regular intervals. For example, as discussed in Chapter 15, banks in most jurisdictions are required by regulation to mark-to-market positions in their trading books daily. Hedge funds are required to mark their books at least monthly in order to arrive at a fund NAV. Other market participants with similar positions may not be subject to such requirements, or only at less frequent intervals. Rule 157 ("FAS 157") issued by the U.S. Financial Accounting Standards Board (FASB), which went into effect after November 15, 2007, expanded the requirements for reporting estimates of FMV even for hard-to-price assets.

Some observers have taken the view that mark-to-market requirements can amplify asset price declines, generally create additional volatility, and, at the extreme, exacerbate financial instability. First, they can abruptly introduce a large gap between market and fundamental value during a period of stress. In this way, mark-to-market requirements make it more difficult for financial intermediaries to avoid "fire sales," selling assets that have experienced or are expected to experience sharp price declines because liquidity and risk premiums are rising, even though their fundamental values, that is, the expected present value of their future cash flows, may not have changed.

Second, by forcing intermediaries to realize losses and making those losses public, their capital bases and confidence in their solvency is reduced, exposing them to greater funding liquidity problems. The negative effects are particularly harsh when transactions liquidity is poor, and only a few or no transactions are being effected, and these only at distressed or hard-to-observe prices. FAS 157 in particular has been held responsible for forcing banks to report large losses early in the subprime crisis, damaging the perception of intermediaries' solvency at a critical moment. Both effects potentially induce contagion via the impact on asset prices and market confidence in the liquidity and solvency of banks.

There are several counterarguments to these concerns. It is not clear, first of all, whether banks have in fact been required under FAS 157 to report unrealistically depressed market values. Moreover, transparency can itself play an important positive role in enhancing financial stability. Finally, as we discuss in Chapter 15, capital and other regulatory standards can be set so as to mitigate any impact of mark-to-market rules in amplifying volatility, for example by requiring higher capital ratios, and are a more appropriate tool for doing so than suspension of mark-to-market accounting.

14.3 BEHAVIOR OF ASSET PRICES DURING CRISES

In this section, we explore the impact of financial crises on asset return behavior. There are, as we've already seen, myriad examples of dramatic changes in returns around crises. But low-frequency changes in prices and spreads are also important in understanding return behavior in crises.

The most immediately visible characteristic of financial crises is an increase in return volatility. Not only do asset price fluctuations increase drastically, but the character of volatility changes. In particular, the volatility of volatility, or "vol of vol," increases unpredictably and fluctuates widely. New information becomes much more important, but also much harder to interpret. Traders generally like volatility, since they can't profit without changes in asset prices, but in crises, the increase in vol of vol makes volatility hard to profit from and induces traders to "pull in their horns." Reluctance to put on positions and to trade contributes to asset liquidity difficulties.

High realized volatility, and the other alarming phenomena seen in crises, also affect the level of implied volatility and the shape of the implied volatility surface. Crises, finally, see sharp changes in some correlations among asset returns.

Increased volatility during crises is preceded, by definition, by lower volatility during the precrisis period. But volatility also displays important low-frequency fluctuations; pre-crisis volatility tends to be lower not only by comparison with the crisis, but also with long-term average volatility. Lower volatility before the onset of crisis is also associated with rising asset prices and an attendant reduction in *ex ante* risk premiums. Real estate returns are particularly prone to large low-frequency fluctuations.

The behavior of asset prices during crises is closely connected to the credit contraction typical of crises. During a crisis, market participants are obliged to repay debts they expected to extend or roll over. They will not be able to use some assets as collateral, or will be able to borrow much less against the collateral as haircuts and margin requirements are increased. They may also be forced to sell unpledged assets.

Financial crises also bring about a *flight to quality*, that is, an increase in the values of less risky asset relative to more risky ones. Investors also favor more liquid assets in a flight to quality. A flight to quality may also take the form of *safe haven* buying, in which currencies perceived as less geopolitically risky, such as the Swiss franc and U.S. dollar, appreciate relative to others.

In an inflation crisis, the flight may take the form of a *flight into real assets*, that is, assets such as commodities, real estate, and art works. The nominal prices of these assets tend to rise at the same pace as the general level of prices in normal times and to outpace the general price level during more extreme inflations, providing an inflation hedge.

14.3.1　Credit Spreads

As concern about rising defaults increases in a crisis, credit spreads move wider. Figure 14.14 displays credit spreads for three types of bonds, U.S. investment-grade and high-yield corporate bonds, and highly rated credit card asset-based securities (ABS). They move wider during recessions and periods of increased concern about credit quality, such as that following the Enron bankruptcy in late 2001 and following the downgrades of the major U.S. automobile manufacturers in 2005.

Spreads declined steadily after the credit scare of 2005, as did virtually all other risk spreads. Higher-rated bonds reached their tights in mid-February

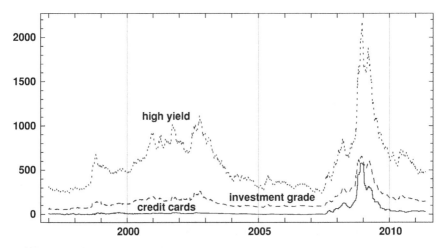

FIGURE 14.14　U.S. Credit Spreads 1997–2011
Spreads over swaps, basis points, daily, December 31, 1996, to May 19, 2011.
Investment grade: BofA Merrill Lynch U.S. Corporate Index (C0A0); high yield:
BofA Merrill Lynch U.S. High Yield Index (H0A0); credit cards: five year AAA U.S.
credit-card ABS.
Source: Bloomberg Financial LP, JPMorgan Chase.

2007, and high-yield somewhat later, in May 2007. But during the subprime crisis, all spreads quickly widened to record levels.

The tightness of credit spreads just before the crisis began is a similar phenomenon to low precrisis volatility. It reflects low risk aversion, "search for yield," and low risk premiums. An open question regarding the origin of crises is: Do low spreads and volatility merely contrast sharply with asset price behavior during the crisis? Or do they also play some role in causing the crisis?

All three bond categories reached their wides at the end of 2008. Among the worst-hit bonds were structured credit products such as asset-backed securities (ABS) backed by auto loans and credit-card receivables. They were affected not only by the increased fear about the economy and risk aversion that caused all risk assets to sell off. They were also affected by aversion to securitized credit markets as the mechanisms and off-balance sheet vehicles built up to invest in them collapsed. Highly rated bonds backed by credit cards were by no means the hardest-hit among ABS; residential MBS prices fell even more sharply. Moreover, even after it became clear that not only financial markets, but also the real economy would be severely impact by the crisis, credit losses on senior nonmortgage ABS were not expected to be large. Nonetheless, they sold off much more severely than corporate bonds, relative to their tightest spreads before the crisis. This table displays values on selected dates from Figure 14.14:

Date	C0A0	H0A0	AAA Cards
15Feb2007	87	259	1
01Jun2007	94	241	3
15Dec2008	651	2,182	580

The wildly disproportionate widening of ABS spreads relative to corporate bonds with arguably comparable credit risk represents a large premium, with components of general risk aversion, specific aversion to the ABS asset class, and a substantial liquidity risk component. The liquidity risk premium, in turn, was generated by the disappearance of both funding and market liquidity for senior nonmortgage ABS.

Another type of credit spread, the swap spread, also widens dramatically during crises. The swap spread is the spread between U.S. Treasury notes and plain-vanilla swap rates with the same maturity, and are a widely used barometer of market anxiety. Both swaps and Treasuries trade daily in highly liquid markets. U.S. Treasury yields drop in times of heightened risk aversion, especially during more extreme episodes of flight to quality and liquidity by investors. Swaps, in contrast, are not free of credit risk, and widen relative to Treasuries when concerns about the fragility of the banking system grow more pronounced. Figure 14.15 displays 10-year swap spreads over the past two decades. Swap spreads were above-average during stress periods such as the currency crisis period of the early 1990s, and the dot-com bust.

Swap spreads, however, are also driven by supply and demand factors that are not closely related to financial distress. The highest swap spreads observed during the past two decades were driven by the declining supply of U.S. Treasuries at a time of rapidly shrinking U.S. budget deficits in the late 1990s. The U.S. Treasury conducted a series of reverse auctions to repurchase outstanding debt between 2000 and 2002, following an announcement on January 13, 2000, and announced the suspension of 30-year bond issuance on October 31, 2001. No auctions of 30-year bonds took place between August 2001 and February 2006. Anxiety on the part of institutional investors about the possible disappearance of a security type, U.S. government bonds, to which a significant fraction of their portfolios are allocated, depressed Treasury yields. The decline in U.S. federal deficits thus contributed to the general decline in yields and risk premiums attributed to the so-called "savings glut" of the late 1990s and early 2000s, which we will discuss further below in the context of the causes of financial crises.

As can be seen in Figure 14.15, swap spreads widened more sharply in response to these market-specific pressures than to financial crises. Swap spreads initially widened during the earliest phase of the subprime crisis, but then, following the Lehman bankruptcy, collapsed and ultimately turned negative for the first time in 30-odd years of swap history. Among the reasons were expectations of large-scale Treasury issuance and institutional investors' desire to receive fixed, locking in yields as interest rates dropped rapidly. Hedging of swaptions may also have played a part. But lack of risk capital was likely the key factor, as in the similar widening of cash-CDS spreads described at the end of Chapter 13 and the increase in convertible bond cheapness displayed in Figure 12.2. This mechanism must be taken into account in using the swap spread as a gauge of overall market sentiment. As we have seen, the focus of the panic from 2007 to 2009 was on short-maturity borrowing, and the widening of credit and term spreads was greatest at maturities of a few months.

14.3.2 Extreme Volatility

To begin our discussion of extreme volatility, let's look more closely at S&P 500 return volatility, as illustrated in Figure 10.2. It is useful to look also at Figure 14.16, which displays logarithmic prices for the same period, 1927

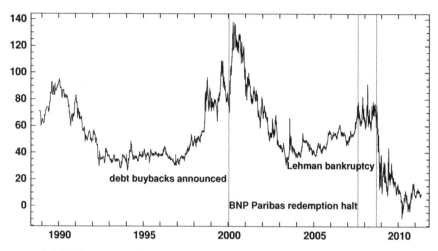

FIGURE 14.15   U.S. Dollar Swap Spreads 1988–2011
Spread between 10-year plain vanilla interest-rate swap spreads and the yield to
maturity of the on-the-run 10-year U.S. Treasury note, daily, November 1, 1988 to
May 11, 2011.
Source: Bloomberg Financial L.P.

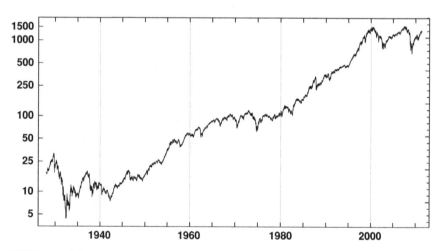

FIGURE 14.16   S&P 500 Prices 1927–2011
Logarithm of the S&P 500 index closing prices, daily, December 30, 1927, to April
14, 2011. The level of the index rather than its log is indicated on the *y*-axis.
Source: Bloomberg Financial L.P.

to date. The solid plots in Figure 10.2 indicate the 99.8 percent confidence interval for the next day's return, based on recent returns, using the EWMA approach (see the caption of Figure 10.2 for details). The horizontal grid lines mark the 99.8 percent confidence interval, using the standard deviation of daily returns of 1.2 percent over the entire period. That return volatility is just about 19 percent annually and corresponds to a 99.8 percent confidence interval for daily returns of ±3.7 percent.

Before the onset of the subprime crisis, there had only been one sustained, long-lasting episode of volatility far in excess of the long-term average: subsequent to the Great Crash of 1929. It lasted until the beginning of U.S. participation in World War II, or well over a decade.

Another episode of extreme volatility, but much shorter in duration, took place in October 1987. The S&P 500 fell over 20 percent on October 19, about double the magnitude of the next-largest daily return in either direction. Relative to the conditional return forecast, it was an even larger outlier, as we see later in this chapter. But this increase in volatility remained an isolated episode. Volatilities may go up or correlations change in the absence of a crisis, due to events in local markets. But isolated increases in volatility tend not to endure long.

The increased volatility since the onset of the subprime crisis, in contrast, has been sustained, though as of early 2011, it had not been as extreme as either the 1929 or 1987 crashes, and its duration is yet to be determined. Since conditional volatility forecasts increased gradually, it displayed fewer extreme outliers; the S&P 500 index "eased itself in" to extreme volatility, in contrast to 1929 and after. Figure 10.2 shows that the amplitude of the price swings has also thus far in the subprime crisis been smaller than during the Great Crash.

Periods of low volatility are also important. The most pronounced occurred between the recovery from the 1987 crash and the onset of the subprime crisis. It is interrupted by higher, though not extreme, volatility between 1997 and 2002, a period that covers the Asian and Russian crises, the end of the NASDAQ bubble, September 11, 2001, and the Enron bankruptcy. The period from the late 1980s to early 2007 is otherwise the longest in the historical record of sustained low volatility.

Pegged currencies show particularly dramatic increases in volatility. On the one hand, their volatility will have been dampened by monetary and exchange-rate policy, as long as the peg is maintained. On the other, once the peg is broken, large capital flows often lead to extreme changes in the exchange rate. We will look at such episodes in more detail later in this chapter.

Implied Volatility   At least for the past few decades, with the growth of options markets, it has become possible to observe not only realized volatility, but also expectations of future volatility via option implied volatility. As discussed in Chapters 2 and 10, option prices contain information about risk-neutral probabilities, a probability measure that contains a mix of information about the probabilities market participants assign to different future price outcomes, and which future price outcomes they most want to protect themselves against. Implied volatility, like any market price, may contain a risk premium; the expectations expressed in it are risk-neutral, not the subjective but unobservable expectations of market participants. Nonetheless, they are informative about market participants' view of future risks.

Implied volatilities rise very quickly with the onset of a crisis or market disturbance. The term structure of implied volatility inverts, with longer-term vols rising, but not as sharply as shorter-term vols. As we see later, there is some evidence that implied vol can anticipate disturbances to some extent. Figure 14.17 displays the VIX volatility index, an important measure of stock market implied volatility, over the past two decades, covering a number of periods of significant stress, including the subprime crisis. The VIX is a composite of implied volatilities of options on the constituents of the S&P 500 with different strike prices and tenors.

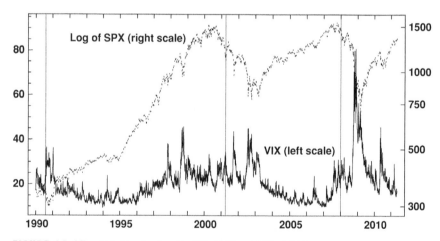

FIGURE 14.17   U.S. Equity Implied Volatility 1990–2011
VIX volatility index, percent per annum, left axis, and the S&P index, plotted on a logarithmic scale. Vertical right-axis tick labels are expressed as levels. Daily data, January 2, 1990 to May 13, 2011. Vertical grid lines represent the dates of NBER business cycle peaks.
Source: Bloomberg Financial L.P.

The spikes in the VIX are the most evident feature of the plot. There are five episodes of a VIX reading above 40, coinciding with the episodes of greatest financial market turmoil over the past two decades. The triggers were

1. The second phase of the 1997–1999 Asian crisis, during which Russia defaulted on its sovereign debt and the Long Term Capital Management hedge fund collapsed.
2. The 9/11 terrorist attack.
3. The post-Enron accounting scandals and final phase of the technology stock bust in 2002. Geopolitical stress and the rise in oil prices also played a role.
4. The Lehman bankruptcy filing, which caused by far the largest spike, to an unprecedented 80 percent.
5. The European debt crisis, which became acute in April 2010.

These spikes all coincide with sharp declines in the S&P 500 index and with some degree of market turmoil. Rising markets are associated with a low VIX. The only occasions on which the VIX recorded a closing value below 10 percent were at the end of 2006 and in January 2007, just before the subprime crisis began.

Volatility of Volatility   Not only the level of volatility, but its variability, increases during crises. Since a great deal of risk management depends on accurately measuring volatility, this presents market participants with tremendous difficulties and contributes to risk aversion and the desire to hold smaller positions, that is, to delever, during a crisis.

Extreme fluctuations affect implied as well as actual volatility, signaling, unsettled expectations, or a period in which market participants expect important news to arrive at an accelerated pace. As seen in Figure 14.17, implied volatility can double in a matter of a few trading sessions, as one would expect when surprising news arrives and more is expected. For example, the VIX index doubled in one month, August 1998, as the Russian debt crisis unfolded, from a level of just over 22 to over 44. It more than tripled from its level of about 26 the Friday before the Lehman bankruptcy (September 12, 2008), to its all-time high, over 80, on October 27, 2008.

In addition to the volatility of implied volatility over time, there is typically a cross-sectional rise in the dispersion of implied volatilities of the individual assets within an asset class. Figure 14.18 illustrates for the U.S. stock market. It displays the cross-section variance of the implied volatilities largest 193 constituents of the S&P 500 index. This measure is closely related to the equity implied correlation, discussed in Chapter 10, and measures

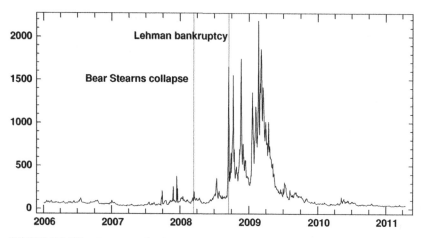

FIGURE 14.18 Equity Volatility Dispersion
Standard deviation of the implied volatilities of the largest 193 constituents of the
S&P 500 index, using market-capitalization weights. The included stocks
accounted for about 80 percent of the total market capitalization of the index in
May 2011.
Data source: Bloomberg Financial L.P.

the dispersion of the implied vols among one another each day. Volatility
dispersion rose sharply during the subprime crisis, reaching a peak in March
2009, as the equity index reached its crisis low.

14.3.3 Correlations

Correlation between asset returns can change abruptly during crises. Typical
patterns of what "moves together" break down, potentially wreaking havoc
with the prices of correlation-sensitive securities and with hedging strategies.
We look next at the behavior of realized and implied correlations during
crises and extreme events.

Historical Correlations   During crises and episodes of stress, realized correlation, that is, correlations of historical returns, can change rapidly. This
can have a large impact on the settings and performance of hedges based on
correlations, and on portfolio allocations based on closely related statistics
such as beta. Historical correlations and betas, like volatilities, are generally
sensitive to such measurement choices as the number of days of historical returns included. This sensitivity of results can increase greatly during periods
of stress.

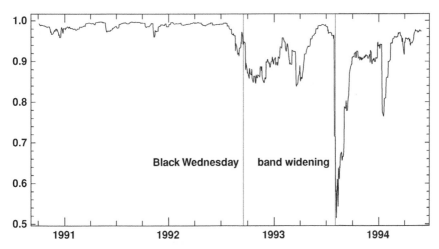

FIGURE 14.19 Proxy Hedging and the ERM Crisis 1992–1993
Daily correlation between logarithmic changes in the USD-DEM and USD-FRF
exchange rates, computed using EWMA model with decay factor 0.94, October 5,
1990, to May 31, 1995.
Data source: Bloomberg Financial L.P.

A dramatic example of the potential for changes in correlation to affect
hedging occurred during the European Monetary System's Exchange Rate
Mechanism (ERM) crisis of 1992 and 1993. As noted above, "weak" currencies typically have higher interest rates than strong ones. The French franc
was generally perceived as weak relative to the deutsche mark, and therefore
had higher international money market rates. In consequence, the practice
became widespread for European importers and exporters to hedge franc-
denominated payables against the U.S. dollar with marks rather than francs.
Because the U.S. dollar is the predominant vehicle currency in international
trade, a substantial portion of French export trade made use of "proxy hedging." The correlation between the two currencies' exchange rates against the
dollar were highly correlated under the ERM fixed exchange-rate system, as
seen in Figure 14.19, so proxy hedging appeared to be a safe practice until
the 1992 crisis. Since it effectively was a short mark/long franc position,
proxy hedgers suffered losses in 1992–1993 when the franc/mark exchange
rate first became more volatile and eventually, in August 1993, depreciated
sharply against the mark.

Another example occurred during the second phase of the 1997–1998
Asian crisis, following Russia's default on its foreign debt in August 1998
and the failure of the hedge fund Long Term Capital Management (LTCM)
the next month. Among the many calamities that befell LTCM were losses

on trades involving recently issued U.S. Treasury bonds. The most recently issued bond or note is called *on-the-run*, while those issued earlier are called *off-the-run*. Typically, on-the-run securities trade slightly tighter than off-the-run, since their market liquidity is somewhat better. LTCM had exploited this phenomenon and its apparent stability to earn the small spread between on- and off-the-run bonds, taking long positions in off-the-run and short positions in on-the-run notes and bonds. Because the spread is so narrow, large positions are needed to earn a significant returns in dollars; to earn $1,000,000 per year with a spread of 6 basis points, for example, requires long and short positions of $1,000,000,000. High leverage is needed to earn a significant rate of return.

High leverage, however, also significantly increases risk. The on- versus off-the-run spread can widen sharply during a crisis. In a flight to quality, the difference in the market liquidity of on- and off-the-run bonds increases, and the value of liquidity to investors rises, causing investors to shun off-the-run bonds unless there is a larger discount relative to on-the-run. When this occurs, the correlation between the yields drops from nearly 1, and the risk of the long-short "arbitrage" as well as the value of the short position increase dramatically, as occured in September 1998 (see Figure 14.20). For LTCM, the losses were magnified by its high leverage in this trade.

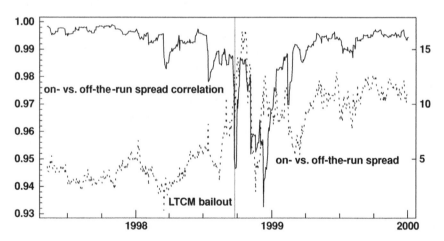

FIGURE 14.20   On- vs. Off-the-Run Rate Correlation
Correlation coefficient of daily changes in (solid line, left axis) and spread between (in basis points, dotted line, right axis) the yields to maturity of the on-the-run and first off-the-run 30-year Treasury bond. Correlation computed using EWMA model with decay factor 0.94, May 7, 1995, to December 31, 1999.
Data source: Bloomberg Financial L.P.

Betas are a function of both the volatilities and correlations of individual equities and equity indexes, and therefore can also fluctuate widely during crises. Asset managers using equity betas as a measure of risk or as a tool to determine the amount to invest in a stock can find this challenging.

An example is provided by the behavior of SLM Corp. ("Sallie Mae," ticker symbol SLM) stock price over the period 2007 to 2009. SLM is a student loan originator that began as a government-sponsored enterprise, but was entirely privatized in the mid-1990s. Its business model is heavily dependent on securitization markets: It originates loans, but then sells them into ABS rather than financing the loans permanently on its own balance sheet. In the spring of 2007, before the full breakout of the subprime crisis, a purchase of SLM by private equity firm J.C. Flowers was announced, leading to an immediate 20 percent increase in SLM's stock price. When the crisis deepened, Flowers withdrew from the leveraged buyout, and SLM's stock price, like those of other financial firms, dropped sharply. Its decline from its high point in the summer of 2007 to its low in early 2009 was about 95 percent.

Until the buyout deal was announced, SLM had a beta to the S&P 500 of close to 1, as seen in Figure 14.21. When the deal was announced, its beta was initially driven higher, in excess of 3, by higher volatility. It then traded

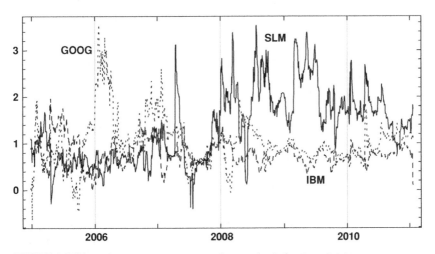

FIGURE 14.21 Changing Equity Betas during the Subprime Crisis
Rolling betas of IBM Corp (IBM), Google (GOOG) and SLM Corp. to the S&P 500 equity index, Dec. 27, 2004 to Jan. 21, 2011. The betas on each day are computed using the EWMA covariance matrix with a decay factor of 0.94.
Data source: Bloomberg Financial L.P.

like a typical "deal stock," more responsive to idiosyncratic news about the firm than to economy-wide news that moved the index, with a beta close to zero. As the buyout deal began to unravel, SLM began to trade more on general news about the financial system and the state of the economy, and its beta gravitated back toward unity. Finally, with the onset of the sub-prime crisis, SLM's beta again rose past 3. As an intermediary particularly dependent on the financing of its student loans through securitization, it was subject to high systematic risk, but also to increased idiosyncratic risk presented by the fragility of its funding.

By comparison, IBM Corp., an established blue-chip company, has had a beta within a fairly narrow range close to one throughout the pre-crisis and crisis periods. A different contrast is provided by Google Inc. (GOOG), a new technology company, and generally a high-beta stock. It has a more variable beta that tends to rise in excess of one during rallies and declines when the broad market is declining. The betas of both stocks were much lower and less variable than of SLM at most times during the crisis.

An old saw in trading and risk measurement states that, during crises, "all correlations go to one." Caution is warranted in interpreting this. While historical correlations do rise in stress periods, it may not be because of a regime switch to a higher-correlation joint return distribution. Boyer, Gibson, and Loretan (1997) and Loretan and English (2000) point out that sample correlation from an unchanged distribution can be much higher when estimated in periods of higher subsample volatility.

The Impact of High Correlation in Crises   Not only sample asset return correlations, but also correlations implied by options and other derivative securities can change dramatically during crises. We have discussed implied correlations in credit markets in Chapters 9 and 11 and equity implied correlation in Chapter 10. Both these measures of systematic risk rise sharply during crises.

Equity base correlation is the most common measure of implied credit correlation, and is a measure of the extent to which the market believes defaults will coincide. It is derived from the prices of the equity (0–3%) standard tranche of credit index CDS, and the prices of CDS on individual companies' senior unsecured debt. Suppose equity tranche prices are relatively high and single-firm CDS spreads are wide. In other words, the market is willing to pay a relatively high amount for a lottery ticket–like security, the equity tranche, that survives only in the low-likelihood event that almost no firms default, and is at the same time willing to pay a wide spread to protect against default by any individual firm. The market is then implicitly betting that not only does each firm have a high default probability viewed

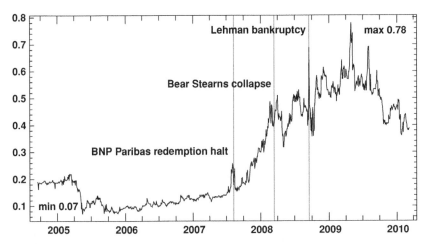

FIGURE 14.22 Implied Credit Correlation 2004–2010
Base correlation of equity (0–3%) tranche of the five year CDX.NA.IG.
Source: JPMorgan Chase.

in isolation, but that there is a high likelihood that, if even a few firms default, many will default. Conversely, the market implicitly believes there is at least a small chance that widespread defaults will be avoided, and the equity tranche return will thus be high. This is essentially a view that systematic credit and systemic risks are high.

Suppose, in contrast, that equity tranche prices are a bit lower, but spreads are relatively wide. This would indicate that the market believes it likely that, even if there are surprisingly few defaults, there will be at least enough to wipe out the equity tranche. In other words, it views default as less likely to cluster and systematic risk as low. Wide spreads of individual firm CDS then reflect firm-specific more than economy-wide drivers of default.

Figure 14.22 displays equity base correlation of the benchmark 125-name investment-grade CDS index over the past six years. Prior to the crisis, implied correlation was relatively low, always below 0.25 and generally in the low teens. We described the 2005 episode of extremely low base correlation in Chapter 11. As the crisis took hold, implied correlation rose steadily. Interestingly, it spiked just prior to the Paribas redemption halt, as markets worried about "hung loans" on large intermediaries' balance sheets. It reached a high of 0.78 just after the nadir of most asset prices in the early spring of 2009.

High correlation in crises drastically reduces diversification benefits and increases return volatility in investment portfolios. It is not surprising that a diversified long equity portfolio suffers losses during a crisis, since the high correlation will make it trade like an equivalent amount of the declining broad equity market. However, diversified high-grade credit portfolios such as traditional bond portfolios can also suffer large mark-to-market losses, but low or no credit writedowns. Even though the portfolio is diversified from a credit point of view, the *spread correlation* may approach unity. Some institutional investors do not have to report mark-to-market losses, and do not rely on short-term borrowing to finance portfolios, and will be relatively unaffected by such an event, as long as the credit of the portfolio remains largely unimpaired. Other investors may have to report losses.

Long-short equity portfolios can have high idiosyncratic risk, even if their net exposure to the market is small. Although the systematic risk of the portfolio will remain low, the increase in idiosyncratic risk can lead to much higher volatility than expected during a crisis.

Implied credit correlations provided some surprises during the subprime crisis. In Chapter 11, we saw that ignoring potential changes in implied correlation led to losses for certain CDX trades. Placing too much reliance on implied correlation has also led to problems, in this case for investors selling equity standard tranches to protect portfolios against widespread defaults. The hedging effect was muted by the failure of equity tranches to fall as much as expected when credit spreads widened.

14.4 CAUSES OF FINANCIAL CRISES

Financial crises are a phenomenon at least as old as commercial banking, and the analysis of financial crises is nearly as old as crises themselves. It is impossible to adequately summarize the vast literature on crises, known in an earlier day as business cycle theory. Most contemporary debates on the origins of financial crises have echoes and roots in similar debates dating back, in some cases, centuries. In this section, we look at some macroeconomic policies and phenomena that have been identified as typical causes of crises.

The macroeconomic causes—or at least antecedents—of crises can be categorized under four main headings. We use the term "macroeconomic" to distinguish these factors from financial factors and credit conditions, but they are, of course, closely interrelated:

- Excessive government debt
- Imbalances in international payments
- Excessively loose or stringent money and credit emission
- Large shocks to the real economy

The macroeconomic causes of crises are among the most controversial areas in economics and economic history. The debate, for example, on the causes of the Depression crisis that began in 1929 remains unresolved. The theses advanced include monetary policy errors, international imbalances related to the U.S. net creditor position, and a widespread, sharp fall in commodity prices during the late 1920s. Few students of crises take a monocausal view, but most emphasize certain factors. We look at a few examples of the macroeconomic background to crises, and briefly describe some approaches to modelling financial crises.

The study of crises is fraught with difficulties of measurement and definition. Most of these difficulties are aspects of the fact that crises are unusual, comparatively rare, large-scale events that happen in history, rather than in a laboratory, and are therefore hard to capture statistically. They are unique, like unhappy families. There is neither a standard definition of crises, nor a standard measure of their duration or intensity. And while there are a number of models of crises, there is no generally agreed view on their causes. The study of crises remains an area in which researchers spend a relatively high amount of effort on the orderly presentation of facts rather than unitary theories.

14.4.1 Debt, International Payments, and Crises

Many, if not most, financial crises have an important international aspect. These problems include default or difficulty servicing private or public debts to foreigners, currency crises, and international transmission of banking crises.

Debt and International Crises Public debt and monetary policies are related, and have an ancient history, long preceding the advent of central banks and bond markets. The recurrence of financial crises has long been attributed to excessive borrowing by governments, and their mismanagement of money and credit. In centuries preceding the establishment of central banks, sovereigns controlled the money supply directly through the monopoly of coinage rights. Sovereigns had two paths to spending in excess of tax revenues and income from their private domains. They could subject the money they issued to *debasement*, that is, issue coins with less precious metal than their nominal value called for, or borrow from banks, which began to emerge in their modern form during the High Middle Ages. Fiscally motivated extreme debasement occurred in ancient times, for example, under the late Roman emperor Diocletian, and until the advent of paper and book-entry monetary systems. Crises occasioned by debasement took a simple form; by impeding monetary exchange and throwing society back on barter, debasements drastically reduced the gains from trade and special-ization. They reduced standards of living until indirect exchange could be rebuilt.

True financial crises have occurred since the origins of modern banking. Bank runs and failures were frequent in the High Middle Ages. Episodes of widespread bank failures, particularly those affecting a wide geographical area, were often associated with defaults on sovereign borrowing. A general banking crisis took place in Florence and Venice in the 1340s. Edward III of England and the Florentine city-state had borrowed on a large scale for war finance and were unable to repay in full. The crisis began in Venice, where a number of banks were weakened by large fluctuations in the relative values of gold and silver coinage, and then spread to Florence, where the much larger Bardi and Peruzzi banking houses were forced into bankruptcy.

In the modern era, a public-debt background to many crises can be iden-tified. Foreign-currency indebtedness, whether public or private, is particu-larly prominent. The Barings crisis of 1890, the Mexican peso ("Tequila") crisis of 1994–1995, and the Asian crises of 1997–1999 are examples.

We can draw a few observations from a vast historical and analytical literature on international capital markets, debt, and financial crises:

- Countries incur large public-sector debts appear to be more prone to financial crises.
- International financial crises are frequently associated with large imbal-ances in international payments. Large public-sector debts often coin-cide with large international net debtor positions. Apart from govern-ment debts, countries that have run protracted current account deficits have a greater propensity to experience crises. The exception has been the United States, which, as issuer of the world's primary reserve cur-rency, has had greater leeway, termed in the 1960s the "exorbitant privilege," to run balance-of-payments deficits.
- Just as with private debtors, when public-sector imbalances have been financed at short-term, a crisis is more likely to occur and to coincide with banking-sector stress. Countries as well as financial intermediaries can face credit difficulties arising from short-term financing. A typical trigger of foreign-exchange crises is sudden difficulty in rolling over short-term foreign-currency funding of capital-account deficits. This phenomenon was at work, for example, in the Mexican peso crisis and in the Russian crisis of 1998. In both cases, the governments involved faced a rollover risk event in financing short-term dollar-denominated government bonds.
- International transmission or contagion is an important aspect of inter-national crises. For example, sovereign defaults by a number of countries

tend to coincide. Large public-sector debt of some highly-indebted governments appears to make international financial crises that affect less indebted countries more likely. The East Asian crisis of 1997 began with the Thai baht devaluation of July 1997, but spread very rapidly to other countries in the region. The next year, Russia defaulted on its debts and devalued. In the very last phase of the extended crisis, in early 1999, some Latin American countries' debt and currencies came under pressure: Brazil abandoned its peg of the real to the dollar on February 1.

An important mechanism of international transmission is *wrong-way exposure*, in which a local enterprise borrows in a foreign currency that can be expected to appreciate when the local economy is weak. The local borrower is then obligated to pay more local currency to meet debt obligations just as its local currency revenues are declining. Foreign banks may have significant losses on such exposures and become an additional contagion vector.

- Domestic banking crises or stresses, such as runs and widespread bank failures, are closely associated with international crises. The "twin crises" literature focuses on interactions between currency crises and banking system weakness. Bank holdings of sovereign debt contributed to financial crises in the Middle Ages, as we have seen. Awareness of the large holdings of European sovereign debt by both local and foreign banks was among the factors behind the strong increase in liquidity preference and risk aversion in response to the European debt crisis in 2010.

- A number of crises with international ramifications are associated with *financial liberalization*. A number of countries with strict capital controls began in the 1980s to permit free flows of capital. This was often associated with the privatization of government-owned enterprises, including banks. Another wave of financial liberalization occurred when formerly socialist countries introduced private ownership and market economies in the late 1980s and 1990s. As experience with liberalization accumulated, policy makers began somewhat belatedly to recognize that the sequence of liberalization of a financially repressed economy was crucial to the success of the project.

Speculative Attacks on Fixed Exchange-Rate Systems Currency crises have played a disproportionate role in postwar crises, though only a minor role in the subprime crisis. Currencies are among the few asset prices that have routinely been subjected to price controls by developed countries. Currencies that are perceived as overvalued are prone to *speculative attack*. These occur when market participants take large long positions in currencies that are expected to appreciate and short positions in currencies that are expected to depreciate. Speculative attacks on currencies are an important example of the peso problem, the phenomenon of large, sudden changes in the "regime" governing asset prices, discussed in Chapter 10.

Currency crises are also prone to contagion. There is a clear channel of transmission among a set of countries in a region with currencies pegged either to one another, such as Europe in the 1980s and 1990s, or to a common anchor currency, such as the East Asian pegs to the dollar prior to 1997. If one or a few countries devalue or break the peg, the countries that do not devalue will immediately be viewed as having overvalued currencies and themselves become vulnerable to speculative attack.

The economics of currency speculation involve interest as well as exchange rates. Suppose an investor takes a short position in a foreign currency that has what he deems to be an unsustainable fixed exchange rate against the domestic currency $\bar{S}$, measured in domestic currency units per foreign currency unit. The investor believes that the exchange rate in τ years will be $E[S_{t+1}]$, with $\bar{S} > E[S_{t+1}]$ and $E[S_{t+1}]$ denoting a subjective expected value. That is, investors expect the foreign currency to become cheaper in domestic currency units. The investor can short the foreign currency by borrowing it for τ years in the international money markets at a rate r^*, exchanging it for the domestic currency, and investing the domestic currency proceeds for τ years at a rate r. If forward foreign exchange markets exist, this position can also be established via a short forward position in the foreign currency.

The expected capital gains from this position, per foreign currency unit shorted, are $\bar{S} - E[S_{t+\tau}]$, the domestic money market proceeds are $\tau r \bar{S}$, and the borrowing cost of one foreign currency unit, measured in domestic currency, is $\tau r^* \bar{S}$. The net interest earned on the position is $(r - r^*)\tau \bar{S}$. This is typically negative, as the interest rate of a weak currency is generally higher than that of a strong one. As we will see later on, this differential is a useful way to identify currencies with the potential for sudden depreciation.

The expected profit on the speculative position, in domestic currency, is

$$\bar{S} - E[S_{t+\tau}] + (r - r^*)\tau \bar{S}$$

The rate of return depends on the capital required to borrow foreign currency. For forward foreign exchange transactions, this can be quite low, providing high leverage and potential returns. The risk of the trade depends on the entire distribution of $S_{t+\tau}$. If the distribution is skewed to higher rather than lower values of $S_{t+\tau}$, that is, if there is a high probability that, conditional on the foreign currency not being devalued, it will appreciate, then a risk-averse investor may choose to stay out of the trade, even though it has positive expected value. Conversely, if the distribution is skewed to lower rather than higher values of $S_{t+\tau}$, a less risk-averse investor may put on the trade, even though it has negative expected value.

The main risk in the trade is that the foreign currency appreciates rather than depreciates. Because of this risk, such a foreign exchange strategy trade is called an "open position." However, this outcome has a low probability in many episodes of exchange rate tension, in which even quite aggressive moves by central banks to defend a parity are patently ineffective. The expected loss in the event the speculative attack doesn't result in devaluation is small; the conditional expected value $E\left[S_{t+\tau}|S_{t+\tau} > \bar{S}\right]$ will only be slightly higher than $\bar{S}$, and the probability of a more-than-trivial appreciation is likely to be low.

In the typical case of a speculative attack, $\bar{S} - E\left[S_{t+\tau}\right]$ is a large positive and $(r - r^*)\tau\bar{S}$ a small negative quantity, especially if the time frame τ within which the devaluation is expected to occur is short. Fixed exchange rates that are widely perceived to be unsustainable are therefore said to offer "one-way bets" to investors shorting the weak currency.

Example 14.1 (Currency Speculation) Suppose the exchange rate is fixed at 1.25 domestic currency units per foreign currency unit, but a devaluation to an exchange rate of 1.00 is expected within a year. If this view proves correct, the capital gains on each unit of foreign currency equal 0.25 domestic currency units. Suppose the domestic and foreign one-year money market rates are 3 and 6 percent. The net cost of maintaining the short position is then $(0.03 - 0.06)1.25 = -0.0375$ domestic currency units per year and the total profit is $0.25 - 0.0375 = 0.2125$. If the exchange rate strengthens to 1.30 instead, the loss on the trade is 0.0875 per foreign currency unit. If the trade horizon is one month, with the same expected conditional future exchange rates of 1.00 and 1.30, the expected gain conditional on devaluation is 0.24685 and the loss conditional on no devaluation is 0.053125, an even more lopsided balance.

Countries maintain pegged exchange rates to foster exchange rate stability and stability of their domestic price levels. But currencies with fixed exchange rates become vulnerable to speculative attack if they are perceived to be conducting expansive monetary and fiscal policies that will make the pegged exchange rate unsustainable. In models of speculative attack in the genre of Krugman (1979), speculative attacks occur when governments peg the exchange rate and in addition run budget deficits financed by either domestic money creation or out of foreign exchange reserves. No finite amount of reserves can stave off the attack indefinitely; at some point, the prospect of reserve exhaustion draws close enough that remaining reserves are depleted instantly.

Exchange rates, via short-term capital flows, affect the banking and financial system in an essential way. Currency crises can be transmitted through international trade and capital flows and interest-rate relationships among currency zone members, and therefore have a particular tendency to spread beyond the initial target of a speculative attack and impact other markets. Countries with a fixed-exchange rate, but somewhat higher interest rates, may experience large short-term capital inflows, which can abruptly reverse in a speculative attack.

We next describe two major episodes of speculative attacks on pegged currencies that created the framework for the contemporary managed floating regime among major currencies. The end of the Bretton Woods system, the framework governing the international financial system in the aftermath of World War II (see Chapter 1), was marked by a speculative attack on the U.S. dollar. The dollar was pegged; that is, it had a fixed price against other currencies, maintained by the central banks involved through currency purchases and sales. The dollar price of gold was also fixed, maintained by the readiness of the U.S. Treasury to sell gold for U.S. dollars to overseas monetary authorities at a fixed price per ounce of $35. But there had long been doubts about the sustainability of these fixed prices, and skepticism grew rampant in the 1960s as U.S. trade and current account surpluses declined and U.S. inflation increased. The United States sold its gold reserves at an accelerating pace at the fixed $35 price, and short-term international claims against the U.S. dollar increased. Foreign central banks could soak these up for a time with the assistance of an occasional modest devaluation of the dollar against their currencies. But this "adjustable peg" system further eroded the credibility of the fixed exchange rates and motivated investors to short the dollar. The system collapsed in two stages: In August 1971, the United States ended gold convertibility, and in March 1973, following an attempt to stabilize rates with another large dollar devaluation, fixed exchange rates were abandoned (see Figure 14.23).

As described in Chapter 1, West European countries, for which international trade is a much higher fraction of output than for the United States, were quite uncomfortable with the end of the Bretton Woods system and of fixed exchange rates. Their major experiment in attaining intra-European exchange rate stability, the *European Monetary System* (EMS), lasted from 1979 until the introduction of a common currency in 1999. The EMS employed fluctuation limits around the pegged exchange rates, called "central parities." If an exchange rate reached one of the fluctuation limits, both central banks were obliged to intervene to support the weakening currency. This system experienced a series of large scale-speculative attacks in 1992 and 1993.

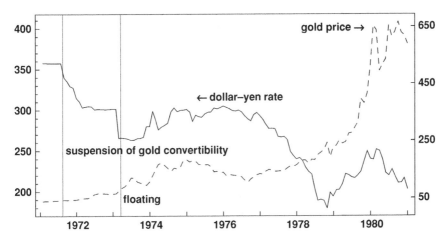

FIGURE 14.23   Gold and the U.S. Dollar at the End of Bretton Woods
The dollar-yen exchange rate (left *y*-axis) and the U.S. dollar price of gold (right
y-axis), month-end, 1971 to 1980.
Source: Bloomberg Financial L.P.

The system had periodically undertaken changes in the central parities, as divergent macroeconomic performance created selling pressure on
currencies of countries with higher inflation rates than the "core" countries, West Germany and the Netherlands. German reunification in 1989
committed Germany to large public expenditures and a potential increase
in the domestic price level stemming from its commitment to convert East
German nominal wages to deutsche mark at a ratio of 1:1. The Bundesbank,
Germany's central bank, in an effort to offset the inflationary consequences,
raised interest rates sharply, and the central parities began to appear unsustainable.

Speculative attacks began on EMS currencies other than the mark and
the guilder, as well as on Scandinavian currencies such as the Swedish krona
which, while not part of the EMS, had pegged rates. In an ultimately unsuc-
cessful effort to stem the pressure, the Riksbank raised its overnight lending
rate to 500 percent before devaluing. We referred earlier to Sweden's guarantee of bank liabilities to stem the attendant banking crisis. To avert a
devaluation of sterling, the Bank of England intervened massively in foreign exchange markets, and eventually raised rates twice in one day, before
withdrawing sterling from the EMS on the same day, September 16, 1992,
or "Black Wednesday." The subsequent exchange rate volatility was aston-
ishing. By the close of the following day, the pound had depreciated over

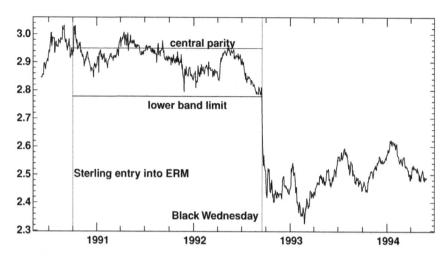

FIGURE 14.24 Sterling in the European Monetary System
The sterling-mark exchange rate, deutsche mark per pound sterling, daily close,
June 1, 1990, to May 31, 1995.
Source: Exchange rate data from Bloomberg Financial L.P.

5 percent below its lower fluctuation limit; by the end of February 1993, it
had lost almost 20 percent of its value against the mark (see Figure 14.24).

14.4.2 Interest Rates and Credit Expansion

Apart from debt and international imbalances, credit and monetary policies
are the most frequently-cited causes or background factors of financial and
the economic expansions that precede them. Sweden's Riksbank, established
in 1668, and the Bank of England, founded in 1694, are among the world's
first central banks, though city-states such as Amsterdam and Hamburg had
established similar institutions earlier in the seventeenth century. Central
banks gradually assumed responsibility for management of internal and
external monetary policies.

At the risk of drastic oversimplification, two frameworks for thinking
about these issues had been formulated by the turn of the twentieth century.
The first, associated with Irving Fisher focused on the demand and supply of
money, and is ancestrally related to *monetarism*. In this view, the demand
for money is generally stable, and booms and busts are caused primarily by
fluctuations in the money supply. A recognized exception is that, during a
crisis, the demand for money may suddenly rise sharply.

A second framework, formulated by Knut Wicksell, was based on a distinction between the *natural* and the *money rate of interest*. The natural rate of interest, expressed in real rather than nominal terms, is the rate of interest that equilibrates the supply of savings and demand for investment capital. At the natural rate, the capital market would clear in the present, and the markets for the future goods produced would clear in the future, with no disappointments and no surprises. The money rate of interest is that actually set by the banking system. Unsustainable booms are set off when the money rate is set below the natural rate, and deflationary spirals when the money rate is set to high.

Wicksell's paradigm remains as a ghostly presence, identifiable behind the scenes in the *Taylor rule*, but is not an explicit element of most models of fluctuations and crises. The Taylor rule states a central bank operating procedure: They should—or actually do, in another interpretation of the rule and of the post-1970s consensus approach to monetary policy—set short-term nominal interest rates equal to a constant related to the long-term equilibrium real interest rate, the real rate consistent with sustainable non-inflationary long-term growth, plus the current inflation rate. The real rate is commonly estimated at 2 to 3 percent. But the central bank should temporarily raise or lower rates if inflation or output growth deviate from their target rates. The parameters of the Taylor rule are set so that, when inflation is not at its target level, policy makers follow a *feedback rule*, "leaning against the wind" by raising the real interest rate. Implicit application of this approach, and its impact on expectations, was considered key to success in reducing inflation at a surprisingly low output cost from 1979 on.

The Taylor rule is challenging to estimate for a number of reasons: its dual interpretation as both descriptive and prescriptive, the variety of ways in which the gap between actual and potential output or employment, and current or forecast inflation can be measured, and because the Federal Reserve is seen as carrying out *interest-rate smoothing*, changing target interest rates incrementally and over longer periods of time.

During the "Great Moderation," discussed in Chapter 1, both short- and long-term interest rates were quite low. Two stories predominate about the role of low interest rates in the macroeconomic background to the subprime crisis: in one, interest rates at a four-decade low were at least a contributing factor to the crisis; in the *global savings glut* story, they were the result of an unusual combination of international asset market imbalances and historical circumstances.

The low interest rate story begins by noting that that, according to many estimates, the short-term interest rates set by policy fell below Taylor rule levels during the decade preceding the subprime crisis. Central banks generally operate via short-term interest rates, as long as they are above zero, but long-term interest rates also fell to unusually low levels. In fact, long-term rates kept falling even after short-term rates began rising from mid-2004. This unusual phenomenon was dubbed the "yield curve conundrum."

Low interest rates didn't, however, lead to rising inflation, the crucial signal that rates were "too low." As we saw in Figure 1.11, U.S. core CPI dropped below 5 percent in 1991 and below 3 percent in 1996, and hasn't returned to those levels since. Economists were divided even at the time about the reasons for the apparently benign economic climate. Some considered it a success of economic policy, while others remained uncomfortable with very low interest rates, in spite of low inflation. Yet others felt the reports of moderation of volatility were greatly exaggerated, observing, for example, that a reduction in the volatility of a single output sector, inventory investment in durable goods, appeared to be responsible for the entire reduction in GDP growth volatility seen in Figure 1.15.

The undercurrent of discomfort with low interest rates focused on credit expansion and rising asset prices. The low volatility of macroeconomic variables we noted in Chapter 1 also extended to asset returns; spreads and yield levels fell as well. We have seen that low volatility can increase fragility by increasing asset values and risk limits on positions, and, in this view, may have played a role in fostering instability. Concerns had been raised before the crises that, while volatility might have declined, financial instability had become more pervasive. These concerns were supported by the rising frequency of larger and smaller financial crises from about 1970 onwards.

In the half-decade prior to the subprime crisis, Federal Reserve policy makers articulated a "risk management approach" to monetary policy, sometimes explicitly couched in terms of a policy maker loss function. It meant that the Federal Reserve would act more aggressively to avert low-probability events with severe consequences. In the low-interest rate view, the risk management approach, combined with low consumer price inflation, contributed to an asymmetry of policy response, in which monetary policy was not tightened in periods of expanding credit and rising asset prices, but loosened in periods of declining credit aggregates and valuations. The perception of asymmetric macroeconomic policy contributed, in this interpretation, to the compression of risk premiums.

Several related channels have been noted by which low interest rates might increase the fragility of the financial system:

First, low rates increase the incentive to enter into leveraged trades. We described how this incentive works in Chapter 12. Low interest rates encourage trades in expectation of rising asset prices, such as housing purchases with low down payments. Low rates, by facilitating maturity and liquidity transformation, also encourage carry trades and leveraged positions in modestly higher-yielding securities, such as senior structured credit products funded at money market rates or hedged with lower-yielding securities.

Interest rate smoothing is also thought to have played a role: Any increases in the level of short-term rates would proceed gradually, limiting the downside and liquidity risks of investments that depended on leverage via short-term funding.

Second, by reducing all-in bond yields, low rates increase the incentives of some market participants to seek out riskier investments to attain return targets. At the same time, it drives risk premiums narrower, so that tail risks, such as the systematic risks of senior securitization bonds, are priced low. This effect is important because it encompasses important market participants, such as insurance companies funding fixed-rate annuities and defined-benefit pension funds. This "search for yield," or "yield panic" reflects agency cost and externality problems, as the institutional investor increases the probability of being able to meet return requirements, but also increases systematic risk and system fragility. Low rates also strengthen market participants' financial positions by increasing the value of their assets and lead them to expand leverage and balance sheets. Finally, and particularly in its interaction with interest-rate smoothing, the perception that central bank policy seeks to avoiding bear markets can diminish the perception of risk by market participants.

These effects of low interest rates have been called the *risk-taking channel*. Diamond and Rajan (2011) present a formal model in which banks are incentivized to fund themselves to some extent with short-term debt because it adds to discipline over borrowers and because the banks anticipate low interest rates in crises. Tighter monetary policy reduces the banks' short-term funding incentive and thus the probability of crises. The increase in risk-taking induced by low rates can manifest itself in increasing balance-sheet leverage, but also in off-balance-sheet transactions that are more difficult to observe.

U.S. broker-dealers provide an example of how low interest rates work through the risk-taking channel. As we saw in Chapter 12, certain forms of securities lending, for example, particularly where higher-quality securities are exchanged for lower-quality ones ("borrowed versus pledged"), are not necessarily reflected in financial reports, or are at least not easy to discern, though it can be indirectly observed in data such as repo volumes (see Figure 12.3).

Low interest rates may interact with other factors, too. For example, in 2004, the SEC changed regulatory capital requirements for major-broker dealers. This permitted the broker-dealers to take on greater leverage, much of it in short-term forms such as commercial paper, repo and securities lending. The assets being financed often lacked market liquidity. The presumption for broker-dealers, as opposed to commercial banks, is that they can be funded short-term, since the asset side of their balance sheets consists largely of inventories of liquid securities. This presumption was no longer accurate by 2007, as broker-dealers became deeply involved in the process of creating securitized credit products. Their balance sheets were employed in part as warehouses for the illiquid intermediate products of the securitization process, including loans held for future securitizations, and bonds created in recent securitizations, but not yet sold to the broader markets, or held as proprietary investments.[3]

The global savings glut view of low interest rates focuses more on the causes than the potential consequences. In this view, the increase in capital flows and the large volume of investment inflows to developed countries, especially the United States, were important factors in the decline in long-term interest rates in developed countries. These flows have their origin in two underlying phenomena: the low U.S. savings rate and persistent U.S. current account deficit, on the one hand, and the successful export-based development strategy pursued by a number of developing countries, especially in Asia, on the other. Each of these phenomena would be unsustainable for long on its own. Together, they have persisted for several decades and intensified during the decade preceding the subprime crisis.

The current-account deficit could be explained either by U.S. investment outlays in excess of U.S. saving, which would pull capital in and raise interest rates, or eagerness by foreigners to buy U.S. assets, which would push capital into the U.S. and lower interest rates. Proponents of the latter, savings glut, view, point to falling U.S. interest rates as evidence that the "capital push" is predominant.

The U.S. current account deficit is made up primarily by developing countries, particularly in East Asia. This is surprising in itself, since one would expect industrial countries to invest in less-developed countries rather than the reverse. One explanation is that these surpluses are part of an overall development strategy. Though counterintuitive, China is said to run a current account surplus in order to foster internal investment. The key to the apparent contradiction is the role of collateral. By investing surpluses and holding reserves in the form of U.S. assets, China conveys collateral to the U.S. The liability that China collateralizes in this fashion is foreign direct investment in China. This direct investment is valuable because it brings technological progress with it, and is worth obtaining even at the cost of locking up a considerable portion of its net assets as collateral. If it were to expropriate the direct investments made by the industrial countries, it would risk having its dollar-denominated assets frozen. In other words, China runs a large current account surplus in order to facilitate the small

---

[3]See U.S. Securities and Exchange Commission (2004) for the text and background discussion of the change to Rule 15c3-1.

direct-investment deficit embedded in the overall capital flows. The overall development strategy is to build a technologically advanced capital stock that will enable a large rural labor force to eventually be employed at a much higher marginal productivity of labor.

An alternative explanation of the counterintuitive, "uphill" flow of capital from less- to more-developed regions points out that, although emerging markets have grown rapidly, they have not developed financially nearly as rapidly. Investors in these countries need the safe assets issued in advanced countries, depressing their rates of return. This line of reasoning dovetails with the story, laid out in Chapter 12 and earlier in this chapter, pointing out the effect of the demand for collateral in fostering the growth in investment-grade securitized credit products. In all of its variants, the global savings glut view sees limits on the ability of U.S. monetary policy to influence longer-term interest rates and the risk-taking channel.

14.4.3 Procyclicality: Financial Causes of Crises

Earlier in this chapter, we examined the self-reinforcing mechanisms that amplify volatility and the credit and liquidity crunch during financial distress. These mechanisms can be viewed as manifestations of the financial system's tendency to procyclical behavior; booms and busts, once underway, tend to amplify until an unsustainable extreme is reached, at which point the reversal, a recovery or a crash, commences.

The risk-taking channel of monetary policy which we have just described is another source of procyclicality. Attention to possible procyclical tendencies in the financial system is an important part of research on the risk-taking channel of monetary policy: The subprime crisis has many observers asking themselves what they had missed. As noted, there is also evidence that the frequency and severity of crises has been increasing in recent decades.

The wide range of views on procyclicality can be categorized along two dimensions

The strength of procyclicality: Some identify tendencies that can be readily counteracted by appropriate policy, while others see large-amplitude, low-frequency fluctuations in activity and financial aggregates as nearly uncontainable in the modern financial system.

The sources of procyclicality: Some see fluctuations as triggered exogenously, that is, by random shocks or policy errors, while others view procyclicality as endogenous, that is, inherent in the organization and functioning of the financial system.

These views on financial crises can be divided along the lines of perennial issue in debates on crises, and economics generally: How reliable is a market economy's tendency toward equilibrium with full employment of economic resources?

A parallel debate, also dating back centuries, concerns the question of whether the financial system automatically controls the volume of money and credit. In the early nineteenth century, two schools of thought on this subject emerged in the United Kingdom. In the *Currency School* view, the banking system would be prone to excessive issuance of credit without externally-imposed limitations. The *Banking School* taught that credit regulated itself automatically: If banks collectively issued too much credit to business, financed by note issuance, the holders would begin redeeming the notes for gold, nipping excessive credit expansion in the bud. As far as British monetary policy was concern, the debate was settled by Peel's Act of 1844, a milestone in the development of modern central banking, which put note issue into the exclusive hands of the Bank of England and restricted its volume. But the debate around the propensity of the banking system to permit credit aggregates to grow excessively has recurred.

We have seen in this chapter how fluctuations in firms' net worth and in the value of collateral they can offer can amplify crises. Observers have been aware of this mechanism since at least the Great Depression, when it found expression in Fisher's (1933) schema of "debt-deflations." Because it puts firms' net worth in the forefront as a driver of boom and bust, and is attentive to the interactions of net worth and asset prices, the debt-deflation approach has resonated with many post-subprime crisis observers. As we saw earlier in this chapter, leverage in new forms was extremely high for many financial intermediaries prior to the subprime crisis, making net worth a key driver of the crisis. In Fisher's schema, an initial state of excessive leverage leads to liquidations, losses, and a drain of liquidity that reduces net worth, leading to fresh rounds of liquidation. These effects are brought about by the reduction in prices, initially those of assets, but eventually also of commodities and final goods. Apart from lower prices, the debt-deflation process brings about a reduction in output, a reduction in nominal interest rates, and a rise in real interest rates.

Another way in which net worth constraints increase instability is to impair the markets' ability to carry out arbitrage and near-arbitrage. Effecting even a riskless arbitrage generally requires some minimum of capital and time. Investors may withdraw capital from vehicles such as hedge funds that specialize in carrying out arbitrage operations. Investors' as well as lenders' urge to withdraw capital may be spurred by a general desire to regain liquidity rather than avoid capital losses. Chapter 12 illustrated the potential effect of this mechanism of procyclicality with the sharp fluctuations in convertible bond values (see Figure 12.2), Chapter 13 with the extreme bond-CDS basis, and this chapter with negative swap spreads in late 2008.

Withdrawal of capital may also arise as a consequence of asymmetric information. Fund investors, like lenders to banks, have less information than the fund's (or bank's) managers about the investments made with their capital. They may therefore rationally rely on fund returns in order to determine whether the fund managers have skill in carrying out arbitrage. When returns are low or negative, which with some probability is due to lack of skill rather than market conditions, investors withdraw capital more eagerly. The reduction in capital, from both the desire for liquidity and the negative return signal, can amplify asset sales.

A similar effect may occur in asset markets. In Chapter 12, we noted that some investors, called "noise traders," may make investment decisions based at least in part on the prices of the assets themselves, rather than on an analysis of their fundamental values relative to the price. A decline in price may indicate that "someone else" knows something negative about fundamental value, and induce them to sell. Earlier, we saw that dynamic hedging by investors can induce self-perpetuating declines in asset prices. One mechanism by which this can happen is for hedging sales in response to a small initial decline in price, for example by option sellers, to amplify it by incorrectly signaling a change in fundamentals. The price decline is amplified further by market participants selling purely in response to earlier price declines.

These mechanisms are to some extent symmetrical, so price increases can also become self-sustaining. But capital and funding constraints will introduce asymmetries between boom and bust, and make asset price declines more powerful and difficult to arrest.

The view that crises are inevitable is associated with the view that there are large low-frequency fluctuations in risk appetite. Keynes referred to risk appetite as "animal spirits," relating its fluctuations to those of economic activity,[4] and the label has stuck. Characteristically, as in his descriptions of thrift, Keynes found a distanced and ironic phrase for a socially useful but unaesthetic quality. The contrasting expression "irrational exuberance" came into usage in late 1996 to characterize the stock markets of the time.

The view that crises are inevitable starts from the observation that risk aversion is subdued—animal spirits are high—during quiet times. This leads to expansion of business activity and bubbles in asset prices. At some point it

---

[4]See Chapter 12 of Keynes (1936). Keynes' alternative formulations are "spontaneous urge to action rather than inaction," and "the delicate balance of spontaneous optimism."

becomes clear, often after some relatively minor triggering event, that not all these business plans can actually be realized. A panic ensues, risk appetites shrink, asset prices collapse, and business activity remains low until the cycle gradually restarts. No economic forces exist that would bring the system to a steadier equilibrium path.

A formulation that combines the two elements of net worth and risk aversion was put forward by Hyman Minsky in the "financial instability hypothesis." The hypothesis is set out as a three-stage theory of boom and bust, each corresponding to a type of finance and a type of borrower (or "unit") that predominates during that phase:

1. *Hedge finance* can be repaid out of the cash flows of the borrower, and does not need to rolled over or refinanced.
2. *Speculative finance* units can pay interest on debt, but cannot repay principal, out of cash flows, and will have to refinance or sell the investment at a higher price to remain solvent.
3. *Ponzi finance* refers to debt on which even interest cannot be paid out of cash flows. Further borrowing is needed to service existing debt. It will be necessary in addition to sell the asset at a profit to repay the loan.

Only a financial system in which hedge financing predominates can be stable in the Minsky paradigm. Enough elements of speculative or Ponzi finance can—and in a free-market system are likely to—set in motion an endogenous cycle, which will either be contained via public-sector intervention or culminate in a bust. The Minsky paradigm is uncannily similar to the credit creation that preceded the subprime crisis, and has therefore garnered renewed attention.

In macroeconomics, the impact of capital and net worth constraints on economic activity, particularly during crises, is called the *credit channel* of transmission of monetary shocks and policy. It is similar to the risk-taking channel in its focus on the financial condition of market participants. In contrast to the risk-taking channel, which focuses on the encouragement low interest rates give to risk-taking, the credit channel focuses on the impact of monetary policy on firms' balance sheet health.

14.4.4 Models of Bubbles and Crashes

Financial crises are related to, but distinct from *bubbles*. A bubble occurs when asset prices become detached from fundamentals and trade on the basis of expected future capital gains, as in Minsky's Ponzi form of finance. Bubbles have been defined more clearly in models than in history. Even in hindsight, it is hard to be sure that any particular episode of rapid asset price increases constitutes a bubble. Two examples are the *tulip mania* of seventeenth-century Europe and the stock market boom of the 1920s. In both these cases, a rapid and sharp runup in prices was followed by an even more abrupt decline. Yet historians have been able to marshal considerable evidence that the asset price had arguably been rational *ex ante* in view of the fundamentals, even if the view of the bulls was not borne out in retrospect.

It is all the more difficult to identify bubbles, in real time, as they occur, and one of the challenges facing public policy is to determine the best means of addressing them. Should policy attempt to dampen swings in asset prices, or focus on the effects of such swings on economic activity? If the focus is to be on asset prices, by what criteria can we identify "bubbles"? We return to these issues in the next chapter.

Models in which the current asset price depends on expectations of future fundamentals, for example dividend-growth models of stock prices, and which also assume rational expectations, which we define in a moment, generally have an infinite number of solutions. The asset price, in these solutions, is a function of current expectations of all the future fundamentals, and an arbitrary constant. If the constant is not zero, the price may veer off ever further from the fundamentals-based value, and still be consistent with rational expectations and with the model.

We can illustrate this using the basic security pricing model of Chapter 2. We look at asset prices in a discrete-time framework, but with infinitely many periods. The price S_t at time t of any asset is equal to the sum of two components: the expected value of its price next period, and its expected cash flow d_t, set at time t but paid at time $t + 1$, which we call a "dividend." The asset return is

$$\frac{S_{t+1} - S_t + d_t}{S_t} \quad t = 1, 2, \ldots$$

Now, let's assume *rational expectations*, as is common in economics. It sets asset prices equal to their actuarial or "physical" expected values, and abstracts from risk appetites and risk premiums. In a rational expectations model, the asset price must be set so that its expected return is equal to the discretely compounded risk free return r_t:

$$r_t = \mathrm{E}\left[\frac{S_{t+1} - S_t + d_{t+1}}{S_t}\right] \quad t = 1, 2, \ldots$$

The only element that is not known at time t is the future price S_{t+1}, so we can pull everything else out of the expectation notation:

$$r_t S_t = \mathrm{E}\left[S_{t+1}\right] - S_t + d_t \quad t = 1, 2, \ldots$$

to get

$$S_t = \frac{E[S_{t+1}] + d_t}{1 + r_t} \quad t = 1, 2, \ldots \tag{14.1}$$

Now, we can use Equation (14.1) to solve for the expected value of the asset price, from the point of view of time t, in a more distant future than $t + 1$. For convenience, let the risk-free interest rate and the dividend be constant, putting the focus entirely on asset-price risk. The next-period asset price is

$$S_{t+1} = \frac{E[S_{t+2}] + d}{1 + r} \quad t = 1, 2, \ldots$$

so

$$S_t = \frac{1}{1 + r} \left\{ E\left[\frac{E[S_{t+2}] + d}{1 + r} \right] + d \right\} \quad t = 1, 2, \ldots$$

Notice that we have the expected value of an expected value in this expression. A standard trick in solving rational expectations models is to note that, at time t, we know no more about *what we will know in the future* than we know right now about the future.[5] So from the time-t point of view,

$$E[E[S_{t+2}]] = E[S_{t+2}]$$

Make this substitution, and take all the nonstochastic terms out, to obtain

$$S_t = \frac{1}{(1 + r)^2} E[S_{t+2}] + \left[\frac{1}{1 + r} + \frac{1}{(1 + r)^2} \right] d \quad t = 1, 2, \ldots$$

---

[5]Technically, this step relies on a property of conditional expectations known as the *law of iterated expectations* or *tower rule*. In essence, we have been working here with conditional expectations of the future asset price. The law of iterated expectations states that if the conditioning set—the set of possible outcomes in the "outer" expectation—is the same as the conditioning set of the "inner" expectation, we can collapse it into one conditional expectation.

We can now successively substitute out the next period's asset price. After doing so τ times, we get

$$S_t = \frac{1}{(1+r)^\tau} E[S_{t+\tau}] + d \sum_{\theta=1}^{\tau} \frac{1}{(1+r)^\theta}$$

$$= \frac{1}{(1+r)^\tau} E[S_{t+\tau}] + \frac{1}{r}\left[1 - \frac{1}{(1+r)^\tau}\right] d \quad t = 1, 2, \ldots$$

Now, if the asset matures at time T, then we know its terminal value, such as the par amount of a bond, for certain. If we set $S_T = 0$ for simplicity, then S_t is just the present value of the dividend flows:

$$S_t = \frac{1}{r}\left[1 - \frac{1}{(1+r)^\tau}\right] d \approx \frac{d}{r}$$

The approximation holds if the time to maturity τ is long.

But suppose the asset is infinitely lived, such as an equity or a commodity. The time-t asset price is now seen to have two components:

$$S_t = \lim_{\tau \to \infty} \frac{1}{(1+r)^\tau} E[S_{t+\tau}] + \frac{d}{r} \tag{14.2}$$

The first is the present value of the future asset price, and the second, called the *fundamental value* of the asset S^*, is the present value of the future cash flows:

$$S^* = \frac{d}{r}$$

That first component

$$b_t \equiv \lim_{\tau \to \infty} \frac{1}{(1+r)^\tau} E[S_{t+\tau}]$$

is not "nailed down." As long as b_t, the "bubble" component, grows (in expected value) at the risk-free rate, that is,

$$\frac{E[b_{t+1}]}{b_t} = 1 + r$$

it is an equilibrium price, since it is consistent with rational expectations, the absence of arbitrage and with our model of the asset price. This phenomenon is called *nonuniqueness* or *multiple equilibria* and is ubiquitous in economic and financial models in which market participants' expectations are equal to physical expectations of future economic variables or asset prices. Situations in which there are several possible outcomes, depending on what market participants expect to happen, or what impact they expect their actions to have on the expectations and actions of others, are common in such models.

One way to get a unique solution is to simply rule out bubbles via the *transversality condition* $b_t = 0$. Modelers dislike doing this because it's arbitrary and doesn't address the fact that the models admit multiple solutions. This is particularly the case since at least one specification of a bubble is eerily similar to our intuitive notion of bubbles and crashes in financial markets. Suppose

$$b_{t+1} = \left\{ \begin{array}{c} \dfrac{1+r}{1-\pi} \, b_t \\[2ex] 0 \end{array} \right\} \text{ with probability } \left\{ \begin{array}{c} 1-\pi \\[1ex] \pi \end{array} \right\}$$

with $0 < \pi < 1$. Since $\frac{1+r}{1-\pi} > 0$, the bubble component b_t will grow over time, until a crash occurs and it goes instantly to zero. The return on the asset will exceed the risk-free rate by enough to compensate for the possibility of a crash. A crash is not inevitable, but the longer the time horizon, the likelier it is to occur. The lower the probability of a crash, the longer the bubble can last. Once a crash occurs, though, the asset price will remain at its fundamental value forever.

In this specification, which equilibrium is realized is random. Models in which equilibrium is random, but unrelated to economic fundamentals are said to display *self-fulling crises* or *sunspots*. Recall that this is precisely what characterizes endogenous liquidity risk, described earlier in this chapter and in Chapter 12.

There is much controversy over whether sunspots and multiple equilibria are real-world phenomena. But the idea is useful in understanding some of the phenomena we have discussed, such as panics, runs, and the role of animal spirits. In the models of bank runs we've described, for example, a run occurs because depositors are afraid others will run. An equilibrium state in which nobody runs can occur as easily as a run; a state in which asset owners "all hold hands" and refrain from selling can occur as easily as a fire sale. A number of models of balance-of-payments crises and currency crashes, such as that of Krugman (1979), cited above, also display multiple equilibria.

In another class of models of bubbles and crashes, credit is an integral part of the process. In an approach set out in Kiyotaki and Moore (1997, 2002), cycles are generated by the net-worth effect. In periods of rising asset prices, firms are able to borrow more and expand; periods of falling asset price persist analogously. The approach of Kiyotaki and Moore (1997) rests on the risk-shifting impact of credit contracts, in which the borrower keeps most of the upside, but has a limited potential loss. In this type of model, intermediation and the agency problems it can generate play an essential role.

Gennotte and Leland (1990) provide a model in which asymmetric information interacts with market liquidity to amplify price swings. In their model, some investors rely on asset price information to draw inferences about value. This behavior is analogous to that of noise traders, or of the providers of capital in Shleifer and Vishny (1997), who draw inferences about the investment skill of their agent-managers from returns. When uninformed investors see a decline in asset price, they interpret it as a decline in fundamental value, and join the selloff, amplifying it. Gennotte and Leland apply the model to the October 1987 market decline.

14.5 ANTICIPATING FINANCIAL CRISES

Market participants as well as policy makers have a keen and growing interest in identifying the potential for crises and extreme events. This potential can be signaled by macroeconomic indicators, at relatively low frequencies, and by the behavior of asset prices.

14.5.1 Identifying Financial Fragility

Ideally, but perhaps unrealistically in practice, one would like to predict financial crises, or at least identify data that help discern whether financial fragility is growing. For example, identifying sharp or sustained increases in asset prices that are not matched by improvements in fundamentals, so that prospective returns or risk premiums are shrinking, might help identify bubbles. We discuss the difficulties of doing so here and in the next chapter.

Another set of indicators germane to financial fragility are measures of leverage. Figure 14.25 shows one simple measure of leverage for the United States, the ratio of credit market borrowing to GDP, showing the total as well as the contributions of the government, private nonfinancial, and financial sectors to the total. The data are drawn from the U.S. Flow of Funds Accounts, and do not adequately represent leverage generated via derivatives, off-balance-sheet vehicles, and collateral markets along the lines

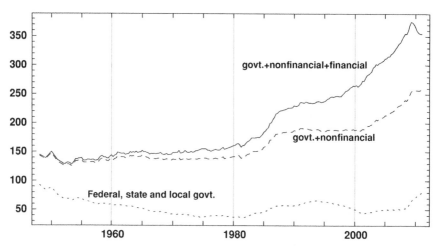

FIGURE 14.25   U.S. Leverage 1947–2010
Ratio of credit market debt outstanding to gross domestic product in current
dollars, percent, quarterly. "Nonfinancial" is the sum of private nonfinancial and
rest of world. "Financial" includes all financial sectors.
Source: Federal Reserve Board, Flow of Funds Accounts of the United States (Z.1),
Table L.1, lines 1–10; U.S. Bureau of Economic Analysis, National Income and
Product Accounts, Table 1.1.5, line 1.

laid out in Chapter 12, but are at least indicative of general trends over the
past few decades.

Leverage increased steadily from the early 1980s until the subprime crisis. Most of the increase in leverage has been in the private sector, especially
households and the financial sector. Household leverage increased particularly rapidly during two phases, the mid-1980s and the decade preceding
the subprime crisis. Financial-sector leverage has been increasing throughout, due primarily to increasing leverage by the nonbank sector. As noted,
banks' rising leverage took forms not reflected clearly in this data set. The
trends reversed with the onset of the panic phase of the crisis. Financial and
private nonfinancial leverage dropped sharply. Government debt rose, but
not enough to offset private-sector deleveraging.

There is no widely accepted standard for what constitutes "high" leverage relative to GDP. One might argue that leverage, as an aspect of financial development, should increase to some extent with economic growth.
Nonetheless, the unabated and rapid rise of the leverage-to-GDP ratio over
the past three decades provided an indicator of excessive credit creation and
fragility.

14.5.2 Macroeconomic Predictors of Financial Crises

The difficulty of generalizing about the nature and causes of crises extends to the search for indicators and warning signals. Macroeconomic data, apart from asset prices, because they have low frequency, pose special problems in this respect. Much work has been done by international organizations such as the International Monetary Fund (IMF) to identify macroeconomic and other low-frequency indicators of financial and balance-of-payments stress, such as data on the condition of the local financial sector. These are especially important for developing countries, which have less well-developed financial markets and a narrower range of observable asset prices. The evidence, however, is weak that such indicators do a good job at predicting crises.

14.5.3 Asset-Price Predictors of Financial Crises

Warning signals of crises may be obtained from asset prices. We've seen many examples throughout this book of asset price dislocations caused by extreme events and crises. Some of these asset price phenomena may appear early enough to serve as useful warning signals. Certain asset prices, particularly the interest-rate term structure and credit spreads, have been used with considerable accuracy to forecast fluctuations in economic activity. For example, the spread between yields on 10-year Treasuries and 3-month T-bills has been a reliable precursor of recessions.

Crises generally coincide with economic downturns, but occur much less frequently, so it is more challenging to identify leading indicators and verify their information content statistically. We can single out three categories of asset prices that appear to move early in response to stresses:

1. "Liquidity spreads," a diffuse group including on-the-run and off-the-run government bond spreads and money-market risk spreads
2. Foreign exchange forward markets
3. Option implied volatilities

Most liquidity spreads, such as those related to the TED spread, the money market spread between a risk-free and credit-risky money market instrument, contain both liquidity and credit risk components. Examples are displayed in Figures 12.4 (repo spreads), 13.4 (the CDS basis), 14.9 (the TED spread), 14.10 (Libor-OIS), 14.11 (Libor-Fed funds), and 14.15 (the swap spread). Liquidity spreads tend to widen out before other credit spreads, such as those on corporate bonds, as some bankers and dealers first become more reticent about granting short-term credit to others. As we have seen, the spread between Libor and OIS began to widen dramatically in August 2007, as concern over banks' liquidity and capital positions began to affect money markets. The behavior of swap spreads, however, was sharply at odds with the past, tightening rather than widening. Credit spreads did not widen out dramatically until 2008.

An interesting example of money market spreads possibly having provided a warning signal of the 1929 stock market crash is presented by Rappoport and White (1993). They obtained time-series data on different types of money market rates: ordinary short-term loans by banks to non-financial customers, commercial paper, and loans to brokers, who in turn used the funding to make secured margin loans to buy stock. In February 1928, the Federal Reserve began to tighten monetary policy to address growing concern about the rising stock market. All money market rates rose, but the spread between margin loans and short-term commercial loans and its volatility rose particularly sharply (see, especially Rappoport and White, 1993, Fig. 2 on p. 555).

Another type of signal is provided by extreme moves in a low-volatility environment, an intriguing example of which occurred in February 2007. Implied volatility, and credit and liquidity spreads were still just barely higher than the all-time lows they had recently touched, but a sense of foreboding about the market had begun to take hold. A number of mortgage lenders had defaulted (though others were still being acquired by large banks and broker-dealers). HSBC had in mid-February made the first announcement by a major banking house of losses due to subprime lending. Toward the end of February, there was a brief spasm of volatility in several markets.[6] It is not clear what was the immediate trigger: in the prior day or two, the Chinese stock market had plunged 9 percent in response to a tightening of policy, Freddie Mac had announced that it would no longer purchase subprime mortgages, and yet another subprime mortgage originator, Fremont General, had signalled distress by delaying its earnings filing. By later standards, the February moves in prices and spreads were quite small, but they represented very large moves relative to the low volatility at the time.

To see how extreme the end-February 2007 episode was, and to put it in context, look again at Figure 10.2. It displays conditional exceedances by the S&P index of a 99.8 percent confidence interval, using a prior-day EWMA volatility estimate. Suppose we set an even higher confidence level, say, 99.99999 percent, so that there is a one-in-10-million chance of an excession on any given day under the normality assumption. This

---

[6]See Vikas Bajaj "Freddie Mac tightens standards," *New York Times*, February 28, 2007.

corresponds to a ±5.32 vol move. There have been only 19 such events since 1928. The following table displays the dates, daily returns, annualized conditional (EWMA) volatility computed via EWMA, and the number of prior-day vols by which the S&P moved, in percent. The last column is computed as the ratio of that day's return to the prior-day estimate of volatility at a daily rate.

Date	Return	Annual vol	Return/daily vol
28Oct1929	−13.9	40.7	−5.4
15Mar1933	15.4	44.7	5.5
23Jan1939	−6.6	19.5	−5.4
05Sep1939	11.2	26.1	6.8
13May1940	−5.7	15.2	−5.9
03Sep1946	−10.4	16.3	−10.2
04Feb1948	−4.3	10.7	−6.4
03Nov1948	−4.7	12.5	−6.0
26Jun1950	−5.5	10.6	−8.3
06Jul1955	3.5	9.8	5.7
26Sep1955	−6.8	9.5	−11.5
28May1962	−6.9	17.6	−6.2
17Aug1982	4.6	13.7	5.4
11Sep1986	−4.9	14.6	−5.3
19Oct1987	−22.9	30.1	−12.1
13Oct1989	−6.3	9.2	−10.9
15Nov1991	−3.7	9.3	−6.4
27Oct1997	−7.1	16.2	−7.0
27Feb2007	−3.5	6.6	−8.5

Viewed this way, February 27, 2007, stands out as exceptional. Only four outliers in over 80 years of data are larger on this normalized basis. One is the October 1987 market crash. Another is the day President Eisenhower suffered a heart attack. Yet the February 2007 event preceeded the onset of the "hot" phase of the crisis by over five months. Other indicators of market fear, such as equity implied correlation, an indicator of concerns about systematic risk (see Chapter 10), also jumped sharply on this date.

There is strong association of these very large outliers with low volatility. The correlation of the volatility with the absolute value of the data in the last column, the ratio of return to volatility, is −18 percent, and if we exclude the great outlier of October 13, 1987, the correlation is −40 percent. This is another bit of evidence that risk managers and policy makers should be wariest when volatility is low.

The Forward and Term Premiums   Perceived risks of large asset price
moves may be reflected in futures and forward prices of those assets. Similarly, anticipations of large changes in interest rates will be reflected in
the behavior of the yield curve, since expectations of short-term rates are
important in the setting of longer-term rates.

An example of information appearing in forward rates has occurred
regularly in currency markets. Selling pressure on currencies with pegged exchange rates is often reflected in the forward premium, which shows a more
pronounced expectation of depreciation, particularly if foreign-exchange intervention keeps spot rates from responding fully to the pressure in the short
term. An implication of this phenomenon is exploited in Svensson's (1991)
"simplest test" of target zone credibility. If the monetary authorities set fluctuation limits for the currency, the currency's forward rate trading outside
those limits is evidence that the limits are not credible.

Another example is the behavior of yield curves during "inflation
scares," episodes in which market participants doubt the credibility of the
central bank's commitment to keep inflation low (see Goodfriend, 1993).
The yield curve tends to steepen sharply in such episodes; the increase in
expected future inflation increases the forward interest rate for longer terms
to maturity.

Option Implied Volatility-Based Crisis Predictors   Option prices are also
potentially useful indicators of financial stress. Like the prices of futures and
forwards—or of any cash asset, for that matter—option values are based on
expectations for the future. Options lend themselves particularly well to this
purpose because their prices are sensitive to the size and likelihood of future
asset returns, and to how risk-averse and ill-positioned to absorb them at
least some market participants are. An extreme return scenario with a low
probability may have little impact on the price of a cash security or a futures,
since these are expected values across all outcomes. But it may have a large
impact on the values of options that pay off if that scenario is realized.
Indicators of the likelihood of an extreme event can be derived from the
option-based risk-neutral probability distributions we studied in Chapter
10, employing options across the exercise price axis. We will focus here on
indicators based solely on time series of at-the-money implied volatility.

In the standard Black-Scholes theory, implied volatility is equal to the
known, constant diffusion volatility parameter. If the theory were true,
but the diffusion parameter happened to be unknown, it would be easy to
estimate and would provide accurate volatility forecasts. Implied volatility is
a Black-Scholes model concept, so if Black-Scholes does not hold, an alternative model is needed to determine the expected relationship between implied
volatility and future volatility. In most empirical work on this relationship,

an alternative model or an ad hoc specification establishes a null hypothesis of unbiasedness, that is, that today's implied volatility is the expected value of future realized volatility.

Such tests of "second-moment efficiency" are the analogue of tests of market efficiency that compare mean realized asset returns to the forecast implied by the current forward or futures price. Futures and forwards are often found to be biased predictors of future prices. For example, as we have seen in Chapter 10 and earlier in this chapter, emerging-market foreign-exchange forward premiums often persistently "forecast" large exchange rate changes that simply don't take place. Rather, the level of the forward rate moves up and down with the spot rate, following a path that is hard to distinguish from a random walk.

The evidence, in contrast, is that options do have some short-term predictive value, at least compared to alternative predictors such as recent historical volatility. In other words, "second-moment efficiency" appears to be rejected less robustly than "first-moment efficiency." However, implied volatilities also appear to be biased upward, that is, they tend to forecast higher volatility than is actually realized, giving rise to the notion of a "volatility risk premium." Implied volatility also seems to have some value for predicting large moves. Implied volatility is typically mean-reverting, so that neither periods of low volatility nor sharp spikes in volatility are expected to persist for very long.

Figure 14.26 illustrates one episode in which options appear to have provided early warning of an extreme event. It compares the warning signals provided by foreign exchange forwards and options prior to the Thai baht float of July 1997. This episode marked the beginning of the Asian financial crisis of 1997. A speculative attack against the baht was initiated on May 14, 1997. Implied volatility began to rise just before the attack, and rose sharply as soon as it began. The forward rate began to rise only some time after the beginning of the attack. It was caught in the tug of war between traders shorting the baht and the Bank of Thailand's interventions in both the spot and forward currency markets. Official intervention inhibited the rise of the forward rate but did not affect the options market and the implied volatility signal.

Once the baht was permitted to float, both historical and implied volatility rose sharply. This behavior was not unusual: In a crisis, implied volatility often leads historical volatility. Realized volatility then spikes much higher than implied, but also "decays" rapidly. Implied volatility continues to rise, and decays slowly.

Asset price–based warning signals can be very useful, but a number of caveats are necessary. One major drawback is the number of false positives or Type II errors. This problem is not unique to derivatives prices, as

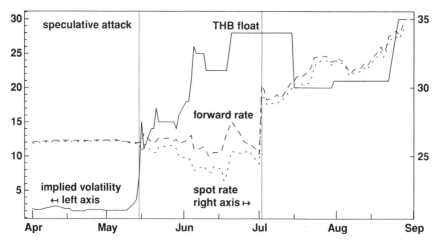

FIGURE 14.26 Behavior of Implied and Historical Volatility in Crises
The plot describes the behavior of the Thai baht (USD-THB) and implied volatility
on USD-THB during the Asian crisis, daily, April through August 1997. Spot rate
in THB per USD. Implied volatility of one month at-the-money forward options.
Historical volatility computed using the EWMA/RiskMetrics approach with decay
factor 0.94 and 90 business days of data.
Data source: Bloomberg Financial L.P.

attested by Paul Samuelson's timeless remark that "the stock market has
predicted nine out of the last five recessions" (quoted in Siegel, 1991, p. 27).
Liquidity spreads widen, and implied volatilities rise, much more often than
crises actually occur. Growing awareness by market participants of the relationship between asset-price indicators and the risk of extreme events may
change their relationship, an example of the operation of Goodhart's Law
(see Chapter 15). Every historical situation is unique, rather than following an unvarying pattern. Warning signals therefore have value only when
used in conjunction with other data and with nonquantitative analyses. It
should, finally, be borne in mind that interpretations of asset prices as signals
of market perceptions share an important limitation: They are risk-neutral
indicators, and can be distorted by changing risk premiums.

This has motivated the development of risk aversion indicators based
on asset prices. These include the VIX, often called a "fear gauge," based on
at-the-money volatilities, and the recently-introduced CBOE Skew Index,
which is based on the prices of at- as well as out-of-the-money options
of S&P 500 constituents. Chapter 10 described equity implied correlation.
Indexes based on other asset prices and on historical volatility, as well as on
implied volatility, have been developed in the trading research departments

of several large banks and dealers, and a number are presented throughout this book.

The search for indicators of crises and extreme events is hardly new, but has become a lively research area in the wake of the subprime crisis. We'll return to this challenging subject in the next chapter, as part of our discussion of public policy to prevent crises.

FURTHER READING

Kindleberger (1978, several subsequent editions) combines a great deal of historical data with an analytical classification of crisis events. Mackay (1962), first published over 150 years ago, is an early work recognizing financial crises as a distinct phenomenon. Grant (1994) is a narrative of selected American banking and capital markets panics. Brown (1987) is a data-rich study of international financial panics, including the interwar era. Kindleberger (1986) and Temin (1989) are a good starting point for studying the macroeconomic background of the Great Depression. Reinhart and Rogoff (2009) is a general history of financial crises, but with a particular focus on crises with sovereign debt and international payments roots. Kaufman (2000*b*) is an analytical survey of systemic risk events.

Although far from ended, there are already a great many valuable studies of the subprime crisis in print and on the Web. Their focus ranges widely, from narratives, to attempts to identify the causes of the crisis, to essays on the implications for financial practitioners. For a detailed chronicle of the crisis, the International Monetary Fund's semiannual *Global Financial Stability Reports* and the Bank for International Settlements' *Annual Reports* and *Quarterly Reviews* issued from mid-2007 onward are invaluable. The U.S. Congress established a number of bodies to study the subprime crisis and report on the public-sector response to it. These bodies maintain web sites with many useful reports and summaries of testimony expressing a wide range of views. The Congressional Oversight Panel home page is http://cop.senate.gov/ and the Office of the Special Inspector General for the Troubled Asset Relief Program home page is http://www.sigtarp.gov/. The Financial Crisis Inquiry Commission has published its final report as U.S. Financial Crisis Inquiry Commission (2011), and maintains its trove of background documentation at http://fcic.law.stanford.edu/. The New York Fed maintains timelines of the crisis at http://www.newyorkfed.org/research/global_economy/policyresponses.html.

Apart from those we cite in reference to specific issues, there are a number of general essays on the crisis worth reading. Crouhy, Jarrow, and Turnbull (2008) and Greenlaw, Hatzius, Kashyap, and Shin (2008) were early assessments. Golub and Crum (2010) discusses risk management implications, with an emphasis on liquidity risk. Swagel (2009) is a narrative by a former senior Treasury official.

Many of the references for Chapter 12 are pertinent to this chapter as well. Pozsar, Adrian, Ashcraft, and Boesky (2010), Adrian and Shin (2009*b*), Tucker (2010), and U.S. Financial Crisis Inquiry Commission (2010) discuss the relationship between the nonbank sector and the subprime crisis. Singh and Aitken (2009*a*, 2009*b*) describe and quantify the decline in credit extension collateralized by securities on the part of banks and broker-dealers during the subprime crisis. Acharya, Cooley, Richardson, and Walter (2009) ties the shadow banking story together with the observation in Chapter 9 that structured products are exposed to hard-to-discern systematic risks. These papers complement the perspective brought by Gorton (2009) and Gorton and Metrick (2010). In addition to the references at the end of Chapter 12 on SIVs and ABCP conduits, see Chapter II of International Monetary Fund (2008a) on the role of these off-balance sheet vehicles and of securitization in the subprime crisis. See also Hördahl and King (2008) on the behavior of repo markets during the subprime crisis.

Bernanke and Lown (1991) and Wojnilower (1980) and (1985) review credit crunch episodes in the postwar U.S. economy. Schularick and Taylor (2009) and Bordo and Haubrich (2010) provide long-term evidence that the severest economic contractions coincide with credit expansions and subsequent credit crises. Ivashina and Scharfstein (2010) details the overall decline in bank lending and "run" on bank lines following the Lehman bankruptcy.

Calomiris and Gorton (1991) uses historical data to better understand the triggers and background of bank runs and panics. Duffie (2010) draws together several new forms a run can take, including the risk of being shut out of the triparty repo system, in describing the collapses of Bear and Lehman. Shin (2009*a*) describes the run on Northern Rock. See also Pedersen (2009). Laeven and Valencia (2008) analyze a database chronicling in detail systemically important banking crises globally from 1970 through 2008.

Longstaff (2004) attempts to estimate the crisis liquidity premium in U.S. Treasury prices. Fleming and Garbade (2002, 2004, 2005) provide institutional and analytical background on settlement fails in repo markets. Liu, McConnell and Saretto (2010) discuss an episode that has been widely interpreted as a failure of market functioning. Kiff, Elliott, Kazarian, Scarlata and Spackman (2009) and Stulz (2010) contribute to the debate over the role of OTC credit derivatives in the crisis.

Brunnermeier (2009), Brunnermeier and Pedersen (2009), and Shleifer and Vishny (2011) discuss self-reinforcing mechanisms in crises. Kaufman (2000*a*) discusses the concept of contagion. Aharony and Swary (1983) is an empirical study of U.S. bank failures and finds no evidence of pure contagion in the data. Krishnamurthy (2010) chronicles the effect of self-propogating mechanisms based on risk and liquidity during the subprime crisis. Danielsson, Shin, and Zigrand (2004) and Chapter II of International Monetary Fund (2007) discuss risk triggers. See Goodhart (2004), Laux and Leuz (2010), Brunnermeier, Crockett, Goodhart, Persaud and Shin (2009), and Chapter III of International Monetary Fund (2008b) on accounting triggers.

Bennett, Keane, and Mosser (1999) describe the phenomenon of mortgage coupon concentration and its potential impact on interest-rate dynamics. Perli and Sack (2003) and Krause (2003) discuss mortgage hedging with Treasuries and its impact on the 2003 Treasury market volatility episode. Kambhu (1998) and Kambhu and Mosser (2001) estimate the effects of interest-rate option hedging on interest-rate volatility. Malz (1995) describes an episode in which exotic option dynamics had a pronounced impact on the spot foreign exchange market.

See Jones (1953) on the Diocletian inflation, and Mueller (1997) and Hunt (1994) on the fourteenth-century financial crisis. Schnabel and Shin (2004) describe an early example of the fire-sale mechanism in crises. Bresciani-Turroni (1937) describes a paradigmatic inflation crisis and the "flight to real values." Solomon (1982) chronicles the decline of the Bretton Woods system. Kaminsky and Schmukler (1999) analyzes the behavior of market prices during the Asian crisis of 1997–1999. Schwert (1990a) notes the increase in equity market volatility during recessions and following extreme negative returns. Longin and Solnik (1995) study correlation behavior in equity markets. Engle (2009) discusses the reasons different asset-return correlations vary in different ways over time.

Kaminsky and Reinhart (1999) and Kaminsky, Reinhart, and Vegh (2003) analyze the causes and interaction of currency and other international financial crises. Garber and Svensson (1995) is a survey of models of speculative attacks on pegged exchange rates. *Brookings Papers on Economic Activity* has published a number of papers offering rich institutional and historical detail on the financial crises of the past three decades within a theoretical framework. For example, Kharas, Pinto, and Ulatov (2001) studies the Russian crisis of 1998; Radelet and Sachs (1998) the East Asian crisis of 1997; and Dornbusch, Goldfajn, Valdés, Edwards, and Bruno (1995) a number of currency crises of the 1980s and 1990s.

A number of other articles and essays cover recent crisis episodes. Desai (2000) summarizes the background of the Russian crisis and provides a critical analysis of the Russian government's response. Committee on the Global Financial System (1999a) is a detailed summary of the 1998 Asian crisis. The LTCM crisis is described in President's Working Group on

Financial Markets (1999). See also the references provided in Chapter 1 for some of the specific episodes listed in Table 1.1.

Calomiris (2004) is a survey on financial fragility and the background of crises. Bernanke (1983) presents evidence for the key role, alongside monetary and other nonfinancial macroeconomic factors, played by loss of access to credit in deepening the Great Depression. As runs and closures caused the banking industry to shrink, nonfinancial firms were thrown back on internally-generated sources of capital. Bernanke and Gertler (1995) discusses the credit channel of monetary policy transmission in modern economies.

The role of collateral markets in the contemporary financial system and in the subprime crisis is explored in Gorton (2009). Data on the contraction of liquidity brought about by the collapse of collateral markets are provided in Gorton (2009) and Gorton and Metrick (2010). Gorton and Metrick (2010) also provides information on available repo data. See also Adrian and Shin (2009*b*).

Still-germane nineteenth-century discussions of interest rates and financial crises are summarized in O'Brien (2007), including the Banking and Currency School controversy. Haberler (1958) covers the early twentieth-century debates that culminated in the Keynesian revolution. Wicksell's approach was originally presented in Wicksell (1907) and Wicksell (1967). These works make fascinating reading in light of the liquidity and credit expansion leading up to the subprime crisis, and also serve as a useful reminder of how old issues in economics resurface again and again in new forms.

On postwar macroeconomic policy generally, consult the references provided at the end of Chapter 1. The original presentation of the Taylor rule is Taylor (1993). Taylor (2007) and Kahn (2010) present the case that interest rates were set below Taylor-rule levels prior to the subprime crisis, and relate leverage and the housing bubble to low rates. Greenspan (2004) and Mishkin (2008) describe the risk management approach in monetary policy. McConnell and Perez-Quiros (2000) present a sectoral analysis of the decline in output volatility in the 1980s. Dooley and Garber (2005), Caballero (2006) and Obstfeld and Rogoff (2010) present three views of the global savings glut hypothesis; the first as a stable, the latter two as an unstable equilibrium. Caballero, Farhi, and Gourinchas (2008), Greenspan (2010), and Bernanke (2011) argue that global payments imbalances and the savings glut were an important cause of the crisis.

Borio, Kennedy, and Prowse (1994) is an important early study of the impact of monetary policy on asset prices and an early document in the literature on the risk-taking channel. Borio and Zhu (2008) and Adrian and Shin (2011) are comprehensive treatments of the risk-taking channel, and Dell'Ariccia, Laeven and Marquez (2010) present a theoretical model of the interaction of leverage, the level of rates, and monitoring in its workings. Gambacorta (2009) is a survey with ample references on this literature. Examinations of the potential for and sources of greater procyclicality in the innovated financial system include Allen and Saunders (2004), Borio and White (2003), and White (2006, 2007, 2010). The relationship between leverage and interest rates is discussed in Adrian and Shin (2009a). Search or reaching for yield is discussed in Rajan (2005) and Hellwig (2009).

Bordo, Eichengreen, Klingebiel, and Martinez-Peria (2001) present evidence that international crises have been more frequent in recent decades. Minsky (1992) is a succinct presentation of Minsky's views. Other presentations include, in the context of the postwar American financial system, Minsky (1986), and, in the context of the boom of the 1920s and subsequent Depression, Minsky (1984).

The basic model of bubbles presented in this chapter is adapted from the Blanchard (1979) and Blanchard and Watson (1982) "generic" version. Camerer (1989) and Brunnermeier (2008) provide surveys of bubble models. Garber (1989, 1990) offer a skeptical analysis, revisiting some classic bubbles and offering evidence that they were considerably less detached from reality than is commonly assumed. In addition to the bubble models based on credit and liquidity discussed in the text, see Allen and Gale (2000) and Geanakoplos (2009).

Friedman and Kuttner (1993) and Estrella and Mishkin (1998) are examples of relatively successful asset-price predictors of business cycle turning points. Kaminsky, Lizondo, and Reinhart (1998) is a survey of macroeconomic warning signals of currency crises. Berg and Patillo (1999) is a statistical study of models intended to help predict crises. Bustelo (2000) takes a skeptical view of the potential of macroeconomic indicators to predict emerging markets crises.

Söderlind and Svensson (1997) provide a survey of market-based warning signals. Coudert and Gex (2008) and Kumar and Persaud (2002) study indicators of risk aversion and their predictive power for financial crises. Chen, Hong, and Stein (2001) and Finger (2008) study crash warning signals in U.S. equity markets. Malz (2001a) provides statistical evidence for the predictive power of implied volatility for extreme asset returns.

Some references to studies of the ability of implied volatility to forecast future realized volatility are provided at the end of Chapter 10. Fleming (1998) summarizes the modeling issues involved. Canina and Figlewski (1993) are more skeptical than most of the literature on second-moment efficiency. Studies of how the risk of financial crises and extreme events might be anticipated by risk-neutral distributions based on option prices include Bates (1991, 1996, 2000), Melick and Thomas (1997), and Malz (1996).

CHAPTER 15

Financial Regulation

L ike most industries, financial services operate in a legal and regulatory framework that privileges some activities and constrains others. The regulatory framework has an enormous impact on financial firms' risk management and on overall financial stability.

As we saw in Chapter 1, the financial services industry has been regulated in recent decades in a less overtly intrusive way than a half-century ago. Certain interest rates were subject to ceilings, fees and commissions for intermediating many financial transactions were set by law or by semipublic authorities, and different types of financial firms were limited in the range of activities permitted to them. In recent decades, and up until the subprime crisis, the trend was away from specific controls and prohibitions. The major regulatory initiatives, rather, focused on setting risk capital standards for banks and other intermediaries.

Public discussion of the subprime crisis has been channeled largely through the topic of financial regulation. Many observers have identified inadequate or faulty regulation as the major cause or enabling factor of the crisis. As a result, the regulatory landscape is in a state of greater flux than at any time in living memory. In the United States, a major legislative bill, the Dodd-Frank Wall Street Reform and Consumer Protection Act (H.R.4173, "Dodd-Frank") was passed in July 2010.

Dodd-Frank left the institutional framework of U.S. regulation largely intact, but ordained major changes in its scope, from consumer protection, to financial stability and *systemic risk*, to the way specific types of financial services are authorized and supervised. But rule making based on Dodd-Frank—and the many technical studies intended to inform rule-making—which will to a large extent determine its impact, will take a number of years to complete: By one estimate, Dodd-Frank mandates 387 new rules. Similar, if less sweeping, legislation and regulatory changes are being carried out in other developed economies. Revisions to capital and liquidity standards by both national and international regulators are slowly taking shape.

Any detailed description of the specifics of regulation of different types of firms in different countries would be a long text, and likely obsolete by the time of publication. We focus in this chapter, rather, on the major issues for firm risk and public policy raised by financial regulation.

15.1 SCOPE AND STRUCTURE OF REGULATION

We begin in this section by summarizing the goals claimed for regulation, and sketch its contemporary institutional framework, in other words, the why and the who of regulation.

15.1.1 The Rationale of Regulation

In Chapter 6, we reviewed the effects, such as moral hazard and risk-shifting, of information and transactions costs on market participants' incentives and on the design and enforcement of credit contracts. These phenomena are also an important but complex part of the rationale for regulation, since regulation can ameliorate as well as amplify these problems. Moreover, the relationship between regulators and the intermediaries they oversee is in some respects similar to that between creditors and borrowers. For example, later in this chapter we discuss deposit insurance, the lender of last resort function, and other ways in which the government or central bank may lend to intermediaries or guarantee certain of their liabilities, either as a matter of course or under certain circumstances.

As we see in this chapter, the intended consequences of regulation are often different from the actual consequences, and the ostensible motivation of regulation often differs from the authentic motivation. With this caveat in mind, broadly speaking, there are three types of rationale or goal for most regulatory measures.

Consumer Protection Individuals consume financial services directly as borrowers and investors. By far the largest part of borrowing by U.S. households is in the form of first- and second-lien mortgages and home equity loans secured by their primary residences, totaling, according to Federal Reserve data, $10.1 trillion at the end of 2010. Other important forms of household borrowing are credit-card debt, auto loans, and student loans; U.S. households' nonmortgage debt totaled $2.4 trillion at end-2010. Households also contract directly with financial intermediaries as retail investors in securities and investment funds, and as clients of financial advisors.

As investors, individuals and households own a large fraction of deposits and money market mutual fund (MMMF) shares; retail accounts owned about one-third of the $2.8 trillion in MMMF assets in early 2011. *Deposit insurance* was created in most countries in large part to protect depositors from loss, as well as to protect the stability of the banking system.

Much regulation is concerned with protecting consumers of financial services. Financial intermediaries are viewed by many as having better information and more market power than individuals, and frequently perpetrating fraud. In addition to these arguments from asymmetric information and market power, behavioral finance has identified certain psychological predispositions that interfere with rational maximizing choice, to the detriment of consumers. Regulation is intended to level the playing field and protect consumers from exploitation rooted in asymmetric information or fraud, or because of their difficulty framing decisions rationally.

Since the onset of the subprime crisis, the prevalence of fraud and deceptive practices by mortgage originators has been debated. A certain type of residential mortgage, the *option adjustable rate mortgage* (ARM), illustrates both the fraud and behavioral-finance consumer-protection rationales for regulation. An option ARM has a below-market initial interest rate that resets to a market-level interest rate after a contractually specified period. The initial interest payments can be so low that there is *negative amortization*; that is, the loan balance increases during the low-rate period. Such mortgages are said to be inappropriate for most households, since they may be unable to stay current on their payments after the initial period if the market-adjusted rate is higher and brings with it a payment shock that the household cannot easily withstand. Option ARMs are, however, well-suited to investors seeking gains from house price appreciation, since they can be refinanced prior to reset.

Regulation might prohibit lenders from offering option ARMs, restrict the terms of such contracts, or require them to provide certain disclosures and explanations. On June 29, 2007, U.S. bank regulators provided guidance on mortgage-lending practices that discouraged banks from offering option ARMs.

A related thread is the protection of retail investors in their interaction with financial advisors, who provide planning services and may recommend investments, and with brokers, who conduct securities transactions with customers. The concern is to protect investors from fraud and conflicts of interest. A key focus of regulatory policy in this area is the standard of care imposed upon financial service providers to retail investors. Dodd-Frank orders the Securities and Exchange Commission (SEC) to study the question of whether brokers, currently subject to a "suitability" or appropriateness standard, should be held to the more stringent *fiduciary responsibility* standard governing advisors. Doing so would oblige brokers to "act solely in the client's interest." The issue is important, apart from the putative beneficiaries, to an array of industry and consumer interest groups, and state and federal regulatory bodies, and remains open. Although insurance agents carry out similar functions, they have not figured in these discussions.

Financial Stability   Another chief concern of financial regulation is financial stability. Much of Chapters 12 and 14 have been devoted to a discussion of the fragility of financial intermediaries. The risk of a financial crisis is important to firms' risk management directly, hence the focus on stress testing by risk managers and regulators. It is now all the more important because averting crises is the overt rationale of many major provisions of Dodd-Frank. Much of the concern with stability focuses on the fragility of financial intermediaries discussed in Chapter 12 and the negative externalities in financial services identified in Chapter 14. Distress of one financial institution can have destabilizing effects on others. At the extreme of these phenomena is systemic risk, the risk of financial crises. In this rationale for regulation, fragility and interconnectedness of financial firms requires the public sector to monitor and restrict their activities, and to provide some form of backstop or support in the event of distress.

The stability rationale intersects with other rationales for regulation, such as consumer protection. For example, the option ARM mortgages we described just above had a potentially destabilizing effect on the financial system: A rise in interest rates might trigger a large increase in the number of households delinquent on their mortgage payments, potentially leading to large losses for lenders and residential mortgage-backed securities (RMBS), as well as to direct negative effects on the economy. In the event, low interest rates during the subprime crisis limited the number of resets.

The stability function has two aspects, which in some countries at some times have been entrusted to separate regulatory bodies. The first, and more traditional, aspect of stability regulation is *safety and soundness* or *prudential supervision*, the responsibility for authorizing and supervising specific financial institutions. The second, newer, aspect is overall monitoring and preservation of financial stability and systemic risk, occasionally described as *macroprudential supervision*. Dodd-Frank ordained the creation of a *Financial Stability Oversight Council* (FSOC), drawn from regulatory authorities and the Federal Reserve, to identify crisis risks and guide systemic risk policy. These two aspects are closely related: Systemic risk is related to the extent and interaction of risk taking by individual market participants, while the perils to any specific firm can only be correctly identified in the context of the externalities generated by the behavior of other intermediaries. A major challenge in financial stability policies, however, is the lack to date of a clear definition of systemic risk, with different approaches emphasizing the possibility of large shocks, the web of credit relationships, or contagion.

Efficiency and Growth Financial services present substantial economies of scale and scope. In consequence, intermediaries themselves, payment and clearing systems, and securities and derivatives exchanges are often large firms or organizations. This raises issues of the microeconomic efficiency of the financial system similar to those raised by public utilities such as the antitrust and competitive implications of natural monopolies or oligopolies. Competitive issues also arise with regard to international capital standards, and were in fact the main initial impetus, in the 1970s, to their formulation. They remain a source of contention today.

Economic growth is not a primary motivation for regulation, but is often a background consideration, and sometimes a constraint. Regulation is often at odds with economic efficiency, or framed as being so. An example from the ongoing debates on financial reform also arises in the context of regulatory capital standards. The banking industry, and at least some public officials and economists, have put forward the view that higher capital requirements raise the cost of capital to banks, and that this higher cost finds its way into loan rates and constrains "credit availability." We return to this highly charged debate later in this chapter.

15.1.2 Regulatory Authorities

The organization of regulatory authority has important consequences for the financial system. In the United States, the regulatory framework is highly fragmented along functional, industry, and regional dimensions. Major changes in the distribution of responsibility are taking place in the wake of the subprime crisis, though not in the direction of simplicity of regulatory structure.

International and National Authorities In a world of highly integrated capital markets, shocks to domestic financial stability can arise in other jurisdictions. Therefore, while only the national and provincial authorities of a country can impose regulations with legal teeth, in key areas, such as capital, risk management, and accounting standards, they do so under heavy guidance from international organizations. Increasing efforts have been made since the late 1970s to coordinate or "harmonize" financial regulation internationally, particularly capital requirements, because the competitive implications are so immediate. But a number of other important cross-border issues became prominent during the subprime crisis. Two examples are:

- Financial intermediaries domiciled in a foreign country can have local subsidiaries or branches, and dense interconnectedness with domestic financial institutions. Domestic financial authorities may then feel obliged to provide various forms of support for the foreign intermediary, even though some part of the benefit goes to its foreign owners, counterparties, and lenders. These benefits are both direct and akin to subsidies, and indirect, via enhanced financial stability.

■ Domestic governments are ultimately responsible for the obligations of deposit insurance schemes to depositors at banks in their jurisdictions, but many of the depositors may be foreign nationals. We look at one extreme episode of this kind, the Icelandic banking crisis, later in this chapter.

Several international organizations have an important, if not legally binding, role in formulating regulatory policy in developed countries. Examples include:

Bank for International Settlements. The BIS, founded in 1930, and located in Basel, is the most important. It carries out banking functions for central banks and provides support for the Basel Committee on Banking Supervision, which has over the past 35 years developed the framework for bank regulation, and particularly regulatory capital standards, adopted by developed countries. The BIS hosts the Financial Stability Board (FSB), an assembly of central bank and finance ministries focusing on a range of institutional and supervisory issues. The Senior Supervisors Group (2009b), cited in Chapters 12 and 14, is organized by the FSB.

International Organization of Securities Commissions (IOSCO) plays a similar role to the BIS for securities regulators. It issues recommendations and standards for the supervision of securities markets and firms.

European Banking Authority (EBA) coordinates activities among European bank regulators. It was established in 2010 as the successor to the Committee of European Banking Supervisors (CEBS) to harmonize banking regulation within the European Union (EU). It has, among other activities, coordinated the EU supervisory stress tests carried out in 2010 and 2011.

Type of Responsibility   In some countries, prudential supervision of banks is carried out by the central bank, while in others, it is entrusted to a separate regulatory body. The reasons for the institutional arrangements in specific countries are largely historical. In the United States, prudential supervision is carried out by both the Federal Reserve and a range of federal and state regulators, depending on the type of intermediary. In the United Kingdom, responsibility for bank supervision was separated from the central bank and placed with a newly created body, the Financial Services Authority (FSA), in 1997. Under current legislation, bank supervision, but not consumer protection responsibilities, will return to the Bank of England in 2012.

An argument advanced for separating prudential supervision from both monetary policy and overall systemic risk monitoring is the potential for conflicts of interest. Central banks, it is said, are overly inclined to provide liquidity or capital support, or to exercise *regulatory forbearance* with respect to large but weak institutions. An important argument in favor of combining these functions in the central bank is that timely and complete supervisory information is required to effectively carry out both the central bank's overall systemic risk monitoring and monetary policy.

Consumer protection has in most industrial countries been part of the overall responsibilities of the bank and securities regulators. In the wake of the subprime crisis, the trend is to separate these functions. In the United States, Dodd-Frank places it, as well as oversight of retail financial products, with a newly created Consumer Financial Protection Bureau (CFPB), though supervision of investment services to retail customers remains in large part with the SEC. A similar separation of responsibility is to take place in the United Kingdom alongside the return of bank supervision responsibility to the central bank.

Type of Firm Supervised Banks, broker-dealers, investment companies, insurance companies, securities exchanges, financial advisors, mortgage lenders, credit card companies, and other consumer lenders have different regulatory authorities in most countries, and most firms have several regulators.

For historical reasons, the U.S. regulatory system distinguishes more deeply between banks and other financial institutions than other national systems do. But a number of other countries have a distinct regulatory authority for broker-dealers similar to the SEC in the United States, and insurance is generally regulated separately. Contrary to expectations, Dodd-Frank did not appreciably simplify the U.S. regulatory structure. Even just in one country, the United States, and for one type of firm, banks, there are several important distinctions that determine which of many regulators have responsibility for a particular firm:

Charter or form of authorization. There has rarely been free entry into the banking industry. Banks must have a charter, an archaic word for license, that permits them to conduct banking business, in particular taking deposits from the general public. *State banks* are chartered by a state banking authority. *National banks* are chartered by the Office of the Comptroller of the Currency (OCC), an agency of the U.S. Treasury.

Form of organization. Banks can be standalone institutions, but large and midsize banks are likely to be subsidiaries of *bank holding companies* (BHCs), which can own one or several banks. Since 1999, under the Gramm-Leach-Bliley Act, financial firms have been able to organize themselves into *financial holding companies* (FHC), which can own brokerage and insurance subsidiaries. Most very large U.S.-domiciled banks are subsidiaries of FHCs.

Federal Reserve membership. Member banks of the Federal Reserve system are required to hold a certain level of reserves in the form of deposits with a Fed district bank. Until the subprime crisis, these reserves did not earn interest. In return, member banks are able to borrow from the Federal Reserve. National banks are all members. State banks become members if they choose and are eligible to do so.

Primary regulator. The OCC is the main regulator of the national banks. State banks are regulated by the state banking authority under which they are chartered. The Federal Reserve is the main regulator for all bank and financial holding companies. Most banks are regulated by several entities. U.S. subsidiaries of foreign banks may, in addition, be regulated by their home-country bank regulator, and vice versa.

Securities markets and securities firms. Apart from the SEC, securities markets have a system of self-regulation through certain quasi-public bodies, most important of which is the National Association of Securities Dealers (NASD).

Some regulation governs firms, regulated by opening their activities and records to inspection, restricting their activities, or obliging them to take certain actions as a condition of doing business. But much regulation governs securities or markets and the process of issuing or trading them. Such regulation is also concerned with market functioning, the ability of markets to clear through smooth price adjustment and without disruption. An important example of regulations on issuance are disclosure requirements for securities to be offered to the general public, discussed in Chapter 1. An example of regulation of trading is the so-called *uptick rule*, which permits short sales of an equity only after an increase in its price has been observed.

The historical accident of dispersion of regulatory authority among different supervisors is frequently criticized. Many critics call for *functional supervision*, which would see a single regulator responsible for supervision of a given set of activities. For example, securities activities would be supervised by the same public body, regardless of whether carried out by banks, broker-dealer, or insurance company. Under Dodd-Frank, the Federal Reserve is charged with regulating so-called Systemically Important Financial

Institutions (SIFIs), regardless of whether they are banks, introducing an additional element of functional regulation into the U.S. framework.

In the United States, some regulatory bodies, such as the Commodities Futures Trading Commission (CFTC), are primarily concerned with the regulation of trading, rather than specific firms. The Securities Exchange Commission (SEC) regulates certain types of firms, for example, broker-dealers and investment companies, but also securities issuance, dealing, and markets. Some supervision is carried out by private-sector firms and organizations, called self-regulatory organization (SROs). Examples include securities exchanges and the supervision of smaller brokers and advisors. The Federal Reserve is responsible mainly for regulating banks, but also for regulating markets, such as those for government securities, which are crucial to the safety and soundness of banks, to monetary and foreign exchange operations, or to its banking services for the U.S. government. In its market and bank regulatory capacity, the Federal Reserve has become involved in issues such as bank liquidity and capital standards, the oversight of CDS markets, and tri-party repo.

15.2 METHODS OF REGULATION

There are several regulatory approaches to mitigating risks to financial institutions. We will discuss these techniques in two parts. In this section, we summarize regulation in normal times, while in the next, we review policies to promote financial stability, and to avert or combat crises when they occur. The first, a more well-established toolkit sometimes referred to as *safety and soundness regulation*, focuses on individual financial firms. The techniques are also sometimes termed *microprudential supervision*, to distinguish it from macroprudential supervision, which focuses on the stability of the financial system as a whole. The second set encompasses tools that are deployed far less frequently, and are the subject of intense debate in the wake of the subprime crisis.

The two sets of tools have the same policy goals outlined earlier, the preservation or restoration of financial stability and market functioning, and they are closely related. Microprudential policy can have a large impact on the likelihood of crises and how they unfold, for example, by keeping supervisors informed about financial firms' vulnerabilities, by inhibiting panic. Public policy actions in crises can influence the behavior of intermediaries in normal times, for example through its impact on policy credibility, or by increasing moral hazard. There is, finally, a close relationship between the conduct of regulatory and monetary policies.

15.2.1 Deposit Insurance

Public deposit insurance is a guarantee by the government that bank deposits, up to some maximum amount, can be redeemed at par. Federal deposit insurance was introduced in the United States in 1933 and is administered by the Federal Deposit Insurance Corporation (FDIC). The key rationales for deposit insurance are, first, to prevent bank runs, and second, to provide a safe investment vehicle to small savers, who are presumed unable to identify prudently-run banks and may be enticed by high interest rates. In its first, financial stability motivation, deposit insurance operates by eliminating the "first-come first-served" incentive; if depositors do not have reason to fear that they will lose part or all of their deposits by delaying redemption, the panic will likely not begin at all.

Deposit insurance, however, also has certain drawbacks:

- Deposits and short-term debt generally can strengthen the monitoring and discipline over borrowers exercised by banks. Deposit insurance reduces due diligence by depositors. If depositors will be made whole by the public insurance fund, they have less incentive to monitor.
- Deposit insurance increases moral hazard by, in essence, writing a put option on the bank's investments. As a result, bankers have an incentive to increase the riskiness of investments, since the losses are borne in part by the public.

  The utility of bank deposits is increased by the insurance, reducing the interest rate that must be offered in order to attract a given volume of deposits. The lower interest rate required on insured deposits increases the net interest margin banks can earn on investments made with insured deposits, increasing the value of the deposit insurance put.

Deposit insurance thus presents a policy tradeoff. If banks' ability to attract insured deposits is not restricted, they may take in a large volume of insured deposits, generating the potential for crises if losses are realized that exhaust banks' capital. The U.S. savings and loan crisis of the mid-1980s is a case in point. The roots of the S&L crisis dated back to the 1960s and 1970s, when changes in interest rates and deposit interest-rate ceilings generated both losses and a decline in business volume. In the early 1980s, deposit rate ceilings (as described in Chapter 1), were lifted, deposit insurance limits were increased, attracting wholesale deposits to S&Ls, and regulatory restrictions on permissible investments were loosened. These changes, together with a thinned-out capital base, created a near-the-money call option-like payoff profile for S&L owners, well-characterized by the Merton model described in Chapter 6. S&Ls were thus provided with incentives to engage in riskier investments, with the owners positioned to reap the gains and the deposit insurance fund bearing much of the risk of loss.

Another example of the pitfalls of deposit insurance is the collapse of the Icelandic banking system in October 2008 as the subprime crisis grew in severity. Landsbanki, an Icelandic bank, operated an Internet banking subsidiary called Icesave, which gathered insured deposits domestically and in other European countries by offering above-market interest rates. The deposit rates it offered were still lower than the rates it would have had to pay in the capital markets. Since not only Landesbanki, but most other Icelandic banks failed simultaneously, the deposit insurance fund was inadequate to meet its obligations to depositors. It remains in dispute whether the Icelandic government alone or also the governments of the depositors' home countries will be obliged to make up any eventual shortfall. This episode illustrates both the incentives to risk taking generated by deposit insurance and the difficulties of international coordination of financial regulation.

To mitigate these risks, deposit insurance can be limited in several ways:

- The amount of deposits insured can be capped by bank account, by household, or by depository institution. U.S. deposit insurance is limited by account, following an increase mandated by Dodd-Frank, to $250,000. Households can, however, own an unlimited amount of insured deposits by holding multiple accounts at different depository institutions. There is, moreover, a tendency for depositors in failed banks to be repaid above the statutory limit, so it is possible that the limits are not perceived as economically meaningful. For example, the increased Dodd-Frank limit was made retroactive so as to apply to depositors of IndyMac and other banks that had failed earlier in the subprime crisis.
- Fees can be assessed on deposit insurance. FDIC-insured banks are assessed a fee related to the volume of insured deposits and to the size of a reserve, out of which insured depositors in failed banks are made whole. A disadvantage of this approach is that fee assessments rise during crises, when the deposit insurance fund is depleted, but banks are weaker and ill-positioned for a fee increase. While fees themselves may reduce incentives to risk-shifting, collecting these fees in an insurance reserve fund may increase them.
- The deposit insurance fee can be related to the risk of the depository institution. The U.S. deposit insurance scheme charges differential fees to participating banks depending on their supervisory risk ratings (see below). Leverage and capital have been among the key criteria used to determine how risky a bank is and therefore how high a fee it will be charged for deposit insurance. Recently, as mandated by the Dodd-Frank Act, the fee has been related more directly to risk by making it a

function of banks' total assets less common equity, rather than of just one form of debt, deposits.

A fee related only to the banks' own risks, however, does not address the externalities in banks' risk-taking that we identified in Chapters 12 and 14. Deposit insurance fees that exceed expected losses have therefore been proposed. Economically, such charges are tantamount to systemic risk charges, to be discussed below.

- It has been argued that in the presence of deposit insurance, some bank activities must be restricted or prohibited outright, particularly *proprietary trading*, or trading by intermediaries with their own capital and for their own account. Such rules can be difficult to implement, since proprietary trades can be difficult to distinguish from market making and from trades on behalf of customers, and because banks routinely hold investment positions as part of their liquidity risk management. Dodd-Frank places new limits on banks' proprietary trading and on their involvement with hedge funds as a share of a bank's capital. These provisions, under the rubric "Volcker Rule," like many other parts of the law, are as yet unspecified and are to be implemented via rule-making. A simple alternative that has been proposed in the past is to require depository institutions to match insured deposits with a dedicated asset position consisting of an equal amount of risk-free bonds.

If, on the other hand, deposit insurance is restricted by these and other methods, disintermediation may reduce the size of the bank sector and accelerate non-bank intermediation, particularly if non-bank intermediaries such as money-market mutual funds (MMMFs) are viewed as enjoying implicit guarantees. Policy makers have generally been uncomfortable with a potential further shift in the center of gravity of intermediation away from banks on financial stability grounds.

15.2.2 Capital Standards

Like deposit insurance, regulatory capital standards are an element of both microprudential and macroprudential supervision. The rationale for regulatory capital standards is that market discipline is inadequate to prevent individual banks and the banking system from taking excessive risk and leverage. The fragility of banking and "information intensiveness," the opaqueness of the quality of a bank's loans and of its skill in monitoring loans and collecting payments, in this view, require regulatory standards for the amount and composition of bank capital. This need is particularly urgent in the presence of deposit insurance and other mechanisms to inhibit bank runs that generate moral hazard, leading to riskier assets and higher leverage. Capital standards are therefore closely related to other elements, and pitfalls, of the regulatory regime.

Capital adequacy of financial intermediaries has come into the forefront of regulatory policy since the formation in 1974 of the Basel Committee on Banking Supervision. Its initial focus was on the international harmonization of capital standards, and grew out of concern that, as the cross-border activities of larger banks grew, national supervisors would come under pressure to impose weak capital standards on—and thus provide a competitive advantage to—their own banks. Thus the effort that eventually culminated in the Basel Capital Accord (1988) has had both an efficiency and a prudential regulation aspect. Basel's focus has been on guaranteeing adequacy of the equity and equity-like capital of banks. The international competitive issues that drove the Basel process at its initiation remain important, as countries whose banks are relatively well-capitalized tend to seek higher capital standards, and countries whose banks are dependent on particular forms of financing seek to have them recognized as regulatory capital.

The original Basel Accord has been amended frequently. The Basel Committee's practice has been to carry out its work in the public eye, publishing consultative and technical papers and absorbing comment on potential capital regulations well in advance of any major changes. A major overhaul called Basel II was announced in 2004, though most of its elements were presented in detail as they were developed over the preceding years. Partly in response to the subprime crisis, another major revision, Basel III, is well advanced, and will substantially increase regulatory capital requirements. A regulatory "leverage ratio," a simple measure based on the size of a bank's balance sheet, putting a floor under regulatory capital ratios, is also under discussion. Finally, regulatory liquidity ratios, which would go beyond capital standards, are contemplated.[1]

The Basel Committee sets standards, but national legislation and regulation put them into legal effect. The Basel I capital standards have been adopted by the U.S. banking authorities and are enshrined in the appendices to Title 12, ¶3 and ¶225 of the Code of Federal Regulations. In jurisdictions within the European Union, all banks have been following Basel II since the beginning of 2008. In the United States, rule-making and other efforts to move to Basel II are underway. Dodd-Frank also contains provisions calling for higher minimum capital ratios, and affecting the use of securities other than common equity as capital.

---

[1] The current proposal was announced in September 2010. The press release outlining it is available at http://www.bis.org/press/p100912.pdf. References to the detailed proposals are at the end of this chapter.

The current Basel Committee framework requires three elements, referred to as "pillars":

1. Minimum capital requirements
2. Supervision of banks
3. Disclosure, leading to stronger market discipline

The most important of these from the risk management standpoint are regulatory capital requirements, which encompass

Definition of capital. The notion of capital underpinning regulatory capital standards, as a buffer against insolvency, is similar to the risk capital concept of Chapter 13. While capital can take a plethora of forms, including common equity, accounting reserves, and other, more debt-like liabilities, common equity is recognized as the most effective loss buffer, but is also the highest-cost type of capital within a given capital structure. Supervisors only want to recognize lower-cost debt as regulatory capital if it is hard to withdraw and is likely to actually take a loss before more senior debt, so Basel III and emerging national standards will restrict the role of certain forms of debt in the regulatory capital mix.

Minimum capital requirements had been set by Basel II at 8 percent of assets (corresponding to leverage of 12.5) in most cases. In the late 1980s, this represented a large increase for most banks in G-10 countries. This level is now seen as inadequate by most observers and will be substantially increased under the new Basel III standard. Some national standards may increase capital ratios further. It has been noted that at one time, bank capital ratios were far higher than the sub-10 percent levels generally seen today, so that even a drastic increase can be viewed as a return to normalcy. U.S. and U.K. banks had capital ratios on the order of 50 percent in the mid-nineteenth century. Capital ratios declined steadily, to about their current levels, up to the end of World War II. The subsequent gentle rise is a but small fluctuation against the longer-term historical decline.

Risk haircuts for assets determine the answer to the question, 8 percent of what? In the Basel approach, regulatory minimum capital is set as a fraction of *risk-weighted assets*, rather than of gross balance sheet assets. Assets with higher risk, such as lending to riskier borrowers, have higher weights, while assets with putatively low risk, such as developed-country bonds, have lower weights. The capital charge is then applied to the total. This has been among the more technically complex parts of the effort. As a simple example, if a bank has $1 billion in assets with a risk weight of 50 percent and $1 billion in assets with a risk weight of 100 percent, its total risk-weighted assets are $1.5 billion. A capital charge of 8 percent of risk-weighted assets would require it to hold a regulatory minimum of $120 million of capital.

Accurate assignment of risk weights is crucial if the capital standards are to provide meaningful constraints on risk-taking. There have been fewer changes under Basel III to the risk-weighting element of the capital standards than to the composition of capital. As we see later in this chapter, the definition of risk-weighted assets played a role in encouraging the development of SIVs and ABCP conduits that proved so damaging during the subprime crisis. Moreover, international differences in the way risk-weighted assets are computed may render international comparisons of banks' capital ratios more difficult.

The Accord permits two approaches to determining the risk haircuts for each of the three risk types, market, credit and operational risk:

- *The standard approach* applies a fixed risk-based haircut to each security type to arrive at total risk-weighted assets.
- *The internal model approach* permits a bank to compute its risk capital using its own models, such as Value-at-Risk (VaR), providing greater recognition of the portfolio context. The bank supervisor is then responsible for vetting the quality of the models. The internal models approach is very different for credit, counterparty credit, and market risk, as we will see in a moment. There are also gradations within the internal model approach, permitting reliance on internal models for fewer or more elements of the risk analysis, depending on the modeling capacity of the bank.

The Accord focuses on three major risk categories:

1. *Credit risk* is considered by regulators to be the quantitatively most important type of risk, and was first to be covered by Basel I. It includes traditional business lending, portfolios of securities, and counterparty risk.
2. *Market risk* includes risk from fluctuations in generic risk factors and "specific" or idiosyncratic risk. As we have seen in Chapter 1, at one time banks were involved primarily in business and real estate lending, and were little exposed to market risk. The emphasis on market risk has grown along with banks' trading activities, and Basel I coverage

was first introduced as a 1993 "Amendment" to the credit risk-focused original Accord of 1988.

3. *Operational risk* is concerned primarily with technology and internal processes in banks. Required capital to support operational risk was introduced as part of Basel II.

Composition of Regulatory Capital　　Capital standards have two sides, like a bank's balance sheet. The asset side of the bank's balance sheet determines how much capital a bank is required to hold. The liability side reflects what type of capital the bank holds. Banks can be undercapitalized even if they hold enough capital in aggregate, if too much of that capital is of the debt-like, "weak" types. The Basel II capital standards stipulate that, of the 8 percent minimum capital, at least 4 percent must be of stronger types such as common equity. This stronger portion of capital is called *Tier I capital*, while the weaker portion is called *Tier II capital*. Because Tier I is expected to absorb losses as long as the firm is solvent, it is also called *going-concern capital*, while Tier II is expected to buffer losses to bondholders in the event of insolvency, hence the term *gone-concern capital*. Basel III shifts the composition toward Tier I, and within Tier I, toward the stronger types of capital.

The main components of the higher-quality Tier I capital are common equity, noncumulative perpetual preferred shares, and retained earnings, all of which are directly exposed to losses in asset value, in that they are junior to all other forms of capital. Common and preferred dividends can be suspended without triggering default.

Even within Tier I, however, there are gradations, with *core capital*, which includes common equity and retained earnings, the strongest form. Much effort has gone into ascertaining whether a particular type of security has enough equity-like characteristics to merit inclusion in Tier I capital. It must share in the essential property of equity, that it absorb losses before and thus genuinely stand in front of other liability-side positions when the firm has losses. *Trust preferred securities*, which permit bank holding companies (BHCs) to issue an equity-like security, but with tax-deductible dividends, are an example of a form of Tier I capital whose loss absorbency has been called into question and whose role will therefore be reduced under Dodd-Frank (the so-called "Collins Amendment") as well as Basel III.

During the subprime crisis, both the market and supervisors began to regard the Tier I capital concept with wariness. Concerns were raised about whether certain components, such as deferred tax assets, goodwill—the value of an acquired firm in excess of its book value—and preferred shares provided a buffer against loss that creditors could rely on. Deferred tax assets, for example, can't be used unless there are profits against which they can be offset. They focused attention instead on a narrower capital concept, *tangible common equity* (TCE), equal to the value of common equity, excluding such intangible items, but including retained earnings. In early 2009, some banks sought to convert preferred into common stock in order to increase TCE with no impact on Tier I. The U.S.-conducted "stress tests," discussed in Chapter 11, also focused on TCE as a measure of capital adequacy.

These events represented both an evolution in the definition of regulatory capital and a sharper distinction by market participants between economic and regulatory capital than they had typically made in normal times. The Basel III standards are to set the minimum for Tier I capital to 6 percent of risk-weighted assets. Within Tier I, Basel III defines Common Equity Tier I, a similar concept to TCE in its exclusion of goodwill and other intangibles, and sets its regulatory minimum to 4.5 percent.

Tier II is a more heterogenous category than Tier I. Its main components are loan loss reserves, cumulative nonperpetual preferred shares, subordinated debt and *hybrid capital*, or securities possessing characteristics of both equity and debt. They are debt-like in paying dividends at a fixed rate, but equity-like in that the dividends can be deferred indefinitely.

The impact of different types of bank capital instruments on market discipline has been an important aspect of the debate about the composition of regulatory capital. The issue has grown more acute with the perception that public policy has introduced additional moral hazard into the banking system. In particular, the market discipline exercised by creditors is weakened if they view a bank as systemically important or too-big-to-fail, terms of art for institutions that are likely to receive liquidity and possibly even capital support in a financial crisis. If the banks are felt to be exposed primarily to systematic rather than idiosyncratic risk, it is then rational for creditors to lend to them at a credit spread that doesn't fully reflect the bank's expected default loss. It has been argued that requiring a bank's capital structure to include subordinated debt helps enforce market discipline on banks. More generally, the heterogeneity of Tier I and II under Basel II proved problematic during the subrime crisis. As we'll see in our discussion of the use of subordinated debt to enhance market discipline, there was some confusion and ambiguity in the market as to where supervisors would draw the line between liabilities to be protected against loss and those to be written down, and the line did not always appear to coincide with the regulatory definition of capital. Tier II was meant to cease paying dividends, absorb losses and behave like equity during a period of financial stress. In many cases, however, supervisors concerned about provoking panic among banks' bondholders treated Tier II securities more like debt and shielded them from loss. Basel III attempts to address the problem of the heterogeneity of capital, particularly across countries.

Regulatory Capital for Credit Risk The original Basel I capital standards put forward a simple approach to computing risk-weighted assets. It encompassed only a standard approach, in which five categories of risk were defined. The categories imposed haircuts between zero, for cash and developed-country sovereign debt, and 100 percent, for most unsecured commercial and real estate loans. The challenge of off-balance-sheet items was recognized even at this early stage. Undrawn but longer-term commitments such as revolving loans and guarantees had a risk weight of 50 percent.

Basel II permits banks to use internal models rather than the fixed-weight standard approach, and introduced rules covering a wider range of financial instruments, in far more detail. It uses credit rating agencies' ratings as a criterion for establishing risk weights. The framework has been left largely intact by Basel III, apart from the treatment of counterparty risk, as we will see in a moment.

The broad conceptual framework of the internal model approach for credit risk is similar to that of the single-factor model we applied to credit portfolios in Chapter 8. The overall level of risk capital is set by imposing a confidence level of 99.9 percent, equivalent, in the single-factor model, to setting the market risk factor to -3.09. It permits banks to estimate using internal models, or otherwise identify, four key parameters of credit risk for each exposure:

1. The probability of default
2. The size of the exposure at the time of default
3. Loss given default
4. The maturity of the exposure

The internal model approach also contains guidelines for taking portfolio effects, that is, default correlation, into account, by relating them to the probability of default. Higher default probabilities are associated with lower correlations, consistent with the Gaussian approach we laid out in Chapters 8, 9, and 11. The approach is subject to some of the same criticisms cited in those chapters, particularly that portfolio credit risk estimates using the model are highly sensitive to a default correlation that is very difficult to estimate.

An innovation of Basel II was to recognize credit-risk mitigants such as credit default swaps and other derivatives. This, however, introduced the necessity of accounting for counterparty risk, treated in Basel II under the rubric "double-default risk." Some banks had material losses when marking to market hedges provided by firms experiencing spread widening or downgrades. Basel III considerably tightens the standards for capitalizing counterparty risk by introducing a capital charge for mark-to-market fluctuation in the counterparty valuation adjustment (CVA), discussed in

Chapter 6. It also encourages banks to use centralized clearing—in essence, exchange-traded CDS—by excluding them from the CVA capital charge. This affects banks that hedge counterparty risk using derivatives or other securities subject to market risk, for example, a bank hedging an exposure to structured credit products by buying CDS protection on the bonds as well as CDS protection on the counterparty in the structured product CDS. If the hedge evidences "wrong-way risk," that is, a high correlation between credit losses on the structured product and the protection seller, the capital charge is increased.

Finally, Basel II contained detailed provisions for securitization and other mechanisms for removing assets from bank balance sheets while retaining an economic interest in the performance of the assets. Some effects of Basel II, such as favorable treatment for securitized credit products with investment-grade ratings, have been highlighted by the subprime crisis; Basel III has increased capital requirements for these securities.

Regulatory Capital for Market Risk   Trading risk as well as traditional lending risk need to be supported by risk capital. The Basel approach requires banks to divide exposures into two portfolios:

1. *The trading book* includes relatively liquid exposures held for a relatively short time. These exposures are covered by the Market Risk Amendment. For the most part, they generate lower capital charges, but it is expected that they will be marked-to-market.

   The trading book consists predominantly of securities, foreign exchange, listed equities, exchange-traded derivatives, and more standard OTC derivatives such as forwards and swaps. The Basel approach makes it possible to apply VaR in measuring trading book capital charges.

   This category roughly coincides with the accounting classification of securities as *trading securities* or as *available-for-sale securities*. These two classes, under U.S. accounting standards, must be marked-to-market on the financial intermediary's balance sheet.

2. *The banking book* includes exposures that are expected to be held to maturity. For the most part, banking book exposures receive higher capital charges, but it is not expected that they will be marked-to-market. Banking book exposures are generally not subject to a market risk capital charge, but under Basel III, certain exposures, particularly securitizations, cannot be subject to lower capital charges in the banking book than in the trading book. These changes are part of Basel III's effort to eradicate regulatory arbitrage between trading and banking book capital treatment, or the "trading book loophole."

   The banking book consists mainly of whole loans to individuals and businesses. As long as the loans are performing, that is, principal and interest are being paid on time, there is generally no requirement to alter their balance sheet valuation to reflect market conditions, or possible changes in their creditworthiness. The banking book, to the extent that it consists of securities rather than loans, roughly coincides with the accounting classification of securities as *held-to-maturity securities*.

Banks may be permitted to use VaR as the basis for calculating required capital for the trading book. This internal model approach is open to banks that can meet criteria related both to model accuracy and the firm's organizational ability to prudently run a model-oriented risk management process. The user-defined parameters (see Chapter 3) are set at

- Confidence level: 99 percent
- Time horizon: 10 days

Banks can choose any mode of computation for VaR, parametric, Monte Carlo, or historical simulation, but must use a minimum of one year of market data in generating simulations or estimating parameters. The data set must be updated at least quarterly.

The VaR measure used for determining regulatory capital is the higher of the average of the past 60 days' VaR estimate, or the prior day's. If the bank uses the average internally computed VaR, it is multiplied by a scalar k between 3 and 4 that depends on the backtest accuracy of the VaR model (see Chapter 11).

If the bank's internal VaR model does not capture specific risk, an additional risk capital requirement is imposed. "Specific risk" is a term Basel uses to cover idiosyncratic, event, default, and other short-term risks of large returns that are not well-captured by generic risk factors. Basel III has also added an *incremental risk capital charge* to cover such issues as tail risk, credit migration risk, and liquidity, and has increased required capital for securitization positions in the trading book.

Under Basel III, the VaR calculation is to incorporate a stress testing element by including a VaR calculation based (in general) on a historical stress period. This *stressed VaR* is to be added to the "normal" VaR and the specific risk charge to compute the minimum required capital for market risk. The overall formula is:

market risk capital$_t$

$$= \max\left[k\frac{1}{60}\sum_{t=1}^{60}\text{VaR}_{t-\tau}\left(0.99, \frac{10}{252}\right)(x_\tau), \text{VaR}_t\left(0.99, \frac{10}{252}\right)(x_t)\right]$$

$+$ stressed VaR$_t$ $+$ charge for specific risk$_t$

Procyclicality of Capital Standards   Capital requirements are meant to enhance bank stability. But they may have a perverse unintended effect if capital requirements tend to be low during expansionary periods and high during contractions and crises. The potential for capital requirements to decline and leverage to increase during booms and vice versa is called procyclicality, the same term used in current discussions to describe the propensity of the entire financial system toward boom and bust cycles. The phenomenon is similar to the potential for VaR estimates to increase with higher volatility, one of the self-reinforcing mechanisms in crises described in Chapter 14. The effects are also similar: Capital may act as an additional constraint on bank lending at times when banks are already seeking to reduce leverage and increase liquidity, because they fear higher loan losses and greater difficulty rolling over short-term funding.

The current Basel III proposal calls for a countercyclical capital charge of up to 2.5 percent, to be composed entirely of common equity. The magnitude of the charge is to be determined by the national banking authorities within each country based on their assessment of whether credit expansion is excessive and systemic risks are building up. Internationally active banks are subject to a countercyclical capital charge that is a weighted average of the charges in the jurisdictions in which they operate. In addition, Basel III calls for a *capital conservation buffer*, an additional 2.5 percent capital requirement over the minimum. When capital falls below the minimum plus the buffer, banks are not required to raise capital immediately, but are obliged to restrict dividends and retain earnings to rebuild the buffer over time.

A particular security type, *contingent capital* (or "CoCos"), has been proposed as a means of introducing greater market discipline into bank capital structures. Contingent capital is a form of subordinated debt that converts into equity or hybrid capital when a certain trigger, such as a Tier I capital ratio, is breached. The appeal of this type of security to regulators is that requiring contingent capital to be issued imposes a market test on the issuer at the time of issuance, and sustains capital ratios automatically in times of stress. It is anticyclical, since it would increase capital and decrease debt in a downturn. Contingent capital's appeal to issuers is that it might have a lower cost of capital than common equity, and would retain the tax advantages of debt. Some national authorities, for example Switzerland's, are contemplating its use as part of an aggressive countercyclical capital charge that goes beyond that of Basel III.

Difficulties arise, however, in designing a security that has clear and unambiguously defined triggers. Ex ante uncertainty about the conversion to common stock reduces the effectiveness of the security. Also, in a way not dissimilar to the effect of hedging strategies on asset prices discussed in the previous chapter, investors could sell a bank's equity short to hedge the risk of conversion if the trigger is approached. By making the trigger event likelier, hedging would generate volatility and thus act pro-, rather than anticyclically. These uncertainties could rob contingent capital of any potential funding cost advantage over common equity. Critics of the proposal also note that, while conversion would add to the buffer against loss, it does not infuse any additional cash into the firm. Later in this chapter, we will discuss another type of security, subordinated debt, that some observers have proposed making a mandatory element of banks' capital structures.

Capital Standards and Reserve Requirements Regulatory capital standards are one way in which regulation directly imposes certain ratios on banks' balance sheets. Another important set of rules are *reserve requirements*. They are similar to regulatory capital rules in that they impose limits on the asset side of the bank's balance sheet relative to certain liability-side accounts, but are more narrowly focused. Reserve requirements oblige banks to hold reserves, in the form of deposits with the central bank or other form of central bank money such as vault cash, in a minimum ratio to deposits. Reserve requirements serve two main functions:

1. They are imposed in order to control the money supply, of which the public's deposit accounts with commercial banks are the largest component, and thus play a role in monetary policy.
2. They also play a role in the regulation of risk-taking by banks. They protect insured deposits and limit banks' risk-taking activities.

The rationale for reserve requirements has evolved and their importance has diminished in most advanced countries over time. Early in the twentieth century—the Federal Reserve System was established in 1913—reserve requirements were viewed as a safeguard of bank liquidity and a means of preventing bank runs. It could be thought of as a form of asset-liability management (ALM), aligning the maturities of at least part of the bank's balance sheet with the short maturities of its deposits. In more recent decades, however, the rationale for reserve requirements has been primarily as a monetary policy tool. Even this function has become less crucial, as, up until the subprime crisis, central banks relied on control of short-term interest rates rather than control of monetary aggregates to implement monetary stance.

Capital requirements, in contrast, oblige banks to limit their risky assets, including not only loans, but also other risky investments, relative to their equity capital. At any point in time, at least one of these constraints is binding. In economic downturns and crises, it is more likely to be capital requirements that bind, as illustrated during the subprime crisis by the large excess reserves held by U.S. banks. Within limits, additional capital or liquidity reserves reduce both solvency and liquidity risk.

The debate on capital standards has become enmeshed with one over the cost, both to individual banks and to society, of higher equity capital requirements. Bankers, some academics, and public officials in countries with relatively highly leveraged banks have pointed out that equity capital must generally be raised at a higher prospective rate of return than debt. It is therefore to be expected that higher equity capital requirements will increase the cost of capital and thus the borrowing rates charged to customers. The result will be to restrict lending and inhibit overall economic growth. The counterarguments are that, while equity is more expensive funding than debt for any given capital structure, increasing equity lowers its risk and increases the buffer below debt liabilities, permitting banks to borrow at lower spreads, so the overall cost of bank capital will not rise. Proponents of higher bank equity have also pointed out that the higher cost of equity is due in substantial part to public subsidies to debt via the tax code, which in many countries permits banks to expense interest, but not dividends. The tax subsidy is a distortion that generates a negative externality by increasing leverage throughout the financial system.

15.2.3 Bank Examinations and Resolution

Apart from capital standards, regulators employ a wide range of tools to promote safety and soundness. A key example are bank examinations. In addition to bank examinations by a state or national supervisor such as the OCC or Federal Reserve, the Federal Reserve inspects bank and financial holding companies.

In the United States, the scope and standards of bank examinations have to some extent been harmonized across regulatory bodies through *CAMELS ratings*, so-called because they focus on

- Capital adequacy
- Asset quality
- Management and administrative ability
- Earnings level and quality
- Liquidity level
- Sensitivity to market risk

The ratings are disclosed only to the bank's management and play an important role in determining what, if any, action a bank will be required to take to address deficiencies. Regulators have various tools for addressing serious safety and soundness issues at regulated institutions. In milder cases, these are referred to as *prompt corrective action*, and can include payment of fines or imposition of cease-and-desist orders. At the extreme is a process called *resolution*, the seizure and orderly liquidation of an institution that has failed or is likely to fail, with the goal of closing the weak institution with minimal loss and risk of damage to others.

Resolution is a difficult issue that touches on a number of others, some of which we will return to in our discussion of the Dodd-Frank approach to systemic risk below:

- Regulators can, instead or resolution, infuse capital into a failing bank temporarily if there is a material probability the firm can work through problems and survive, or can eventually be acquired by a healthier competitor. But there is considerable evidence that this route is more costly than prompt resolution.[2] Since 1991, the FDIC is mandated to pursue "least-cost resolution," that is, resolving failed banks in a way that minimizes the cost to the taxpayer.

- There is debate on the form in which the temporary continuation of the institution takes place. This stage is sometimes called a *bridge bank*, and is contemplated under Dodd-Frank, which calls for the establishment of a process by which the Treasury and the FDIC can liquidate banks and other financial companies deemed insolvent.

- Resolution can occur in ordinary bankruptcy, or as part of a special regime used only for financial institutions. At issue is whether the conventional bankruptcy process can be used for large financial firms, or is too fraught with systemic risk to be used. Uncertainty around the possibility of safely unwinding a failed bank can generate moral hazard by making regulators hesitate to shut it down. The bankruptcy of Lehman has provided arguments in favor of both bankruptcy and resolution. Dodd-Frank maintains the distinction between the financial company resolution and the bankruptcy processes.

- An alternative approach is to require systemically important intermediaries to draw up a *living will*, that is, a plan for the rapid unwinding and resolution of the firm.

- Moral hazard issues arise if creditors and/or shareholders in the failed institution do not suffer losses. This issue is related, of course, to other "safety net" issues, and to the bankruptcy regime.

---

[2]See U.S. Congressional Budget Office (1992) and Gupta and Misra (1999).

A similar tool of safety and soundness regulation to on-site examinations is assessment of the quality of the investment portfolios of supervised intermediaries. Since the 1930s, federal and state regulators have used credit ratings as the basis of this assessment, imposing ratings standards on the portfolios of institutional investors, such as pension funds, mutual funds, MMMFs, insurance companies, banks, broker-dealers, and others. Entry into the ratings business is restricted, in the United States and other countries, to a small number of firms. From 1975 on, the SEC has recognized the ratings of a small group of firms, called Nationally Recognized Statistical Rating Organizations (NRSROs), as acceptable for assessing the quality of credit portfolios. There were only three NRSROs—the major ratings firms—until 2003, when the SEC began to recognize new entrants; as of 2011, there are 10. Dodd-Frank calls for eradicating dependence on ratings of the federal regulatory system.

15.3 PUBLIC POLICY TOWARD FINANCIAL CRISES

The increased frequency and intensity of financial crises in the past few decades, culminating in the subprime crisis, was a surprise to many policy makers, and has led to discussion of new policy approaches to promote financial stability. In Chapter 12, we discussed the fragility of fractional-reserve banking, of intermediaries carrying out liquidity and maturity transformation, and of leveraged intermediaries. Chapter 14 discussed the channels by which crises unfold and gave a number of examples of systemic risk events. Deposit insurance, capital requirements, and other mitigants of the risks arising from the fragility of banking are not foolproof, and have risk-amplifying consequences of their own, for example by increasing moral hazard or risk-shifting. There is therefore a need to take account of financial stability and systemic risk in regulatory as well as monetary and other economic policies, through specific measures as well as a general orientation. The aim of a macroprudential policy orientation is to prevent crises, panics, failures of credit markets to function, and widespread failures of financial institutions from occurring in the first place. An additional, much less frequently applied set of policies, the *lender of last resort* function, is designed to address panics and crises once they have begun.

15.3.1 Financial Stability Policies

Financial stability policies in advance of crises is an evolving discipline that is not yet well defined. A formal mandate to pursue financial stability is (or is on course to become) part of the legal charter of some central banks, such as the Bank of England and the European Central Bank, but not of others. As noted, these policies occupy a zone encompassing macroeconomic as well as regulatory policies.

Asset-Price Targeting One potential, but controversial, element of macroprudential policy is *asset-price targeting*. In most developed countries, monetary policies are intended in part or entirely to maintain price stability. The Federal Reserve has a dual mandate, under the Humphrey-Hawkins Full Employment Act of 1946, to maintain both high employment and price stability. In some countries, the central bank pursues formal *inflation targeting*, in which explicit goals are set for price stability, but not necessarily also for employment or economic growth. Typically, inflation targets are set in terms of the consumer price or some other broad index of final-goods prices. Like the Taylor Rule, discussed in Chapter 14, inflation targeting requires the central bank to tighten monetary policy if it believes inflation is above its desired range.

However, overly accommodative monetary policy or excessive credit creation may not always lead quickly to rising general price levels. Financial imbalances that undermine financial stability can arise without being signaled by higher inflation, as evidenced by the experience of the decade preceding the subprime crisis. Increases in asset prices, particularly long-lived ones that are more dependent on interest rates, may provide an earlier sign of excessive accommodation than rising general price levels. Monetary authorities, in addition to their existing responsibilities for macroeconomic and price stability, have therefore been asked to adopt asset-price targeting, a policy of tightening money to "pop bubbles" when asset prices generally or a specific set of asset prices increases "too fast."

Housing finance played a key role in the credit expansion preceding the subprime crisis. A frequently cited example of an asset-price bubble that might usefully have been thwarted by tighter monetary policy is therefore house prices in the United States during the prior decade. Figure 15.1 displays house prices for U.S. cities as a whole and for one particularly robust market, Las Vegas. The price peak in May 2006 can be considered one of the earliest clear warning signals of the subprime crisis. By that time, the overall index had nearly tripled over the previous 10 years. Prices in Las Vegas had risen even more rapidly during the last few years of the housing boom and were 65 percent higher in April 2006 than at the end of 2003. The increase in house prices coincided with a rapid increase in homeownership rates, a longstanding government objective. Homeownership rates rose from 64 to 69 percent between 1994 and 2006.

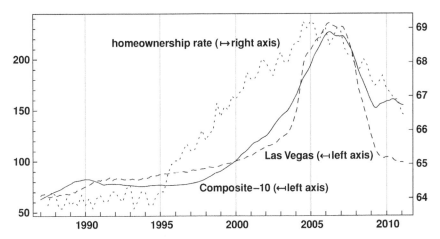

FIGURE 15.1 U.S. House Prices and Homeownership 1987–2011
The solid line plots the S&P/Case-Shiller 10-City Composite Home Price Index, a paired-sale index of house prices in 10 large U.S. Metropolitan Statistical Areas (MSAs). The dotted line plots the S&P/Case-Shiller Home Price Index for one particular MSA, Las Vegas. The dashed line (right axis) plots the U.S. Census Bureau's estimate of U.S. homeownership rates. House price data are monthly from January 1987 to February 2011; homeownership rates are quarterly from 1987 through Q1 2011.

The argument that housing prices were driven in substantial part by low interest rates, and that higher rates would have been an effective tool in addressing housing prices focuses on the incentives to leveraged housing investment. In Example 12.3 and in the discussion of the risk-taking channel of monetary policy in Chapter 14, we saw that for a given expected rate of increase in home prices, lower interest rates increase prospective returns to housing investors. Return prospects with high leverage—low down payments—are particularly attractive because of their option-like character; in most U.S. jurisdictions, the so-called non-recourse states, a homebuyer's exposure is limited to the down payment. House prices were supported by three necessary conditions: Wider availability of credit to homebuyers on increasingly generous terms, the expectation of rising home prices, and low interest rates. As long as prices continued to rise, and refinancing was available, homeowners could capture high capital gains on homes. Once prices stopped rising, returns became negative, and refinancing was no longer possible, making default more likely. There is evidence that a high proportion of terminated but nondefaulting subprime loans were refinanced rather than repaid prior to 2007.[3]

The case against asset-price targeting is that it is difficult to identify bubbles accurately in advance. After a sharp decline in asset values, a bubble may seem blindingly obvious and the skeptics in retrospect to have been prophets. But even after some historical bubbles have burst, it has not always been clear that they were unwarranted by ex ante information on fundamentals. Central banks are therefore not well situated to determine what asset-price increases are excessive.

A second argument against asset-price targeting is that monetary policy will become less accurate and effective, and on balance too tight, if central banks lean against asset-price increases. This argument is often made in the context of formal models of optimal monetary policy. In the risk-management paradigm, discussed in the previous chapter, the central bank in considering its monetary stance against a backdrop of rising asset prices should consider the potential growth and employment costs of a sufficiently tight monetary stance to curtail the asset price rise. The alternative is letting the asset price rise run its course and addressing negative consequences if and when they materialize. The latter approach is referred to as asymmetric monetary policy, and the alternatives sometimes characterized as the "lean or clean" choice. The costs of monetary tightening are high, since it may cause a recession, and likely, if tightening would not otherwise be called for. The costs of letting a putative bubble play itself out are at best speculative.

The discussion of asset-price targeting is often rather narrowly framed, as a shift of "optimal" monetary policy stance in response to a set of specific asset prices being "too high." The crucial symptoms may rather be assets, risk spreads and options that are generally "priced for perfection," and the appropriate monetary policy response, the "lean" prescription, is a bias toward tightness within the range of parameters that are consistent with rule-oriented policy.

Countercyclical Policy Orientation   The arguments against specific targets or policies around asset prices don't therefore vitiate the more general argument for a financial stability orientation of macroeconomic and regulatory policy. As with systemic risk and financial stability, there is no crisp definition of macroprudential supervision, or of countercyclical policy.

The regulatory tools discussed in the last section, such as capital standards, minimum liquidity and leverage ratios, and resolution regimes, also have a macroprudential policy purpose. Some relatively new tools, such

---

[3]See Demyanyk (2009).

as regulatory intervention in the compensation policies of financial firms, have also been proposed. Other tools, such as systemic risk charges, are extensions of risk capital requirements, an existing regulatory method. The discussion has included these elements:

Countercyclical monetary policy. Interest rate and monetary policy can be attentive to general financial conditions and wary of deviations from credit norms without adopting a formal scheme of asset-price targeting, and while retaining a primary orientation toward employment and the price level. This would provide a counterweight to formal and informal inflation targeting, which deemphasize financial and credit conditions. The macroeconomic models used by many central banks to guide monetary policy give only a limited role to financial conditions, posing a challenge to research on the tradeoffs and synergies of macroprudential and macroeconomic policies.

Indicators of financial stability. A countercyclical policy orientation, even if not necessarily targeting specific measures of asset prices, would be required to monitor them, as well as leverage, volatility, and risk premiums. As we saw in Chapters 12 and 14, measuring leverage, particularly the overall degree of leverage in the financial system, and identifying useful indicators of potential financial stress events in asset prices, are difficult topics of ongoing research, and far from solved. Leverage measures would ideally capture economic, rather than more evident balance-sheet leverage, and thus include the collateral markets, off-balance-sheet and derivatives-induced leverage as well. Leverage by sectors, such as households, different types of intermediaries, and nonfinancial corporations, can help identify excessive credit creation. Low volatility, measured by implied as well as realized volatility, and low risk premiums, may provide evidence that risk appetites are high, and that some market participants may be coming under "search for yield" pressure to achieve return targets.

A related potential risk to financial stability that is difficult to define, let alone measure, is that of "crowded trades," or trades attracting large amounts of capital from investors such as hedge funds that can use leverage and can readily change their portfolios. Concern has been raised about the potential for volatility if investors withdraw from "crowded trades" rapidly and has spurred interest in identifying and measuring them as part of financial stability monitoring.

Collecting and aggregating leverage and other data relevant to financial stability in a way that is meaningful for policy makers is challenging, and estimating risk premiums reliably is extraordinarily difficult. In the United States, the Financial Stability Oversight Council (FSOC) established by Dodd-Frank has been tasked with collecting data and carrying out research pertinent to financial stability.

Small items of data can be telling. Consider, for example, the observation that median loan-to-value ratios for subprime mortgage loans extended for the initial purchase of a home that became part of residential mortgage-based securities (RMBS) pools were 100 percent—that is, the homeowner had no equity in the home—in each of the years 2005, 2006, and 2007.[4]

A systemic risk regulator is tasked with overall responsibility for identifying risks to financial stability and coordinating responses among public sector entities. An agency focusing exclusively on the prevention of financial crises, working to that end with other parts of the sprawling regulatory apparatus, is intended to complement the traditional focus of bank supervision on the financial health of specific intermediaries, rather than on the stability of the system as a whole.

Identifying "systemically important" financial firms, or SIFIs, is a major focus of the post-subprime crisis regulatory restructuring effort. In the United States, it is a key task of the FSOC. In the United Kingdom, a Financial Policy Committee of the Bank of England will have overall responsibility for financial regulation and a specific focus on financial stability and macroprudential supervision, and will oversee the microprudential supervisor, the Prudential Regulatory Authority (see HM Treasury, 2011). A proposal has been adopted by the European Union for a European Systemic Risk Board with similar functions.

Systemic risk charges imposed on SIFIs are among the key financial stability policy tools currently under consideration. A variety of systemic risk charges have been proposed, generally designed as taxes, as part of the deposit insurance funding system, as an addition to minimum capital requirements, or as a time-varying addition to capital charges determined in part by overall financial conditions rather than that of the individual bank. Such charges might also vary by the

---

[4]See Mayer, Pence, and Sherlund (2009).

size or composition of balance sheets. The imposition of systemic risk charges is consistent with the idea that systemic risk arises from negative externalities, that is, that an intermediary taking excessive risk does not bear the full cost of its behavior. The costs can be internalized through systemic risk charges, which thereby also act as a counter to moral hazard and the too-big-to-fail problem.

Basel III incorporates a number of elements that can be considered systemic risk charges, most importantly the capital conservation buffer and countercyclical capital charge.

Macroprudential supervision is the idea, noted above, that supervision of banks and other intermediaries should take account not only of the condition of each firm in isolation, but should be carried out with regard to firms' impact on financial stability. An example is attention not only to the exposures of a particular intermediary, but also of the extent to which several intermediaries have the same type of position, which would indicate higher potential for asset price volatility, and could result in losses across firms if they attempted to exit positions simultaneously. Macroprudential supervision is closely related to the proposal for a systemic risk regulator.

As mentioned earlier in this chapter, two new tools, the leverage and liquidity ratios, have been introduced as part of the Basel III capital accord. As with capital adequacy regulation, these new rules have a microprudential function. But are also part of the macroprudential policy response to the lessons of the subprime crisis. There are two liquidity ratios:

- The *liquidity coverage ratio* requires a bank to hold unpledged liquid assets equal to a conservative estimate of the potential 30-day runoff of its short-term funding. Some controversy has been generated by the ratio, particularly by the Basel Committee's blanket acceptance of government bonds as liquid assets.
- The *net stable funding ratio* requires the bank to obtain longer-term funding for relatively illiquid assets.

The Basel III leverage ratio, finally, sets a minimum 2 percent ratio of Tier I regulatory capital to a simplified (compared to the elaborate computation of risk-weighted assets) measure of on- and off-balance sheet exposure.

While the terminology of anticyclical policy and macroprudential supervision is relatively new, the idea is not. As we saw in Chapter 14, during the Great Depression, some observers, such as Irving Fisher, were calling attention to the stability consequences of excessive credit creation. What was new in recent decades is the disparity between the rapid pace of credit creation and its minimal effect on consumer inflation rates, and the ability of market participants to put on leverage in hard-to-discern ways.

Henry Simons, a contemporary of Fisher's who more than shared his aversion for leverage, and particularly for short-term debt, went a step further, proposing policies to gradually extinguish the use of all non-equity financing of private firms, and all non-money financing of government. His prescription is one yardstick by which to measure proposals for macroprudential supervision.

> *The danger of pervasive, synchronous, cumulative maladjustments would be minimized if there were no fixed money contracts at all—if all property were held in a residual-equity or common-stock form. With such a financial structure, no one would be in a position either to create effective money-substitutes (whether for circulation or for hoarding) or to force enterprises into wholesale efforts at liquidation. Hoarding and dishoarding (changes in velocity) would, to be sure, still occur; but the dangers of cumulative maladjustment would be minimized ... [T]he economy becomes exposed to catastrophic disturbances as soon as short-term borrowing develops on a large scale. No real stability of production and employment is possible when short-term lenders are continuously in a position to demand conversion of their investments, amounting in the aggregate to a large multiple of the total available circulating media, into such media.[5]*
>
> *[A]n economy where all private property consisted in pure assets, pure money, and nothing else ... is the financial good-society.[6]*

15.3.2 Lender of Last Resort

The most important policy tool, once a crisis or systemic shock has actually occurred, is the readiness of a large financial institution to act as a *lender of last resort*. In modern times, that institution is typically the central bank, though historically large private intermediaries have also carried out this function. The beginning of most crises is a liquidity crunch, as Simons hints at in the passage just cited. Market participants rapidly change behavior, suddenly seeking to preserve and acquire the largest possible reserves of liquid assets. It is at this point, when liquidity premiums rise rapidly, and

---

[5]Simons (1936, pp. 6–9).
[6]Simons (1946, p. 30).

asset fire sales may already have begun, or are at least anticipated, that the lender of last resort is potentially most effective in containing the crisis.

Standing Lending Facilities We begin by describing facilities maintained by central banks to offer temporary funding to qualified, and not necessarily distressed, individual firms. In normal times, even an appropriately reserved and capitalized financial intermediary can face extraordinary short-term funding needs. A century ago, in an economy still substantially focused on farming, banks faced large seasonal fluctuations in deposits as a result of the agricultural cycle; rural banks typically faced cash shortages in the planting season and surpluses after crops were marketed. Today, seasonal fluctuations are much milder, and banks facing such temporary funding needs can generally borrow in the interbank markets.

Nonetheless, a number of central banks, at least for historical reasons, maintain *standing lending facilities*, geared towards both normal and stress needs of eligible borrowers. U.S. banks that are members of the Federal Reserve System can borrow, against adequate collateral, at the *discount window*. The window serves three main purposes.

1. While U.S. monetary policy is carried out mainly via *open-market operations*, as in most developed countries, the discount window provides an additional mechanism by which unexpected shortages of monetary reserves in the financial system as a whole can be addressed.
2. The discount window provides a channel in addition to the money markets by which individual banks in sound condition, but experiencing unexpected shortages of cash, can borrow. Such shortages typically arise late in a trading day and must be addressed quickly. These first two uses are called the *primary credit facility*.
3. Finally, distressed depository institutions can borrow from the discount window, for a short time and under close monitoring, either to help bridge the institution to soundness, or as part of its resolution and unwinding.

The discount window can be seen as a precursor form of the lender of last resort function, addressing temporary urgent borrowing needs that fall short of distress. With predictable, short-term agricultural seasonality now a historical episode, the discount window has a dual role as both an emergency lending facility for individual distressed institutions in normal times, and a lender of last resort facility during periods of financial distress.

Central Bank Policy During Panics During a financial crisis, or in the presence of bank runs, the function of the lender of last resort is to replace liquidity abruptly draining from the financial intermediation system. The ultimate goal is to prevent immediate and severe harm to the real economy, which is dependent on credit availability, specifically, on the structure of maturity and liquidity transformation that is in place at the moment. Since the payment and credit systems are closely intertwined, a severe disruption of credit intermediation can also impact payments systems, for example, by the collapse of an intermediary that is also an operator of or a large participant in a key component of the payment system. As noted in Chapter 12, the tri-party repo system, in which a large volume of instantly revocable credit is granted during trading hours by a small number of large banks, is perhaps the most important example.

The term "lender of last resort" was first used by the banker Francis Baring in 1797. Referring to the Bank of England's role during a crisis in which credit intermediation had suddenly been interrupted on news of war between Britain and France: "In such cases the Bank are not an intermediary body, or power; there is no resource on their refusal, for they are the *dernier resort*."[7] The role of a lender of last resort in a crisis was classically formulated by Henry Thornton in 1802, and by Walter Bagehot in Chapter 7 of his 1873 *Lombard Street: A Description of the Money Market*: "[A]dvances in time of panic ... are necessary, and must be made by someone." This responsibility falls to the central bank:

> *By painful events and incessant discussions, men of business have now been trained to see that a large banking reserve is necessary, and to understand that, in the curious constitution of the English banking world, the Bank of England is the only body which could effectually keep it* [p. 180] ... [T]*he Bank of England ... is simply in the position of a Bank keeping the Banking reserve of the country* ... [I]*n time of panic it must advance freely and vigorously to the public out of the reserve* [p. 196].

He then puts forth what has come to be known as *Bagehot's Rule*, the two principles by which central bank reserves are to be deployed in a financial crisis, the application of a penalty rate of interest on the loans and the requirement that loans be secured:

> *The end is to stay the panic; and the advances should, if possible, stay the panic. And for this purpose there are two rules: First. That these loans should only be made at a very high rate of interest.*

---

[7]Cited in Wood (2000), p. 203.

> *This will operate as a heavy fine on unreasonable timidity, and will prevent the greatest number of applications by persons who do not require it. The rate should be raised early in the panic, so that the fine may be paid early; that no one may borrow out of idle precaution without paying well for it; that the Banking reserve may be protected as far as possible.*
>
> *Secondly. That at this rate these advances should be made on all good banking securities, and as largely as the public ask for them. . . . If it is known that the Bank of England is freely advancing on what in ordinary times is reckoned a good security—on what is then commonly pledged and easily convertible—the alarm of the solvent merchants and bankers will be stayed. But if securities, really good and usually convertible, are refused by the Bank, the alarm will not abate, the other loans made will fail in obtaining their end, and the panic will become worse and worse* [pp. 197–198].

The lender of last resort function is to be carried out on the largest possible scale, and the policy of doing so is to be clearly announced during normal times, in advance of any crisis. Preannouncement will stabilize expectations, reduce endogenous liquidity risk, and thus make a crisis less likely.

Bagehot asserts that the central bank—and thus the taxpayer—is unlikely, once the crisis has subsided, to have incurred losses in carrying out its lender of last resort function, but is safe from loss only if it lends massively enough to avert a full-scale crisis:

> *The* amount *of the advance is the main consideration for the Bank of England, and not the nature of the security on which the advance is made, always assuming the security to be good. . . . In ordinary times the Bank is only one of many lenders, whereas in a panic it is the sole lender, and we want, as far as we can, to bring back the unusual state of a time of panic to the common state of ordinary times* . . . [p. 205].
>
> *No advances indeed need be made by which the Bank will ultimately lose. The amount of bad business in commercial countries is an infinitesimally small fraction of the whole business. . . . The only safe plan for the Bank is the brave plan, to lend in a panic on every kind of current security, or every sort on which money is ordinarily and usually lent* [p. 198].

In this classic formulation, Bagehot touches on most of the key issues in the debate on the lender of last resort function of central banks. One aspect of the lender of last resort that Bagehot does not address is the term to maturity of loans. Typically, most of a central bank's monetary operations are conducted via short-term loans. But in a crisis, it may see a need to satisfy the desire for longer-term loans, potentially constraining future monetary operations and thus departing from pure liquidity support, in order to ease a panic.

Rationale and Scope of a Lender of Last Resort   Several competing arguments have been voiced for—and against—recognizing the lender of last resort as a legitimate function of central banks. Each argument brings with it a different definition of its scope, that is, when to exercise it.

In the classical view of Bagehot and his successors, the lender of last resort function is necessary and has no substitute in financial panics. The lender of last resort should, however, be exercised only to avert a general panic in financial markets or in some other way respond to the threat or actuality of a systemic risk event. In particular, there must be a genuine threat to the real economy overall, that is, aggregate output, growth, and employment, rather than just to one or several financial firms, or even a branch of the financial industry. An opposing view holds that reducing the deadweight cost of individual bank failures justifies liquidity or even capital support.

In the Bagehot formulation, the central bank should provide liquidity support only, to avert an collapse of velocity and the money supply. Loans must be secured by collateral to the satisfaction of the central bank, and are short-term. In this view, only public treasuries and not central banks should provide credit support or recapitalize banks.

One argument for going beyond pure liquidity support is uncertainty about the solvency of the borrowers. Hemingway described bankruptcy as occurring "gradually and then suddenly," and financial crises typically develop the same two ways, with bewildering phases in which events move rapidly and it is unclear just what is happening. It is difficult then to discriminate between merely illiquid and insolvent financial firms. As we saw in Chapter 14, much of the disfunction in money markets during the subprime crisis was due to uncertainty about the solvency of many banks. Though only a handful were thought insolvent, no one knew for certain which ones.

Moreover, in the early stages of panic, when it is not yet clear how great the dangers to the real economy are, the political cost but also the public benefit of rapid action on a large scale are at their maximum. There is therefore an argument for the central bank at least taking the risk of lending to a possibly, but not probably, insolvent firm. The lender of last resort would in any event be secured by collateral.

A very different view is that the central bank *qua* central bank, as sole issuer of high-powered money, never carries out a distinct lender of last resort function. Rather, the central bank, in seeing to it that the money stock does not collapse in the face of an increase in liquidity preference, hoarding, and depositor withdrawals, is merely conducting stabilizing monetary policy. In crises, it is an appropriate policy for the central bank to offset the sudden increase in the desire for liquidity by providing as much liquidity as the market needs. But it doesn't need any special policy tools to confront an "internal drain"; its ordinary monetary policy instruments, such as the discount window and open-market operations, are sufficient. Only the massive scale of the liquidity operations will be different in a crisis. The liquidity infusion need not be directed to specific intermediaries: Provided only that enough liquidity is provided, the money market will distribute it as needed.

The counterargument is that much of the problem in a crisis is that the distribution mechanism for liquidity becomes impaired. In situations like those described in Chapters 12 and 14, in which banks cease lending to one another, the central bank must concern itself with the distribution of reserves as well as its volume. It may be necessary to lend to borrowers that are atypical for the central bank, as the normal counterparties, the large banks and dealers, will otherwise themselves hoard the proceeds because of the perceived risk of lending to others. Related questions raised in this debate are whether the lender of last resort should accept any credit risk under any circumstances, and whether a panic is essentially a collapse of credit intermediation or a collapse of monetary aggregates.

Issues in the Lender of Last Resort Function Aside from the major controversies just outlined, a number of other important issues surround the lender of last resort function:

> *Terms of support.* Bagehot emphasized the penalty rate charged to banks benefitting directly from emergency liquidity support. The penalty rate is defined as a rate substantially higher than that which would prevail in the absence of a panic, rather than a rate higher than realized during the panic, when it is elevated by risk and liquidity premiums. The penalty rate is a mechanism for reducing the moral hazard of access to emergency liquidity support and for encouraging early repayment of the loans as the panic subsides.
>
> Some have argued that a fee should be paid in advance, and as a condition of access to emergency support. This is the mechanism used by clearinghouses, which then support only their members in difficulty, and then only if solvency criteria are met. In a panic, however, the externalities generated by liquidity problems of institutions that have not paid an access fee in advance may dominate, and the lender of last resort may feel obliged to provide support nonetheless.

A related debate surrounds the quality of the collateral accepted against loans by the lender of last resort. One school of thought holds that the central bank should accept only securities of high credit quality, while another holds that even low-quality collateral is acceptable, provided haircuts high enough to minimize the lender's credit risk are imposed.

Who should provide support? Private support is an alternative to central banks as lender of last resort. For example, we noted the role of clearinghouses in mitigating counterparty risk in futures markets in Chapter 6. There is evidence that, while by no means foolproof, such mechanisms also helped contain and avert banking panics in the late nineteenth and early twentieth centuries. The countervailing view is that private support may be difficult to mobilize because of collective action problems.

Financial innovation and disintermediation. The lender of last resort function may need to be adapted as the financial system evolves. The doctrine was originally formulated for a bank-centered financial system. Market-based intermediation raised new challenges both to the rationale and implementation of lender of last resort policy, requiring operations to provide liquidity support to markets rather than specific intermediaries. An example is the Federal Reserve's Term Asset-Backed Securities Lending Facility (TALF), which was in operation from March 2009 to June 2010. It aimed to preserve the securitization intermediation channel in the face of large liquidity premiums (see Figure 14.14) and the dissolution of an entire investing clientele, by lending broadly to new investors in investment-grade securitization products.

These interpretations of the lender of last resort function as going beyond averting the collapse of the money supply, to maintaining the integrity of the credit intermediation system, have been referred to as "market maker of last resort" (Buiter and Sibert, 2007, and Buiter, 2007) or "dealer of last resort" (Mehrling, 2011). These terms emphasize the recommendation that the central bank act to prevent market-based intermediation from instantaneous collapse. The argument is foreshadowed in Calomiris (1994), a chronicle of the Penn Central bankruptcy, showing that discount window lending to banks averted a credit crunch that would otherwise have been induced by a shutdown of the commercial paper market.

Stigma. A depository institution that accesses the discount window may fear that doing so signals that it is in financial distress. It may thereby cut off its own access to interbank markets. The stigma problem became an issue early in the subprime crisis when it appeared that banks were reluctant to make use of the primary credit facility for fear that they would be stigmatized and become unable to borrow in the private interbank market. One way to mitigate stigma is the use of auctions, rather than standing facilities, for example the Federal Reserve's Term Auction Facility, in operation from December 2007 to March 2010.

Moral hazard. The existence of a lender of last resort increases moral hazard, particularly since the policy, in the classical doctrine, is to be preannounced and thus well-known to market participants. There is a trade-off between the negative effect on financial stability of moral hazard and the higher incentive to risk-taking, and the positive effect on financial stability of reducing endogenous liquidity risk. The moral hazard problem here is closely related to the problem of too-big-to-fail, to be discussed below.

Support for evidently or potentially insolvent institutions increases moral hazard. As noted, the deadweight cost of supporting firms that ultimately fail can be considerable. For these reasons, the liquidity-oriented lender of last resort function, best carried out by central banks, is carefully distinguished from that of capital support, best carried out by finance ministries.

All these issues have played a role in central banks' exercise of the lender of last resort function during the subprime crisis. Due to the extraordinary extent of leverage and short-term borrowing via market-based channels, the crisis presented a sharp challenge to central banks' existing framework for provision of emergency liquidity support to the financial system. The Federal Reserve in particular introduced a number of newly designed mechanisms for carrying out the lender of last resort function, and extended the range of its counterparties, the term to maturity of the loans, and the types of collateral accepted.

15.4 PITFALLS IN REGULATION

The rationale and techniques of regulation we've presented rest primarily on efficiency arguments, that is, flaws in the ability of market mechanisms to achieve either a desirable allocation of credit, or to do so without inducing avoidable disruptions in credit. There are, however, a number of pitfalls in putting regulatory solutions into practice. Many are not unique to finance, but rather apply generally to public policy vis-à-vis markets.

In Chapter 6, we described contracting and transactions cost issues that arise in credit. These issues affect private parties and their incentives in contractual relationships. We've had occasion to refer to these costs in describing, for example, the difficulties of aligning incentives in securitization and bank deposit contracts. But the same issues concerning incentives also create difficulties in designing regulations capable of meeting the goals set for them.

15.4.1 Moral Hazard and Risk Shifting

In regulatory policy, moral hazard describes a situation in which individuals or firms benefit from government guarantees and therefore have reduced incentives to avoid losses. The guarantees may not be expected to be fulfilled with certainty. Moral hazard enables its beneficiaries to borrow more cheaply, and leverage permits market participants to create convex, option-like payoff profiles. As in the insurance case, key elements enabling moral hazard are asymmetrical information; that is, the person or firm enjoying the guarantee has better information about the risk mitigants available than does the provider of the guarantee, and risk shifting, that is, the capacity to impose greater risk of loss on a counterparty after contracting.

Moral Hazard and the Financial Safety Net   Some examples of moral hazard in financial regulation include

Deposit insurance and other explicit investor guarantees reduce the incentives of depositors to scrutinize the efficacy with which the bank carries out its loan monitoring and collection, and other contractual obligations. This problem is one of the key arguments, as noted, in favor of regulatory capital standards.

Too-big-to-fail doctrine, under which systemically important financial institutions are to be supported by public lending rather than be unwound or permitted to file for bankruptcy protection.[8] The term was introduced in 1984 in response to testimony by the Comptroller of the Currency in the aftermath of the Continental Illinois bailout. The policy creates an option-like payoff profile for too-big-to-fail firms, in which the public sector bears some of the risk of loss, while the firms' employees, shareholders, and creditors receive positive returns, thus generating moral hazard.

---

[8]See Tim Carrington, "Won't let 11 biggest banks in nation fail—testimony by Comptroller at House hearing is first policy acknowledgement," *Wall Street Journal*, September 20, 1984.

Too-big-too-fail reduces the incentive for counterparties to manage the risks of their exposures to large intermediaries, except to the extent there is doubt about the policy or whether it applies to a specific firm, thus shoring up if not creating what has been referred to as the "counterparty system" (Einhorn, 2008). Too-big-to-fail similarly enabled large banks under its umbrella to credibly extend their own implicit guarantees to the off-balance sheet vehicles they sponsored.

Too-big-to-fail would be more fairly described as a practice than as a doctrine; a pattern has emerged over several decades from rescues of creditors of large institutions. It may have been fostered also by the shift in corporate governance from shareholder to managerial power over these same decades. Greater imperviousness to outside challenge, together with the ability to borrow at low credit spreads, may have increased the convexity/option value of the payoff profile of too-big-too-fail firms and contributed to moral hazard.

Dodd-Frank attempts to counteract too-big-to-fail by allowing regulators, particularly Treasury and the FDIC, to liquidate such firms. As noted above, the FDIC is charged with developing a process for doing so. Such a process must be credible, as we will see in a moment, in order to weaken too-big-too-fail.

The extent of the moral hazard depends on the nature of the expected bailout. If the policy is perceived, for example, as being particularly protective of creditors, the firms' credit risk premium will be tight and will lower their funding costs compared to competitors that are not too big too fail.

Too-big-to-fail is related, but not identical, to central banks' lender of last resort function. The rationale for rescuing large financial firms in danger of insolvency is that such institutions are so intricately interwoven with the rest of the financial system that a failure would cause or deepen a financial crisis. Financial firms and their investors are aware of this externality and the likely public-sector response, and curtail their own monitoring and due diligence accordingly.

Too-big-to-fail has effects on the cost of capital of large financial firms, but also on the overall arrangements market participants make. For example, payments and settlements systems may incorporate a tacit assumption of a public-sector backstop, and that key participants are covered by too-big-to-fail.

The Dodd-Frank Act addresses the too-big-to-fail problem chiefly through the proposed mechanism, noted above, of designating certain large financial intermediaries as systemically important financial institution (SIFIs). The designation includes all banks with assets in excess of $50 billion and other nonbank intermediaries to be designated by the FSOC. As noted, SIFIs are to be regulated by the Federal Reserve, regardless of whether they are banks. If a SIFI is determined to pose systemic risk, for example because it is in peril of default, the firm is to be resolved or unwound under an Orderly Liquidation Authority (OLA) rather than in bankruptcy. The FDIC is charged with designing and administering the process, which is to include firing management, wiping out equity owners, and imposing haircuts on creditors without absolute deference to the standard rules of seniority, such as equal treatment of unsecured senior debtholders. The Federal Reserve may lend to an individual SIFI only if it is the process of resolution under the OLA or via a facility such as the discount window with broad market eligibility, precluding actions such as those taken in 2008 under Section 13(3) of the Federal Reserve Act (prior to its Dodd-Frank modification) to prevent the collapse of Bear Stearns and AIG.

The "counterparty system" is not what it was prior to the crisis; as noted, the presumption that large dealers collect initial margin from customers has shifted closer to two-way margining. Dodd-Frank, once the pertinent rules are made, such as those on central clearing requirements and on the designation and resolution of SIFIs, will further alter these relationships in OTC derivatives markets in hard-to-predict ways. The impact on intermediaries' credit spreads, and how spreads behave over time, is also hard to predict. The so-called "ratings uplift," the ratings agencies' practice of assigning higher ratings to large banks' debt issues on the assumption that they are too-big-to-fail, also plays a key role in market determination of spreads. Market perception of potential public-sector support, together with the ratings uplift, tends to tighten spreads. Uncertainty about public-sector support, about how resolution will be carried out, and the potential for haircuts on some debt spreads, tend to widen spreads.

Spread behavior if there is an immediate prospect of resolution under the OLA is at least as hard to predict, as there is potential for sparking a sell-off by creditors seeking to avoid supervisor-determined haircuts. Uncertainty about quiet-state as well as stressed-state credit spreads of SIFIs and potential SIFIs will also have been increased by disparate treatment of senior unsecured creditors following major intermediary failures during the subprime crisis, to which we return in our discussion of moral hazard mitigants.

A tough response to the too-big-to-fail problem may be taken in Switzerland, where a federal government-appointed "too-big-to-fail" Commission of Experts has recommended capital standards considerably more stringent than those proposed in Basel III. As noted above, these additional capital requirements may take the form of contingent capital that converts to common under certain triggers. The Swiss proposal has the same structure as Basel III, but ordains a larger capital buffer and explicitly labels the countercyclical component as a surcharge for systemically important banks yet to be identified. Where Basel III may call for a total of 10.5 percent total capital, with a minimum 7 percent consisting of common equity, the Swiss proposal is for 19 percent total capital, with 10 percent in common equity (see Commission of Experts, 2010).

Implicit guarantees were given to the two government sponsored enterprises (GSEs) Fannie Mae and Freddie Mac, permitting these institutions to issue debt and finance the purchase of mortgage assets at lower cost than otherwise. Prior to the subprime crisis, *agency debt*, as their debt issues are called, had tighter spreads than other private corporations. Their low cost of capital was below the spreads paid even by senior RMBS, whether guaranteed by the GSEs or "private label." Together with their mandate to support homeownership, the spread between agency debt and RMBS provided incentives for the GSEs to go beyond their original business of guaranteeing prime mortgages and packaging them into agency RMBS, and make direct investments in a "retained portfolio" of agency and private-label RMBS and whole loans. While the final cost is still not known with certainty, there is a high likelihood that GSE losses will represent the bulk of the direct fiscal costs arising from public support of financial intermediaries during the subprime crisis.

Walter and Weinberg (2002) have attempted to estimate the present value of these various forms of support to U.S. financial firms; they place the total of explicit and implicit guarantees at $9.2 trillion, largely off-balance sheet. While that estimate is based in part on model assumptions, and is in any case now outdated, it gives a sense of the large magnitude of these explicit and implicit guarantees. Haldane and Alessandri (2009) estimate the total "nominal amount" of support provided during the subprime crisis by the U.S. and U.K. central banks and governments, including guarantees, liquidity and capital infusions, at about 75 percent of annual GDP. These totals, like notional swap amounts, are much larger than the amounts at risk or potential taxpayer cost. Veronesi and Zingales (2010) apply the Merton model to estimate the deadweight cost of bankruptcy avoided by the U.S. Treasury's infusion of capital into U.S. banks and broker-dealers and the FDIC's debt guarantees in October 2008 at $130 billion.

Moral hazard can also arise from changes in the situation of households. For example, as we saw in Chapter 1, U.S. households today have far greater exposure than in the past to equity markets, and home ownership is more widespread, even several years into the subprime crisis, than at any earlier time. This is thought by some to place constraints on macroeconomic stabilization policy. Monetary authorities contemplating a tightening of monetary policy would have to take into account the impact of the consequent reduction in household wealth on the real economy. This reluctance might over shorter periods reduce the frequency and severity of large declines; that is, it would foster positive skewness in equity returns, and possibly thereby make equity investment even more attractive to many households. In the long run, it might thereby increase procyclicality by increasing the magnitude of extreme negative returns when they occur. This phenomenon is similar to the effect of securitization in concentrating systematic risk in the seniormost bonds.

Concern about too-big-to-fail is compounded by the pattern of rescues of financial firms, which, though hardly uniform, has confirmed that some form of too-big-too-fail policy has been in place. In the view of some observers, the new resolution authority of the Treasury and FDIC under the Dodd-Frank Act can be expected to mitigate the too-big-to-fail problem. If, however, a credible resolution process is not established, the public perception that too-big-to-fail remains in place may be strengthened. Similar hopes had been invested in the Federal Deposit Insurance Corporation Improvement Act (FDICIA) of 1991. FDICIA mandated rapid "least-cost" resolution of weak banks and risk-based deposit insurance fees, and was an important part of the regulatory response to the S&L crisis.

Mitigating Moral Hazard   One proposed solution to the problem of moral hazard generated by too-big-to-fail and deposit insurance is the requirement that firms that benefit from implicit guarantees issue subordinated debt in proportion to the size of their balance sheets or risk-weighted assets. Subordinated debt has a number of potential benefits: It increases the cost of raising capital and, because of its subordinate position in the capital structure, relates that cost to the riskiness of issuers' balance sheets. The secondary-market spreads on subordinate debt issues provide information to supervisors as well as to markets about the riskiness of the issuers' assets. It also obliges issuers to be more transparent in disclosures about risk, as investors will otherwise be unwilling to purchase the bonds except at higher spreads. A similar, but somewhat narrower, proposal is to tie regulatory actions to firms' CDS spreads in the marketplace.

It is not clear, however, that required subordinated debt issuance can solve the moral hazard problem. If the perceived solicitude for creditors in a financial crisis is great enough, spreads even of subordinated debt of highly leveraged intermediaries may stay "too tight." As we saw earlier in this chapter, poor loss absorbency of Tier II regulatory capital, of which subordinated debt is the main component, was a key motivation for the Basel III revisions. The ratings uplift may also tighten sub spreads.

The experience of the subprime crisis has left this issue ambiguous. Apart from Lehman, most failures of large U.S. banks and broker-dealers during the crisis have resulted in an acquisition in which the acquired firms' bondholders suffered no losses, reducing the value of sub spreads as an early-warning signal. The major exception were senior and subordinated debt of Washington Mutual ("WaMu"), a commercial bank particularly active in subprime residential mortgage lending. Its assets and deposits, but not its senior unsecured and subordinated debt, were assumed by J.P. Morgan Chase on September 25, 2008. Recovery on the subordinated debt was zero.

Moreover, the revisions to the regulatory definition of capital described above, regulatory questioning of the appropriateness of including subordinated debt in Tier II regulatory capital under the Basel II rules, and the emphasis on common equity at the expense of other components of capital during the Supervisory Capital Assessment Program (SCAP) discussed in Chapter 13 indicated reticence about viewing subordinated debt as fully at risk of loss. Finally, infusions of capital by the United States and a number of other governments in the form of common and preferred shares, which are junior to subordinated debt, as well as debt guarantees, effectively shielded subordinated debt from loss. The failure of junior capital in some cases to take losses impairs the monitoring function of such capital.

The behavior of subordinated debt during the subprime crisis is illustrated in Figure 15.2 with the example of Citigroup. The graph displays the spread between its long-term senior unsecured and subordinated bond yields. The spread remained close to zero, generally around 10 bps, until the fall of 2007. The senior-sub spread exploded following the Lehman collapse, reaching a wide of nearly 1,200 bps, and collapsed after results of the supervisory capital adequacy tests were released in early May 2009. The most recent spreads are somewhat wider than prior to the subprime crisis, and certainly more volatile. But its overall tightness during most of the subprime crisis, apart from the nine months or so of the 2008–2009 panic, casts some doubt on its efficacy as an early warning signal and on its loss absorbency.

Moral Hazard and Time Consistency *Credibility* and *time consistency* problems contribute to moral hazard. Credibility refers to the extent to which the policy commitments of regulators are believed by market participants. Most financial regulatory policies rely to at least some extent on credibility, which arises particulalry frequently in systemic risk problems. For example, suppose the public sector sets certain conditions, such as tests of solvency, for providing liquidity or credit support for financial firms. If it then provides support for firms that have not met these criteria, the credibility of the criteria will be called into question, increasing moral hazard.

An important aspect of credibility is the ability to establish time-consistent policies. The focus on time consistency initially arose in monetary policy, where policy makers face the following dilemma: Suppose low inflation and unemployment are both desirable, and can best be achieved by keeping inflation expectations low, but that large increases in employment can be achieved by increasing inflation precisely when it is expected to be low. Lower inflation expectations then increase the temptation of policy makers to raise employment with surprise inflation. Policy makers consequently find it more difficult to persuade markets that they will keep inflation low. The result is a worse outcome, with both higher inflation and unemployment, than if there were no time-consistency problem.

A similar dilemma arises in the case of systemic risk policies. The public knows that in extremis the central bank will likely provide liquidity and possibly credit support to troubled intermediaries. This increases the willingness of financial firms to take risk, particularly systematic risks, since then the probability of a systemic risk event, and thus public-sector support, conditional on the distress of the individual risk taker, is higher.

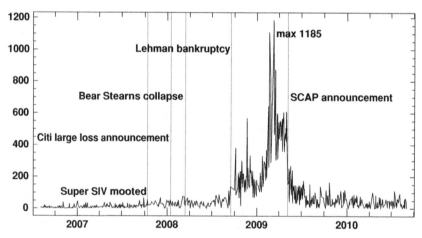

FIGURE 15.2   Citigroup Credit Spreads during the Subprime Crisis
Difference between yields to maturity of Citigroup Inc. senior unsecured and subordinated bonds with maturities of about 10 years, daily, in bps, August 2, 2006, to September 2, 2010. The construction of the senior unsecured bond data is analogous to that described for z-spreads in the caption to Figure 13.4. The subordinated bond yields are for the 4.875% issue maturing May 7, 2015.
Source: Bloomberg Financial L.P.

Another example of the time consistency problem are legislative and regulatory initiatives to reduce residential mortgage loan balances following the decline in U.S. home prices from 2007, by legislative fiat or by increasing the latitude of judges in bankruptcy courts. The individual and economy-wide benefits of reduction in debt balances would be immediate. However, future mortgage lenders would have to factor the possibility of debt forgiveness into the interest rates demanded of borrowers, since it would be difficult to credibly frame any such measure as "one time only."

The classic solution to the problem of time inconsistency in monetary policy is the adoption of rules to govern and constrain policy makers. However, it is more difficult to apply rules to the management of systemic risk, because systemic risk events are rare and very different from one another. Also, as Bagehot noted, policy in panics must be "brave," and therefore resourceful and tailored to the situation as it stands, characteristics of policy that are difficult to define thorough rules.

15.4.2 Regulatory Evasion

In advanced countries, regulation is enshrined in two types of source document, legislation and rule-making. Market participants can often find mechanisms that adhere to the "letter of the law"—while substantively avoiding the restrictions. Texts are subject to interpretation, so case law developed through lawsuits and regulatory appeals tends to lag behind techiques of evasion.

An early example of regulatory evasion is the *bill of exchange*, a medieval money market instrument. Usury laws prevented lending money at interest. The bill of exchange permitted merchants to buy and sell merchandise on credit and charge interest. The proceeds due at the maturity of a bill of exchange were generally payable in a different location and currency from the initial loan, concealing the embedded interest payments within a forward foreign exchange transaction.[9]

A more recent example is the development of swap markets, which began with the introduction of currency swaps. As described in Hodgson (2009), one purpose of these contracts was to evade controls, still prevalent in the early 1970s, on international capital flows.

A milder form of regulatory evasion is *regulatory arbitrage*. Among the most important forms of regulatory arbitrage are those involving capital standards and securitization. The simple risk weights under Basel I and the standardized approach of Basel II provided strong incentives to reduce

---

[9]See Neal (1990), ch. 1.

required capital by securitizing certain assets. A bank issuing loans with a risk weight of 100 percent could securitize those loans rather than hold them in whole loan form. The junior tranches might still have a risk weight of 100 percent, but the senior tranche, if rated AAA, would have a much lower, if not zero, risk weight. Even if the bank retained all tranches on its own balance sheet, it would have drastically lowered the regulatory capital required against the assets. Yet the securitization has the same risks as the original loans.

Two examples of regulatory arbitrage involving securitization were particularly important in increasing the fragility of large banks in the years preceding the subprime crisis:

1. Regulatory capital for investments in non-sovereign bonds were determined by the ratings of the bonds. Risk weights and capital requirements for AAA bonds were the lowest. This provided an incentive for banks to invest in the AAA bonds with the highest yields available, AAA RMBS and CDOs. The bank then earned the spread between the yields on the AAA RMBS and CDOs, and the cost of capital, which included lower-yielding deposits and senior debt of the bank.

   One bank, UBS, was particular hard hit by these investments, many of which it had made in the very last phase of the buildup of mortgage debt. These losses were among the motivations for the aggressive increase in minimum capital requirements, mentioned above, now under discussion in Switzerland.

2. We described off-balance-sheet ABCP conduits at length in Chapters 12 and 14. These vehicles had lower capital charges than if the same securitization and whole loan assets had been held on the balance sheet. The bank earned the spread between the assets and its cost of capital, which was close to the low yield on the ABCP.

In both of these examples, banks chose the path that, within the regulatory capital rules, permitted them to take on the greatest economic leverage. In each case, a relatively narrow spread between the returns of the assets and the cost of capital was enhanced by conducting the trade in size and with high leverage.

Regulatory arbitrage can be carried out by individual households as well as by intermediaries. An example is the use of multiple bank accounts by well-to-do households to increase the amount of insured deposits they hold; deposit insurance is limited by account, not by account owner. Intermediaries have introduced a financial innovation, the Certificate of Deposit Accounts Registry Service (CDARS), to facilitate the process of obtaining deposit insurance coverage for large balances.

15.4.3 Unintended Consequences

The economic and financial systems are complex, and public policies often have unintended consequences. An example in monetary policy is *Goodhart's Law*, which states that when central banks employ specific money aggregates as instruments of monetary policy, based on relationships to macroeconomic variables, those relationships will change and the targeted effects will not be achieved. Intermediaries also adapt the degree and type of risk they assume to the regulatory environment. The form in which risks are taken, for example, via cash positions or expressed through derivatives and structured products, is heavily influenced by regulation. As we can see from the example of ABCP conduits, this often occurs in ways quite different from the rulemakers' intentions.

Myriad examples can be brought. Under Dodd-Frank, risk-conscious deposit insurance fees are based on a bank's entire liability base rather than just on deposit volume. The new fees have prompted some banks to withdraw from the repo and Fed funds markets, drastically reducing money market rates, and with potential further consequences for the money market mutual fund industry.[10]

Bills of exchange and the development of the swap market, and our examples of regulatory arbitrage of capital standards, also illustrate how financial regulation, together with the factors described in Chapter 1, drives financial innovation. The increase in complexity and decrease in transparency in derivatives and other securities, in financial transactions, and in market participants' balance sheets and disclosures, are in part such an unintended consequence. Similarly, regulatory arbitrage is a driver of the long intermediation chains noted in Chapter 12's discussion of "interconnectedness," as illustrated by banks' use of off-balance sheet vehicles to finance mortgages and consumer loans.

Another example is the evolution of the credit ratings business and its impact on capital markets. As we have seen, the effects of ratings standards for the investment portfolios of regulated intermediaries, and the development of the ratings industry generally, are to a large extent historical artifacts. Entry into the ratings business is restricted, but institutional investors have been required to use the product. The ratings business itself has changed dramatically in recent decades:

- The ratings business model has evolved from selling ratings information to bond investors to one in which the bond issuer pays for ratings, called

---

[10] See Michael Mackenzie, "Repo fee hits money market funds," *Financial Times*, April 11, 2011.

the *issuer-pays model*. This change was driven by the introduction of photocopiers and, later, the Internet, which made it difficult to keep ratings private information and permitted free riders to use ratings they hadn't paid for.

■ The structured credit product market created new demand for ratings. In contrast to ratings of corporate bonds, structured credit ratings are part of the process of creating the bonds, since they determine the size of the senior bond tranche and thus the cost of capital of the liabilities. Ratings firms have thereby become involved in structuring deals.

Regulation has interacted with these historical developments. Securitization issuers are said to have used competitive pressures among rating agencies to obtain larger senior bond tranches (lower credit enhancement levels) and improve deal economics, a phenomenon known as *ratings shopping*. Ratings shopping creates incentives for ratings firms to use models that underestimate systematic risk by, for example, underestimating mortgage default correlation. Bond investors' incentives are also aligned with this process. Many institutional investors have high demand for investment-grade bonds that yield even a small spread premium over corporate bonds with the same ratings. An example, mentioned in Chapter 14's discussion of "search for yield" as a source of financial fragility, are public pension funds seeking to meet return targets driven by liability growth. Moreover, regulatory validation of the credit quality of their portfolios based on ratings provides a legal and reputational safe harbor protecting investment managers if there are losses.

Proposals to reform ratings have focused on the issuer-pays model. One variant seeks to counter ratings shopping by having a regulatory body choose the ratings firm for each bond issue. This direction of reform has the disadvantages of reliance on regulators for the accuracy of ratings and further entrenching the NRSROs in the investment process. An alternative approach seeks to remove ratings as a regulatory criterion and place greater reliance on investors themselves to ascertain and demonstrate to regulators the credit quality of their portfolios. Both approaches have found expression in Dodd-Frank.

A final example of unintended consequences is the impact of too-big-to-fail on large intermediaries in early 2009. On the one hand assurances to creditors enabled the firms to maintain access to credit markets and inhibited forced asset liquidations. On the other hand, ambiguity about seniority was generated by the government's purchases of preferred shares in a number of large banks. The possibility that preferred shares might be treated as creditors increased the perceived risk to the common shareholders and made it more difficult for a time for the firms to raise additional equity capital.

Regulation may inhibit competition and protect incumbents, for example through large banks' funding cost advantage. Unintended consequences, at least from the standpoint of the overt intentions of regulation, may also arise from *regulatory capture*, which occurs when regulators exercise their powers at least partly in the interest of the regulated industry. In Stigler's (1971) formulation, "as a rule, regulation is acquired by the industry and is designed and operated primarily for its benefit." It can affect both the formulation and implementation of policy. A related problem is that of coordination among multiple regulators with possibly differing goals and priorities. This is particularly the case for large complex intermediaries in a holding company structure, which often have subsidiaries subject to supervision by different regulators. Macroprudential regulation may face even greater challenges of coordinating the actions of different regulators. Under the Dodd-Frank Act, coordination is to occur through the FSOC, but different agencies must also cooperate in the formulation of the numerous complex rules the Act mandates.

This chapter has focused on how regulation influences financial firms' approach to risk management, how they adapt to regulation in the degree of risk they take, and the impact of regulation on systemic risk, that is, risk to the financial system as a whole. Financial regulation confronts excruciating tradeoffs: It is far more costly, complex and problematic to deal with the consequences of large credit expansions than to limit them ex ante. But attempts to remove risk and volatility from some areas of economic and financial life, or from some market participants, displace those risks elsewhere. It will be some time before risk managers, market participants and policy makers learn what balance has emerged from the revised regulatory framework.

FURTHER READING

Brunnermeier, Crockett, Goodhart, Persaud and Shin (2009), NYU Stern Working Group on Financial Reform (2009), and French et al. (2010) are surveys of and proposals on regulatory issues brought to the fore by the subprime crisis. Counterparty Risk Management Policy Group (2008) is a similar survey by a predominantly private-sector group. Zingales (2009) focuses on securities regulation issues arising from the subprime crisis. The text of the Dodd-Frank Act is available at http://www.gpo.gov/fdsys/pkg/PLAW-111publ203/pdf/PLAW-111publ203.pdf. Davis Polk and Wardwell LLP (2010) is a detailed summary and analysis by a prominent law firm that also maintains a Web page tracking Dodd-Frank rulemaking at http://www.davispolk.com/Dodd-Frank-Rulemaking-Progress-Report/. Skeel (2011) provides commentary on some of the Act's major titles.

Spong (2000) and U.S. Congressional Research Service (2010) provide surveys of U.S. financial regulation and supervision. Goodhart and Schoenmaker (1995) and Calomiris (2006) presents contrasting arguments in the debate on the appropriate bank supervision role of central banks. Black, Miller, and Posner (1978) applies a creditor-borrower template to the relationship between regulators and the financial firms they regulate.

Ayotte and Skeel (2010) provide a defense of bankruptcy, in contrast to special forms of resolution, for insolvent financial firms. See also Bliss (2003) and Bliss and Kaufman (2006) on resolution.

Merton and Bodie (1993) and Benston and Kaufman (1997) discuss deposit insurance as part of the post–S&L crisis banking reform initiatives. Pennacchi (2009) and Acharya, Santos, and Yorulmazer (2010) discuss the pricing of deposit insurance and current reform proposals. Demirgüç-Kunt, Kane, and Laeven (2008) is a collection of essays on experience with deposit insurance in several countries and on the role of deposit insurance within the overall regulatory framework. The editors' introductory essay summarizes cross-country empirical evidence that deposit insurance increases rather than decreasing the likelihood of banking crises and points out the complex effects on market discipline of deposit insurance fees. Daníelsson (2010) describes the Icesave episode.

See Berger, Herring, and Szegö (1995) and Santos (2001) on the economic rationale for capital standards. Berger, Herring, and Szegö (1995) and Haldane (2010) document the decline in bank capital ratios over the past 150 years. Gordy (2000, 2003) and Saidenberg and Schuermann (2003) present the modeling approach underpinning the Basel capital adequacy standards for credit risk. Basel Committee (2006) is the reference work on the Basel II capital standards. The Basel III updates to the capital standards, including the leverage ratio, are presented in Basel Committee (2010*b*) in the form of edits and additions to Basel Committee (2006). The liquidity standards are presented in Basel Committee (2010*c*). Blundell-Wignall and Atkinson (2010) is a critical summary of Basel III. Admati, DeMarzo, Hellwig and Pfleiderer (2010) is a critical survey of the debate on the cost to firms and the economy of higher capital requirements. De Mooij (2011) reviews the impact of tax-deductibility of interest costs on leverage. Bliss and Kaufman (2003) discusses the relationship between regulatory capital and reserve requirements.

DeBandt and Hartmann (2000) discusses the concept of systemic risk. Tarullo (2011) is a regulator's articulation of financial stability policy. Galati and Moessner (2011) is a survey of the macroprudential supervision literature. Haldane, Hall, and Pezzini (2007) focuses on stability risk assessment. Some difficulties in defining these concepts are discussed in Borio and Drehmann (2009). Bernanke and Gertler (2001), Cecchetti, Genberg and Wadhwani (2002), Kohn (2002), Roubini (2006), Posen (2006) and White (2009) present contrasting views on asset price targeting and monetary policy. Demirgüç-Kunt and Servén (2010) contains a critical review of the debate. Acharya, Cooley, Richardson and Walter (2010) discuss the Dodd-Frank approach to systemic risk regulation and provide a survey of systemic risk measures.

Eichner, Kohn, and Palumbo (2010) discusses the difficulties of gathering data useful for assessing financial fragility for the United States, but with implications for other industrialized countries. Pojarliev and Levich (2011) propose a technique for detecting crowded trades in currency markets. A number of central banks and international organizations, including the European Central Bank, the Bank of England, and the International Monetary Fund, publish regular reports and working paper series on financial stability. Some of this work is cited in the references to this chapter and Chapter 14. Acharya, Cooley, Richardson, and Walter (2009) discusses systemic risk charges.

We cited several key sources on RMBS securitization in Chapter 9. On the relationship among credit standards, leverage, house prices and the securitization channel in the background to the subprime crisis, see also Gerardi, Lehnert, Sherlund, and Willen (2008), Kiff and Mills (2007), Demyanyk (2009), Demyanyk and Hemert (2011), Mayer Pence and Sherlund (2009), and Geanakoplos (2010).

The early history of the lender of last resort concept is surveyed in O'Brien (2007), particularly Chapters 7 and 8. Goodhart (1988) discusses the key role of the lender of last resort in the historical development of central banking. Bordo (1990) and Miron (1986) provide historical surveys of the issues surrounding the lender of last resort function. White (1983) and Miron (1986) chronicle the importance of smoothing seasonal fluctuations in credit demand to reduce the frequency of financial panics, and the part played in it by the Federal Reserve, in the early twentieth century.

Madigan and Nelson (2002) describes the functioning and rationale of the Fed's discount window. McAndrews and Potter (2002) discusses a rare example of emergency liquidity provision for purely operational, but extraordinary, reasons. Freixas, Giannini, Hoggarth, and Soussa (1999, 2000) provide surveys of the issues in lender of last resort policy. Goodhart (1987, 1988) relates lender of last resort to the unique role of banks and discuss the problem of accurately discerning solvency in real time. Goodhart (2008) discusses the relationships among financial firms' liquidity risk management, moral hazard, and the lender of last resort function. Wood (2000) is a critique of more expansive interpretations of the lender of last resort function.

Bordo (2000) distinguishes in this context between real crises, in which exercise of the lender of last resort is genuinely needed, and "pseudo-crises."

Goodfriend and King (1988) and Borio and Nelson (2008) present contrasting views on the need for the lender of last resort to lend to specific institutions, rather than to the market as a whole, during crises. White (1983, pp. 74ff.), Timberlake (1984) and Kroszner (2000) describe the role and functioning of private bank clearinghouses in nineteenth and early twentieth century financial crises. The problem of stigma in lender of last resort operations is discussed in Furfine (2003), Klee (2011) and in the references they provide. Madigan (2009) discusses the lender of last resort function and financial innovation in the context of the Federal Reserve response to the the subprime crisis. Group of Ten (1996) discusses issues in public policy during sovereign debt crises.

Hetzel (2009) and Haldane and Alessandri (2009) discusses the moral hazard issues arising from the financial safety net in historical perspective. The latter paper discusses specific channels by which banks can exploit moral hazard and shift risks to the public. Akerlof and Romer (1993) describes some distasteful consequences of moral hazard during the U.S. savings and loan crisis. Laeven and Valencia (2008) documents the prevalence of recapitalization as a response to banking crises.

A comprehensive treatment of too-big-to-fail is given in Stern and Feldman (2004). Its historical background in the United States is described in Hetzel (1991, 2009). Ötker-Robe , Narain, Ilyina, and Surti (2011) is a recent internationally-aware survey of the extent of and proposed solutions to the too-big-to-fail policy. Schnabel (2009) documents preferential treatment of large banks in Germany during its Great Depression banking crisis." Flannery (1999) discusses the displacement of private monitoring and the role of payments systems in too-big-to-fail.

Board of Governors of the Federal Reserve System (2000), Calomiris (1999), Ashcraft (2006), and White (2009) discuss the role of bank-issued subordinated debt in prudential regulation. Hart and Zingales (2009) and Caprio, Demirgüç-Kunt and Kane (2010) propose the use of the CDS spreads of large intermediaries to provide market discipline and market-based triggers of regulatory action. Basel Committee on Banking Supervision (2010a) reviews the experience with subordinated debt during the subprime crisis.

Stigler (1971) and Posner (1974) discuss regulatory capture, while Peltzman (1989) provides a survey of the "economic theory of regulation" analysis of regulation as the outcome of political competition. Caprio, Demirgüç-Kunt and Kane (2010) and Demirgüç-Kunt and Servén (2010) review the regulatory issues raised by the subprime crisis, emphasizing the role of regulatory arbitrage and incentives. UBS (2008) and Swiss Federal Banking

Commission (2008) provide a detailed analysis of the UBS losses on investment-grade structured products. White (2009) discusses problems arising from the use of ratings in supervision. Acharya and Richardson (2009) and Acharya and Schnabl (2010) give examples of regulatory arbitrage in the securitization process. Calomiris and Mason (2004) examine credit card securitization and find no definitive evidence of regulatory arbitrage.

Technical Notes

A.1 BINOMIAL DISTRIBUTION

A coin toss is an example of a *Bernoulli trial*, a random experiment with two possible outcomes. The coin is not necessarily stipulated to be "fair." The probability of heads can be equal to any $\pi \in [0, 1]$. If we assign the value $Y = 1$ to one of the outcomes of the Bernoulli trial and the value $Y = 0$ to the other, we say that Y follows a *Bernoulli distribution* with parameter π.

Suppose we repeat a Bernoulli trial n times and add up the resulting values of $Y_i, i = 1, \ldots, n$. Successive trials are independent. The random variable $X = \sum_{i=1}^{n} Y_i$ is said to follow a *binomial distribution* with parameters π and n. We have

$$E[X] = n\pi$$

$$\mathrm{Var}[X] = n\pi(1 - \pi)$$

The Bernoulli and binomial distributions are both discrete distributions. But the binomial distribution converges to the normal distribution as the number of trials n grows larger. This convergence result is an application of the *central limit theorem*. Specifically, if we standardize a binomially distributed random variable X, we can get its probability distribution arbitrarily close to that of a standard normal variate by increasing n enough:

$$P\left[\frac{X - n\pi}{\sqrt{n\pi(1 - \pi)}} \leq z\right] \to \Phi(z) \quad \text{as} \quad n \to \infty$$

This book uses the binomial distribution in two applications, to analyze the probability distribution of the terminal state of a random walk (Chapter 2) and to characterize the distribution of credit losses in a portfolio of identical, uncorrelated credits (Chapter 8). In the case of the random walk,

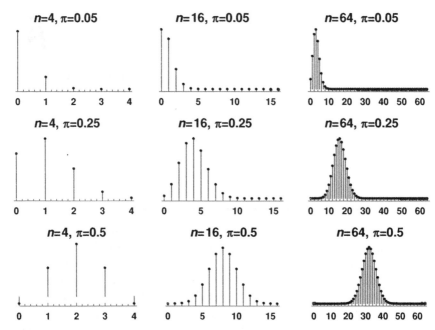

FIGURE A.1 Convergence of Binomial to Normal Distribution
The plots display the probability density of X_n, the terminal position of a random walk over an interval of length 1, with $n = 4, 16, 64$ time steps. The upper two rows of graphs set $\pi = 0.05$ and $\pi = \frac{1}{4}$. The distributions are not symmetrical, but converge to a symmetrical normal distribution. The lower row of graphs uses $\pi = \frac{1}{2}$, and all three distributions in the row are symmetrical.

we use convergence to the normal distribution to show that the discrete-step random walk converges to a continuous Brownian motion. Figure A.1 illustrates. Notice that if the probability of the Bernoulli trial is not equal to 0.5, the binomial distribution is skewed for small n. But as n grows larger, the skewness disappears. In the credit context, convergence is used to derive an approximation to the distribution of losses in a credit portfolio.

A.2 QUANTILES AND QUANTILE TRANSFORMATIONS

Suppose we have a random variable X. A p-th *quantile* of X is a number $Q_p(X)$ such that $\mathbf{P}\left[X < Q_p(X)\right] \leq p$. We can define quantiles in terms of the cumulative distribution function $F(X)$. The p-th quantile is the value of

X such that, for any $x < Q_p(X)$,

$$F(x) \le p$$

Every probability distribution has an *inverse probability distribution function* or *quantile function*. If X is a continuous random variable, with a cumulative distribution function (CDF) that is monotone increasing in X, we can define the quantile more simply. The p-th quantile is then a number $Q_p(X)$ such that $\mathbf{P}\left[X < Q_p(X)\right] = p$. It is equal to the value of the inverse function of the CDF, evaluated at p:

$$Q_p(X) = F^{-1}(p)$$

The most commonly mentioned quantile is the 0.5 quantile, or the *median*. If X is a random variable, there is a probability of $\frac{1}{2}$ of realizing a value of X less than or equal to the median. The "p" in "p-th quantile" is commonly expressed as a percent, and the quantile is then called a *percentile*. A familiar example comes from the standard normal distribution. The median of the standard normal is zero, equal to its mean. The 0.01 quantile or first percentile of the standard normal is about 2.33.

We use quantile functions in a number of applications, including simulation, in applying copulas (Chapters 8 and 9), and in understanding risk neutral probability distributions (Chapter 10). The probability distribution tells us, for any value x of a random variable X, what the probability is of X having a realization that is less than or equal to x, that is, $\mathbf{P}[X \le x]$. The quantile function tells us, for any $p \in [0, 1]$, what is the value of x such that $p = \mathbf{P}[X \le x]$.

The most common approach to obtaining random variates with a desired probability distribution applies the *quantile transformation* or *inversion principle*. This principle exploits the fact that the cumulative probabilities $F(X)$ of a random variable X are uniform-$[0, 1]$ distributed.

By the same token, values of the quantile function, applied to the uniform-$[0, 1]$ variates, have the original distribution. Both the domain of a uniform random variable and the probabilities lie on $[0, 1]$; the domain of the uniform random variable happens to be the range of any cumulative distribution function. The inversion principle states: If we have a uniform distribution value, we can transform it into the value of another distribution $F(X)$ by finding the value for which that other distribution has a probability equal to the uniform distribution value. If U represents a uniform-$[0, 1]$ variate, the random variable $F^{-1}(U)$ has the same distribution function as X, namely $F(X)$.

A.3   NORMAL AND LOGNORMAL DISTRIBUTIONS

A.3.1   Relationship between Asset Price Levels and Returns

The *lognormal distribution* is defined as the probability distribution of a random variable y with a logarithm that is normally distributed. If $\log(y) \sim N(a, b)$, then y has a lognormal distribution with parameters a and b. Those parameters, though, are not the mean and standard deviation of y.

We use the lognormal distribution to relate changes in the level of an asset price to its logarithmic returns. We want to find the probability distributions, at some future time $t + \tau$, of

- the asset price level $S_{t+\tau}$
- the change in price $S_t - S_{t+\tau}$
- the logarithmic return $\log\left(\frac{S_{t+\tau}}{S_t}\right)$

Typically, we have a reasonable assumption about the mean of the future price $E[S_{t+\tau}]$, based on the forward or futures price, or on a price forecast, and a reasonable assumption about the annualized volatility σ of the logarithmic return, based on historical or implied volatility.

How do we match these distributions and parameters? The expected discrete rate of return that "grows" $\log(S_t)$ to its time $t + \tau$ mean $E[S_{t+\tau}]$ in a straight line is the μ that satisfies

$$E[S_{t+\tau}] = S_t e^{\mu\tau}$$

But there is noise along the path; S_t has a volatility. The expected constant logarithmic rate of return that gets S_t to $E[S_{t+\tau}]$ is *not* μ, but $\mu - \frac{\sigma^2}{2}$:

$$\frac{1}{\tau} \log\left(\frac{E[S_{t+\tau}]}{S_t}\right) = \mu - \frac{\sigma^2}{2}$$

Reducing the rate of return by $\frac{\sigma^2}{2}$ just offsets the asymmetric, growth-increasing impact of volatility combined with compounding described in Chapter 2. The logarithmic rate of return is therefore distributed as

$$\log\left(\frac{S_{t+\tau}}{S_t}\right) \sim N\left[\left(\mu - \frac{\sigma^2}{2}\right)\tau, \sigma\sqrt{\tau}\right]$$

implying that

$$\frac{\log\left(\frac{S_{t+\tau}}{S_t}\right) - \left(\mu - \frac{\sigma^2}{2}\right)\tau}{\sigma\sqrt{\tau}} \sim N(0, 1)$$

By the definition of a lognormal random variable, we thereby establish that the distribution of $S_{t+\tau} - S_t$ is lognormal with parameters $\left(\mu - \frac{\sigma^2}{2}\right)\tau$ and $\sigma\sqrt{\tau}$. Shifting the mean of the logarithmic return by $\log(S_t)$, the distribution of $S_{t+\tau}$ is lognormal with parameters $\log(S_t) + \left(\mu - \frac{\sigma^2}{2}\right)\tau$ and $\sigma\sqrt{\tau}$.

In general, if y has a lognormal distribution with parameters a and b, then $E[y] = e^{a+\frac{b^2}{2}}$. The mean of the distribution of $S_{t+\tau} - S_t$ is therefore $e^{\mu\tau}$ and that of $S_{t+\tau}$ is $S_t e^{\mu\tau}$.

We can also match up the *quantiles* of these distributions. The p-th quantile of the lognormal distribution equals S_t times the exponential of the p-th quantile of the corresponding normal distribution, or

$$S_t e^{\left(\mu - \frac{\sigma^2}{2}\right)\tau + \sigma\sqrt{\tau}z} \quad \text{with} \quad \Phi(z) = p$$

The cumulative probability distribution function of $\log\left(\frac{S_{t+\tau}}{S_t}\right)$ is

$$\Phi\left[\frac{\log\left(\frac{S_{t+\tau}}{S_t}\right) - \left(\mu - \frac{\sigma^2}{2}\right)\tau}{\sigma\sqrt{\tau}}\right]$$

A.3.2 The Black-Scholes Distribution Function

We can use these relationships to interpret the Black-Scholes delta and other sensitivities under the risk-neutral probability distribution. In the Black-Scholes model, the future asset price follows a lognormal distribution, and the logarithmic return $\log\left(\frac{S_{t+\tau}}{S_t}\right)$ follows a normal distribution. What are the parameters of those risk-neutral distributions?

Suppose we have an asset with a current price of S_t, paying a risk-free, constant, and continuous dividend at a rate q. The constant and continuously compounded risk-free rate is r. The forward price $F_{t,\tau}$ is equal to the mean of the future price under the risk-neutral distribution:

$$\tilde{E}[S_{t+\tau}] = S_t e^{(r-q)\tau} = F_{t,\tau}$$

If σ is the implied volatility, $r - q - \frac{\sigma^2}{2}$ is the risk-neutral mean of the logarithmic return and $\sigma \sqrt{\tau}$ its risk-neutral standard deviation. This sets the parameters of the risk-neutral time $t + \tau$ asset price and return distributions, which we can express as

$$\frac{\log\left(\frac{S_{t+\tau}}{S_t}\right) - \left(r - q - \frac{\sigma^2}{2}\right)\tau}{\sigma \sqrt{\tau}} \sim N(0, 1)$$

With the derivations just above, we can summarize as follows:

- The risk-neutral probability distribution of the future asset price level $S_{t+\tau}$ is lognormal, with parameters $\log(S_t) + \left(r - q - \frac{\sigma^2}{2}\right)\tau$ and $\sigma \sqrt{\tau}$.
- The risk-neutral probability distribution of the change in price $S_t - S_{t+\tau}$ is lognormal, with parameters $\left(r - q - \frac{\sigma^2}{2}\right)\tau$ and $\sigma \sqrt{\tau}$.
- The risk-neutral probability distribution of the logarithmic return $\log\left(\frac{S_{t+\tau}}{S_t}\right)$ is normal, with mean $\left(r - q - \frac{\sigma^2}{2}\right)\tau$ and standard deviation $\sigma \sqrt{\tau}$.

How do these distributions relate to the Black-Scholes formulas? The Black-Scholes model values for European puts and calls are:

$$v(S_t, \sigma, r, q) = S_t e^{-q\tau} \Phi\left[\frac{\log\left(\frac{S_t}{X}\right) + \left(r - q + \frac{\sigma^2}{2}\right)\tau}{\sigma \sqrt{\tau}}\right]$$

$$- Xe^{-r\tau} \Phi\left[\frac{\log\left(\frac{S_t}{X}\right) + \left(r - q - \frac{\sigma^2}{2}\right)\tau}{\sigma \sqrt{\tau}}\right]$$

$$w(S_t, \tau, X, \sigma, r, q) = Xe^{-r\tau} \Phi\left[-\frac{\log\left(\frac{S_t}{X}\right) + \left(r - q - \frac{\sigma^2}{2}\right)\tau}{\sigma \sqrt{\tau}}\right]$$

$$- S_t e^{-q\tau} \Phi\left[-\frac{\log\left(\frac{S_t}{X}\right) + \left(r - q + \frac{\sigma^2}{2}\right)\tau}{\sigma \sqrt{\tau}}\right]$$

The Black-Scholes call delta is

$$\delta_{c,t} \equiv \frac{\partial}{\partial S_t} v(S_t, \tau, X, \sigma, r, q) = e^{-q\tau} \Phi \left[\frac{\log\left(\frac{S_t}{X}\right) + \left(r - q + \frac{\sigma^2}{2}\right)\tau}{\sigma\sqrt{\tau}} \right]$$

The derivative of the Black-Scholes formula for the value of a European call with respect to the exercise price is less commonly used than the delta. We'll denote this "exercise price delta" by $\chi_{c,t}$:

$$\chi_{c,t} \equiv \frac{\partial}{\partial X} v(S_t, \tau, X, \sigma, r, q) = -e^{-r\tau} \Phi \left[\frac{\log\left(\frac{S_t}{X}\right) + \left(r - q - \frac{\sigma^2}{2}\right)\tau}{\sigma\sqrt{\tau}} \right]$$

Multiplying the value at which the normal CDF is evaluated by -1, we have

$$e^{r\tau} \chi_{c,t} = - \left\{ 1 - \Phi \left[\frac{\log\left(\frac{X}{S_t}\right) - \left(r - q - \frac{\sigma^2}{2}\right)\tau}{\sigma\sqrt{\tau}} \right] \right\}$$

We showed in Chapter 10 that $\chi_{c,t}$ is related to the risk-neutral CDF by

$$\tilde{\Pi}(X) = 1 + e^{r\tau} \chi_{c,t}$$

Now we can see that in the specific case of the Black-Scholes model, the risk-neutral distribution of $S_{t+\tau}$ is lognormal, and that $\log\left(\frac{S_{t+\tau}}{S_t}\right)$ is a normally distributed random variable with CDF

$$\tilde{\Pi}(X) = \Phi \left[\frac{\log\left(\frac{X}{S_t}\right) - \left(r - q - \frac{\sigma^2}{2}\right)\tau}{\sigma\sqrt{\tau}} \right]$$

Example A.1 Let's take the dollar-euro exchange rate as an example. Suppose the current spot rate is 1.25 per euro, that the dollar and euro one-year funding rates are both 1 percent, and that the one-year implied volatility

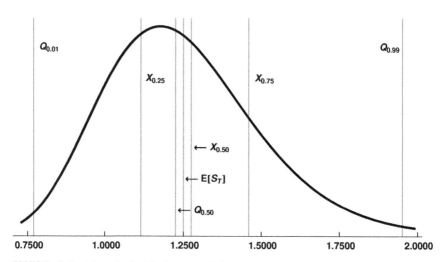

FIGURE A.2 The Black-Scholes Probability Density Function
The market-based parameters are as given in Example A.1. The grid lines are

$Q_{0.01}$	0.01 quantile of $S_{t+\tau}$	0.769414
$X_{0.25}$	Exercise price of 25-δ call	1.45942
$Q_{0.50}$	Median or 0.50 quantile of $S_{t+\tau}$	1.22525
$\tilde{E}[S_{t+\tau}]$	Expected value of $S_{t+\tau}$	1.25
$X_{0.50}$	Exercise price of 50-δ call, or expected value of $S_{t+\tau}$ conditional on exceeding 0.50 quantile	1.27525
$X_{0.75}$	Exercise price of 75-δ call	1.11432
$Q_{0.99}$	0.99 quantile of $S_{t+\tau}$	1.95114

is 20 percent. What is the risk-neutral distribution of the exchange rate in one year?

The one-year forward rate and the risk-neutral mean are both 1.25. The quantiles of the distribution are

Probability	Quantile
0.001	0.6604
0.01	0.7694
0.5	1.2253
0.99	1.9511
0.999	2.2732

Figure A.2 plots the exchange rate distribution in one year. Note that the median is below the mean. This is typical for continuous unimodal ("one-humped") probability distributions. We've assumed a lognormal distribution, which is skewed to the right, so the mean is to the right of the median.

A.4 HYPOTHESIS TESTING

In the standard approach to statistical hypothesis testing, we start with a statement about the parameters of a statistical distribution, called the *null hypothesis*, denoted $\mathfrak{H}_0$. The null hypothesis is then tested against the *alternative hypothesis*, which can be the statement that the null hypothesis is not true, or a more specific hypothesis. The null or the alternative hypothesis is called a *simple* or *point hypothesis* if it states that the parameter is equal to a particular value.

For example, we might stipulate that the physical heights of a human population are normally distributed with a standard deviation of 5 inches, and formulate the simple null hypothesis that the mean height is 72 inches. The next step is then to devise a test procedure for determining whether we will accept the null hypothesis. Typically, using a sample of data from the population, we can calculate a *test statistic*. The test procedure is framed so that, if the null hypothesis is true, we can determine the probability distribution of the test statistic. Given the distribution of the test statistic, we can determine the probability with which the test statistic takes on any particular value. If the sample leads to a value of the test statistic that is highly unlikely, we will be inclined to reject the null hypothesis.

Continuing our physical height example, we can calculate a sample mean $N^{-1} \sum_{n=1}^{N} h_n$ by measuring the heights h_n of N randomly chosen individuals. Since we have stipulated that the population's distributional family is normal and its standard deviation is $\sigma = 5$ inches, the test statistic

$$\frac{\sqrt{N} N^{-1} \sum_{n=1}^{N} (h_n - \mu)}{\sigma}$$

where μ is the hypothesized population mean, is a standard normal variate. Note that the distributional family and standard deviation are *maintained hypotheses*, which we are *not* testing. The maintained hypotheses drive the probability distribution of the test statistic, while the data drive the value it takes on in our particular case. The z-test, which uses a standard normal as a test statistic, is appropriate here; if we used the sample rather than population standard deviation, and had a relatively small sample, we would prefer to use a *t*-test. The null hypothesis is

$$\mathfrak{H}_0 : \mu = 72$$

We'll test the null against the alternative hypothesis that the mean is

$$\mathfrak{H}_1 : \mu \neq 72$$

Suppose our sample consists of $N = 10$ individuals, with a sample mean of 70 inches. The value of the test statistic is then

$$\frac{\sqrt{10}(70 - 72)}{5} = -1.265$$

To complete the test procedure, we need to establish criteria for accepting or rejecting the null hypothesis. This is not a matter of mathematics or science, but rather of the relative penalty we want to place on two types of error, mistakenly accepting the null even though it is false, or mistakenly rejecting the null even though it is true, known respectively as *Type I* and *Type II errors*. There is an unavoidable trade-off: If we reduce the probability of a Type I error, we increase the probability of a Type II error, and vice versa.

The test criteria can be expressed by dividing the range of possible values of the test statistic we are testing into two regions. If the test statistic falls in the *critical region*, we reject the null hypothesis, and if the test statistic falls in the *acceptance region*, we do not reject the null hypothesis. In our example, we are carrying out a *two-sided test*, since the alternative hypothesis is an inequality. At a conventional significance level of, say, 5 percent, we would reject the null is the test statistic fell outside the range $(-1.96, +1.96)$. Our test statistic value of -1.265 is comfortably within the range, so we do not reject the null.

A.5   MONTE CARLO SIMULATION

Once we have a probability distribution, we could in principle use it to describe random outcomes algebraically. This is not, however, the way it is actually done in practice. More often than not, quantitative results are derived by simulation.

Why? Often, the random variables involved, say, asset returns or default times, are complicated functions of the underlying random drivers that we are confident we can model. The algebra needed to describe the distribution we are interested in may be too complicated.

Simulation is in a way a brute-force approach that cuts through the algebra and goes straight from what we think we know about the underlying drivers to the distribution of the random outcomes. It is often easier or more accurate. In this appendix, we outline the basics of how this is done. In Chapters 3 through 6, 8, and 9, we apply simulation to concrete market and credit risk measurement problems.

Monte Carlo simulation is one approach to estimating distributions. It comprises three stages:

1. We *generate random variates* according to the distributional hypotheses that we believe govern the terminal value of the portfolio.
2. The *model* transforms the raw random data in some way. In market risk applications, we may have a pricing model. In credit risk applications, we may have a model that values the outcomes of credit events.
3. The *results* of the simulation are a set of Monte Carlo *realizations* (also called *replications* or *threads*). The realizations have a distribution that can be described by its sample statistics, such as mean and variance. In risk measurement, we are usually interested in low quantiles such as the first percentile or the 0.01 quantile.

A.5.1 Fooled by Nonrandomness: Random Variable Generation

The first step in generating random variates is to generate uniformly distributed random numbers, that is, equiprobable real numbers on [0, 1]. In a later step, we transform these into random variates that follow other distributions.

There are two ways to generate uniform randoms. The first is to use a physical process, such as radioactive decay or flipping a coin. It is unusual to use physical techniques, because we often need many random numbers and it is both expensive and time-consuming to accurately generate and record physically generated ones.

The second, more typical, approach is to use *pseudo random numbers*. As the name indicates, pseudo random numbers are not truly random, the way the results of physical random processes can be. Rather, they are deterministic, since they are generated by algorithms. The main advantage of pseudo random numbers is that, since computing power is now so cheap, they are cheap to produce.

An example of a pseudo random number generator is

$$I_{j+1} = \frac{1}{2^{31} - 1} [7^5 I_j \mod (2^{31} - 1)]$$

where $x \mod (y)$ denotes the remainder obtained on dividing x by y. For example, $3 \mod (3) = 0$ and $4 \mod (3) = 1$. This type of pseudo random number generator is called a *linear congruential generator*.

The initial value I_0 is provided by the user (or automatically by the computer or the high-level application, for example, by setting it equal to the computer's internal clock time) and is called the *random seed*. Because the pseudo random number generator is deterministic, for a given seed, a sequence of N random numbers will always be identical. This is another advantage of pseudo random numbers: The results can always be replicated exactly, realization by realization, by reusing the seed.

Pseudo random number generators can be evaluated by testing their outputs for whether they are close to truly random: for example, to see if there is repetition or if the realizations are serially correlated.

A.5.2 Generating Nonuniform Random Variates

Once we have a set of uniform random numbers, we turn them into random numbers drawn from the distribution we are really interested in. The inversion or transformation principle cited above tells us that the range of a distribution function follows a uniform distribution. Therefore, if we have a uniform distribution value, we can transform it into the value of another distribution by finding its quantile, that is, the value for which that other distribution has a probability equal to the uniform distribution value. In this way, once we have generated a set of uniform-[0, 1] variates, we can use the results to generate a random sample from any other distribution.

Figure A.3 illustrates this approach for the standard normal distribution. It plots the quantile function $z = \Phi^{-1}(u)$, which maps real numbers on [0, 1] to a real number on $(-\infty, \infty)$ such that $u = \Phi(z)$. The graph also displays 200 pseudo random uniform-[0, 1] variates. As the number of simulations grows, the simulations trace out the target, normal, distribution as precisely as desired.

A.6 HOMOGENEOUS FUNCTIONS

A function $f(x_1, \ldots, x_n N)$ is *homogeneous of degree p* if $\forall t \geq 0$,

$$f(tx_1, \ldots, tx_N) = t^p f(x_1, \ldots, x_N) \tag{A.1}$$

The partial derivatives of functions homogeneous of degree p are homogeneous of degree $p - 1$:

$$\frac{\partial f(x_1, \ldots, x_N)}{\partial x_n} = t^{p-1} \frac{\partial f(x_1, \ldots, x_N)}{\partial x_n}, \qquad n = 1, \ldots, N$$

To see this, differentiate (A.1) w.r.t. any of the x_n:

$$\frac{\partial f(tx_1, \ldots, tx_N)}{\partial x_n} = t \frac{\partial f(tx_1, \ldots, tx_N)}{\partial x_n} = t^p \frac{\partial f(x_1, \ldots, x_N)}{\partial x_n} \qquad n = 1, \ldots, N$$

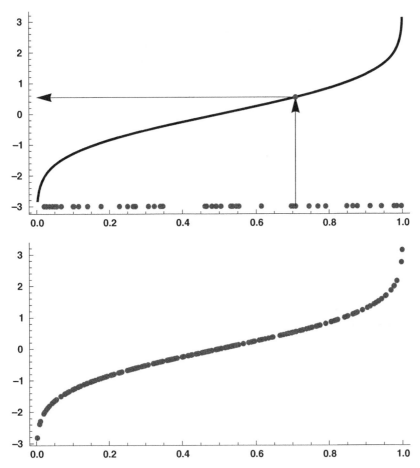

FIGURE A.3 Transforming Uniform into Normal Variates
The plot in the upper panel represents the inverse standard normal distribution. The points represent 50 simulated values of the uniform distribution. The lower panel plots the results of generating 200 standard normal variates. Each point has coordinates u_i, $\Phi^{-1}(u_i)$, $i = i, \ldots, 200$.

The first equality differentiates the left-hand side of Equation (A.1) using the chain rule, while the expression following the second equality is the derivative of the right-hand side. Dividing both sides by t gives the result.

Homogeneous functions of degree p have the *Euler property*:

$$\sum_{n=1}^{N} x_n \frac{\partial f(x_1, \ldots, x_N)}{\partial x_n} = p f(x_1, \ldots, x_N)$$

For example, the weighted sum of the partial first derivatives of a linearly homogeneous function, with the weights set equal to the value of the function's arguments, is equal to the value of the function itself.

To prove this, differentiate (A.1) w.r.t. t. Using the chain rule to differentiate w.r.t. the tx_n, we have

$$\frac{\partial f(tx_1, \ldots, tx_N)}{\partial t} = \frac{\partial f(tx_1, \ldots, tx_N)}{\partial tx_n} \frac{\partial (tx_n)}{\partial t} = x_n \frac{\partial f(tx_1, \ldots, tx_N)}{\partial x_n}$$

$$n = 1, \ldots, N$$

Therefore, differentiating both sides of (A.1) w.r.t. t gives

$$\sum_{n=1}^{N} x_n \frac{\partial f(tx_1, \ldots, tx_N)}{\partial x_n} = pt^{p-1} f(x_1, \ldots, x_N)$$

Since this is true for all t, it is also true for $t = 1$, giving the result.

FURTHER READING

Most of the material in this Appendix is reviewed in intermediate textbooks on probability and statistics. Pfeiffer (1990) and Wasserman (2004) stand out for clarity of presentation. The lognormal distribution is covered in option textbooks such as Hull (2000). The explication in Jarrow and Rudd (1983) is particularly lucid. Numerical techniques and simulation are covered in Stoer and Bulirsch (1993).

Abbreviations

ABCP	Asset-backed commercial paper
ABS	Asset-backed securities
ALM	Asset-liability management
AMLF	Asset-Backed Commercial Paper Money Market Mutual Fund Liquidity Facility
APT	Arbitrage pricing theory
ARM	Adjustable rate mortgage
ATM	At-the-money
ATMF	At-the-money forward
BBA	British Bankers' Association
BHC	Bank holding company
BIS	Bank for International Settlements
BISTRO	Broad Index Secured Trust Offering
bps	basis points
CAPM	Capital asset pricing model
CD	Certificate of deposit
CDF	Cumulative probability distribution function
CDO	Collateralized debt obligation
CDS	Credit default swap
CEBS	Committee of European Banking Supervisors
CFPB	Consumer Financial Protection Bureau
CFTC	Commodities Futures Trading Commission
CLO	Collateralized loan obligation
CMBS	Commercial mortgage-backed security
CME	Chicago Mercantile Exchange
CPFF	Commercial Paper Funding Facility
CVA	Counterparty valuation adjustment
CVaR	Conditional value-at-risk
EL	Expected Loss
EMS	European monetary system

ERM	Exchange Rate Mechanism
ES	Expected shortfall (conditional value-at-risk)
ETF	Exchange-traded fund
EVT	Extreme value theory
EWMA	Exponentially weighted moving average
FDIC	Federal Deposit Insurance Corporation
FHC	Financial holding company
FMV	Fair market value
FRN	Floating-rate note
FSA	Financial Services Authority
FSOC	Financial Stability Oversight Council
GDP	Gross domestic product
GNMA	Government National Mortgage Association
GSE	Government-sponsored enterprise
IRR	Internal rate of return
LBO	Leveraged buyout
LGD	Loss given default
Libor	London Interbank Offered Rate
MBS	Mortgage-backed security
MMMF	Money market mutual fund
MTM	Mark-to-market
MTN	Medium-term note
NASD	National Association of Securities Dealers
NAV	Net asset value
NBER	National Bureau of Economic Research
NPV	Net present value
NRSRO	Nationally Recognized Statistical Rating Organization
OCC	Office of the Comptroller of the Currency
OIS	Overnight interest rate swaps
OLA	Orderly Liquidation Authority
OTC	Over-the-counter
PDCF	Primary Dealer Credit Facility
PDF	Probability density function
PIK	Payment-in-kind (bond)
P&L	Profit and loss
RMBS	Residential mortgage-backed security
RMS	Root mean square
S&L	Savings and loan association
SEC	Securities and Exchange Commission
SRO	Self-regulatory organization
SDE	Stochastic differential equation
SDF	Stochastic discount factor

SIFI	Systemically Important Financial Institution
SIV	Structured investment vehicle
SPE	Special-purpose entity
SPV	Special-purpose vehicle
SRO	Self-regulatory organization
SWF	Sovereign wealth fund
TALF	Term Asset-Backed Securities Lending Facility
TCE	Tangible common equity
TRS	Total return swap
VaR	Value-at-Risk
WAL	Weighted average life

APPENDIX C

References

Acerbi, C. and Finger, C. C. (2010). The value of liquidity: can it be measured? RiskMetrics Group, Working paper, RiskMetrics Group. http://www.rbcdexia.com/documents/en/Misc/The%20value%20of%20liquidity.pdf.

Acerbi, C. and Tasche, D. (2002). On the coherence of expected shortfall, *Journal of Banking and Finance* **26**(7), 1487–1503.

Acharya, V. V., Cooley, T. F., Richardson, M. and Walter, I. (2009). Manufacturing tail risk: a perspective on the financial crisis of 2007–09, *Foundations and Trends in Finance* **4**(4), 247–325.

Acharya, V. V., Cooley, T. F., Richardson, M. P., and Walter, I. (2010). Measuring systemic risk, in *Regulating Wall Street: the Dodd-Frank Act and the new architecture of global finance*, Hoboken, NJ: John Wiley & Sons.

Acharya, V. V., Gale, D. and Yorulmazer, T. (2009). Rollover risk and market freezes, New York University, Stern School of Business, Finance Working Paper FIN-08-030.

Acharya, V. V. and Richardson, M. (2009). Causes of the financial crisis, *Critical Review* **21**(2–3), 195–210.

Acharya, V. V., Santos, J. A. C. and Yorulmazer, T. (2010). Systemic risk and deposit insurance premiums, Federal Reserve Bank of New York, *Economic Policy Review* **16**(1), 89–99.

Acharya, V. V. and Schnabl, P. (2010). Do global banks spread global imbalances? Asset-backed commercial paper during the financial crisis of 2007–09, *IMF Economic Review* **58**(1), 37–73.

Admati, A. R., DeMarzo, P. M., Hellwig, M. F. and Pfleiderer, P. (2010). Fallacies, irrelevant facts, and myths in the discussion of capital regulation: why bank equity is not expensive, Rock Center for Corporate Governance at Stanford University Working Paper 86. http://papers.ssrn.com/sol3/papers.cfm?abstract_id=1669704.

Adrian, T., Kimbrough, K. and Marchioni, D. (2010). The Federal Reserve's Commercial Paper Funding Facility, Federal Reserve Bank of New York, Staff Report 423.

Adrian, T. and Shin, H. S. (2009a). Money, liquidity, and monetary policy, *American Economic Review* **99**(2), 600–605.

Adrian, T. and Shin, H. S. (2009b). The shadow banking system: implications for financial regulation, Banque de France, *Financial Stability Review* 13, 1–10.

Adrian, T. and Shin, H. S. (2010). Financial intermediaries and monetary economics, in Friedman, B. M. and Woodford, M., eds., *Handbook of Monetary Economics* 3, Amsterdam: Elsevier B.V., 601–650.

Agarwal, V. and Naik, N. (2005). Hedge funds, *Foundations and Trends in Finance* 1(2), 103–169.

Aharony, J. and Swary, I. (1983). Contagion effects of bank failures: evidence from capital markets, *Journal of Business* 56(3), 305–322.

Aït-Sahalia, Y. and Lo, A. W. (2000). Nonparametric risk management and implied risk aversion, *Journal of Econometrics* 94(1-2), 9–51.

Akerlof, G. A. (1970). The market for "lemons": quality uncertainty and the market mechanism, *Quarterly Journal of Economics* 84(3), 488–500.

Akerlof, G. A. and Romer, P. M. (1993). Looting: the economic underworld of bankruptcy for profit, *Brookings Papers on Economic Activity* (2), 1–73.

Akgiray, V. and Booth, G. G. (1988). Mixed diffusion-jump process modeling of exchange rate movements, *Review of Economics and Statistics* 70(2), 631–637.

Alessandri, P. and Haldane, A. G. (2009). Banking on the state, based on a presentation delivered at the Federal Reserve Bank of Chicago Twelfth Annual International Banking Conference, Sep. http://www.bis.org/review/r091111e.pdf.

Alfaro, R. and Drehmann, M. (2009). Macro stress tests and crises: what can we learn?, *BIS Quarterly Review*, Dec., 29–41.

Allen, F. and Gale, D. (2000). Bubbles and crises, *Economic Journal* 110(460), 236–255.

Allen, F. and Santomero, A. M. (1997). The theory of financial intermediation, *Journal of Banking and Finance* 21(11-12), 1461–1485.

Allen, F. and Santomero, A. M. (2001). What do financial intermediaries do?, *Journal of Banking and Finance* 25(2), 271–444.

Allen, L. and Saunders, A. (2004). Incorporating systemic influences into risk measurements: a survey of the literature, *Journal of Financial Services Research* 26(2), 161–191.

Allen, S. (2003). *Financial risk management: a practitioner's guide to managing market and credit risk*, Hoboken, NJ: John Wiley & Sons.

Almgren, R. and Chriss, N. (2000/2001). Optimal execution of portfolio transactions, *Journal of Risk* 3(2), 5–39.

Altman, E. I. (1968). Financial ratios, discriminant analysis and the prediction of corporate bankruptcy, *Journal of Finance* 23(4), 589–609.

Altman, E. I. and Kishore, V. M. (1996). Almost everything you wanted to know about recoveries on defaulted bonds, *Financial Analysts Journal*, Vol. 52(6), 57–64.

Amato, J. and Gyntelberg, J. (2005). CDS index tranches and the pricing of credit risk correlations, *BIS Quarterly Review*, Mar., 73–87.

Amato, J. and Remolona, E. M. (2005). The pricing of unexpected credit losses, Bank for International Settlements, Working Paper 190.

Amihud, Y. and Mendelson, H. (1986). Asset pricing and the bid-ask spread, *Journal of Financial Economics* 17(2), 223–249.

Amihud, Y., Mendelson, H. and Pedersen, L. H. (2005). Liquidity and asset prices, *Foundations and Trends in Finance* 1(4), 269–364.

Amin, K. I. and Ng, V. (1997). Inferring future volatility from the information in implied volatility in Eurodollar options: a new approach, *Review of Financial Studies* 10(2), 333–367.

Andersen, T. G., Bollerslev, T., Christoffersen, P. F. and Diebold, F. X. (2010). Volatility and correlation forecasting, in G. Elliott, C. Granger, and A. Timmermann, eds., *Handbook of Economic Forecasting* 1, Amsterdam: Elsevier, 777–878.

Anderson, R. G. and Gascon, C. S. (2009). The commercial paper market, the Fed, and the 2007–2009 financial crisis, Federal Reserve Bank of St. Louis *Review*, 91(6), 589–612.

Aragon, G. O. and Strahan, P. E. (2009). Hedge funds as liquidity providers: evidence from the Lehman bankruptcy, 1870–2008, National Bureau of Economic Research, NBER Working Paper 15336.

Arrow, K. J. (1963). Uncertainty and the welfare economics of medical care, *American Economic Review* 53(5), 941–973.

Arteta, C., Carey, M., Correa, R. and Kotter, J. (2010). Revenge of the steamroller: ABCP as a window on risk choices, Board of Governors of the Federal Reserve System. http://webuser.bus.umich.edu/jkotter/papers/revengesteamroller.pdf.

Artzner, P., Delbaen, F., Eber, J.-M. and Heath, D. (1999). Coherent measures of risk, *Mathematical Finance* 9(3), 203–228.

Ashcraft, A. B. (2006). Does the market discipline banks? New evidence from the regulatory capital mix, Federal Reserve Bank of New York, Staff Report 244.

Ashcraft, A. B. and Schuermann, T. (2008). Understanding the securitization of subprime mortgage credit, *Foundations and Trends in Finance* 2(3), 191–309.

Asness, C. S., Liew, J. M. and Krail, R. J. (2001). Alternative investments: do hedge funds hedge?, *Journal of Portfolio Management* 28(1), 6–19.

Ayotte, K. and Skeel, D. A. J. (2010). Bankruptcy or bailouts, *Journal of Corporation Law* 35(3), 469–498.

Bagehot, W. (1873). *Lombard Street: a description of the Money Market*, 3rd ed., Cambridge, UK: Henry S. King & Co. http://files.libertyfund.org/files/128/0184_Bk.pdf.

Bahra, B. (1996). Probability distributions of future asset prices implied by option prices, Bank of England, *Quarterly Bulletin* 36(3), 299–311.

Ball, C. A. and Torous, W. N. (1985). On jumps in common stock prices and their impact on call option pricing, *Journal of Finance* 40(1), 155–173.

Bangia, A., Diebold, F. X., Schuermann, T. and Stroughair, J. D. (1999). Modeling liquidity risk with implications for traditional market risk measurement and management, Wharton Financial Institutions Center, Working Paper 99-06. http://fic.wharton.upenn.edu/fic/papers/99/p9906.html.

Barberis, N. and Thaler, R. (2003). A survey of behavioral finance, in G. Constantinides, in M. Harris and R. Stulz, eds., *Handbook of the Economics of Finance*, 1B, Amsterdam: Elsevier, 1053–1128.

Basel Committee on Banking Supervision (1999). Credit risk modelling: current practices and applications, Bank for International Settlements, BCBS Publications 49. http://www.bis.org/publ/bcbs49.pdf.

Basel Committee on Banking Supervision (2000). Sound practices for managing liquidity in banking organisations, Bank for International Settlements, BCBS Publications 69. http://www.bis.org/publ/bcbs69.pdf.

Basel Committee on Banking Supervision (2006). Basel II: International convergence of capital measurement and capital standards: a revised framework – comprehensive version, Bank for International Settlements, BCBS Publications 128. http://www.bis.org/publ/bcbs128.pdf.

Basel Committee on Banking Supervision (2010a). Proposal to ensure the loss absorbency of regulatory capital at the point of non-viability, *consultative document*, Bank for International Settlements, BCBS Publications 174. http://www.bis.org/publ/bcbs174.pdf.

Basel Committee on Banking Supervision (2010b). Basel III: A global regulatory framework for more resilient banks and banking systems, Bank for International Settlements, BCBS Publications 189. http://www.bis.org/publ/bcbs189.pdf.

Basel Committee on Banking Supervision (2010c). Basel III: International framework for liquidity risk measurement, standards and monitoring, Bank for International Settlements, BCBS Publications 188. http://www.bis.org/publ/bcbs188.pdf.

Basel Committee on Banking Supervision (2011). Messages from the academic literature on risk measurement for the trading book. Bank for International Settlements, Working Paper 19. http://www.bis.org/publ/bcbs_wp19.pdf.

Baskin, J. B. and Miranti, P. J., Jr. (1997). *A history of corporate finance*, Cambridge, UK and New York: Cambridge University Press.

Bates, D. S. (1991). The Crash of '87: was it expected? The evidence from options markets, *Journal of Finance* 46(3), 1009–1044.

Bates, D. S. (1996). Dollar jump fears, 1984-1992: distributional abnormalities implicit in currency futures options, *Journal of International Money and Finance* 15(1), 65–93.

Bates, D. S. (2000). Post-'87 crash fears in the S&P 500 futures option market, *Journal of Econometrics* 94(1/2), 181–238.

Baxter, M. and Rennie, A. (1996). *Financial calculus: an introduction to derivative pricing*, Cambridge, UK: Cambridge University Press.

Beder, T. S. (1995). VAR: seductive but dangerous, *Financial Analysts Journal* 51(5), 12–24.

Belsham, T., Vause, N. and Wells, S. (2005). Credit correlation: interpretation and risks, *Financial Stability Review* (19), 103–115.

Benmelech, E. and Dlugosz, J. (2009). The alchemy of CDO credit ratings, *Journal of Monetary Economics* 56(5), 617–634.

Bennett, P., Keane, F. and Mosser, P. C. (1999). Mortgage refinancing and the concentration of mortgage coupons, Federal Reserve Bank of New York, *Current Issues in Economics and Finance* 5(4).

Benston, G. J. (1993). Market discipline: the role of uninsured depositors and other market participants, in Randall, R. E., ed., *Safeguarding the banking system in an environment of financial cycles*, Federal Reserve Bank of Boston, Research Conference Series. http://www.bos.frb.org/economic/conf/conf37/conf37c.pdf.

Benston, G. J. and Kaufman, G. G. (1997). FDICIA after five years, *Journal of Economic Perspectives* **11**(3), 139–158.

Berd, A. M., Mashal, R. and Wang, P. (2003). Estimating implied default probabilities from credit bond prices, Lehman Brothers, *Quantitative Credit Research Quarterly*, (Q3), 45–53.

Berg, A. and Patillo, C. (1999). Are currency crises predictable? A test, *IMF Staff Papers* **46**(2), 107–138.

Berger, A. N., Herring, R. J., Szegö, G. P. (1995). The role of capital in financial institutions, *Journal of Banking and Finance* **19**(3-4), 393–430.

Berkowitz, J. (2001). Testing density forecasts, with applications to risk management, *Journal of Business and Economic Statistics* **19**(4), 465–474.

Berkowitz, J. and O'Brien, J. (2002). How accurate are value-at-risk models at commercial banks?, *Journal of Finance* **57**(3), 1093–1111.

Bernanke, B. S. (1983). Nonmonetary effects of the financial crisis in propagation of the Great Depression, *American Economic Review* **73**(3), 257–276.

Bernanke, B. S. (1990). Clearing and settlement during the crash, *Review of Financial Studies* **3**(1), 133–151.

Bernanke, B. S. (2011). International capital flows and the returns to safe assets in the United States 2003–2007, Banque de France, *Financial Stability Review* **15**, 13–26.

Bernanke, B. S. and Gertler, M. (1995). Inside the black box: the credit channel of monetary policy transmission, *Journal of Economic Perspectives* **9**(4), 27–48.

Bernanke, B. S. and Gertler, M. (2001). Should central banks respond to movements in asset prices? *American Economic Review* **91**(2), 253–257.

Bernanke, B. S. and Lown, C. S. (1991). The credit crunch, *Brookings Papers on Economic Activity* (2), 205–247.

Bernstein, P. L. (1996). *Against the gods: the remarkable story of risk*, New York: John Wiley & Sons.

Black, F. (1986). Noise, *Journal of Finance* **41**(3), 529–543.

Black, F. (1993). Estimating expected return, *Financial Analysts Journal* **49**(5), 36–38.

Black, F., Miller, M. H., and Posner, R. A. (1978). An approach to the regulation of bank holding companies, *Journal of Business* **51**(3), 379–412.

Blanchard, O. J. (1979). Speculative bubbles, crashes and rational expectations, *Economics Letters*, **3**(4), 387–389.

Blanchard, O. J. and Watson, M. W. (1982). Bubbles, rational expectations, and financial markets, in P. Wachtel, ed., *Crisis in the economic and financial structure*, Lexington, MA: Lexington Books, 295–315.

Bliss, R. R. (2003). Bankruptcy law and large complex financial organizations: a primer, Federal Reserve Bank of Chicago, *Economic Perspectives* **27**(1), 48–58.

Bliss, R. R. and Kaufman, G. G. (2003). Bank procyclicality, credit crunches, and asymmetric monetary policy effects: a unifying model, *Journal of Applied Finance* **13**(2), 23–31.

Bliss, R. R. and Kaufman, G. (2006). A comparison of U.S. corporate and bank insolvency resolution, Federal Reserve Bank of Chicago, *Economic Perspectives* **30**(2), 44–55.

Bliss, R. R. and Panigirtzoglou, N. (2002). Testing the stability of implied probability density functions, *Journal of Banking and Finance* 26(2–3), 381–422.

Bliss, R. R. and Panigirtzoglou, N. (2004). Option-implied risk aversion estimates, *Journal of Finance* 59(1), 407–446.

Blume, M. (2002). The structure of the U.S. equity markets, *Brookings-Wharton Papers on Financial Services*, 35–59.

Blundell-Wignall, A. and Atkinson, P. (2010). Thinking beyond Basel III: Necessary solutions for capital and liquidity, *OECD Journal: Financial Market Trends* 1, 9–33.

Board of Governors of the Federal Reserve System (2000). *Feasibility and desirability of mandatory subordinated debt*, Report to the Congress. http://www.federalreserve.gov/boarddocs/rptcongress/debt/subord_debt_2000.pdf.

Bogle, J. C. (2008). Black Monday and black swans, *Financial Analysts Journal* 64(2).

Bordo, M. D. (1990). The lender of last resort: alternative views and historical experience, Federal Reserve Bank of Richmond, *Economic Review* 76(1), 18–29.

Bordo, M. D. (2000). Sound money and sound financial policy, *Journal of Financial Services Research* 18(2–3), 129–155.

Bordo, M., Eichengreen, B., Klingebiel, D. and Martinez-Peria, M. S. (2001). Is the crisis problem growing more severe?, *Economic Policy* 16(32), 53–82.

Bordo, M. D. and Haubrich, J. G. (2010). Credit crises, money and contractions: an historical view, *Journal of Monetary Economics* 57(1), 1–18.

Borio, C. and Drehmann, M. (2009). Towards an operational framework for financial stability: "fuzzy" measurement and its consequences, Bank for International Settlements, Working Paper 284. http://www.bis.org/publ/work284.pdf.

Borio, C., Kennedy, N. and Prowse, S. (1994). Exploring aggregate asset price fluctuations across countries: measurement, determinants and monetary policy implications, Bank for International Settlements, Economic Paper 40.

Borio, C. and Nelson, W. (2008). Monetary operations and the financial turmoil, *BIS Quarterly Review*, Mar., 31–46.

Borio, C. and White, W. R. (2003). Whither monetary and financial stability: the implications of evolving policy regimes, in *Monetary policy and uncertainty: adapting to a changing economy*, Jackson Hole Symposium, Federal Reserve Bank of Kansas City, 131–211. http://www.kc.frb.org/publicat/sympos/2003/pdf/Boriowhite2003.pdf.

Borio, C. and Zhu, H. (2008). Capital regulation, risk-taking and monetary policy: a missing link in the transmission mechanism?, Bank for International Settlements, Working Paper 268. http://www.bis.org/publ/work268.pdf.

Boudoukh, J., Richardson, M. P. and Whitelaw, R. (1997). The best of both worlds: a hybrid approach to calculating value at risk. http://papers.ssrn.com/sol3/papers.cfm?abstract_id=51420.

Boyer, B. H., Gibson, M. S. and Loretan, M. (1997). Pitfalls in tests for changes in correlations, Board of Governors of the Federal Reserve System, International Finance Discussion Paper 597. http://www.federalreserve.gov/pubs/ifdp/1997/597/ifdp597.pdf.

Brailsford, T. J. and Faff, R. W. (1996). An evaluation of volatility forecasting techniques, *Journal of Banking and Finance* 20(3), 419–438.

Breeden, D. T. and Litzenberger, R. H. (1978). Prices of state-contingent claims implicit in option prices, *Journal of Business* 51(4), 621–651.

Bresciani-Turroni, C. (1937). *The economics of inflation: a study of currency depreciation in post-war Germany*, London: George Allen and Unwin.

Breuer, P. (2002). Measuring off-balance-sheet leverage, *Journal of Banking and Finance* 26(2-3), 223–242.

Breuer, T., Jandačka, M., Rheinberger, K. and Summer, M. (2009). How to find plausible, severe, and useful stress scenarios, *International Journal of Central Banking* 5(3), 205–223.

Britten-Jones, M. and Schaefer, S. M. (1999). Non-linear value-at-risk, *European Finance Review* 2(2), 161–187.

Brooks, C. and Persand, G. (2003). Volatility forecasting for risk management, *Journal of Forecasting* 22(2), 1–22.

Brown, B. (1987). *Flight of international capital: a contemporary history*, Croom Helm, London, New York.

Brown, S. J. and Goetzmann, W. N. (2003). Hedge funds with style, *Journal of Portfolio Management* 29(2), 101–112.

Brunnermeier, M. K. (2008). Bubbles, in S. N. Durlauf and L. E. Blume, eds. *The New Palgrave Dictionary of Economics*, 2nd ed., Basingstoke: Palgrave Macmillan.

Brunnermeier, M. K. (2009). Deciphering the liquidity and credit crunch 2007–2008, *Journal of Economic Perspectives* 23(1), 77–100.

Brunnermeier, M. K., Crockett, A., Goodhart, C. A., Persaud, A. and Shin, H. S. (2009). The fundamental principles of financial regulation, Centre for Economic PolicyResearch, Technical Report 49. http://www.bis.org/publ/bcbs49.pdf.

Brunnermeier, M. K., Nagel, S. and Pedersen, L. H. (2009). Carry trades and currency crashes, *NBER Macroeconomics Annual* 22(6), 313–347.

Brunnermeier, M. K. and Pedersen, L. H. (2009). Market liquidity and funding liquidity, *Review of Financial Studies* 22(6), 2201–2238.

Buiter, W. H. and Sibert, A. C. (2007). The central bank as market maker of last resort 1, Maverecon, August 12, http://blogs.ft.com/maverecon/2007/08/the-central-banhtml/.

Buiter, W. H. (2007). The central bank as market maker of last resort 2, Maverecon, August 12, http://blogs.ft.com/maverecon/2007/08/central-banks-ahtml/.

Burghardt, G. D. and Belton, T. (2005). *The Treasury bond basis: an in-depth analysis for hedgers, speculators, and arbitrageurs*, 3rd ed., New York: McGraw-Hill.

Bustelo, P. (2000). Novelties of financial crises in the 1990s and the search for new indicators, *Emerging Markets Review* 1(3), 229–251.

Butt, S., Shivdasani, A., Stendevad, C. and Wyman, A. (2008). Sovereign wealth funds: a growing global force in corporate finance, *Journal of Applied Corporate Finance* 20(1), 73–83.

Caballero, R. J. (2006). On the macroeconomics of asset shortages, National Bureau of Economic Research, NBER Working Paper 12753.

Caballero, R. J., Farhi, E. and Gourinchas, P.-O. (2008). Financial crash, commodity prices, and global imbalances, *Brookings Papers on Economic Activity* (2), 1–55.

Calomiris, C. W. (1994). Is the discount window necessary? A Penn Central perspective, Federal Reserve Bank of St. Louis, *Review* 76(3), 31–55.

Calomiris, C. W. (1999). Building an incentive-compatible safety net, *Journal of Banking and Finance* 23(10), 1499–1519.

Calomiris, C. W. (2004). Financial fragility: issues and policy implications, *Journal of Financial Services Research* 9(3–4), 241–257.

Calomiris, C. W. (2006). The regulatory record of the Greenspan Fed, *American Economic Review* 96(2), 170–173.

Calomiris, C. W. and Gorton, G. (1991). The origins of banking panics: models, facts, and bank regulation, in R. G. Hubbard, ed., *Financial markets and financial crises*, Chicago: University of Chicago Press, 109–173.

Calomiris, C. W. and Kahn, C. M. (1991). The role of demandable debt in structuring optimal banking arrangements, *American Economic Review* 81(3), 497–513.

Calomiris, C. W. and Mason, J. R. (2004). Credit card securitization and regulatory arbitrage, *Journal of Financial Services Research* 26(1), 5–27.

Camerer, C. (1989). Bubbles and fads in asset prices, *Journal of Economic Surveys* 3(1), 3–41.

Campa, J. M. and Chang, P. K. (1998). The forecasting ability of correlations implied in foreign exchange options, *Journal of International Money and Finance* 17(6), 855–880.

Campbell, J. Y. (2000). Asset pricing at the millennium, *Journal of Finance* 55(4), 1515–1567.

Canina, L. and Figlewski, S. (1993). The informational content of implied volatility, *Review of Financial Studies*, 6(3), 659–681.

Caprio, G., Demirgüç-Kunt, A. and Kane, E. J. (2010). The 2007 meltdown in structured securitization: Searching for lessons, not scapegoats, *World Bank Research Observer* 25(1), 125–155.

Cecchetti, S. G., Genberg, H. and Wadhwani, S. (2003). Asset prices in a flexible inflation targeting framework, in W. Hunter, G. Kaufman, and M. Pomerleano, eds., *Asset Price Bubbles*, Cambridge, MA: MIT Press.

Černý, A. (2004). *Mathematical techniques in finance: tools for incomplete markets*, Princeton, NJ: Princeton University Press.

Chance, D. M. and Jordan, J. V. (1996). Duration, convexity, and time as components of bond returns, *Journal of Fixed Income* 6(2), 88–96.

Chen, J., Hong, H. and Stein, J. C. (2001). Forecasting crashes: trading volume, past returns, and conditional skewness in stock prices, *Journal of Financial Economics* 61(3), 345–381.

Chordia, T., Roll, R. and Subrahmanyam, A. (2001). Market liquidity and trading activity, *Journal of Finance* 56(2), 501–530.

Christensen, B. and Prabhala, N. (1998). The relation between implied and realized volatility, *Journal of Financial Economics* 50(3), 125–150.

Christoffersen, P. F. and Diebold, F. X. (2000). How relevant is volatility forecasting for financial risk management?, *Review of Economics and Statistics* 82(1), 12–22.

Clarida, R., Davis, J. and Pedersen, N. (2009). Currency carry trade regimes: Beyond the Fama regression, *Journal of International Money and Finance* **28**(8), 1375–1389.

Clarida, R., Gali, J. and Gertler, M. (1999). The science of monetary policy: a New Keynesian perspective, *Journal of Economic Literature* **37**(4), 1661–1707.

Clarida, R., Gali, J. and Gertler, M. (2000). Monetary policy rules and macroeconomic stability: evidence and some theory, *Quarterly Journal of Economics* **115**(1), 147–80.

Clews, R., Panigirtzoglou, N. and Proudman, J. (2000). Recent developments in extracting information from options markets, Bank of England, *Quarterly Bulletin* **40**(1), 50–60.

Cochrane, J. H. (2005). *Asset pricing*, rev. ed., Princeton, NJ: Princeton University Press.

Collin-Dufresne, P. (2009). A short introduction to correlation markets, *Journal of Financial Econometrics* **7**(1), 12–29.

Commission of Experts (2010). Final report of the Commission of Experts for limiting the economic risks posed by large companies. http://www.sif.admin.ch/dokumentation/00514/00519/00592/index.html.

Committee of European Banking Supervisors (2010). Aggregate outcome of the 2010 EU wide stress test exercise coordinated by CEBS in cooperation with the ECB. http://stress-test.c-ebs.org/documents/Summaryreport.pdf.

Committee on the Global Financial System (1999a). A review of financial market events in Autumn 1998, Bank for International Settlements, CGFS Publications 12. http://www.bis.org/publ/cgfs12.pdf.

Committee on the Global Financial System (1999b). Market liquidity: research findings and selected policy implications, Bank for International Settlements, CGFS Publications 11. http://www.bis.org/publ/cgfs11.pdf.

Committee on the Global Financial System (2005). Stress testing at major financial institutions: survey results and practice, Bank for International Settlements, CGFS Publications 24. http://www.bis.org/publ/cgfs24.pdf.

Cont, R. (2001). Empirical properties of asset returns: stylized facts and statistical issues, *Quantitative Finance* **1**(2), 223–236.

Cont, R. and da Fonseca, J. (2002). Dynamics of implied volatility surfaces, *Quantitative Finance* **2**(1), 45–59.

Copeland, A., Martin, A. and Walker, M. (2010). The tri-party repo market before the 2010 reforms, Federal Reserve Bank of New York, Staff Report 477.

Coudert, V. and Gex, M. (2008). Does risk aversion drive financial crises? Testing the predictive power of empirical indicators, *Journal of Empirical Finance* **15**(2), 167–184.

Coudert, V. and Gex, M. (2010). Contagion inside the credit default swaps market: the case of the GM and Ford crisis in 2005, *Journal of International Financial Markets, Institutions and Money* **20**(2), 109–134.

Counterparty Risk Management Policy Group (2008). Containing systemic risk: the road to reform. http://www.crmpolicygroup.org/docs/CRMPG-III.pdf.

Coval, J., Jurek, J. and Stafford, E. (2009). The economics of structured finance, *Journal of Economic Perspectives* **23**(1), 3–25.

Covitz, D. M., Liang, N. and Suarez, G. A. (2009). The evolution of a financial crisis: panic in the asset-backed commercial paper market, Board of Governors of the Federal Reserve System, Finance and Economics Discussion Series 2009-36.

Cowen, T. and Kroszner, R. (1990). Mutual fund banking: A market approach, *Cato Journal* 10(1), 223–237.

Credit Suisse First Boston (2004). *Credit portfolio modeling handbook.*

Crouhy, M., Jarrow, R. A. and Turnbull, S. M. (2008). The subprime credit crisis of 2007, *Journal of Derivatives* 16(1), 81–110.

Crouhy, M., Mark, R. and Galai, D. (2000a). A comparative analysis of current credit risk models, *Journal of Banking and Finance* 24(1-2), 59–117.

Crouhy, M., Mark, R. and Galai, D. (2000b). *Risk management,* New York: McGraw–Hill.

Culp, C. L., Miller, M. H. and Neves, A. M. P. (1998). Value at risk: uses and abuses, *Journal of Applied Corporate Finance* 10(4), 26–38.

Daglish, T., Hull, J. and Suo, W. (2007). Volatility surfaces: theory, rules of thumb, and empirical evidence, *Quantitative Finance* 7(5), 507–524.

Daníelsson, J. (2002). The emperor has no clothes: limits to risk modelling, *Journal of Banking and Finance* 26(7), 1273–1296.

Daníelsson, J. (2008). Blame the models, *Journal of Financial Stability* 4(4), 321–328.

Daníelsson, J. (2010). The saga of Icesave, Centre for Economic Policy Research, Technical Report 44.

Daníelsson, J., Shin, H. S. and Zigrand, J.-P. (2004). The impact of risk regulation on price dynamics, *Journal of Banking and Finance* 28(5), 1069–1087.

Danthine, J.-P. and Donaldson, J. B. (2005). *Intermediate financial theory,* 2nd ed., Academic Press, Amsterdam.

Davis Polk and Wardwell LLP (2010). Summary of the Dodd-Frank Wall Street Reform and Consumer Protection Act, Enacted into Law on July 21, 2010. http://www.davispolk.com/files/Publication/7084f9fe-6580-413b-b870 -b7c025ed2ecf/Presentation/PublicationAttachment/1d4495c7-0be0-4e9a- ba77-f786fb90464a/070910_Financial_Reform_Summary.pdf.

D'Avolio, G. (2002). The market for borrowing stock, *Journal of Financial Economics* 66(2–3), 271–306.

De Bandt, O. and Hartmann, P. (2000). Systemic risk: a survey, European Central Bank, Working Paper 35. http://www.ecb.int/pub/pdf/scpwps/ecbwp035.pdf.

De Vries, C. G. (1994). Stylized facts of nominal exchange rate returns, in F. van der Ploeg, ed., *The handbook of international macroeconomics,* Oxford and Cambridge, MA: Blackwell Publishers.

Dell'Ariccia, G., Laeven, L. and Marquez, R. (2010). Monetary policy, leverage, and bank risk-taking, IMF Working Paper 276.

Demirgüç-Kunt, A., Kane, E. J. and Laeven, L. (2008). *Deposit insurance around the world,* Cambridge, MA: MIT Press.

Demirgüç-Kunt, A. and Servén, L. (2010). Are all the sacred cows dead? Implications of the financial crisis for macro- and financial policies, *World Bank Research Observer* 25(1), 91–124.

De Mooij, R. A. (2011). Tax biases to debt finance: assessing the problem, finding solutions, International Monetary Fund, Staff Discussion Note 2011/11.

Demsetz, H. (1968). The cost of transacting, *Quarterly Journal of Economics* 82(1), 33–53.

Demyanyk, Y. (2009). Quick exits of subprime mortgages, Federal Reserve Bank of St. Louis, *Review* 91(2), 79–94.

Demyanyk, Y. and Hemert, O. V. (2011). Understanding the subprime mortgage crisis, *Review of Financial Studies* 24(6), 1848–1880.

Derman, E. (1996). Model risk, Goldman Sachs and Co., Quantitative Strategies Research Notes. http://www.ederman.com/new/docs/gs-model_risk.pdf.

Derman, E. (1999). Regimes of volatility, Goldman Sachs and Co., Quantitative Strategies Research Notes. http://www.ederman.com/new/docs/risk-regimes_of_volatility.pdf.

Derman, E. (2009). Models, *Financial Analysts Journal* 65(1), 28–33.

Derman, E. and Kani, I. (1994). Riding on a smile, *Risk* 7(2), 32–39.

Desai, P. (2000). Why did the ruble collapse in August 1998?, *American Economic Review* 90(2), 48–52.

Diamond, D. W. (1984). Financial intermediation and delegated monitoring, *Review of Economic Studies* 51(3), 393–414.

Diamond, D. W. (1996). Financial intermediation as delegated monitoring: a simple example, Federal Reserve Bank of Richmond, *Economic Quarterly* 82(3), 51–66.

Diamond, D. W. (2007). Banks and liquidity creation: a simple exposition of the diamond-dybvig model, Federal Reserve Bank of Richmond, *Economic Quarterly* 93(2), 189–200.

Diamond, D. W. and Dybvig, P. H. (1983). Bank runs, deposit insurance, and liquidity, *Journal of Political Economy* 91(3), 401–419.

Diamond, D. W. and Rajan, R. G. (2010). Fear of fire sales and the credit freeze, Bank for International Settlements, Working Paper 305.

Diamond, D. W. and Rajan, R. G. (2011). Illiquid banks, financial stability, and interest rate policy, National Bureau of Economic Research, NBER Working Paper 16994, http://papers.ssrn.com/sol3/ papers.cfm?abstract id=1020396.

Diebold, F. X. and Li, C. (2006). Forecasting the term structure of government bond yields, *Journal of Econometrics* 130(2), 337–364.

Dixit, A. K. and Pindyck, R. S. (1994). *Investment under uncertainty*, Princeton, NJ: Princeton University Press.

Dooley, M. and Garber, P. (2005). Is it 1958 or 1968? Three notes on the longevity of the revived Bretton Woods system, *Brookings Papers on Economic Activity* (2), 147–187.

Dornbusch, R., Goldfajn, I., Valdés, R. O., Edwards, S. and Bruno, M. (1995). Currency crises and collapses, *Brookings Papers on Economic Activity* (2), 219–293.

Dowd, K. (1992). Models of banking instability: a partial review of the literature, *Journal of Economic Surveys* 6(2), 107–132.

Dowd, K. (2005). *Measuring market risk*, 2nd ed., Hoboken, NJ: John Wiley & Sons.

Drèze, J. H. (1970). Market allocation under uncertainty, *European Economic Review* 2(2), 133–165.

Duffie, D. (1996). *Dynamic asset pricing theory*, 2nd ed., Princeton, NJ: Princeton University Press.

Duffie, D. (1999). Credit swap valuation, *Financial Analysts Journal* 55(1), 73–87.

Duffie, D. (2010). The failure mechanics of dealer banks, *Journal of Economic Perspectives* 24(1), 51–72.

Duffie, D. and Gârleanu, N. (2001). Risk and valuation of collateralized debt obligations, *Financial Analysts Journal* 57(1), 41–59.

Duffie, D. and Pan, J. (1997). An overview of value at risk, *Journal of Derivatives* 4(3), 7–49.

Duffie, D. and Singleton, K. J. (1999). Modeling term structures of defaultable bonds, *Review of Financial Studies* 12(4), 7–49.

Duffie, D. and Singleton, K. J. (2003). *Credit risk: pricing, measurement, and management*, Princeton, NJ: Princeton University Press.

Duffie, D. and Ziegler, A. (2003). Liquidation risk, *Financial Analysts Journal* 59(3), 42–51.

Dumas, B., Fleming, J. and Whaley, R. E. (1997). Implied volatility functions: empirical tests, *Journal of Finance* 53(6), 2059–2106.

Dybvig, P. H. and Ross, S. A. (2003). Arbitrage, state prices and portfolio theory, in G. Constantinides, M. Harris and R. Stulz, eds., *Handbook of the Economics of Finance* 1(2), Amsterdam: Elsevier, 605–637.

Eichengreen, B. (2008). *Globalizing capital: a history of the international monetary system*, 2nd ed., Princeton, NJ: Princeton University Press.

Eichner, M. J., Kohn, D. L., and Palumbo, M. G. (2010). Financial statistics for the United States and the crisis: what did they get right, what did they miss, and how should they change?, Board of Governors of the Federal Reserve System, Finance and Economics Discussion Series 2010-20.

Einhorn, D. (2008). Private profits and socialized risks, speech at Grant's Spring Investment Conference, April 8. http://manualofideas.com/files/blog/einhornspeech200804.pdf.

Elton, E. J. and Gruber, M. J. (2003). *Modern portfolio theory and investment analysis*, 6th ed., New York: John Wiley & Sons.

Embrechts, P., Klüppelberg, C., and Mikosch, T. (1997). *Modelling extremal events for insurance and finance*, New York: Springer.

Engle, R. F. (2009). *Anticipating correlations: a new paradigm for risk management*, Princeton, NJ: Princeton University Press.

Engle, R. F. and Manganelli, S. (2001). Value at risk models in finance, European Central Bank, Working Paper 75. http://www.ecb.int/pub/pdf/scpwps/ecbwp075.pdf.

Engle, R. F. and Patton, A. J. (2001). What good is a volatility model?, *Quantitative Finance* 1(2), 237–245.

Estrella, A. and Mishkin, F. S. (1998). Predicting U.S. recessions: financial variables as leading indicators, *Review of Economics and Statistics* 80(1), 45–61.

Evans, M. D. (1996). Peso problems: their theoretical and empirical implications, in G. Maddala and C. Rao, eds. *Handbook of statistics*, 14, Amsterdam: Elsevier Science B.V., 613–646.

Fama, E. F. (1965). The behavior of stock-market prices, *Journal of Business* 38(1), 34–105.

Fama, E. F. and French, K. R. (1992). The cross-section of expected stock returns, *Journal of Financial Economics* 47(2), 427–465.

Fama, E. F. and French, K. R. (1993). Common risk factors in the returns on stocks and bonds, *Journal of Financial Economics* 33(1), 3–56.

Finger, C. C. (1999). Conditional approaches for CreditMetrics portfolio distributions, *CreditMetrics Monitor* pp. 14–33.

Finger, C. C. (2001). The one-factor CreditMetrics model in the New Basel Capital Accord, *RiskMetrics Journal* 2(1), 9–18.

Finger, C. C., ed. (2002). *CreditGrades Technical Document*, RiskMetrics Group.

Finger, C. C. (2005). Eating our own cooking, RiskMetrics Group *Research Monthly*, June.

Finger, C. C. (2008). Doomed to repeat it? RiskMetrics Group, *Research Monthly* Nov.

Fisher, I. (1933). The debt-deflation theory of great depressions, *Econometrica* 1(4), 337–357.

Flannery, M. J. (1999). Modernizing financial regulation: the relation between interbank transactions and supervisory reform, *Journal of Financial Services Research* 16(2–3), 101–116.

Fleming. J. (1998). The quality of market volatility forecasts implied by S&P 100 index option prices, *Journal of Empirical Finance* 5(4), 317–345.

Fleming, J., Kirby, C. and Ostdiek, B. (2001). The economic value of volatility timing, *Journal of Finance* 56(1), 329–352.

Fleming, M. J. and Garbade, K. D. (2002). When the back office moved to the front burner: settlement fails in the Treasury market after 9/11, Federal Reserve Bank of New York, *Economic Policy Review* 8(2), 35–57.

Fleming, M. J. and Garbade, K. D. (2004). Repurchase agreements with negative interest rates, Federal Reserve Bank of New York, *Current Issues in Economics and Finance* 10(5).

Fleming, M. J. and Garbade, K. D. (2005). Explaining settlement fails, Federal Reserve Bank of New York, *Current Issues in Economics and Finance* 11(5).

Frederiksen, D. M. (1894). Mortgage banking in Germany, *Quarterly Journal of Economics* 9(1), 47–76.

Frees, E. W. and Valdez, E. A. (1998). Understanding relationships using copulas, *North American Actuarial Journal* 2(1), 1–25.

Freixas, X., Giannini, C., Hoggarth, G. and Soussa, F. (1999). Lender of last resort: a review of the literature, Bank of England, *Financial Stability Review* (7), 151–167.

Freixas, X., Giannini, C., Hoggarth, G. and Soussa, F. (2000). Lender of last resort: what have we learned since Bagehot?, *Journal of Financial Services Research* 18(1), 63–84.

French, K. R., Baily, M. N., Campbell, J. Y., Cochrane, J. H., Diamond, D. W., Duffie, D., Kashyap, A. K., Mishkin, F. S., Rajan, R. G., Scharfstein, D. S., Shiller, R. J., Shin, H. S., Slaughter, M. J., Stein, J. C. and Stulz, R. M. (2010). *The Squam Lake report: fixing the financial system*, Princeton, NJ: Princeton University Press.

Friedman, B. M. and Kuttner, K. N. (1993). Why does the paper-bill spread predict real economic activity, in J. H. Stock and M. W. Watson, eds., *Business cycles, indicators, and forecasting*, Chicago: University of Chicago Press, 213–249.

Friedman, M. (1953). *Essays in positive economics*, Chicago: University of Chicago Press.

Froot, K. A. and Stein, J. C. (1998). Risk management, capital budgeting, and capital structure policy for financial institutions: an integrated approach, *Journal of Financial Economics* 47(1), 55–82.

Frye, J. (2000). Collateral damage, *Risk* 13(4), 91–94.

Frye, J. (2001). Weighting for risk, *Risk* 14(5), 91–94.

Fung, W. and Hsieh, D. A. (1997). Empirical characteristics of dynamic trading strategies: the case of hedge funds, *Review of Financial Studies* 10(2), 275–302.

Fung, W. and Hsieh, D. A. (1999). A primer on hedge funds, *Journal of Empirical Finance* 6(3), 309–331.

Fung, W. and Hsieh, D. A. (2001). The risk in hedge fund strategies: theory and evidence from trend followers, *Review of Financial Studies* 14(2), 313–341.

Furfine, C. (2003). Standing facilities and interbank borrowing: Evidence from the Federal Reserve's new discount window, *International Finance* 6(3), 329–347.

Gabaix, X. (2009). Power laws in economics and finance, *Review of Financial Studies* 1, 255–293.

Galati, G. and Moessner R. (2011). Macroprudential policy—a literature review, Bank for International Settlements, Working Paper 337, http://www.bis.org/publ/work337.pdf.

Gambacorta, L. (2008). Monetary policy and the risk-taking channel, *BIS Quarterly Review*, December, 43–53.

Garber, P. M. (1989). Tulipmania, *Journal of Political Economy* 97(3), 535–560.

Garber, P. M. (1990). Famous first bubbles, *Journal of Economic Perspectives* 4(2), 35–54.

Garber, P. M. and Svensson, L. E. (1995). The operation and collapse of fixed exchange rate regimes, in G. M. Grossman and K. Rogoff, eds., *Handbook of international economics*, 3, Amsterdam: Elsevier Science B.V., 1865–1911.

Gatheral, J. (2006). *The volatility surface: a practitioner's guide*, New York: John Wiley & Sons.

Geanakoplos, J. (2009). The leverage cycle, *NBER Macroeconomics Annual* 24, 1–65.

Geanakoplos, J. (2010). Solving the present crisis and managing the leverage cycle, Federal Reserve Bank of New York, *Economic Policy Review* 16(1), 101–131.

Gennotte, G. and Leland, H. (1990). Market liquidity, hedging, and crashes, *American Economic Review* 80(5), 999–1021.

Gerardi, K., Lehnert, A., Sherlund, S. M. and Willen, P. (2008). Making sense of the subprime crisis, *Brookings Papers on Economic Activity* 2, 69–159.

Gertler, M. (1988). Financial structure and aggregate economic activity: an overview, *Journal of Money, Credit, and Banking* 20(3), 559–588.

Gibson, M. S. (2004). Understanding the risk of synthetic CDOs, Board of Governors of the Federal Reserve System, Finance and Economics Discussion Series 2004-36.

Glasserman, P., Heidelberger, P. and Shahabuddin, P. (2002). Portfolio value-at-risk with heavy-tailed risk factors, *Mathematical Finance* 12(3), 239–269.

Glosten, L. R., Jagannathan, R. and Runkle, D. E. (1993). On the relation between the expected value and the volatility of the nominal excess return on stocks, *Journal of Finance* 48(5), 1779–1801.

Goldman Sachs Group, Inc. (2010). 2009 Annual Report. http://www2. goldmansachs.com/our-firm/investors/financials/current/annual-reports/ 2009-complete-annual.pdf.

Golub, B. W. and Crum, C. C. (2010). Risk management lessons worth remembering from the credit crisis of 2007–2009, *Journal of Portfolio Management* 36(3), 21–44.

Goodfriend, M. (1993). Interest rate policy and the inflation scare problem: 1979–1992, Federal Reserve Bank of Richmond, *Economic Quarterly* 79(1), 1–24.

Goodfriend, M. (2007). How the world achieved consensus on monetary policy, *Journal of Economic Perspectives* 21(4), 47–68.

Goodfriend, M. and King, R. G. (1988). Financial deregulation, monetary policy, and central banking, Federal Reserve Bank of Richmond, *Economic Review* 74(3), 3–22.

Goodhart, C. A. E. (2004). Some new directions for financial stability? Per Jacobsson Foundation, Per Jacobsson Foundation Lectures. http://www.perjacobsson. org/lectures/062704.pdf.

Goodhart, C. A. E. (2008). Liquidity risk management, Banque de France, *Financial Stability Review* (11), 39–44.

Goodhart, C. A. E. (1987). Why do banks need a central bank?, *Oxford Economic Papers*, new ser. 39(1), 75–89.

Goodhart, C. A. E. (1988). *The evolution of central banks*, Cambridge, MA: MIT Press.

Goodhart, C. A. E. and Schoenmaker, D. (1995). Should the functions of monetary policy and banking supervision be separated?, *Oxford Economic Papers*, new ser. 47(4), 539–560.

Gordy, M. B. (2000). A comparative anatomy of credit risk models, *Journal of Banking and Finance* 24(1–2), 199–232.

Gordy, M. B. (2003). A risk-factor model foundation for ratings-based bank capital rules, *Journal of Financial Intermediation* 12(3), 199–232.

Gorton, G. B. (2008). The Panic of 2007, in *Maintaining stability in a changing financial system*, Jackson Hole Symposium, Federal Reserve Bank of Kansas City, 131–262. http://www.kc.frb.org/publicat/sympos/2008/Gorton.03.12.09.pdf.

Gorton, G. B. (2009). Slapped in the face by the invisible hand: banking and the Panic of 2007. http://papers.ssrn.com/sol3/papers.cfm?abstract_id=1401882.

Gorton, G. B. and Metrick, A. (2010). Securitized banking and the run on repo. http://papers.ssrn.com/sol3/papers.cfm?abstract_id=1440752.

Gourieroux, C. and Jasiak, J. (2010). Value at Risk, in Aït-Sahalia, Y. and Hansen, L. P., eds., *Handbook of Financial Econometrics: Tools and Techniques*, Amsterdam: Elsevier B.V., 553–615.

Grant, J. (1994). *Money of the mind: borrowing and lending in America from the Civil War to Michael Milken*, Noonday Press, New York.

Greenbaum, S. I. and Thakor, A. V. (2007). *Contemporary financial intermediation*, 2nd ed., Amsterdam: Elsevier Academic Press.

Greenlaw, D., Hatzius, J., Kashyap, A. K. and Shin, H. S. (2008). Leveraged losses: lessons from the mortgage market meltdown. http://www.chicagogsb.edu/usmpf/docs/usmpf2008confdraft.pdf.

Greenspan, A. (2004). Risk and uncertainty in monetary policy, remarks at the Meetings of the American Economic Association, San Diego, California. http://www.federalreserve.gov/boarddocs/speeches/2004/20040103/default.htm.

Greenspan, A. (2010). The crisis, *Brookings Papers on Economic Activity* (1), 201–261.

Group of Ten (1996). The resolution of sovereign liquidity crises. http://www.bis.org/publ/gten03.pdf.

Gupta A. and Misra L. (1999). Failure and failure resolution in the US thrift and banking industries, *Financial Management* 28(4), 87–105.

Gupton, G. M., Finger, C. C. and Bhatia, M. (2007). *CreditMetrics—Technical Document*, RiskMetrics Group. First published in 1997 by J.P. Morgan & Co.

Haberler, G. (1958). *Prosperity and depression: a theoretical analysis of cyclical movements*, 4th ed., Cambridge, MA: Harvard University Press.

Haldane, A., Hall S., Pezzini, S. (2007). A new approach to assessing risks to financial stability, Bank of England, Financial Stability Paper 2, http://www.bankofengland.co.uk/publications/fsr/fs_paper02.pdf.

Hart, O. and Zingales, L. (2009). A new capital regulation for large financial institutions, University of Chicago Booth School of Business, Chicago Booth Research Paper 09-36. http://papers.ssrn.com/sol3/papers.cfm?abstract_id=1481779.

Hellwig, M. F. (2009). Systemic risk in the financial sector: an analysis of the subprime-mortgage financial crisis, *De Economist* 157(2), 129–207.

Hendricks, D. (1996). Evaluation of value-at-risk models using historical data, *Economic Policy Review* 2(1), 39–69.

HM Treasury (2011). *A new approach to financial regulation: building a stronger system*, http://www.hm-treasury.gov.uk/d/consult_newfinancial_regulation170211.pdf.

Hetzel, R. L. (1991). Too big to fail: origins, consequences, and outlook, Federal Reserve Bank of Richmond, *Economic Review* 77(6), 3–15.

Hetzel, R. L. (2009). Should increased regulation of bank risk-taking come from regulators or from the market?, Federal Reserve Bank of Richmond, *Economic Review* 95(2), 161–200.

Hicks, J. R. (1962). Liquidity, *Economic Journal* 72(288), 787–802.

Hirtle, B., Schuermann, T. and Stiroh, K. (2009). Macroprudential supervision of financial institutions: lessons from the SCAP, Federal Reserve Bank of New York, Staff Report 409.

Hodgson, R. (2009). The birth of the swap, *Financial Analysts Journal* 65(3), 32–35.

Hördahl, P. and King, M. (2008). Developments in repo markets during the financial turmoil, *BIS Quarterly Review*, Dec., 37–53.

Houweling, P. and Vorst, T. (2005). Pricing default swaps: empirical evidence, *Journal of International Money and Finance* 24(8), 1200–1225.

Huberman, G. and Wang, Z. (2008). Arbitrage pricing theory, in S. N. Durlauf and L. E. Blume, eds., *New Palgrave Dictionary of Economics*, 2nd ed., Palgrave Macmillan, Basingstoke.

Hull, J. C. (2000). *Options, futures and other derivative securities*, 4th ed., Englewood Cliffs, NJ: Prentice–Hall.

Hull, J. C. (2006). *Risk management and financial institutions*, Upper Saddle River, NJ: Pearson/Prentice–Hall.

Hull, J. C. and White, A. D. (1998). Value at risk when daily changes in market variables are not normally distributed, *Journal of Derivatives* 5(3), 9–19.

Hull, J. C. and White, A. D. (2000). Valuing credit default swaps I: no counterparty default risk, *Journal of Derivatives* 8(1), 29–40.

Hull, J. C. and White, A. D. (2001). Valuing credit default swaps II: modeling default correlations, *Journal of Derivatives* 8(3), 12–21.

Hunt, E. S. (1994). *The medieval super-companies: a study of the Peruzzi Company of Florence*, Cambridge, UK: Cambridge University Press.

International Monetary Fund (2007). Financial market turbulence: causes, consequences, and policies, Global Financial Stability Report 2. http://www.imf.org/External/Pubs/FT/GFSR/2007/02/pdf/text.pdf.

International Monetary Fund (2008a), Containing systemic risks and restoring financial soundness, Global Financial Stability Report 1. http://www.imf.org/External/Pubs/FT/GFSR/2008/01/pdf/text.pdf.

International Monetary Fund (2008b). Financial stress and deleveraging: macro-financial implications and policy, Global Financial Stability Report 2. http://www.imf.org/External/Pubs/FT/GFSR/2008/02/pdf/text.pdf.

Ivashina, V. and Scharfstein, D. (2010). Bank lending during the financial crisis of 2008, *Journal of Financial Economics* 97(3), 319–338.

Jackwerth, J. C. (1999). Option-implied risk-neutral distributions and implied binomial trees: a literature review, *Journal of Derivatives* 7(2), 66–82.

Jackwerth, J. C. (2004). *Option-implied risk-neutral distributions and risk aversion*, Research Foundation of CFA Institute. http://www.cfapubs.org/doi/pdf/10.2470/rf.v2004.n1.3925.

Jarrow, R. A. and Rudd, A. (1983). *Option pricing*, Homewood, IL: Dow Jones-Irwin.

Jen, S. (2006). Sovereign wealth funds and official FX reserves, Morgan Stanley Research.

Jen, S. (2007). Sovereign wealth funds: what they are and what's happening, *World Economics* 8(4), 1–7.

Jensen, M. C. and Meckling, W. H. (1976). Theory of the firm: managerial behavior, agency costs and ownership structure, *Journal of Financial Economics* 3(4), 305–360.

Johnson, C. A. (1997). Derivatives and rehypothecation failure: it's 3:00 p.m., do you know where your collateral is?, *Arizona Law Review* 39(3), 949–1001.

Jones, A. H. M. (1953). Inflation under the Roman Empire, *Economic History Review*, 2nd ser., 5(3), 293–318.

Jorion, P. (1988). On jump processes in the foreign exchange and stock markets, *Review of Financial Studies* 1(4), 427–445.

Jorion, P. (1996a). Lessons from the Orange County bankruptcy, *Journal of Derivatives* 4(4), 61–66.

Jorion, P. (1996b). Risk²: measuring the risk in value at risk, *Financial Analysts Journal* 52(6), 47–56.

Jorion, P. (2007). *Value at risk: the new benchmark for managing financial risk*, 3rd ed., New York: McGraw-Hill.

Kahn, G. A. (2010). Taylor rule deviations and financial imbalances, Federal Reserve Bank of Kansas City, *Economic Review* 95(2), 63–99.

Kakodkar, A., Galiani, S. and Shchetkovskiy, M. (2004). Base correlations: overcoming the limitations of tranche implied correlations, Merrill Lynch, Nov.

Kambhu, J. (1998). Dealers hedging of interest rate options in the U.S. dollar fixed-income market, Federal Reserve Bank of New York, Bank for International Settlements, *Economic Policy Review* 4(2), 35–57.

Kambhu, J. and Mosser, P. C. (2001). The effect of interest rate options hedging on term-structure dynamics, Federal Reserve Bank of New York, *Economic Policy Review* 7(3), 51–70.

Kaminsky, G., Lizondo, S. and Reinhart, C. (1998). Leading indicators of currency crises, *IMF Staff Papers* 45(1), 1–48.

Kaminsky, G. and Reinhart, C. (1999). The twin crises: the causes of banking and balance-of-payments problems, *American Economic Review* 89(3), 473–500.

Kaminsky, G., Reinhart, C. and Vegh, C. A. (2003). The unholy trinity of financial contagion, *Journal of Economic Perspectives* 17(4), 51–74.

Kaminsky, G. and Schmukler, S. L. (1999). What triggers market jitters? A chronicle of the Asian crisis, *Journal of International Money and Finance* 18(4), 537–560.

Kaplan, S. N. and Stromberg, P. (2009). Leveraged buyouts and private equity, *Journal of Economic Perspectives* 23(1), 121–146.

Kaufman, G. G. (2000a). Bank contagion: a review of the theory and evidence, *Journal of Financial Services Research* 8(2), 123–150.

Kaufman, G. G. (2000b). Banking and currency crises and systemic risk: a taxonomy and review, *Financial Markets, Institutions and Instruments* 9(2), 69–131.

Keynes, J. M. (1920). *The economic consequences of the peace*, New York: Harcourt, Brace and Howe, New York.

Keynes, J. M. (1936). *The general theory of employment, interest and money*, Macmillan, London.

Keynes, J. M. (1937). The general theory of employment, *Quarterly Journal of Economics* 51(2), 209–223.

Khandani, A. E. and Lo, A. W. (2008). What happened to the quants in August 2007? Evidence from factors and transactions data. papers.ssrn.com/sol3/papers.cfm?abstract_id=1015987.

Kharas, H., Pinto, B. and Ulatov, S. (2001). An analysis of Russia's 1998 meltdown: fundamentals and market signals, *Brookings Papers on Economic Activity* (1), 1–50.

Kiff, J., Elliott, J. A., Kazarian, E. G., Scarlata, J. G. and Spackman, C. (2009). Credit derivatives: systemic risks and policy options, International Monetary Fund, Working Paper 09/254.

Kiff, J. and Mills, P. S. (2007). Money for nothing and checks for free: recent developments in U.S. subprime mortgage markets, International Monetary Fund, Working Paper 07/188.

Kim, J. and Finger, C. C. (2000). A stress test to incorporate correlation breakdown, *Journal of Risk* 2(3), 5–19.

Kindleberger, C. P. (1978). *Manias, panics and crashes: a history of financial crises*, Basic Books, New York.

Kindleberger, C. P. (1986). *The world in depression, 1929–1939*, rev. ed., Berkeley: University of California Press.

Kindleberger, C. P. (1993). *A financial history of western Europe*, 2nd ed., New York: Oxford University Press.

King, M. (2008). Are the brokers broken?, Citigroup Global Markets, Sep.

Kiyotaki, N. and Moore, J. (1997). Credit cycles, *Journal of Political Economy* 105(2), 211–248.

Kiyotaki, N. and Moore, J. (2002). Balance-sheet contagion, *American Economic Review* 92(2), 46–50.

Klee, E. (2011). The first line of defense: the discount window during the early stages of the financial crisis, Federal Reserve Board, Finance and Economics Discussion Series 2011-23.

Klugman, S. A., Panjer, H. H. and Willmot, G. E. (2008). *Loss models: from data to decisions*, 3rd ed., Hoboken, NJ: John Wiley & Sons.

Knight, F. H. (1921). *Risk, uncertainty and profit*, Boston, New York: Houghton Mifflin Company.

Kohn, D. L. (2002). Monetary policy and asset prices revisited, *Cato Journal* 29(1), 31–44.

Kothari, V. (2006). *Securitization: the financial instrument of the future*, Hoboken, NJ: John Wiley & Sons.

Kothari, V. (2009). *Credit derivatives and structured credit trading*, rev. ed., Singapore: John Wiley & Sons.

Krasker, W. S. (1980). The "peso problem" in testing the efficiency of forward exchange markets, *Journal of Monetary Economics* 6(2), 269–276.

Krause, A. (2003). Crashes in bond markets and the hedging of mortgage-backed securities, *Journal of Fixed Income* 13(3), 19–32.

Krishnamurthy, A. (2010). How debt markets have malfunctioned in the crisis, *Journal of Economic Perspectives*, 24(1), 3–28.

Kroszner, R. S. (2000). Lessons from financial crises: the role of clearinghouses, *Journal of Financial Services Research* 18(2–3), 157–171.

Krugman, P. (1979). A model of balance-of-payments crises, *Journal of Money, Credit and Banking* 11(3), 311–325.

Kuester, K., Mittnik, S. and Paolella, M. S. (2006). Value-at-risk prediction: a comparison of alternative strategies, *Journal of Financial Econometrics* 4(1), 53–89.

Kumar, M. and Persaud, A. (2002). Pure contagion and shifting risk appetite: analytical issues and empirical evidence, *International Finance* 5(3), 401–436.

Kupiec, P. H. (1995a). Stress testing in a value at risk framework, *Journal of Derivatives* 6(1), 73–84.

Kupiec, P. H. (1995b). Techniques for verifying the accuracy of risk measurement models, *Journal of Derivatives* 3(2), 7–24.

Kupiec, P. H. (2002). What exactly does credit VaR measure?, *Journal of Derivatives* 9(3), 46–59.

Kyle, A. S. (1985). Continuous auctions and insider trading, *Econometrica* 53(6), 1315–1335.

Laeven, L. and Valencia, F. (2008). Systemic banking crises: a new database, International Monetary Fund, Working Paper 224.

Landes, D. S. (1998). *The wealth and poverty of nations: why some are so rich and some so poor*, New York: W.W. Norton.

Lando, D. (2004). *Credit risk modeling: theory and applications*, Princeton, NJ: Princeton University Press.

Laux, C. and Leuz, C. (2010). Did fair-value accounting contribute to the financial crisis?, *Journal of Economic Perspectives* 24(1), 93–118.

Lehman Brothers (2003). *The Lehman Brothers guide to exotic credit derivatives.*

Levine, R. (2005). Finance and growth: theory and evidence, in P. Aghion and S. N. Durlauf, eds., *Handbook of Economic Growth*, 1(1), Amsterdam: Elsevier, 865–934.

Lhabitant, F.-S. (2001). Assessing market risk for hedge funds and hedge fund portfolios, *Journal of Risk Finance* 2(4), 16–32.

Li, D. X. (2000). On default correlation: a copula function approach, *Journal of Fixed Income* 9(4), 43–54.

Litterman, R. (1996). Hot Spots and hedges, Goldman Sachs and Co., Risk Management Series.

Litterman, R. B. and Iben, T. (1991). Corporate bond valuation and the term structure of credit spreads, *Journal of Portfolio Management* 17(3), 52–64.

Liu, B., McConnell, J. J. and Saretto, A. (2010). Why did auction rate bond auctions fail during 2007–2008?, *Journal of Fixed Income* 20(2), 5–18.

Lo, A. W. (1999). The three Ps of Total Risk Management, *Financial Analysts Journal* 55(1), 13–26.

Lo, A. W. (2001). Risk management for hedge funds: introduction and overview, *Financial Analysts Journal* 57(6), 16–33.

Lo, A. W. (2005). *The dynamics of the hedge fund industry*, Research Foundation of CFA Institute. http://www.cfapubs. org/doi/pdf/10.2470/rf.v2005.n3.3932.

Longin, F. (2000). From value at risk to stress testing: the extreme value approach, *Journal of Banking and Finance* 24(7), 1097–1130.

Longin, F. and Solnik, B. (1995). Is the correlation in international equity returns constant: 1960–1990?, *Journal of International Money and Finance* 14(1), 3–26.

Longstaff, F. A. (2004). The flight-to-liquidity premium in U.S. Treasury bond prices, *Journal of Business* 77(3), 511–526.

Lopez, J. A. (1999). Methods for evaluating value-at-risk estimates, Federal Reserve Bank of San Francisco, *Economic Review* (2), 3–17.

Lopez, J. A. and Walter, C. A. (2000). Is implied correlation worth calculating? Evidence from foreign exchange options, *Journal of Derivatives* 7(3), 65–82.

Loretan, M. and English, W. B. (2000). Evaluating "correlation breakdowns" during periods of market volatility, Board of Governors of the Federal Reserve System,

International Finance Discussion Paper 658. http://www.federalreserve.gov/pubs/ifdp/2000/658/ifdp658.pdf.

Lucas, D. J. (1995). Default correlation and credit analysis, *Journal of Fixed Income* 4(4), 76–87.

Mackay, C. (1962). *Extraordinary popular delusions: and the madness of crowds*, New York: Noonday Press.

Madhavan, A. (2000). Market microstructure: a survey, *Journal of Financial Markets* 3(3), 205–258.

Madhavan, A. (2002). Market microstructure: a practitioner's guide, *Financial Analysts Journal* 58(5), 28–42.

Madigan, B. F. (2009). Bagehot's dictum in practice: formulating and implementing policies to combat the financial crisis, in *Financial stability and macroeconomic policy*, Jackson Hole Symposium, Federal Reserve Bank of Kansas City, 169–189. http://www.kc.frb.org/publicat/sympos/2009/papers/Madigan-2009.pdf.

Madigan, B. F. and Nelson, W. R. (2002). Proposed revision to the Federal Reserve's discount window lending programs, *Federal Reserve Bulletin* 88(7), 313–319. http://www.federalreserve.gov/pubs/bulletin/2002/0702lead.pdf.

Malz, A. M. (1995). Currency option markets and exchange rates: a case study of the U.S. dollar in March 1995, Federal Reserve Bank of New York, *Current Issues in Economics and Finance* 1(4).

Malz, A. M. (1996). Using option prices to estimate realignment probabilities in the European Monetary System: the case of sterling-mark, *Journal of International Money and Finance* 15(5), 717–748.

Malz, A. M. (1997). Estimating the probability distributions of the future exchange rate from option prices, *Journal of Derivatives* 5(2), 18–36.

Malz, A. M. (2000/2001b). Vega risk and the smile, *Journal of Risk* 3(2), 41–63.

Malz, A. M. (2001a). Crises and volatility, *Risk* 14(11), 105–108.

Mandelbrot, B. (1963). The variation of certain speculative prices, *Journal of Business* 36(4), 394–419.

Mandler, M. (2003). *Market expectations and option prices: techniques and applications*, Heidelberg and New York: Physica-Verlag.

Markit Partners (2009). The CDS Big Bang: understanding the changes to the global CDS contract and North American conventions, Mar. http://www.markit.com/cds/announcements/resource/cds_big_bang.pdf.

Marrison, C. (2002). *The fundamentals of risk measurement*, New York: McGraw-Hill.

Marshall, C. and Siegel, M. (1997). Value at risk: implementing a risk measurement standard, *Journal of Derivatives* 4(3), 91–111.

Mayer, C., Pence, K. and Sherlund, S. M. (2009). The rise in mortgage defaults, *Journal of Economic Perspectives* 23(1), 27–50.

McAndrews, J. J. and Potter, S. M. (2002). Liquidity effects of the events of September 11, 2001, Federal Reserve Bank of New York, *Economic Policy Review* 8(2), 59–79.

McConnell, M. M. and Perez-Quiros, G. (2000). Output fluctuations in the United States: what has changed since the early 1980's?, *American Economic Review*, 90(5), 1464–1476.

Mehran, H. and Stulz, R. M. (2007). The economics of conflicts of interest in financial institutions, *Journal of Financial Economics* 85(2), 267–296.

Mehrling, P. (2011). *The new Lombard Street: how the Fed became the dealer of last resort*, Princeton, NJ: Princeton University Press.

Meissner, G., ed. (2008). *Definitive guide to CDOs: market, application, valuation and hedging*, London: Risk Books.

Melick, W. R. and Thomas, C. P. (1997). Recovering an asset's implied PDF from option prices: an application to oil prices during the Gulf Crisis, *Journal of Financial and Quantitative Analysis* 32(1), 91–115.

Merton, R. C. (1974). On the pricing of corporate debt: the risk structure of interest rates, *Journal of Finance* 29(2), 449–470.

Merton, R. C. (1976). Option pricing when underlying stock returns are discontinuous, *Journal of Financial Economics* 3(1–2), 125–144.

Merton, R. C. (1980). On estimating the expected return on the market: an exploratory investigation, *Journal of Financial Economics* 8(4), 323–361.

Merton, R. C. and Bodie, Z. (1993). Deposit insurance reform: a functional approach, *Carnegie-Rochester Conference Series on Public Policy* 38, 1–34.

Merton, R. C. and Perold, A. (1993). Theory of risk capital in financial firms, *Journal of Applied Corporate Finance* 6(3), 16–32.

Mina, J. (1999). Improved cash-flow map, RiskMetrics Group, Working paper.

Mina, J. (2000). Calculating VaR through quadratic approximation, *RiskMetrics Journal* 1, 23–33.

Mina, J. and Ulmer, A. (1999). Delta-gamma four ways, RiskMetrics Group, Working paper.

Mina, J. and Xiao, J. (2001). *Return to RiskMetrics: the evolution of a standard*, RiskMetrics Group.

Minsky, H. P. (1984). Banking and industry between the two wars: the United States, *Journal of European Economic History* 13(2), 235–272.

Minsky, H. P. (1986). *Stabilizing an unstable economy*, New Haven: Yale University Press.

Minsky, H. P. (1992). The financial instability hypothesis, Levy Economics Institute, Working Paper 74.

Miron, J. A. (1986). Financial panics, the seasonality of the nominal interest rate, and the founding of the Fed, *American Economic Review* 76(1), 125–140.

Mishkin, F. S. (2008). Monetary policy flexibility, risk management, and financial disruptions, speech delivered at the Federal Reserve Bank of New York. http://www.federalreserve.gov/newsevents/speech/mishkin20080111a.htm.

Mitchell, M., Pedersen, L. H. and Pulvino, T. (2007). Slow moving capital, *American Economic Review* 97(2), 215–220.

Modarres, M. (2006). *Risk analysis in engineering: techniques, tools, and trends*, Boca Raton, FL: Taylor & Francis.

Moody's Investors Service (2011). Corporate default and recovery rates, 1920–2010, Special Comment, Feb.

Moody's Investors Service (2010). Structured finance rating transitions: 1983–2009, Special Comment, Mar.

Morgan Guaranty Trust Company (1996). *RiskMetrics Technical Document*, 4th ed.

Mounfield, C. (2009). *Synthetic CDOs: modelling, valuation and risk management*, Cambridge, UK: Cambridge University Press.

Moyer, S. G. (2005). *Distressed debt analysis: strategies for speculative investors*, Boca Raton, FL: J. Ross.

Mueller, R. C. (1997). *The Venetian money market: banks, panics, and the public debt, 1200-1500*, Baltimore, MD: John Hopkins University Press.

Neal, L. (1990). *The rise of financial capitalism: international capital markets in the Age of Reason*, Cambridge, UK: Cambridge University Press.

Neftci, S. N. (2000). Value at risk calculations, extreme events, and tail estimation, *Journal of Derivatives* 7(3), 23–37.

Nelson, C. R. and Siegel, A. F. (1987). Parsimonious modeling of yield curves, *Journal of Business* 60(4), 473–489.

Nieuwland, F. G., Verschoor, W. F. and Wolff, C. C. (1994). Stochastic trends and jumps in EMS exchange rates, *Journal of International Money and Finance* **13**, 699–727.

NYU Stern Working Group on Financial Reform (2009). Real time solutions for financial reform. http://govtpolicyrecs.stern.nyu.edu/home.html.

O'Brien, D. (2007). *The development of monetary economics: a modern perspective on monetary controversies*, Cheltenham, UK and Northampton, MA: Edward Elgar.

Obstfeld, M. and Rogoff, K. (2010). Global imbalances and the financial crisis: products of common causes, in *Asia and the global financial crisis*, Federal Reserve Bank of San Francisco, 131–172. http://www.frbsf.org/economics/conferences/aepc/2009/Obstfeld_Rogoff.pdf.

O'Hara, M. (1995). *Market microstructure theory*, Cambridge, MA: Blackwell Publishers.

O'Kane, D. and Livesey, M. (2004). Base correlation explained, Lehman Brothers, *Quantitative Credit Research Quarterly* (Q3–Q4), 3–20.

O'Kane, D. and Schloegl, L. (2001). Modelling credit: theory and practice, Lehman Brothers, Advanced Research Series.

O'Kane, D. and Sen, S. (2004). Credit spreads explained, Lehman Brothers, *Quantitative Credit Research Quarterly* (Q1), 48–65.

O'Kane, D. and Turnbull, S. (2003). Valuation of credit default swaps, Lehman Brothers, *Quantitative Credit Research Quarterly* (Q1–Q2), 28–44.

Ötker-Robe, İ., Narain, A., Ilyina, A. and Surti, J. (2011). The too-important-to-fail conundrum: impossible to ignore and difficult to resolve, International Monetary Fund, Staff Discussion Note 2011/12.

Overdahl, J. and Schachter, B. (1995). Derivatives regulation and financial management: lessons from Gibson Greetings, *Financial Management* **24**(1), 68–78.

Pearson, N. D. and Smithson, C. (2002). VaR: the state of play, *Review of Financial Economics* **11**(3), 175–189.

Pedersen, L. H. (2009). When everyone runs for the exit, *International Journal of Central Banking* **5**(4), 177–199.

Peltzman, S. (1989). The economic theory of regulation after a decade of deregulation, *Brookings Papers on Economic Activity: Microeconomics* 1–41.

Pennacchi, G. G. (2009). Deposit insurance, Working paper. http://business. illinois.edu/gpennacc/DepInsGP.pdf.

Perli, R. and Sack, B. (2003). Does mortgage hedging amplify movements in long-term interest rates?, *Journal of Fixed Income* 13(3), 7–17.

Perold, A. (2005). Capital allocation in financial firms, *Journal of Applied Corporate Finance* 17(3), 110–118.

Pfeiffer, P. E. (1990). *Probability for applications*, New York: Springer-Verlag.

Plosser, C. I. (2009). Financial econometrics, financial innovation, and financial stability, *Journal of Financial Econometrics* 7(1), 3–11.

Pojarliev, M. and Levich, R. M. (2011). Detecting crowded trades in currency funds, *Financial Analysts Journal* 67(1), 26–39.

Poon, S.-H. and Granger, C. (2003). Forecasting volatility in financial markets: a review, *Journal of Economic Literature* 41(2), 478–539.

Poon, S.-H. and Granger, C. (2005). Practical issues in forecasting volatility, *Financial Analysts Journal* 61(1), 45–56.

Posen, A. S. (2006). Why central banks should not burst bubbles, *International Finance* 9(1), 109–124.

Posner, R. A. (1974). Theories of economic regulation, *Bell Journal of Economics and Management Science* 5(2), 335–358.

Pownall, R. A. J. and Koedijk, K. G. (1999). Capturing downside risk in financial markets: the case of the Asian Crisis, *Journal of International Money and Finance* 18(6), 853–870.

Pozsar, Z., Adrian, T., Ashcraft, A., and Boesky, H. (2010). Shadow banking, Federal Reserve Bank of New York, Staff Report 458.

Pritsker, M. (1997). Evaluating value at risk methodologies: accuracy versus computational time, *Journal of Financial Services Research* 12(2–3), 201–242.

Pyle, D. H. (1995). The U.S. savings and loan crisis, in R. Jarrow, V. Maksimovic and W. Ziemba, eds., *Handbooks in Operations Research and Management Science: Finance* 9, Amsterdam: Elsevier, 1105–1125.

Radelet, S. and Sachs, J. D. (1998). The East Asian financial crisis: diagnosis, remedies, prospects, *Brookings Papers on Economic Activity* (1), 1–90.

Rajan, R. G. (2005). Has financial development made the world riskier? in *The Greenspan era: lessons for the future*, Jackson Hole Symposium, Federal Reserve Bank of Kansas City, 313–397. http://www.kansascityfed.org/Publicat/sympos/2005/PDF/Rajan2005.pdf.

Rappoport, P. and White, E. N. (1993). Was there a bubble in the 1929 stock market? *Journal of Economic History* 53(3), 549–574.

Reinhart, C. M. and Rogoff, K. S. (2009). *This time is different: eight centuries of financial folly*, Princeton, NJ: Princeton University Press.

Rosenberg, J. V. and Engle, R. F. (2002). Empirical pricing kernels, *Journal of Financial Economics* 64(3), 341–372.

Rosenberg, J. V. and Schuermann, T. (2006). A general approach to integrated risk management with skewed, fat-tailed risks, *Journal of Financial Economics* 79(3), 569–614.

Ross, S. A. (1976). The arbitrage theory of capital asset pricing, *Journal of Economic Theory* **13**(3), 341–360.

Ross, S. A. (2005). *Neoclassical finance*, Princeton, NJ: Princeton University Press.

Roubini, N. (2006). Why central banks should burst bubbles, *International Finance* **9**(1), 87–107.

Royal Swedish Academy of Sciences (2003). The Prize in Economic Sciences 2003– advanced information. http://nobelprize.org/nobel_prizes/economics/laureates/2003/ecoadv.pdf.

Rubinstein, M. (1994). Implied binomial trees, *Journal of Finance* **49**(3), 771–818.

Rutledge, A. and Raynes, S. (2010). *Elements of structured finance*, Oxford and New York: Oxford University Press.

Saidenberg, M. R. and Schuermann, T. (2003). The new Basel Accord and questions for research, Working Paper 03-14, Wharton Financial Institutions Center. http://fic.wharton.upenn.edu/fic/papers/03/0314.pdf.

Santos, J. A. C. (2001). Bank capital regulation in contemporary banking theory: a review of the literature, *Financial Markets, Institutions and Instruments* **10**(2), 41–84.

Schachter, B. (2010). Stress testing, in R. Cont, ed., *Encyclopedia of quantitative finance* **4**, Hoboken, NJ: John Wiley & Sons.

Schloegl, L. and Greenberg, A. (2003). Understanding deltas of synthetic CDO tranches, Lehman Brothers, *Quantitative Credit Research Quarterly* (Q4), 45–54.

Schnabel, I. (2009). The role of liquidity and implicit guarantees in the German twin crisis of 1931, *Journal of International Money and Finance* **28**(1), 1–25.

Schnabel, I. and Shin, H. S. (2004). Liquidity and contagion: the crisis of 1763, *Journal of the European Economic Association*, **2**(6), 929–968.

Schönbucher, P. J. (2003). *Credit derivatives pricing models: models, pricing and implementation*, Hoboken, NJ: John Wiley & Sons.

Schularick, M. and Taylor, A. M. (2009). Credit booms gone bust: monetary policy, leverage cycles and financial crises, 1870–2008, National Bureau of Economic Research, NBER Working Paper 15512.

Schwarcz, S. L. (1994). The alchemy of asset securitization, *Stanford Journal of Law, Business and Finance* **1**(1), 133–154.

Schwert, G. W. (1990a). Stock market volatility, *Financial Analysts Journal* **46**(1), 23–34.

Schwert, G. W. (1990b). Stock volatility and the crash of '87, *Review of Financial Studies* **3**(1), 77–102.

Segoviano Basurto, M. A. and Singh, M. (2008). Counterparty risk in the over-the-counter derivatives market, International Monetary Fund, Working Paper 8.

Senior Supervisors Group (2009a), Observations on management of recent credit default swap credit events. http://www.newyorkfed.org/newsevents/news/markets/2009/SSG_030909.pdf.

Senior Supervisors Group (2009b). Risk management lessons from the global banking crisis of 2008. Oct. http://www.ny.frb.org/newsevents/news/banking/2009/SSG_report.pdf.

Sharpe, W. F. (2002). Budgeting and monitoring pension fund risk, *Financial Analysts Journal* 58(5), 74–86.

Shiller, R. J. and McCulloch, J. H. (1990). The term structure of interest rates, in B. M. Friedman and F. H. Hahn, eds., *Handbook of monetary economics* 1, Amsterdam: North-Holland, 627–722.

Shimko, D. (1993). Bounds of probability, *Risk* 6(4), 33–37.

Shin, H. S. (2009a). Reflections on Northern Rock: the bank run that heralded the global financial crisis, *Journal of Economic Perspectives* 23(1), 101–119.

Shin, H. S. (2009b). Securitisation and financial stability, *Economic Journal* 119(536), 309–332.

Shleifer, A. and Summers, L. H. (1990). The noise trader approach to finance, *Journal of Economic Perspectives* (4)2, 19–33.

Shleifer, A. and Vishny, R. W. (1997). The limits of arbitrage, *Journal of Finance* 52(1), 737–783.

Shleifer, A., and Vishny, R. (2011). Fire sales in finance and macroeconomics, *Journal of Economic Perspectives* 25(1), 29–48.

Siegel, J. J. (1991). Does it pay stock investors to forecast the business cycle?, *Journal of Portfolio Management*, 18(1), 27–34.

Silverman, B. (1986). *Density estimation for statistics and data analysis*, London: Chapman and Hall.

Simons, H. C. (1936). Rules versus authorities in monetary policy, *Journal of Political Economy* 44(1), 1–30.

Simons, H. C. (1946). Debt policy and banking policy, *Review of Economics and Statistics* 28(2), 85–89.

Singh, M. and Aitken, J. (2009a). Counterparty risk, impact on collateral flows and role for central counterparties, International Monetary Fund, Working Paper 173.

Singh, M. and Aitken, J. (2009b). Deleveraging after Lehman—evidence from reduced rehypothecation, International Monetary Fund, Working Paper 42.

Singh, M. and Aitken, J. (2010). The (sizable) role of rehypothecation in the shadow banking system, International Monetary Fund, Working Paper 172.

Skeel, D. (2011). *The New Financial Deal: understanding the Dodd-Frank Act and its (unintended) consequences*, Hoboken, NJ: John Wiley & Sons.

Söderlind, P. and Svensson, L. E. (1997). New techniques to extract market expectations from financial instruments, *Journal of Monetary Economics* 40(1), 383–429.

Solomon, R. (1982). *The international monetary system, 1945–1981*, updated ed., New York: Harper & Row.

Spong, K. (2000). *Banking regulation: its purposes, implementation, and effects*, 5th ed. Federal Reserve Bank of Kansas City. http://www.kc.frb.org/BS&S/Publicat/PDF/RegsBook2000.pdf.

Standard & Poor's (2006). Annual 2005 global corporate default study and rating transitions, Global Fixed Income Research, Jan.

Standard & Poor's (2010). 2009 U.S. corporate default study and rating transitions.

Stern, G. H. and Feldman, R. J. (2004). *Too big to fail: the hazards of bank bailouts*, Washington, DC: Brookings Institution Press.

Stigler, G. J. (1971). The theory of economic regulation, *Bell Journal of Economics and Management Science* 2(1), 3–21.

Stoer, J. and Bulirsch, R. (1993). *Introduction to numerical analysis*, 2nd ed., New York, Berlin, and Heidelberg: Springer-Verlag.

Stoll, H. R. (2003). Market microstructure, in G. Constantinides, M. Harris and R. Stulz, eds., *Handbook of the Economics of Finance* 1(1), Amsterdam: Elsevier B.V., 553–604.

Stulz, R. (2010). Credit default swaps and the credit crisis, *Journal of Economic Perspectives* 24(1), 73–92.

Svensson, L. E. (1991). The simplest test of target zone credibility, *IMF Staff Papers* 38(3), 655–665.

Swagel, P. (2009). The financial crisis: an inside view, *Brookings Papers on Economic Activity* (1), 1–78.

Swiss Federal Banking Commission (2008). Subprime crisis: SFBC investigation into the causes of the write-downs of UBS AG. http://www.finma.ch/archiv/ebk/e/publik/medienmit/20081016/ubs-subprime-bericht-ebk-e.pdf.

Taleb, N. (1997). *Dynamic hedging: managing vanilla and exotic options*, New York: John Wiley & Sons.

Tarullo, D. K. (2011). Regulating systemic risk, speech at the 2011 Credit Markets Symposium, Charlotte, North Carolina. http://www.federalreserve.gov/newsevents/speech/tarullo20110331a.pdf.

Task Force of the Market Operations Committee of the European System of Central Banks (2007). The use of portfolio credit risk models in central banks, European Central Bank, Occasional Paper 64. http://www.ecb.int/pub/pdf/scpops/ecbocp64.pdf.

Tay, A. S. and Wallis, K. F. (2000). Density forecasting: a survey, *Journal of Forecasting* 19(4), 235–254.

Taylor, J. B. (1993). Discretion versus policy rules in practice, *Carnegie-Rochester Conference Series on Public Policy* 39, 195–214.

Taylor, J. B. (2007). Housing and monetary policy, in *Housing, housing finance, and monetary policy*, Jackson Hole Symposium, Federal Reserve Bank of Kansas City, 463–476. http://www.kansascityfed.org/PUBLICAT/SYMPOS/2007/PDF/Taylor_0415.pdf.

Temin, P. (1989). *Lessons from the Great Depression*, Cambridge, MA: MIT Press.

Timberlake, R. H. (1984). The central banking role of clearinghouse associations, *Journal of Money, Credit, and Banking* 16(1), 1–15.

Tobin, J. (1958). Liquidity preference as behavior towards risk, *Review of Economic Studies* 25(2), 65–86.

Tucker, P. (2010). Shadow banking, financing markets and financial stability, speech at a BGC Partners Seminar, London. http://www.bankofengland.co.uk/publications/speeches/2010/speech420.pdf.

Tuckman, B. (2002). *Fixed income securities: tools for today's markets*, 2nd ed., Hoboken, NJ: John Wiley & Sons.

UBS (2008). Shareholder Report on UBS's Write-Downs. http://www.ubs.com/1/ShowMedia/investors/releases?contentId=140331&name=080418ShareholderReport.pdf.

U.S. Congressional Budget Office (1992). The cost of forbearance during the thrift crisis, CBO Staff Memorandum. http://www.cbo.gov/doc.cfm?index=9927.

U.S. Congressional Research Service (2010). Who regulates whom? An overview of U.S. financial supervision, by M. Jickling and E.V. Murphy, R40249, April 21. http://assets.opencrs.com/rpts/R40249_20101208.pdf.

U.S. Financial Crisis Inquiry Commission (2010). Shadow banking and the financial crisis. http://fcic-static.law.stanford.edu/cdn_media/fcic-reports/2010-0505-Shadow-Banking.pdf.

U.S. Financial Crisis Inquiry Commission (2011). *The financial crisis inquiry report: final report of the National Commission on the Causes of the Financial and Economic Crisis in the United States*, Washington, DC: Financial Crisis Inquiry Commission. http://fcic-static.law.stanford.edu/cdn_media/fcic-reports/fcic_final_report_full.pdf.

U.S. President's Working Group on Financial Markets (1999). Hedge funds, leverage, and the lessons of Long-Term Capital Management. http://www.treasury.gov/resource-center/fin-mkts/Documents/hedgfund.pdf.

U.S. Securities and Exchange Commission (2004). Final rule: alternative net capital requirements for broker-dealers that are part of consolidated supervised entities. http://www.sec.gov/rules/final/34-49830.htm.

Vasicek, O. (1991). Limiting loan loss probability distribution, Moody's KMV.

Veronesi, P. and Zingales, L. (2010). Paulson's gift, *Journal of Financial Economics* **97**(3), 339–368.

Walter, J. R. and Weinberg, J. A. (2002). How large is the Federal financial safety net?, *Cato Journal* **21**(3), 369–393.

Wasserman, L. (2004). *All of statistics: a concise course in statistical inference*, New York: Springer.

Weiss, D. M. (2006). *After the trade is made: processing securities transactions*, 2nd rev. ed., New York: Portfolio.

White, E. N. (1983). *The regulation and reform of the American banking system*, 1900–1929, Princeton, NJ: Princeton University Press.

White, L. J. (2009). The credit-rating agencies and the subprime debacle, *Critical Review* **21**(2–3), 389–399.

White, W. R. (2006). Is price stability enough?, Bank for International Settlements, Working Paper 205. http://www.bis.org/publ/work205.pdf.

White, W. R. (2007). The need for a longer policy horizon: A less orthodox approach, in *Global imbalances and developing countries: Remedies for a failing international financial system*, Amsterdam: FONDAD, 57–92. http://www.fondad.org/uploaded/Fondad-GlobalImbalancesRemedies/Fondad-GlobalImbalances Remedies-Chapter06.pdf.

White, W. R. (2009). Should monetary policy "lean or clean"?, Globalization and Monetary Policy Institute, Federal Reserve Bank of Dallas, Working Paper 34. http://www.dallasfed.org/institute/wpapers/2009/0034.pdf.

White, W. R. (2010). Some alternative perspectives on macroeconomic theory and some policy implications, Globalization and Monetary Policy Institute, Federal Reserve Bank of Dallas, Working Paper 54. http://dallasfed.org/institute/wpapers/2010/0054.pdf.

Wicksell, K. (1907). The influence of the rate of interest on prices, *Economic Journal* 17(66), 213–220.

Wicksell, K. (1967). *Lectures on political economy*, 2, New York: A. M. Kelley.

Williams, J. (1986). *The economic function of futures markets*, Cambridge, UK: Cambridge University Press.

Williamson, O. E. (1985). *The economic institutions of capitalism: firms, markets, relational contracting*, New York: Free Press.

Willis, P. B. (1972). *The federal funds market: its origin and development*, 5th ed., Federal Reserve Bank of Boston.

Wojnilower, A. M. (1980). The central role of credit crunches in recent financial history, *Brookings Papers on Economic Activity* (2), 277–339.

Wojnilower, A. M. (1985). Private credit demand, supply, and crunches—how different are the 1980s? *American Economic Review* 73(2), 351–356.

Wood, G. E. (2000). The lender of last resort reconsidered, *Journal of Financial Services Research* 18(2–3), 203–227.

Zangari, P. (2003). Equity risk factor models, in Litterman, R.B., ed., *Modern investment management: an equilibrium approach*, Hoboken, NJ: John Wiley & Sons, 368–395.

Zhou, C. (2001). An analysis of default correlations and multiple defaults, *Review of Financial Studies* 14(4), 555–576.

Zimmerman, T. (2007). The Great Subprime Meltdown of 2007, *Journal of Structured Finance* 13(3), 7–20.

Zingales, L. (2009). The future of securities regulation, *Journal of Accounting Research* 47(2), 391–426.

Zweig, S. (1944). *Die Welt von Gestern: Erinnerungen eines Europäers*, Stockholm: Bermann-Fischer.

Index

ABCP conduits. *See* Asset-backed commercial paper (ABCP) conduits
ABX index family, 406–407
Acceptance region, 662
Accounting balance sheet, 193
Accounting triggers, 547
Adverse price impact, 463, 467
Adverse selection, 198, 462
Agency debt, 639
Agency MBS, 298, 446
Agency securities lending, 441
Aggregate credit, 517
Alternative hypothesis, 661
Amaranth (hedge fund), 505
American International Group (AIG), 211
American option, 121
Analytical approach, 123–126
Arbitrage, regulatory, 644
Arbitrage CDOs, 343
Arbitrage pricing theory (APT), 81–82. *See also* Multiple risk factors
Arithmetic rate of return, 44–49
Arithmetic return approximation, 164, 165–166
Arranger. *See* Underwriters/underwriting
Asian financial crisis of 1997, 42–43, 588
Asset and default correlation, 279–281
Asset-backed commercial paper (ABCP) conduits, 299, 431–432, 524–525, 528–529, 644–645
Asset-Backed Commercial Paper Money Market Mutual Fund Liquidity Facility (AMLF), 429

Asset-backed securities (ABS), 10, 299–309, 431–432
spreads, 550
Asset-liability management (ALM), 464
Asset-price targeting, 622–624
Asset return correlation, *see* Correlation
Asset prices and returns. *See also* Kurtosis, Skewness, Volatility
and default correlation, 279–281
behavior, 43, 72, 349–363, 514
return correlation, 343
statistical behavior of, 43
statistical properties of, 356, 358
time variation of distribution of, 352
Asset-swap spread, 232
Asymmetric information, 197, 583, 599
Asymptotic behavior, 142
Attachment point, 303
At-the-money-forward, 122
Automotive industry, 402–405
Available-for-sale securities, 615
AXA Rosenberg, 394

Backtesting, 407–413
Bagehot's rule, 630–631
Balance sheet CDOs, 343
Balance sheet of firm, 216
Balance sheet risk, 422
Bank examinations, 619–621
Bank for International Settlements, 8, 602
Bank of America, 260
Bank runs, 428, 523–524, 528–535, 617

Printed and bound by CPI Group (UK) Ltd, Croydon, CR0 4YY

23/04/2025

14660904-0003